Red Hat®
Enterprise Linux® 6 Administration
Real World Skills for Red Hat Administrators

Sander van Vugt

WILEY
John Wiley & Sons, Inc.

Senior Acquisitions Editor: Jeff Kellum
Development Editor: Gary Schwartz
Technical Editors: Floris Meester, Erno de Korte
Production Editor: Rebecca Anderson
Copy Editor: Kim Wimpsett
Editorial Manager: Pete Gaughan
Production Manager: Tim Tate
Vice President and Executive Group Publisher: Richard Swadley
Vice President and Publisher: Neil Edde
Book Designer: Judy Fung and Bill Gibson
Proofreaders: Louise Watson and Jennifer Bennett, Word One New York
Indexer: J & J Indexing
Project Coordinator, Cover: Katherine Crocker
Cover Designer: Ryan Sneed
Cover Image: © Jacob Wackerhausen / iStockPhoto
Copyright © 2013 by John Wiley & Sons, Inc., Indianapolis, Indiana

Published simultaneously in Canada

ISBN: 978-1-118-30129-6
ISBN: 978-1-118-62045-8 (ebk.)
ISBN: 978-1-118-42143-7 (ebk.)
ISBN: 978-1-118-57091-3 (ebk.)

Dear Reader,

Thank you for choosing *Red Hat Enterprise Linux 6 Administration: Real World Skills for Red Hat Administrators*. This book is part of a family of premium-quality Sybex books, all of which are written by outstanding authors who combine practical experience with a gift for teaching.

Sybex was founded in 1976. More than 30 years later, we're still committed to producing consistently exceptional books. With each of our titles, we're working hard to set a new standard for the industry. From the paper we print on to the authors we work with, our goal is to bring you the best books available.

I hope you see all that reflected in these pages. I'd be very interested to hear your comments and get your feedback on how we're doing. Feel free to let me know what you think about this or any other Sybex book by sending me an email at nedde@wiley.com. If you think you've found a technical error in this book, please visit http://sybex.custhelp.com. Customer feedback is critical to our efforts at Sybex.

Best regards,

Neil Edde
Vice President and Publisher
Sybex, an Imprint of Wiley

To Florence, my loving wife of 20 years who supports me and believes in everything I do. Chérie, I'm looking forward to spending the next 60 years of our lives together.

About the Author

Sander van Vugt is an author of more than 50 technical books. Most of these books are in his native language of Dutch. Sander is also a technical instructor who works directly for major Linux vendors, such as Red Hat and SUSE. He specializes in high availability and performance issues in Linux. He has also built up a lot of experience in securing servers with SELinux, especially on platforms that don't support it natively. Sander has applied his skills in helping many companies all over the world who are using Linux. His work has taken him to amazing places like Greenland, Utah, Malaysia, and more.

When not working, Sander likes to spend time with his two sons, Franck and Alex, and his beautiful wife, Florence. He also likes outdoor sports, in particular running, hiking, kayaking, and ice-skating. During these long hours of participating in sports, he thinks through the ideas for his next book and the projects on which he is currently working, which makes the actual writing process a lot easier and the project go more smoothly.

Acknowledgments

Books of this size and depth succeed because of all the hard work put in by a team of professionals. I'm grateful for all the hard work put in by several people at Sybex on this project. Gary Schwartz was a great developmental editor. He helped keep things on track and provided excellent editorial guidance. The technical editors, Floris Meester and Erno de Korte, provided insightful input throughout the book. I appreciated the meticulous attention to detail provided by Rebecca Anderson, the production editor for this book. Last, but certainly not least, I want to thank Jeff Kellum, the acquisitions editor, for having the faith in me to write this book for Sybex.

Contents at a Glance

Contents

Table of Exercises

Introduction

Red Hat is the number-one Linux vendor on the planet. Even though official figures have never been released, as the first open source, one-billion dollar company, Red Hat is quite successful in enterprise Linux. More and more companies are installing Red Hat servers every day, and with that, there's an increasing need for Red Hat skills. That is why I wrote this book.

This book is a complete guide that contains real-world examples of how Red Hat Enterprise Linux should be administered. It targets a broad audience of both beginning and advanced Red Hat Enterprise Linux administrators who need a reference guide to learn how to perform complicated tasks.

This book was also written as a study guide, which is why there are many exercises included in the book. Within each chapter, you'll find step-by-step exercises that lead you through specific procedures. Also, in Appendix A at the end of the book, you'll find lab exercises that help you wrap up everything you've learned in the chapter.

Red Hat offers two certifications that are relevant for system administrators: Red Hat Certified System Administrator (RHCSA) and Red Hat Certified Engineer (RHCE). This book does not prepare for either the Red Hat RHCSA or RHCE exams, but it does cover most of the objectives of both exams. For those interested in taking RHCSA and RHCE exams, it is recommended that you also attend a Red Hat training course, where the learner risks meeting the author of this book who has been a Red Hat Certified Instructor for many years now.

Who Should Read This Book?

This book was written for Red Hat administrators. The book is for beginning administrators as well as those who already have a couple of years of experience working with Red Hat systems. For the advanced administrators, it is written as a reference guide that helps them set up services such as web servers, DNS and DHCP, clustering, and more. It also contains advanced information, such as a long chapter on performance optimization.

What You Need

To work with this book, you need a dedicated computer on which you can install Red Hat Enterprise Linux. If this is not feasible, a virtual machine can be used as an alternative, however this is absolutely not recommended, as you won't be able to do all the exercises on virtualization. To install Red Hat Enterprise Linux and use it as a host for KVM virtualization, make sure that your computer meets the following minimum criteria:

- 64-bit CPU with support for virtualization.
- At least 2GB of RAM is recommended. (It will probably work with 1GB, but this is not recommended.)

- A DVD drive.
- A hard disk that is completely available and at least 40GB in size.
- A network card and connection to a network switch.

What Is Covered in This Book?

Red Hat Linux Enterprise 6 Administration is organized to provide the knowledge that you'll need to administer Red Hat Enterprise Linux 6. It includes the following chapters:

Part I: Getting Familiar with Red Hat Enterprise Linux

Chapter 1, "Getting Started with Red Hat Enterprise Linux"   This chapter introduces Red Hat Enterprise Linux and explains its particulars. You'll also learn about the value added by this commercial Linux distribution as compared to free Linux distributions. In the second part of this chapter, you'll learn how to install Red Hat Enterprise Linux. You'll also get a quick introduction to the workings of the graphical user interface.

Chapter 2, "Finding Your Way on the Command Line"   This chapter introduces you to working on the command line, the most important interface you'll use to manage your Red Hat Enterprise Linux server.

Part II: Administering Red Hat Enterprise Linux

Chapter 3, "Performing Daily System Administration Tasks"   In this chapter, you'll learn about some common system administration tasks. This includes mounting and unmounting file systems, setting up and managing a printing environment, and scheduling jobs with cron. You'll also learn how to do process administration and make backups.

Chapter 4, "Managing Software"   In this chapter, you'll learn how to install software. You'll also read how to manage software, which includes querying software packages to find out everything you need to know about installed software. You'll also read how to set up the repositories that you'll need for an easy way to install and manage software.

Chapter 5, "Configuring and Managing Storage"   This chapter teaches you how to set up storage. It includes information about managing partitions, logical volumes, and encrypted volumes. You'll also learn how to set up automatic mounting of volumes through fstab and how to create and manage swap space.

Chapter 6, "Connecting to the Network"   Here you'll learn how to connect your server to the network. The chapter addresses setting up the network interface, both from the command line and from the configuration files. You'll set up normal network connections, and you will also learn how to create a bonded network interface. Finally, you'll learn how to test your network using common utilities such as ping and dig.

Part III: Securing Red Hat Enterprise Linux

Chapter 7, "Working with Users, Groups, and Permissions"   To manage who can do what on your system, you'll need to create users and put them in groups. In this chapter, you'll learn how to do that and how to add users to primary and secondary groups. You'll also learn how to work with basic and advanced permissions and set up access control lists.

Chapter 8, "Understanding and Configuring SELinux"   This chapter teaches you how to make your Red Hat Enterprise Linux server really secure using SELinux. You'll learn about the different modes that are available and how to set file system context labels and Booleans to tune SELinux exactly to your needs.

Chapter 9, "Working with KVM Virtualization"   Red Hat Enterprise Linux offers virtualization capabilities by default. In this chapter, you'll learn how to set these up using KVM virtualization. You'll learn what your server needs to be a KVM host, and you'll read how to create and manage virtual machines.

Chapter 10, "Securing Your Server with iptables"   iptables is a kernel-provided firewall, which blocks or allows access to services configured to listen at specific ports. In this chapter, you'll learn how to set up the iptables firewall from the command line.

Chapter 11, "Setting Up Cryptographic Services"   In this chapter, you'll learn how to set up cryptographic services on Red Hat Enterprise Linux. You'll learn how to configure SSL certificates and have them signed by a certificate authority. You'll also learn how to use GPG for file and email encryption and security.

Part IV: Networking Red Hat Enterprise Linux

Chapter 12, "Configuring OpenLDAP"   If you really need to manage more than just a few users, using a directory service such as OpenLDAP can be handy. In this chapter, you'll learn how to set up OpenLDAP on your server. You'll also learn how to add user objects to the OpenLDAP server and how to configure your server to authenticate on OpenLDAP.

Chapter 13, "Configuring Your Server for File Sharing"   This chapter teaches you how to set up your server for file sharing. You'll learn about common file sharing solutions, such as FTP, NFS, and Samba. You'll also learn how to connect to servers offering these services from Red Hat Enterprise Linux.

Chapter 14, "Configuring DNS and DHCP"   In this chapter, you'll read how to set up a Dynamic Host Configuration Protocol (DHCP) server to automate providing computers in your network with IP addresses and related information. You'll also learn how to set up Domain Name System (DNS) on your servers, configuring them as primary and secondary servers, as well as cache-only servers.

Chapter 15, "Setting Up a Mail Server"   Postfix is the default mail server on Red Hat Enterprise Linux. In this chapter, you'll learn how to set up Postfix to send and receive email on your server. You'll also learn how to set up Dovecot to make email accessible for clients using POP or IMAP.

Chapter 16, "Configuring Apache on Red Hat Enterprise Linux"   In this chapter, you'll learn how to set up Apache on your server. You'll learn how to configure basic hosts, virtual hosts, and SSL secured hosts. The chapter also teaches you how to set up file-based or LDAP-based user authentication.

Part V: Advanced Red Hat Enterprise Linux Configuration

Chapter 17, "Monitoring and Optimizing Performance"   For your server to function properly, it is important that it performs well. In this chapter, you'll learn how to analyze server performance and how to fix it if there are problems. You'll also read some hints about setting up the server in a way that minimizes the chance of having performance-related problems.

Chapter 18, "Introducing Bash Shell Scripting"   Every Linux administrator should at least know the basics of shell scripting. This chapter teaches you how it works. You'll learn how to set up a shell script and how to use common shell scripting structures to handle jobs in the most ideal manner.

Chapter 19, "Understanding and Troubleshooting the Boot Procedure"   Many tasks are executed sequentially when your server boots. In this chapter, you'll learn about everything that happens during server startup, including GRUB configuration and the way Upstart is used. You'll also learn how to troubleshoot common issues that you may encounter while booting your server.

Chapter 20, "Introducing High-Availability Clustering"   In a mission-critical environment, the Red Hat High Availability add-on can be a valuable addition to your datacenter. In this chapter, you'll learn how to design and set up high availability on Red Hat Enterprise Linux.

Chapter 21, "Setting Up an Installation Server"   In a datacenter environment, you don't want to set up every server manually. This is why it makes sense to set up an installation server. This chapter teaches you how to automate the installation of Red Hat Enterprise Linux completely. It includes setting up a network installation server and configuring a TFTP server that hands out boot images to clients that perform a PXE boot. You'll also learn how to create a kickstart configuration file, which passes all parameters that are to be used for the installation.

Glossary   This contains definitions of the relevant vocabulary terms in this book.

How to Contact the Author

If you want to provide feedback about the contents of this book or if you're seeking a helping hand in setting up an environment or fixing problems, you can contact me directly. The easiest way to get in touch with me is by sending an email to mail@sandervanvugt.nl. You can also visit my website at www.sandervanvugt.com. If you're interested in the person behind the book, you're also more than welcome to visit my hobby site at www.sandervanvugt.org.

Sybex strives to keep you supplied with the latest tools and information you need for your work. Please check their website at www.sybex.com, where we'll post additional content and updates that supplement this book if the need arises. Enter search terms in the Search box (or type the book's ISBN: 978-1-118-30129-6), and click Go to get to the book's update page.

Getting Familiar with Red Hat Enterprise Linux

Chapter 1

Getting Started with Red Hat Enterprise Linux

TOPICS COVERED IN THIS CHAPTER:

- ✓ Linux, Open Source, and Red Hat
- ✓ Red Hat Enterprise Linux and Related Products
- ✓ Installing Red Hat Enterprise Linux Server
- ✓ Exploring the GNOME User Interface

Red Hat Enterprise Linux is in use at most Fortune 500 companies, and it takes care of mission-critical tasks in many of them. This chapter introduces Red Hat Enterprise Linux. It begins with a brief history, where you'll learn about Linux in general and the role of Red Hat in the Linux story. Following that, it provides an overview of Red Hat Enterprise Linux (RHEL) and its related products. Finally, you'll learn how to install RHEL so that you can start building your RHEL skills.

Linux, Open Source, and Red Hat

If you want to work with Red Hat, it helps to understand a little bit about its background. In this introduction, you'll learn about the rise of UNIX, the Linux kernel and open source, and the founding of Red Hat.

Origins of Linux

The late 1960s and early 1970s were the dawn of the modern computing era. It was the period of proprietary stacks, where a vendor would build a "closed" computer system and create the operating software to run on it. Computers were extremely expensive and rare among businesses. In that period, scientists were still looking for the best way to operate a computer, and that included developing the best programming language. It was normal for computer programmers to address the hardware directly, using very complex assembly programming languages.

An important step forward was the development of the general-purpose programming language C by Dennis Richie at Bell Telephone Laboratories in 1969. This language was developed for use with the UNIX operating system.

The UNIX operating system was the first operating system where people from different companies tried to work together to build instead of competing with each other, keeping their efforts secret. This spirit brought UNIX to scientific, government, and higher-education institutions. There it also became the basis for the rise of another phenomenon, the Internet Protocol (IP) and the Internet. One of the huge contributors to the success of UNIX was the spirit of openness of the operating system. Everyone could contribute to it, and the specifications were freely available to anyone.

Because of the huge success of UNIX, companies started claiming parts of this operating system in the 1970s. They succeeded fairly well, and that was the beginning of the development of different flavors of UNIX, such as BSD, Sun Solaris, and HP AIX. Instead of working together, these UNIX flavors worked beside one another, with each sponsoring organization trying to develop the best version for a specific solution.

As a reaction to the closing of UNIX, Richard Stallman of MIT announced in 1984 the GNU operating system project. The goal of this project was to develop "a sufficient body of free software [...] to get along without any software that is not free."

During the 1980s, many common Unix commands, tools, and applications were developed until, in 1991, the last gap was filled in with the launch of the Linux kernel by a student at the University of Helsinki in Finland, Linus Torvalds. The interesting fact about the Linux kernel is that it was never developed to be part of the GNU project. Rather, it was an independent initiative. Torvalds just needed a license to ensure that the Linux kernel would be free software forever, and he chose to use the GNU General Public License (GPL) for this purpose. The GPL is a *copyleft license*, which means that derived works can be distributed only under the same license terms. Using GPL made it possible to publish open source software where others could freely add to or modify lines of code.

Torvalds also made an announcement on Usenet, a very popular news network that was used to communicate information about certain projects in the early 1990s. In his Usenet message, Torvalds asked others to join him working on the Linux kernel, a challenge that was very soon taken up by many programmers around the world.

Distributions

With the adoption of the Linux kernel, finally everything that was needed to create a complete operating system was in place. There were many GNU utilities to choose from, and those tools, together with a kernel, made a complete operating system. The only thing enthusiastic users still needed to do was to gather this software, compile it from source code, and install the working parts on a computer. Because this was a rather complicated task, some initiatives started soon to provide ready-to-install Linux distributions. Among the first was MCC Interim Linux, a distribution made available for public download in February 1992, shortly after the release of the Linux kernel itself. In 1993, Patrick Volkerding released a distribution called Slackware, a distribution that could be downloaded to floppy disk images in the early days. It is still available and actively being developed today.

In 1993, Marc Ewing and Bob Young founded Red Hat, the first Linux distributor operating as a business. Since then, Red Hat has acquired other companies to integrate specific Linux-related technologies.

Red Hat went public in 1999, thus becoming the first Linux-based company on Wall Street. Because of the publicity stemming from its IPO, Red Hat and Linux received great exposure, and many companies started using it for their enterprise IT environments. It was initially used for applications, such as intranet web servers running Apache software. Soon Linux was also used for core financial applications.

Today Linux in general and Red Hat Linux in particular is at the heart of the IT organization in many companies. Large parts of the Internet operate on Linux, using popular applications such as the Apache web server or the Squid proxy server. Stock exchanges use Linux in their real-time calculation systems, and large Linux servers are running essential business applications on top of Oracle and SAP. Linux has largely replaced UNIX, and Red Hat is a leading force in Linux.

One reason why Red Hat has been so successful since the beginning is the level of support the company provides. Red Hat offers three types of support, and this gives companies the confidence they need to run vital business applications on Linux.

The three types of Linux support provided by Red Hat are as follows:

Hardware Support   Red Hat has agreements with every major server hardware vendor to make sure that whatever server a customer buys, the hardware vendor will assist them in fixing hardware issues, when Red Hat is installed on it.

Software Support   Red Hat has agreements with every major enterprise software vendor to make sure that their software runs properly on top of the Red Hat Linux operating system and that the enterprise software is also guaranteed to run on Red Hat Linux by the vendor of the operating system.

Hands-on Support   This means that if a customer is experiencing problems accomplishing tasks with Red Hat software, the Red Hat Global Support organization is there to help them by fixing bugs and providing technical assistance.

It is also important to realize that Red Hat is doing much more than just gathering the software pieces and putting them together on the installation media. Red Hat employs hundreds of developers who work on developing new solutions that will run on Red Hat Enterprise Linux in the near future.

Fedora

Even as Red Hat is actively developing software to be part of Red Hat Linux, it still is largely involved in the open source community. The most important approach to do this is by sponsoring the Fedora project. Fedora is a freely available Linux distribution that is completely comprised of open source software, and Red Hat is providing the funds and people to tackle this project. Both Red Hat and Fedora are free of charge; with Red Hat you pay only for updates and support.

Fedora is used as a development platform for the latest and greatest version of Linux, which is provided free of charge for users who are interested. As such, Fedora can be used as a test platform for features that will eventually be included in Red Hat Enterprise Linux. If you want to know what will be included in future versions of Red Hat Linux, Fedora is the best place to look. Also, Fedora makes an excellent choice to install on your personal computer, because it offers all the functions you would expect from a modern operating system—even some functions that are of interest only to home users.

Red Hat Enterprise Linux and Related Products

Red Hat offers several products, of which Red Hat Enterprise Linux and JBoss are the most important solutions. There are other offerings in the product catalog as well. In the following sections, you can read about these products and their typical application.

Red Hat Enterprise Linux Server Edition

The core of the Red Hat offering is Red Hat Enterprise Linux. This is the basis for two editions: a server edition and a workstation edition. The RHEL Server edition is the highly successful Red Hat product that is used in companies around the globe.

 At the time of this writing, the current RHEL release is version 6.2.

With the Red Hat Enterprise Linux Server edition, there is a major new release about every three to four years. In between the major updates, there are minor ones, represented by the number after the dot in the version number. Apart from these releases, Red Hat provides patches to fix bugs and to apply security updates. Typically, these patches are applied by using the Red Hat Network, a certified collection of repositories where Red Hat makes patches available after verifying them.

To download and install repositories from the Red Hat Network (RHN), a current subscription is required. Without a current subscription, you can still run RHEL, but no updates will be installed through RHN. As an alternative to connecting each server directly to RHN, Red Hat provides a solution called Satellite. Satellite works as a proxy to RHN, and just the Satellite server is configured to fetch updates from RHN, after which the Red Hat nodes in the network connect to Satellite to access their updates. Be aware that there is also a product called RHN Proxy, which is a real caching proxy, whereas Satellite is a versioning and deployment tool.

Red Hat Enterprise Linux for Free

If you want updates and support, you have to pay for Red Hat Enterprise Linux, so how come people have to buy licenses for GPL software that is supposed to be available for free? Well, the fact is that the sources of all the software in RHEL are indeed available for free. As with any other Linux vendor, Red Hat provides source code for the software in RHEL. What customers typically buy, however, is a subscription to the compiled version of the software that is in RHEL. In the compiled version, the Red Hat logo is included.

This is more than just a logo; it's the guarantee of quality that customers expect from the leader in Linux software.

Still, the fact is that the sources of the software contained in RHEL are available for free. Some Linux distributions have used these sources to create their own distributions. The two most important distributions are CentOS (short for Community Enterprise Operating System) and Scientific Linux. Because these distributions are built upon Red Hat Linux with the Red Hat logo removed, the software is basically the same. However, small binary differences do exist, such as the integration of the software with RHN. The most important difference, however, is that these distributions don't offer the same level of support as in in RHEL. So, you're better off going for the real thing.

You can download a free version of RHEL with 30 days of access to RHN at www.redhat.com. Alternatively, you can download CentOS at www.centos.org or Scientific Linux at www.scientificlinux.org.

Red Hat Enterprise Linux Workstation Edition

The other product that falls under Red Hat Enterprise Linux is the Workstation edition. This solution is based on the same code as RHEL Server. Also, the same license conditions apply for RHEL Workstation as for RHEL Server, and you need a current subscription to access and install updates from RHN. To date, Red Hat Linux Workstation hasn't experienced the same level of success as Red Hat Linux Enterprise Server.

Red Hat Add-Ons

RHEL includes everything most people need to run a Linux server. Some components require an extra effort, though, and for that reason they are offered as add-ons in RHEL. The two most significant kinds of add-on are the Enterprise File System (XFS) and Red Hat Cluster Services.

Enterprise File System (XFS)   The Enterprise File System offers full scalability for large environments where many files or very large files have to be handled on large file systems. Even though ext4, the default file system in Red Hat Enterprise Linux, has been optimized significantly over time, it still doesn't fit well in environments that have very specific storage needs, such as the need to stream multimedia files or to handle hundreds of thousands of files per day.

Red Hat Cluster Services (RHCS)   RHCS offers high-availability clustering to vital services in the network. In an RHCS cluster, you run specialized cluster software on multiple nodes that are involved in the cluster, and that software monitors the availability of vital services. If anything goes down with such a service, Red Hat Cluster Services takes over and makes sure that the service is launched on another node.

Red Hat Directory Server

In a corporate environment where many user accounts have to be managed, it doesn't make sense to manage these accounts in stand-alone databases on individual servers. One solution is to have servers handle their authentication on external directory servers. An example of this approach is to connect RHEL to Microsoft Active Directory, an approach that is used frequently by many Red Hat customers. Another approach is to use Red Hat Directory Server, a dedicated LDAP directory service that can be used to store and manage corporate identities.

Red Hat Enterprise Virtualization

Red Hat Enterprise Virtualization (RHEV) provides a virtualization platform that can be compared with other solutions, such as VMware vSphere. In RHEV, several dedicated servers running the KVM hypervisor are managed through RHEV-M, the management server for the virtual environment. In the RHEV infrastructure, fully installed RHEL servers as well as dedicated on-iron hypervisors (the RHEV-H) can be used. A major reason why companies around the world are using RHEV is because it offers the same functionality as VMware vSphere, but for a fraction of the price.

JBoss Enterprise Middleware

JBoss Enterprise Middleware is an application layer that can be installed on top of any operating system, including RHEL. The platform is used to build custom-made applications which can offer their services to perform any tasks you can think of. JBoss is an open platform, and therefore its adoption level is high. Red Hat has had huge success selling JBoss solutions on top of Red Hat Enterprise Linux.

Red Hat Cloud

Red Hat Cloud is the solution where everything comes together. In the lower layers of the cloud infrastructure, Red Hat can offer Platform as a Service services that are based on RHEV or any other virtualization platform. At the PaaS layer, Red Hat Cloud helps deploy virtual machines on demand easily. In the higher layers of the cloud, combined with JBoss Enterprise Middleware, Red Hat Cloud delivers software as a service, thus helping customers build a complete cloud infrastructure on top of Red Hat software.

Installing Red Hat Enterprise Linux Server

There is a version of RHEL Server for almost any hardware platform. That means you can install it on a mainframe computer, a mid-range system, or PC-based server hardware using a 64- or 32-bit architecture. Currently, the 64-bit version of Red Hat Enterprise Linux is the most used version, and that is why, in this chapter, you can read about how to install this software version on your computer. The exact version you need is Red Hat Enterprise Linux Server for 64-bit x86_64. If you don't have the software yet, you can download a free evaluation copy at www.redhat.com.

The ideal installation is on server-grade hardware. However, you don't have to buy actual server hardware if you just want to learn how to work with Red Hat Enterprise Linux. Basically, any PC will do as long as it meets the following minimum requirements:

- A CPU capable of handling 64-bit instructions
- 1GB of RAM
- 20GB of available hard disk space
- A DVD drive
- A network card

Make sure your computer meets these minimum requirements. To work your way through the exercises in this book, I'll assume you have a computer or virtual machine that meets them.

You can run Red Hat Enterprise Linux with less than this, but if you do, you'll miss certain functionality. For instance, you can install RHEL on a machine that has 512MB of RAM, but you'll lose the graphical user interface. You could also install RHEL on a 32-bit CPU or on a VMware or VirtualBox virtual machine, but within these environments you cannot configure KVM virtualization. Because this book includes some exercises that work directly on the hard disk of your computer and you don't want to risk destroying all of your data by accident, it is strongly recommended that you do not install a dual-boot RHEL and other OS configuration.

If you don't have a dedicated computer on which to install RHEL, a virtual machine is the second-best choice. RHEL can be installed in most virtual environments. If you want to run it on your own computer, VMware Workstation (fee-based software) or VMware Player (free software but with fewer options) works fine. You can download this software from www.vmware.com. Alternatively, you can use VirtualBox, a free virtualization solution provided by Oracle. You can download it from www.virtualbox.org.

You'll be working with Red Hat Enterprise Linux in a graphical environment in this book. RHEL offers some very good graphical tools, and for now, you'll need a graphical environment to run them. A typical Linux server that provides services in a datacenter does not offer a graphical environment. Rather, it runs in console mode. That is because servers in a datacenter normally are accessed only remotely. The administrator of such a server can still use graphical tools with it but will start them over an SSH session, accessing the server remotely. Later in this book, you will learn how to configure such an environment.

In Exercise 1.1, you will install Red Hat Linux on your computer.

Installing Linux on Your Machine

This procedure describes how to install Red Hat Enterprise Linux on your computer. This is an important exercise, because you will use it to set up the demo system that you'll use throughout this book. It is important that you perform the steps exactly as described here, to match the descriptions in later exercises in this book.

To perform this exercise successfully, you'll need to install on a physical computer that meets the following requirements:

- An entire computer that can be dedicated to using Red Hat Enterprise Linux

- A minimum of 1GB of RAM (2GB is recommended)

- A dedicated hard disk of 40GB or more

- A DVD drive

- A network card

Apart from these requirements, other requirements relate to KVM virtualization as well. The most important of these is that the CPU on your computer needs virtualization support. If you can enable virtualization from the computer BIOS, you are probably OK. Read Chapter 6, "Connecting to the Network," for more details about the requirements for virtualization.

1. Put the RHEL 6 installation disc in the optical drive of your computer, and boot from the installation disc. If the DVD drive is not in the default boot order on your computer, you'll have to go into the setup and instruct your computer to boot from the optical drive. After booting from the installation DVD successfully, you'll see the Welcome to Red Hat Enterprise Linux screen.

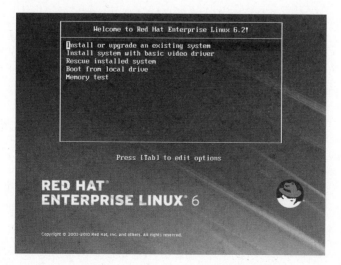

2. From the graphical installation screen, select Install Or Upgrade An Existing System. In case you're experiencing problems with the graphical display, you can choose to install using the basic video driver. However, in most cases that isn't necessary. The other options are for troubleshooting purposes only and will be discussed in later chapters in this book.

3. After beginning the installation procedure, a Linux kernel is started, and the hardware is detected. This normally takes about a minute.

4. Once the Linux kernel has been loaded, you will see a nongraphical screen that tells you that a disc was found. (Nongraphical menus like the one in the following image are referred to as *ncurses interfaces*. *Ncurses* refers to the programming library that was used to create the interface.)

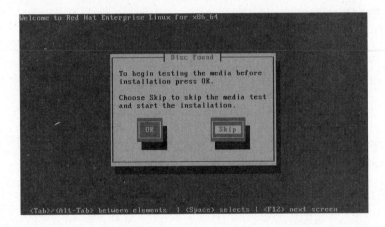

From this screen, you can start a check of the integrity of the installation media. Don't do this by default; the media check can easily take 10 minutes or more! Press the Tab key once to navigate to the Skip button, and press Enter to proceed to the next step.

5. If the graphical hardware in your computer is supported, you'll next see a graphical screen with only a Next button on it. Click this button to continue. If you don't see the graphical screen at this point, restart the installation procedure by rebooting your computer from the installation disc. From the menu, select Install System With Basic Video Driver.

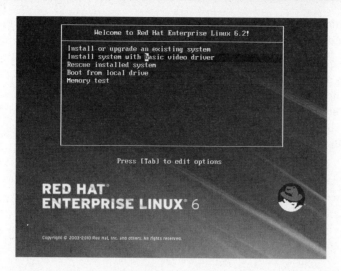

6. On the next screen, you can select the language you want to use during the installation process. This is just the installation language. At the end of the installation, you'll be offered another option to select the language you want to use on your Red Hat server. Many languages are supported; in this book I'm using English.

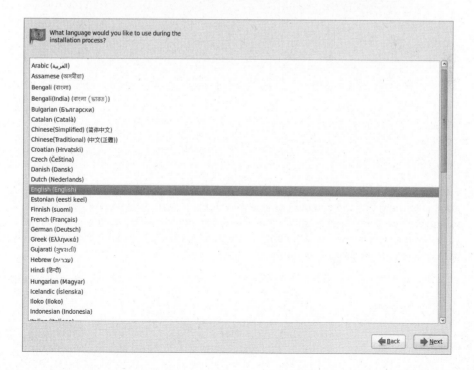

EXERCISE 1.1 *(continued)*

7. After selecting the installation language, on the next screen, select the appropriate keyboard layout, and then click Next to continue.

8. Once you've selected the keyboard layout you want to use, you need to select the storage devices with which you are working. To install on a local hard drive in your computer, select Basic Storage Devices. If you're installing RHEL in an enterprise environment and want to write all files to a SAN device, you should select the Specialized Storage Devices option. If you're unsure about what to do, select Basic Storage Devices and click Next to proceed.

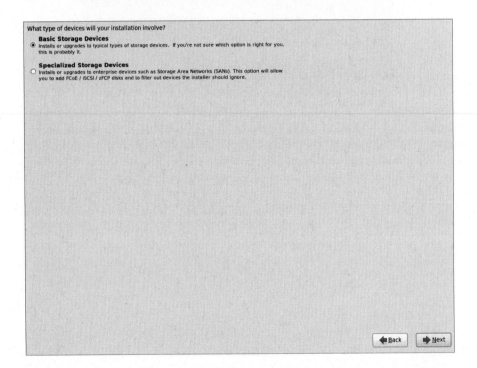

9. After you have selected the storage device to be used, the installation program may issue a warning that the selected device may contain data. This warning is displayed to prevent you from deleting all the data on the selected disk by accident. If you're sure that the installer can use the entire selected hard disk, click Yes, and discard any data before clicking Next to continue.

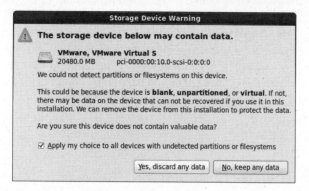

10. On the next screen, you can enter the hostname you want to use on the computer. Also on this screen is the Configure Network button, which you'll use to change the current network settings for the server. Start by entering the hostname you want to use. Typically, this is a fully qualified domain name that includes the DNS suffix. If you don't have a DNS domain in which to install the server, you can use example.com. This name is available for test environments, and it won't be visible to others on the Internet.

11. After setting the hostname, you have to click the Configure Network button on the same screen to change the network settings. If you don't do this, your server will be configured to get the network configuration from a DHCP server. There's nothing wrong with that if you're installing a personal desktop where it doesn't matter if the IP address it is using changes, but for servers in general, it's better to work with a fixed IP address. To set this fixed address, click Configure Network now.

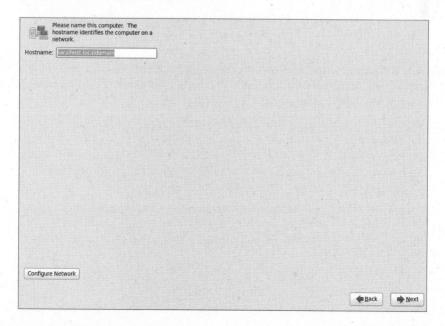

12. You'll see the Network Connections window. This window comes from the NetworkManager tool, and it allows you to set and change all different kinds of network connections. In this window, select the Wired tab and, on that tab, click the System eth0 network card. Notice that depending on the hardware you are using, a different name may be used. Next click Edit to change its properties.

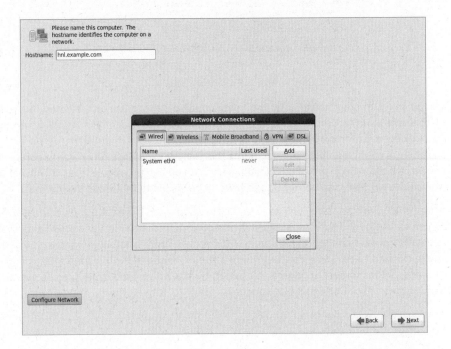

13. You'll now see the properties of the eth0 network card. First make sure that the option Connect Automatically is selected. If it isn't, your network card won't be activated when you boot the server.

Editing System eth0

Connection name: | System eth0
☑ Connect automatically

Wired | 802.1x Security | IPv4 Settings | IPv6 Settings

Method: | Manual

Addresses

Address	Netmask	Gateway	
192.168.1.99	24	192.168.1.1	Add
			Delete

DNS servers: | 192.168.1.1

Search domains: |

DHCP client ID: |

☑ Require IPv4 addressing for this connection to complete

Routes...

☑ Available to all users   Cancel   Apply...

14. Select the IPv4 Settings tab, and in the Method drop-down list, select Manual.

15. Click Add to enter the IP address you want to use. You need at least an IP address and a netmask. Make sure that the address and netmask you're using here do not conflict with anything else that is in use on the network to which you are connecting. In this book I'll assume your server uses the IP address 192.168.0.70. If you want to communicate with other computers and the Internet, you'll have to enter the address of the gateway and the address of at least one DNS server. You need to consult the documentation of the network to which you're connecting to find out which addresses to use here. For the moment, you don't have to enter anything here.

16. After entering the required parameters, click Apply to save and apply these settings.

17. Click Close to close the NetworkManager window. Back on the main screen where you set the hostname, click Next to continue.

18. At this point, you'll configure the time settings for your server. The easiest way to do this is just to click the city nearest to your location on the world map that is displayed. Alternatively, you can choose the city that is nearest to you from the drop-down list.

19. You'll also need to specify whether your computer is using UTC for its internal clock. UTC is Coordinated Universal Time, a time standard by which the world regulates clocks and time. It is one of several successors to Greenwich Mean Time, without Daylight Saving Time settings. Most servers have their hardware clocks set to UTC, but most PCs don't. If the hardware clock is set to UTC, the server uses the time zone settings to calculate the local software time. If your computer has its hardware clock set to UTC, select the option System Clock Uses UTC, and click Next to continue. If not, deselect this option and proceed with the installation.

20. Next you'll specify the password that is to be used by the user root. The root account is used for system administration tasks, and its possibilities are nearly unlimited. Therefore, you should set the root password to something that's not easy for possible intruders to guess.

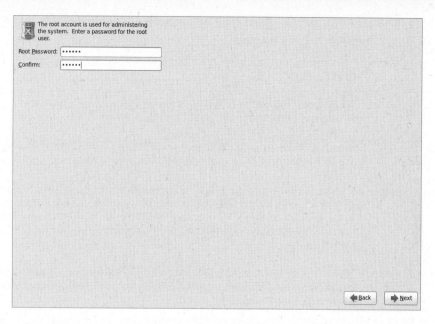

21. The next screen you'll see is used to specify how you'd like to use the storage devices on which you'll install Red Hat Enterprise Linux. If you want to go for the easiest solution, select Use All Space. This will remove everything currently installed on the selected hard disk (which typically isn't a bad idea anyway). Table 1.1 gives an overview of all the available options.

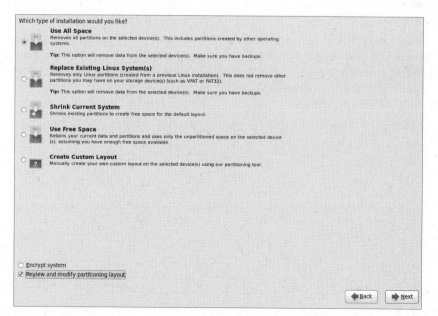

EXERCISE 1.1 *(continued)*

TABLE 1.1:   Available storage options

Option	Description
Use All Space	Wipes everything that is currently on your computer's hard disk to use all available disk space. This is typically the best option for a server.
Replace Existing Linux System(s)	Removes existing Linux systems only if found. This option doesn't touch Windows or other partitions if they exist on your computer.
Shrink Current System	Tries to shrink existing partitions so that free space is made available to install Linux. Using this option typically results in a dual-boot computer. Using a dual-boot computer is a bad idea in general, and more specifically, this option often has problems shrinking NTFS partitions. Don't use it.
Use Free Space	Use this option to install Linux in the free, unpartitioned disk space on your computer. This option assumes that you've used external tools to make disk space available.
Create Custom Layout	The most difficult but also the most flexible option available. Using this option assumes you'll manually create all the partitions and logical volumes that you want to use on your computer.

22. To make sure you're using a setup that allows you to do all exercises that come later in this book, you'll need to select the Create Custom Layout option.

23. After selecting the Create Custom Layout option, click Next to continue. You'll now see a window in which your hard drive is shown with a name like sda or hda on old IDE-based computers below it. Under that appears one more item with the name Free that indicates all available disk space.

24. To configure your hard disk, you first have to create two partitions. Click Create to start the Create Storage interface. For the first partition, you'll select the Standard Partition option. Select this option, and click Create.

EXERCISE 1.1 *(continued)*

25. You'll now see the Add Partition interface in which you have to specify the proper-
    ties of the partitions you want to create. The first partition is a rather small one that is
    used for booting only. Make sure to use the following properties:

    ```
    Mount Point: /boot
    File System Type: ext4
    Size: 200 MB
    Additional Size Options: Fixed size
    Force to be a primary partition
    ```

26. After creating the boot partition, you'll need to create a partition that's going to be
    used as an LVM physical volume. From the main partitioning screen, click Create, and
    in the Create Storage options box, select LVM Physical Volume. Next click Create.

EXERCISE 1.1 *(continued)*

 At this point, the purpose is to get you up and running as fast as possible. Therefore, you'll read how to configure your disk, without overwhelming you with too many details on exactly what it is you're doing. In Chapter 5, "Configuring and Managing Storage," you'll read more about partitions and logical volumes and what exactly they are.

27. In the Add Partition window, you now have to enter the properties of the physical volume you've just created. Use the following values:

```
File System Type: Physical Volume (LVM)
Size: 40000
Additional Size Options: Fixed size
Force to be a primary partition
```

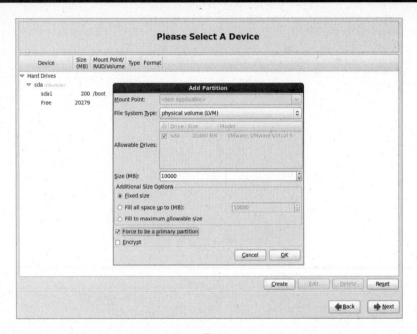

28. At this point, you have created an LVM physical volume, but you can't do anything useful with it yet. You now need to create a volume group on top of it. To do this, click Create, and under the Create LVM option, select LVM Volume Group. Next click Create.

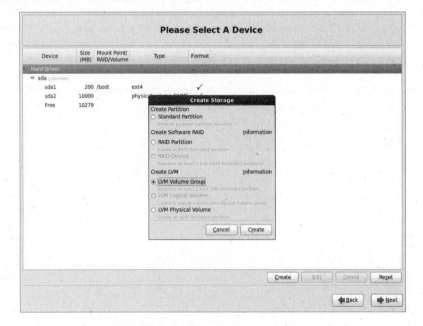

EXERCISE 1.1 *(continued)*

29. You'll now see the properties of the LVM volume group. The only relevant parameter is the name, which is set to vg_yourhostname, which is perfectly fine. Change nothing, and click Add to add logical volumes in the volume group. The logical volumes are what you're going to put your files on, and you'll need three of them:

    - One 20GB volume that contains the root directory

    - One 512MB volume to use for a swap

    - One 2GB volume that contains the /var directory

    To start creating the logical volumes, click Add.

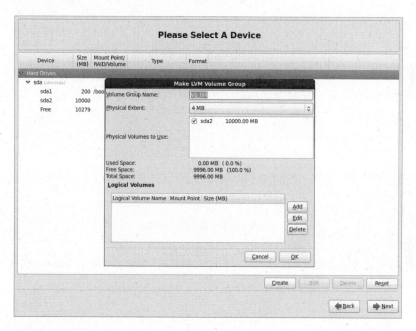

30. You need to add three logical volumes using the following parameters:

```
The root volume:
Mount Point: /
File System Type: Ext4
Logical Volume Name: root
Size: 20000
The swap volume:
File System Type: swap
Logical Volume Name: swap
Size: 512
The var volume:
Mount Point: /var
File System Type: Ext4
Logical Volume Name: var
Size: 2000
```

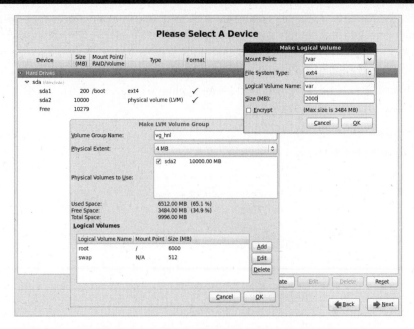

Once you've finished configuring storage devices on your computer, the disk layout should look like this:

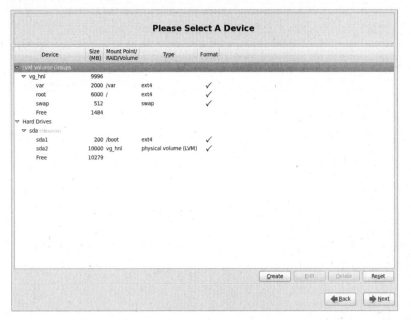

31. Now click Next to continue. In the Format Warning window that you now see, click Format to start the formatting process. Next, confirm that you really want to do this by selecting the Write Changes To Disk option.

32. At this point, the partitions and logical volumes have been created, and you're ready to continue with the installation procedure. On the following screen, the installer asks what you want to do with the boot loader. Select the default option, which installs it on the master boot record of your primary hard drive, and click Next.

33. You now have to specify what type of installation you want to perform. The only thing that counts at this moment is that you'll need to select the Desktop option. If you don't, you'll end up with a server that, by default, doesn't have a graphical environment, and that is hard to fix if you're just taking your first steps into the world of Red Hat Enterprise Linux. After selecting the Desktop option, click Next to continue.

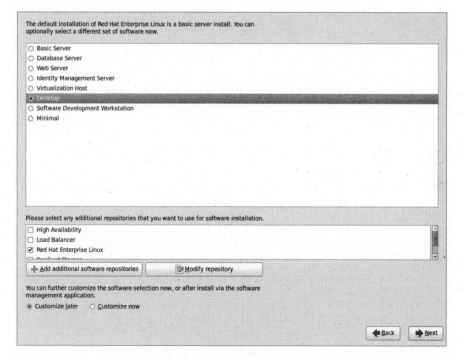

34. The installation process is now started, and the files will be copied to your computer. This will take about 10 minutes on an average system, so it's now time to have a cup of coffee.

35. Once the installation has completed, you'll see the Congratulations message telling you that your server is ready. On this screen, click Reboot to stop the installation program and start your server.

EXERCISE 1.1 *(continued)*

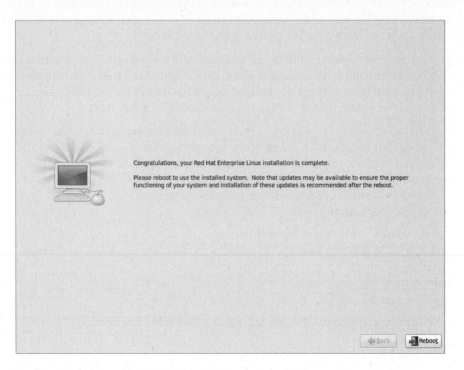

Congratulations, your Red Hat Enterprise Linux installation is complete.

Please reboot to use the installed system. Note that updates may be available to ensure the proper functioning of your system and installation of these updates is recommended after the reboot.

36. Once the server has successfully started for the first time, you'll see the Welcome screen that guides you through the remainder of the installation procedure. From this screen, click Forward. Next you'll see the License Information screen in which you have to agree to the license agreement. After doing so, click Forward to proceed.

39. Now you'll see the Set Up Software Updates screen where you can connect to the Red Hat Network.

   a. If you have credentials for Red Hat Network, you can connect now.

   b. If you don't and just want to install a system that cannot download patches and updates from Red Hat Network, select the No, I Prefer To Register At A Later Time option, and click Forward.

   In this book, RHN access is not required, so select No, I Prefer To Register At A Later Time. You'll see a window informing you about all the good things you'll miss without RHN. In this window, click No Thanks, I'll Connect Later to confirm your selection. Now click Forward once more to proceed to the next step.

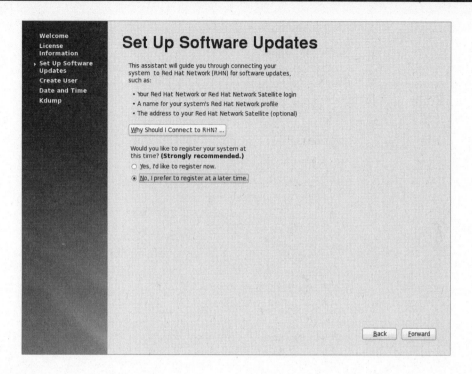

If you don't connect your server to RHN, you cannot update it. This means it's not a good idea to use this server as a production system and provide services to external users; you'll be vulnerable if you do. If you need to configure a Red Hat system that does provide public services, you have to purchase a subscription to Red Hat Enterprise Linux. If you don't want to do that, use Scientific Linux or CentOS instead.

40. At this point, you'll need to create a user account. In this book, we'll create the user "student," with the full name "student" and the password "redhat" (all lowercase). You can safely ignore the message that informs you that you've selected a weak password.

EXERCISE 1.1 *(continued)*

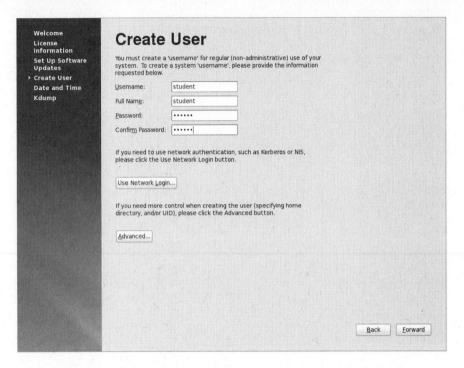

41. During the installation, you already indicated your time zone and whether your server is using UTC on the hardware clock. At this point, you need to finalize the Date And Time settings.

    a. Specify the current time.

    b. Indicate whether you want to synchronize the date and time over the network.

    c. Because time is an essential factor for the functioning of many services on your server, it is a very good idea to synchronize time with an NTP time server on the Internet. Therefore, on the Date And Time screen, select Synchronize Date And Time Over The Network. This will show a list containing three NTP servers on the Internet. In many cases, it doesn't really matter which NTP servers you're using, as long as you're using some NTP servers, so you can leave the servers in this list.

d. Open Advanced Options, and select the Speed Up Initial Synchronization and Use Local Time Source options. The first option makes sure that, if a difference is detected between your server and the NTP time server it is synchronizing with, your server will synchronize its time as fast as it can. If you are installing your server in a VMware virtual environment, it is important to use this option to prevent problems in time synchronization. The second option tells your server to use the local hardware clock in your server as a backup option. It is a good idea to enable this option on all servers in your network, because it creates a backup in case the connection to the Internet is lost for a long period of time.

e. After enabling the advanced options, click Forward to continue.

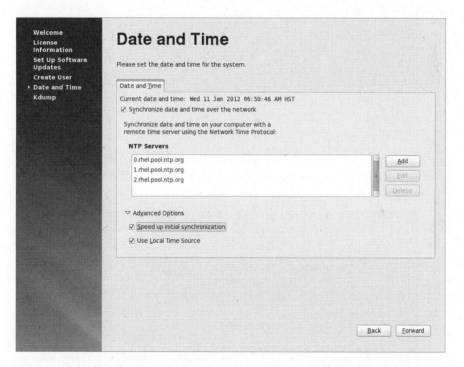

42. In the final part of the configuration, you can enable the Kdump settings. *Kdump* refers to crash dump. It allows a dedicated kernel to activate on the rare occasion that your server crashes. To use this feature, you need at least 2GB of available RAM. If you're using less, you'll see an error message indicating that you have insufficient memory to configure Kdump. You can safely ignore this message.

EXERCISE 1.1 *(continued)*

43. On the next and final screen of the installation program, click Finish. This completes the installation procedure and starts your system. You'll now see a login window where you can select the user account you'll use to log in.

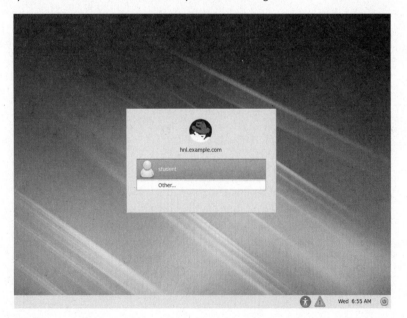

Exploring the GNOME User Interface

Now that your server is installed, it's time to get a bit familiar with the GNOME user interface. As indicated, on most servers, the graphical user interface (GUI) is not enabled. However, to get familiar with RHEL, it is a good idea to use the GNOME interface anyway.

To make yourself known to your Red Hat server, you can choose between two options. The best option is to click the name of the user account that you've created while installing the server and enter the password of that user. It's easy to pick the username—a list of all user accounts that exist on your server is displayed on the graphical login screen. Selecting a username from the graphical login screen connects you with normal user credentials to the server. That means you'll enter the server as a nonprivileged user, who faces several restrictions on the server.

Alternatively, from the graphical login screen, you can click Other to enter the name of another user you want to use to log in. You can follow this approach if you want to log in as user root. Because there are no limitations to what the user root can do, it is a very bad idea to log in as root by default. So, at this point, click the name of the user that you've created, and enter the password. After successful authentication, this shows the default GNOME desktop with its common screen elements, as shown in Figure 1.1.

FIGURE 1.1   The default GNOME graphical desktop

In the GNOME desktop, there are a few default elements with which you should be familiar. First, in the upper-left part of the desktop, there is the GNOME menu bar. There are three menu options: Applications, Places, and System.

Exploring the Applications Menu

In the Applications menu, you'll find a limited number of common desktop applications. The most useful applications are in the System Tools submenu. The Terminal Application is the single most important application in the graphical desktop because it gives you access to a shell window in which you can enter all the commands you'll need to configure your server (see Figure 1.2). Because it is so important, it's a good idea to add the icon to start this application to the panel. The panel is the bar which, by default, is at the top of the graphical screen. The following procedure describes how to do this:

1. Open the Applications menu, and select System Tools. You see the contents of the System Tools submenu.

2. Right-click the Terminal icon, and select Add This Launcher To Panel.

3. You'll now see a launcher icon that enables you to start the Terminal application in a quick and easy way from the panel.

FIGURE 1.2   The Terminal application gives access to a shell interface.

Another rather useful application in the System Tools submenu of the Applications menu is the file browser. Selecting this application starts Nautilus, the default file browser on a Red Hat system. Nautilus organizes your computer in Places, which allow you to browse the content of your computer in a convenient way.

After opening Nautilus, you'll see the contents of your home directory, as shown in Figure 1.3. This is your personal folder where you can store your files so that other users have no access. By using the Places sidebar, you can navigate to other folders on your computer, or by using the Network option, you can even navigate to folders that are shared by other computers on the network.

FIGURE 1.3   After opening Nautilus, you'll get access to your home folder.

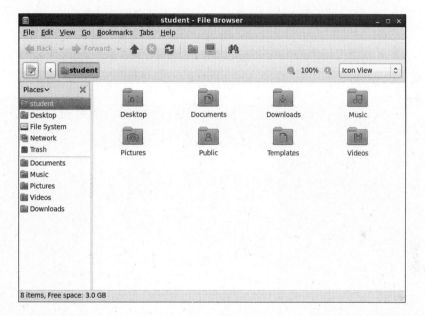

The file system is among the most useful places that you'll see in Nautilus. This gives you access to the root of the Linux file system, which allows you to see all the folders that exist on your computer. Be aware that, as an ordinary user without root permissions, you won't have access to all folders or files. To get access to everything, you should run Nautilus as root.

From Nautilus, you can access properties of files and folders by right-clicking them. This gives you access to the most important properties, including permissions that are assigned to a file or folder. However, this is not the way that you would normally change permissions or other file attributes. In subsequent chapters of this book, you'll learn how to perform these tasks from the command line.

Exploring the Places Menu

Now let's get back to the main menus in the GNOME interface. There you'll notice that the name of the second menu is Places. This menu, in fact, shows more or less the same options as Places in Nautilus; that is, it includes all the options you need to connect to certain folders or computers easily on the network. It also includes a Search For Files option, which may be useful for locating files on your computer. However, you will probably not be interested in the Search For Files option once you've become familiar with the powers of the Find command.

Exploring the System Menu

The third of the default GNOME menus, the System menu, gives you access to the most interesting items. First you'll find the Preferences submenu, which has tools such as the Screensaver and Display tools. You'll use the Display Preferences window (see Figure 1.4) to change the settings of the graphical display. This is useful in configuring external monitors or projectors or just to correct the screen resolution if the default resolution doesn't work for you.

FIGURE 1.4 The Display Preferences menu helps you optimize properties of the graphical display hardware.

In the Screensaver tool, you can set the properties of the screensaver, which by default activates after five minutes of inactivity. It will lock the screen so that you get access to it again only after entering the correct password. This is very useful in terms of security, but it can also be annoying. To disable the automatic locking of the screensaver, select System ➢ Preferences ➢ Screensaver and make sure the option Lock Screen When Screensaver Is Active option is unchecked.

In the Administration submenu under System, you'll get access to some common administration utilities. These are the *system-config* utilities that allow you to perform common administration tasks in a convenient way. These tools relate more to system administration tasks than the tools in any of the other GNOME submenus.

You'll learn how to use the system-config utilities in later chapters.

The upper-right part of the GNOME panel displays some apps that give access to common tools, including the Network Manager utility, which gives you easy access to the screens that help you configure the network cards in your computer. You'll also find the name of the current user in the upper-right corner of the screen. You can click on it and then Account Information to get access to personal information about this user, as well as the option to change the user's password (see Figure 1.5).

FIGURE 1.5   Click the name of the current user to get access to account information about that user.

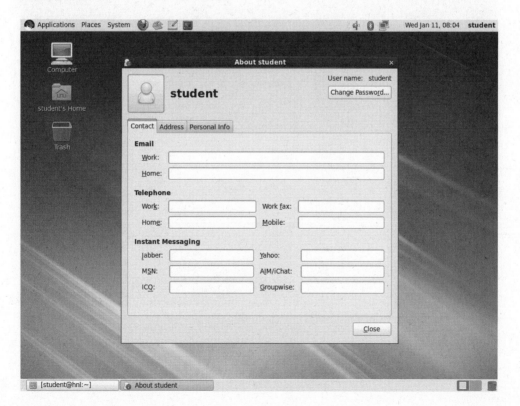

The menu associated with the current user also gives you access to the Lock Screen tool. Use it whenever you walk away from the server to lock the desktop in order to make sure that no one can access the files on the server without your supervision. Another useful tool is Switch User, which allows you to switch between two different user accounts that are both logged in.

The last part of the screen gives access to all open applications. Just click the application that you want to use to access it again. A very useful element in this taskbar is the Workspace Switcher (see Figure 1.6). This screen is one of the two workspaces that are activated by default. If you want to open many applications, you can use multiple workspaces to work in a more organized way. You can put specific application windows on those workspaces where you really need them. By default, Red Hat Enterprise Linux shows two workspaces, but you can increase the number of workspaces to an amount that is convenient for you. To activate another workspace, just click the miniature of the workspace as it is shown in the taskbar.

FIGURE 1.6   Increasing the number of workspaces

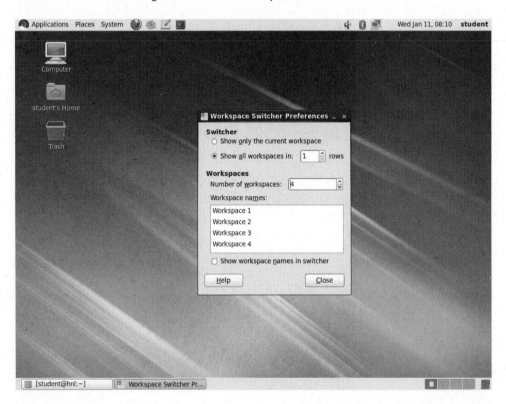

Summary

In this chapter, you became familiar with Red Hat Enterprise Linux (RHEL). You learned about what Linux is and where it comes from. You read that Linux comes from a tradition of open source software, and it is currently in use in most of the Fortune 500 companies. Next you will read about the Red Hat company and its product offerings.

You then learned how to install Red Hat Enterprise Linux on your computer. If all went well, you now have a usable version of RHEL that is available to you while working your way through this book.

Finally, the chapter introduced you to the GNOME graphical desktop. You learned that using it makes the process of learning Linux easier. You also saw where some of the most interesting applications are located in the different menus of the GNOME interface.

Chapter 2

Finding Your Way on the Command Line

TOPICS COVERED IN THIS CHAPTER:

✓ Working with the Bash Shell

✓ Performing Basic File System Management Tasks

✓ Piping and Redirection

✓ Finding Files

✓ Working with an Editor

✓ Getting Help

Although Red Hat Enterprise Linux provides the system-config tools as a convenient way to change parameters on your server, as a Linux administrator you will need to work from the command line from time to time. Even today, the most advanced management jobs are issued from the command line. For this reason, this chapter introduces you to the basic skills needed to work with the command line.

Working with the Bash Shell

To communicate commands to the operating system kernel, an interface is needed that sits between the kernel and the end user issuing these commands. This interface is known as the *shell*. Several shells are available on RHEL. *Bash* (short for the Bourne Again Shell) is the one that is used in most situations. This is because it is compatible with the Bourne shell, which is commonly found on UNIX servers. You should, however, be aware that Bash is not the only shell that can be used. A partial list of other shells follows:

tcsh   A shell with a scripting language that works like the C programming language. It is very popular with C programmers.

zsh   A shell that is compatible with Bash but offers even more features.

sash   This stands for stand-alone shell. This is a minimal-feature shell that runs in almost all environments. Therefore, it is very well suited for system troubleshooting.

Getting the Best of Bash

Basically, from the Bash environment, an administrator is working with commands. An example of such a command is `ls`, which can be used to display a list of files in a given directory. To make working with these commands as easy as possible, Bash has some useful features to offer. Some of the most used Bash features are automatic completion and the history mechanism.

In this chapter, you need a Terminal window to enter the commands with which you'd like to work. To open a Terminal window, from the Applications menu in the GNOME interface, select System Tools ➤ Terminal.

Some shells offer the option to complete a command automatically. Bash also has this feature, but it goes beyond the option of simply completing commands. Bash can complete almost everything, not just commands. It can also complete filenames and shell variables.

Variables

A *shell variable* is a common value that is used often by the shell and commands that work from that shell, and it is stored with a given name. An example of such a variable is PATH, which stores a list of directories that should be searched when a user enters a command. To refer to the contents of a variable, prepend a $ sign before the name of the variable. For example, the command echo $PATH would display the contents of the current search path that Bash is using.

To use this nice feature of completion, use the Tab key. An example of how this works follows. In this example, the cat command is used to display the contents of an ASCII text file. The name of this file, which is in the current directory, is this_is_a_file. To open this file, the user can type cat thi and then immediately hit the Tab key. If there is just one file that starts with the letters thi, Bash will automatically complete the name of the file. If there are more options, Bash will complete the name of the file as far as possible. This happens, for example, when in the current directory there is a file with the name this_is_a_text_file and thisAlsoIsAFile. Since both files start with this, Bash completes only up to this and doesn't go any further. To display a list of possibilities, you can then hit the Tab key again. This allows you to enter more information manually. Of course, you can then use the Tab key to use the completion feature again.

Useful Bash Key Sequences

Sometimes, you will enter a command from the Bash command line and nothing, or something totally unexpected, will happen. If that occurs, it is good to know that some key sequences are available to perform basic Bash management tasks. Here is a short list of the most useful of these key sequences:

Ctrl+C   Use this key sequence to quit a command that is not responding (or simply is taking too long to complete). This key sequence works in most scenarios where the command is active and producing screen output.

Ctrl+D   This key sequence is used to send the end-of-file (EOF) signal to a command. Use this when the command is waiting for more input. It will indicate this by displaying the secondary prompt >.

Ctrl+R   This is the reverse search feature. When used, it will open the reverse-i-search prompt. This feature helps you locate commands you have used previously. The feature is especially useful when working with longer commands. Type the first characters of the command, and you will immediately see the last command you used that started with the same characters.

Ctrl+Z   Some people use Ctrl+Z to stop a command. In fact, it does stop your command, but it does not terminate it. A command that is interrupted with Ctrl+Z is just halted until it is started again with the `fg` command as a foreground job or with the `bg` command as a background job.

Ctrl+A   The Ctrl+A keystroke brings the cursor to the beginning of the current command line.

Ctrl+B   The Ctrl+B keystroke moves the cursor to the end of the current command line.

Working with Bash History

Another useful aspect of the Bash shell is the history feature. The history mechanism helps you remember the last commands you used. By default, the last 1,000 commands of any user are remembered. History allows you to use the up and down arrow keys to navigate through the list of commands that you used previously. You can see an overview of these remembered commands when using the history command from the Bash command line. This command shows a list of all of the recently used commands. From this list, a command can also be restarted. For example, if you see command 5 in the list of commands, you can easily rerun this command by using its number preceded by an exclamation mark, or `!5` in this example.

Using ! to Run Recent Commands

You can also repeat commands from history using !. Using !, you can repeat the most recent command you used that started with the same string. For example, if you recently used `useradd linda` to create a user with the name linda, just entering the characters `!us` would repeat the same command for you.

```
                          root@hnl:/etc                        _ □ ×
File  Edit  View  Search  Terminal  Help
[root@hnl etc]# history
    1  cd
    2  vi users
    3  useradd < users
    4  history
    5  cd /etc
    6  cat hosts
    7  cp hosts /tmp
    8  history
[root@hnl etc]# !ca
cat hosts
127.0.0.1    localhost localhost.localdomain localhost4 localhost4.localdomain4
::1          localhost localhost.localdomain localhost6 localhost6.localdomain6
[root@hnl etc]#
```

As an administrator, you sometimes need to manage the commands that are in the history list. There are two ways of doing this.

- First you can manage the file .bash_history (note that the name of this file starts with a dot), which stores all of the commands you have used before. Every user has such a file, which is stored in the home directory of the user. If, for example, you want to delete this file for the user joyce, just remove it with the command rm /home/joyce/.bash_history. Notice that you must be at the root to do this. Since the name of the file begins with a dot, it is a hidden file, and normal users cannot see hidden files.

- A second way of administering history files, which can be accomplished by regular users, is by using the history command. The most important option offered by this Bash internal command is the option -c. This will clear the history list for the user who uses this command. So, use history -c to make sure that your history is cleared. In that case, however, you cannot use the up arrow key to access commands used previously.

WARNING   In the command history, everything you enter from the command line is saved. Even passwords that are typed in plain text are saved in the command history. For this reason, I recommend never typing a plain-text password on the command line because someone else might be able to see it.

Performing Basic File System Management Tasks

Essentially, everything on your RHEL server is stored in a text or ASCII file. Therefore, working with files is a very important task when administering Linux. In this section, you learn about file system management basics.

Working with Directories

Since files are normally organized within directories, it is important that you know how to handle these directories. This involves a few commands.

cd   Use this command to change the current working directory. When using cd, make sure to use proper syntax. First, names of commands and directories are case-sensitive; therefore, /bin is not the same as /BIN. Next, you should be aware that Linux uses a forward slash instead of a backslash. So, use cd /bin and not cd \bin to change the current directory to /bin.

pwd   The pwd command stands for Print Working Directory. You can often see your current directory from the command line, but not always. If the latter is the case, pwd offers help.

mkdir   If you need to create a new directory, use `mkdir`. With Linux `mkdir`, it is possible to create a complete directory structure in one command using the -p option, something that you cannot do on other operating systems. For example, the command `mkdir/some /directory` will fail if /some does not exist beforehand. In that case, you can force `mkdir` to create /some as well if it doesn't already exist. Do this by using the `mkdir -p /some /directory` command.

rmdir   The `rmdir` command is used to remove directories. Be aware, however, that it is not the most useful command available, because it will work only on directories that are already empty. If the directory still has files and/or subdirectories in it, use `rm -r` instead, as explained below.

Working with Files

An important command-line task is managing the files in the directories. A description of the four important commands used for this purpose follows.

Using ls to List Files

To manage files on your server, you must first know what files are available. For this purpose, the `ls` command is used. If you just use `ls` to show the contents of a given directory, it will display a list of files. These files, however, also have properties. For example, every file has a user who is the owner of the file, some permissions, a size that is stored in the file system, and more. To see this information, use `ls -l`.

`ls` has many other options as well. One useful option is -d. The example that follows shows clearly why this option is so useful. Wildcards can be used when working with the `ls` command. For example, `ls *` will show a list of all files in the current directory, `ls /etc/*a.*` will show a list of all files in the directory /etc that have an a followed by a . (dot) somewhere in the filename, and `ls [abc]*` will show a list of all files where the name starts with either a, b, or c in the current directory. Now without the option -d, something strange will happen. If a directory matches the wildcard pattern, the entire contents of that directory are displayed as well. This isn't very useful, and for that reason, the -d option should always be used with the `ls` command when using wildcards.

When displaying files using `ls`, note that some files are created as hidden files. These are files where the name starts with a dot. By default, hidden files are not shown. To display hidden files, use the `ls -a` command.

A *hidden file* is one where the name starts with a dot. Most configuration files that are stored in user home directories are created as hidden files. This prevents the user from deleting the file by accident.

Removing Files with rm

Cleaning up the file system is a task that also needs to be performed on a regular basis. The `rm` command is used for this purpose. For example, use `rm /tmp/`*somefile* to remove *somefile* from the /tmp directory. If you are at the root and have all the proper permissions for this file (or if you *are* the root), you will succeed without any problem. Since removing files can be delicate (imagine removing the wrong files), the shell will ask your permission by default (see Figure 2.1). Therefore, it may be necessary to push the rm command a little. You can do this by using the -f (force) switch. For example, use rm -f *somefile* if the command states that some file cannot be removed for some reason.

In fact, on Red Hat, the rm command is an alias for the command rm -i, which makes rm interactive and prompts for confirmation for each file that is going to be removed. This means that any time you use rm, the option -i is used automatically. You'll learn how to create an alias later in this chapter.

FIGURE 2.1   By default, rm asks for confirmation before it removes files.

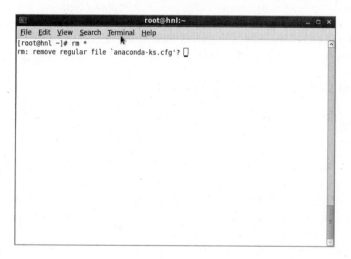

The rm command can also be used to wipe entire directory structures. In this case, the -r option has to be used. When this option is combined with the -f option, the command becomes very powerful. For example, use rm -rf /*somedir/** to clear out the entire contents of /*somedir*. This command doesn't remove the directory itself, however. If you want to remove the directory in addition to the contents of the directory, use rm -rf /*somedir*.

You should be very careful when using rm this way, especially since a small typing mistake can result in very serious consequences. Imagine, for example, that you type rm -rf / *somedir* (with a space between / and *somedir*) instead of rm -rf /*somedir*. As a result, the rm command will first remove everything in /, and when it is finished with that, it will remove *somedir* as well. Note that the second part of the command is actually no longer required once the first part of the command has completed.

Copying Files with cp

If you need to copy files from one location on the file system to another location, use the cp command. This straightforward command is easy to use. For example, use cp ~/* / tmp to copy all files from your home directory (which is referred to with the ~ sign) to the directory /tmp. If subdirectories and their contents need to be included in the copy command, use the option -r. You should, however, be aware that cp normally does not copy hidden files where the name starts with a dot. If you need to copy hidden files as well, make sure to use a pattern that starts with a .(dot). For example, use cp ~/.* /tmp to copy all files where the name starts with a dot from your home directory to the directory /tmp.

Moving Files with mv

An alternative method for copying files is to move them. In this case, the file is removed from its source location and placed in the target location. For example, use mv ~/somefile /tmp/otherfile to move the filename somefile to /tmp. If a subdirectory with the name otherfile exists in /tmp, somefile will be created in this subdirectory. If, however, no directory with this name exists in /tmp, the command will save the contents of the original file somefile under its new name, otherfile, in the directory /tmp.

The mv command is not just used to move files. You can also use it to rename directories or files, regardless of whether there are any files in those directories. For example, if you need to rename the directory /somedir to /somethingelse, use mv /somedir /somethingelse.

Viewing the Contents of Text Files

When administering your RHEL server, you will very often find that you are modifying configuration files, which are all ASCII text files. Therefore, the ability to browse the content of these files is very important. Different methods exist to perform this task.

cat   This command displays the contents of a file by dumping it to the screen. This can be useful if the contents of the file do not fit on the screen. You will see some text scrolling by, and as the final result, you will see only the last lines of the file being displayed on the screen.

tac   This command does the same thing as cat but inverts the result; that is, not only is the name of tac the opposite of cat, but the result is the opposite as well. This command will dump the contents of a file to the screen, but with the last line first and the first line last.

tail   This command shows only the last lines of a text file. If no options are used, this command will show the last 10 lines of a text file. The command can also be modified to show any number of lines on the bottom of a file. For example, tail -n 2 /etc/passwd will show you the last two lines of the configuration file where usernames are stored. The option to keep tail open on a given log file is also very useful for monitoring what happens on your system. For example, if you use tail -f /var/log/messages, the most generic log file on your system is opened, and when a new line is written to the bottom of that file, you will see it immediately, as shown in Figure 2.2.

head   This command is the opposite of tail. It displays the first lines of a text file.

less   The last command used to monitor the contents of text files is less. This command will open a plain-text file viewer. In the viewer, you can browse the file using the Page Down key, Page Up key, or spacebar. It also offers a search capability. From within the less viewer, use /sometext to find *sometext* in the file. To quit less, use q.

more   This command is similar to less but not as advanced.

FIGURE 2.2   With `tail -f`, you can follow lines as they are added to your text file.

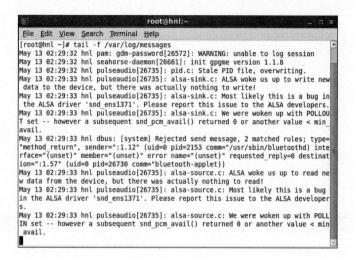

Creating Empty Files

It is often useful to create files on a file system. This is a useful test to check to see whether a file system is writable. The `touch` command helps you do this. For example, use `touch somefile` to create a zero-byte file with the name `somefile` in the current directory.

It was never the purpose of `touch` to create empty files. The main purpose of the `touch` command is to open a file so that the last access date and time of the file displayed by `ls` is modified to the current date and time. For example, `touch *` will set the time stamp to the present time on all files in the current directory. If `touch` is used with the name of a file that doesn't exist as its argument, it will create this file as an empty file.

  Real World Scenario

Unleashing the Power of Linux Using the Command Line

The ability to use pipes and redirects to combine Linux commands in an efficient way can save administrators lots of time. Imagine that you need to create a list of all existing users on your server. Because these users are defined in the /etc/passwd file, it would be easy to do if you could just get them out of this file. The starting point is the command cat /etc/passwd, which dumps all the content of /etc/passwd to the screen. Next pipe it to cut -d : -f 1 to filter out the usernames only. You can even sort it if you want, creating a pipe to the sort command. In upcoming sections, you'll learn how to use these commands and how to use pipes to connect them.

Piping and Redirection

The piping and redirection options are among the most powerful features of the Linux command line. *Piping* is used to send the result of a command to another command, and *redirection* sends the output of a command to a file. This file doesn't necessarily need to be a regular file, but it can also be a device file, as you will see in the following examples.

Piping

The goal of piping is to execute a command and send the output of that command to the next command so that it can do something with it. See the example described in Exercise 2.1.

EXERCISE 2.1

Discovering the Use of Pipes

In this exercise, you'll see how a pipe is used to add functionality to a command. First you'll execute a command where the output doesn't fit on the screen. Next, by piping this output through less, you can see the output screen by screen.

1. Open a shell, and use su - to become the root. Enter the root password when prompted.

2. Type the command ps aux. This command provides a list of all the processes that are currently running on your computer. You'll notice that the list doesn't fit on the screen.

3. To make sure you can see the complete result page by page, use ps aux | less. The output of ps is now sent to less, which outputs it so that you can browse it page by page.

Another very useful command that is often used in a pipe construction is grep. This command is used as a filter to show just the information that you want to see and nothing else. Imagine, for example, that you want to check whether a user with the name linda exists in the user database /etc/passwd. One solution is to open the file with a viewer like cat or less and then browse the contents of the file to check whether the string you are seeking is present in the file. However, that's a lot of work. A much easier solution is to pipe the contents of the file to the filter grep, which would select all of the lines that contain the string mentioned as an argument of grep. This command would read cat /etc/passwd | grep linda.

In Exercise 2.2, I will show you how to use grep and pipes together.

EXERCISE 2.2

Using grep in Pipes

In this procedure, you'll use the ps aux command again to show a list of all processes on your system, but this time you'll pipe the output of the command through the grep utility, which selects the information you're seeking.

1. Type ps aux to display the list of all the processes that are running on your computer. As you see, it's not easy to find the exact information you need.

2. Now use ps aux | grep blue to select only the lines that contain the text *blue*. You'll now see two lines, one displaying the name of the grep command you used and another one showing you the name of the Bluetooth applet.

3. In this step, you're going to make sure you don't see the grep command itself. To do this, the command grep -v grep is added to the pipe. The grep option -v excludes all lines containing a specific string. The command you'll enter to get this result is ps aux | grep blue | grep -v grep.

Redirection

Whereas piping is used to send the result of a command to another command, redirection sends the result of a command to a file. While this file can be a text file, it can also be a special file, such as a device file. The following exercise shows an example of how redirection is used to redirect the standard output (STDOUT), which is normally written to the current console to a file.

In Exercise 2.3, first you'll use the ps aux command without redirection. The results of the command will be written to the terminal window in which you are working. In the next step, you'll redirect the output of the command to a file. In the final step, you'll display the contents of the file using the less utility.

EXERCISE 2.3

Redirecting Output to a File

1. From a console window, use the command ps aux. You'll see the output of the command on the current console.

2. Now use ps aux > ~/psoutput.txt. You don't see the actual output of the command, because it is written to a file that is created in your home directory, which is designated by the ~ sign.

3. To show the contents of the file, use the command less ~/psoutput.txt.

Do not use the single redirector sign (>) if you don't want to overwrite the content of existing files. Instead, use a double redirector sign (>>). For example, who > myfile will put the result of the who command (which displays a list of users currently logged in) in a file called myfile. If then you want to append the result of another command, for example the free command (which shows information about memory usage on your system), to the same file myfile, then use free >> myfile.

Aside from redirecting output of commands to files, the opposite is also possible with redirection. For example, you may redirect the content of a text file to a command that will use that content as its input. You won't use this as often as redirection of the STDOUT, but it can be useful in some cases. The next exercise provides an example of how you can use it.

In Exercise 2.4, you'll run the mail command twice. This command allows you to send email from the command line. At first, you'll use it interactively, typing a . (dot) on a line to tell mail that it has reached the end of its input. In the second example, you'll feed the dot using input redirection.

EXERCISE 2.4

Using Redirection of STDIN

1. From a console, type **mail root**. This opens the command-line mail program to send a message to the user root.

2. When mail prompts for a subject, type **Test message** as the subject text, and press Enter.

3. The mail command displays a blank line where you can type the message body. In a real message, here is where you would type your message. In this exercise, however, you don't need a message body, and you want to close the input immediately. To do this, type a . (dot) and press Enter. The mail message has now been sent to the user root.

4. Now you're going to specify the subject as a command-line option using the command mail -s test message 2. The mail command immediately returns a blank line, where you'll enter a . (dot) again to tell the mail client that you're done.

5. In the third attempt, you enter everything in one command, which is useful if you want to use commands like this in automated shell scripts. Type this command: **mail -s test message 3** <. As you can see, when using redirection of the STDIN, the dot is fed to the mail command immediately, and you don't have to do anything else to send the message.

EXERCISE 2.4 *(continued)*

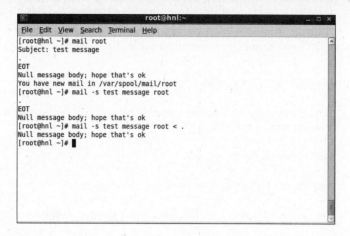

When using redirection, you should be aware that it is possible not only to redirect STDOUT and STDIN. Commands can also produce error output. This error output is technically referred to as STDERR. To redirect STDERR, use the 2> construction to indicate that you are interested only in redirecting error output. This means that you won't see errors anymore on your current console, which is very helpful if your command produces error messages as well as normal output. The next exercise demonstrates how redirecting STDERR can be useful for commands that produce a lot of error messages.

In Exercise 2.5, you'll use redirection of STDERR to send the error message somewhere else. Using this technique makes it much easier to work with commands that show a clean output.

EXERCISE 2.5

Separating STDERR from STDOUT

1. Open a terminal session, and make sure you are not currently logged in as root.

2. Use the command find / -name root, which starts at the root of the file system and tries to find files with the name root. Because regular users don't have read permission on all files, this command generates lots of permission denied errors.

3. Now run the command again using redirection of STDERR. This time the command reads as follows: find / -name root > ~/find_errors.txt. You won't see any errors now.

4. Quickly dump the contents of the file you've created using cat ~/find_errors.txt. As you can see, all error messages have been redirected to a text file.

One of the interesting features of redirection is that, not only it is possible to redirect to regular files, but you can also redirect output to device files. In many cases, however, this works only if you're at the root. One of the nice features of Linux is that any device connected to your system can be addressed by addressing a file. Before discussing how that works, here is a partial list of some important device files that can be used:

/dev/null	The null device. Use this device to redirect to nothing.
/dev/zero	A device that can be used to generate zeros. This can be useful when creating large empty files.
/dev/ttyS0	The first serial port.
/dev/lp0	The first legacy LPT printer port.
/dev/hda	The master IDE device on IDE interface 0 (typically your hard drive).
/dev/hdb	The slave IDE device on IDE interface 0 (not always in use).
/dev/hdc	The master device on IDE interface 1 (typically your optical drive).
/dev/sda	The first SCSI, SAS, serial ATA, or USB disk device in your computer.
/dev/sdb	The second SCSI or serial ATA device in your computer.
/dev/vda	The name of your hard disk if you're working on a virtual machine in a KVM virtual environment.
/dev/sda1	The first partition on the first SCSI or serial ATA device in your computer.
/dev/tty1	The name of the first text-based console that is active on your computer. These ttys are available from tty1 up to tty12.

One way to use redirection together with a device name is by redirecting error output of a given command to the null device. To do this, you would modify the previous command to grep root * 2> /dev/null. Of course, there is always the possibility that your command is not working well for a serious reason. In that case, use the command grep root * 2> /dev/tty12, for example. This will log all error output to tty12. To view the error messages later, you can use the Ctrl+F12 key sequence. (Use Ctrl+Alt+F12 if you are working in a graphical environment.)

Another cool feature you can use is redirecting the output from one device to another. To understand how this works, let's first take a look at what happens when you are using cat on a device, as in cat /dev/sda. As you can see in Figure 2.3, this displays the complete content of the sda device in the standard output, which is not very useful.

FIGURE 2.3 By default, output is sent to the current terminal window

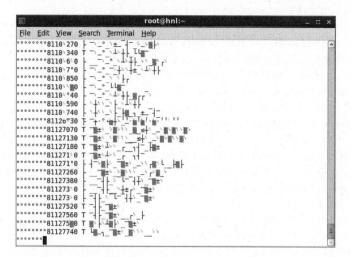

Cloning Devices Using Output Redirection

The interesting thing about displaying the contents of a storage device such as this is that you can redirect it. Imagine the situation where you have a /dev/sdb as well and this sdb device, which is at least as large as /dev/sda. In that case, you can clone the disk just by using cat /dev/sda > /dev/sdb!

Redirecting to devices, however, can also be very dangerous. Imagine what would happen if you use the command cat /etc/passwd > /dev/sda. It would simply dump the content of the passwd file to the beginning of the /dev/sda device. Since you are working on the raw device, no file system information is used, so this command would overwrite all important administrative information stored at the beginning of the device. If such an accident ever occurs, you'll need a specialist to reboot your computer.

A more efficient way to clone devices is to use the dd command. The advantage of using dd is that it handles I/O in a much more efficient way. To clone a device using dd, use dd if=/dev/sda of=/dev/sdb. Before you press Enter, however, make sure there is nothing you want to keep on the /dev/sdb device!

Finding Files

Finding files is another useful task you can perform on your server. Of course, you can use the available facility for this from the graphical interface. When you are working on the command line, however, you probably don't want to start a graphical environment just to find some files. In that case, use the find command instead. This is a very powerful command that helps you find files based on any property the file may have.

You can use find to search for files based on any file property, such as their names; the access, creation, or modification date; the user who created them; the permissions set on the file; and much more. If, for example, you want to find all files whose name begins with hosts, use find / -name "hosts*". I recommend that you always put the string of the item for which you are searching between quotes. This prevents Bash from expanding * before sending it to the find command.

Another example where find is useful is to locate files that belong to a specific user. For example, use find / -user "linda" to locate all files created by user linda. The fun part about find is that you can execute a command on the result of the find by using the -exec option. If, for example, you want to copy all files of user linda to the null device (a rather senseless example, I realize, but it's the technique that counts here), use find / -user "linda" -exec cp {} /dev/null \;.

If you're using -exec in your find commands, you should pay special attention to two specific elements used in the command. First there is the {} construction, which is used to refer to the result of the previous find command. Next there is the \; element, which is used to tell find that this is the end of the part that began with -exec.

Working with an Editor

For your day-to-day management tasks from the command line, you will often need to work with an editor. Many Linux editors are available, but vi is the only one you should use. Unfortunately, using vi isn't always easy. You may think "why bother using such a difficult editor?" The answer is simple: vi is always available no matter what Linux or UNIX system you are using. The good news is that vi is even available for Windows under the name of winvi, so there is no longer a reason to use the Notepad editor with its limited functionality. In fact, once you've absorbed the vi learning curve, you'll find that it is not that difficult. Once you're past that, you'll appreciate vi because it gets the job done faster than most other editors.

Another important reason why you should become familiar with vi is that some other commands are based on it. For example, to edit quota for the end users on your server, you would use edquota, which is a macro built on vi. If you want to set permissions for the sudo command, use visudo, which, as you can guess, is also a macro built on top of vi.

It looks as though visudo is built on top of vi, and by default it is. In Linux, the $EDITOR shell variable is used to accomplish this. If you don't like vi and want to use another editor for sudo and many other commands that by default rely on vi, you could also change the $EDITOR shell variable. To do this for your user account, create a file with the name .bashrc in your home directory and put in the line EDITOR=youreditorofchoice.

If you find that vi is hard to use, there is some good news: RHEL uses a user-friendly version of vi called vim, for "vi improved." To start vim, just use the vi command. In this section, I will provide you with the bare essentials that are needed to work with vi.

Vi Modes

One of the hardest things to get used to when working with vi is that it uses two modes.

In fact, vi uses three modes. The third mode is the ex mode. Because the ex mode can also be considered a type of command mode, I won't distinguish between ex mode and command mode in this book.

After starting a vi editor session, you first have to enter *insert mode* (also referred to as *input mode*) before you can start entering text. Next there is the command mode, which is used to enter new commands. The nice thing about vi, however, is that it offers you a lot of choices. For example, you can choose between several methods to enter insert mode.

- Use i to insert text at the current cursor position.
- Use a to append text after the current position of the cursor.
- Use o to open a new line under the current position of the cursor
- Use 0 to open a new line above the current position of the cursor.

After entering insert mode, you can enter text, and vi will work just like any other editor. To save your work, go back to command mode and use the appropriate commands. The magic key to go back to the command mode from insert mode is Esc.

When starting vi, always use the file you want to create or the name of an existing file you want to modify as an argument. If you don't do that, vi will display the relevant help text screen, which you will have to exit (unless you really need help).

Saving and Quitting

After activating command mode, you use the appropriate command to save your work. The most common command is :wq!

With this command, you'll actually do two different things. First the command begins with a : (colon). Then w saves the text you have typed thus far. If no filename is specified after the w, the text will be saved under the same filename that was used when the file was opened. If you want to save it under a new filename, just enter the new name after the w command. Next the q will ensure that the editor is quit as well. Finally, the exclamation mark is used to tell vi not to issue any warnings and just do its work. Using an ! at the end of a command is potentially dangerous; if a previous file with the same name already exists, vi will overwrite it without any further warning.

As you have just learned, you can use :wq! to write and to quit vi. You can also use just parts of this command. For example, use :w if you just want to write the changes you made while working on a file without quitting it, or you can use :q! to quit the file without writing the changes. The latter is a nice panic option if you've done something that you absolutely don't want to store on your system. This is useful because vi will sometimes do mysterious things to the contents of your file when you have hit the wrong keys by accident. There is, however, a good alternative; use the u command to *undo* the last changes you made to the file.

Cut, Copy, and Paste

You do not need a graphical interface to use the cut, copy, and paste features. To cut and copy the contents of a file in a simple way, you can use the v command, which enters visual mode. In visual mode, you can select a block of text using the arrow keys. After selecting the block, you can cut, copy, and paste it.

- Use d to cut the selection. This will remove the selection and place it in a buffer in memory.
- Use y to copy the selection to the designated area reserved for that purpose in your server's memory.
- Use p to paste the selection underneath the current line, or use P if you want to paste it above the current line. This will copy the selection you have just placed in the reserved area of your server's memory back into your document. For this purpose, it will always use your cursor's current position.

Deleting Text

Another action you will often do when working with vi is deleting text. There are many methods that can be used to delete text with vi. The easiest is from insert mode: just use the Delete and Backspace keys to get rid of any text you like. This works just like a word processor. Some options are available from vi command mode as well.

- Use x to delete a single character. This has the same effect as using the Delete key while in insert mode.
- Use dw to delete the rest of the word. That is, dw will delete anything from the current position of the cursor to the end of the word.
- Use D to delete from the current cursor position up to the end of the line.
- Use dd to delete a complete line.

Replacing Text

When working with ASCII text configuration files, you'll often need to replace parts of some text. Even if it's just one character you want to change, you'll appreciate the r command. This allows you to change a single character from command mode without entering input mode.

A more powerful method of replacing text is by using the :%s/oldtext/newtext/g command, which replaces *oldtext* with *newtext* in the current file. This is very convenient if you want to change a sample configuration file in which the sample server name needs to be changed to your own server name. The next exercise provides you with some practice doing this.

In Exercise 2.6, you'll create a small sample file. Next you'll learn how to change a single character and to replace multiple occurrences of a string with new text.

EXERCISE 2.6

Replacing Text with vi

1. Open a terminal, and make sure you're in your home directory. Use the cd command without any arguments to go to your home directory.

2. Type vi example, which starts vi in a newly created file with the name *example*. Press i to open insert mode, and enter the following text:

   ```
   Linda Thomsen       sales      San Francisco
   Michelle Escalante  marketing  Salt Lake City
   Lori Smith          sales      Honolulu
   Zeina Klink         marketing  San Francisco
   Anja de Vries       sales      Eindhoven
   Susan Menyrop       marketing  Eindhoven
   ```

3. Press c to enter command mode, and use :w to write the document.

4. In the name Menyrop, you've made an error. Using the r command, it is easy to replace that one character. Without entering insert mode, put the cursor on the letter *y* and press **r**. Next type a **t** as a replacement for the letter *y*. You have just changed one single character.

5. As the Eindhoven department is closing down, all staff that works there will be relocated to Amsterdam. So, all occurrences of *Eindhoven* in the file need to be replaced with *Amsterdam*. To do this, use :%s/Eindhoven/Amsterdam/g from vi command mode.

6. Verify that all of the intended changes have been applied, and close this vi session by using :wq! from command mode.

Using sed for the Replacement of Text

In the previous procedure, you learned how to change text in vi. In some cases, you will need a more powerful tool to do this. The *Streamline Editor* (*sed*) is a perfect candidate. sed is also an extremely versatile tool, and many different kinds of operations can be performed with it. The number of sed operations is so large, however, that many administrators don't use sed simply because they don't know where to begin. In this section, you'll learn how to get started with sed.

Standard editors like vi are capable of making straightforward modifications to text files. The difference between these editors and sed is that sed is much more efficient when handling multiple files simultaneously. In particular, sed's ability to filter text in a pipe is not found in any other editor. sed's default behavior is that it will walk through input files line by line, apply its commands to these lines, and write the result to the standard output. To perform these commands, sed uses regular expressions. Let's look at some sample expressions that are applied to the example file users that you see in the following listing:

```
my-computer:~> cat users
lori:x:1006:100::/home/lori:/bin/bash
linda:x:1007:100::/home/linda:/bin/bash
lydia:x:1008:100::/home/lydia:/bin/bash
lisa:x:1009:100::/home/lisa:/bin/bash
leonora:x:1010:100:/home/leonora:/bin/bash
```

To begin, the following command displays the first two lines from the users file and exits:

```
sed 2q users
```

Much more useful, however, is the following command, which prints all lines containing the text *or*:

```
sed -n /or/p users
```

In this example, consider -n a mandatory option, followed by the string you are looking for, or. The p command then gives the instruction to print the result. In this example, you've been searching for the literal text or. sed also works with regular expressions, the powerful search patterns that you can use in Linux and UNIX environments to make your searches more flexible. Here are some examples in which regular expressions are used:

sed -n /^or/p users   Shows all lines that don't contain the text or

sed -n /./p users   Shows all lines that contain at least one character

sed -n /\./p users   Shows all lines that contain a dot

Just printing lines, however, isn't what makes sed so powerful. You can also substitute characters using sed. The base syntax to do this is summarized in the following command where s/ is referring to the substitute command:

```
sed s/leo/lea/g users
```

This command replaces the string leo with the string lea and writes the results to the standard output. Writing it to the standard output is very secure, but it doesn't apply a single change to the file itself. If you want to do that, add the -i option to the command.

```
sed -i s/leo/lea/g users
```

The changes are now applied immediately to the file, which is useful if you know exactly what you are doing. If you don't, just have sed send the results to the standard output first so that you can check it before writing it.

At this stage, you've seen enough to unleash the full power of sed, which reveals its full glory if combined with shell scripting. Imagine that you have four files named file1, file2, file3, and file4 in the current directory and you need to replace the text *one* in each of these files with the text *ONE*. The following small scripting line that includes sed will perform this task perfectly for you. (Much more coverage of scripting appears later in this book.)

```
for i in file[1-4]; do sed -i s/one/ONE/g $i; done
```

Imagine the power of this in a datacenter where you need to change all configuration files that contain the ID of a storage device that has just been replaced, or where you want to modify a template file to make sure that the name of a placeholder service is replaced by the real name of the service you are now using. The possibilities of sed are unlimited, even though this section has shown you only the basics.

Getting Help

Linux offers many ways to get help. Let's start with a short overview.

- The man command offers documentation for most commands that are available on your system.

- Almost all commands listen to the --help argument as well. This will display a short overview of available options that can be used with the command on which you use the --help option.

- For Bash internal commands, there is the help command. This command can be used with the name of the Bash internal command about which you want to know more. For example, use help for to get more information about the Bash internal command for.

 An *internal command* is a command that is part of the shell and does not exist as a program file on disk. To get an overview of all internal commands that are available, just type help on the command line.

- For almost all programs that are installed on your server, extensive documentation is available in the directory /usr/share/doc.

Using man to Get Help

The most important source information available for use of Linux commands is man, which is short for the system programmer's "manual." Think of it as nine different books in which all parts of the Linux operating system are documented. That's how the man system started in the early days of UNIX. This structure of several different books (nowadays called *sections*) is still present in the man command; therefore, you will find a list of the available sections and the type of help you can find in each section.

     Looking for a quick introduction to the topics handled in any of these sections? Use man n intro. This displays the introduction page for the section you've selected. Table 2.1 provides an overview of the sections that are used in man.

TABLE 2.1   Overview of man sections

Section	Type	Description
0	Header files	These are files that are typically in /usr/include and contain generic code that can be used by your programs.
1	Executable programs or shell commands	For the end user, this is the most important section. Normally all commands that can be used by end users are documented here.
2	System calls	As an administrator, you won't use this section frequently. The system calls are functions that are provided by the kernel. This is very interesting if you are a kernel debugger or if you want to do advanced troubleshooting of your system. Normal administrators, however, do not need this information.
3	Library calls	A *library* is a piece of shared code that can be used by several different programs. Typically, you don't often need the information here to do your work as a system administrator.
4	Special files	The device files in the directory /dev are documented in here. It can be useful to use this section to find out more about the workings of specific devices.
5	Configuration files	Here you'll find the proper format that you can use for most configuration files on your server. If, for example, you want to know more about the way /etc/passwd is organized, use the entry for passwd in this section by issuing the command man 5 passwd.
6	Games	Historically, Linux and UNIX systems were limited in the number of games that could be installed. On a modern server, this is hardly ever the case, but man section 6 still exists as a reminder of this old habit.

Section	Type	Description
7	Miscellaneous	This section contains some information on macro packages used on your server.
8	System administration commands	This section does contain important information about the commands you will use on a frequent basis as a system administrator.
9	Kernel routines	This documentation isn't part of a standard install. It contains information about kernel routines.

The most important information that you will use as a system administrator is in sections 1, 5, and 8. Sometimes an entry can exist in more than one section. For example, there is information on passwd in section 1 and in section 5. If you just use man passwd, man would show the content of the first entry it finds. If you want to make sure that all the information you need is displayed, use man -a yourcommand. This ensures that man browses all sections to see whether it can find anything about your command. If you know beforehand the specific section to search, specify that section number as well, as in man 5 passwd, which will open the passwd item from section 5 directly.

The basic structure for using man is to type man followed directly by the command about which you seek information. For example, type man passwd to get more information about the passwd item. This will show a man page, as shown in Figure 2.4.

FIGURE 2.4   Showing help with man

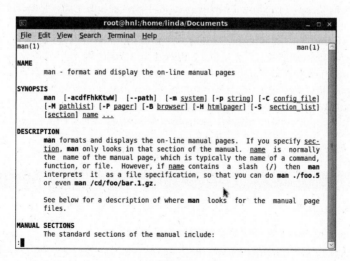

Man pages are organized in a very structured way that helps you find the information you need as quickly as possible. The following structural elements are often available:

Name   This is the name of the command. It describes in one or two lines what the command is used for.

Synopsis   Here you can find short usage information about the command. It will show all available options and indicate whether it is optional (it will be between square brackets) or mandatory (it will not be between brackets).

Description   The description gives a long explanation of what the command is doing. Read it to get a clear and complete picture of the purpose of the command.

Options   This is a complete list of all options that are available. It documents the use of all of them.

Files   This section provides a brief list of files, if any, that are related to the command about which you want more information.

See Also   A list of related commands.

Author   The author and also the email address of the person who wrote the man page.

Man is a very useful way to get more information on how to use a given command. The problem is that it works only if you know the exact name of the command about which you want to know more. If you don't, you can use man -k, which is also available as the alias apropos. The -k option allows you to locate the command you need by looking at keywords. This will often show a very long list of commands from all sections of the man pages. In most cases, you don't need to see all of this information; the commands that are relevant for the system administrator are in sections 1 and 8. Occasionally, when you are looking for a configuration file, section 5 should be browsed. Therefore, it is useful to pipe the output of man -k through the grep utility that can be used for filtering. For example, use man -k time | grep 1 to show only lines from man section 1 that have the word *time* in the description.

To use man, you rely on the whatis database that exists on your system. If it doesn't, you'll see a "nothing appropriate" message on everything you try to do—even if you're using a command that should always give a result, such as man -k user. If you get this message, use the makewhatis command. It can take a few minutes to complete, but once it does, you have a whatis database, and man -k can be used as the invaluable tool that it is.

In Exercise 2.7, you'll work with man -k to find the information you need about a command.

EXERCISE 2.7

Working with man -k

1.   Open a console, and make sure you are the root.

2.   Type **makewhatis** to create the whatis database. If it already exists, that's not a problem. makewhatis just creates an updated version in that case.

3.   Use man -k as a password. You'll see a long list of commands that match the keyword password in their description.

4. To obtain a more useful result, make an educated guess about which section of the man pages the command you're looking for is most likely documented in. If you're looking for a password item, you probably are looking for the command that a user would use to change their password. So, section 1 is appropriate here.

5. Use `man -k password | grep 1` to filter the result of your man command a bit more.

To finish this section about man, there are a few more things of which you should be aware.

- The `man` command has many things in common with `less`. Things that work in `less` also often work in `man`. Think of searching for text using /, going to the top of a document using g, going to the end of it using G, and using q to quit man.

- There is much interesting information near the end of the man page. In some of the more complicated man pages, this includes examples. There is also a section that lists related commands.

- If you still can't find out how a command works, most man pages list the email address of the person who maintains the page.

Using the --help Option

The `--help` option can be used with most commands. It is pretty straightforward. Most commands listen to this option, although not all commands recognize it. The nice thing, however, is that if your command doesn't recognize the option, it will give you a short summary of how to use the command when it doesn't understand what you want it to do. You should be aware that, although the purpose of the command is to give a short overview of the way it should be used, the information is very often still too long to fit on one screen. In that case, pipe it through `less` to view the information page by page. In Figure 2.5, you can see an example of the output provided by using the `--help` option.

Getting Information on Installed Packages

Another good option for getting help that is often overlooked is the documentation that is installed for most software packages in the /usr/share/doc directory. In this directory, you will find a long list of subdirectories that contain some useful information. In some cases, the information is very brief; in other cases, extensive information is available. This information is often available in ASCII text format and can be viewed with `less` or any other utility that is capable of handling clear text. In other situations, the information is in HTML format and can be displayed properly only with a web browser. If this is the case, you don't necessarily need to start a graphical environment to see the contents of the HTML file. RHEL comes with the elinks browser, which was especially developed to run from a nongraphical environment. In elinks, you can use the arrow keys to browse between hyperlinks. To quit the elinks browser, use the q command.

FIGURE 2.5 With --help you can display a usage summary.

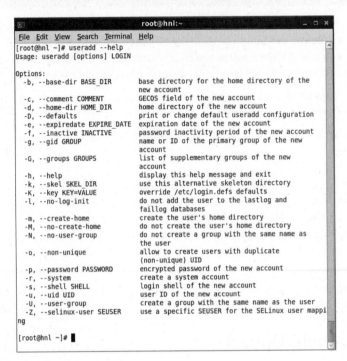

```
                              root@hnl:~                        _  □  ×
 File  Edit  View  Search  Terminal  Help
[root@hnl ~]# useradd --help
Usage: useradd [options] LOGIN

Options:
  -b, --base-dir BASE_DIR       base directory for the home directory of the
                                new account
  -c, --comment COMMENT         GECOS field of the new account
  -d, --home-dir HOME_DIR       home directory of the new account
  -D, --defaults                print or change default useradd configuration
  -e, --expiredate EXPIRE_DATE  expiration date of the new account
  -f, --inactive INACTIVE       password inactivity period of the new account
  -g, --gid GROUP               name or ID of the primary group of the new
                                account
  -G, --groups GROUPS           list of supplementary groups of the new
                                account
  -h, --help                    display this help message and exit
  -k, --skel SKEL_DIR           use this alternative skeleton directory
  -K, --key KEY=VALUE           override /etc/login.defs defaults
  -l, --no-log-init             do not add the user to the lastlog and
                                faillog databases
  -m, --create-home             create the user's home directory
  -M, --no-create-home          do not create the user's home directory
  -N, --no-user-group           do not create a group with the same name as
                                the user
  -o, --non-unique              allow to create users with duplicate
                                (non-unique) UID
  -p, --password PASSWORD       encrypted password of the new account
  -r, --system                  create a system account
  -s, --shell SHELL             login shell of the new account
  -u, --uid UID                 user ID of the new account
  -U, --user-group              create a group with the same name as the user
  -Z, --selinux-user SEUSER     use a specific SEUSER for the SELinux user mappi
ng
[root@hnl ~]# █
```

Summary

This chapter prepared you for the work you will be doing from the command line. Because even a modern Linux distribution like Red Hat Enterprise Linux still relies heavily on its configuration files, this is indeed important information. In the next chapter, you'll read about some of the most common system administration tasks.

Administering
Red Hat
Enterprise Linux

Chapter

3

Performing Daily System Administration Tasks

TOPICS COVERED IN THIS CHAPTER:

✓ Performing Job Management Tasks

✓ Monitoring and Managing Systems and Processess

✓ Scheduling Jobs

✓ Mounting Devices

✓ Working with Links

✓ Creating Backups

✓ Managing Printers

✓ Setting Up System Logging

In the previous chapter, you learned how to start a terminal window. As an administrator, you start many tasks from a terminal window. To start a task, you type a specific command. For example, you type ls to display a listing of files in the current directory. Every command you type from the perspective of the shell is started as a job. Most commands are started as a job in the foreground. In other words, once the command is started, it shows the result on the terminal window, and then it exits.

Performing Job Management Tasks

Because many commands take only a brief moment to complete their work, you don't have to do any specific job management on them. While some commands take only a few seconds or less to finish, other commands may take much longer. Imagine, for example, the makewhatis command that is going to update the database used by the man -k command. This command can easily take a few minutes to complete. For commands like this, it makes sense to start them as a background job by putting an & sign at the end of the command, as in the following example:

makewhatis &

By putting an & sign at the end of a command, you start it as a background job. When starting a command this way, the shell provides a job number (between square brackets) and a unique process identification number (the *PID*), as shown in Figure 3.1. You can then use these numbers to manage your background jobs.

FIGURE 3.1 If you start a job as a background job, its job ID and PID are displayed.

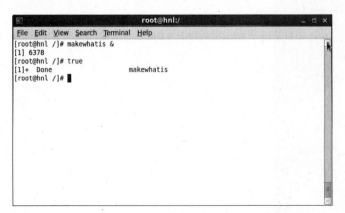

The benefit of starting a job in the background is that the terminal is still available for you to launch other commands. At the moment, the background job is finished; you'll see a message that it has completed, but this message is displayed only after you've entered another command to start.

To manage jobs that are started in the background, there are a few commands and key sequences that you can use, as listed in Table 3.1.

TABLE 3.1   Managing foreground and background jobs

Command	Use
Ctrl+Z	Use this to pause a job. Once paused, you can put it in the foreground or in the background.
fg	Use this to start a paused job as a foreground job.
bg	Use this to start a paused job as a background job.
jobs	Use this to show a list of all current jobs.

Normally, you won't need to do too much in the way of job management, but in some cases it makes sense to move a job you've started into the background so that you can make the terminal available for other tasks. Exercise 3.1 shows you how to do this.

EXERCISE 3.1

Managing Jobs

In this exercise, you'll learn how to move a job that was started as a foreground job into the background. This can be especially useful for graphical programs that were started as a foreground job and that occupy your terminal until they're finished.

1. From a graphical user interface, open a terminal, and from that terminal, start the system-config-users program. You will see that the terminal is now occupied by the graphical program you've just started and that you cannot start any other programs.

2. Click in the terminal where you started system-config-users, and use the Ctrl+Z key sequence. This temporarily stops the graphical program and returns the prompt on your terminal.

3. Use the bg command to move the job you started by entering the system-config-users command to the background. You can now continue using the graphical user interface and, at the same time, have access to the terminal where you can start other jobs by entering new commands.

EXERCISE 3.1 *(continued)*

4.   From the terminal window, type the jobs command. This shows a list of all jobs that
     are started from this terminal. You should see just the system-config-users com-
     mand. Every job has a unique job number in the list displayed by the jobs command.
     If you have just one job, it will always be job 1.

5.   To put a background job back into the foreground, use the fg command.
     By default, this command will put the last command you started in the background
     into the foreground. If you want to put another background job into the foreground,
     use fg followed by the job number of the job you want to manage; for instance,
     use fg 1.

Job numbers are specific for the shell in which you've started the job. This
means if you have multiple terminals that are open, you can manage jobs
in each of those terminals.

System and Process Monitoring
and Management

In the preceding section, you learned how to manage jobs that you started from a shell. As
mentioned, every command that you start from the shell can be managed as a job. There
are, however, many more tasks that are running at any given moment on your Red Hat
Enterprise Linux Server. These tasks are referred to as *processes*.

Every job that you start is not only a job but also a process. In addition, when your
server boots, many other processes are started to provide services on your server. These are
the *daemons*, which are processes that are always started in the background and provide
services on your server. If, for instance, your server starts an Apache web server, this server
is started as a daemon.

Managing processes is an important task for a system administrator. You may need to
send a specific signal to a process that doesn't respond properly anymore. Otherwise, on a
very busy system, it is important to get an overview of the system and check exactly what it
is doing. You will use a few commands to manage and monitor processes on your system,
as shown in Table 3.2.

TABLE 3.2 Commands for process management

Command	Use
ps	Used to show all current processes
kill	Used to send signals to processes, such as asking or forcing a process to stop
pstree	Used to get an overview of all processes, including the relationship between parent and child processes
killall	Used to kill all processes, based on the name of the process
top	Used to get an overview of current system activity

Managing Processes with ps

As an administrator, you might need to find out what a specific process is doing on your server. The ps command helps you do that. If run as root with the appropriate options, ps shows information about the current status of processes. For historical reasons, the ps command can be used in two different modes: the BSD mode, in which options are not preceded by a – (minus) sign, and the System V mode, in which all options are preceded by a – (minus) sign. Between these two modes, there are options with overlapping functionality. Two of the most useful ways to use the ps commands are in the command ps afx, which yields a treelike overview of all current processes, and ps aux, which provides an overview with a lot of usage information for every process. You can see what the output of the ps aux command looks like in Figure 3.2.

FIGURE 3.2 Displaying process information using ps aux

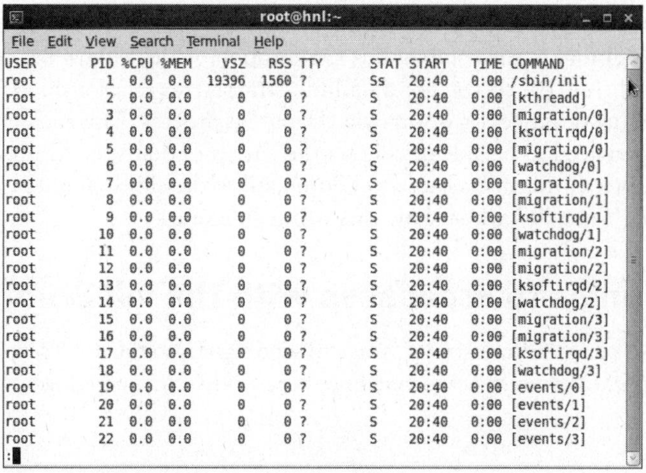

When using ps aux, process information is shown in different columns:

USER
: The name of the user whose identity is used to run the process.

PID
: The process identification number, which is a unique number that is needed to manage processes.

%CPU
: The percentage of CPU cycles used by a process.

%MEM
: The percentage of memory used by a process.

VSZ
: The virtual memory size. This is the total amount of memory that is claimed by a process. It is common for processes to claim much more memory than they actually need. This is referred to as *memory over allocation.*

RSS
: The resident memory size. This is the total amount of memory that a process is actually using.

TTY
: If the process is started from a terminal, the device name of the terminal is mentioned in this column.

STAT
: The current status of the process. The top three most common status indicators are S for sleeping, R for running, or Z for a process that has entered the zombie state.

START
: The time that the process started.

TIME
: The real time in seconds that a process has used CPU cycles since it was started.

COMMAND
: The name of the command file that was used to start a process. If the name of this file is between brackets, it is a *kernel* process.

Another common way to show process information is by using the command ps afx. The most useful addition in this command is the f option, which shows the relationship between parent and child processes. For an administrator, this relationship is important because the managing of processes occurs via the parent process. This means that in order to kill a process, you need to be able to contact the parent of that specific process. Also, if you kill a process that currently has active children, all of the children of the process are terminated as well. You will find out how this works in Exercise 3.2.

Sending Signals to Processes with the kill Command

To manage processes as an administrator, you can send signals to the process in question. According to the *POSIX standard*, which defines how UNIX-like operating systems should behave, different signals can be used. In practice, only a few of these signals are continuously available. It is up to the person who writes the program to determine those signals that are available and those that are not.

A well-known example of a command that offers more than the default signals is the dd command. When this command is operational, you can send SIGUSR1 to the command to show details about the current progress of the dd command.

Three signals are available at all times: SIGHUP (1), SIGKILL (9), and SIGTERM (15). Each of these signals can be referred to by the name of the signal or by the number when managing processes. You can, for instance, use either `kill -9 123` or `kill -SIGKILL 123` to send the SIGKILL signal to the process with PID 123.

Among these signals, SIGTERM is the best way to ask a process to stop its activity. If, as an administrator, you request closure of a program using the SIGTERM signal, the process in question can still close all open files and stop using its resources.

A more brutal way of terminating a process is by sending it SIGKILL, which doesn't allow the process any time at all to cease its activity; that is, the process is simply cut off, and you risk damaging open files.

Another way of managing a process is by using the SIGHUP signal. SIGHUP tells a process that it should reinitialize and read its configuration files again.

To send signals to processes, you will use the `kill` command. This command typically has two arguments. The first argument is the number of the signal you want to send to the process, and the second argument is the PID of the process to which you want to send a signal. For instance, the command `kill -9 1234` will send the SIGKILL signal to the process with PID 1234.

When using the `kill` command, you can use the PIDs of multiple processes to send specific signals to multiple processes simultaneously. Another convenient way to send a signal to multiple processes simultaneously is by using the `killall` command, which takes the name of a process as its argument. For example, the command `killall -SIGTERM hpptd` would send the SIGTERM signal to all active httpd processes. Exercise 3.2 shows you how to manage processes with `ps` and `kill`.

EXERCISE 3.2

Managing Processes with ps and kill

In this exercise, you will start a few processes to make the parent-child relationship between these processes visible. Then you will kill the parent process, and you will see that all related child processes also disappear.

1. Open a terminal window (right-click the graphical desktop, and select Open In Terminal).

2. Use the bash command to start Bash as a subshell in the current terminal window.

3. Use ssh -X localhost to start ssh as a subshell in the Bash shell you just opened. When asked if you want to permanently add localhost to the list of known hosts, enter **yes**. Next enter the password of the user root.

4. Type **gedit &** to start gedit as a background job.

5. Type **ps afx** to show a listing of all current processes, including the parent-child relationship between the commands you just entered.

6. Find the PID of the SSH shell you just started. If you can't find it, use ps aux | grep ssh. One of the output lines shows the ssh -X localhost command you just entered. Note the PID that you see in that output line.

7. Use **kill** followed by the PID number you just found to close the ssh shell. Because the ssh environment is the parent of the gedit command, killing ssh will also kill the gedit window.

Using top to Show Current System Activity

The top program offers a convenient interface in which you can monitor current process activity and also perform some basic management tasks. Figure 3.3 shows what a top window looks like.

FIGURE 3.3   Showing current system activity with top

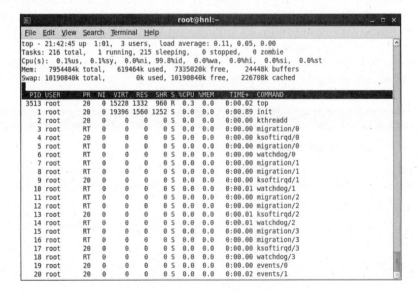

In the upper five lines of the top interface, you can see information about the current system activity. The lower part of the top window shows a list of the most active processes at the moment. This window is refreshed every five seconds. If you notice that a process is very busy, you can press the k key from within the top interface to terminate that process. The top program will first ask for the PID of the process to which you want to send a signal (PID to kill). After you enter this, it will ask which signal you want to send to that PID, and then it will immediately operate on the requested PID.

In the upper five lines of the top screen, you'll find a status indicator of current system performance. The most important information you'll find in the first line is the *load average*. This gives the load average of the last minute, the last 5 minutes, and the last 15 minutes.

To understand the load average parameter, you should know that it reflects the average number of processes in the run queue, which is the queue where processes wait before they can be handled by the scheduler. The *scheduler* is the kernel component that makes sure that a process is handled by any of the CPU cores in your server. One rough estimate of whether your system can handle the workload is that the number of processes waiting in the run queue should never be higher than the total number of CPU cores in your server.

A quick way to find out how many CPU cores are in your server is by pressing the 1 key from the top interface. This will show you one line for every CPU core in your server.

In the second line of the top window, you'll see how many tasks your server is currently handling and what each of these tasks is doing. In this line, you may find four status indications.

running   The number of active processes in the last polling loop.

sleeping   The number of processes currently loaded in memory, which haven't issued any activity in the last polling loop.

stopped   The number of processes that have been sent a stop signal but haven't yet freed all of the resources they were using.

zombie   The number of processes that are in a zombie state. This is an unmanageable process state because the parent of the zombie process has disappeared and the child still exists but cannot no longer be managed because the parent is needed to manage that process.

A zombie process normally is the result of bad programming. If you're lucky, zombie processes will go away by themselves. Sometimes they don't, and that can be an annoyance. In that case, the only way to clean up your current zombie processes is by rebooting your server.

In the third line of top, you get an overview of the current processor activity. If you're experiencing a problem (which is typically expressed by a high load average), the CPU(s) line tells you exactly what the CPUs in your server are doing. This line will help you understand current system activity because it summarizes all the CPUs in your system. For a per-CPU overview of current activity, press the **1** key from the top interface (see Figure 3.4).

FIGURE 3.4   From top, type 1 to get a CPU line for every CPU core in your server.

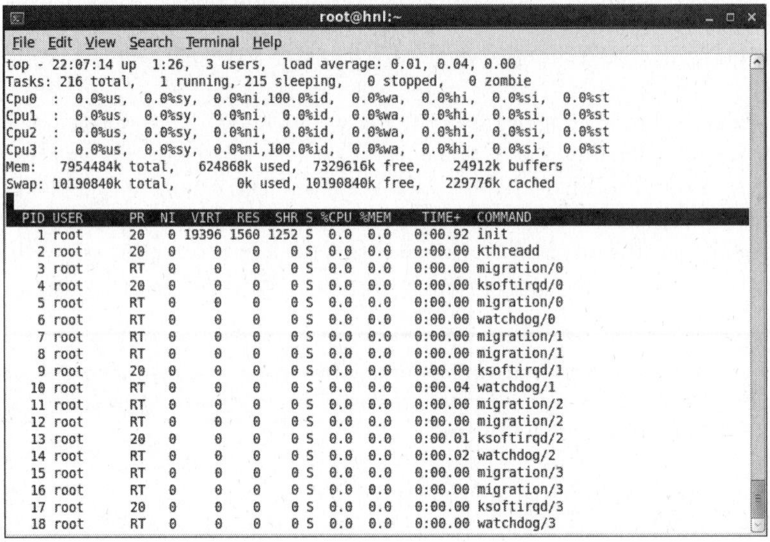

```
                              root@hnl:~                              _  □ ×
File  Edit  View  Search  Terminal  Help
top - 22:07:14 up  1:26,  3 users,  load average: 0.01, 0.04, 0.00
Tasks: 216 total,   1 running, 215 sleeping,   0 stopped,   0 zombie
Cpu0  :  0.0%us,  0.0%sy,  0.0%ni,100.0%id,  0.0%wa,  0.0%hi,  0.0%si,  0.0%st
Cpu1  :  0.0%us,  0.0%sy,  0.0%ni,  0.0%id,  0.0%wa,  0.0%hi,  0.0%si,  0.0%st
Cpu2  :  0.0%us,  0.0%sy,  0.0%ni,  0.0%id,  0.0%wa,  0.0%hi,  0.0%si,  0.0%st
Cpu3  :  0.0%us,  0.0%sy,  0.0%ni,100.0%id,  0.0%wa,  0.0%hi,  0.0%si,  0.0%st
Mem:   7954484k total,   624868k used,  7329616k free,    24912k buffers
Swap: 10190840k total,        0k used, 10190840k free,   229776k cached

  PID USER      PR  NI  VIRT  RES  SHR S %CPU %MEM    TIME+  COMMAND
    1 root      20   0 19396 1560 1252 S  0.0  0.0   0:00.92 init
    2 root      20   0     0    0    0 S  0.0  0.0   0:00.00 kthreadd
    3 root      RT   0     0    0    0 S  0.0  0.0   0:00.00 migration/0
    4 root      20   0     0    0    0 S  0.0  0.0   0:00.00 ksoftirqd/0
    5 root      RT   0     0    0    0 S  0.0  0.0   0:00.00 migration/0
    6 root      RT   0     0    0    0 S  0.0  0.0   0:00.00 watchdog/0
    7 root      RT   0     0    0    0 S  0.0  0.0   0:00.00 migration/1
    8 root      RT   0     0    0    0 S  0.0  0.0   0:00.00 migration/1
    9 root      20   0     0    0    0 S  0.0  0.0   0:00.00 ksoftirqd/1
   10 root      RT   0     0    0    0 S  0.0  0.0   0:00.04 watchdog/1
   11 root      RT   0     0    0    0 S  0.0  0.0   0:00.00 migration/2
   12 root      RT   0     0    0    0 S  0.0  0.0   0:00.00 migration/2
   13 root      20   0     0    0    0 S  0.0  0.0   0:00.01 ksoftirqd/2
   14 root      RT   0     0    0    0 S  0.0  0.0   0:00.02 watchdog/2
   15 root      RT   0     0    0    0 S  0.0  0.0   0:00.00 migration/3
   16 root      RT   0     0    0    0 S  0.0  0.0   0:00.00 migration/3
   17 root      20   0     0    0    0 S  0.0  0.0   0:00.00 ksoftirqd/3
   18 root      RT   0     0    0    0 S  0.0  0.0   0:00.00 watchdog/3
```

In the CPU(s) line, you'll find the following information about CPU states:

us   The percentage of time your system is spending in *user space*, which is the amount of time your system is handling user-related tasks.

sy   The percentage of time your system is working on kernel-related tasks in system space. On average, this should be (much) lower than the amount of time spent in user space.

ni   The amount of time your system has worked on handling tasks of which the nice value has been changed (see the next section on the nice command).

id   The amount of time the CPU has been idle.

wa   The amount of time the CPU has been waiting for I/O requests. This is a very common indicator of performance problems. If you see an elevated value here, you can make your system faster by optimizing disk performance.

hi   The amount of time the CPU has been handling hardware interrupts.

si   The amount of time the CPU has been handling software interrupts.

st   The amount of time that has been stolen from this CPU. You'll see this only if
          your server is a virtualization hypervisor host, and this value will increase at the
          moment that a virtual machine running on this host requests more CPU cycles.

You'll find current information about memory usage in the last two lines of the top status. The first line contains information about memory usage, and the second line has information about the usage of swap space. The formatting is not ideal, though. The last item on the second line provides information that is really about the usage of memory. The following parameters show how memory currently is used:

Mem   The total amount of memory that is available to the Linux kernel.

used   The total amount of memory that currently is used.

free   The total amount of memory that is available for starting new processes.

buffers   The amount of memory that is used for buffers. In buffers, essential system
          tables are stored in memory, as well as data that still has to be committed to
          disk.

cached   The amount of memory that is currently used for cache.

The Linux kernel tries to use system memory as efficiently as possible. To accomplish this goal, the kernel caches a lot. When a user requests a file from disk, it is first read from disk and then copied to RAM. Fetching a file from disk is an extremely slow process compared to fetching the file from RAM. For that reason, once the file is copied in RAM, the kernel tries to keep it there as long as possible. This process is referred to as *caching*. From top, you can see the amount of RAM that is currently used for caching of data. You'll notice that the longer your server is up, the more memory is allocated to cache. This is good because the alternative to using memory for caching would be to do nothing at all with it. When the kernel needs memory that currently is allocated to cache for something else, it can claim this memory back immediately.

The memory in buffers is related to cache. The kernel caches tables and indexes that it needs in order to allocate files and caches data that still has to be committed to disk in buffers. Like cache, buffer memory can also be claimed back immediately by the kernel when needed.

WARNING   As an administrator, you can tell the kernel to free all memory in buffers
                and cache immediately. However, make sure that you do this on test serv-
                ers only because, in some cases, it may lead to a crash of the server. To
                free the memory in buffers and cache immediately, as root, use the com-
                mand echo 3 > /proc/sys/vm/drop_caches.

Managing Process Niceness

By default, every process is started with the same priority. On occasion, some processes may need additional time, or they can cede some of their time because the particular processes are not that important. In those cases, you can change the priority of a process by using the nice command.

> In general, nice isn't used very often because the Linux scheduler knows how to handle and prioritize jobs. But if, for example, you want to run a large batch job on a desktop computer that doesn't need the highest priority, using nice can be useful.

When using the nice command, you can adjust the process niceness from -20, which is good for the most favorable scheduling, to 19 for the least favorable scheduling. By default, all processes are started with a *niceness* of 0. The following sample code line shows how to start the dd command with an adjusted niceness of -10, which makes it more favorable and therefore allows it to finish its work faster:

```
nice -n -10 dd if=/dev/sda of=/dev/sdb
```

Aside from specifying which niceness setting to use when starting a process, you can also use the renice command to adjust the niceness of a command that has already started. By default, renice works on the PID of the process whose priority you want to adjust. Thus, you have to find this PID before using renice. The ps command described earlier in this chapter is used to do this.

If, for example, you want to adjust the niceness of the find command that you just started, you would begin by using ps aux | grep find, which gives you the PID of the command. Assuming that would give you the PID 1234, you can use renice -10 1234 to adjust the niceness of the command.

Another method of adjusting process niceness is to do it from top. The convenience of using top for this purpose is that top shows only the busiest processes on your server, which are typically the processes whose niceness you want to adjust anyway. After identifying the PID of the process you want to adjust, from the top interface press **r**. You'll now see the PID to renice message on the sixth line of the top window. Now enter the PID of the process you want to adjust. The top program then prompts you with Renice PID 3284 to value. Here you enter the positive or negative nice value you want to use. Finally, press Enter to apply the niceness to the selected process. Exercise 3.3 shows how to use nice to change process priority.

EXERCISE 3.3

Using nice to Change Process Priority

In this exercise, you'll start four dd processes, which, by default, will go on forever. You'll see that all of them are started with the same priority and receive about the same amount of CPU time and capacity. Next you'll adjust the niceness of two of these processes from within top, which immediately shows the effect of using nice on these commands.

EXERCISE 3.3 *(continued)*

1. Open a terminal window, and use **su** – to escalate to a root shell.

2. Type the command **dd if=/dev/zero of=/dev/null &**, and repeat this four times.

3. Now start top. You'll see the four dd commands listed at the top. In the PR column, you can see that the priority of all of these processes is set to 20. The NI column, which shows the actual process niceness, indicates a value of 0 for all of the dd processes, and, in the TIME column, you can see that all of the processes use about the same amount of processor time.

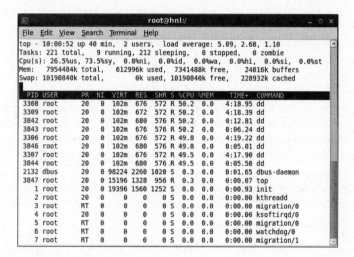

4. Now, from within the top interface, press **r**. On the PID to renice prompt, type the PID of one of the four dd processes, and press Enter. When asked Renice PID 3309 to value:, type **5**, and press Enter.

5. With the previous action, you lowered the priority of one of the dd commands. You should immediately start seeing the result in top, because one of the dd processes will receive a significantly lower amount of CPU time.

6. Repeat the procedure to adjust the niceness of one of the other dd processes. Now use a niceness value of -15. You will notice that this process now tends to consume all of the available resources on your computer. Thus, you should avoid the extremes when working with nice.

7. Use the k command from the top interface to stop all processes where you adjusted the niceness.

Scheduling Jobs

Up to now, you have been learning how to start processes from a terminal window. For some tasks, it makes sense to have them started automatically. Think, for example, of a backup job that you want to execute automatically every night. To start jobs automatically, you can use cron.

cron consists of two parts. First there is the *cron daemon*, a process that starts automatically when your server boots. The second part is the cron configuration. This is a set of different configuration files that tell cron what to do. The cron daemon checks its configuration every minute to see whether there are any new tasks that should be executed.

Some cron jobs are started from the directories /etc/cron.hourly, /etc/cron.daily, /etc/cron.weekly, and /etc/cron.monthly. Typically, as an administrator, you're not involved in managing these jobs. Programs and services that need some tasks to be executed on a regular basis just put a script in the directory where they need it, which makes sure that the task is automatically executed.

There are two ways you can start a cron job as a specific user: you can log in as that specific user or use su - to start a subshell as that particular user. After doing that, you'll use the command crontab -e, which starts the crontab editor, which by default is a vi interface. That means you work from crontab -e in a similar way that you are used to working in vi. As root, you can also use crontab -u user -e to create a cron job for a specific user.

In a crontab file created with crontab -e, you'll specify which command is to be executed and when on separate lines. Here is an example of a crontab line:

```
0 2 * * *    /root/bin/runscript.sh
```

In the definition of cron jobs, it is very important that you specify to have it start at the right moment. To do that, five different positions are used to specify date and time. You can use the following time and date indicators:

Field	Allowed value
Minute	0–59
Hour	0–23
Day of month	1–31
Month	1–12
Day of week	0–7 (0 and 7 are Sunday)

This means that, in a crontab specification, the time indicator 0 2 3 4 * indicates that a cron job will start on minute 0 of hour 2 (which is 2 a.m.) on the third day of the fourth month. Day of week in this example is not specified, which means the job would run on any day of the week.

In a cron job definition, you can use ranges as well. For instance, the line */5 * * * 1-5 means that a job has to run every five minutes, but only on Monday through Friday. Alternatively, you can also supply a list of comma-separated values, like 0 14,18 * * *, to run a job at 2 p.m. and at 6 p.m.

After creating the cron configuration file, the cron daemon automatically picks up the changes, and it will make sure that the job runs at the time indicated. Exercise 3.4 shows how to run a task from cron.

EXERCISE 3.4

Running a Task from cron

In this exercise, you'll learn how to schedule a cron job. You'll use your own user account to run a cron job that sends an email message to user root on your system. In the final step, you'll verify that root has indeed received the message.

1. Open a terminal, and make sure you are logged in with your normal user account.

2. Type **crontab -e** to open the crontab editor.

3. Type the following line, which will send an email message every five minutes:

   `*/5 * * * * mail -s "hello root" root <`

4. Use the vi command :wq! to close the crontab editor and save your changes.

5. Wait five minutes. Then, in a root terminal, type **mail** to start the command-line mail program. You should see a message with the subject hello root that was sent by your normal user account. Type **q** to quit the mail interface.

6. Go back to the terminal where you are logged in with the normal user account, and type **crontab -r**. This deletes the current crontab file for your user account.

Mounting Devices

As an administrator, you'll occasionally need to make storage devices like USB flash drives, hard drives, or network shares available. To do this, you need to connect the device to a directory in the root file system. This process is known as *mounting* the device.

If you're working from the graphical desktop, you'll notice that devices are mounted automatically. That is, if you take a USB flash drive that is formatted with a supported file system like Ext4 or FAT, the graphical interface will create a subdirectory in the folder /media and make the contents of the USB drive accessible in that subdirectory. The problem, however, is that this works only from a graphical environment. If you're behind a server that was started in text mode, you'll need to mount your devices manually.

To mount a storage device, you first need to find out two things: what is the name of the device you want to mount, and on which directory do you want to mount it? Normally, the primary hard drive in your server is known as /dev/sda. However, if your server is connected to a SAN, you might have many additional sd devices. lsscsi is a convenient command you can use to find out the current configuration for your server, but it isn't installed by default. To install it, use yum install lsscsi.

If the yum install command fails, you first need to set up a repository. You'll learn how to do that in Chapter 4, "Managing Software."

The commands blkid and dmesg are alternative ways to find out the names of storage devices. blkid provides an overview of all block devices currently connected to your computer. The last few lines of dmesg show the names of devices that were recently connected to your computer. In Listing 3.1, you can see how dmesg shows that the USB drive that was connected to this computer is now known as sdb. So, /dev/sdb is the name of the device in this case. Just stick in the key, and run dmesg; it will show you the device name that is assigned.

Listing 3.1: dmesg shows the name of recently connected block devices

```
usb 2-1.2: New USB device strings: Mfr=1, Product=2, SerialNumber=3
usb 2-1.2: Product: Flash Disk
usb 2-1.2: Manufacturer: Usb 2
usb 2-1.2: SerialNumber: 00005655851111ED
usb 2-1.2: configuration #1 chosen from 1 choice
Initializing USB Mass Storage driver...
scsi6 : SCSI emulation for USB Mass Storage devices
usbcore: registered new interface driver usb-storage
USB Mass Storage support registered.
usb-storage: device found at 3
usb-storage: waiting for device to settle before scanning
usb-storage: device scan complete
scsi 6:0:0:0: Direct-Access     Usb 2.0  Flash Disk      2.10 PQ: 0 ANSI: 2
sd 6:0:0:0: Attached scsi generic sg2 type 0
sd 6:0:0:0: [sdb] 4072448 512-byte logical blocks: (2.08 GB/1.94 GiB)
sd 6:0:0:0: [sdb] Write Protect is off
sd 6:0:0:0: [sdb] Mode Sense: 0b 00 00 08
sd 6:0:0:0: [sdb] Assuming drive cache: write through
sd 6:0:0:0: [sdb] Assuming drive cache: write through
 sdb:
sd 6:0:0:0: [sdb] Assuming drive cache: write through
sd 6:0:0:0: [sdb] Attached SCSI removable disk
SELinux: initialized (dev sdb, type vfat), uses genfs_contexts
[root@hnl ~]#
```

After finding the device name of your USB drive, you also need to find out whether there are any partitions on the device. The `fdisk -cul` command will help you with that. Assuming that your USB drive is known to your server by the name /dev/sdb, you have to use `fdisk -cul dev/sdb` to see the current partitioning of the USB drive. Listing 3.2 shows what this looks like.

Listing 3.2: Use `fdisk -cul` to show partition information

```
[root@hnl ~]# fdisk -cul /dev/sdb

Disk /dev/sdb: 4127 MB, 4127195136 bytes
94 heads, 60 sectors/track, 1429 cylinders, total 8060928 sectors
Units = sectors of 1 * 512 = 512 bytes
Sector size (logical/physical): 512 bytes / 512 bytes
I/O size (minimum/optimal): 512 bytes / 512 bytes
Disk identifier: 0x84556ad2

   Device Boot     Start         End      Blocks   Id  System
/dev/sdb1            2048     8060927     4029440   83  Linux
[root@hnl ~]#
```

In Listing 3.2, you can see that there is one partition only on /dev/sdb, and it is called /dev/sdb1. Now that you know the name of the partition, you can mount it on a directory. If you want to mount the partition just once, the directory /mnt is an excellent one to host the temporary mount. If you think you're going to use the mount more than once, you might want to use `mkdir` to create a dedicated directory for your device. To mount the device /dev/sdb1 on the directory /mnt, you would use the following command:
`mount /dev/sdb1 /mnt`

At this point, if you use `cd` to go into the /mnt directory, you'll see there the contents of the USB drive. You can now treat it as an integrated part of the local file system. Also, you can check that it is actually mounted using the `mount` command (see Listing 3.3). The device you've just mounted will be shown last in the list.

Listing 3.3: Use the `mount` command to display all current mounts

```
[root@hnl ~]# mount
/dev/mapper/vg_hnl-lv_root on / type ext4 (rw)
proc on /proc type proc (rw)
sysfs on /sys type sysfs (rw)
devpts on /dev/pts type devpts (rw,gid=5,mode=620)
tmpfs on /dev/shm type tmpfs (rw,rootcontext="system_u:object_r:tmpfs_t:s0")
/dev/sda1 on /boot type ext4 (rw)
/dev/mapper/vg_hnl-lv_home on /home type ext4 (rw)
none on /proc/sys/fs/binfmt_misc type binfmt_misc (rw)
sunrpc on /var/lib/nfs/rpc_pipefs type rpc_pipefs (rw)
gvfs-fuse-daemon on /root/.gvfs type fuse.gvfs-fuse-daemon (rw,nosuid,nodev)
```

```
/dev/sdb1 on /media/EA36-30C4 type vfat (rw,nosuid,nodev,uhelper=udisks,uid=0,
gid=0,shortname=mixed,dmask=0077,utf8=1,flush)
[root@hnl ~]#
```

Once you've stopped working with the device you've just mounted, you need to dis-mount it. To do this, use the umount command. This works only if there are no files on the mounted device currently in use. It also means you cannot be in the directory you used as a mount point. After verifying this, use umount followed either by the name of the device that you want to unmount or by the name of the directory you used as a mount point. For instance, to unmount a device that currently is mounted on /mnt, use umount /mnt. Exercise 3.5 shows how to mount a USB flash drive.

EXERCISE 3.5

Mounting a USB Flash Drive

In this exercise, you'll learn how to mount a USB flash drive. After mounting it success-fully on the /mnt directory, you'll then dismount it. You'll also see what happens if there are files currently in use while dismounting the device.

1. Open a terminal, and make sure you have root privileges.

2. Insert a USB flash drive in the USB port of your computer.

3. Use dmesg to find the device name of the USB flash drive. (I'll assume it is /dev/sdb for the remainder of this exercise.)

4. Use fdisk -cul /dev/sdb to find current partitions on the USB flash drive. I'll assume you'll find one partition with the name of /dev/sdb1.

5. Use mount /dev/sdb1 /mnt to mount the USB flash drive on the /mnt directory.

6. Use cd /mnt to go into the /mnt directory.

7. Type ls to verify that you see the contents of the USB flash drive.

8. Now use umount /dev/sdb1 to try to dismount the USB flash drive. This won't work because you still are in the /mnt directory. You'll see the "device is busy" error mes-sage.

9. Use cd without any arguments. This takes your current shell out of the /mnt directory and back to your home directory.

10. At this point, you'll be able to dismount the USB flash drive successfully using umount /dev/sdb1.

Working with Links

In a Linux file system, it is very useful to be able to access a single file from different locations. This discourages you from copying a file to different locations, where subsequently different versions of the file may come to exist. In a Linux file system, you can use links for this purpose. A *link* appears to be a regular file, but it's more like a pointer that exists in one location to show you how to get to another location.

In Linux, there are two different types of links. A *symbolic link* is the most flexible link type you can use. It points to any other file and any other directory, no matter where it is. A *hard link* can be used only to point to a file that exists on the same device.

With symbolic links, there is a difference between the original file and the link. If you remove the original file, the symbolic link won't work anymore and thus is invalid.

A hard link is more like an additional name you'd give to a file. To understand hard links, you have to appreciate how Linux file systems work with inodes. The *inode* is the administration of a file. To get to a file, the file system reads the file's inode in the file system metadata, and from there it learns how to access the block where the actual data of the file is stored. To get to the inode, the file system uses the filename that exists somewhere in a directory. A hard link is an additional filename that you can create anywhere in a directory on the same device that gives access to the same file system metadata. With hard links, you only need the original filename to create the hard link. Once it has been created, it isn't needed anymore, and the original filename can be removed. In general, you'll use symbolic links, not hard links, because hard links have some serious limitations.

To create a link, you need the ln command. Use the option -s to create a symbolic link. Without this option, you'll automatically create a hard link. First you'll put the name of the original file directly after the ln command. Next you'll specify the name of the link you want to create. For instance, the command ln -s /etc/passwd ~/users creates a symbolic link with the name users in your home directory. This link points to the original file /etc/passwd. Exercise 3.6 shows how to create links.

Creating Links

In this exercise, you'll learn how to create links. You'll create a hard link as well as a symbolic link to the file /etc/hosts, and you will see how both behave differently.

1. Open a terminal, and make sure you have root permissions.

2. Use the command ln -s /etc/hosts ~/symhosts. This creates a symbolic link with the name symhosts in your home directory.

3. Use the command ln /etc/hosts ~/hardhosts. This creates a hard link with the name hardhosts in your home directory.

4. Use the command echo 10.0.0.10 dummyhost >> /etc/hosts. Verify that you can see this addition in all three files: /etc/hosts, ~/symhosts, and ~/hardhosts.

5. Use the command ls -il /etc/hosts ~/symhosts ~/hardhosts. The option -I shows the inode number. You can see that it is the same for /etc/hosts and ~/hardhosts, like all other properties of the file.

6. Use rm /etc/hosts. Try to read the contents of ~/symhosts. What happens? Now try to access the contents of ~/hardhosts. Do you see the difference?

7. Restore the original situation by re-creating the /etc/hosts file. You can do that easily by making a new hard link using ln ~/hardhosts /etc/hosts.

Creating Backups

Occasionally, you might want to make a backup of important files on your computer. The tar command is the most common way of creating and extracting backups on Linux. The tar command has many arguments, and for someone who's not used to them, they appear overwhelming at first. If, however, you take a task-oriented approach to using tar, you'll find it much easier to use.

Three major tasks are involved in using tar: creating an archive, verifying the contents of an archive, and extracting an archive. You can write the archive to multiple destinations, but the most common procedure is to write it to a file. While using tar, use the f option to specify which file to work with.

To create an archive of all configuration files in the /etc directory, for example, you would use tar cvf /tmp/etc.tar /etc. Notice that the options are not preceded by a – (minus) sign in this command (which is common behavior in tar). Also, the order of the options is specific. If, for instance, you used the command tar fvc /tmp/etc.tar /etc, it wouldn't work as the f option, and its argument /tmp/etc.tar would be separated. Also, notice that you specify the location where to write the archive before specifying what to put into the archive.

Once you have created an archive file using the tar command, you can verify its contents. The only thing that changes in the command is the c (create) option. This is replaced by the t (test) option. So, `tar tvf /tmp/etc.tar` yields the content of the previously created archive.

Finally, the third task to accomplish with tar is the extraction of an archive. In this process, you get the files out of the archive and write them to the file system of your computer. To do this, you can use the `tar xvf /tmp/etc.tar` command.

When working with tar, you can also specify that the archive should be compressed or decompressed. To compress a tar archive, use either the z or j option. The z option tells tar to use the gzip compression utility, and the j option tells it to use bzip2. It doesn't really matter which one you use because both yield comparable results. Exercise 3.7 shows how to archive and extract with tar.

EXERCISE 3.7

Archiving and Extracting with tar

In this exercise, you'll learn how to archive the contents of the /etc directory into a tar file. Next you'll check the contents of the archive, and as the last step, you'll extract the archive into the /tmp directory.

1. Open a terminal, and use the following command to write an archive of the /etc directory to /tmp/etc.tar: `tar zxvf /tmp/etc.tar /etc`.

2. After a short while, you'll have a tar archive in the /tmp directory.

3. Use the command `file /tmp/etc.tar` to verify that it is indeed a tar archive.

4. Now show the contents of the archive using `tar tvf /tmp/etc.tar`.

5. Extract the archive in the /tmp directory using `tar xvf /tmp/etc.tar`. Once finished, the extracted archive is created in the /tmp directory, which means you'll find the directory /tmp/etc. From there, you can copy the files to any location you choose.

Managing Printers

On occasion, you'll need to set up printers as well. The easiest way to accomplish this task is by using the graphical system-config-printer utility. This utility helps in setting up a local printer that is connected directly to your computer. It also gives you access to remote print queues.

CUPS (Common UNIX Print System) uses the Internet Printing Protocol (IPP), a generic standard for printer management. You can also manage your CUPS environment using a web-based interface that is available at `http://localhost:631`.

Before delving into how to use `system-config-printer` to set up a print environment, it helps to understand exactly which components are involved. To handle printing in a Linux environment, CUPS is used. CUPS consists of a local print process, the CUPS daemon `cupsd`, and a queue. The *queue* is a spool directory where print jobs are created. The `cupsd` process makes sure that print jobs are serviced and printed on the associated printer.

From a print queue, a print job can go in two directions. It is either handled by a printer that is connected locally or forwarded to a remote printer. With `system-config-printer`, it is easy to set up either of these scenarios. Connecting a local printer is really easy. Just attach the printer to your server, and start `system-config-printer`. After clicking the New button, the tool automatically detects your locally connected printers, which makes it easy to connect to them. Since most servers nowadays are hidden in datacenters that aren't easily accessible, you probably won't use this option very often. More frequently, you will set up remote printers.

To set up a remote printer, start `system-config-printer` and click Network Printer. Chances are that you will see a list of all network printers that have been detected on the local network. Printers send packets over the network on a regular basis to announce their availability, which generally makes it very easy to connect to the network printer you need (see Figure 3.5).

FIGURE 3.5   In general, network printers are detected automatically.

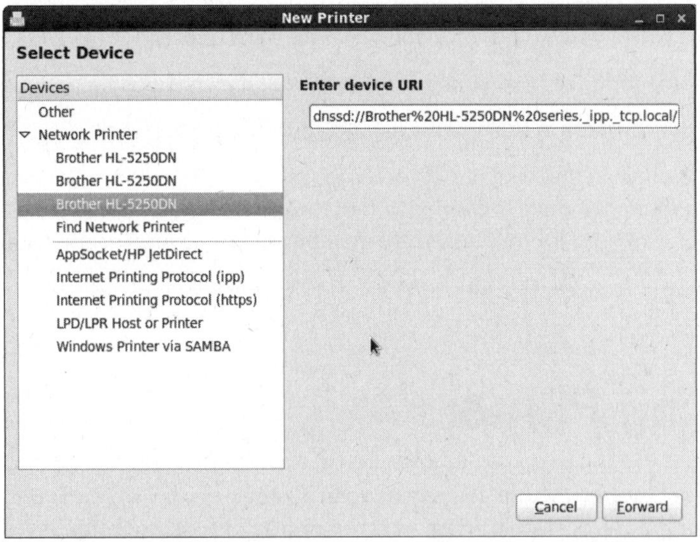

If your network printer wasn't detected automatically, you can set it up manually. The `system-config-printer` tool offers different ways to connect to remote printers.

AppSocket/HP JetDirect   Use this to access printers that have an HP JetDirect card inserted.

Internet Printing Protocol (ipp)   Use this to provide access to printers that offer access on the ipp port.

Internet Printing Protocol (http)   Use this to provide access to printers that offer access on the https port.

LPD/LPR Host or Printer   Use this for printers connected to a UNIX or Linux system.

Windows Printer via Samba   Use this for printers that are connected to a Windows Server or workstation or to a Linux server offering Samba shared printers.

After setting up a print queue on your server, you can start sending print jobs to it. Normally, the CUPS process takes care of forwarding these jobs to the appropriate printer. To send a job to a printer, you can either use the Print option provided by the program you're using or use a command to send a file directly to the printer. Table 3.3 provides an overview of the commands you can use to manage your printing environment.

TABLE 3.3 Commands for printer management

Command	Use
Lpr	Used to send a file directly to a printer
Lpq	Shows all jobs currently waiting to be serviced in the print queue
Lprm	Used to remove print jobs from the print queue
Lpstat	Gives status information about current jobs and printers

Setting Up System Logging

If problems arise on your server, it is important for you to be able to find out what happened and why. To help with that, you need to set up logging on your server. On Red Hat Enterprise Linux, the Rsyslog service is used for this purpose. In this section, you'll learn how to set up Rsyslog, you'll become familiar with the most commonly used log files, and you'll learn how to set up logrotate to make sure that your server doesn't get flooded with log messages.

Setting Up Rsyslog

Even if you don't do anything to set it up, your server will log automatically. On every Red Hat server, the *rsyslogd process* is started automatically to log all important events to log files and other log destinations, most of which exist in the /var/log directory.

Rsyslogd uses its main configuration file, /etc/rsyslog.conf, to determine what it has to do. To be able to change the default logging behavior on your server, you need to understand how this file is used. In Listing 3.4 you see part of the default rsyslog.conf file as it is created while installing Red Hat Enterprise Linux.

Listing 3.4: Part of rsyslog.conf

```
#### RULES ####

# Log all kernel messages to the console.
# Logging much else clutters up the screen.
#kern.*                                          /dev/console

# Log anything (except mail) of level info or higher.
# Don't log private authentication messages!
*.info;mail.none;authpriv.none;cron.none         /var/log/messages

# The authpriv file has restricted access.
authpriv.*                                       /var/log/secure
authpriv.*                                       root

# Log all the mail messages in one place.
mail.*                                           -/var/log/maillog


# Log cron stuff
cron.*                                           /var/log/cron

# Everybody gets emergency messages
*.emerg                                                    *
30 fewer lines
```

In the /etc/rsyslog.conf file, you'll set up how to handle the logging of different events. To set this up properly, you need to be able to identify the different components that occur in every log. The first part of the lines of code in rsyslog.conf define the facility. In Linux, you work with a fixed set of predefined facilities, which are summarized in Table 3.4.

TABLE 3.4   Predefined syslog facilities

Facility	Description
auth and authpriv	This is the facility that relates to authentication. auth has been deprecated. Use authpriv instead.
cron	Logs messages related to the cron scheduler.
daemon	A generic facility that can be used by different processes.
kern	A facility used for kernel-related messages.
lpr	Printer-related messages.
mail	Everything that relates to the handling of email messages.
mark	A generic facility that can be used to place markers in syslog.
news	Messages that are related to the NNTP news system.
syslog	Messages that are generated by Rsyslog itself.
user	A generic facility that can be used to log user-related messages.
uucp	An old facility that is used to refer to the legacy UUCP protocol.
local0-local7	Eight different local facilities, which can be used by processes and daemons that don't have a dedicated facility.

Most daemons and processes used on your system will be configured to use one of the facilities listed in Table 3.4 by default. Sometimes, the configuration file of the daemon will allow you to specify which facility the daemon is going to use.

The second part of the lines of code in rsyslog.conf specifies the priority that should be used for this facility. *Priorities* are used to define the severity of the message. In ascending order, the following priorities can be used:

1. debug
2. info
3. notice
4. warning
5. err

6. crit

7. alert

8. emerg

If any of these priorities is used, the default behavior is such that anything that matches that priority and higher will be logged. To log only a specific priority, the name of the priority should be preceded by an = sign.

Instead of using the specific name of a facility or a priority, you can also use * for all or none. It is also possible to specify multiple facilities and/or priorities by separating them with a semicolon. For instance, the following line ensures that, for all facilities, everything that is logged with a priority of info and higher is written to /var/log/messages. However, for the mail, authpriv, and cron facilities, nothing is written to this file.

```
*.info;mail.none;authpriv.none;cron.none    /var/log/messages
```

The preceding example brings me to the last part of the lines of code in rsyslog.conf, which contain the destination. In most cases, the messages are written to a file in the /var/log directory. However, it is possible to write to a logged-in user, a specific device, or just everywhere. The following three lines show you how all messages related to the kern facility are written to /dev/console, the console of your server. Next you can see how all authentication-related messages are sent to root, and finally, you can see how all facilities that generate a message with an emerg status or higher send that message to all destinations.

```
kern.*      /dev/console
authpriv.*   root
*.emerg       *
```

Common Log Files

As mentioned earlier, the default rsyslog.conf configuration works quite well in most situations, and it ensures that all important messages are written to different log files in the /var/log directory. The most important file that you'll find in this directory is /var/log/messages, which contains nearly all of the messages that pass through syslog. Listing 3.5 shows a portion of the contents of this file on the test server that was used to write this book.

Listing 3.5: Sample code from /var/log/messages

```
[root@hnl ~]# tail /var/log/messages
Mar 13 14:38:41 hnl udev-configure-printer: Failed to get parent
Mar 13 14:46:06 hnl rhsmd: This system is missing one or more valid
entitlement certificates. Please run subscription-manager for more information.
Mar 13 15:06:55 hnl kernel: usb 2-1.2: USB disconnect, address 3
Mar 13 18:33:35 hnl kernel: packagekitd[5420] general protection
ip:337c257e13 sp:7fff2954e930 error:0 in libglib-2.0.so.0.2200.5[337c200000+e4000]
```

```
Mar 13 18:33:35 hnl abrt[5424]: saved core dump of pid 5420 (/usr/sbin/
packagekitd) to /var/spool/abrt/ccpp-2012-03-13-18:33:35-5420.new/coredump
(1552384 bytes)
Mar 13 18:33:35 hnl abrtd: Directory 'ccpp-2012-03-13-18:33:35-5420' creation
detected
Mar 13 18:33:36 hnl kernel: Bridge firewalling registered
Mar 13 18:33:48 hnl abrtd: Sending an email...
Mar 13 18:33:48 hnl abrtd: Email was sent to: root@localhost
Mar 13 18:33:49 hnl abrtd: New dump directory /var/spool/abrt/ccpp-2012-03-13-
18:33:35-5420, processing
[root@hnl ~]#
```

Listing 3.5 shows messages generated from different sources. Every line in this log file is composed of a few standard components. To start with, there's the date and time when the message was logged. Next you can see the name of the server (hnl in this example). After that, the name of the process is mentioned, and after the name of the process, you can see the actual messages that were logged.

You will recognize the same structure in all log files. Consider the sample code shown in Listing 3.6, which was created using the tail -f /var/log/secure command. The file /var/log/secure is where you'll find all messages that are related to authentication. The tail -f command opens the last 10 lines in this file and shows new lines while they are added. This gives you a very convenient way to monitor a log file and to find out what is going on with your server.

Listing 3.6: Sample code from /var/log/secure

```
[root@hnl ~]# tail -f /var/log/secure
Mar 13 13:33:20 hnl runuser: pam_unix(runuser:session): session opened for user
qpidd by (uid=0)
Mar 13 13:33:20 hnl runuser: pam_unix(runuser:session): session closed for user
qpidd
Mar 13 13:33:20 hnl runuser: pam_unix(runuser-1:session): session opened for user
qpidd by (uid=0)
Mar 13 13:33:21 hnl runuser: pam_unix(runuser-1:session): session closed for user
qpidd
Mar 13 13:33:28 hnl polkitd(authority=local): Registered Authentication Agent
for session /org/freedesktop/ConsoleKit/Session1 (system bus name :1.25 [/usr/
libexec/polkit-gnome-authentication-agent-1], object path /org/gnome/PolicyKit1/
AuthenticationAgent, locale en_US.UTF-8)
Mar 13 14:27:59 hnl pam: gdm-password[2872]: pam_unix(gdm-password:session):
session opened for user root by (uid=0)
Mar 13 14:27:59 hnl polkitd(authority=local): Unregistered Authentication Agent
for session /org/freedesktop/ConsoleKit/Session1 (system bus name :1.25, object
path /org/gnome/PolicyKit1/AuthenticationAgent, locale en_US.UTF-8) (disconnected
from bus)
Mar 13 14:28:27 hnl polkitd(authority=local): Registered Authentication Agent
for session /org/freedesktop/ConsoleKit/Session2 (system bus name :1.48 [/usr/
libexec/polkit-gnome-authentication-agent-1], object path /org/gnome/PolicyKit1/
AuthenticationAgent, locale en_US.UTF-8)
```

```
Mar 13 15:20:02 hnl sshd[4433]: Accepted password for root from 192.168.1.53 port
55429 ssh2
Mar 13 15:20:02 hnl sshd[4433]: pam_unix(sshd:session): session opened for user
root by (uid=0)
```

Setting Up Logrotate

On a very busy server, you may find that entries get added to your log files really fast. This poses a risk—your server may quickly become filled with log messages, leaving little space for regular files. There are two solutions to this problem. First, the directory /var/log should be on a dedicated partition or logical volume. In Chapter 1, you read about how to install a server with multiple volumes. If the directory /var/log is on a dedicated partition or logical volume, your server's file system will never be completely filled, even if too much information is written to the log files.

Another solution that you can use to prevent your server from being completely filled by log files is using logrotate. By default, the logrotate command runs as a cron job once a day from /etc/cron.daily, and it helps you define a policy where log files that grow beyond a certain age or size are rotated.

Rotating a log file basically means that the old log file is closed and a new log file is opened. In most cases, logrotate keeps a certain number of the old logged files, often stored as compressed files on disk. In the logrotate configuration, you can define exactly how you want to handle the rotation of log files. When the maximum amount of old log files is reached, logrotate removes them automatically.

The configuration of logrotate is spread out between two different locations. The main logrotate file is /etc/logrotate.conf. In this file, some generic parameters are stored in addition to specific parameters that define how particular files should be handled.

The logrotate configuration for specific services is stored in the directory /etc/logrotate.d. These scripts are typically put there when you install the service, but you can modify them as you like. The logrotate file for the sssd services provides a good example that you can use if you want to create your own logrotate file. Listing 3.7 shows the contents of this logrotate file.

Listing 3.7: Sample logrotate configuration file

```
[root@hnl ~]# cat /etc/logrotate.d/sssd
/var/log/sssd/*.log {
    weekly
    missingok
    notifempty
    sharedscripts
    rotate 2
    compress
```

```
    postrotate
        /bin/kill -HUP `cat /var/run/sssd.pid 2>/dev/null` 2> /dev/null || true
    endscript
}  .
[root@hnl ~]#
```

To start, the sample file tells logrotate which files to rotate. In this example, it applies
to all files in /var/log/sssd where the name ends in log. The interesting parameters in this
file are weekly, rotate 2, and compress. The parameter weekly tells logrotate to rotate
the files once every week. Next rotate 2 tells logrotate to keep the two last versions of
the file and remove everything that is older. The compress parameter tells logrotate to
compress the old files so that they take up less disk space. Exercise 3.8 shows how to configure logging.

> You don't have to decompress a log file that is compressed. Just use
> the zcat or zless command to view the contents of a compressed file
> immediately.

EXERCISE 3.8

Configuring Logging

In this exercise, you'll learn how to configure logging on your server. First you'll set up
rsyslogd to send all messages that relate to authentication to the /var/log/auth file.
Next you'll set up logrotate to rotate this file on a daily basis and keep just one old
version of the file.

1. Open a terminal, and make sure you have root permissions by opening a root shell
   using su -.

2. Open the /etc/rsyslog.conf file in an editor, and scroll down to the RULES section.
   Under the line that starts with authpriv, add the following line:

   authpriv.* /var/log/auth

3. Close the log file, and make sure to save the changes. Now use the command service
   rsyslog restart to ensure that rsyslog uses the new configuration.

4. Use the Ctrl+Alt+F4 key sequence to log in as a user. It doesn't really matter which
   user account you're using for this.

5. Switch back to the graphical user interface using Ctrl+Alt+F1. From here, use tail
   -f /var/log/auth. This should show the contents of the newly created file that contains authentication messages. Use Ctrl+C to close tail -f.

6. Create a file with the name /etc/logrotate.d/auth, and make sure it has the following contents:

    ```
    /var/log/auth
        daily
        rotate 1
        compress
    ```

7. Normally, you would have to wait a day until logrotate is started from /etc/cron .daily. As an alternative, you can run it from the command line using the following command:

    /usr/sbin/logrotate /etc/logrotate.conf.

8. Now check the contents of the /var/log directory. You should see the rotated /var/ log/auth file.

Summary

In this chapter, you read about some of the most common administrative tasks. You learned how to manage jobs and processes, mount disk devices, set up printers, and handle log files. In the next chapter, you'll learn how to manage software on your Red Hat Enterprise Server.

Chapter

4

Managing Software

TOPICS COVERED IN THIS CHAPTER:

- ✓ Understanding RPM
- ✓ Understanding Meta Package Handlers
- ✓ Installing Software with yum
- ✓ Querying Software
- ✓ Extracting Files from RPM Packages

Managing Red Hat software is no longer the challenge it was in the past. Now everything is efficiently organized. In this chapter, first you'll learn about RPMs, the basic package format that is used for software installation. After that, you'll learn how software is organized in repositories and how yum is used to manage software from these repositories.

Understanding RPM

In the early days of Linux, the "tar ball" was the default method for installing software. A *tar ball* is an archive that contains files that need to be installed. Unfortunately, there were no rules for exactly what needed to be in the tar ball; neither were there any specifications of how the software in the tar ball was to be installed.

Working with tar balls was inconvenient for several reasons.

- There was no standardization.
- When using tar balls, there was no way to track what was installed.
- Updating and de-installing tar balls was difficult to do.

In some cases, the tar ball contained source files that still needed to be compiled. In other cases, the tar ball had a nice installation script. In other situations still, the tar ball would just include a bunch of files including a README file explaining what to do with the software.

The ability to trace software was needed to overcome the disadvantages of tar balls. The *Red Hat Package Manager (RPM)* is one of the standards designed to fulfill this need.

An RPM is basically an archive file. It is created with the cpio command. However, it's no ordinary archive. With RPM, there is also metadata describing what is in the package and where those different files should be installed. Because RPM is so well organized, it is easy for an administrator to query exactly what is happening in it.

Another benefit of using RPM is that its database is created in the /var/lib/rpm directory. This database keeps track of the exact version of files that are installed on the computer. Thus, for an administrator, it is possible to query individual RPM files to see their contents. You can also query the database to see where a specific file comes from or what exactly is in the RPM. As you will learn later in this chapter, these query options make it really easy to find the exact package or files you need to manage.

Understanding Meta Package Handlers

Even though RPM is a great step forward in managing software, there is still one inconvenience that must be dealt with—software dependency.

To standardize software, many programs used on Linux use libraries and other common components provided by other software packages. That means to install package A, package B is required to be present. This way of dealing with software is known as a *software dependency.*

Though working with common components provided from other packages is a good thing—even if only for the uniformity of appearance of a Linux distribution—in practice doing so could lead to real problems. Imagine an administrator who wants to install a given package downloaded from the Internet. It's possible that in order to install this package, the administrator would first have to install several other packages. This would be indicated by the infamous "Failed dependencies" message (see Listing 4.1). Sometimes the situation can get so bad that a real dependency hell can occur where, after downloading all of the missing dependencies, each of the downloaded packages would have its own set of dependencies!

Listing 4.1: While working with rpm, you will see dependency messages

```
[root@hnl Packages]# rpm -ivh createrepo-0.9.8-4.el6.noarch.rpm
warning: createrepo-0.9.8-4.el6.noarch.rpm: Header V3 RSA/SHA256
Signature, key ID fd431d51: NOKEY
error: Failed dependencies:
        deltarpm is needed by createrepo-0.9.8-4.el6.noarch
        python-deltarpm is needed by createrepo-0.9.8-4.el6.noarch
[root@hnl Packages]#
```

The solution for dependency hell is the Meta Package Handler. *Meta Package Handler,* which in Red Hat is known as *yum* (Yellowdog Update Manager), works with *repositories,* which are the installation sources that are consulted whenever a user wants to install a software package. In the repositories, all software packages of your distribution are typically available.

While installing a software package using yum install somepackage, yum first checks to see whether there are any dependencies. If there are, yum checks the repositories to see whether the required software is available in the repositories, and if it is, the administrator will see a list of software that yum wants to install as the required dependencies. So, using a yum is really the solution for dependency hell. In Listing 4.2 you can see that yum is checking dependencies for everything it installs.

Listing 4.2: Using yum provides a solution for dependency hell

```
[root@hnl ~]# yum install nmap
Loaded plugins: product-id, refresh-packagekit, security, subscription-manager
Updating certificate-based repositories.
Setting up Install Process
Resolving Dependencies
--> Running transaction check
---> Package nmap.x86_64 2:5.21-4.el6 will be installed
--> Finished Dependency Resolution

Dependencies Resolved

================================================================================
 Package         Arch           Version            Repository        Size
================================================================================
Installing:
 nmap            x86_64         2:5.21-4.el6        repo             2.2 M

Transaction Summary
================================================================================
Install      1 Package(s)

Total download size: 2.2 M
Installed size: 7.3 M
Is this ok [y/N]: n
Exiting on user Command
[root@hnl ~]#
[root@hnl ~]# yum install libvirt
Loaded plugins: product-id, refresh-packagekit, security, subscription-manager
Updating certificate-based repositories.
Setting up Install Process
Resolving Dependencies
--> Running transaction check
---> Package libvirt.x86_64 0:0.9.4-23.el6 will be installed
--> Processing Dependency: libvirt-client = 0.9.4-23.el6 for package:
 libvirt-0.9.4-23.el6.x86_64
--> Processing Dependency: radvd for package: libvirt-0.9.4-23.el6.x86_64
--> Processing Dependency: lzop for package: libvirt-0.9.4-23.el6.x86_64
--> Processing Dependency: libvirt.so.0(LIBVIRT_PRIVATE_0.9.4)(64bit)
for package: libvirt-0.9.4-23.el6.x86_64
--> Processing Dependency: libvirt.so.0(LIBVIRT_0.9.4)(64bit) for package:
 libvirt-0.9.4-23.el6.x86_64
...
```

If you installed Red Hat Enterprise Linux with a valid registration key, the installation process sets up repositories at the Red Hat Network (RHN) server automatically for you. With these repositories, you'll always be sure that you're using the latest version of the RPM available. If you installed a test system that cannot connect to RHN, you need to create your own repositories. In the following sections, you'll first read how to set up your own repositories. Then you'll learn how to include repositories in your configuration.

Creating Your Own Repositories

If you have a Red Hat server installed that doesn't have access to the official RHN repositories, you'll need to set up your own repositories. This procedure is also useful if you want to copy all of your RPMs to a directory and use that directory as a repository. Exercise 4.1 describes how to do this.

EXERCISE 4.1

Setting Up Your Own Repository

In this exercise, you'll learn how to set up your own repository and mark it as a repository. First you'll copy all of the RPM files from the Red Hat installation DVD to a directory that you'll create on disk. Next you'll install and run the createrepo package and its dependencies. This package is used to create the metadata that yum uses while installing the software packages. While installing the createrepo package, you'll see that some dependency problems have to be handled as well.

1. Use mkdir /repo to create a directory that you can use as a repository in the root of your server's file system.

2. Insert the Red Hat installation DVD in the optical drive of your server. Assuming that you run the server in graphical mode, the DVD will be mounted automatically.

3. Use the cd /media/RHEL[Tab] command to go into the mounted DVD. Next use cd Packages, which brings you to the directory where all RPMs are by default. Now use cp * /repo to copy all of them to the /repo directory you just created. Once this is finished, you don't need the DVD anymore.

4. Now use cd /repo to go to the /repo directory. From this directory, type **rpm -ivh createrepo[Tab]**. This doesn't work, and it gives you a "Failed dependencies" error. To install createrepo, you first need to install the deltarpm and python-deltarpm packages. Use rpm -ivh deltarpm[Tab] python-deltarpm[Tab] to install both of them. Next, use rpm -ivh createrepo[Tab] again to install the createrepo package.

5. Once the createrepo package has been installed, use createrepo /repo, which creates the metadata that allows you to use the /repo directory as a repository. This will take a few minutes. When this procedure is finished, your repository is ready for use.

Managing Repositories

In the preceding section, you learned how to turn a directory that contains RPMs into a repository. However, just marking a directory as a repository isn't enough. To use your newly created repository, you'll have to tell your server where it can find it. To do this, you need to create a repository file in the directory /etc/yum.repos.d. You'll probably already have some repository files in this directory. In Listing 4.3, you can see the content of the rhel-source.repo file that is created by default.

Listing 4.3: Sample repository file

```
[root@hnl ~]# cat /etc/yum.repos.d/rhel-source.repo
[rhel-source]
name=Red Hat Enterprise Linux $releasever - $basearch - Source
baseurl=ftp://ftp.redhat.com/pub/redhat/linux/enterprise/$releasever/en/os/SRPMS/
enabled=0
gpgcheck=1
gpgkey=file:///etc/pki/rpm-gpg/RPM-GPG-KEY-redhat-release
[rhel-source-beta]
name=Red Hat Enterprise Linux $releasever Beta - $basearch - Source
baseurl=ftp://ftp.redhat.com/pub/redhat/linux/beta/$releasever/en/os/SRPMS/
enabled=0
gpgcheck=1
gpgkey=file:///etc/pki/rpm-gpg/RPM-GPG-KEY-redhat-beta,file:///etc/pki/rpm
-gpg/RPM-GPG-KEY-redhat-release
[root@hnl ~]#
```

In the sample file in Listing 4.3, you'll find all elements that a repository file should contain. First, between square brackets there is an identifier for the repository. It doesn't really matter what you use here; the identifier just allows you to recognize the repository easily later, and it's used on your computer only. The same goes for the name parameter; it gives a name to the repository.

The really important parameter is baseurl. It tells where the repository can be found in URL format. As you can see in this example, an FTP server at Red Hat is specified. Alternatively, you can also use URLs that refer to a website or to a directory that is local on your server's hard drive. In the latter case, the repository format looks like file:///yourrepository. Some people are confused about the third slash in the URL, but it really has to be there. The file:// part is the URI, which tells yum that it has to look at a file, and after that, you need a complete path to the file or directory, which in this case is /yourrepository.

Next the parameter enabled specifies whether this repository is enabled. A 0 indicates that it is not, and if you really want to use this repository, this parameter should have 1 as its value.

The last part of the repository specifies if a GPG file is available. Because RPM packages are installed as root and can contain scripts that will be executed as root without any warning, it really is important that you are confident that the RPMs you are installing can be trusted. GPG helps in guaranteeing the integrity of software packages you are installing.

To check whether packages have been tampered with, a GPG check is done on each package that you'll install. To do this check, you need the GPG files installed locally on your computer. As you can see, some GPG files that are used by Red Hat are installed on your computer by default. Their location is specified using the gpgkey option. Next the option gpgcheck=1 tells yum that it has to perform the GPG integrity check. If you're having a hard time configuring the GPG check, you can change this parameter to gpgcheck=0, which completely disables the GPG check for RPMs that are found in this repository.

In Exercise 4.2 you'll learn how to enable the repository that you created in the preceding exercise by creating a repository file for it.

EXERCISE 4.2

Working with yum

In this exercise, you'll start by using some yum commands, which are explained in the next section of this chapter. The purpose of using these commands is that at the start of this exercise, yum doesn't show anything. Next you'll enable the repository that you created in the preceding exercise, and you'll repeat the yum commands. You will see that after enabling the repositories, the yum commands now work.

1. Use the command yum repolist. In its output (repolist: 0), the command tells you that currently no repositories are configured.

2. Use the command yum search nmap. The result of this command is the message No Matches found.

3. Now use vi to create a file with the name /etc/yum.repos.d/myrepo.repo. Note that it is important that the file has the extension .repo. Without it, yum will completely ignore it! The file should have the following contents:

    ```
    [myrepo]
    name=myrepo
    baseurl=file:///repo
    gpgcheck=0
    ```

4. Now use the commands yum repolist and yum search nmap again. Listing 4.4 shows the result of these commands.

Listing 4.4: After enabling the repository, yum commands will work

```
[root@hn1 ~]# yum repolist
Loaded plugins: product-id, refresh-packagekit, security, subscription-manager
Updating certificate-based repositories.
repo id                         repo name                          status
myrepo                          myrepo                             3,596
```

```
repolist: 3,596
[root@hn1 ~]# yum search nmap
Loaded plugins: product-id, refresh-packagekit, security, subscription-manager
Updating certificate-based repositories.
============================= N/S Matched: nmap =============================
nmap.x86_64 : Network exploration tool and security scanner
  Name and summary matches only, use "search all" for everything.
[root@hn1 ~]#
```

At this point, your repositories are enabled, and you can use yum to manage software packages on your server.

RHN and Satellite

In the preceding sections, you learned how to create and manage your own repository. This procedure is useful on test servers that aren't connected to RHN. In a corporate environment, your server will be connected either directly to RHN or to a Red Hat Satellite or Red Hat Proxy server, which both can be used to provide RHN packages from within your own site.

Taking Advantage of RHN

In small environments with only a few Red Hat servers, your server is likely to be connected directly to the RHN network. There are just two requirements.

- You need a key for the server that you want to connect to.
- You need direct access from that server to the Internet.

From RHN, you can see all servers that are managed through your RHN account (see Figure 4.1). To see these servers, go to http://rhn.redhat.com, log in with your RHN user credentials, and go to the systems link.

From RHN, you can directly access patches for your server and perform other management tasks.

RHN is convenient for small environments. However, if your environment has hundreds of Red Hat servers that need to be managed, RHN is not the best approach. In that case, you're better off using Satellite. Red Hat Satellite server provides a proxy to RHN. It will also allow for basic deployment and versioning. You configure Satellite with your RHN credentials, and Satellite fetches the patches and updates for you. Next you'll register your server with Satellite while setting it up.

FIGURE 4.1   If your server is registered through RHN, you can see it in your RHN account.

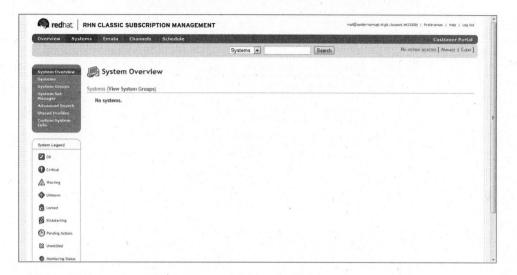

Registering a Server with RHN

To register a server with RHN, you can use the rhn_register tool. This tool runs from a graphical as well as a text-based interface. After starting the rhn_register tool, it shows an introduction screen on which you just click Forward. Next the tool shows a screen in which you can choose what you want to do. You can indicate that you want to download updates from the Red Hat Network, or you can indicate that you have access to a Red Hat Network Satellite, if there is a Satellite server in your network (see Figure 4.2).

To connect your server to RHN, enter your login credentials on the next screen.

> If you can't afford to pay for Red Hat Enterprise Linux, you can get a free 30-day access code at www.redhat.com. Your server will continue to work after the 30-day period; however, you won't be able to install updates any longer.

After a successful registration with RHN, the rhn_register tool will ask if you want limited updates or all available updates. This is an important choice. By default, you'll get all available updates, which will give you the latest version of all software for Red Hat Enterprise Linux. Some software, however, is supported on a specific subversion of Red Hat Enterprise Linux only. If this is the case for your environment, you're better off selecting limited updates (see Figure 4.3).

FIGURE 4.2   Specify whether you want to connect to RHN or to a Satellite server.

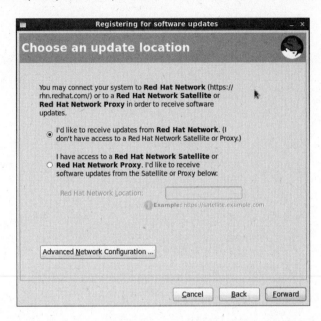

FIGURE 4.3   Select limited updates if your software is supported on a specific subversion of RHEL.

In the next step, the program asks for your system name and profile data (see Figure 4.4). This information will be sent to RHN, and it makes it possible to register your system with RHN. Normally, there is no need to change any of the options in this window.

FIGURE 4.4   Specifying what information to send to RHN

After clicking Forward, your system information is sent to RHN. This will take a while. After a successful registration, you can start installing updates and patches from RHN. To verify that you really are on RHN, you can use the yum repolist command, which provides an overview of all of the repositories your system is currently configured to use.

Installing Software with Yum

After configuring the repositories, you can install, query, update, and remove software with the meta package handler yum. This tool is easy to understand and intuitive.

Searching Packages with Yum

To manage software with yum, the first step is often to search for the software you're seeking. The command yum search will do this for you. If you're looking for a package with the name nmap, for example, you'd use yum search nmap. Yum will come back with a list of all packages that match the search string, but it looks for it only in the package name and summary. If this doesn't give you what you were seeking, you can try yum search all, which will also look in the package description (but not in the list of files that are in the package).

If you are looking for the name of a specific file, use yum provides or its equivalent, yum whatprovides. This command also checks the repository metadata for files that are in a package, and it tells you exactly which package you need to find a specific file. There is one peculiarity, though, when using yum provides. You don't just specify the name of the file you're seeking. Rather, you have to specify it as */nameofthefile. For example, the following command searches in yum for the package that contains the file zcat:
yum provides */zcat.

Listing 4.5 shows the result of this command.

Listing 4.5: Use yum provides to search packages containing a specific file

```
[root@hnl ~]# yum provides */zcat
Loaded plugins: product-id, refresh-packagekit, rhnplugin, security,
                : subscription-manager
Updating certificate-based repositories.
gzip-1.3.12-18.el6.x86_64 : The GNU data compression program
Repo        : myrepo
Matched from:
Filename    : /bin/zcat
gzip-1.3.12-18.el6.x86_64 : The GNU data compression program
Repo        : rhel-x86_64-server-6
Matched from:
Filename    : /bin/zcat
gzip-1.3.12-18.el6.x86_64 : The GNU data compression program
Repo        : installed
Matched from:
Filename    : /bin/zcat
```

You'll notice that sometimes it takes a while to search for packages with yum. This is because yum works with indexes that it has to download and update periodically from the repositories. Once these indexes are downloaded, yum will work a bit faster, but it may miss the latest updates that have been applied in the repositories. You can force yum to clear everything it has cached and download new index files by using yum clean all.

Installing and Updating Packages

Once you've found the package you were seeking, you can install it using yum install. For instance, if you want to install the network analysis tool nmap, after verifying that the name of the package is indeed nmap, you'd use yum install nmap to install the tool. Yum will then check the repositories to find out where it can find the most recent version of the program you're seeking, and after finding it, yum shows you what it wants to install. If there are no dependencies, it will show just one package. However, if there are dependencies, it displays a list of all the packages it needs to install in order to give you what you want. Next, type **Y** to confirm that you really want to install what yum has proposed, and the software will be installed.

There are two useful options when working with yum install. The first option, -y, can be used to automate things a bit. If you don't use it, yum will first display a summary of what it wants to install. Next it will prompt you to confirm, after which it will start the installation. Use yum install -y to proceed immediately, without any additional prompts for confirmation.

Another useful yum option is --nogpgcheck. If you occasionally don't want to perform a GPG check to install a package, just add --nogpgcheck to your yum install command. For instance, use yum install -y --nogpgcheck xinetd if you want to install the xinetd package without performing a GPG check and without having to confirm the installation. See Listing 4.6 for an example of how to install a package using yum install.

Listing 4.6: Installing packages with yum install

```
rhel-x86_64-server-6                                                  6989/6989
Setting up Install Process
Resolving Dependencies
--> Running transaction check
---> Package nmap.x86_64 2:5.21-4.el6 will be installed
--> Finished Dependency Resolution
Dependencies Resolved

================================================================================
 Package        Arch          Version           Repository        Size
================================================================================
Installing:
 nmap           x86_64        2:5.21-4.el6      myrepo            2.2 M
Transaction Summary
================================================================================
Install      1 Package(s)
Total download size: 2.2 M
Installed size: 7.3 M
Is this ok [y/N]: y
Downloading Packages:
Running rpm_check_debug
Running Transaction Test
Transaction Test Succeeded
Running Transaction
Warning: RPMDB altered outside of yum.
  Installing : 2:nmap-5.21-4.el6.x86_64                                     1/1
Installed products updated.
```

```
Installed:
  nmap.x86_64 2:5.21-4.el6
Complete!
You have new mail in /var/spool/mail/root
[root@hnl ~]#
```

In some cases, you may need to install an individual software package that is not in a repository but that you've downloaded as an RPM package. To install such packages, you could use the command rpm -ivh packagename.rpm. However, this command doesn't update the yum database, and therefore it's not a good idea to install packages using the rpm command. Use yum localinstall instead. This will update the yum database and also check the repositories to try to fix all potential dependency problems automatically, like you are used to when using yum install.

If a package has already been installed, you can use yum update to update it. Use this command with the name of the specific package you want to update, or just use yum update to check all repositories and find out whether more recent versions of the packages you're updating are available.

Normally, updating a package will remove the older version of a package, replacing it completely with the latest version. An exception occurs when you want to update the kernel. The command yum update kernel will install the newer version of the kernel, while keeping the older version on your server. It is useful because it allows you to boot the old kernel in case the new kernel is giving you problems.

Removing Packages

As is the case for installing packages, removing is also easy to do with yum. Just use yum remove followed by the name of the package you want to uninstall. For instance, to remove the package nmap, use yum remove nmap. The yum remove command will first provide an overview of what exactly it intends to do. In this overview, it will display the name of the package it intends to remove and all packages that depend on this package.

It is very important that you read carefully what yum intends to do. If the package you want to remove has many dependencies, by default yum will remove these dependencies as well. In some cases, it is not a good idea to proceed with the default setting. See Listing 4.7, for example, where the command yum remove bash is used. Fortunately, this command fails at the moment that yum wants to remove bash, because so many packages depend on it to be operational. It would really be a bad idea to remove bash!

Listing 4.7: Be careful when using yum remove

```
--> Processing Dependency: m17n-contrib-malayalam >= 1.1.3 for package:
m17n-db-malayalam-1.5.5-1.1.el6.noarch
---> Package m17n-contrib-marathi.noarch 0:1.1.10-4.el6_1.1 will be erased
---> Package m17n-contrib-oriya.noarch 0:1.1.10-4.el6_1.1 will be
erased
```

```
--> Processing Dependency: m17n-contrib-oriya >= 1.1.3 for package: m17n-db-
oriya-1.5.5-1.1.el6.noarch
---> Package m17n-contrib-punjabi.noarch 0:1.1.10-4.el6_1.1 will be erased
--> Processing Dependency: m17n-contrib-punjabi >= 1.1.3 for package:
m17n-db-punjabi-1.5.5-1.1.el6.noarch
---> Package m17n-contrib-sinhala.noarch 0:1.1.10-4.el6_1.1 will be erased
--> Processing Dependency: m17n-contrib-sinhala >= 1.1.3 for package:
m17n-db-sinhala-1.5.5-1.1.el6.noarch
---> Package m17n-contrib-tamil.noarch 0:1.1.10-4.el6_1.1 will be erased
--> Processing Dependency: m17n-contrib-tamil >= 1.1.3 for package:
m17n-db-tamil-1.5.5-1.1.el6.noarch
---> Package m17n-contrib-telugu.noarch 0:1.1.10-4.el6_1.1 will be erased
--> Processing Dependency: m17n-contrib-telugu >= 1.1.3 for package:
m17n-db-telugu-1.5.5-1.1.el6.noarch
---> Package m17n-contrib-urdu.noarch 0:1.1.10-4.el6_1.1 will be erased
--> Running transaction check
---> Package m17n-db-assamese.noarch 0:1.5.5-1.1.el6 will be erased
---> Package m17n-db-bengali.noarch 0:1.5.5-1.1.el6 will be erased
---> Package m17n-db-gujarati.noarch 0:1.5.5-1.1.el6 will be erased
---> Package m17n-db-hindi.noarch 0:1.5.5-1.1.el6 will be erased
---> Package m17n-db-kannada.noarch 0:1.5.5-1.1.el6 will be erased
---> Package m17n-db-malayalam.noarch 0:1.5.5-1.1.el6 will be erased
---> Package m17n-db-oriya.noarch 0:1.5.5-1.1.el6 will be erased
---> Package m17n-db-punjabi.noarch 0:1.5.5-1.1.el6 will be erased
---> Package m17n-db-sinhala.noarch 0:1.5.5-1.1.el6 will be erased
---> Package m17n-db-tamil.noarch 0:1.5.5-1.1.el6 will be erased
---> Package m17n-db-telugu.noarch 0:1.5.5-1.1.el6 will be erased
--> Processing Dependency: /sbin/new-kernel-pkg for package: kernel-2.6.32-220.
el6.x86_64
Skipping the running kernel: kernel-2.6.32-220.el6.x86_64
--> Processing Dependency: /bin/sh for package: kernel-2.6.32-220.el6.x86_64
Skipping the running kernel: kernel-2.6.32-220.el6.x86_64
--> Restarting Dependency Resolution with new changes.
--> Running transaction check
--> Finished Dependency Resolution
Error: Trying to remove "yum", which is protected
 You could try using --skip-broken to work around the problem
 You could try running: rpm -Va --nofiles --nodigest
[root@hnl ~]#
```

If you're courageous, you can use the option -y with yum remove to tell yum that it shouldn't ask for any confirmation. I hope the preceding example has shown that this is an extremely bad idea, though. Make sure you never do this!

Working with Package Groups

To simplify installing software, yum works with the concept of package groups. In a package group, you'll find all software that relates to specific functionality, as in the package group Virtualization, which contains all packages that are used to implement a virtualization solution on your server.

To get more information about the packages in a yum group, use the yum groupinfo command. For instance, yum groupinfo Virtualization displays a list of all packages within this group. Next use yum groupinstall Virtualization to install all packages in the group.

In Table 4.1, you can find an overview of the most common yum commands. After this table you'll find Exercise 4.3, where you can practice your yum skills.

TABLE 4.1   Overview of common yum commands

Command	Use
yum search	Search for a package based on its name or a word in the package summary.
yum provides */filename	Search in yum packages to find the package that contains a filename.
yum install	Install packages from the repositories.
yum update [packagename]	Update all packages on your server or a specific one, if you include a package name.
yum localinstall	Install a package that is not in the repositories but available as an RPM file.
yum remove	Remove a package.
yum list installed	Provide a list of all packages that are installed. This is useful in combination with grep or to check whether a specific package has been installed.
yum grouplist	Provide a list of all yum package groups.
yum groupinstall	Install all packages in a package group.

EXERCISE 4.3

Installing Software with Yum

In this exercise, you will install the xeyes program. First, you'll learn how to locate the package that contains xeyes. After that, you'll request more information about this package and install it.

1. Use yum provides */xeyes to find the name of the package that contains the xeyes file. It will indicate that the xorg-x11-apps package contains this file.

2. Use yum info xorg-x11-apps to request more information about the xeyes package. It will display a short description of the package content and metadata, such as the installation size.

3. To get an exact list of the contents of the package, use repoquery -ql x11-xorg-apps. You'll see a list of all files that are in the package and that it also contains some other neat utilities, such as xkill and xload. (I recommend you run them and see what they do—they really are cool!)

4. Use yum install xorg-x11-apps to install the package to your system. The command provides you with an overview of the package and its dependencies, and it asks whether you want to install it. Answer by typing **y** on your keyboard.

5. Once the software has been installed, use yum update xorg-x11-apps. You probably understand why that doesn't work, but at least it gives you a taste for updating installed packages!

Querying Software

Once installed, it can be quite useful to query software. This helps you in a generic way to get more information about software installed on your computer. Moreover, querying RPM packages also helps you fix specific problems with packages, as you will discover in Exercise 4.4.

There are many ways to query software packages. Before finding out more about your currently installed software, be aware that there are two ways to perform a query. You can query packages that are currently installed on your system, and it's also possible to install package files that haven't yet been installed. To query an installed package, you can use one of the rpm -q options discussed next. To get information about a package that hasn't yet been installed, you need to add the -p option.

To request a list of files that are in the samba-common RPM file, for example, you can use the rpm -ql samba-common command, if this package is installed. In case it hasn't yet been installed, you need to use rpm -qpl samba-common-[version-number].rpm, where you also need to refer to the exact location of the samba-common file. If you omit it, you'll get an error message stating that the samba-common package hasn't yet been installed.

A very common way to query RPM packages is by using rpm -qa. This command generates a list of all RPM packages that are installed on your server and thus provides a useful means for finding out whether some software has been installed. For instance, if you want to check whether the media-player package is installed, you can use rpm -qa | grep mediaplayer.

A useful modification to rpm -qa is the -V option, which shows you if a package has been modified from its original version. Using rpm -qVa thus allows you to perform a basic integrity check on the software you have on your server. Every file that is shown in the output of this command has been modified since it was originally installed. Note that this command will take a long time to complete. Also note that it's not the best way, nor the only one, to perform an integrity check on your server. Tripwire offers better and more advanced options. Listing 4.8 displays the output of rpm -qVa.

Listing 4.8: rpm -qVa shows which packages have been modified since installation

```
[root@hn1 ~]# rpm -qVa
.M....G..    /var/log/gdm
.M.......    /var/run/gdm
missing      /var/run/gdm/greeter
SM5....T. c /etc/sysconfig/rhn/up2date
.M....... c /etc/cups/subscriptions.conf
..5....T. c /etc/yum/pluginconf.d/rhnplugin.conf
S.5....T. c /etc/rsyslog.conf
....L.... c /etc/pam.d/fingerprint-auth
....L.... c /etc/pam.d/password-auth
....L.... c /etc/pam.d/smartcard-auth
....L.... c /etc/pam.d/system-auth
..5....T. c /etc/inittab
.M...UG..    /var/run/abrt
```

The different query options that allow you to obtain information about installed packages, or about packages you are about to install, is also very useful. In particular, the query options in Table 4.2 are useful.

TABLE 4.2   Query options for installed packages

Query command	Result
rpm -ql packagename	Lists all files in packagename
rpm -qc packagename	Lists all configuration files in packagename
rpm -qd packagename	Lists all documentation files in packagename

To query packages that you haven't installed yet, you need to add the option -p. (Exercise 4.4 provides a nice sample walk-through of how this works.)

A particularly useful query option is the --scripts option. Use rpm -q --scripts packagename to apply this option. This option is useful because it shows the scripts that are executed when a package is installed. Because every RPM package is installed with root privileges, things can terribly go wrong if you install a package that contains a script that wants to do harm. For this reason, it is essential that you install packages only from sources that you really trust. If you need to install a package from an unverified source, use the --script option. Listing 4.9 shows the results of the --script option when applied to the httpd package, which is normally used to install the Apache web server.

Listing 4.9: Querying packages for scripts

```
[root@hnl Packages]# rpm -q --scripts httpd
preinstall scriptlet (using /bin/sh):
# Add the "apache" user
getent group apache >/dev/null || groupadd -g 48 -r apache
getent passwd apache >/dev/null || \
  useradd -r -u 48 -g apache -s /sbin/nologin \
    -d /var/www -c "Apache" apache
exit 0
postinstall scriptlet (using /bin/sh):
# Register the httpd service
/sbin/chkconfig --add httpd
preuninstall scriptlet (using /bin/sh):
if [ $1 = 0 ]; then
        /sbin/service httpd stop > /dev/null 2>&1
        /sbin/chkconfig --del httpd
fi
posttrans scriptlet (using /bin/sh):
/sbin/service httpd condrestart >/dev/null 2>&1 || :
[root@hnl Packages]#
```

As you can see, it requires a bit of knowledge of shell scripting to gauge the value of these scripts. You'll learn about this later in this book.

Finally, there is one more useful query option: rpm -qf. You can use this option to find out from which file a package originated. In Exercise 4.4, you'll see how this option is used to find out more about a package.

Use repoquery to query packages from the repositories. This command has the same options as rpm -q but is much more efficient for packages that haven't yet been installed and that are available from the repositories.

EXERCISE 4.4

Finding More Information About Installed Software

In this exercise, you'll walk through a scenario that often occurs while working with Linux servers. You want to configure a service, but you don't know where to find its configuration files. As an example, you'll use the `/usr/sbin/wpa_supplicant` program.

1. Use `rpm -qf /usr/sbin/wpa_supplicant` to find out from what package the `wpa_supplicant` file originated. It should show you the `wpa_supplicant` package.

2. Use `rpm -ql wpa_supplicant` to show a list of all the files in this package. As you can see, the names of numerous files are displayed, and this isn't very useful.

3. Now use `rpm -qc wpa_supplicant` to show just the configuration files used by this package. This yields a list of three files only and gives you an idea of where to start configuring the service.

 Real World Scenario

Using RPM Queries to Find a Configuration File

Imagine that you need to configure a new service. All you know is the name of the service and nothing else. Based on the name of the service and rpm query options, you can probably find everything you need to know. Let's imagine that you know the name of the service is `blah`. The first step would be to use `find / -name blah`, which gives an overview of all matching filenames. This would normally show a result as `/usr/bin/blah`. Based on that filename, you can now find the RPM it comes from: `rpm -qf /usr/bin/blah`. Now that you've found the name of the RPM, you can query it to find out which configuration files it uses (`rpm -qc blah`) or which documentation is available (`rpm -qd blah`). I often use this approach when starting to work with software I've never used before.

Extracting Files from RPM Packages

Software installed on your computer may become damaged. If this happens, it's good to know that you can extract files from the packages and copy them to the original location of the file.

Every RPM package consists of two parts: the metadata part that describes what is in the package and a `cpio` archive that contains the actual files in the package. If a file has been damaged, you can start with the `rpm -qf` query option to find out from what package the file originated. Next use `rpm2cpio | cpio -idmv` to extract the files from the package to a temporary location. In Exercise 4.5, you'll learn how to do this.

EXERCISE 4.5

Extracting Files from RPM Packages

In this exercise, you'll learn how to identify from which package a file originated. Next you'll extract the package to the /tmp directory, which allows you to copy the original file from the extracted RPM to the location where it's supposed to exist.

1. Use rm -f /usr/sbin/modem-manager. Oops! You've just deleted a file from your system! (It normally doesn't do any harm to delete modem-manager, because it's hardly ever used anymore.

2. Use rpm -qf /usr/sbin/modem-manager. This command shows that the file comes from the ModemManager package.

3. Copy the ModemManager package file from the repository you created in Exercise 4.1 to the /tmp directory by using the cp /repo/ModemM[Tab] /tmp command.

4. Change the directory to the /tmp command, and use rpm2cpio |cpio -idmv to extract the package.

5. The command you used in step 4 created a few subdirectories in /tmp. Activate the directory /tmp/usr/sbin, where you can find the modem-manager file. You can now copy it to its original location in /usr/sbin.

Summary

In this chapter, you learned how to install, query, and manage software on your Red Hat server. You also learned how you can use the RPM tool to get extensive information about the software installed on your server. In the next chapter, you'll learn how to manage storage on your server.

Chapter

5

Configuring and Managing Storage

TOPICS COVERED IN THIS CHAPTER:

- ✓ Understanding Partitions and Logical Volumes
- ✓ Creating Partitions
- ✓ Creating File Systems
- ✓ Mounting File Systems Automatically through fstab
- ✓ Working with Logical Volumes
- ✓ Creating Swap Space
- ✓ Working with Encrypted Volumes

In this chapter, you'll learn how to configure storage on your server. In Chapter 1, you learned how to create partitions and logical volumes from the Red Hat installation program. In this chapter, you'll learn about the command-line tools that are available to configure storage on a server that already has been installed.

First you'll read how to create partitions and logical volumes on your server, which allows you to create file systems on these volumes later. You'll read about the way to configure /etc/fstab to mount these file systems automatically. Also, in the section about logical volumes, you'll learn how to grow and shrink logical volumes and how to work with snapshots.

At the end of this chapter, you'll read about some advanced techniques that relate to working with storage. First, you'll learn how to set up *automount*, which helps you make storage available automatically when a user needs access to storage. Finally, you'll read how to set up encrypted volumes on your server. This helps you achieve a higher level of protection to prevent unauthorized access of files on your server.

Understanding Partitions and Logical Volumes

In Chapter 1, "Getting Started with Red Hat Enterprise Linux," you learned about partitions and logical volumes. You know that partitions offer a rather static way to configure storage on a server, whereas logical volumes offer a much more dynamic way to configure storage. However, all Red Hat servers have at least one partition that is used to boot the server, because the boot loader GRUB can't read data from logical volumes.

If you need only basic storage features, you'll use partitions on the storage devices. In all other cases, it is better to use logical volumes. The *Logical Volume Manager (LVM)* offers many benefits. The following are its most interesting features:

- LVM makes resizing of volumes possible.

- In LVM, you can work with snapshots, which are useful in making a reliable backup.

- In LVM, you can easily replace failing storage devices.

As previously noted, sometimes you just need to configure access to storage where you know that the storage configuration is never going to change. In that case, you can use partitions instead of LVM. Using partitions has one major benefit: it is much easier to create and manage partitions. Therefore, in the next section you'll learn how to create partitions on your server.

Creating Partitions

There are two ways to create and manage partitions on a Red Hat server. You can use the graphical *Palimpsest tool*, which you can start by selecting Applications ➤ System Tools ➤ Disk Utility (see Figure 5.1). Using this tool is somewhat easier than working with fdisk on the command line, but it has the disadvantage that not all Red Hat servers offer access to the graphical tools. Therefore, you're better off using command-line tools.

FIGURE 5.1   Creating partitions with Palimpsest

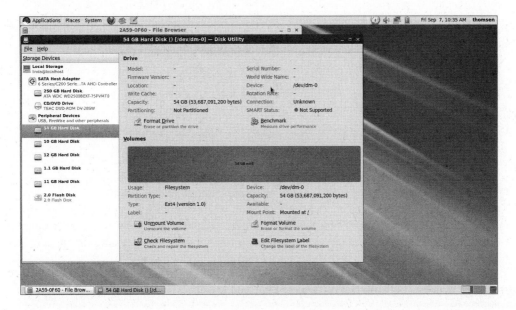

Two popular command-line tools are used to create partitions on RHEL. The *fdisk tool* is available on every Linux server. Alternatively, you can use the newer parted tool. In this book, you will be working with fdisk. There is good reason to focus on fdisk; it will always be available, even if you start a minimal rescue environment.

Creating a partition with fdisk is easy to do. After starting fdisk, you simply indicate you want to create a new partition. You can then create three kinds of partitions.

Primary Partitions   These are written directly to the master boot record of your hard drive. After creating four primary partitions, you can't add any more partitions—even if there is still a lot of disk space available. There's space for just four partitions in the partition table and no more than four.

Extended Partition   Every hard drive can have one extended partition. You cannot create a file system in an extended partition. The only thing you can do with it is to create logical partitions. You'll use an extended partition if you intend to use more than four partitions in total on a hard drive.

Logical Partitions   A logical partition (not to be confused with a logical volume) is created inside an extended partition. You can have a maximum of 11 logical partitions per disk, and you can create file systems on top of logical partitions.

No matter what kind of partition you're using, you can create a maximum of four partitions in the partition table. If you need more than four partitions, make sure to create one extended partition, which allows you to create 11 additional logical partitions.

After selecting between primary, extended, or logical partitions, you need to select a partition type. This is an indication to the operating system what the partition is to be used for. On RHEL servers, the following are the most common partition types:

83   This is the default partition type. It is used for any partition that is formatted with a Linux file system.

82   This type is used to indicate that the partition is used as swap space.

05   This partition type is used to indicate that it is an extended partition.

8e   Use this partition type if you want to use the partition as an LVM physical volume.

Many additional partition types are available, but you'll hardly ever use them.

Once you've created the partition, you'll write the changes to disk. Writing the new partition table to disk doesn't automatically mean your server can start using it right away. In many cases, you'll get an error message indicating that the device on which you've created the partition is busy. If this happens, you'll need to restart your server to activate the new partition. Exercise 5.1 shows how to create a partition.

EXERCISE 5.1

Creating Partitions

In this exercise, you'll create three partitions: a primary partition, an extended partition, and, within the latter, one logical partition. You can perform this exercise on the remaining free space on your hard drive. If you followed the procedures described in Chapter 1, you should have free and unallocated disk space. However, it is better to perform this procedure on an external storage device, such as a USB flash drive. Any 1GB or greater USB flash drive allows you to perform this procedure.

In this exercise, I'll describe how to work with an external medium, which is known to this server as /dev/sdb. You will learn how to recognize the device so that you do not mess up your current installation of Red Hat Enterprise Linux.

EXERCISE 5.1 *(continued)*

1. Insert the USB flash drive that you want to use with your server. If a window opens showing you the contents of the USB flash drive, close it.

2. Open a root shell, and type the command **dmesg**. You should see messages indicating that a new device has been found, and you should also see the device name of the USB flash drive. Listing 5.1 shows what these messages look like. In this listing, you can see that the name of this device is sdb.

Listing 5.1:   Verifying the device name with dmesg

```
VFS: busy inodes on changed media or resized disk sdb
VFS: busy inodes on changed media or resized disk sdb
usb 2-1.4: new high speed USB device using ehci_hcd and address 4
usb 2-1.4: New USB device found, idVendor=0951, idProduct=1603
usb 2-1.4: New USB device strings: Mfr=1, Product=2, SerialNumber=3
usb 2-1.4: Product: DataTraveler 2.0
usb 2-1.4: Manufacturer: Kingston
usb 2-1.4: SerialNumber: 899000000000000000000185
usb 2-1.4: configuration #1 chosen from 1 choice
scsi7 : SCSI emulation for USB Mass Storage devices
usb-storage: device found at 4
usb-storage: waiting for device to settle before scanning
usb-storage: device scan complete
scsi 7:0:0:0: Direct-Access     Kingston DataTraveler 2.0 1.00 PQ: 0 ANSI: 2
sd 7:0:0:0: Attached scsi generic sg2 type 0
sd 7:0:0:0: [sdb] 2007040 512-byte logical blocks: (1.02 GB/980 MiB)
sd 7:0:0:0: [sdb] Write Protect is off
sd 7:0:0:0: [sdb] Mode Sense: 23 00 00 00
sd 7:0:0:0: [sdb] Assuming drive cache: write through
sd 7:0:0:0: [sdb] Assuming drive cache: write through
 sdb: unknown partition table
sd 7:0:0:0: [sdb] Assuming drive cache: write through
sd 7:0:0:0: [sdb] Attached SCSI removable disk
[root@hnl ~]#
```

3. Now that you have found the name of the USB flash drive, use the following command to wipe out its contents completely: dd if=/dev/zero of=/dev/sdb.

The dd if=/dev/zero of=/dev/sdb command assumes that the USB flash drive with which you are working has the device name /dev/sdb. Make sure you are working with the right device before executing this command! If you are not sure, do not continue; you risk wiping all data on your computer if it is the wrong device. There is no way to recover your data after overwriting it with dd!

EXERCISE 5.1 *(continued)*

4. At this point, the USB flash drive is completely empty. Use **fdisk -cu /dev/sdb** to open fdisk on the device, and create new partitions on it. Listing 5.2 shows the fdisk output.

Listing 5.2: Opening the device in fdisk

```
[root@hnl ~]# fdisk -cu /dev/sdb
Device contains neither a valid DOS partition table, nor Sun, SGI or
OSF disklabel
Building a new DOS disklabel with disk identifier 0x3f075c76.
Changes will remain in memory only, until you decide to write them.
After that, of course, the previous content won't be recoverable.

Warning: invalid flag 0x0000 of partition table 4 will be corrected by w(rite)

Command (m for help):
```

5. From within the fdisk menu-driven interface, type **m** to see an overview of all commands that are available in fdisk. Listing 5.3 shows the results of this action.

Listing 5.3: Showing fdisk commands

```
Warning: invalid flag 0x0000 of partition table 4 will be corrected by w(rite)

Command (m for help): m
Command action
   a   toggle a bootable flag
   b   edit bsd disklabel
   c   toggle the dos compatibility flag
   d   delete a partition
   l   list known partition types
   m   print this menu
   n   add a new partition
   o   create a new empty DOS partition table
   p   print the partition table
   q   quit without saving changes
   s   create a new empty Sun disklabel
   t   change a partition's system id
   u   change display/entry units
   v   verify the partition table
   w   write table to disk and exit
   x   extra functionality (experts only)

Command (m for help):
```

6. Now type **n** to indicate you want to create a new partition. fdisk then asks you to choose between a primary and an extended partition. Type **p** for primary. Now you have to enter a partition number. Because there are no partitions currently on the USB flash drive, you can use partition 1. Next you have to enter the first sector of the partition. Press Enter to accept the default value of sector 2048. When asked for the last sector, type **+256M** and press Enter. At this point, you have created the new partition, but, by default, fdisk doesn't provide any confirmation. Type **p** to print a list of current partitions. Listing 5.4 shows all steps you performed.

Listing 5.4: Creating a new partition in fdisk

```
Command (m for help): n
Command action
   e   extended
   p   primary partition (1-4)
p
Partition number (1-4): 1
First sector (2048-2007039, default 2048):
Using default value 2048
Last sector, +sectors or +size{K,M,G} (2048-2007039, default 2007039): +256M

Command (m for help): p

Disk /dev/sdb: 1027 MB, 1027604480 bytes
32 heads, 62 sectors/track, 1011 cylinders, total 2007040 sectors
Units = sectors of 1 * 512 = 512 bytes
Sector size (logical/physical): 512 bytes / 512 bytes
I/O size (minimum/optimal): 512 bytes / 512 bytes
Disk identifier: 0x3f075c76

   Device Boot      Start         End      Blocks   Id  System
/dev/sdb1            2048      526335      262144   83  Linux

Command (m for help):
```

7. You have now created a primary partition. Let's continue and create an extended partition with a logical partition inside. Type **n** again to add this new partition. Now choose option **e** to indicate that you want to add an extended partition. When asked for the partition number, enter **2**. Next press Enter to accept the default starting sector that fdisk suggests for this partition. When asked for the last sector, hit Enter to accept the default. This will claim the rest of the available disk space for the extended partition. This is a good idea in general, because you are going to fill the extended partition with logical partitions anyway. You have now created the extended partition.

8. Since an extended partition by itself is useful only for holding logical partitions, press **n** again from the fdisk interface to add another partition. fdisk displays two different options: p to create another primary partition and 1 to create a logical partition. Because you have no more disk space available to add another primary partition, you have to enter **1** to create a logical partition. When asked for the first sector to use, press Enter. Next enter **+100M** to specify the size of the partition. At this point, it's a good idea to use the **p** command to print the current partition overview. Listing 5.5 shows what this all should look like.

Listing 5.5:   Verifying current partitioning

```
Command (m for help): n
Command action
   e   extended
   p   primary partition (1-4)
e
Partition number (1-4): 2
First sector (526336-2007039, default 526336):
Using default value 526336
Last sector, +sectors or +size{K,M,G} (526336-2007039, default 2007039):
Using default value 2007039

Command (m for help): n
Command action
   1   logical (5 or over)
   p   primary partition (1-4)
1
First sector (528384-2007039, default 528384):
Using default value 528384
Last sector, +sectors or +size{K,M,G} (528384-2007039, default 2007039): +100M

Command (m for help): p

Disk /dev/sdb: 1027 MB, 1027604480 bytes
32 heads, 62 sectors/track, 1011 cylinders, total 2007040 sectors
Units = sectors of 1 * 512 = 512 bytes
Sector size (logical/physical): 512 bytes / 512 bytes
I/O size (minimum/optimal): 512 bytes / 512 bytes
Disk identifier: 0x3f075c76
```

EXERCISE 5.1 *(continued)*

```
    Device Boot     Start        End    Blocks   Id  System
/dev/sdb1           2048     526335    262144   83  Linux
/dev/sdb2         526336    2007039    740352    5  Extended
/dev/sdb5         528384     733183    102400   83  Linux
```

Command (m for help):

9. If you are happy with the current partitioning, type the **w** command to write the new partitions to disk and exit. If you think something has gone wrong, type **x** to exit without saving and to keep the original configuration. In case you have any doubt, using x is a good idea because it won't change the original partitioning scheme in any way.

10. If you see a message indicating an error while activating the new partitions, reboot your server.

Red Hat suggests that you need to reboot your server to activate new partitions if they cannot be activated automatically. There is an unsupported alternative, though: use command partx -a /dev/sdb to update the kernel partition table. You should be aware, however, that this is an unsupported option and you risk losing data!

At this point, you have added partitions to your system. The next step is to do something with them. Since you created normal partitions, you would now typically go ahead and format them. In the next section, you'll learn how to do just that.

Creating File Systems

Once you have created one or more partitions or logical volumes (covered in the next section), most likely you'll put a file system on them next. In this section, you'll learn which file systems are available, how to format your partitions with these file systems, and how to set properties for the Ext4 file system.

File Systems Overview

Several file systems are available on Red Hat Enterprise Linux, but Ext4 is used as the default file system. Sometimes you may want to consider using another file system, however. Table 5.1 provides an overview of all the relevant file systems to consider.

TABLE 5.1   File system overview

File system	Use
Ext4	The default file system on RHEL. Use it if you're not sure which file system to use, because it's an excellent general-purpose file system.
Ext2/3	The predecessors of the Ext4 file system. Since Ext4 is much better, there is really no good reason to use Ext2 or Ext3, with one exception: Ext2 doesn't use a file system journal, and therefore it is a good choice for very small partitions (less than 100MB).
XFS	XFS must be purchased separately. It offers good performance for very large file systems and very large files. Ext4 has improved a lot recently, however, and therefore you should conduct proper performance tests to see whether you really need XFS.
Btrfs	Btrfs is the next generation of Linux file systems. It is organized in a completely different manner. An important difference is that it is based on a B-tree database, which makes the file system faster. It also has cool features like Copy on Write, which makes it very easy to revert to a previous version of a file. Apart from that, there are many more features that make Btrfs a versatile file system that is easy to grow and shrink. In RHEL 6.2 and newer, Btrfs is available as a tech preview version only, which means that it is not supported and not yet ready for production.
VFAT and MS-DOS	Sometimes it's useful to put files on a USB drive to exchange them among Windows users. This is the purpose of the VFAT and MS-DOS file systems. There is no need whatsoever to format partitions on your server with one of these file systems.
GFS	GFS is Red Hat's Global File System. It is designed for use in high availability clusters where multiple nodes need to be able to write to the same file system simultaneously.

As you can see, Red Hat offers several file systems so that you can use the one that is most appropriate for your environment. However, Ext4 is a good choice for almost any situation. For that reason, I will cover the use and configuration of the Ext4 file system exclusively in this book.

Before starting to format partitions and putting file systems on them, there is one file system feature of which you need to be aware—the file system journal. Modern Linux file systems offer journaling as a standard feature. The journal works as a transaction log in which the file system keeps records of files that are open for modification at any given time. The benefit of using a file system journal is that, if the server crashes, it can check to see what files were open at the time of the crash and immediately indicate which files are potentially damaged. Because using a journal helps protect your server, you would normally want to use it by default. There is one drawback to using a journal, however: a file system journal takes up disk space—an average of 50MB normally on Ext4. That means it's not a good idea to create a journal on very small file systems because it might leave insufficient space to hold your files. If this situation applies to some of your partitions, use the Ext2 file system.

Creating File Systems

To create a file system, you can use the *mkfs utility*. There are different versions of this utility—one for every file system type that is supported on your server. To create an ext4 file system, you use the `mkfs.ext4` command or, alternatively, the command `mkfs -t ext4`. It doesn't matter which of these you use because they both do the same thing.

Formatting a partition is straightforward. Although `mkfs.ext4` offers many different options, you won't need them in most cases, and you can run the command without additional arguments. In Exercise 5.2, you'll learn how to make an Ext4 file system on one of the partitions you created in Exercise 5.1.

EXERCISE 5.2

Creating a File System

In this exercise, you'll learn how to format a partition with the Ext4 file system.

1. Use the `fdisk -cul /dev/sdb` command to generate a list of all partitions that currently exist on the /dev/sdb device. You will see that /dev/sdb1 is available as a primary partition that has a type of 83. This is the partition on which you will create a file system.

2. Before creating the file system, you probably want to check that there is nothing already on the partition. To verify this, use the command `mount /dev/sdb1 /mnt`. If this command fails, everything is good. If the command succeeds, check that there are no files you want to keep on the partition by verifying the contents of the /mnt directory.

3. Assuming that you are able to create the file system, use `mkfs.ext4 /dev/sdb1` to format the sdb1 device. You'll see output similar to Listing 5.6.

4. Once you are finished, use `mount /dev/sdb1 /mnt` to check that you can mount it.

Listing 5.6: Making a file system

```
[root@hnl ~]# mkfs.ext4 /dev/sdb1
mke2fs 1.41.12 (17-May-2010)
Filesystem label=
OS type: Linux
Block size=1024 (log=0)
```

```
Fragment size=1024 (log=0)
Stride=0 blocks, Stripe width=0 blocks
65536 inodes, 262144 blocks
13107 blocks (5.00%) reserved for the super user
First data block=1
Maximum filesystem blocks=67371008
32 block groups
8192 blocks per group, 8192 fragments per group
2048 inodes per group
Superblock backups stored on blocks:
        8193, 24577, 40961, 57345, 73729, 204801, 221185

Writing inode tables: done
Creating journal (8192 blocks): done
Writing superblocks and filesystem accounting information: done

This filesystem will be automatically checked every 27 mounts or
180 days, whichever comes first.  Use tune2fs -c or -i to override.
```

Changing File System Properties

In most cases, you won't need to change any of the properties of your file systems. In some cases, however, it can be useful to change them anyway. The tune2fs command allows you to change properties, and with dumpe2fs, you can check the properties that are currently in use. Table 5.2 lists the most useful properties. You'll also see the tune2fs option to set the property in the list.

TABLE 5.2 Ext file system properties

Property	Use
-c max_mounts_count	Occasionally, an Ext file system must be checked. One way to force a periodic check is by setting the maximum mount count. Don't set it too low, because you'll have to wait a while for the file system check to finish. On large SAN disks, it's a good idea to disable the automated check completely to prevent unexpected checks after an emergency reboot.

Property	Use
`-i interval`	Setting a maximum mount count is one way to make sure that you'll see an occasional file system check. Another way to accomplish the same task is by setting an interface in days, months, or weeks.
`-m reserved_blocks_percent`	By default, 5 percent of an Ext file system is reserved for the user root. Use this option to change this percentage, but don't go below 5 percent.
`-L volume_label`	You can create a *file system label,* which is a name that is in the file system. Using file system labels makes it easier to mount the file system. Instead of using the device name, you can use `label=labelname`.
`-o mount_options`	Any option that you can use with `mount -o` can also be embedded in the file system as a default option using `-o option-name`.

Before setting file system properties, it's a good idea to check the properties that are currently in use. You can find this out using the `dumpe2fs` command. Listing 5.7 shows what the partial output of this command looks like. The `dumpe2fs` command provides a lot of output; only the first part of it, however, is really interesting because it shows current file system properties.

Listing 5.7: Showing file system properties with `dumpe2fs`

```
[root@hnl ~]# dumpe2fs /dev/sdb1 | less
Filesystem volume name:    <none>
Last mounted on:           <not available>
Filesystem UUID:           a9a9b28d-ec08-4f8c-9632-9e09942d5c4b
Filesystem magic number:   0xEF53
Filesystem revision #:     1 (dynamic)
Filesystem features:       has_journal ext_attr resize_inode dir_index
 filetype extent flex_bg sparse_super huge_file uninit_bg dir_nlink
 extra_isize
Filesystem flags:          signed_directory_hash
Default mount options:     (none)
Filesystem state:          clean
Errors behavior:           Continue
Filesystem OS type:        Linux
Inode count:               65536
Block count:               262144
```

Reserved block count:	13107
Free blocks:	243617
Free inodes:	65525
First block:	1
Block size:	1024
Fragment size:	1024
Reserved GDT blocks:	256
Blocks per group:	8192
Fragments per group:	8192

To change current file system properties, you can use the `tune2fs` command. The procedure in Exercise 5.3 shows you how to use this command to set a label for the file system you just created.

EXERCISE 5.3

Setting a File System Label

In this exercise, you'll use tune2fs to set a file system label. Next you'll verify that you have succeeded using the dumpe2fs command. After verifying this, you'll mount the file system using the file system label. This exercise is performed on the /dev/sdb1 file system that you created in the previous exercise.

1. Make sure the /dev/sdb1 device is not currently mounted by using umount /dev/sdb1.

2. Set the label to mylabel using tune2fs -L mylabel /dev/sdb1.

3. Use dumpe2fs /dev/sdb1 | less to verify that the label is set. It is listed as the file system volume name on the first line of the dumpe2fs output.

4. Use mount label=mylabel /mnt. The /dev/sdb1 device is now mounted on the /mnt directory.

Checking the File System Integrity

The integrity of your file systems will be thoroughly checked every so many boots (depending on the file system options settings) using the `fsck` command. A quick check is performed on every boot, and this will indicate whether your file system is in a healthy state. Thus, you shouldn't have to start a file system check yourself.

WARNING   If you suspect that something is wrong with your file system, you can run the `fsck` command manually. Make sure, however, that you run this command only on a file system that is not currently mounted.

You may also encounter a situation where, when you reboot your server, it prompts you to enter the password of the user root because something has gone wrong during the automatic file system check. In such cases, it may be necessary to perform a manual file system check.

The fsck command has a few useful options. You may try the -p option, which attempts to perform an automatic repair, without further prompting. If something is wrong with a file system, you may find that you have to respond to numerous prompts. Because it doesn't make any sense to press Y hundreds of times for confirmation, try using the -y option, which assumes yes as the answer to all prompts.

Mounting File Systems Automatically through fstab

In the previous section, you learned how to create partitions and how to format them using the Ext4 file system. At this point, you can mount them manually. As you can imagine, this isn't very handy if you want the file system to come up again after a reboot. To make sure that the file system is mounted automatically across reboots, you should put it in the /etc/fstab file. Listing 5.8 provides an example of the contents of this important configuration file.

Listing 5.8: Put file systems to be mounted automatically in /etc/fstab

```
[root@hnl ~]# cat /etc/fstab

#
# /etc/fstab
# Created by anaconda on Sun Jan 29 14:11:48 2012
#
# Accessible filesystems, by reference, are maintained under '/dev/disk'
# See man pages fstab(5), findfs(8), mount(8) and/or blkid(8) for more info
#
/dev/mapper/vg_hnl-lv_root /                     ext4      defaults        1 1
UUID=cc890fc9-a6a8-4c7c-8cc1-65f3f43037cb /boot             ext4
    defaults        1 2
/dev/mapper/vg_hnl-lv_home /home                 ext4      defaults        1 2
/dev/mapper/vg_hnl-lv_swap swap                  swap      defaults        0 0
tmpfs                 /dev/shm           tmpfs    defaults        0 0
devpts                /dev/pts           devpts   gid=5,mode=620  0 0
sysfs                 /sys               sysfs    defaults        0 0
proc                  /proc              proc     defaults        0 0
```

The /etc/fstab file is used to mount two different kinds of devices: you can mount file systems and system devices. In Listing 5.8, the first four lines are used to mount file systems, and the last four lines are used to mount specific system devices.

To specify how the mounts should be performed, six different columns are used:

- The name of the device to be mounted.

- The directory where this device should be mounted.

- The file system that should be used to mount the device.

- Specific mount options: use defaults if you want to perform the mount without any specific options.

- Dump support: use 1 if you want the dump backup utility to be able to make a backup of this device, and use 0 if you don't. It's good practice to enable dump support for all real file systems.

- fsck support: use 0 if you never want this file system to be checked automatically while booting. Use 1 for the root file system. This ensures that it will be checked before anything else takes place. Use 2 for all other file systems.

When creating the /etc/fstab file, you need to refer to the device you want to mount. There are several different ways of doing that. The easiest way is to use the device name, like /dev/sdb1, to indicate you want to mount the first partition on the second disk. The disadvantage of this approach is that the names of these devices depend on the order in which they were detected while booting, and this order can change. Some servers detect external USB hard drives before detecting internal devices that are connected to the SCSI bus. This means you might normally address the internal hard drive as /dev/sda. However, if someone forgets to remove an external USB drive while booting, the internal drive might be known as /dev/sdb after a reboot.

To avoid issues with the device names, Red Hat Enterprise Linux partitions are normally mounted by using the UUID that is assigned to every partition. To find out the UUIDs of the devices on your server, you can use the blkid command. Listing 5.9 shows the result of this command.

Listing 5.9: Finding block IDs with blkid

```
[root@hn1 ~]# blkid
/dev/sda1: UUID="cc890fc9-a6a8-4c7c-8cc1-65f3f43037cb" TYPE="ext4"
/dev/sda2: UUID="VDaoOy-ckKR-1U6f-6t0n-qzQr-vdxJ-c5HOv1" TYPE="LVM2_member"
/dev/mapper/vg_hn1-lv_root: UUID="961998c5-4aa9-4e8a-90b5-47a982041130"
 TYPE="ext4"
/dev/mapper/vg_hn1-lv_swap: UUID="5d47bfca-654e-4a59-9c4f-a5b0a8f5732d"
 TYPE="swap"
```

```
/dev/mapper/vg_hn1-lv_home: UUID="9574901d-4559-4f19-abce-b2bbe149f2a0"
 TYPE="ext4"
/dev/sdb1: LABEL="mylabel" UUID="a9a9b28d-ec08-4f8c-9632-9e09942d5c4b"
 TYPE="ext4"
```

In Listing 5.9, you can see the UUIDs of the partitions on this server as well as the LVM logical volumes, which are discussed in the next section. For mounting partitions, it is essential that you use the UUIDs, because the device names of partitions may change. For LVM logical volumes, it's not important because the LVM names are detected automatically when your server boots.

Another method for addressing devices with a name that doesn't change is to use the names in the /dev/disk directory. In this directory, you'll find four different subdirectories where the Linux kernel creates persistent names for devices. In SAN environments where iSCSI is used to connect to the SAN, the /dev/disk/by-path directory specifically provides useful names that make it easy to see the exact iSCSI identifier of the device.

> *iSCSI* is a method for connecting external partitions on a SAN to a server. This practice is very common in data center environments. You'll learn more about this technique in Chapter 15, "Setting Up a Mail Server."

Even though using persistent device names is useful for avoiding problems, you should eschew this method if you're working on machines that you want to clone, such as virtual machines in a VMware ESXi environment. The disadvantage of persistent device names is that these names are bound to the specific hardware, which means you'll get into trouble after restoring a cloned image to different hardware. Exercise 5.4 shows how to mount a device.

EXERCISE 5.4

Mounting Devices through /etc/fstab

In this exercise, you'll learn how to create an entry in /etc/fstab to mount the file system that you created in Exercise 5.3. You will use the UUID of the device to make sure that it also works if you restart your machine using another external disk device that is connected to it.

1. Open a root shell, and use the blkid command to find the UUID of the /dev/sdb1 device you created. If you're in a graphical environment, copy the UUID to the clipboard.

2. Every device should be mounted on a dedicated directory. In this exercise, you'll create a directory called/mounts/usb for this purpose. Use mkdir -p /mounts/usb to create this directory.

EXERCISE 5.4 *(continued)*

3. Open /etc/fstab in vi using vi /etc/fstab, and add a line with the following con-
    tents. Make sure to replace the UUID in the example line with the UUID that you
    found for your device.

    UUID= a9a9b28d-ec08-4f8c-9632-9e09942d5c4b /mounts/usb ext4 defaults 1 2.

4. Use the vi command :wq! to save and apply the changes to /etc/fstab.

5. Use mount -a to verify that the device can be mounted from /etc/fstab. The mount
    -a command tries to mount everything that has a line in /etc/fstab that hasn't been
    mounted already.

You are now able to add lines to /etc/fstab, and you've added a line that automatically
tries to mount your USB flash drive when your server reboots. This might not be a very
good idea because you will run into problems at reboot if the USB flash drive isn't present.
Because it's always good to be prepared, you'll see what happens in the next exercise where
you will reboot your computer without the USB flash drive inserted. In short, because the
boot procedure checks the integrity of the USB flash drive file system, this will not work
because the USB flash drive isn't available. This further means that fsck fails, which is considered a fatal condition in the boot procedure. For that reason, you'll drop into an emergency repair shell where you can fix the problem manually. In this case, the best solution is
to remove the line that tries to mount /etc/fstab completely.

You will encounter another problem, however. As you dropped into the emergency
repair shell, the root file system is not yet mounted in a read-write mode, and you cannot
apply changes to /etc/fstab. To apply the changes anyway, you'll first remount the root
file system in read-write mode using mount -o remount,rw /. This allows you to make all
of the required changes to the configuration file. Exercise 5.5 shows how to fix /etc/fstab
problems.

EXERCISE 5.5

Fixing /etc/fstab **Problems**

In this exercise, you'll remove the USB flash drive that you added for automatic mount in
/etc/fstab in the previous exercise. This will drop you into a root shell. Next you'll apply
the required procedure to fix this problem. Make sure you understand this procedure
because, sooner or later, you'll experience this situation for real.

1. Unplug the USB flash drive from your server and from a root shell, and type **reboot**
    to restart it.

2. You'll see that your server is stopping all services, after which it can restart. After
    a while, the graphical screen that normally displays while booting disappears, and

you'll see error messages. Read all of the messages on your computer below the line Checking filesystems. You'll see a message that starts with fsck.ext4: Unable to resolve 'UUID=... and ends with the text FAILED. On the last two lines, you'll see the message Give root password for maintenance (or type Control-D to continue).

3. Now enter the root password to open the Repair filesystem shell. Use the command **touch /somefile**, and you'll see a message that the file cannot be touched: Read-only file system.

4. Mount the root file system in read-write mode using **mount -o remount,rw /**.

5. Use **vi /etc/fstab** to open the fstab file, and move your cursor to the line on which you try to mount the USB file system. Without switching to Input mode, use the **vi dd** command to delete this line. Once it has been deleted, use the **vi :wq!** command to save the modifications and quit vi.

6. Use the Ctrl+D key sequence to reboot your server. It should now boot without any problems.

Working with Logical Volumes

In the previous sections, you learned how to create partitions and then how to create file systems on them. You'll now learn how to work with LVM logical volumes. First you'll learn how to create them. Then you'll read how to resize them and how to work with snapshots. In the last subsection, you'll learn how to remove a failing device using pvmove.

Creating Logical Volumes

To create logical volumes, you need to set up three different parts. The first part is the physical volume (PV). The *physical volume* is the actual storage device you want to use in your LVM configuration. This can be a LUN on the SAN, an entire disk, or a partition. If it is a partition, you'll need to create it as one marked with the 8e partition type. After that, you can use pvcreate to create the physical volume. Using this command is easy: the only mandatory argument specifies the name of the device you want to use, as in pvcreate /dev/sdb3.

The next step consists of setting up the volume group (VG). The *volume group* is the collection of all the storage devices you want to use in an LVM configuration. You'll see the total amount of storage in the volume group while you create the logical volumes in the next step. You'll use the vgcreate command to create the volume group. For example, use vgcreate mygroup /dev/sdb3 to set up a volume group that uses /dev/sdb3 as its physical volume.

The last step consists of creating the LVM volumes. To do this, you'll need to use the lvcreate command. This command needs to know which volume group to use and what size to stipulate for the logical volume. To specify the size, you can use -L to specify the size in kilo, mega, giga, tera, exa, or petabytes. Alternatively, you can use -l to specify the size in extents. The *extent* is the basic building block of the LVM logical volume, and it typically has a size of 4MB. Another very handy way to specify the size of the volume is by using -l 100%FREE, which uses all available extents in the volume group. An example of the command lvcreate is lvcreate -n myvol -L 100M mygroup, which creates a 100MB volume in the group mygroup.

In Figure 5.2, you can see a schematic overview of the way LVM is organized.

FIGURE 5.2 LVM schematic overview

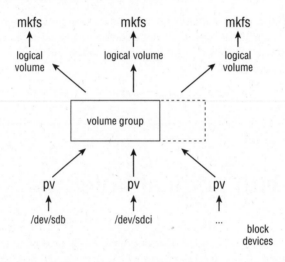

Exercise 5.6 shows how to create LVM logical volumes.

EXERCISE 5.6

Creating LVM Logical Volumes

In this exercise, you'll learn how to create LVM logical volumes. First you'll create a partition of partition type 8e. Next you'll use pvcreate to mark this partition as an LVM physical volume. After doing that, you can use vgcreate to create the volume group. As the last step of the procedure, you'll use lvcreate to set up the LVM logical volume. In this exercise, you'll continue to work on the /dev/sdb device you worked with in previous exercises in this chapter.

1. From a root shell, type **fdisk -cul /dev/sdb**. This should show the current partitioning of /dev/sdb, as in the example shown in Listing 5.10. You should have available disk space in the extended partition that you can see because the last sector in the extended partition is far beyond the last sector of the logical partition /dev/sdb5.

Listing 5.10: Displaying current partitioning

```
[root@hnl ~]# fdisk -cul /dev/sdb

Disk /dev/sdb: 1027 MB, 1027604480 bytes
32 heads, 62 sectors/track, 1011 cylinders, total 2007040 sectors
Units = sectors of 1 * 512 = 512 bytes
Sector size (logical/physical): 512 bytes / 512 bytes
I/O size (minimum/optimal): 512 bytes / 512 bytes
Disk identifier: 0x3f075c76

   Device Boot      Start         End      Blocks   Id  System
/dev/sdb1             2048      526335      262144   83  Linux
/dev/sdb2           526336     2007039      740352    5  Extended
/dev/sdb5           528384      733183      102400   83  Linux
[root@hnl ~]#
```

2. Type **fdisk -cu /dev/sdb** to open the fdisk interface. Now type **n** to create a new
    partition, and choose **1** for a logical partition. Next press Enter to select the default
    starting sector for this partition, and then type **+500M** to make this a 500MB partition.

3. Before writing the changes to disk, type **t** to change the partition type. When asked
    for the partition number, enter **6**. When asked for the partition type, enter **8e**. Next
    type **p** to print the current partitioning. Then type **w** to write the changes to disk. If
    you get an error message, reboot your server to update the kernel with the changes.
    In Listing 5.11 below you can see the entire procedure of adding a logical partition
    with the LVM partition type.

Listing 5.11: Adding a logical partition with the LVM partition type

```
[root@hnl ~]# fdisk -cu /dev/sdb

Command (m for help): n
Command action
   l   logical (5 or over)
   p   primary partition (1-4)
l
First sector (735232-2007039, default 735232):
Using default value 735232
Last sector, +sectors or +size{K,M,G} (735232-2007039, default
2007039): +200M

Command (m for help): t
Partition number (1-6): 6
```

EXERCISE 5.6 *(continued)*

Hex code (type L to list codes): 8e
Changed system type of partition 6 to 8e (Linux LVM)

Command (m for help): p

Disk /dev/sdb: 1027 MB, 1027604480 bytes
32 heads, 62 sectors/track, 1011 cylinders, total 2007040 sectors
Units = sectors of 1 * 512 = 512 bytes
Sector size (logical/physical): 512 bytes / 512 bytes
I/O size (minimum/optimal): 512 bytes / 512 bytes
Disk identifier: 0x3f075c76

Device Boot	Start	End	Blocks	Id	System
/dev/sdb1	2048	526335	262144	83	Linux
/dev/sdb2	526336	2007039	740352	5	Extended
/dev/sdb5	528384	733183	102400	83	Linux
/dev/sdb6	735232	1144831	204800	8e	Linux LVM

Command (m for help): w
The partition table has been altered!

Calling ioctl() to re-read partition table.
Syncing disks.

3. Now that you have created a partition and marked it as partition type 8e, use **pvcreate /dev/sdb** to convert it into an LVM physical volume. You will now see a message that the physical volume has been created successfully.

4. To create a volume group with the name usbvg and to put the physical volume /dev/sdb6 in it, use the command **vgcreate usbvg /dev/sdb6**.

5. Now that you have created a volume group that contains the physical volume on /dev/sdb6, use **lvcreate -n usbvol -L 100M usbvg**. This creates a logical volume that uses 50 percent of available disk space in the volume group.

6. To confirm that the logical volume has been created successfully, you can type the **lvs** command, which summarizes all currently existing logical volumes. Listing 5.12 shows the result of this command.

EXERCISE 5.6 *(continued)*

Listing 5.12: Displaying currently existing LVM logical volumes

```
[root@hnl ~]# lvcreate -n usbvol -L 100M usbvg
  Logical volume "usbvol" created
[root@hnl ~]# lvs
  LV       VG      Attr    LSize    Origin Snap% Move Log Copy% Convert
  usbvol   usbvg   -wi-a-  100.00m
  lv_home  vg_hnl  -wi-ao   11.00g
  lv_root  vg_hnl  -wi-ao   50.00g
  lv_swap  vg_hnl  -wi-ao    9.72g
```

7. Now that you have created the logical volume, you're ready to put a file system on it. Use `mkfs.ext4 /dev/usbvg/usbvol` to format the volume with an Ext4 file system.

While working with logical volumes, it is important to know which device name to use. By default, every LVM logical volume has a device name that is structured as /dev/name-of-vg/name-of-lv, like /dev/usbvg/usbvol in the preceding exercise.

An alternative name that exists by default for every LVM volume is in the /dev/mapper directory. There you'll find every logical volume with a name that is structured as /dev/mapper/vgname_lvname. This means the volume you created in the exercise will also be visible as /dev/mapper/usbvg-subvol. You can use either of these names to address the logical volume.

While managing LVM from the command line gives you many more options and possibilities, you can also use the graphical tool system-config-lvm, which offers an easy-to-use graphical interface for LVM management. You will probably miss some features, however, when you use this tool. Figure 5.3 shows the system-config-lvm interface.

Resizing Logical Volumes

One of the advantages of working with LVM is that you can resize volumes if you're out of disk space. That goes both ways: you can extend a volume that has become too small, and you can shrink a volume if you need to offer some of the disk space somewhere else.

When resizing logical volumes, you always have to resize the file system that is on it as well. If you are extending a logical volume, you will first extend the volume itself, and then you can extend the file system that is on it. When you reduce a logical volume, you first need to reduce the file system before you can reduce the size of the logical volume. To resize any Ext file system (Ext2, Ext3, or Ext4), you can use `resize2fs`.

Sometimes you'll need to extend the volume group before you can extend a logical volume. This occurs when you have allocated all available disk space in the volume group previously. To extend a volume group, you have to add new physical volumes to it.

The three common scenarios for resizing a logical volume are as follows:

- Extending a logical volume if there are still unallocated extents in the volume group.

- Extending a logical volume if there are no longer any unallocated extents in the volume group. When this occurs, you'll need to extend the volume group first.

- Shrinking a logical volume.

FIGURE 5.3 The system-config-lvm tool allows you to manage LVM from a graphical interface.

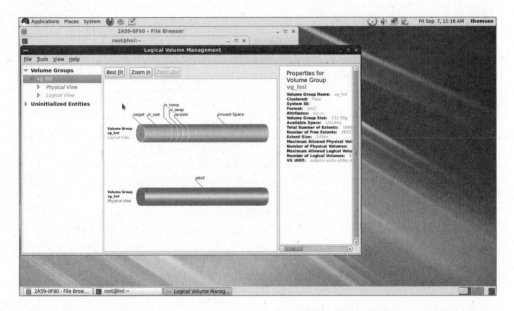

In the following three exercises (Exercises 5.7 through 5.9), you'll learn how to perform these procedures.

EXERCISE 5.7

Extending a Logical Volume

In this exercise, you'll extend the logical volume you created in Exercise 5.6. At this point, there still is unallocated space available in the volume group, so you just have to grow the logical volume. After that, you need to extend the Ext file system as well.

1. Type **vgs** to get an overview of the current volume groups. If you've succeeded in the preceding exercises, you'll have a VG with the name usbvg that still has 96MB of unassigned disk space. Listing 5.13 shows the result of this.

EXERCISE 5.7 *(continued)*

Listing 5.13: Checking available disk space in volume groups

```
[root@hnl ~]# vgs
  VG      #PV #LV #SN Attr   VSize    VFree
  usbvg    1   1   0 wz--n- 196.00m  96.00m
  vg_hnl   1   3   0 wz--n- 232.39g 161.68g
[root@hnl ~]#
```

2. Use **lvextend -l +100%FREE /dev/usbvg/usbvol**. This command adds 100 percent of all free extents to the usbvol logical volume and tells you that it now has a size of 196MB.

3. Type **resize2fs /dev/usbvg/usbvol**. This extends the file system on the logical volume to the current size of the logical volume.

In the previous exercise, you learned how to extend a logical volume that is in a VG that still has unallocated extents. Unfortunately, it won't be always that easy. In many cases, the volume group will no longer have unallocated extents, which means you first need to extend it by adding a physical volume to it. The next procedure shows how to do this.

EXERCISE 5.8

Extending a Volume Group

If you want to extend a logical volume and you don't have unallocated extents in the volume group, you first need to create a physical volume and add that to the volume group. This exercise describes how to do this.

1. Use the vgs command to confirm that VFree indicates that no unallocated disk space is available.

2. Use the procedure that you learned earlier to create a logical partition called /dev/sdb7 that has a size of 100MB. Remember to set the partition type to 8e. Write the changes to disk, and when fdisk indicates that rereading the partition table has failed, reboot your server.

3. Use **vgextend usbvg /dev/sdb7** to extend the volume group with the physical volume you just created. To confirm that you were successful, type **vgs**, which now shows that there are 96MB of available disk space within the VG. Listing 5.14 shows the results of performing these steps.

Listing 5.14: Extending a volume group

```
[root@hnl ~]# vgextend usbvg /dev/sdb7
 No physical volume label read from /dev/sdb7
```

EXERCISE 5.8 *(continued)*

```
Writing physical volume data to disk "/dev/sdb7"
Physical volume "/dev/sdb7" successfully created
Volume group "usbvg" successfully extended
[root@hn1 ~]# vgs
  VG      #PV #LV #SN Attr   VSize    VFree
  usbvg    2   1   0 wz--n- 292.00m  96.00m
  vg_hn1   1   3   0 wz--n- 232.39g 161.68g
```

In the preceding exercise, you extended a volume group. At this point, you can grow any of the logical volumes in the volume group. You learned how to do that in Exercise 5.8, and therefore that procedure won't be repeated here.

EXERCISE 5.9

Reducing a Logical Volume

If you need to reduce a logical volume, you first have to reduce the file system that is on it. You can do that only on an unmounted file system that has been checked previously. This exercise describes the procedure that you have to apply in this situation.

1. Before shrinking an LVM logical volume, you first must reduce the size of the file system. Before reducing the size of the file system, you must unmount the file system and check its integrity. To do so, use **umount /dev/usbvg/usbvol** and use **e2fsck -f /dev/usbvg/usbvol** to check its integrity.

2. Once the check is completed, use **resize2fs /dev/usbvg/usbvol 100M** to shrink the file system on the volume to 100MB.

3. Use **lvreduce -L 100M /dev/usbvg/usbvol** to reduce the size of the volume to 100MB as well. Once completed, you can now safely mount the reduced volume.

Working with Snapshots

Using an LVM *snapshot* allows you to freeze the current state of an LVM volume. Creating a snapshot allows you to keep the current state of a volume and gives you an easy option for reverting to this state later if that becomes necessary. Snapshots are also commonly used to create backups safely. Instead of making a backup of the normal LVM volume where files may be opened, you can create a backup from the snapshot volume, where no file will be open at any time.

To appreciate what happens while creating snapshots, you need to understand that a volume consists of two essential parts: the file system metadata and the actual blocks containing data in a file. The file system uses the metadata pointers to find the file's data blocks.

When initially creating a snapshot, the file system metadata is copied to the newly created snapshot volume. The file blocks stay on the original volume, however, and as long as nothing has changed in the snapshot metadata, all pointers to the blocks on the original volume remain correct. When a file changes on the original volume, the original blocks are copied to the snapshot volume before the change is committed to the file system. This means that the longer the snapshot exists, the bigger it will become. This also means you have to estimate the number of changes that are going to take place on the original volume in order to create the right size snapshot. If only a few changes are expected for a snapshot that you'll use to create a backup, 5 percent of the size of the original volume may be enough. If you're using snapshots to be able to revert to the original state before you start a large test, you will need much more than just 5 percent.

Every snapshot has a life cycle; that is, it's not meant to exist forever. If you no longer need the snapshot, you can delete it using the `lvremove` command. In Exercise 5.10, you'll learn how to create and work with a snapshot.

EXERCISE 5.10

Managing Snapshots

In this exercise, you'll start by creating a few dummy files on the original volume you created in earlier exercises. Then you'll create a snapshot volume and mount it to see whether it contains the same files as the original volume. Next you'll delete all files from the original volume to find out whether they are still available on the snapshot. Then you'll revert the snapshot to the original volume to restore the original state of this volume. At the end of this exercise, you'll delete the snapshot, a task that you always have to perform to end the snapshot life cycle.

1. Use **vgs** to get an overview of current use of disk space in your volume groups. This shows that usbvg has enough available disk space to create a snapshot. For this test, 50MB will be enough for the snapshot.

2. Use **mount /dev/usbvg/usbvol /mnt** to mount the original volume on the /mnt directory. Next use **cp /etc/* /mnt** to copy some files to the original volume.

3. Use **lvcreate -s -L 50M -n usbvol_snap /dev/usbvg/usbvol**. You'll see that the size is rounded up to 52MB because a basic allocation unit of 4MB is used to create logical volumes.

4. Use **lvs** to verify the creation of the snapshot volume. You'll see that the snapshot volume is clearly listed as the snapshot of the original volume (see Listing 5.15).

Listing 5.15: Verifying the creation of the snapshot

```
[root@hnl mnt]# lvcreate -s -L 50M -n usbvol_snap /dev/usbvg/usbvol
  Rounding up size to full physical extent 52.00 MiB
```

```
  Logical volume "usbvol_snap" created
[root@hnl mnt]# lvs
  LV           VG      Attr   LSize   Origin Snap%  Move Log Copy%  Convert
  usbvol       usbvg   owi-ao 100.00m
  usbvol_snap  usbvg   swi-a-  52.00m usbvol  0.02
  lv_home      vg_hnl  -wi-ao  11.00g
  lv_root      vg_hnl  -wi-ao  50.00g
  lv_swap      vg_hnl  -wi-ao   9.72g
```

4. Use **mkdir /mnt2** to create a temporary mounting point for the snapshot, and mount it there using **mount /dev/usbvg/usbvol_snap /mnt2**. Switch to the /mnt2 directory to check to see that the contents are similar to the contents of the /mnt directory where the original usbvol volume is mounted.

5. Change to the /mnt directory, and use **rm -f** *. This removes all files from the /mnt directory. Change back to the /mnt2 directory to see that all files still exist there.

6. Use **lvconvert --merge /dev/usbvg/usbvol_snap** to schedule the merge of the snapshot back into the original volume at the next volume activation. You'll see some error messages that you can safely ignore. Now unmount the snapshot using **umount /mnt2**.

7. Unmount the original volume using **umount /mnt**. Next use **lvchange -a n /dev/usbvg/usbvol; lvchange -a y /dev/usbvg/usbvol**. This deactivates and then activates the original volume, which is a required step in merging the snapshot back into the original volume. If you see an error relating to the /var/lock directory, ignore it.

8. Use **ls /mnt** to show the contents of the /mnt directory, which verifies that you succeeded in performing this procedure.

9. You don't need to remove the snapshot. By converting the snapshot back into the original volume, you've automatically removed the snapshot volume. In Listing 5.16 you can see what happens when merging snapshots back into the original volume.

Listing 5.16: Merging snapshots back into the original volume

```
[root@hnl /]# lvconvert --merge /dev/usbvg/usbvol_snap
  Can't merge over open origin volume
  Can't merge when snapshot is open
  Merging of snapshot usbvol_snap will start next activation.
[root@hnl /]# umount /mnt2
[root@hnl /]# umount /mnt
```

```
[root@hn1 /]# lvchange -a n /dev/usbvg/usbvol; lvchange -a y /dev/usbvg/usbvol
  /var/lock/lvm/V_usbvg: unlink failed: No such file or directory
[root@hn1 /]# mount /dev/usbvg/usbvol /mnt
```

Replacing Failing Storage Devices

On occasion, you may see errors in your syslog relating to a device that you're using in LVM. If that happens, you can pvmove all physical extents from the failing device to another device in the same VG. This frees up the failing device, which allows you to remove it and replace it with a new physical volume.

Although this technique doesn't make much sense in an environment where you have only one hard disk in your server, it is indeed very useful in a typical datacenter environment where storage is spread among different volumes on the SAN. Using a SAN and pvmove allows you to be very flexible in regard to storage in LVM.

There is just one requirement before you can start using pvmove: you need replacement disk space. Typically, that means you need to add a new volume of the same size as the one you're about to remove before you can start using pvmove to move the physical volume out of your volume group. Once you've done that, moving out a physical volume really is easy: just type pvmove followed by the name of the volume you need to replace, for instance, pvmove /dev/sdb7.

Creating Swap Space

Every server needs swap space, even if it's never going to use it. *Swap space* is allocated when your server is completely out of memory, and using swap space allows your server to continue to offer its services. Therefore, you should always have at least a minimal amount of swap space available.

In many cases, it's enough to allocate just 1GB of swap space, just in case the server is out of memory. There are some scenarios in which you need more swap space. Here are some examples:

- If you install on a laptop, you need RAM + 1GB to be able to close the lid of the laptop to suspend it. Typically, however, you don't use laptops for RHEL servers.

- If you install an application that has specific demands in regard to the amount of swap space, make sure to honor these requirements. If you don't, you may no longer be supported. Oracle databases and SAP Netweaver are well-known examples of such applications.

You would normally create swap space while installing the server, but you can also add it later. Adding swap space is a four-step procedure.

1. Make sure to create a device you're going to use as the swap device. Typically, this would be a partition or a logical volume, but you can also use dd to create a large empty file. For the Linux kernel it doesn't matter—the kernel addresses swap space directly, no matter where it is.

2. Use mkswap to format the swap device. This is similar to the creation of a file system on a storage device.

3. Use swapon to activate the swap space. You can compare this to the mounting of the file system, which ensures you can actually put files on it.

4. Create a line in /etc/fstab to activate the swap space automatically the next time you reboot your server.

In Exercise 5.11, you'll learn how to add a swap file to your system and mount it automatically through fstab.

EXERCISE 5.11

Creating a Swap File

In this exercise, you'll learn how to use dd to create a file that is filled with all zeroes, which you can use as a swap file. Next you'll use mkswap and swapon on this file to format it as a swap file and to start using it. Finally, you'll put it in /etc/fstab to make sure it is activated automatically the next time you restart your server.

1. Use **dd if=/dev/zero of=/swapfile bs=1M count=1024**. This command creates a 1GB swap file in the root directory of your server.

2. Use **mkswap /swapfile** to mark this file as swap space.

3. Type **free -m** to verify the current amount of swap space on your server. This amount is expressed in megabytes.

4. Type **swapon /swapfile** to activate the swap file.

5. Type **free -m** again to verify that you just added 1GB of swap space.

6. Open /etc/fstab with an editor, and put in the following line: **/swapfile   swap   swap   defaults   0 0.** In Listing 5.17 you can see the entire procedure of adding swap space to a system.

Listing 5.17: Creating swap space

```
[root@hnl /]# dd if=/dev/zero of=/swapfile bs=1M count=1024
1024+0 records in
1024+0 records out
```

```
1073741824 bytes (1.1 GB) copied, 0.650588 s, 1.7 GB/s
[root@hnl /]# mkswap /swapfile
mkswap: /swapfile: warning: don't erase bootbits sectors
        on whole disk. Use -f to force.
Setting up swapspace version 1, size = 1048572 KiB
no label, UUID=204fb22f-ba2d-4240-a4a4-5edf953257ba
[root@hnl /]# free -m
             total       used       free     shared    buffers     cached
Mem:          7768       1662       6105          0         28       1246
-/+ buffers/cache:        388       7379
Swap:         9951          0       9951
[root@hnl /]# swapon /swapfile
[root@hnl /]# free -m
             total       used       free     shared    buffers     cached
Mem:          7768       1659       6108          0         28       1246
-/+ buffers/cache:        385       7382
Swap:        10975          0      10975
```

Working with Encrypted Volumes

Normally, files on servers must be protected from people who are trying to get unauthorized access to them remotely. However, if someone succeeds in getting physical access to your server, the situation is different. Once logged in as root, access to all files on the servers is available. In the next chapter, you'll learn that it's not hard at all to log in as root—even if you don't have the root password.

Normally a server is well protected, and unauthorized people are not allowed access to it. But if Linux is installed on a laptop, it's even worse because you might forget the laptop on the train or any other public location where a skilled person can easily gain access to all data on the laptop. That's why encrypted drives can be useful.

In this section, you'll learn how to use *LUKS (Linux Unified Key Setup)* to create an encrypted volume. Follow along with this six-step procedure:

1. First you'll need to create the device you want to encrypt. This can be an LVM logical volume or a partition.

2. After creating the device, you need to format it as an encrypted device. To do that, use the **cryptsetup luksFormat /dev/yourdevice** command. While doing this, you'll also set the decryption password. Make sure to remember this password, because it is the only way to get access to a device once it has been encrypted!

3. Once the device is formatted as an encrypted device, you need to open it before you can do anything with it. When opening it, you assign a name to the encrypted device. This name occurs in the /dev/mapper directory, because this entire procedure is managed by Device Mapper. Use **cryptsetup luksOpen /dev/yourdevice cryptdevicename**, for example, to create the device /dev/mapper/cryptdevicename.

4. Now that you've opened the encrypted device and made it accessible through the /dev/mapper/cryptdevice device, you can create a file system on it. To do this, use mkfs: **mkfs.ext4 /dev/mapper/cryptdevicename**.

5. At this point, you can mount the encrypted device and put files on it. Use **mount /dev/mapper/cryptdevicename /somewhere** to mount it, and do whatever else you want to do to it.

6. After using the encrypted device, use umount to unmount. This doesn't close the encrypted device. To close it, also (which ensures that it is accessible only after entering the password), use **cryptsetup luksClose cryptdevicename**.

In Exercise 5.12, you will create the encrypted device.

EXERCISE 5.12

Creating an Encrypted Device

In this exercise, you'll learn how to create an encrypted device. You'll use the luksFormat and luksOpen commands in cryptsetup to create and open the device. Next you'll put a file system on it using mkfs.ext4. After verifying that it works, you'll unmount the file system and use luksClose to close the device to make sure it is closed to unauthorized access.

1. Create a new partition on the USB flash drive you used in earlier exercises in this chapter. Create it as a 250MB logical partition. If you've done all of the preceding exercises, the partition will be created as /dev/sdb8.

You know that you have to reboot to activate a new partition. There is also another way, but it is unsupported, so use it at your own risk! To update the kernel with the new partitions you just created on /dev/sdb, you can also use partx -a /dev/sdb.

2. Use **cryptsetup luksFormat /dev/sdb8** to format the newly created partition as an encrypted one. When asked if you really want to do this, type **YES** (all in uppercase). Next, enter the password you're going to use. Type it a second time, and wait a few seconds while the encrypted partition is formatted.

3. Now type **cryptsetup luksOpen /dev/sdb8 confidential** to open the encrypted volume and make it accessible as the device /dev/mapper/confidential. Use **ls /dev/mapper** to verify that the device has been created correctly. Listing 5.18 shows what has occurred so far.

EXERCISE 5.12 *(continued)*

Listing 5.18: Creating and opening an encrypted volume

```
[root@hnl /]# cryptsetup luksFormat /dev/sdb8

WARNING!
========
This will overwrite data on /dev/sdb8 irrevocably.

Are you sure? (Type uppercase yes): YES
Enter LUKS passphrase:
Verify passphrase:
[root@hnl /]# cryptsetup luksOpen /dev/sdb8 confidential
Enter passphrase for /dev/sdb8:
[root@hnl /]# cd /dev/mapper
[root@hnl mapper]# ls
confidential  usbvg-usbvol    vg_hnl-lv_root
control       vg_hnl-lv_home  vg_hnl-lv_swap
[root@hnl mapper]#
```

4. Now use **mkfs.ext4 /dev/mapper/confidential** to put a file system on the encrypted device you've just opened.

5. Mount the device using **mount /dev/mapper/confidential /mnt**. Copy some files to it from the /etc directory by using **cp /etc/[ps][ah]* /mnt**.

6. Unmount the encrypted device using **umount /mnt**, and close it using **cryptsetup luksClose confidential**. This locks all content on the device. You can also see that the device /dev/mapper/confidential no longer exists.

In the preceding exercise, you learned how to create an encrypted device and mount it manually. That's nice, but if the encrypted device is on your hard drive, you might want to mount it automatically while your server boots. To do this, you need to put it in /etc/fstab, as you learned previously in this chapter.

However, you can't just put an encrypted device in /etc/fstab if it hasn't been created first. To create the encrypted device, you need another file with the name /etc/crypttab. You put three fields in this file.

- The name of the encrypted device in the way that you want to use it.
- The name of the real physical device you want to open.
- Optionally, you can also refer to a password file.

Using a password file on an encrypted device is kind of weird: it automatically enters the password while you are booting. Because this makes it kind of silly to encrypt the device anyway, you'd better completely forget about the password file. This means you just need two fields in /etc/crypttab: the name of the encrypted device once it is opened and the name of the real underlying device, as in the following example:

```
confidential /dev/sdb8
```

After making sure you've created the /etc/crypttab file, you can put a line in /etc/fstab that mounts the encrypted device as it exists after opening in the /dev/mapper directory. This means you won't mount /dev/sdb8, but you'll mount /dev/mapper/confidential instead. The following line shows what the line in /etc/fstab should look like:

```
/dev/mapper/confidential /confidential ext4 defaults 1 2
```

In Exercise 5.13, you'll learn how to create these two files.

EXERCISE 5.13

Mounting an Encrypted Device Automatically

In this exercise, you'll automatically mount the encrypted device you created in Exercise 5.12. First you'll create /etc/crypttab, containing one line that automates the crypt-setup luksOpen command. After doing this, you can add a line to /etc/fstab to mount the encrypted device automatically. Even though you won't be using a password file, you'll be prompted while booting to enter a password.

1. Use **vi /etc/crypttab** to open the file /etc/crypttab. Put the following line in it:

    ```
    confidential /dev/sdb8
    ```

2. Use **mkdir /confidential** to create a directory with the name /confidential.

3. Use **vi /etc/fstab**, and put the following line in it:

    ```
    /dev/mapper/confidential    /confidential    ext4    defaults    1 2
    ```

4. Restart your server using the reboot command. Notice that you'll need to enter the password while rebooting.

Summary

In this chapter, you learned how to work with storage. You created partitions and logical volumes, and you learned how to mount them automatically using /etc/fstab. You also learned about the many possibilities that LVM logical volumes offer. Beyond that, you learned how to analyze file systems using fsck and set up encrypted volumes for increased protection of files on your server. In the next chapter, you'll learn what happens when your Linux server boots.

Chapter

6

Connecting to the Network

TOPICS COVERED IN THIS CHAPTER:

✓ Understanding NetworkManager

✓ Configuring Networking from the Command Line

✓ Troubleshooting Networking

✓ Setting Up IPv6

✓ Configuring SSH

✓ Configuring VNC Server Access

In the previous chapter, you learned how to configure storage on your server. In this chapter, you'll learn about the last essential task of Red Hat Server administration—configuring the network.

Understanding NetworkManager

In Red Hat Enterprise Linux 6, the *NetworkManager service* is used to start the network. This service is conveniently available from the graphical desktop as an icon that indicates the current status of the network.

Also, if your server doesn't employ a graphical desktop by default, it still uses NetworkManager as a service. This service reads its configuration files during start-up. In this section, you'll learn how to configure the service, focusing on the configuration files behind the service. Before you study NetworkManager itself, it's a good idea to look at how Red Hat Enterprise Linux deals with services in general.

Working with Services and Runlevels

Many services are typically offered in a Red Hat Enterprise Linux environment. A service starts as your server boots. The exact services start-up process is determined by the runlevel in which the server boots. The *runlevel* defines the state in which the server boots. Every runlevel is referenced by number. Common runlevels are runlevel 3 and runlevel 5. Runlevel 3 is used to start services that are needed on a server that starts without a graphical user interface, and runlevel 5 is used to define a mode where the runlevel starts with a graphical interface. In each runlevel, service scripts are started. These service scripts are installed in the /etc/init.d directory and managed with the service command.

Most services provided by a Red Hat Enterprise Linux server are offered by a service script that starts when your server boots. These Bash shell scripts are written in a generic way, which allows your server to handle them all in the same manner. You can find the scripts in the /etc/init.d directory.

A service script doesn't contain any variable parameters. All variable parameters are read while the service script starts, either from its configuration file in the /etc directory or from a configuration file that it uses, which is stored in the /etc/sysconfig directory.

Typically, the configuration files in the /etc/sysconfig directory contain parameters that are required at the very first stage of the service start process; the configuration files in /etc are read once the server has started, and they determine exactly what the service should do.

To manage service scripts, two commands are relevant. First there is the service command, which you can use to start, stop, and monitor all of the service scripts in the /etc/init.d directory. Next there is the chkconfig command, which you can use to enable the service in the runlevel. In Exercise 6.1, you'll learn how to use both commands on the ntpd service, the process that is used for NTP time synchronization. (For more information about this, read Chapter 11, "Setting Up Cryptographic Services.")

EXERCISE 6.1

Working with Services

In this exercise, you'll learn how to work with services. You'll use the ntpd service as a sample service. First you'll learn how to monitor the current state of the service and how to start it. Then, once you've accomplished that, you'll learn how to enable the service so that it will automatically be started the next time you boot your server.

1. Open a root shell, and use **cd** to go to the directory /etc/init.d. Type **ls** to get a list of all service scripts currently in existence on your server.

2. Type **service ntpd status**. This should tell you that the ntpd service is currently stopped.

3. Type **service ntpd start** to start the ntpd service. You'll see the message starting ntpd, followed by the text [OK] to confirm that ntpd has started successfully.

4. At this moment, you've started ntpd, but after a reboot it won't be started automatically. Use **chkconfig ntpd on** to add the ntpd service to the runlevels of your server.

5. To verify that ntpd has indeed been added to your server's runlevels, type **chkconfig --list** (see also Listing 6.1). This command lists all services and their current status. If you want, you can filter the results by adding **grep ntpd** to the chkconfig --list command.

Listing 6.1: Displaying current service enablement using chkconfig --list

```
[root@hnl ~]# chkconfig --list
NetworkManager  0:off  1:off  2:on   3:on   4:on   5:on   6:off
abrt-ccpp       0:off  1:off  2:off  3:on   4:off  5:on   6:off
abrt-oops       0:off  1:off  2:off  3:on   4:off  5:on   6:off
```

EXERCISE 6.1 *(continued)*

```
abrtd            0:off   1:off   2:off   3:on    4:off   5:on    6:off
acpid            0:off   1:off   2:on    3:on    4:on    5:on    6:off
atd              0:off   1:off   2:off   3:on    4:on    5:on    6:off
auditd           0:off   1:off   2:on    3:on    4:on    5:off   6:off
autofs           0:off   1:off   2:off   3:on    4:on    5:on    6:off
...
sshd             0:off   1:off   2:on    3:on    4:on    5:on    6:off
sssd             0:off   1:off   2:off   3:off   4:off   5:off   6:off
sysstat          0:off   1:on    2:on    3:on    4:on    5:on    6:off
udev-post        0:off   1:on    2:on    3:on    4:on    5:on    6:off
wdaemon          0:off   1:off   2:off   3:off   4:off   5:off   6:off
wpa_supplicant   0:off   1:off   2:off   3:off   4:off   5:off   6:off
xinetd           0:off   1:off   2:off   3:on    4:on    5:on    6:off
ypbind           0:off   1:off   2:off   3:off   4:off   5:off   6:off
xinetd based services:
        chargen-dgram:   off
        chargen-stream:  off
        cvs:             off
        daytime-dgram:   off
        daytime-stream:  off
        discard-dgram:   off
        discard-stream:  off
        echo-dgram:      off
        echo-stream:     off
        rsync:           off
        tcpmux-server:   off
        time-dgram:      off
        time-stream:     off
[root@hnl ~]#
```

Configuring the Network with NetworkManager

Now that you know how to work with services in Red Hat Enterprise Linux, it's time to get familiar with NetworkManager. The easiest way to configure the network is by clicking the NetworkManager icon on the graphical desktop of your server. In this section, you'll learn how to set network parameters using the graphical tool.

You can find the NetworkManager icon in the upper-right corner of the graphical desktop. If you click it, it provides an overview of all currently available network connections, including Wi-Fi networks to which your server is not connected. This interface is convenient if you're using Linux on a laptop that roams from one Wi-Fi network to another, but it's not as useful for servers.

If you right-click the NetworkManager icon, you can select Edit Connections to set the properties for your server's network connections. You'll find all of the wired network connections on the Wired tab. The name of the connection you're using depends on the physical location of the device. Whereas in older versions of RHEL names like `eth0` and `eth1` were used, Red Hat Enterprise Linux 6.2 and newer uses device-dependent names like `p6p1`. On servers with many network cards, it can be hard to find the specific device you need. However, if your server has only one network card installed, it is not that hard. Just select the network card that is listed on the Wired tab (see Figure 6.1).

FIGURE 6.1 Network Connections dialog box

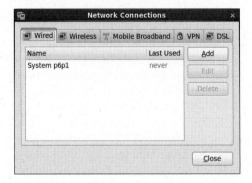

To configure the network card, select it on the Wired tab, and click Edit. You'll see a window that has four tabs. The most important tab is IPv4 Settings. On this tab, you'll see the current settings for the IPv4 protocol that is used to connect to the network. By default, your network card is configured to obtain an address from a DHCP server. As an administrator, you'll need to know how to set the address you want to use manually, so select Manual from the drop-down list (see Figure 6.2).

FIGURE 6.2 Setting an IPv4 address manually

Now click Add to insert a fixed IPv4 address. Type the IP address, and then follow this by typing the netmask that is needed for your network as well as the gateway address. Note that you need to enter the netmask address in CIDR format and not in the dotted format. That is, instead of 255.255.255.0, you need to use 24. If you don't know which address you can use, ask your network administrator. Next enter the IP address of the DNS server that is used in your network, and click Apply. You can now close the NetworkManager interface to write the configuration to the configuration files and activate the new address immediately.

Working with system-config-network

On Red Hat Enterprise Linux, many management tools whose name starts with **system-config** are available. For a complete overview of all tools currently installed on your server, type **system-config** and press the Tab key twice. The Bash automatic command-line completion feature will show you a list of all the commands that start with system-config. For network configuration, there is the system-config-network interface, a text user interface that works from a nongraphical runlevel.

In the system-config-network tool, you'll be presented two options. The Device Configuration option helps you set the address and other properties of the network card, and the DNS Configuration option allows you to specify which DNS configuration to use. These options offer the same possibilities as those provided by the graphical NetworkManager tool but are presented in a different way.

After selecting Device Configuration, you'll see a list of all network cards available on your server. Select the network card you want to configure, and press Enter. This opens the Network Configuration interface in which you can enter all of the configuration parameters that are needed to obtain a working network (see Figure 6.3).

FIGURE 6.3   system-config-network main screen

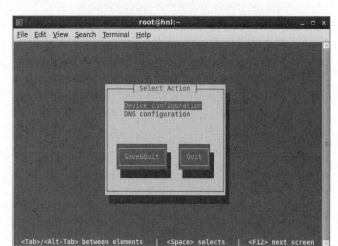

After entering all the required parameters, as shown in Figure 6.4, use the Tab key to navigate to the OK button and press Enter. This brings you back to the screen on which all network interfaces are listed. Use the Tab key to navigate to the Save button and press Enter. This brings you back to the main interface, where you select Save & Quit to apply all changes and exit the tool.

FIGURE 6.4   Entering network parameters in system-config-network

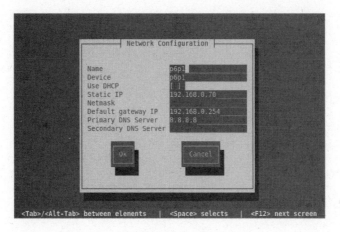

Understanding NetworkManager Configuration Files

Whether you use the graphical NetworkManager or the text-based system-config-network, the changes you make are written to the same configuration files. In the directory /etc/sysconfig/network-scripts, you'll find a configuration file for each network interface on your server. The names of all of these files start with ifcfg- and are followed by the names of the specific network cards. If your network card is known as p6p1, for example, its configuration is stored in /etc/sysconfig/network-scripts/ifcfg-p6p1. Listing 6.2 shows what the content of the network-scripts directory might look like. (The exact content depends on the configuration of your server.)

Listing 6.2: Network configuration files are stored in /etc/sysconfig/network-script.

```
[root@hn1 network-scripts]# ls
ifcfg-lo       ifdown-ipv6     ifup           ifup-plip      ifup-wireless
ifcfg-p6p1     ifdown-isdn     ifup-aliases   ifup-plusb     init.ipv6-global
ifcfg-wlan0    ifdown-post     ifup-bnep      ifup-post      net.hotplug
ifdown         ifdown-ppp      ifup-eth       ifup-ppp       network-functions
ifdown-bnep    ifdown-routes   ifup-ippp      ifup-routes    network-functions-ipv6
ifdown-eth     ifdown-sit      ifup-ipv6      ifup-sit
ifdown-ippp    ifdown-tunnel   ifup-isdn      ifup-tunnel
[root@hn1 network-scripts]#
```

In the network configuration scripts, variables are used to define different network settings. Listing 6.3 provides an example of a configuration script. There you can see the configuration for the network card p6p1 that was configured in the preceding sections.

Listing 6.3: Sample contents of a network configuration file

```
[root@hn1 network-scripts]# cat ifcfg-p6p1
DEVICE=p6p1
NM_CONTROLLED=yes
ONBOOT=yes
TYPE=Ethernet
BOOTPROTO=none
DEFROUTE=yes
IPV4_FAILURE_FATAL=yes
IPV6INIT=no
NAME="System p6p1"
UUID=131a1c02-1aee-2884-a8f2-05cc5cd849d9
HWADDR=b8:ac:6f:c9:35:25
IPADDR=192.168.0.70
PREFIX=24
GATEWAY=192.168.0.254
DNS1=8.8.8.8
USERCTL=no
```

Different variables are defined in the configuration file. Table 6.1 lists all these variables.

TABLE 6.1   Common ifcfg configuration file variables

Parameter	Value
DEVICE	Specifies the name of the device, as it is known on this server.
NM_CONTROLLED	Specifies whether the device is controlled by the NetworkManager service, which is the case by default.
ONBOOT	Indicates that this device is started when the server boots.
TYPE	Indicates the device type, which typically is Ethernet.
BOOTPROTO	Set to dhcp if the device needs to get an IP address and additional configuration from a DHCP server. If set to anything else, a fixed IP address is used.

Parameter	Value
DEFROUTE	If set to yes, the gateway that is set in this device is also used as the default route.
IPV4_FAILURE_FATAL	Indicates whether the device should fail to come up if there is an error in the IPv4 configuration.
IPV6INIT	Set to yes if you want to use IPv6.
NAME	Use this to set a device name.
UUID	As names of devices can change according to hardware configuration, it might make sense to set a universal unique ID (UUID). This UUID can then be used as a unique identifier for the device.
HWADDR	Specifies the MAC address to be used. If you want to use a different MAC address than the one configured on your network card, this is where you should change it.
IPADDR	Defines the IP address to be used on this interface.
PREFIX	This variable defines the subnet mask in CIDR format. The CIDR format defines the number of bits in the sub-net mask and not the dotted decimal number, so use 24 instead of 255.255.255.0.
GATEWAY	Use this to set the gateway that is used for traffic on this network card. If the variable DEFROUTER is also set to yes, the router specified here is also used as the default router.
DNS1	This parameter specifies the IP address of the first DNS server that should be used. To use additional DNS servers, use the variables DNS2 and, if you like, DNS3 as well.
USERCTL	Set to yes if you want end users to be able to change the network configuration. Typically, this is not a very good idea on servers.

Normally, you probably want to set the network configuration by using tools like NetworkManager or system-config-network. However, you also can change all parameters from the configuration files. Because the NetworkManager service monitors these configuration files, all changes you make in the files are picked up and applied immediately.

Understanding Network Service Scripts

The network configuration on Red Hat Enterprise Linux is managed by the NetworkManager service. This service doesn't require much management, because it is enabled by default. Also, in contrast to many other services that you might use on Linux, it picks up changes in configuration automatically. While it is commonly necessary to restart a service after changing the configuration, this is not the case for NetworkManager.

    Apart from the NetworkManager service (/etc/init.d/NetworkManager), there's also the network service (/etc/init.d/network). The *network service* is what enables all network cards on your server. If you stop it, all networking on your server will be ceased. The NetworkManager service is used for managing the network cards. Stopping the NetworkManager service doesn't stop networking; it just stops the NetworkManager program, which means you need to fall back to manual management of the network interfaces on your server.

Configuring Networking from the Command Line

In all cases, your server should be configured to start the network interfaces automatically. In many cases, however, it's also useful if you can manually create a configuration for a network card. This is especially useful if you're experiencing problems and want to test whether a given configuration works before writing it out to a configuration file.

    The classic tool for manual network configuration and monitoring is ifconfig. This command conveniently provides an overview of the current configuration of all network cards, including some usage statistics that show how much traffic has been handled by a network card since it was activated. Listing 6.4 shows a typical output of ifconfig.

Listing 6.4: ifconfig output

```
[root@hnl ~]# ifconfig
lo        Link encap:Local Loopback
          inet addr:127.0.0.1  Mask:255.0.0.0
          inet6 addr: ::1/128 Scope:Host
          UP LOOPBACK RUNNING  MTU:16436  Metric:1
          RX packets:212 errors:0 dropped:0 overruns:0 frame:0
          TX packets:212 errors:0 dropped:0 overruns:0 carrier:0
          collisions:0 txqueuelen:0
          RX bytes:16246 (15.8 KiB)  TX bytes:16246 (15.8 KiB)
```

```
p6p1      Link encap:Ethernet  HWaddr B8:AC:6F:C9:35:25
          inet addr:192.168.0.70  Bcast:192.168.0.255  Mask:255.255.255.0
          inet6 addr: fe80::baac:6fff:fec9:3525/64 Scope:Link
          UP BROADCAST RUNNING MULTICAST  MTU:1500  Metric:1
          RX packets:4600 errors:0 dropped:0 overruns:0 frame:0
          TX packets:340 errors:0 dropped:0 overruns:0 carrier:0
          collisions:0 txqueuelen:1000
          RX bytes:454115 (443.4 KiB)  TX bytes:40018 (39.0 KiB)
          Interrupt:18
wlan0     Link encap:Ethernet  HWaddr A0:88:B4:20:CE:24
          UP BROADCAST MULTICAST  MTU:1500  Metric:1
          RX packets:0 errors:0 dropped:0 overruns:0 frame:0
          TX packets:0 errors:0 dropped:0 overruns:0 carrier:0
          collisions:0 txqueuelen:1000
          RX bytes:0 (0.0 b)  TX bytes:0 (0.0 b)
```

Even if the ifconfig output is easy to read, you shouldn't use ifconfig anymore on modern Linux distributions such as Red Hat Enterprise Linux. For about 10 years now, the ip tool is the default instrument for manual network configuration and monitoring. Exercise 6.2 shows you how to use this tool and why you should no longer use ifconfig.

EXERCISE 6.2

Configuring a Network Interface with ip

In this exercise, you'll add a secondary IP address to a network card using the ip tool. Using secondary IP addresses can be beneficial if you have multiple services running on your server and you want to make a unique IP address available for each of these services. You will check your network configuration with ifconfig and see that the secondary IP address is not visible. Next you'll use the ip tool to display the current network configuration. You will see that this tool shows you the secondary IP address you've just added.

1. Open a terminal, and make sure you have root permissions.

2. Use the command **ip addr show** to display the current IP address configuration (see Listing 6.5). Find the name of the network card.

Listing 6.5: Showing current network configuration with ip addr show

```
[root@hnl ~]# ip addr show
1: lo: <LOOPBACK,UP,LOWER_UP> mtu 16436 qdisc noqueue state UNKNOWN
    link/loopback 00:00:00:00:00:00 brd 00:00:00:00:00:00
```

```
     inet 127.0.0.1/8 scope host lo
     inet6 ::1/128 scope host
        valid_lft forever preferred_lft forever
2: p6p1: <BROADCAST,MULTICAST,UP,LOWER_UP> mtu 1500 qdisc mq state UP qlen 1000
     link/ether b8:ac:6f:c9:35:25 brd ff:ff:ff:ff:ff:ff
     inet 192.168.0.70/24 brd 192.168.0.255 scope global p6p1
     inet6 fe80::baac:6fff:fec9:3525/64 scope link
        valid_lft forever preferred_lft forever
3: wlan0: <NO-CARRIER,BROADCAST,MULTICAST,UP> mtu 1500 qdisc mq state DOWN qlen
1000
     link/ether a0:88:b4:20:ce:24 brd ff:ff:ff:ff:ff:ff
```

3. As shown in Listing 6.5, the network card name is p6p1. Knowing this, you can now add an IP address to this network card using the command **ip addr add dev p6p1 192.168.0.71/24**. (Make sure you're using a unique IP address!)

4. Now use the command **ping 192.168.0.71** to check the availability of the IP address you've just added. You should see the echo reply packets coming in.

5. Use **ifconfig** to check the current network configuration. You won't see the secondary IP address you just added.

6. Use **ip addr show** to display the current network configuration. This will show you the secondary IP address.

One reason why many administrators who have been using Linux for years dislike the ip command is because it's not very easy to use. This is because the ip command works with subcommands, known as *objects* in the help for the command. Using these objects makes the ip command very versatile but complex at the same time.

If you type ip help, you'll see a help message showing all the objects that are available with the ip command (see Listing 6.6).

Listing 6.6: Use ip help to get an overview of all available objects

```
[root@hnl ~]# ip help
Usage: ip [ OPTIONS ] OBJECT { COMMAND | help }
       ip [ -force ] -batch filename
where  OBJECT := { link | addr | addrlabel | route | rule | neigh |
  ntable | tunnel | maddr | mroute | monitor | xfrm }
       OPTIONS := { -V[ersion] | -s[tatistics] | -d[etails] | -r[esolve] |
                    -f[amily] { inet | inet6 | ipx | dnet | link } |
                    -o[neline] | -t[imestamp] | -b[atch] [filename] |
                    -rc[vbuf] [size]}
```

As you can see, many objects are available, but only three are interesting:

- `ip link` is used to show link statistics.
- `ip addr` is used to show and manipulate the IP addresses of network interfaces.
- `ip route` can be used to show and manage routes on your server.

Managing Device Settings

Let's start by taking a look at `ip link`. With this command, you can set device properties and monitor the current state of a device. If you use the command `ip link help`, you'll get a nice overview of all the available options, as you can see in Listing 6.7.

Listing 6.7: Use `ip link help` to show all available ip link options

```
[root@hnl ~]# ip link help
Usage: ip link add link DEV [ name ] NAME
                    [ txqueuelen PACKETS ]
                    [ address LLADDR ]
                    [ broadcast LLADDR ]
                    [ mtu MTU ]
                    type TYPE [ ARGS ]
        ip link delete DEV type TYPE [ ARGS ]
        ip link set DEVICE [ { up | down } ]
                            [ arp { on | off } ]
                            [ dynamic { on | off } ]
                            [ multicast { on | off } ]
                            [ allmulticast { on | off } ]
                            [ promisc { on | off } ]
                            [ trailers { on | off } ]
                            [ txqueuelen PACKETS ]
                            [ name NEWNAME ]
                            [ address LLADDR ]
                            [ broadcast LLADDR ]
                            [ mtu MTU ]
                            [ netns PID ]
                            [ alias NAME ]
                            [ vf NUM [ mac LLADDR ]
                                     [ vlan VLANID [ qos VLAN-QOS ] ]
                                     [ rate TXRATE ] ]
        ip link show [ DEVICE ]
TYPE := { vlan | veth | vcan | dummy | ifb | macvlan | can }
```

To begin, ip link show lists all current parameters on the specified device or on all devices if no specific device has been named. If you don't like some of the options you see, you can use ip link set on a device to change its properties. For example, a rather common option is ip link set p6p1 mtu 9000, which sets the maximum size of packets sent on the device at 9,000 bytes. This is particularly useful if the device connects to an iSCSI SAN.

Be sure, however, to check that your device supports the setting you intend to make. If it doesn't, you'll see an invalid argument error and the setting won't be changed.

Managing Address Configuration

To manage the current address allocation of a device, you use ip addr. If used without any arguments, this command shows the current address configuration, as is the case if you use the command ip addr show (see also Listing 6.5).

To set an IP address, you need ip addr add followed by the name of the device and the address you want to set. Make sure the address is always specified with the subnet mask you want to use. If it isn't, a 32-bit subnet mask is used, and that makes it impossible to communicate with any other node on the same network. As you've seen before, to add an IP address such as 192.168.0.72 to the network device with the name p6p1, you would use ip addr add dev p6p1 192.168.0.72/24.

Another common task you may want to perform is deleting an IP address. This is very similar to adding an IP address. To delete the IP address 192.168.0.72, for instance, use ip addr del dev p6p1 192.168.0.72/24.

Managing Routes

To communicate on a network, your server needs to know which node to use as the *default gateway*, also known as the *default router*. To see the current settings, use ip route show (see Listing 6.8).

Listing 6.8: Use ip route show to display the current routing configuration

```
[root@hnl ~]# ip route show
192.168.0.0/24 dev p6p1  proto kernel  scope link  src 192.168.0.70  metric 1
default via 192.168.0.254 dev p6p1  proto static
```

On a typical server, you won't see much routing information. There's only one direct route for the networks to which your server is directly connected. This is shown in the first line in Listing 6.8, where the network 192.168.0.0 is identified with the scope link (which means that it is directly attached) and accessible through the network card p6p1.

Apart from the directly connected routers, there should be a default route on every server. In Listing 6.8, you can see that the default route is the node with IP address 192.168.0.254. This means that all traffic to networks that are not directly connected to this server are sent to IP address 192.168.0.254.

As a server administrator, you occasionally need to set a route from the command line. You can do this using the ip route add command. This must be followed by the required routing information. Typically, you need to specify in this routing information which host is identified as a router and which network card is used on this server to reach this host.

Thus, if there is a network 10.0.0.0 that can be reached through IP address 192.168.0.253, which is accessible through the network card p6p2, you can add the route using ip route add 10.0.0.0 via 192.168.0.253 dev p6p2.

 Nothing you do with the ip command is automatically saved. This means that if you restart a network card, you will lose all the information you've manually set using ip.

Troubleshooting Networking

When using a network, you may experience many different configuration problems. In this section, you'll learn how to work with some common tools that help you fix these problems.

Checking the Network Card

Before using any tool to fix a problem, you must know what exactly is wrong. A common approach is to work from the network interface to a remote host on the Internet. This means you must first check the configuration of the network card by seeing whether it is up at all and whether it has an IP address currently assigned to it. The ip addr command shows this. In Listing 6.9, for example, you can see that the interface wlan0 is currently down (state DOWN), which means you have to activate it before it can do anything.

Listing 6.9: Checking the current state of a network interface

```
[root@hnl ~]# ip addr
1: lo: <LOOPBACK,UP,LOWER_UP> mtu 16436 qdisc noqueue state UNKNOWN
    link/loopback 00:00:00:00:00:00 brd 00:00:00:00:00:00
    inet 127.0.0.1/8 scope host lo
    inet6 ::1/128 scope host
       valid_lft forever preferred_lft forever
2: p6p1: <BROADCAST,MULTICAST,UP,LOWER_UP> mtu 1500 qdisc mq state UP qlen 1000
    link/ether b8:ac:6f:c9:35:25 brd ff:ff:ff:ff:ff:ff
    inet 192.168.0.70/24 brd 192.168.0.255 scope global p6p1
    inet6 fe80::baac:6fff:fec9:3525/64 scope link
       valid_lft forever preferred_lft forever
3: wlan0: <NO-CARRIER,BROADCAST,MULTICAST,UP> mtu 1500 qdisc mq state DOWN qlen 1000
    link/ether a0:88:b4:20:ce:24 brd ff:ff:ff:ff:ff:ff
```

If you have confirmed that the problem is related to the local network card, it's a good idea to see whether you can fix it without changing the actual configuration files. The following tips will help you do that:

- Use `ifup` on your network card to try to change its status to up. If that fails, check the physical connection; that is, is the network cable plugged in?

- Use `ip addr add` to add an IP address manually to the network card. If this fixes the problem, you probably have a DHCP server that's not working properly or a misconfiguration in the network card's configuration file.

After fixing the problem, you should perform a simple test to see that you can truly communicate to an outside host. To do this, pinging the default gateway is a very good idea. Just use the `ping` command, followed by the IP address of the node you want to ping, such as `ping 192.168.0.254`.

Once the network card is up again, you should check its configuration files. You may have a misconfiguration in the configuration file, or else the DHCP server might be down.

Checking Routing

If the local network card is not the problem, you should check external hosts. The first step is to ping the default gateway. If that works, you can ping a host on the Internet, if possible, by using its IP address. My favorite ping host is `137.65.1.1`, which has never failed me in my more than 20 years in IT.

In case your favorite ping host on the Internet doesn't reply, it's time to check routing. The following three steps generally give a result:

1. Use **`ip route show`** to display your current routing configuration. You should see a line that indicates which node is used as the default gateway. If you don't, you should add it manually.

2. If you have a default router set, verify that there is no local firewall blocking access. To do this, use **`iptables -L`** as root. If it gives you lots of output, then you do have a firewall that's blocking access. In that case, use **`service iptables stop`** to stop it and repeat your test. If you're still experiencing problems, something might be wrong with your firewall configuration. If this is the case, read Chapter 10, "Securing Your Server with IPtables," as soon as possible to make sure that the firewall is configured correctly. If possible, turn the firewall on again (after all, it does protect you!) by using **`service iptables start`**.

3. If you don't have a firewall issue, there might be something wrong between your default gateway and the host on the Internet you're trying to reach. Use **`traceroute`**, followed by the IP address of the target host (for example, `traceroute 137.65.1.1`). This command shows just how far you get and may indicate where the fault occurs. However, if the error is at your Internet provider, there's nothing you can do.

Checking DNS

The third usual suspect in network communications errors is DNS. A useful command to check DNS configuration is `dig`. Using `dig`, you can find out whether a DNS server is capable of finding an authoritative answer for your query about DNS hosts.

The problem that many users have with the dig command is that it provides a huge amount of information. Consider the example in Listing 6.10, which is the answer dig gave to the command dig www.redhat.com. The most important aspect of this example is the Got answer section. This means that the DNS server was able to provide an answer. In the line directly below the Got answer line, you can see that the status of the answer is NOERROR. This is good because you didn't only get an answer but also determined that there was no error in the answer. What follows this are lots of details about the answer.

In the question section, you can see the original request was for www.redhat.com. In the answer section, you can see exactly what comprised the answer. This section provides details in which you probably aren't interested, but it enables the eager administrator to analyze exactly which DNS server provided the answer and how it got there.

Listing 6.10: dig answer for a known host

```
; <<>> DiG 9.5.0-P2 <<>> www.redhat.com
;; global options: printcmd
;; Got answer:
;; ->>HEADER<<- opcode: QUERY, status: NOERROR, id: 56745
;; flags: qr rd ra; QUERY: 1, ANSWER: 4, AUTHORITY: 0, ADDITIONAL: 0
;; QUESTION SECTION:
;www.redhat.com.                        IN      A
;; ANSWER SECTION:
www.redhat.com.         60      IN      CNAME
wildcard.redhat.com.edgekey.net.
wildcard.redhat.com.edgekey.net. 21600 IN CNAME
wildcard.redhat.com.edgekey.net.globalredir.akadns.net.
wildcard.redhat.com.edgekey.net.globalredir.akadns.net.
 900 IN CNAME e1890.b.akamaiedge.net.
e1890.b.akamaiedge.net. 20      IN      A       95.101.247.214
;; Query time: 339 msec
;; SERVER: 80.69.66.67#53(80.69.66.67)
;; WHEN: Wed Apr 25 19:47:43 2012
;; MSG SIZE  rcvd: 191
```

In the example in Listing 6.11, a request was made for the address of a nonexisting server: hweg.skdhv.df. The important part, again, is in the Got answer section. This means that a DNS server did give an answer; it just wasn't very useful. This can be seen from the line that starts with HEADER. The status, indicated as NXDOMAIN, is especially important. This means no such domain exists. From the answer that the dig command provides, you can see that a DNS server could be contacted. In the authority section, you can even see that a DNS server of the DNS root domain was queried. However, no useful answer resulted from this query.

Listing 6.11: dig answer for a nonexisting host

```
sander@web:~> dig hweg.skdhv.df
; <<>> DiG 9.5.0-P2 <<>> hweg.skdhv.df
;; global options: printcmd
```

```
;; Got answer:
;; ->>HEADER<<- opcode: QUERY, status: NXDOMAIN, id: 32123
;; flags: qr rd ra; QUERY: 1, ANSWER: 0, AUTHORITY: 1, ADDITIONAL: 0
;; QUESTION SECTION:
;hweg.skdhv.df.              IN      A
;; AUTHORITY SECTION:
.                       86400   IN      SOA     a.root-servers.net.
   nstld.verisign-grs.com. 2012042501 1800 900 604800 86400
;; Query time: 90 msec
;; SERVER: 80.69.66.67#53(80.69.66.67)
;; WHEN: Wed Apr 25 19:49:29 2012
;; MSG SIZE   rcvd: 106
```

In the following two dig examples, a DNS server has been reached. You might also encounter situations where no DNS server could be reached. If that happens, the answer dig gives is much shorter, as you can see in Listing 6.12.

Listing 6.12: dig answer when DNS is not available

```
[root@hnl ~]# dig www.redhat.com
; <<>> DiG 9.7.3-P3-RedHat-9.7.3-8.P3.el6 <<>> www.redhat.com
;; global options: +cmd
;; connection timed out; no servers could be reached
[root@hnl ~]#
```

The answer is loud and clear here: no DNS servers could be reached, which means that the error is probably in the local DNS configuration. This means you have to check the /etc/resolv.conf file, which typically contains a list of DNS servers to be contacted. Listing 6.13 shows an example of what this file should look like.

Listing 6.13: Example /etc/resolv.conf file

```
# Generated by NetworkManager
search example.com
nameserver 192.168.0.70
nameserver 8.8.8.8
```

In the example file in Listing 6.13, you can see that two name servers are used. This means that if the first name server cannot be contacted, your server tries to contact the second DNS server. In the error shown in Listing 6.12, no servers could be reached. That indicates a problem in the local network configuration. It is very unlikely that two DNS name servers are experiencing an error at the same time.

Setting Up IPv6

Configuring IPv6 is typically not hard to do. This is because of the nature of the IPv6 protocol. In IPv6, it's not necessary to set an IP address for every node in the network. IPv6 uses the *Neighbor Discovery Protocol (NDP)*. This means that a node in an IPv6 network is capable of setting its own IPv6 address.

In NDP, the IPv6 node detects the IPv6 address that is in use on its network. This means that, in every network, you need just one node to be configured with a reliable IPv6 address. This address consists of two parts: the first part is the network address, and the second part is the node ID on that network. In Listing 6.14, you can see the IPv6 address configuration as shown by the `ip a` command.

Listing 6.14: Showing IPv6 configuration

```
web:~ # ip a
1: lo: <LOOPBACK,UP,LOWER_UP> mtu 16436 qdisc noqueue state UNKNOWN
    link/loopback 00:00:00:00:00:00 brd 00:00:00:00:00:00
    inet 127.0.0.1/8 brd 127.255.255.255 scope host lo
    inet 127.0.0.2/8 brd 127.255.255.255 scope host secondary lo
    inet6 ::1/128 scope host
       valid_lft forever preferred_lft forever
2: eth0: <BROADCAST,MULTICAST,UP,LOWER_UP> mtu 1500 qdisc pfifo_fast
  state UNKNOWN qlen 1000
    link/ether 00:16:3e:37:ea:cd brd ff:ff:ff:ff:ff:ff
    inet 87.253.155.186/25 brd 87.253.155.255 scope global eth0
    inet6 2a01:7c8:c127:1216::3/64 scope global
       valid_lft forever preferred_lft forever
    inet6 fe80::216:3eff:fe37:eacd/64 scope link
       valid_lft forever preferred_lft forever
```

As you can see in Listing 6.14, in interface eth0, two IPv6 addresses are set. First there is the address that starts with 2a01, and then there is the address starting with fe80. The first address is a unique, worldwide address handed out by an Internet provider. The address starting with fe80 is an IPv6 address that is for internal use only. You will note that on every node that has IPv6 configured, you will see one of these addresses.

In IPv6 addresses, a total of 128 bits are used to create an address that consists of eight groups of 2 bytes, written in hexadecimal. Since IPv6 has an enormous available address space, there is no need to use subnet masks: the first half of the address is used for the network, and the second half of the address is used for the node portion. This means that in the imaginary address fe80:1234:bad:cafe:216:3eff:fe37:eacd, the part up to cafe is the network address, and the part that starts with 216 is the node ID on the network.

If you look carefully at the node ID of the IPv6 address, you will see that it includes the MAC address of the network card on which the IPv6 address is set. You can see this in Listing 6.14, where the MAC address 00:16:3e:37:ea:cd is easily recognized in the node part of the fe80 address, which is 216:3eff:fe:37:eacd. Because the MAC address is just 6 bytes by default, the node ID is padded with the bytes ff:fe to make it an 8-byte address in the 16-byte IPv6 address.

Now that you know how IPv6 uses the MAC address in the node ID of the address, it's easy to imagine how NDP works. NDP detects the network address in use on this network and just adds the node ID to this network.

As for servers, it might be convenient to use a node ID that is easier to recognize. You can also set it manually. Exercise 6.3 shows you how to do this.

EXERCISE 6.3

Setting a Fixed IPv6 Address

In this exercise, you will use NetworkManager to set a fixed IPv6 address. To avoid any conflicts, you'll use an address from the fe80 network address range. This range is reserved for use in your own LAN environment.

1. Right-click the NetworkManager icon, and select the Wired tab. From there, select your server's network interface, and click Edit to modify its properties.

2. From the Editing System window, select the IPv6 Settings tab. From the Method drop-down list, select Manual and then click Add to open the interface that allows you to add an IPv6 address.

3. Enter the address **fe80::10**. The fact that you're using :: in the address means that between the ::, the address consists of all 0s. This means that this address could also have been written as fe80:0:0:0:0:0:0:10.

4. Click Apply to save and apply the IPv6 settings to your server.

After completing the procedure in Exercise 6.3, you've configured your server as an IPv6 host. This means that using the Neighbor Discovery Protocol, it is now able to hand out IPv6 addresses to other nodes in the network that are trying to find out which address to use.

To complete the IPv6 configuration of your network, you should also configure the DNS server to enable address resolution for node names to IPv6 addresses and IPv6 addresses into node names.

Configuring SSH

Most servers are in datacenters—hostile environments that are noisy and cold. This means that as an administrator of a Red Hat Enterprise Linux Server, you probably want to access the server from a distance. The Secure Shell (SSH) protocol is the default service to obtain remote access to a server.

To use SSH, you need an SSH server and an SSH client. SSH server is a process that runs on your server. On most Linux distributions, the name of this process is sshd. To connect to it from a client computer, you can use the ssh client utility if the client is Linux, or you can use PuTTY if you're on a Windows client.

Enabling the SSH Server

The SSH service is installed on your Red Hat Enterprise Linux server. It isn't enabled by default, however, so you should make sure to start it manually using the service sshd start command. After doing that, make sure that it is also started after a reboot of your server by using chkconfig sshd on. After performing these tasks, you can first do a basic connection test and connect to it using the ssh command. Exercise 6.4 lets you practice these steps.

EXERCISE 6.4

Enabling and Testing the SSH Server

In this exercise, you'll enable the SSH server and test its connectivity from your own local server.

1. From a terminal with root permissions, use the command **service sshd start**. In the unlikely event that this command shows an error, use yum install openssh-server to install the ssh server package.

2. Use the **chkconfig sshd on** command to enable the SSH service, and add it to your server's runlevels. This ensures that the SSH server also comes up after rebooting the server.

3. Now it's time to test the SSH server. Open a new terminal window, and use **ssh root@localhost** to open an SSH session where you're logging in as root. Enter the password when prompted.

4. You're now in an SSH session. In this example, you tested the connection from your own local machine. You can also test the connection from a remote machine. This will be discussed further in the sections that follow.

5. Type **exit** to close the SSH sessions.

You've seen that it's not hard to enable SSH on your server. An SSH server that has been enabled with all the default settings isn't a secure SSH server, however. To make the SSH server secure, there are at least two modifications you should make to the /etc/ssh/sshd_config file: the Port setting and the AllowRootLogin parameter.

There are two configuration files: /etc/ssh/ssh_config is the configuration file in which you put default settings for the ssh client utility, and you specify default settings for the Secure Shell server in /etc/ssh/sshd_config.

Make sure you consider at least the following SSH security settings:

Port   By default, SSH listens on port 22. Every hacker knows this. This means that if you offer SSH services on port 22 of your server and it is connected directly to the Internet, you will see the first brute-force attack, launching a dictionary attack against your server within minutes. So if you're directly connected to the Internet, change the SSH port to something less obvious. I like putting it on port 443 (the average hacker expects HTTPS to be offered on that port and therefore will launch an HTTPS attack that will not work). The disadvantage of using port 443, however, is that you can't use HTTPS anymore. So, use any port you like, as long as it's not port 22.

ListenAddress   By default, your SSH server offers its services on all IP addresses. In some cases, you might want to restrict this to only the IP addresses that are visible from the internal network and not from the Internet. If this is the case, change 0.0.0.0 to the specific IP address on which your SSH server should offer its services.

PermitRootLogin   By default, this parameter allows the user root to log in to your SSH server. This is not a good idea. If root is permitted to log in, the potential hacker only has to guess the root password. It's better to switch off root login by giving this parameter the value no. This means you'll have to connect as an ordinary user, and once connected, you'll have to use su - to escalate your privileges to the root level.

PasswordAuthentication   By default, this parameter allows users to log in using passwords. If you have created public/private key pairs, you might consider switching off password authentication completely. Be careful, though: switching off password authentication also makes it difficult for you to log in from an unknown machine where your private key is not available.

AllowUsers   This is a very nice parameter that is not in sshd_config by default. Everyone should use it and add a list of only those users you want to allow to log in to your SSH server. This makes it really hard for hackers, because they will have to guess the name of that user before starting this evil work!

You can change the default sshd behavior using many other parameters. However, the parameters discussed are generally considered the most important parameters. In Exercise 6.5, you'll learn how to change some of these important parameters.

EXERCISE 6.5

Securing the SSH Server

In this exercise, you'll change some parameters that help you secure the SSH server. You'll also create two user accounts to test the AllowUsers parameter.

1. Open a root shell on your server, and use the commands **useradd linda** and **useradd lisa** to add two users to your server. Next set the password for these users to password by using **passwd linda** and **passwd lisa.**

2. Use **vi /etc/ssh/sshd_config** to open the sshd configuration file.

3. Change the Port parameter, and give it a value 443. Next set the PermitRootLogin parameter value to **no**, and add the parameter **AllowUsers**, giving it the value **linda.**

4. Close the vi editor using the **:wq!** command, and restart the sshd process using **service sshd restart.**

5. Connect as root on SSH port 443 using **ssh -p 443 root@localhost.** Access should be denied. Try to connect as lisa using **ssh -p 443 lisa@localhost.** Access should also be denied. Now try to connect as linda using **ssh -p 443 linda@localhost.** You should be granted access.

Using the SSH Client

An SSH client is available on every Linux computer. Using it is easy—just use the name of the server you'd like to connect to as the argument, and a connection will be established. For example, use ssh 192.168.0.1 to establish an SSH session with SSH host 192.168.0.1.

By default, SSH connects with the same user ID as the one with which you are currently logged in. You can specifically tell the SSH client to connect as a different user, using username@servername as the argument while using the SSH command. For instance, to connect as user linda to server 192.168.0.1, you can use ssh linda@192.168.0.1.

Using PuTTY on Windows Machines

Every Linux computer has an SSH client by default. If you're working in a Windows environment, you can also establish SSH sessions using PuTTY. You can download a free copy of PuTTY from www.putty.org and install it on your Windows computer. After starting PuTTY, you'll see the interface shown in Figure 6.5. From there, you can enter the IP address or name of the server with which you want to connect and click Open to establish the connection.

Alternatively, you can enter different properties of the SSH session you want to establish using PuTTY, including font sizes and other parameters, and you can specify a name under Saved Sessions. Next click Save to save the parameters, which creates an entry in the list of saved sessions. By using these, you can easily reestablish a session to a host that you frequently use.

FIGURE 6.5   PuTTY Configuration dialog box

Configuring Key-Based SSH Authentication

The default authentication method in SSH is password based, which means when connecting to a server, you need to enter the password of the user with whom you are connecting. There are two reasons why this might not be ideal.

- There is a risk that someone can guess your password.

- If you frequently need to connect to the same server, it's a waste of time to enter the identical password over and over.

There is an alternative, however; you can use *key-based authentication*. When SSH key-based authentication is used, you have to make sure the public key is available on the servers to all users who need to use this technology where they want to log in. When logging in, the user creates an authentication request that is signed with their private key. This authentication request is matched to the public key of the same user on the server where that user wants to authenticate. If it matches, the user is allowed to enter; if it doesn't, the user is denied access.

Authentication based on public/private keys is enabled by default on Red Hat Enterprise Linux. Therefore, the server will prompt the user for a password only when no keys are present.

Here is a summary of what happens when a user is trying to establish an SSH session with a server:

1. If public key authentication is enabled (which is the default), SSH checks the `.ssh` directory in the user's home directory to see whether a private key is present.

2. If a private key is found, ssh creates a packet containing some data (the salt), encrypts that packet with the private key, and sends it to the server. The public key is also sent with this packet.

3. The server then checks whether a file with the name `authorized_keys` exists in the home directory of the user. If it does not, the user cannot authenticate with their keys. If this file does exist and the public key is an allowed key that is also identical to the key that was previously stored on the server, the server uses this key to check the signature.

4. If the signature can be verified, the user is granted access. If it cannot, the server will prompt the user, who tries to connect for their password.

In Exercise 6.6, you'll learn how to set up key-based authentication.

EXERCISE 6.6

Setting Up Key-Based Authentication

To use key-based authentication, you first need to create a key pair. Next you have to copy the key you want to use to the host to which you want to create a connection. You would normally do this between two hosts. This means that in order to perform this exercise, you need a second host that has Red Hat Enterprise Linux installed. In this exercise, the remote host is referred to as the *server*. If you don't have a second host on which you can work, replace the host name server with localhost, and it will also work.

1. Open a root shell, and from there use **ssh server**. You will be prompted for a password.

2. Type **exit** to close the SSH session.

3. Now generate the public-private key pair using **ssh-keygen**. You will be prompted for the file in which you want to save the private key, as you can see in Listing 6.15. Press Enter to accept the default, which saves the key in /root/.ssh/id_rsa. Next press Enter twice to save the key without a passphrase. This completes the procedure and creates two files: id_rsa and id_rsa.pub. The private key is stored in id_rsa, and the public key is stored in id_rsa.pub.

Listing 6.15: Creating a public/private key pair

```
[root@hnl ~]# ssh-keygen
Generating public/private rsa key pair.
Enter file in which to save the key (/root/.ssh/id_rsa):
Enter passphrase (empty for no passphrase):
```

EXERCISE 6.6 *(continued)*

```
Enter same passphrase again:
Your identification has been saved in /root/.ssh/id_rsa.
Your public key has been saved in /root/.ssh/id_rsa.pub.
The key fingerprint is:
3e:af:28:f2:41:09:1f:31:46:05:10:f5:22:37:f3:3e root@hnl.example.com
The key's randomart image is:
+--[ RSA 2048]----+
|   o=Bo.         |
|    . +          |
|   o * .         |
|    = B          |
|    + . S        |
|     . . .       |
|     . E o       |
|    . ... o o    |
|    o... ...     |
+-----------------+
```

4. Now you need to copy the public key to the server where you want to use it. Use **ssh_copy_id** server to do this. This copies the public key to the server and generates some messages.

5. Use **ssh server** to connect to the server again. You'll notice that you won't be prompted for a password because the SSH keys are used to establish the connection.

   In the previous exercise, you established a key-based session where no further protection was used for the keys. When prompted to enter a passphrase for the key, you just pressed Enter. This is convenient for use in a trusted environment, but it is not very secure.

   If you create a public/private key pair to make a connection to a server easier, you should consider using a passphrase. Without a passphrase, anyone who copies your private key can fake your identity. With a passphrase, no one can use your private key without knowing the passphrase as well. To use a passphrase, just enter it when prompted by ssh-keygen.

   There is an inconvenience when using a passphrase, however. You will have to enter it every time you connect to the server. To make this a bit easier for you, you can use ssh-agent to cache the passphrase for the duration of the session. To do this, run ssh-agent with the name of the shell for which you want to cache the passphrase. For instance, run ssh-agent /bin/bash. Next you need to run ssh-add, a command that will add the key to the agent and also ask for a password. Enter the passphrase, and it will be cached as long as you keep on working in the same shell. When you type exit, the passphrase will be forgotten, and you'll have to repeat the same procedure if you want to start caching your passphrase again. In Exercise 6.7, you'll create a private key that is secured with a passphrase, and next you will use ssh-agent to cache this passphrase.

Setting Up Key-Based SSH Authentication Protected with a Passphrase

In this exercise, you'll generate an SSH public/private key pair. You'll protect the private key by adding a passphrase. Next you will start ssh-agent to cache the passphrase.

1. Open a root shell, and type **ssh-keygen**. When asked where to save the file, press Enter. You will be prompted that the file /root/.ssh/id_rsa already exists. Type **Y** to confirm that you want to overwrite this file.

2. Now enter a passphrase, and press Enter to confirm. Type the same passphrase again, and once more press Enter. The key will now be saved.

3. Copy the new public key to your server using **ssh-copy-id server**. You need to enter your password once to perform this operation.

4. Establish an SSH session to your server using **ssh server**. Enter the passphrase when prompted. Next type **exit** to close this session.

5. Type **ssh-agent /bin/bash**. Next type **ssh-add** to add your current passphrase. Enter the passphrase, and you will see a confirmation prompting **Identity added**.

6. Type **ssh server**. At this point, you'll notice that you can enter a session without entering a passphrase.

7. Type **exit** to close the current ssh session.

8. Type **exit** to close the ssh-agent session. When you do this, the passphrase is forgotten.

9. Type **ssh server** to establish a new session. Notice that you are prompted to enter the passphrase again.

Using Graphical Applications with SSH

By default, you cannot use graphical programs over an SSH session. To use them in spite of this, you need to enable X-Forwarding on the SSH client. To do this, use ssh -X instead of just ssh when establishing a connection.

As an alternative, you can also set X-Forwarding to on for all users. To do this, you have to modify the /etc/ssh/ssh_config file. This file contains the parameter ForwardX11.

Make sure to enable this parameter, and give it a value of Yes. The next time you start a graphical program from an SSH session, it will work automatically.

Using SSH Port Forwarding

SSH can also be used for port forwarding. This means you connect a local port on your server to a remote port on some other machine.

In the sample network that you see in Figure 6.6, there are three nodes. AMS is the node where the administrator is working. ATL is the node that runs an ssh process used for SSH forwarding. AMS has a direct connection to ATL but not to SLC, which is behind a firewall. ATL has a direct connection to SLC that is not hindered by a firewall.

FIGURE 6.6 Three-node sample network

A simple example of port forwarding is provided in the following command:

```
linda@AMS:~> ssh -L 4444:ATL:110 linda@ATL
```

In this example, user linda forwards connections to port 4444 on her local host to port 110 on the host ATL as user linda on that host. This is what you would use, for example, to establish a secure session to the insecure POP service on that host. The local host first establishes a connection to the SSH server running on ATL. This SSH server connects to port 110 at ATL, whereas ssh binds to port 4444 on the local host. An encrypted session is now established between local port 4444 and server port 110. Everything sent to port 4444 on the local host really goes to port 110 on the server. If, for example, you configure your POP mail client to get its mail from local port 4444, it would actually get it from port 110 at ATL. Notice in this example that a nonprivileged port is used. Only user root can connect to a privileged port with a port number lower than 1024. No matter what port you are connecting to, you should always check in the service's configuration file /etc/services, where port numbers are matched to names of services, to see what the port is normally used for (if used), and you should use netstat -patune | grep <your-intended-port> to make sure that the port is not already in use.

A little variation on the local port forwarding described earlier is *remote port forwarding*. To do this, you forward all connections to a given port on the remote port to a local port on your computer. To do this, use the -R option, as shown in the following example:

```
linda@AMS:-> ssh -R 4444:AMS:110 linda@ATL.
```

In this code, user linda connects to host ATL (at the end of the command). Port 4444 is addressed by using the construction -R 4444 on this host. This remote port is redirected to port 110 on the local host. As a result, anything going to port 4444 on ATL is redirected to port 110 on AMS. This example would be useful if ATL is the client and AMS is the server running a POP mail server to which linda wants to connect.

Another common occurrence is when the host that you want to forward cannot be reached directly because it is behind a firewall. In this case, you can establish a tunnel to another host that is reachable with SSH. Imagine that in the example in Figure 6.5, the host SLC is running a POP mail server to which user linda wants to connect. This user would enter the following command:

```
linda@AMS:~> ssh -L 4444:SLC:110 linda@ATL
```

In this example, user linda forwards connections to port 4444 on her local host to server ATL that is running ssh. This server in turn would forward the connection to port 110 on server SLC. Note that, in this scenario, the only requirement is that ATL has the SSH service activated and no sshd is needed on SLC for this to work. Also note that there is no need for host AMS to have direct contact with SLC because this would happen from host ATL onward.

In the previous examples, you learned how to use the SSH command to do port forwarding. The SSH command isn't your only option for doing this, however. If a port forwarding connection needs to be established continuously, you can put it in the ssh configuration file at the client computer. Put it in .ssh/config in your home directory if you want it to work for your user account only. Alternatively, you can put it in /etc/ssh/ssh_config if you want it to apply to all users on your machine. The parameter that should be used as an alternative to ssh -L 4444:ATL:110 is as follows:

```
LocalForward 4444 ATL:110
```

Configuring VNC Server Access

In most cases, SSH gives you everything you need to establish a session to a remote server. Most administration programs are text-based. In some cases, though, you may want to establish a connection to a full graphical desktop. For such cases, VNC provides a useful solution.

To configure VNC on Red Hat Enterprise Linux, first you install the tigervnc package. This package has a configuration file in /etc/sysconfig/vncservers. You need to predefine every VNS session you want to enable for specific users in this configuration file. The contents of the file may appear as follows:

```
VNCSERVERS="1:root"
VNCSERVERARGS[1]="-geometry 800x600 -nolisten tcp -localhost"
```

In the previous configuration example, VNC session 1 is defined and assigned to user root on the first line. The parameters for this session are defined after that. The session number to which the parameters apply is shown between square brackets, and following that is a list of arguments that apply to this session. The most important argument in this list is -localhost. This specifies that VNC clients are allowed only from localhost, which means they have to establish a secured session with the VNC server first. To establish a secured session with the VNC Server, SSH tunneling is used.

Before starting the VNC server, VNC passwords must be generated for all users to whom a session is assigned. To set the password, you must log in as that user and use the command vncpasswd to set the password. Setting the password creates the file ~/.vnc/passwd, and if this file doesn't exist, the VNC server refuses to start. Only once the password has been specified can the VNC server be started.

Once started, a connection to the VNC server is created using the vncviewer VNC client. For example, the command vncviewer -via root@server localhost:1 would connect to the VNC session defined in the example configuration file shown earlier. In Exercise 6.8, you will set up a VNC server yourself.

EXERCISE 6.8

Setting Up a VNC Server

In this exercise, you will set up a VNC Server. To do this exercise, you'll need two machines. If you don't have two machines available, refer to Chapter 8, "Understanding and Configuring SELinux," about KVM virtualization before getting started. In this chapter, you will install a second Red Hat Server as a virtual machine. The two machines are referred to as *client* and *server* in this exercise.

1. Use **yum install tigervnc-server** to install the VNC package on the server.

2. Edit the configuration file /etc/sysconfig/vncservers, and include the following two lines:

   VNCSERVERS="1:linda"
   VNCSERVERARGS[1]="-geometry 800x600 -nolisten tcp -localhost"

3. Use **su - linda** on the server to switch to the user account linda. From there, type **vncpasswd** to set the VNC password for this user.

4. Start the vncserver, and put it in the runlevels of your server using **service vncserver start** followed by **chkconfig vncserver on.**

5. From the client, use **vncviewer -via linda@server localhost:1**. This establishes the VNC session from the client to the server.

Summary

In this chapter, you learned how to configure networking on Red Hat Enterprise Linux. You read how to set up your network card with IPv4 and IPv6, and you discovered the services that are related to managing the network. You also learned how to configure SSH and VNC for connecting remotely to your server. In the next chapter, you'll learn how to work with user and group accounts on your server.

Securing Red Hat Enterprise Linux

Chapter

7

Working with Users, Groups, and Permissions

TOPICS COVERED IN THIS CHAPTER:

- ✓ Managing Users and Groups
- ✓ Using Graphical Tools for User and Group Management
- ✓ Using External Authentication Sources
- ✓ Understanding the Authentication Process
- ✓ Understanding nsswitch
- ✓ Managing Permissions

Managing Users and Groups

To create users from a command-line environment, you can use the useradd command. Alternatively, it is possible to add users to the relevant configuration files manually. The latter may be useful in an environment where users are added from a custom-made shell script, but normally it is not recommended. The reason for this is obvious—an error in the main user configuration files might cause problems for all users on your server.

In this section, you will learn how to add users from the command line using useradd, how the relevant configuration files are modified for these users, and how users can be added using the system-config-users utility.

Commands for User Management

If you want to add users from the command line, useradd is the command to use. Some other commands are available as well. Here are the most important commands for managing the user environment:

useradd This command is used for adding users to the local authentication system.

usermod This command is used to modify properties for existing users.

userdel This command is used to delete users properly from a system.

Using useradd is simple. In its easiest form, it just takes the name of a user as its argument, so useradd linda will create a user called linda on your server.

The useradd command has a few options. If an option is not specified, useradd will read its configuration file in /etc/default/useradd. In this configuration file, useradd finds some default values (see Listing 7.1). These specify the groups the user will become a member of, where to create the user's home directory, and more.

Listing 7.1: Setting default values in /etc/default/useradd

```
[root@hnl ~]# cat /etc/default/useradd
# useradd defaults file
```

```
GROUP=100
HOME=/home
INACTIVE=-1
EXPIRE=
SHELL=/bin/bash
SKEL=/etc/skel
CREATE_MAIL_SPOOL=yes
```

You can set different properties to manage users. To set up an efficient server, it's important to know the purpose of the settings. For every user, the group membership, UID, and shell default properties are set.

Group Membership

In any UNIX environment, a user can be a member of two different kinds of groups: the primary group and all other groups. Every user must be a member of a primary group. If one user on your system does not have a primary group setting, no one will be able to log in, so membership in a primary group is vital. On a Red Hat server, all users are by default a member of a group that has the same name as the user. This is done for security reasons to make sure that no files are shared with other users by accident.

Users can be members of more than just the primary group, and they will automatically have access to the rights granted to these other groups. The most important difference between a primary group and other groups is that the primary group will automatically become group owner of a new file that a user creates.

You now know the relation between the primary group and the other groups of which a user is a member. You will learn how to apply this knowledge in the sections covering group management later in this chapter.

UID

Another major type of information used when creating a user is the user ID (UID). For your server, this is the only way to identify a user. (Usernames are just a convenience because we, as humans, tend not to handle being identified by numbers well.) In general, all users need a unique UID. Red Hat Enterprise Linux starts generating local UIDs at 500, as explained in a moment. The highest UID available by default is 60000. This is because of a restriction that is defined in /etc/login.defs, which can be changed if needed.

Typically, UIDs below 500 are reserved for system accounts that are needed to start services. The UID 0 is also special—the user who has it has complete administrative permissions to the server. UID 0 is typically reserved for the user root.

Shell

To log in to a server, every user needs a shell. The *shell* will enable interpretation of commands the user enters from their console. The default shell in Linux is /bin/bash, but several other shells are available. One of the more common alternative shells is /bin/tcsh, which has a scripting language similar to the C programming language, which makes tcsh the perfect shell for C programmers.

You should, however, be aware that not all users need shells. Users with a shell are allowed to log in locally to your system and access any files and directories stored on that system, as far as their permissions allow such access. If you are using your system as a mail server where users only need to access their mailboxes using the POP protocol, it makes no sense to give them a login shell. Therefore, you could choose to specify an alternative command to be used as the shell. For example, /sbin/nologin can be used if you don't want to allow the user any interaction with your system locally. It may make sense to use other commands as shell. If, for example, you want the Midnight Commander to be started automatically when a user logs in to your system, make sure that /usr/bin/mc is specified as the shell for that user.

Be sure to include the complete path to the command you want to execute as the shell environment for a user. No clue about the complete path for your favorite command? Use the command which. For example, which mc will display a line showing exactly where the program file you are seeking is located.

Managing Passwords

To access the system, a user needs a password. By default, login is denied for the users you create, and passwords are not assigned automatically. Thus, your newly created users can't do anything on the server. To enable these users, assign passwords using the passwd command.

The passwd command is easy to use. A user can use it to change his password. If that happens, the passwd command will first prompt for the old password and then for the new one. Some complexity requirements, however, have to be met. This means, in essence, that the password cannot be a word that is also in the dictionary.

The root user can change passwords as well. To set the password for a user, root can use passwd followed by the name of the user whose password needs to be changed. For example, passwd linda would change the password for user linda.

The user root can use the passwd command in three generic ways. First, you can use it for password maintenance—to change a password, for example. Second, it can also be used to set password expiry information, which dictates that a password will expire at a particular date. Lastly, the passwd command can be used for account maintenance. For example, an administrator can use passwd to lock an account so that login is disabled temporarily.

Performing Account Maintenance with passwd

In an environment where many users are using the same server, it is important to perform some basic account maintenance tasks. These include locking accounts when they are unneeded for a long time, unlocking an account, and reporting the password status. An administrator can also force a user to change their password on first use. To perform these tasks, the passwd command has some options available.

-l   Enables an administrator to lock an account. For example, passwd -l lucy will lock the account for user lucy.

-u   Unlocks an account that has been locked before.

-S   Reports the status of the password for a given account.

-e   Forces the user to change their password on next login.

Managing Password Expiry

In a server environment, it makes sense to change passwords occasionally. The passwd command has some options to manage account expiry.

-n min   This rarely used option is applied to set the minimum number of days that a user must use their password. If this option is not used, a user can change their password at any time.

-x max   This option is used to set the maximum number of days a user can use a password without changing it.

-c warn   When a password is about to expire, you can use this option to send a warning to the user. The argument for this option specifies the number of days before expiry of the password that the user will receive the warning.

-i inact   Use this option to expire an account automatically when it hasn't been used for a given period of time. The argument for this option is used to specify the exact duration of this period.

Apart from the passwd command, you can also use chage to manage account expiry. Consult the man page for more details on its usage.

Modifying and Deleting User Accounts

If you already know how to create a user, modifying an existing user account is no big deal. The usermod command is used for this purpose. It employs many of the same options that are used with useradd. For example, use usermod -g 101 linda to set the new primary group of user linda to a group with the unique ID 101. The usermod command has many other options. For a complete overview, consult its man page.

Another command that you will occasionally need is userdel. Use this command to delete accounts from your server. userdel is a very simple command: userdel linda deletes user linda from your system, for example. However, if used this way, userdel will leave the home directory of your user untouched. This may be necessary to ensure that your company still has access to the work of a user; however, it may be necessary to delete the user's home directory as well. If there is no more useful data in the user home directory, it makes sense to delete it as well.

If you want to delete a user's home directory and not just the user, use the -r option with userdel. However, if there are files that are not owned by user linda in this home directory, userdel can't remove it. If this is the case, add the option -f. This will make sure that all files are removed from the home directory, even if the specific user being deleted does not own them. That also includes the directory where the user's mail is stored. Thus, to make sure user linda is removed, including all files in her home directory, use userdel -rf linda.

You now know how to remove a user, including their home directory. But what about other files the user may have created in other directories on your system? If you want to make sure these other files are removed as well, the find command is very useful. With find, you can search for all of the files owned by a given user and remove them automatically. For example, to locate all files on your system that are created by linda and remove them automatically, you can use find / -user "linda" -exec rm {} \;.

Removing a user, including all files that were owned by that user, may lead to problems on your server. Imagine the environment where linda was a very active user of the group sales and she had created a lot of files in the directory /home/sales. These files will all be removed as well, and this could lead to serious problems. Therefore, I recommend you do not use the -exec option to remove files immediately but rather copy them to a safe place instead. If no one has complained after a couple of months, you can remove them at that time (with linda's supervisor's permission). To move all files owned by linda to a directory called /trash/linda (which must have been created beforehand), use find / -user linda -exec mv {} /trash/linda \;.

Behind the Commands: Configuration Files

In the previous section, you learned all of the commands required to manage users from a console environment. These commands also put all user-related information in some configuration files. A configuration file is also used for default settings that are applied when managing the user environment. The aim of this section is to give you some insight into the use of these files.

/etc/passwd

The first, and probably the most important, of all user-related configuration files is /etc/passwd. This file is the primary database where user information is stored. That is, the most important user properties are stored in this file. Listing 7.2 will give you an impression of what the fields in this file look like.

Listing 7.2: Users in /etc/passwd

```
[root@hn1 ~]# cat /etc/passwd
root:x:0:0:root:/root:/bin/bash
bin:x:1:1:bin:/bin:/sbin/nologin
daemon:x:2:2:daemon:/sbin:/sbin/nologin
```

```
adm:x:3:4:adm:/var/adm:/sbin/nologin
lp:x:4:7:lp:/var/spool/lpd:/sbin/nologin
sync:x:5:0:sync:/sbin:/bin/sync
shutdown:x:6:0:shutdown:/sbin:/sbin/shutdown
vcsa:x:69:69:virtual console memory owner:/dev:/sbin/nologin
rpc:x:32:32:Rpcbind Daemon:/var/cache/rpcbind:/sbin/nologin
rtkit:x:499:497:RealtimeKit:/proc:/sbin/nologin
abrt:x:173:173::/etc/abrt:/sbin/nologin
sshd:x:74:74:Privilege-separated SSH:/var/empty/sshd:/sbin/nologin
tcpdump:x:72:72::/:/sbin/nologin
linda:x:500:500:johnson:/home/linda:/bin/bash
qemu:x:107:107:qemu user:/:/sbin/nologin
```

Different fields are used in /etc/passwd. The fields are separated with a colon. Here is a short explanation of all the fields used in /etc/passwd.

Username   The user's login name is stored in the first field in /etc/passwd. In older UNIX versions, there was a maximum-length limitation on login names, which was eight characters. In modern Linux distributions, such as Red Hat Enterprise Linux, this limitation no longer exists.

Password   In the old days of UNIX, encrypted passwords were stored in this file. There is, however, one big problem with passwords stored here—even if the password has been hashed, everyone is allowed to read /etc/passwd. Since this poses a security risk, passwords are stored in the configuration file /etc/shadow nowadays, which is discussed in the next section.

UID   As you have already learned, every user has a unique user ID. Red Hat Enterprise Linux starts numbering local user IDs at 500, and typically the highest number that is used is 60000 (the highest numbers are reserved for special-purpose accounts).

GID   As discussed in the previous section, every user has a primary group. The group ID of this primary group is listed there. On Red Hat Enterprise Linux, every user is also a member of a private group that has the name of the user.

GECOS   The General Electric Comprehensive Operating System (GECOS) field is used to include some additional information about the user. The field can contain anything you like, such as the department where the user works, the user's phone number, or anything else. This makes identifying a user easier for an administrator. The GECOS field is optional, and often you will see that it is not used at all.

Home Directory   This field points to the directory of the user's home directory.

Shell   The last field in /etc/passwd is used to refer to the program that is started automatically when a user logs in. Most often, this will be /bin/bash, but as discussed previously, every binary program can be referred to here as long as the complete path name is used.

For an administrator, it is perfectly acceptable to edit /etc/passwd and the related file /etc/shadow manually. Make sure to use the vipw command to edit the files in order to prevent locking issues if other users or commands are editing the files at the same time.

If an error is made, the consequences can be serious. It can even completely prevent logging in on a system. Therefore, if manual changes are made to any of these files, you should check their integrity. To do this, use the pwck command. You can run this command without any options, and it will tell you whether there are any serious problems that need to be fixed.

/etc/shadow

The encrypted user passwords are stored in /etc/shadow. Information relating to password expiry is also kept in this file. Listing 7.3 shows an example of its contents.

Listing 7.3: Displaying user information in /etc/shadow

```
[root@hn1 ~]# cat /etc/shadow
root:$6$4U.GRa4hziUW51nk$gAbbcEBNFThzAc.GaQTuZUXYR/dJbhsoVWzzexkN
 AIYviyp5QlgUWTdf3tQot8jMYkUagI.rP3WtapObyFyIS1:15368:0:99999:7:::
bin:*:15155:0:99999:7:::
daemon:*:15155:0:99999:7:::
adm:*:15155:0:99999:7:::
lp:*:15155:0:99999:7:::
sync:*:15155:0:99999:7:::
shutdown:*:15155:0:99999:7:::
halt:*:15155:0:99999:7:::
mail:*:15155:0:99999:7:::
uucp:*:15155:0:99999:7:::
gdm:!!:15368::::::
sshd:!!:15368::::::
tcpdump:!!:15368::::::
linda:$6$TKn8du1TQxvjoo4K$jU9fByqHINOrb5q1zsH6vfIDR5b75V8kkBO6MqrQ
 uBwSFEyWJlXxkNTegpKwy6ch8.v6z/n2q0LBKCAL9LKd1.:15368:0:99999:7:::
qemu:!!:15424::::::
```

As in /etc/passwd, the lines in /etc/shadow are also organized in different fields. For most administrators, only the first two fields matter. The first field is used to store the name of the user, and the second field is used to store the encrypted password.

In the encrypted password field, an ! and an * can be used. If an ! is used, login is currently disabled. If an * is used, it is a system account that can be used to start services, but that is not allowed for interactive shell login. Also, note that, by default, an encrypted password is stored there, but it is also possible to store a nonencrypted password.

Here are the fields used in the lines in /etc/shadow:

- Login name
- Encrypted password
- Days since January 1, 1970 that password was last changed
- Days before password may be changed
- Days after which password must be changed
- Days before password is to expire that user is warned
- Days after password expires that account is disabled
- Days since January 1, 1970, that account is disabled
- Reserve field, not currently used

/etc/login.defs

/etc/login.defs is a configuration file that relates to the user environment but is used completely in the background. Some generic settings are defined in this configuration file. These settings determine all kinds of information relating to the creation of users. In login.defs, you'll find variables. These variables specify the default values used when users are created. Listing 7.4 shows you part of this configuration file.

Listing 7.4: login.defs contains variables that are used when users are created.

```
# It should remove any at/cron/print jobs etc. owned by
# the user to be removed (passed as the first argument).
#
#USERDEL_CMD    /usr/sbin/userdel_local
#
# If useradd should create home directories for users by default
# On RH systems, we do. This option is overridden with the -m flag on
# useradd command line.
#
CREATE_HOME     yes
# The permission mask is initialized to this value. If not specified,
# the permission mask will be initialized to 022.
UMASK           077
# This enables userdel to remove user groups if no members exist.
#
USERGROUPS_ENAB yes
# Use SHA512 to encrypt password.
ENCRYPT_METHOD SHA512
```

Now that you have read about all ingredients that play a part in user management, in Exercise 7.1 you will create some user accounts.

EXERCISE 7.1

Creating Users

In this exercise, you'll learn how to create user accounts. You'll also see how these user accounts are written to the related configuration files.

1. Open a root shell, and use the command **useradd lisa**.

2. Use the command **su - lisa**. This opens a shell in which you are logged in as the user lisa. The command also brings you to the home directory of this user. You can use **pwd** to verify this.

3. Use **exit** to close the shell in which you are user lisa.

4. Open the file /etc/login.defs with an editor. Locate the variable CREATE_HOME and change its value to no. Close the file and save the changes to disk.

5. Still as root, use the command **useradd lori** to create a user lori.

6. Use **su - lori** to open a subshell as the user lori. You should get an error message that lori doesn't have a home directory.

7. Close the lori subshell, and as root, use **cat /etc/passwd** to see how users lisa and lori have been defined. As you can see, even if lori doesn't have a home directory, there is a field that refers to the location of her home directory.

8. Use **userdel lori** to remove lori from your system.

9. Restore the CREATE_HOME variable in /etc/login.defs to its original value.

10. Create user lori again. At this point, you should have three users: linda, lisa, and lori.

11. As root, use the passwd command to set the password for each of the three users.

Creating Groups

As you already learned, all users require a group membership. You have read about the differences between the primary group and the other groups; however, you have yet to learn how to create these groups. In this section, you'll learn how to use the command-line tools that are available to create groups.

Commands for Group Management

There are three commands to manage the groups in your environment: groupadd, groupdel, and groupmod. As you see, group management follows the same patterns as user management. There also is some overlap between the commands that you'll use to manage groups and those that are used to manage users. For example, usermod as well as groupmod can be used to make a user a member of some group. The basic structure for using the groupadd command is simple: groupadd somegroup, where somegroup is the name of the group you want to create. When creating groups, the first available group ID (GID) is assigned automatically. If you want to specify the GID yourself, you can use the option -g.

Behind the Commands: /etc/group

All groups on your system are defined in the configuration file /etc/group. Listing 7.5 shows a rather simple file that has just four fields for each group definition.

Listing 7.5: Groups are written to /etc/group.

```
[root@hn1 ~]# cat /etc/group
root:x:0:root
bin:x:1:root,bin,daemon
daemon:x:2:root,bin,daemon
sys:x:3:root,bin,adm
adm:x:4:root,adm,daemon
tty:x:5:
vcsa:x:69:
rpc:x:32:
rtkit:x:497:
abrt:x:173:
cdrom:x:11:
tape:x:33:
sshd:x:74:
tcpdump:x:72:
slocate:x:21:
linda:x:500:
kvm:x:36:qemu
qemu:x:107:
cgred:x:490:
```

The first field in /etc/group is reserved for the name of the group. The password for the group, or an exclamation mark that signifies that no password is allowed for this group, is stored in the second field. Just ignore this field, because group passwords are not used anymore.

A unique group ID is provided in the third field of /etc/group, and finally, the names of the members of the group are present in the last field. These names are required only for users for whom this is not the primary group. Primary group membership itself is managed from the /etc/passwd configuration file.

Managing Group Membership

To manage group membership, you can use the usermod and groupmod commands. The available usermod options provide three different choices to manipulate group membership.

-g, --gid GROUP   This option is used to set the primary group for the user.

-G, --groups GROUPS   Use this option to define a new list of supplementary groups. Notice that this option replaces the old list of supplementary groups with the list of new supplementary groups defined here.

-a, --append   Use this option together with -G to add new supplementary groups to the current list of supplementary groups.

Thus, if you want to add supplementary group sales to user linda, use usermod -Ga sales linda, not usermod -G sales linda. You can create and modify groups yourself in Exercise 7.2.

To verify that you've done your work correctly, use the id command. This command shows properties of users, including the current group assignment. Listing 7.6 shows a sample result of this command.

Listing 7.6: Use id to show user properties.

```
[root@hnl ~]# id linda
uid=500(linda) gid=500(linda) groups=500(linda)
```

EXERCISE 7.2

Creating and Managing Groups

In this exercise, you'll create two groups. Next, you'll change the current group assignments for some of your existing users.

1. Use **groupadd sales** and **groupadd account** to create the groups sales and account.

2. Use **id linda** to view the current group assignment for user linda. She should be a member just of the group linda.

3. Use **usermod -aG sales linda** to add user linda to the group sales as a secondary group. Use **id linda** to confirm that she has been added to this group.

4. Repeat this procedure to add users lori and linda to the group account as a secondary group and to add user lisa to the group sales as well.

Using Graphical Tools for User and Group Management

Until now, you've worked with command-line tools for user and group management only. Red Hat Enterprise Linux provides the system-config tools that offer a graphical solution as an alternative to the command-line tools. For user and group management, the name of the tool is *system-config-users*. You can see what this tool looks like in Figure 7.1.

FIGURE 7.1   system-config-users provides a convenient interface for user and group management.

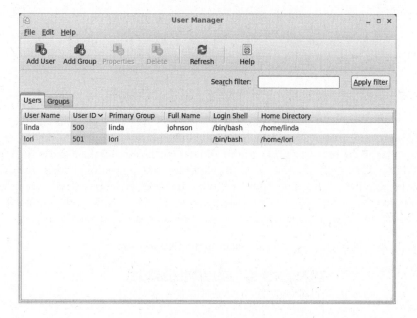

The system-config-users tool was developed to simplify managing users and groups. To create a new user, click Add User. This opens the Add New User window in which you can specify all of the properties you want when creating a new user. It is also easy to add new groups. Just click Add Group, and you'll see a window prompting you for all of the properties that are needed to add a new group, as shown in Figure 7.2.

FIGURE 7.2   To add a new user, just enter all of the required properties in the Add New User window.

After creating the user or group, you can select it to set the properties that aren't shown in the main interface. Just click the user, and in the button bar at the top of the screen, click Properties. You'll then see a window containing four tabs on which you can set all of the required properties for your user.

You can change the properties that you've entered when creating the user on the User Data tab. Select Account Info if you want to enable account expiration, and set the data on which the account expires. The Password Info tab is used to set password expiration, and you can manage membership of secondary groups for your users on the Groups tab. In Figure 7.3 you can see how to change user properties using system-config-users.

FIGURE 7.3   Changing user properties in system-config-users

Using External Authentication Sources

The local user database in /etc/passwd and /etc/shadow is used in a default installation of Red Hat Enterprise Linux. In a corporate environment, it is likely that an external source of authentication is used, such as an LDAP directory server or an Active Directory service that is offered by Windows servers on the network. To configure your server to use these sources, you can use the system-config-authentication tool or authconfig as an alternative.

After starting the system-config-authentication tool, you'll see two tabs. On the Identity & Authentication tab, you can specify how authentication should happen. By default, the tool is set to use local accounts only as the user account database. On the Advanced Options tab, you can enable advanced authentication methods, such as the use of a fingerprint reader (see Figure 7.4).

FIGURE 7.4   Enabling advanced authentication options

If an external authentication source is used on your network, you can select this by using the User Account Database drop-down list on the Identity & Authentication tab. Four options are offered by default:

Local Accounts Only   Use this option to use the local user databases in /etc/passwd and /etc/shadow.

LDAP   This option allows you to log in using an external LDAP directory server.

NIS   In old UNIX environments, NIS might be in use as an authentication service. Use this to connect to a NIS authentication service.

Winbind   This option allows you to authenticate on Windows networks.

Of the options that are listed here, LDAP and Winbind are commonly used. To practice these solutions fully, you would need an external LDAP or Active Directory services. Setting these up is beyond the scope of this book, but in the following subsections you'll become familiar with the procedures that you would normally use to connect to these services.

Red Hat offers the Red Hat Directory Service as an add-on service. That means this service is not available as a default option in Red Hat Enterprise Linux but is available only through additional purchase. An alternative solution is to use OpenLDAP, which is in the default Red Hat Enterprise Linux repositories.

Connecting to an LDAP Server

An LDAP server is organized as a hierarchical structure, which looks a bit like the structure of domains and subdomains that is used in DNS. In many cases, the DNS structure is mapped one-to-one to the LDAP database—only the way it is written is different. The DNS domain referred to as example.com is referred to as dc=example,dc=com in LDAP.

To connect to LDAP, you need to specify at a minimum what is used as the LDAP base DN. This is the branch of the hierarchical structure in which you would expect to find user accounts. Also, you need to specify which LDAP server is used. This LDAP server provides access to the user database.

To connect to the LDAP server, it is good practice to use TLS to encrypt connections. This is possible only if certificates are provided as well. Normally, every LDAP server is able to hand out its own certificates. As an administrator, you just have to specify where these certificates can be found.

The second part of the configuration of LDAP authentication consists of selecting an authentication method. For best security, Kerberos passwords are used. As an alternative, you may also elect to use LDAP passwords. To log in using Kerberos, you need at least three parameters.

Realm   This is like a domain, but in Kerberos the domain name is referred to as a *realm*. The realm specifies where authentication should be handled.

KDCs   In Kerberos, a *key distribution center (KDC)* is used to hand out tickets that are needed while authenticating. This KDC is a specific server that has been configured as such.

Admin Servers   The admin server is the server that is used for administration tasks in a Kerberos environment. It is often the same as the KDC.

Instead of entering these parameters manually, a Kerberos environment can also be set up to use DNS. DNS can be used to locate the KDC for a realm and also to resolve hosts to realms. This is typically the case when connecting to Kerberos in an Active Directory environment. In Exercise 7.3 you'll learn how to configure your server for login on an LDAP Directory Server.

EXERCISE 7.3

Logging in Using an LDAP Directory Server

In this exercise, you'll learn how to connect to an LDAP directory server. You'll use fake settings, because there is no real LDAP directory service available in the course environment.

1.   Start system-config-authentication, and on the Identity & Authentication tab, select LDAP. This opens a window in which you can enter all the parameters that are required to connect to an LDAP server.

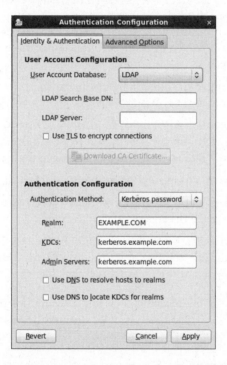

2.   In the User Account Configuration section, enter the LDAP search base DN. In this example, you'll use dc=example,dc=com.

3.   In the LDAP Server field, enter the IP address or—if DNS has been set up properly—use the DNS name of the LDAP Server. For this exercise, use **127.0.0.1**.

4.   Select TLS, and click Download CA Certificate. This opens a browser that allows you to specify the URL from where the TLS certificate can be downloaded. Skip this task, because no TLS certificate is available for this exercise.

5. Under Authentication Method, make sure that Kerberos password is selected. Enter the names of the realm, the KDC, and the admin servers you want to use. For each of these, you can keep the settings that are used by default.

6. Click Save to apply the settings. You'll notice that the system-config-authentication tool is now closed, and back in the terminal window, you can see that the sssd service is started.

Connecting to an Active Directory Server

Active Directory has become the standard for authentication in corporate networks. To have your users authenticate on Active Directory, you need Winbind.

Once Winbind has been installed, you can specify the required parameters in system-config-authentication that allows you to connect to the Windows environment. The following parameters can be used:

Winbind Domain The name of the domain to which you want to connect. This is an Active Directory domain or a classical Windows NT domain.

Security Model Choose between ADS, domain, server, and user to specify how you want to connect to the Windows environment. To connect to Active Directory, select ADS. All other options are for legacy Windows versions, and it's better not to use them.

Windows ADS Realm Use this to specify the Kerberos realm to use.

Winbind Domain Controllers This parameter is used to specify where the domain controllers that are required to make the connection can be found.

Template Shell Use this to indicate which shell should be used for the users at local login on the Linux machine. By default, the shell is set to /bin/false, which doesn't allow shell login for Winbind users. To change this, select a real shell like /bin/bash.

After setting the connection parameters, click Join Domain to join your Red Hat server to the domain (see Figure 7.5). To do this, you need to enter the Administrator password, after which the server will be joined to the domain.

Configuring Authentication Sources with authconfig

The graphical system-config-authentication offers a convenient method to set the authentication sources for your server. On servers where no graphical interface is available, authconfig can be used. There are two versions of this tool. authconfig-tui provides a menu-driven interface where you can select the authentication source you want to use. Alternatively, you can use the authconfig command-line tool, but this requires you to specify many options about how exactly you want to connect to an LDAP server, for instance. In Figure 7.6, you can see what the `authconfig-tui` tool interface looks like.

FIGURE 7.5 Joining your server to a Windows domain

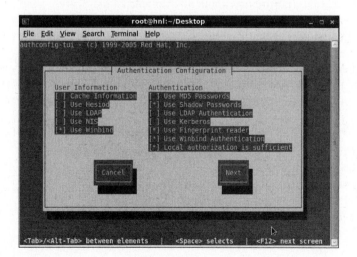

FIGURE 7.6 The text-driven `authconfig-tui` menu interface

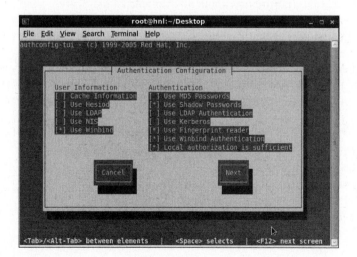

If you need a tool that can be scripted, `authconfig` is the solution for you. Don't be afraid, however, of typing commands like the following, which enables secure LDAP authentication where Kerberos is used (all is one command!):

```
authconfig --enableldap --enableldapauth --ldapserver=ldap.example.com
  --ldapbasedn=dc=example,dc=com --enabletls
  --ldaploadcert=http://ldap.example.com/certificate --enablekrb5
  --krb5kdc=krb.example.com --krb5realm=examplecom --update
```

As you can imagine, there are good reasons why some prefer using graphical or menu-driven tools like the system-config-authentication tool!

Understanding the Authentication Process

When a user authenticates to your server, the local user database as defined in the files /etc/passwd and /etc/shadow is used on a default configuration. If you've used one of the tools described in the previous section to configure authentication against an external authentication server, the sssd service is involved as well. Apart from sssd, PAM and /etc/nsswitch.conf also play a role. You'll learn how these are used in the upcoming subsections.

Understanding sssd

The sssd service provides information about all available authentication sources, and it is also capable of providing offline authentication. This means that if you're on a laptop that is temporarily disconnected from the network, you can still authenticate against the external authentication service using the sssd cache.

Using sssd doesn't require much information. The configuration parameters you've specified are written to the configuration file /etc/sssd/sssd.conf. Listing 7.7 shows the part of the configuration that was written to this file when LDAP authentication was enabled.

Listing 7.7: LDAP authentication parameters in /etc/sssd/sssd.conf

```
# ldap_user_object_class = user
# ldap_group_object_class = group
# ldap_user_home_directory = unixHomeDirectory
# ldap_user_principal = userPrincipalName
# ldap_account_expire_policy = ad
# ldap_force_upper_case_realm = true
```

```
#
# krb5_server = your.ad.example.com
# krb5_realm = EXAMPLE.COM
[domain/default]
ldap_id_use_start_tls = False
krb5_realm = EXAMPLE.COM
ldap_search_base = dc=example,dc=com
id_provider = ldap
auth_provider = krb5
chpass_provider = krb5
ldap_uri = ldap://127.0.0.1/
krb5_kpasswd = kerberos.example.com
krb5_kdcip = kerberos.example.com
cache_credentials = True
ldap_tls_cacertdir = /etc/openldap/cacerts
```

As mentioned, you won't need to modify the sssd configuration manually very often. However, the enumerate parameter can be rather useful. By default, if information about available users is requested with a command like getent, sssd doesn't list LDAP users as well. This is for performance reasons. If you also want those users to be listed, add the line enumerate = True to the [domain/default] section in /etc/sssd/sssd.conf. Don't forget to restart the sssd service after this modification; otherwise, it won't work!

Understanding nsswitch

The /etc/nsswitch file is used to determine where different services on a computer are looking for configuration information. The different sources of information are specified in this file. Listing 7.8 provides an overview of the most relevant parameters used in this file.

Listing 7.8: Specifying sources of information in /etc/nsswitch.conf

```
passwd:     files sssd
shadow:     files sssd
group:      files sssd
bootparams: nisplus [NOTFOUND=return] files
ethers:     files
netmasks:   files
networks:   files
protocols:  files
rpc:        files
services:   files
```

```
netgroup: files
publickey: nisplus
automount: files
aliases:  files nisplus
```

The passwd and shadow files are relevant for authentication. They specify that the local files are always checked first, prior to the authentication mechanism that is offered through sssd.

Understanding Pluggable Authentication Modules

On Linux, *pluggable authentication modules (PAM)* are what is used to make authentication pluggable. Every modern service that needs to handle authentication passes through PAM.

There are two parts in PAM. First there are the configuration files in use. Every service has its own configuration file in the directory /etc/pam.d. For instance, the login service uses the configuration file /etc/pam.d/login. Listing 7.9 shows the contents of this file.

Listing 7.9: The PAM file for login defines how to handle login.

```
[root@hnl ~]# cat /etc/pam.d/login
#%PAM-1.0
auth [user_unknown=ignore success=ok ignore=ignore default=bad] pam_securetty.so
auth       include      system-auth
account    required     pam_nologin.so
account    include      system-auth
password   include      system-auth
# pam_selinux.so close should be the first session rule
session    required     pam_selinux.so close
session    required     pam_loginuid.so
session    optional     pam_console.so
# pam_selinux.so open should only be followed by sessions to be
 executed in the user context
session    required     pam_selinux.so open
session    required     pam_namespace.so
session    optional     pam_keyinit.so force revoke
session    include      system-auth
-session   optional     pam_ck_connector.so
```

In the sample PAM file, you can see that three columns are used to define what should happen. In the first column, the authentication process is split into four different phases: auth, account, password, and session. These are the stages that are typically passed through in the authentication process, but in the end, the writer of the PAM module decides which of these to implement.

A PAM module is called on each line in a PAM configuration file. The PAM modules define exactly what should happen while authenticating. If, for example, you need the authentication procedure to use an LDAP server, you can include the pam_ldap.so module that tells the service how to contact LDAP. The second column specifies how this PAM module should be handled.

To use PAM, it is important to know which modules are available and what exactly is the purpose of each of these modules. You can find out all this information in the Linux-PAM_SAG.txt file in the directory /usr/share/doc/pam<version>. This file contains an extensive description of all the default PAM modules.

As you can see, the /etc/pam.d/login file includes some common parameters that are found in /etc/pam.d/system-auth. This file contains generic parameters that should be included by other services that are related to authentication, such as the PAM files for su and sudo.

The general system-auth file is useful for services that need to be included by many programs. Imagine that you want to have your server authenticate through LDAP. Just put a line in /etc/pam.d/system-auth that calls the LDAP module, and it will be included by all login-related services, such as login, passwd, su, and many more. In Exercise 7.4, you'll discover how to use PAM.

EXERCISE 7.4

Configuring PAM

In this exercise, you'll work with PAM and the /etc/securetty file. The /etc/securetty file defines the terminals on which it is secure for user root to log in. By default, this file is used by the PAM configuration file for login and not for su. In this exercise, you'll define /dev/tty4 as an insecure tty. Next you'll include it in the PAM file for su to disable root login through su on tty4 as well.

1. Open a root shell. Using vi, modify the /etc/securetty file in this root shell and remove the line that contains the text tty4.

2. Use the Ctrl+Alt+F4 key sequence to open the virtual console tty4. Log in as root. You'll notice this doesn't work. Now use the Ctrl+Alt+F3 key sequence, and check to see whether you can perform a root login on this tty. You'll notice this works.

3. Open the /etc/pam.d/login file. You'll notice that, on the first line of this file, the pam_securetty file is called, which means that all authentication passes through the restrictions that are defined in /etc/securetty.

4. Open tty4 again, and now log in as user linda using the password **password**. Next, use **su - to** escalate to root permissions. You'll notice that this works without any restriction.

5. Open the /etc/pam.d/su file, and add the following on the first line:

   auth required   pam_securetty.so

6. Save the changes, and close the file.

7. Type **exit** until you see a login prompt on tty4. Now log in as linda. This should still work. Escalate your privileges using **su** -. You'll now get an access denied message, coming from the security module.

Managing Permissions

At the beginning of this chapter, you learned how to create users and groups. In this section, you'll learn how to apply permissions to these users and groups.

Understanding the Role of Ownership

Before I talk about permissions, you must know about the role of file and directory ownership. File and directory ownership is vital for working with permissions. First you'll learn how you can see ownership. Next you'll learn how to change user and group ownership for files and directories.

Displaying Ownership

Every file and every directory has an owner on Linux. To determine whether you, as a user, have permissions to a file or a directory, the kernel checks ownership. First it will see whether you are the *user owner*, which is also referred to as the *user* of the file. If you are the user, you will get the permissions that are set for the user, and the shell looks no further. If you are not the user owner, the shell will check whether you are a member of the *group owner*, which is also referred to as the *group* of the file. If you are a member of the group, you will get access to the file with the permissions of the group, and the shell looks no further. If you are neither the user owner nor the group owner, you'll get the permissions of others.

With 1s, you can display ownership for files in a given directory. To see current ownership assignments, you can use the 1s -1 command. This command shows the user as well as the group owner. Listing 7.10 shows the ownership settings for directories in the directory /home on a system that uses the public group approach, where all users are members of the same group called *users*.

Listing 7.10: Displaying current file ownership

```
[root@hn1 home]# ls -l
total 32
```

```
drwx------. 4 laura laura  4096 Apr 30 16:54 laura
drwx------. 27 linda linda  4096 Apr 28 11:07 linda
drwx------. 4 lisa  lisa   4096 Apr 30 16:54 lisa
drwx------. 4 lori  lori   4096 Apr 30 16:54 lori
drwx------. 2 root  root  16384 Jan 29 14:10 lost+found
```

Occasionally, it may be useful to get a list of all files that have a given user or group as owner. To do this, use the find command with the argument -user. For example, the command find / -user linda shows all files that have user linda as their owner.

You can also use find to search for files that have a specific group as their owner. For instance, the command find / -group users searches all files that are owned by the group *users*.

Changing User Ownership

When working with permissions, it is important to know how to change them. The chown command is used to do this. The syntax of this command is easy to understand, as in chown who what.

For instance, the command chown linda account would change ownership for the file *account* to user linda.

The chown command has one important option: -R. You can guess its function, because this option is available for many other commands. -R allows you to set ownership *recursively*. In other words, it allows you to set ownership of the current directory and everything below it. The command chown -R linda /home changes ownership for the directory /home and everything beneath it to user linda (which is typically not a very good idea because there may be files in there that have a different file ownership on purpose).

Changing Group Ownership

There are actually two ways to change group ownership. You can do it using chown, but the chgrp command does the job specifically. If you want to use the chown command, use a : in front of the group name. For example, the command chown :account /home/account would change the group owner of directory /home/account to the group account.

You can also use the chgrp command for the same purpose. The command chgrp account /home/account can be used to set group ownership for the directory /home/account to the group account. As is the case for chown, you can use the option -R with chgrp to change group ownership recursively.

Default Ownership

You may have noticed that when a user creates a file, default ownership is applied. The user who creates the file will automatically become user owner, and the primary group automatically becomes group owner. This will normally be the group that is set in the /etc/passwd file as the user's primary group. If, however, the user is a member of more groups, they can change the effective primary group.

To show the current effective primary group, a user can use the groups command as follows:

```
linda@nuuk:~> groups
users dialout video
```

One way to change default group ownership for new files is to change the primary group. If the current user linda wants to change the effective primary group, she can use the newgrp command followed by the name of the group she wants to set as the new effective primary group. Listing 7.11 shows how user linda uses this command to make sales her effective primary group.

Listing 7.11: Using newgrp to change the effective primary group

```
linda@nuuk:~> groups
users dialout video sales
linda@nuuk:~> newgrp sales
linda@nuuk:~> groups
sales dialout video users
linda@nuuk:~>
```

After changing the effective primary group, all new files that the user creates will have this group as their group owner. To return to the original primary group setting, use exit. This will bring you back to the previous effective primary group setting.

Basic Permissions: Read, Write, and Execute

The Linux permissions system was invented in the 1970s. Since computing needs were limited in those years, the basic permission system created then was a bit limited as well. Because of backward compatibility reasons, this system is still in place today, though. This basic system consists of three permissions that can be applied to files and directories. In this section, you'll learn how the system works and how to modify these permissions.

Understanding Read, Write, and Execute Permissions

The three basic permissions allow you to read, write, and execute files. The effect of these permissions is different if applied to files vs. directories. If applied to a file, the *read permission* gives you the right to open the file for reading. That means you can read its contents, and it also means your computer can open the file to do something with it. A program file that needs access to a library, for example, requires read access to that library. From this it follows that the read permission is the most basic permission you will need to work with files.

If applied to a directory, read allows you to list the contents of that directory. You should be aware, however, that this permission does not allow you to read files in the directory. The Linux permission system does not know inheritance, and the only way to read a file is by using the read permission on that file. To open a file for reading, however, you do need read permission for the directory, because you wouldn't see the file otherwise.

As you can probably guess, if applied to a file, the write permission allows you to write to that file. Stated otherwise, *write permission* allows you to modify the contents of existing files. It does not, however, allow you to create or delete new files. To do that, you need write permission on the directory where you want to create the file. In directories, this permission also allows you to create and remove new subdirectories and files, but you need execute as well to descend into the directory.

Execute permission is required to execute a file. It is never set by default, which makes Linux almost completely immune to viruses. Only someone with administrative rights to a directory will be capable of applying the execute permission. Typically this would be the user root. However, a user who is owner of a directory also has the right to change permissions in that directory.

While the execute permission on files means you are allowed to run a program file, when applied to a directory, it indicates that the user can use the cd command to go to that directory. This means that execute is an important permission for directories, and you will see that it is normally applied as the default permission to them. Without it, there is no way to change to a particular directory or create files in that directory.

Table 7.1 summarizes the use of the basic permissions.

TABLE 7.1   Use of read, write, and execute permissions

Permission	Applied to files	Applied to directories
Read	Open a file	List contents of a directory
Write	Change contents of a file	Create and delete files
Execute	Run a program file	Change to the directory

Applying Read, Write, and Execute Permissions

Use the chmod command to apply permissions. When using chmod, you can set permissions for user, group, and others. You can use this command in two modes: relative and absolute. In the absolute mode, three digits are used to set the basic permissions. Table 7.2 provides an overview of the permissions and their numerical representation.

TABLE 7.2   Numerical representation of permissions

Permission	Numerical representation
Read	4
Write	2
Execute	1

When setting permissions, calculate the value you need. For example, if you want to set read, write, execute for the user, read and execute for the group, and read and execute for others on the file /somefile, you would use the chmod command chmod 755 /somefile.

When using chmod this way, all current permissions are replaced by the permissions you set. If you want to modify permissions relative to the current permissions, you can use chmod in relative mode. When using chmod in relative mode, you work with three indicators to specify what you want to do. First you'll specify for whom you want to change permissions. To do this, you can choose between user (u), group (g), and others (o). Next you use an operator to add or remove permissions from the current mode or set them in an absolute way. At the end, you use r, w, and x to specify the permissions you want to set. When changing permissions in relative mode, you may omit the "to whom" part to add or remove a permission for all entities. For example, chmod +x somefile would add the execute permission for all users.

When working in relative mode, you may use more complex commands as well. For instance, chmod g+w,o-r somefile would add the write permission to the group and remove read for others. In Exercise 7.5 you'll learn how to apply permissions on your file system.

Advanced Permissions

Linux also has a set of advanced permissions. These are not permissions you would set by default, but in some instances they provide a useful addition. In this section, you'll learn what the advanced permissions are and how to set them.

EXERCISE 7.5

Setting Permissions for Users and Groups

In this exercise, you'll create a directory structure for the groups you created earlier. You'll also assign the correct permissions to these directories.

1.   From a root shell, type **mkdir -p /data/sales /data/account**.

2. Before setting the permissions, change the owners of these directories using **chown linda.sales /data/sales** and **chown linda.account /data/account**.

3. Set the permissions to enable the user and group owners to write files to these directories and deny all access for all others.

   chmod 770 /data/sales, and next chmod 770 /data/account

4. Use **su - lisa** to become user lisa, and change into the directory /data/account. Use **touch emptyfile** to create a file in this directory. Does this work?

5. Still as user lisa, use **cd /data/sales** and **touch emptyfile** to create a file in this directory. Does this work?

Understanding Advanced Permissions

There are three advanced permissions. The first of them is the *set user ID (SUID) permission*. On some very specific occasions, you may want to apply this permission to executable files. By default, a user who runs an executable file runs this file with their own permissions. For standard users, this normally means the use of the program is restricted. In some cases, however, the user needs special permissions for the execution of a certain task.

Consider the situation where a user needs to change their password. To do this, the user needs to write the new password to the /etc/shadow file. This file, however, is not writable for users who don't have root permissions:

```
[root@hnl ~]# ls -l /etc/shadow
----------. 1 root root 1184 Apr 30 16:54 /etc/shadow
```

The SUID permission offers a solution for this problem. On the /usr/bin/passwd utility, this permission is applied by default. This means that when changing a password, the user temporarily has root permissions, which allow the user to write to the /etc/shadow file. You can see the SUID permission with ls -l as an s at the position where normally you would expect to see the x for the user permissions.

```
[root@hnl ~]# ls -l /usr/bin/passwd
-rwsr-xr-x. 1 root root 32680 Jan 28  2010 /usr/bin/passwd
```

The SUID permission may look useful, and it is in rare cases. At the same time, however, it is potentially dangerous. If applied incorrectly, you can give away root permissions by accident. I therefore recommend using it with the greatest care only.

The second special permission is *set group ID (SGID)*. This permission has two effects. If applied on an executable file, it gives the user who executes the file the permissions of the group owner of that file. Thus, SGID can accomplish more or less the same thing that SUID does. However, SGID is hardly ever used for this purpose.

When applied to a directory, SGID may be used to set default group ownership on files and subdirectories created in that directory. By default, when a user creates a file, the user's effective primary group is set as the group owner for that file. That's not always very useful.

Imagine a situation where users linda and lori work for the accounting department and are both members of the group account. By default, these users are members of the private group of which they are the only members. Both users, however, are also members of the accounting group but as a secondary group setting.

The default situation is that when either of these users creates a file, the primary group becomes owner. However, if you create a shared group directory, say /groups/account, and you apply the SGID permission to that directory and set the group accounting as the group owner for that directory, all files created in this directory and all of its subdirectories would also have group accounting as the default group owner.

The SGID permission shows in the output of ls -l as an s at the position where you would normally find the group execute permission.

```
[root@hnl data]# ls -ld account
drwxr-sr-x. 2 root account 4096 Apr 30 21:28 account
```

The third of the special permissions is called *sticky bit*. *Sticky bit permission* is used to protect files against accidental deletion in an environment where multiple users have write permissions in the same directory. For that reason, it is applied as a default permission to the /tmp directory, and it can be useful on shared group directories as well.

Without sticky bit, if a user can create files in a directory, the user can also delete files from that directory. In a shared group environment, this may be annoying. Imagine users linda and lori again, both of whom have write permissions to the directory /data/account and who have these permissions because of their membership of the group accounting. That means that linda is capable of deleting files that lori has created, and vice versa.

When applying sticky bit, a user can delete files only if either of the following is true:

- The user is owner of the file
- The user is owner of the directory where the file exists

When using ls -l, you can see sticky bit as a t at the position where you would normally see the execute permission for others.

```
[root@hnl data]# ls -ld account/
drwxr-sr-t. 2 root account 4096 Apr 30 21:28 account/
```

Applying Advanced Permissions

To apply SUID, SGID, and sticky bit, you can use the chmod command. SUID has numerical value of 4, SGID has numerical value of 2, and sticky bit has numerical value of 1. If you want to apply these permissions, you need to add a four-digit argument to chmod, where the first digit refers to the special permissions. For example, the command chmod 2755 /some-dir would add the SGID permission to a directory and set rwx for user and rx for group and others.

It is impractical to look up the current permissions that are set before working with chmod in absolute mode. However, you would risk overwriting permissions if you didn't. Therefore, I recommend working in relative mode if you need to apply any of the special permissions.

- For SUID, use chmod u+s.

- For SGID, use chmod g+s.

- For sticky bit, use chmod +t, followed by the name of the file or the directory on which you want to set the permissions.

Table 7.3 summarizes all you need to know about special permissions. In Exercise 7.6 you'll learn how to apply advanced permissions to your system.

TABLE 7.3   Working with SUID, SGID, and sticky bit

Permission	Numerical value	Relative value	On files	On directories
SUID	4	u+s	User executes file with permissions of file owner	No meaning
SGID	2	g+s	User executes file with permissions of group owner	Files created in directory get the same group owner
Sticky bit	1	+t	No meaning	Prevents users from deleting files of other users

EXERCISE 7.6

Working with Special Permissions

In this exercise, you'll use special permissions to make it easier for members of a group to share files in a shared group directory. You'll assign the set group ID bit and sticky bit. After setting these, you'll see that features are added that make it easier for group members to work together.

1. Open a terminal in which you are user linda.

2. Use **cd /data/sales** to go to the sales directory. Use **touch linda1** and **touch linda2** to create two files of which linda is the owner.

3. Use **su - lisa** to switch the current user identity to user lisa, who is also a member of the sales group.

4. Use **cd /data/sales** and, from that directory, use **ls -l**. You'll see the two files that were created by user linda, which are group-owned by the group linda. Use **rm -f linda***. This will remove both files.

5. Use the command **touch lisa1** and **touch lisa2** to create two files that are owned by user lisa.

6. Use **su -** to escalate your current permissions to root level.

7. Use **chmod g+s,o+t /data/sales** to set the set group ID bit and sticky bit on the shared group directory.

8. Use **su - linda**. First use **touch linda3** and **touch linda4**. You should now see that the two files you have created are owned by the group sales, which is group owner of the directory /data/sales.

9. Use **rm -rf lisa***. Sticky bit will prevent you from removing these files as user linda, because you are not the owner of the files. Note that if user linda is directory owner of /data/sales, she can remove the files in question.

Working with Access Control Lists

Even if the advanced permissions that were discussed in the previous section add useful functionality to the way Linux works with permissions, it doesn't allow you to give permissions to more than one user or one group on the same file. This feature is offered through access control lists (ACLs). Aside from that, they allow administrators to set default permissions in a sophisticated way, where the permissions that are set can be different on different directories.

Understanding ACLs

Although the ACL subsystem adds great functionality to your server, there is one drawback: not all utilities support it. This means you may lose ACL settings when copying or moving files and also that your backup software may not be capable of backing up ACL settings.

The tar utility hasn't supported ACLs for a long time. To make sure your ACL settings aren't lost when you make a backup, use star instead of tar. The star utility works with the same options as tar, but it adds support for ACL settings. Alternatively, you can use the `--acls` option with tar.

The lack of support for permissions doesn't have to be a problem, however. ACLs are often applied to directories as a structural measure and not on individual files. This means you won't have lots of them but rather just a few applied to smart places in the file system. Hence, it will be relatively easy to restore the original ACLs with which you were working, even if your backup software doesn't support them.

Preparing Your File System for ACLs

Before starting to work with ACLs, you must prepare your file system for ACL support. Because the file system metadata needs to be extended, ACLs are not always supported by default in the file system.

There are two ways to add file system support for permissions. First, if you're using the Ext4 file system (which is the default file system on Red Hat Enterprise Linux), ACL support is added to all file systems that were created while installing the system. You can verify this is the case by using the dumpe2fs utility on the device you want to check. For example, use dumpe2fs /dev/sda1 to check to see whether ACLs are supported on the file system on the device /dev/sda1 (see Listing 7.12). The `Default mount options` line shows the current default mount options for your file system. As an alternative, support for ACLs can be added as a mount option in /etc/fstab.

Listing 7.12: If your file system has default support for permissions, dumpe2fs shows it.

```
[root@hnl ~]# dumpe2fs /dev/sda1 | less
Filesystem volume name:   <none>
Last mounted on:          /boot
Filesystem UUID:          cc890fc9-a6a8-4c7c-8cc1-65f3f43037cb
Filesystem magic number:  0xEF53
Filesystem revision #:    1 (dynamic)
Filesystem features:      has_journal ext_attr resize_inode dir_index
 filetype needs_recovery extent flex_bg sparse_super huge_file
 uninit_bg dir_nlink extra_isize
Filesystem flags:         signed_directory_hash
Default mount options:    user_xattr acl
Filesystem state:         clean
Errors behavior:          Continue
Filesystem OS type:       Linux
```

```
Inode count:            128016
Block count:            512000
Reserved block count:   25600
Free blocks:            456166
Free inodes:            127976
First block:            1
Block size:             1024
Fragment size:          1024
Reserved GDT blocks:    256
Blocks per group:       8192
:
```

If your file system doesn't offer support for permissions, you can use `tune2fs` to add support to it, or you can use `acl` as a mount option in `fstab` to activate it on every mount. To add `acl` support by using `tune2fs`, use the command `tune2fs -o acl,user_xattr /dev/yourdevice`.

> On file systems that you've added yourself, ACLs are not added as a default mount option. So, for every file system you've added where you want to be able to use ACLs, you'll have to set them yourself.

Another option is to put the ACL option in `fstab` so that it is activated every time your system reboots. Just make sure that in `/etc/fstab`, the fourth column reads `acl,user_xattr`. Once your file system is remounted with ACL support, you can use the `setfacl` command to set ACLs.

> In fact, file systems that have been created while installing your server have ACL support by default, so you don't need the defaults option in /etc/fstab. File systems that have been created later don't have this option set. In that case, you do need the `acl` option. Use `dumpe2fs` to see the properties of the file system, and look for the Default mount option. If that has `acl` set, you don't need to put the `acl` option in `fstab`.

Changing and Viewing ACL Settings with setfacl and getfacl

To set ACLs, you need to use the `setfacl` command. To see your current ACL settings, you need to use `getfacl`. Before setting ACLs, it's always a good idea to show the current ACL settings using `getfacl`. Listing 7.13 shows the current permissions as shown with `ls -l` and as shown with `getfacl`. If you look closely, you'll see that the information shown is exactly the same.

Listing 7.13: Checking permissions with ls -l and getfacl

```
[root@hnl /]# ls -l /data
total 4
drwxr-sr-t. 2 root account 4096 Apr 30 21:28 account
[root@hnl /]# getfacl /data
getfacl: Removing leading '/' from absolute path names
# file: data
# owner: root
# group: root
user::rwx
group::r-x
other::r-x
```

Listing 7.13 shows the result of the getfacl command. You can see that the permissions are shown for three different entities: the user, the group, and others. Now let's add an ACL to give read and execute permissions to the group sales as well. The command to use for this is setfacl -m g:sales:rx /data. In this command, -m indicates that the current ACL settings need to be modified. After that, g:sales:rx tells the command to set the ACL to read and execute (rx) for the group (g) sales. Listing 7.14 shows what the command looks like and the output of the getfacl command after changing the current ACL settings.

Listing 7.14: Changing group ACLs using setfacl

```
[root@hnl /]# setfacl -m g:sales:rx /data
[root@hnl /]# getfacl /data
getfacl: Removing leading '/' from absolute path names
# file: data
# owner: root
# group: root
user::rwx
group::r-x
group:sales:r-x
mask::r-x
other::r-x
```

Now that you understand how to set a group ACL, it's easy to understand other ACLs as well. For example, the command setfacl -m u:linda:rwx /data gives permissions to user linda on the /data directory without making her the owner and without changing the current owner assignment.

The setfacl command has many possibilities and options. The -R option is particularly important. When used, the option makes the ACL setting for all files and subdirectories currently existing in the directory where you set the ACL. It is a good idea always to use this option when changing ACLs for existing directories.

Working with Default ACLs

One benefit of using ACLs is that you can give permissions to more than one user or group at a directory. Another benefit is that you can enable inheritance by working with default ACLs. By setting a default ACL, you'll determine the permissions that will be set for all new items that are created in the directory. Be aware, however, that a default ACL does not change the permissions for existing files and subdirectories. To change those as well, you'll need to add a standard ACL.

To set a default ACL, you have to add the option d after the option -m. (The order does matter.) Use `setfacl -m d:g:sales:rx /data` if you want group sales to have read and execute permissions on everything that will ever be created in the /data directory.

When using default ACLs, it can also be useful to set an ACL for others. Normally this doesn't make much sense, because you can change the permissions for others by using chmod. What you can't do with chmod, however, is to specify the permissions that should be given to others on every new file that will ever be created. For example, if you want others not to get any permissions on anything that is created in /data, use `setfacl -m d:o::-` /data. In Exercise 7.7 you'll learn how to apply ACLs to your file system.

EXERCISE 7.7

Refining Permissions Using ACLs

In this exercise, you'll continue to work on the /data/account and /data/sales directories that you created earlier. In previous exercises, you ensured that the group sales has permissions on /data/sales and that the group account has permissions on /data/account. Up to now, you haven't been able to refine the design, which you will do in this exercise. First you'll make sure that the group account gets read permissions on the /data/sales directory and that group sales gets read permissions on the /data/account directory. Next you'll set default ACLs to make sure that the permissions are properly set for all new items on all new files.

1. Open a root terminal.

2. Use **setfacl -m g:account:rx /data/sales** and **setfacl -m g:sales:rx /data/account**.

3. Use **getfacl** to verify that the permissions have been set the way you intend.

4. Use **setfacl -m d:g:account:rwx,g:sales:rx /data/sales** to set the default ACL for the directory sales.

5. Add the default ACL for the directory /data/account by using **setfacl -m d:g:sales:rwx,g:account:rx /data/account**.

6. Verify that the ACL settings are effective by adding a new file in /data/sales; use **touch /data/sales/newfile** and use **getfacl /data/sales/newfile** to check the current permission assignments.

Setting Default Permissions with umask

In the previous section, you learned how to work with default ACLs. umask is a shell setting that determines the default permissions that you will get if you don't use ACLs. In this section, you'll learn how to modify default permissions using umask.

You probably have noticed that when creating a new file, some default permissions are set. These permissions are determined by the umask setting. This is a shell setting that is applied to all users when logging in to the system. The umask setting contains a numeric value that is subtracted from the maximum permissions that can be set automatically to a file. The maximum setting for files is 666 and for directories is 777. There are, however, some exceptions to this rule. You can find a complete overview of umask settings in Table 7.4.

Of the digits used in the umask, as with the numeric arguments for the chmod command, the first digit refers to end-user permissions, the second digit refers to the group permissions, and the last refers to default permissions set for others. The default umask setting of 022 gives 644 for all new files and 755 for all new directories that are created on your server. You can find a complete overview of all umask numeric values and their results after the table.

TABLE 7.4   umask values and their results

Value	Applied to files	Applied to directories
0	Read and write	Everything
1	Read and write	Read and write
2	Read	Read and execute
3	Read	Read
4	Write	Write and execute
5	Write	Write
6	Nothing	Execute
7	Nothing	Nothing

There are two ways to change the umask setting: one for all users and one for individual users. If you want to set umask for all users, you must make sure the umask setting is entered in the configuration file /etc/profile. If the umask is changed in this file, it applies to all users after logging in to your server.

An alternative to setting the umask setting in /etc/profile, where it is applied to all users logging in to the system, is to change the umask settings in a file with the name .profile, which is created in the home directory of an individual user. Settings applied in this file are for the individual user only. Therefore, this is a good method if you need more granularity.

Working with Attributes

When working with permissions, there is always a relationship between a user or group object and the permissions these user or group objects have on a file or directory. An alternative method of securing files on a Linux server is by working with attributes. Attributes do their work, regardless of the user who accesses the file.

As is the case for ACLs, a mount option must also be enabled for file attributes. This is the user_xattr option. Some attributes are available but not yet implemented. Don't use them because they bring you nothing. Here is a list of the most useful attributes that can be applied:

A   This attribute ensures that the file access time of the file is not modified. Normally, every time a file is opened, the file access time is written to the file's metadata. This affects performance in a negative way. Therefore, on files that are accessed on a regular basis, the A attribute is used to disable this feature.

a   This attribute allows a file to be added to but not to be removed.

c   If you are using a file system where volume-level compression is supported, this file attribute makes sure that the file is compressed the first time that the compression engine becomes active.

D   This attribute makes sure that changes to files are written to disk immediately and not to cache first. This is a useful attribute on important database files to make sure they don't get lost between file cache and hard disk.

d   This attribute makes sure the file is not backed up in backups where the dump utility is used.

I   This attribute enables indexing for the directory where it is enabled. It allows faster file access for primitive file systems like ext3 that don't use a B-tree database for fast access to files.

i   This attribute makes the file immutable. This means that no changes can be made to the file, which is useful for files that need a bit of extra protection.

j   This attribute ensures that, on an ext3 file system, the file is first written to the journal and only after that to the data blocks on the hard drive.

s   This attribute overwrites the blocks where the file was stored with zeros after the file has been deleted. It makes sure that recovery of the file is not possible after it has been deleted.

u   This attribute saves undelete information. This allows a utility to salvage deleted files.

Although there are quite a few attributes that can be used, be aware that most attributes are rather experimental and are useful only if an application is used that works with the given attribute. For example, it doesn't make sense to apply the u attribute if no utility has been developed to use this attribute to recover deleted files.

If you want to apply attributes, you can use the `chattr` command. For example, use `chattr +s somefile` to apply the attribute s to `somefile`. What if you need to remove the attribute again? Then use `chattr -s somefile`, and it will be removed. To get an overview of all attributes that are currently applied, use the `lsattr` command.

Summary

In this chapter, you learned how to set up your server with users and groups. You also learned how to use permissions and attributes to make sure these users and groups can do what they need to do. In the next chapter, you'll learn how to use SELinux to add an extra layer of protection to your server.

Chapter

8

Understanding and Configuring SELinux

TOPICS COVERED IN THIS CHAPTER:

- ✓ Understanding SELinux
- ✓ Selecting the SELinux Mode
- ✓ Working with SELinux Context Types
- ✓ Configuring SELinux Policies
- ✓ Working with SELinux Modules
- ✓ Setting up SELinux with system-config-selinux
- ✓ Troubleshooting SELinux

To keep a server really secure, you'll need to make sure that services are monitored and limited in what they can do. That is what SELinux is used for. In this chapter you'll read how to manage SELinux to add more security to your server and limit the chances of security incidents happening.

Understanding SELinux

Permissions are the foundation of all security on your Red Hat Enterprise Linux server. Just using permissions, however, isn't sufficient if you really want to protect your server. Let's start with a real-life example that happened to me in 2011.

 Real World Scenario

SELinux in Real Life

In 2011, I was running a server that was hosting the Apache web server. The server had been operational since late 2004, and since it worked well and nothing bad had ever happened to it, I had basically left it to its own devices, so to speak. Then one morning I discovered several email messages coming from the hosting provider. The last of them stated that I was at 250 percent of my monthly bandwidth!

So, what happened? On this server, the Apache web server was running with the permissions of a dedicated user account. This user account had some permissions in the Apache-related directories, but as is the case for all users, read, write, and execute was in the /tmp directory. So, a hacker had used a flaw in the Apache process to enter my server and place some Python scripts in the /tmp directory that were sending lots of data to victims all over the world.

Now, the interesting thing is how to resolve such a problem. My first approach was rather naïve: I created a firewall rule that blocked all traffic on this server that wasn't an answer to an incoming connection request. That worked for about a week, until the hacker came back and applied a much more sophisticated hack where a client and server part of his script worked together so that my firewall considered it normal and allowed network traffic. After that, I reached 350 percent of my monthly bandwidth.

The question is how a firewall and permissions can be applied to prevent a hacker from doing this. The answer is they can't, unless you are willing to restrict the permissions of the Apache user severely and thus brutally limit the functionality of your server. SELinux was implemented this way to prevent situations like this from ever happening.

What Is SELinux?

In SELinux, an additional set of rules is used to define exactly which process or user can access which files, directories, or ports.

 SELinux uses rules to define what processes and users can do to objects. These objects include files, directories, and processes, and also system objects such as Interprocess Communication channels, sockets, and even remote hosts. For what you need to understand to achieve an RHCE level, it's good enough to know that SELinux adds a context to files, directories, and ports.

To do this, SELinux applies a *context* to every file, directory, process, and port. This is a security label that defines how this file, directory, process, or port should be treated. These context labels are used by the SELinux policy, which defines exactly what should be done with the context labels. By default, the policy blocks all nondefault access, which means that, as an administrator, you have to enable all features that are nondefault on your server.

Understanding the Type Context

As mentioned, files, folders, and ports can be labeled. Within each label, different contexts are used. To be able to perform your daily administration work, you will be most interested in the type context. In this book, I'll ignore the user and role contexts. Many commands allow you to use the -Z option to show a list of current context settings. Listing 8.1 shows the context settings for the directories in the root directory.

Listing 8.1: The default context for directories in the root directory

```
[root@hnl /]# ls -Z
dr-xr-xr-x. root root system_u:object_r:bin_t:s0        bin
dr-xr-xr-x. root root system_u:object_r:boot_t:s0       boot
drwxr-xr-x. root root system_u:object_r:cgroup_t:s0     cgroup
drwxr-xr-x+ root root unconfined_u:object_r:default_t:s0 data
drwxr-xr-x. root root system_u:object_r:device_t:s0     dev
drwxr-xr-x. root root system_u:object_r:etc_t:s0        etc
drwxr-xr-x. root root system_u:object_r:home_root_t:s0 home
dr-xr-xr-x. root root system_u:object_r:lib_t:s0        lib
dr-xr-xr-x. root root system_u:object_r:lib_t:s0        lib64
```

```
drwx------.  root root system_u:object_r:lost_found_t:s0 lost+found
drwxr-xr-x.  root root system_u:object_r:mnt_t:s0         media
drwxr-xr-x.  root root system_u:object_r:autofs_t:s0      misc
drwxr-xr-x.  root root system_u:object_r:mnt_t:s0         mnt
drwxr-xr-x.  root root unconfined_u:object_r:default_t:s0 mnt2
drwxr-xr-x.  root root unconfined_u:object_r:default_t:s0 mounts
drwxr-xr-x.  root root system_u:object_r:autofs_t:s0      net
drwxr-xr-x.  root root system_u:object_r:usr_t:s0         opt
dr-xr-xr-x.  root root system_u:object_r:proc_t:s0        proc
drwxr-xr-x.  root root unconfined_u:object_r:default_t:s0 repo
dr-xr-x---.  root root system_u:object_r:admin_home_t:s0  root
dr-xr-xr-x.  root root system_u:object_r:bin_t:s0         sbin
drwxr-xr-x.  root root system_u:object_r:security_t:s0    selinux
drwxr-xr-x.  root root system_u:object_r:var_t:s0         srv
-rw-r--r--.  root root unconfined_u:object_r:swapfile_t:s0 swapfile
drwxr-xr-x.  root root system_u:object_r:sysfs_t:s0       sys
drwxrwxrwt.  root root system_u:object_r:tmp_t:s0         tmp
-rw-r--r--.  root root unconfined_u:object_r:etc_runtime_t:s0 tmp2.tar
-rw-r--r--.  root root unconfined_u:object_r:etc_runtime_t:s0 tmp.tar
drwxr-xr-x.  root root system_u:object_r:usr_t:s0         usr
drwxr-xr-x.  root root system_u:object_r:var_t:s0         var
```

You can see the complete context for all directories in Listing 8.1. It consists of a user, a role, and a type. The context type defines what kind of activity is permitted in the directory. Compare, for example, the /root directory, which has the admin_home_t context type, and the /home directory, which has the home_root_t context type. In the SELinux policy, different kinds of access are defined for these context types. In Exercise 8.1 you'll learn how to display SELinux Type Context.

EXERCISE 8.1

Displaying SELinux Type Context

In this exercise, you'll learn how to display SELinux contexts. The goal is to get familiar with how to display contexts. I'll give more information about their specific use later in this chapter.

1. Open a root shell. Use **cd /etc** to go to the /etc directory. Type **ls -Z** to show the default context settings for the files in this directory. Notice that many of the files have a specific context setting according to their function.

2. Activate the home directory of user linda using **cd /home/linda**. Use **ls -Z** to show the context settings for files in this directory. Notice that they all have the user_home_t context type.

3. While still in the directory /home/linda, use **touch newfile** to create a new file. You can see that this file also gets the user_home_t context type.

4. Type **ps aux**. This shows a list of current processes on your server. Type **ps Zaux**. This adds the context listing for each of these processes.

5. Type **netstat -tulpen**. This shows a list of all ports that are available to other computers on your network. Type **netstat -tulpenZ**. You'll now see that the context is displayed as well.

Selecting the SELinux Mode

Three different modes can be used in SELinux.

Enforcing This is the default mode. SELinux protects your server according to the rules in the policy, and SELinux logs all of its activity to the audit log.

Permissive This mode is useful for troubleshooting. If set to Permissive, SELinux does not protect your server, but it still logs everything that happens to the log files. Also, in permissive mode, the Linux kernel still maintains the SELinux labels in the file system. This is good, because this prevents your system from relabeling everything after turning SELinux on again.

Disabled This mode is to be inactivated. In disabled mode, SELinux is switched off completely, and no logging occurs.

There are different ways of managing the current SELinux mode. First you can switch between Enforcing and Permissive using the setenforce command as root. You cannot switch to Disabled mode using setenforce. Switching to Disabled mode completely requires a reboot. To monitor the current SELinux mode, you can use the getenforce command.

To set the SELinux mode while booting, you can put it in the /etc/sysconfig/selinux file. You can see an example of this in Listing 8.2.

Listing 8.2: Setting SELinux mode in /etc/sysconfig/selinux

```
[root@hn1 ~]# cat /etc/sysconfig/selinux

# This file controls the state of SELinux on the system.
# SELINUX= can take one of these three values:
#     enforcing - SELinux security policy is enforced.
#     permissive - SELinux prints warnings instead of enforcing.
#     disabled - No SELinux policy is loaded.
SELINUX=enforcing
# SELINUXTYPE= can take one of these two values:
#     targeted - Targeted processes are protected,
#     mls - Multi Level Security protection.
SELINUXTYPE=targeted
```

You can also set the current SELinux mode on the GRUB prompt while booting. See Chapter 19, "Understanding and Troubleshooting the Boot Procedure," for more details about the boot procedure.) On the GRUB prompt, use selinux=0 to disable SELinux while booting, and use selinux=1 if you want it to be enabled.

In general, you want SELinux to be enabled at all times. There are some products, however, that specifically mention they cannot work with SELinux. If you have software that specifically mentions an incompatibility with SELinux, you have to turn off SELinux. If you suspect that SELinux is preventing your service from functioning the way it should, don't just turn it off. Instead, analyze the log files as described in the "Troubleshooting SELinux" section in this chapter. It can be useful, however, to test whether your server works if SELinux is switched off. To perform this temporary test, use setenforce Permissive. Exercise 8.2 provides an example of why this might be useful.

EXERCISE 8.2

Switching between SELinux Modes

In this exercise, you'll install an Apache web server and configure it for nondefault behavior, which will be denied by SELinux. Next you'll set SELinux to Permissive mode, which shows that the nondefault behavior is then accepted. Then you'll change the /etc /sysconfig/selinux file to set SELinux to disabled. Following that, you'll create an empty file, set SELinux to Enforcing again, and reboot your server. You'll notice that, after the reboot, a relabeling procedure is started, which takes a lot of time to complete.

1. Use **yum install httpd** to install the Apache web server. If yum says that it's already installed, that's OK; just continue with the exercise.

2. Once installed, use **service httpd start** to verify that your Apache server does indeed start. Once verified, use **service httpd stop** to stop it again.

3. With your editor, open the /etc/httpd/conf/httpd.conf file and find the line that reads Listen 80. Change this to Listen 81. This tries to start the Apache web server on port 81. Now use **service httpd start** to start the Apache web server again. You will get a Permission denied message.

4. Type **setenforce Permissive**, and try to start the Apache server again. You'll see that it now works. Open the httpd.conf file, and change the default listen port back to 80.

5. Open the file /etc/sysconfig/selinux in your editor, and change the SELINUX parameter to disabled. Reboot your server.

6. After the reboot, log in as root and use **touch disabledfile** to create a new file in your home directory.

7. Use **ls -Z** to check the context that was set for this file. You will see that no context is set for this file.

8. Modify the /etc/sysconfig/selinux file again, and set SELINUX back to enabled. Reboot your server. When the Red Hat logo is displayed, press Esc to display boot messages. You'll see this message: Warning -- SELinux targeted policy label is required. It will take at least a few minutes before this message disappears and the relabeling has been completed. This is exactly why you should normally try to avoid Disabled SELinux mode completely.

Working with SELinux Context Types

You have already learned how the -Z option is used with many commands, including ls, ps, and netstat, to display the current context type. In this section, you'll learn how to set a context type for new files and directories.

If a file is created within a specific directory, it inherits the context type of the parent directory by default. You witnessed this in Exercise 8.1. If, however, a file is moved from one location to another, it retains the context type that it had in the old location. This is because the SELinux context is stored in the user-extended attributes of the file system. To set the context type for files, you can use the semanage fcontext command. With this command, you write the new context type to the policy, but it doesn't change the actual context type immediately. To apply the context types that are in the policy, you need to run the restorecon command afterward.

The semanage command is not installed by default. To use it, make sure the policycoreutils and policycoreutils-python packages are installed on your server. Alternatively, just use yum whatprovides */semanage if you don't want to remember the names of these packages.

The big challenge when working with semanage fcontext is to find out which context you actually need. You can use semanage fcontext -l to show a list of all contexts in the policy, but it still might be a bit hard to find out the actual context you need from that list. In Listing 8.3 you can see what the output of the command looks like.

Listing 8.3: Displaying default file contexts with semanage fcontext -l

```
[root@hnl ~]# semanage fcontext -l | less
SELinux fcontext                          type            Context

/                        directory        system_u:object_r:root_t:s0
```

```
/.*                     all files       system_u:object_r:default_t:s0
/[^/]+                  regular file    system_u:object_r:etc_runtime_t:s0
/\.autofsck             regular file    system_u:object_r:etc_runtime_t:s0
/\.autorelabel          regular file    system_u:object_r:etc_runtime_t:s0
/\.journal              all files       <<None>>
/\.suspended            regular file    system_u:object_r:etc_runtime_t:s0
/a?quota\.(user|group)  regular file    system_u:object_r:quota_db_t:s0
/afs                    directory       system_u:object_r:mnt_t:s0
/bin                    directory       system_u:object_r:bin_t:s0
/bin/.*                 all files       system_u:object_r:bin_t:s0
:
```

There are two ways to find out which context settings are available for your services:

- Install the service and look at the default context settings that are used.

- Consult the man page for the specific service. Many services have a man page that ends in _selinux, which contains all the information you need to find the correct context settings.

After finding the specific context setting you need, you just have to apply it. To do this, semanage fcontext takes -t contexttype as its first argument, followed by the name of the directory or file to which you want to apply the context settings. To apply the context to everything that already exists in the directory where you want to apply the context, you add the regular expression (/.*)? to the name of the directory. This means, optionally, match a slash followed by any character.

> If you're having a hard time remembering the syntax of the semanage fcontext command, just look at the man page. You'll find a list of examples near the end of the man page showing you exactly how to use the command.

You will never be able to memorize all of the available type contexts. More than 3,000 are available by default! You can retrieve an overview of all of these using the seinfo -t command. In Exercise 8.3 you'll learn how to apply file contexts to your server.

EXERCISE 8.3

Applying File Contexts

In this exercise, you'll apply file contexts using semanage fcontext and restorecon. You will notice that at first attempt, the web server with a nondefault document root doesn't work. After changing the SELinux context, it will work properly.

1. Make sure the packages containing semanage and restorecon are installed by using **yum install policycoreutils policycoreutils-python**.

EXERCISE 8.3 *(continued)*

2. Use **mkdir /web**, and then activate that directory using **cd /web**.

3. Use your editor to create the file /web/index.html that contains the text *welcome to my website*.

4. Open the file /etc/httpd/conf/httpd.conf with an editor, and change the DocumentRoot line to **DocumentRoot "/web"**.

5. Start the Apache web server using **service httpd start**.

6. Use elinks localhost to open a session to your local web server. You will receive a Connection refused message. Press Enter and then q to quit elinks.

7. Use **ls -Z /var/www** to find the current type context for the default Apache DocumentRoot, which is /var/www/html. It should be set to httpd_sys_content_t.

8. Use **semanage fcontext -a -f ""-t httpd_sys_content_t '/web(/.*) ?'** and press Enter.

9. Now use **restorecon /web** to apply the new type context.

10. Use **ls -Z /web** to show the context of the files in the directory /web. Can you see what has gone wrong?

11. Use **restorecon -R /web** to apply the new context recursively to the /web directory. The type context has now been set correctly.

12. Restart the web server using **service httpd restart**. You should now be able to access the content of the /web directory.

13. Open the /etc/httpd/conf/httpd.conf file with an editor, and make sure the DocumentRoot parameter is set to /var/www/html.

Configuring SELinux Policies

Writing a policy is the work of a specialist, and it would merit a book in itself. An easy way to change the behavior of the policy is by working with Booleans. *Booleans* are switches that you can use to change the settings in the policy.

To find out what Booleans can do for you, here are three options:

- Use the man page for the service you want to configure to find out about Booleans that are specific to that service. Many services have a man page that ends in _selinux and contain exactly the information you need.

- Use getsebool -a to show a list of all Booleans that are currently available. Use grep to filter the list for Booleans that are specific to the service you want to configure. The name of the Boolean often provides a good indication of its purpose.

- Use semanage Boolean -l to show a list of all Booleans. The output of this command is similar to the output of getsebool -a, with the difference being that the description is usually a bit longer.

Once you have found the Boolean you want to set, you can use `setsebool -P`. It is important to use the `-P` option at all times when using `setsebool`. This option writes the setting to the policy file on disk, and this is the only way to make sure that the Boolean is applied automatically after a reboot. In Exercise 8.4, you will learn how to work with SELinux Booleans.

EXERCISE 8.4

Working with SELinux Booleans

In this exercise, you'll learn how to work with Booleans. You will explore Booleans that are available for the vsftpd FTP server, and you will enable the FTP server for anonymous writes.

1. From a root shell, type **getsebool -a | grep ftp**. This displays a list of Booleans that are related to FTP servers.

2. Use the command semanage **boolean -1 | grep ftp**. Compare the result to that of the getsebool command you used in the first step of this exercise.

3. Use **man -k _selinux**. This shows a short list of services that have their own man pages that relate to SELinux. As you can see, there is a man page for ftpd_selinux as well.

4. Use **setsebool allow_ftpd_anon_write on** to switch on this Boolean. Notice that it doesn't take much time to write the change. Use **getsebool -a |grep ftpd_anon** to verify that the Boolean is indeed turned on.

5. Reboot your server.

6. Check again to see whether the allow_ftpd_anon_write Boolean is still turned on. Because it hasn't yet been written to the policy, you'll see that it is off right now.

7. Use **setsebool -P allow_ftpd_anon_write on** to switch the Boolean on and write the setting to the policy.

Working with SELinux Modules

The current implementation of SELinux on Red Hat Enterprise Linux is modular. This means that the policy that implements SELinux features is not a single large policy but one that consists of many smaller modules. Each module covers a specific part of the SELinux configuration.

The concept of SELinux module was introduced to make it easy for third-party vendors to make their services compatible with SELinux. To get an overview of SELinux modules, you can use the `semodule -1` command.

It is also possible for an administrator to switch modules on or off. This can be useful if you want to disable a single part of SELinux to run a specific service without SELinux protection. To switch off a SELinux module, use `selinux -d modulename`. If you want to switch it on again, use `selinux -e modulename.`

Setting Up SELinux with system-config-selinux

You've read about some of the most useful command-line tools. In case you don't like working with the command-line interface, there is a graphical tool as well, known as system-config-selinux. This tool is in the package policycoreutils-gui, so make sure it is installed before you try to launch it.

The system-config-selinux tool conveniently offers most of the options you learned how to use from the command line. There is one important drawback to using it, though; everything you want to write to the policy from system-config-selinux is written to the policy immediately after selecting it. This means you can't click dozens of options one after another because, after selecting an option, the policy is immediately updated and you have to wait a minute for that. So, my advice on this is simple: don't use it!

Troubleshooting SELinux

As you read earlier in this chapter, many administrators turn off SELinux because it prevents them from doing what they want to do. By turning off SELinux, you take a huge risk, however. It is much better to keep it on and then to analyze what needs to be done if it is preventing you from performing a specific task. The setroubleshoot-server package makes it a lot easier to analyze what has gone wrong by providing a set of tools that spell out what you need to do to make it work. Use `yum install -y setroubleshoot` to install the server and all of the utilities you need.

By default, if SELinux is the reason why something isn't working, a log message to this effect is sent to the /var/log/audit/audit.log file (that is, *if* the auditd service is running). If you see an empty /var/log/audit, check that the auditd service is running (`service auditd status`) and enabled (`chkconfig --list | grep auditd`). Also, you need the package setroubleshoot-server to be installed before anything appears in the audit.log file. The messages in the audit.log file, unfortunately, are hard to read. Listing 8.4 shows an example of this.

Listing 8.4: Example lines from /etc/audit/audit.log

```
type=USER_START msg=audit(1336057801.202:14): user pid=2943 uid=0
 auid=500 ses=4 subj=system_u:system_r:crond_t:s0-s0:c0.c1023
msg='op=PAM:session_open acct="linda" exe="/usr/sbin/crond" hostname=?
 addr=? terminal=cron res=success'
type=CRED_DISP msg=audit(1336057801.325:15): user pid=2942 uid=0 auid=0
```

```
ses=3 subj=system_u:system_r:crond_t:s0-s0:c0.c1023 msg='op=PAM:setcred
acct="root" exe="/usr/sbin/crond" hostname=? addr=? terminal=cron
 res=success'
type=USER_END msg=audit(1336057801.326:16): user pid=2942 uid=0 auid=0
 ses=3 subj=system_u:system_r:crond_t:s0-s0:c0.c1023 msg='op=PAM:session_close
acct="root" exe="/usr/sbin/crond" hostname=?
 addr=? terminal=cron res=success'
type=CRED_DISP msg=audit(1336057801.390:17): user pid=2943 uid=500 auid=500
 ses=4 subj=system_u:system_r:crond_t:s0-s0:c0.c1023 msg='op=PAM:setcred
 acct="linda" exe="/usr/sbin/crond" hostname=? addr=? terminal=cron
 res=success'
type=USER_END msg=audit(1336057801.390:18): user pid=2943 uid=500 auid=500
 ses=4 subj=system_u:system_r:crond_t:s0-s0:c0.c1023
 msg='op=PAM:session_close acct="linda" exe="/usr/sbin/crond"
 hostname=? addr=? terminal=cron res=success'
type=AVC msg=audit(1336057812.508:19): avc:  denied  { getattr } for
  pid=2823 comm="httpd" path="/webb/index.html" dev=dm-0 ino=2228227 scontext=un
confined_u:system_r:httpd_t:s0
  tcontext=unconfined_u:object_r:default_t:s0 tclass=file
type=AVC msg=audit(1336057812.508:20): avc:  denied  { getattr } for
  pid=2823 comm="httpd" path="/webb/index.html" dev=dm-0 ino=2228227
  scontext=unconfined_u:system_r:httpd_t:s0
  tcontext=unconfined_u:object_r:default_t:s0 tclass=file
```

If you're really motivated, you'll get the information you need out of the audit.log file. Take, for example, the last line that starts with type=AVC. It is followed by an ID that is used by auditd, after which you can see that the httpd process with PID 2823 is denied access to the file /webb/index.html. There is another way of understanding what's happening, though. Look at the last lines of /var/log/messages in Listing 8.5. After installing setroubleshoot-server, it logs the same event.

Listing 8.5: The same message as seen in /var/log/messages

```
[root@hnl audit]# tail /var/log/messages
May  3 17:01:59 hnl kernel: hda-intel: Invalid position buffer, using LPIB read
method instead.
May  3 17:02:00 hnl kernel: hda-intel: IRQ timing workaround is activated
 for card #0. Suggest a bigger bdl_pos_adj.
May  3 17:02:07 hnl avahi-daemon[2121]: Invalid query packet.
May  3 17:02:34 hnl avahi-daemon[2121]: Invalid query packet.
May  3 17:04:43 hnl kernel: type=1400 audit(1336057483.276:4): avc:  denied
  { getattr } for  pid=2822 comm="httpd" path="/webb/index.html" dev=dm-0
 ino=2228227 scontext=unconfined_u:system_r:httpd_t:s0
```

```
tcontext=unconfined_u:object_r:default_t:s0 tclass=file

May  3 17:04:43 hnl kernel: type=1400 audit(1336057483.276:5): avc:  denied
 { getattr } for  pid=2822 comm="httpd" path="/webb/index.html" dev=dm-0
 ino=2228227 scontext=unconfined_u:system_r:httpd_t:s0
 tcontext=unconfined_u:object_r:default_t:s0 tclass=file

May  3 17:10:00 hnl auditd[2929]: Started dispatcher: /sbin/audispd pid:
 2931
May  3 17:10:00 hnl audispd: audispd initialized with q_depth=120 and 1
 active plugins
May  3 17:10:00 hnl auditd[2929]: Init complete, auditd 2.1.3 listening for
 events (startup state enable)
May  3 17:10:15 hnl setroubleshoot: SELinux is preventing httpd from
 getattr access on the file /webb/index.html. For complete SELinux messages. run
sealert -l bedbcf59-9bc0-4425-b4fd-e45b8f4e3369
```

As you can see from /var/log/messages, it is loud and clear what is happening. Even better, you can run the sealert command followed by a specific ID to find an even more detailed explanation of what's going on. You can see the complete explanation for this event in Listing 8.6.

Listing 8.6: The sealert command tells you what to do

```
[root@hnl ~]# sealert -l bedbcf59-9bc0-4425-b4fd-e45b8f4e3369
SELinux is preventing httpd from getattr access on the file /webb/index.html.

*****  Plugin catchall_labels (83.8 confidence) suggests   *********************

If you want to allow httpd to have getattr access on the index.html file
Then you need to change the label on /webb/index.html
Do
# semanage fcontext -a -t FILE_TYPE '/webb/index.html'
where FILE_TYPE is one of the following: net_conf_t, textrel_shlib_t,
 public_content_t, cert_type, etc_runtime_t, anon_inodefs_t,
 dirsrv_var_run_t, sysctl_kernel_t, httpd_modules_t, fail2ban_var_lib_t,
 puppet_var_lib_t, httpd_var_lib_t, httpd_var_run_t, rpm_script_tmp_t,
 httpd_awstats_htaccess_t, httpd_dirsrvadmin_htaccess_t,
 httpd_suexec_exec_t, httpd_user_htaccess_t, application_exec_type,
chroot_exec_t, httpd_nutups_cgi_htaccess_t, mailman_cgi_exec_t,

 gitosis_var_lib_t, httpd_sys_content_t, public_content_rw_t,
dirsrvadmin_config_t, user_cron_spool_t, httpd_squid_htaccess_t,
```

httpd_bugzilla_htaccess_t, httpd_cobbler_htaccess_t, httpd_munin_htaccess_t, rpm_tmp_t, mailman_data_t,

dirsrvadmin_unconfined_script_exec_t, httpd_apcupsd_cgi_htaccess_t, mailman_archive_t, system_dbusd_var_lib_t, httpd_cvs_htaccess_t,

httpd_git_htaccess_t, httpd_sys_htaccess_t, squirrelmail_spool_t, ld_so_cache_t, bin_t, httpd_prewikka_htaccess_t, httpd_t, lib_t,

abrt_var_cache_t, passenger_var_lib_t, passenger_var_run_t, cobbler_var_lib_t, usr_t, httpd_rotatelogs_exec_t,

httpd_smokeping_cgi_htaccess_t, nagios_etc_t, nagios_log_t, sssd_public_t, httpd_keytab_t, locale_t, httpd_unconfined_script_exec_t, etc_t, fonts_t,

logfile, cluster_conf_t, proc_t, sysfs_t, krb5_keytab_t, fonts_cache_t, httpd_exec_t, httpd_lock_t, passenger_exec_t, httpd_log_t, dirsrv_config_t,

httpd_config_t, krb5_conf_t, user_tmp_t, abrt_var_run_t, httpd_mediawiki_htaccess_t, udev_tbl_t, httpd_tmp_t, calamaris_www_t,

smokeping_var_lib_t, shell_exec_t, httpd_w3c_validator_htaccess_t, httpd_cache_t, httpd_tmpfs_t, mysqld_etc_t, sysctl_crypto_t, cvs_data_t,

iso9660_t, dirsrvadmin_tmp_t, cobbler_etc_t, puppet_tmp_t, var_lib_t, httpd_helper_exec_t, dbusd_etc_t, user_home_t, dirsrv_share_t, configfile,

abrt_t, lib_t, httpd_squirrelmail_t, httpd_php_exec_t, httpd_nagios_htaccess_t, abrt_helper_exec_t, httpd_mediawiki_tmp_t,

samba_var_t, dirsrv_var_log_t, ld_so_t, zarafa_var_lib_t, httpd_cvs_ra_content_t, httpd_cvs_rw_content_t, httpd_git_ra_content_t,

httpd_git_rw_content_t, httpd_nagios_content_t, httpd_sys_ra_content_t, httpd_sys_rw_content_t, httpd_sys_rw_content_t,

httpd_w3c_validator_content_t, httpd_nagios_ra_content_t, httpd_nagios_rw_content_t, httpd_nutups_cgi_ra_content_t,

httpd_nutups_cgi_rw_content_t, httpd_cobbler_script_exec_t, httpd_mediawiki_script_exec_t, httpd_smokeping_cgi_script_exec_t,

httpd_git_content_t, httpd_user_content_t, httpd_apcupsd_cgi_content_t, httpd_mediawiki_ra_content_t, httpd_mediawiki_rw_content_t,

httpd_apcupsd_cgi_ra_content_t, httpd_apcupsd_cgi_rw_content_t, httpd_squid_ra_content_t, httpd_squid_rw_content_t,

httpd_prewikka_content_t, httpd_smokeping_cgi_content_t, httpd_smokeping_cgi_ra_content_t, httpd_smokeping_cgi_rw_content_t,

httpd_cvs_content_t, httpd_sys_content_t, httpd_munin_content_t, httpd_squid_content_t, httpd_awstats_script_exec_t,

httpd_munin_script_exec_t, httpd_dirsrvadmin_ra_content_t, httpd_dirsrvadmin_rw_content_t, httpd_w3c_validator_script_exec_t,

httpd_prewikka_ra_content_t, httpd_prewikka_rw_content_t, httpd_user_script_exec_t, httpd_bugzilla_content_t,

httpd_mediawiki_content_t, krb5_host_rcache_t, httpd_cobbler_content_t, httpd_apcupsd_cgi_script_exec_t, root_t, httpd_dirsrvadmin_content_t,

httpd_squid_script_exec_t, httpd_nagios_script_exec_t, httpd_w3c_validator_ra_content_t, httpd_w3c_validator_rw_content_t,

httpd_awstats_ra_content_t, httpd_awstats_rw_content_t, httpd_awstats_content_t, httpd_bugzilla_script_exec_t,

httpd_user_ra_content_t, httpd_user_rw_content_t, httpdcontent, httpd_cobbler_ra_content_t, httpd_cobbler_rw_content_t,

httpd_prewikka_script_exec_t, httpd_nutups_cgi_content_t, httpd_munin_ra_
content_t, httpd_munin_rw_content_t,
 httpd_sys_script_exec_t, httpd_git_script_exec_t, httpd_cvs_script_exec_t,
httpd_dirsrvadmin_script_exec_t, httpd_bugzilla_ra_content_t,
 httpd_bugzilla_rw_content_t, httpd_nutups_cgi_script_exec_t.
Then execute:
restorecon -v '/webb/index.html'

***** Plugin catchall (17.1 confidence) suggests ***************************

If you believe that httpd should be allowed getattr access on the
 index.html file by default.
Then you should report this as a bug.
You can generate a local policy module to allow this access.
Do
allow this access for now by executing:
grep httpd /var/log/audit/audit.log | audit2allow -M mypol
semodule -i mypol.pp

The amount of information that is shown by sealert may strike you as being over-whelming, but if you know where to look, it's not that bad. As you can see right at the beginning, it tells you to run the semanage fcontext command, followed by a type context. It is not exactly sure which one to use, so for your convenience, it shows just those type contexts that are relevant to this scenario instead of the more than 3,000 type contexts that exist. After the list of all relevant type contexts, it tells you to run restorecon to apply the final fix. Just follow the procedure that is indicated here, and you'll fix the issue right away. In Exercise 8.5 you'll learn how to enable sealert messages.

EXERCISE 8.5

Enabling sealert Message Analysis

In this exercise, once again you'll modify the Apache web server to force it to do something that SELinux doesn't like. To analyze what is happening, you'll use the tools that are available from the setroubleshoot-server package.

1. Use **yum -y install setroubleshoot-server** to install the setroubleshoot-server package.

2. Create a directory with the name **/web2**, put an index.html file in the directory that contains some text, and change the httpd DocumentRoot setting in /etc/httpd/conf/httpd.conf to refer to /web2 as the default DocumentRoot. After making those changes, restart Apache using **service httpd restart**.

EXERCISE 8.5 *(continued)*

3. Make sure that auditd is started; if it's not, use **service auditd start** and **chkconfig auditd on** to start auditd and put it in your server's runlevels.

4. Use elinks to try to get to the new DocumentRoot, which obviously will be forbidden. (Use elinks **http://localhost**.)

5. Use **tail /var/log/audit/audit.log** to read the messages that were written by SELinux to the audit.log. You'll notice they are a bit hard to read.

6. Use **tail /var/log/messages** to read about the same event. You'll see that it's much easier to do from this file.

7. Copy the sealert -l command from /var/log/messages, including the full ID after the -l option, and run the command from the command line.

8. Follow the directions given by sealert -l to fix the issue.

Summary

In this chapter, you learned how to work with SELinux. You learned only the basics—the real work begins when you start installing and configuring services that need SELinux to allow them to do what you need them to do. Therefore, in many of the chapters that follow, you'll encounter SELinux again and explore some practical cases where you really need to configure SELinux before you can start a service.

Chapter

9

Working with KVM Virtualization

TOPICS COVERED IN THIS CHAPTER:

- ✓ Understanding the KVM Virtualization Architecture
- ✓ Preparing Your Host for KVM Virtualization
- ✓ Installing a KVM Virtual Machine
- ✓ Managing KVM Virtual Machines
- ✓ Understanding KVM Networking

Virtualization is a popular solution to use system resources in a more efficient way. In Red Hat Enterprise Linux, KVM is available to offer datacenter-ready virtualization. In this chapter, you'll learn everything you need to know about KVM to build a versatile virtualized environment on top of it.

Understanding the KVM Virtualization Architecture

In many datacenters today, virtualization techniques are employed to use hardware more efficiently. Virtualization allows you to run several virtual machines on one physical server and thus makes each server more cost-effective to run.

Red Hat KVM Virtualization

In its 64-bit version, Red Hat Enterprise Linux Server includes KVM virtualization by default. KVM stands for *Kernel Virtual Machine*. This is *hypervisor type 1 virtualization*; a hypervisor offers the most efficient way to install virtualized operating systems. In this section, you'll learn how to set up a KVM virtual machine and perform basic management tasks on it.

To run KVM on your server, there are just two requirements:

- The server must be running a 64-bit version of Red Hat Enterprise Linux.

- The CPU must offer virtualization support.

In Exercise 9.1, you'll learn how to determine whether your server meets these conditions.

EXERCISE 9.1

Determining Whether Your Server Meets KVM Virtualization Requirements

In this exercise, you'll use two commands to determine whether your server meets KVM virtualization requirements.

1. Log in to your server using the username *root* and the password *password*.

2. Right-click the graphical desktop, and select the option Open In Terminal.

3. Type the command **arch**. If it answers x86_64, you're using a 64-bit architecture.

4. Type **cat /proc/cpuinfo**, and locate the flags section of the output. With Intel microprocessors, you will see *vmx*, and on AMD microprocessors, you will see *svm* to indicate that virtualization is supported on your CPU. If you also see the lm flag on your CPU, this indicates you have a 64-bit processor.

5. Reboot your server, and enter the BIOS settings. The exact procedure to do this is different on different server models. Check the CPU features to ensure that virtualization is enabled.

To use your server as a KVM virtualization host, you'll also need to install the required software. The easiest way to do this is by selecting the Virtualization host package while installing the server. Alternatively, you can add the required packages once the installation is completed. In Exercise 9.2 later in the chapter, you'll learn how to do this.

An essential part of the KVM configuration on your server is libvirt. *Libvirt* is a generic interface that communicates to the KVM hypervisor and makes it possible to manage KVM and other virtualization solutions that may run on Linux. The advantage of using libvirt is that it provides a library against which different management programs can be used. On Red Hat Enterprise Linux, the Virtual Machine Manager graphical tool and the virsh command provide the main management interfaces that use libvirt. In Figure 9.1 you see an overview of how libvirt integrates in virtualization on Red Hat Enterprise Linux.

FIGURE 9.1   Libvirt overview

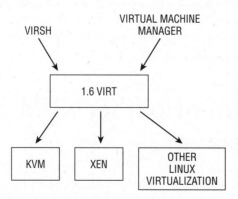

Red Hat Enterprise Virtualization

The default KVM virtualization in Red Hat Enterprise Linux works fine as far as it goes, but it's not a solution that would allow administrators to virtualize a large datacenter and manage many virtual machines from a central location. To provide such a solution, Red Hat created *Red Hat Enterprise Virtualization (RHEV)*.

In Red Hat Enterprise Virtualization, the *RHEV Manager (RHEV-M)* is used to manage *RHEV-H* hosts, which are hosts running a thin Red Hat–based hypervisor. The RHEV-M host runs the management platform, to which the administrator will connect to manage the RHEV-H hosts. A browser is used to manage the RHEV-H host. At the time of this writing, Internet Explorer is the only supported browser. However, in upcoming versions of RHEV (versions 3.1 and newer), other browsers will be supported. Figure 9.2 provides an example of the RHEV management interface.

FIGURE 9.2   The RHEV management interface

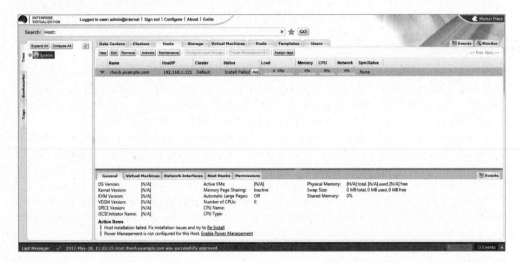

RHEV allows administrators to create a virtualization solution with simple and accessible management for a price that is significantly less than competing products such as VMware vSphere or Citrix XenServer. Check the following site for more details on RHEV:

www.redhat.com/products/virtualization/server/

Preparing Your Host for KVM Virtualization

The easiest way to turn your server into a KVM virtualization host is by installing the "Virtualization host" package group while installing your server. If you didn't install this software when you installed your server, you can install the required software packages later. Exercise 9.2 shows you exactly how to do this.

EXERCISE 9.2

Preparing Your Server to Function as a KVM Hypervisor

In this exercise, you'll install all of the software that is needed to turn your server into a KVM virtualization host. You'll also start the required services and kernel modules and do a test run to verify that KVM support is indeed enabled.

1. Open a root shell on your server, and type **yum -y groupinstall virtualization**. This installs all of the packages that are required for KVM virtualization and its management.

2. To use libvirt, you need libvirtd. Use **service libvirtd start** and **chkconfig libvirtd on** to start and enable this service.

3. Load the KVM kernel module using **modprobe kvm**. Next, use **lsmod | grep kvm** to verify that the kvm kernel module and the platform-specific support modules are loaded. Your server is now ready to start installing KVM virtual machines (see Listing 9.1).

Listing 9.1: Verifying that the KVM kernel module is loaded

```
[root@hnl ~]# lsmod | grep kvm
kvm_intel              50380  0
kvm                   305113  1 kvm_intel
```

Installing a KVM Virtual Machine

After ensuring you've met all of the requirements to install virtual machines, you can use the Virtual Machine Manager to start the installation. In Exercise 9.3, you'll use the Virtual Machine Manager utility to install a virtual machine, and you'll become familiar with some of the most important features of Virtual Machine Manager.

Before starting the installation of a virtual machine, consider how you will handle storage. KVM offers two options:

- Create a disk image file as the backend for the virtual hard drive.
- Use an LVM logical volume.

There is a major benefit to using LVM logical volumes. Doing so allows you to create a snapshot of the current state of the virtual machine.

EXERCISE 9.3

Installing a KVM Virtual Machine

In this exercise, you'll install a KVM virtual machine. This exercise is mandatory; you'll need the KVM virtual machine in many of the exercises and labs that follow throughout the rest of this book. The focus of the exercise is on installing the virtual machine. Thus, only minimal details are provided about the installation.

To perform the steps described in this exercise, you'll need 10GB of available hard disk space. The CPU in your server also needs to offer the virtualization extensions that have been described previously.

If your hardware prevents you from using KVM virtualization, it is recommended that you create a virtual machine in another virtualization solution, such as a VMware workstation. For the exercises in subsequent chapters, you do need a second machine to test network functionality.

1. Log in as root on your Linux server. Right-click the graphical desktop, and click Open In Terminal.

2. Type **modprobe kvm** to load the KVM kernel module.

3. Open the Applications menu on the graphical desktop, and select System Tools ➢ Virtual Machine Manager.

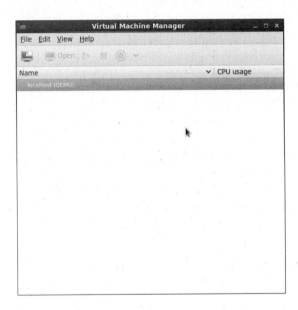

4.   In the Virtual Machine Manager, click the Create A New Virtual Machine button (the left-most button on the toolbar) to start the process of creating a new virtual machine. When asked to enter the virtual machine details, give it the name **testvm**. Also, select Local Install Media to install the virtual machine from your Red Hat Linux installation disc. Make sure that the Red Hat installation DVD is in the optical drive before you click Forward.

5.   On the second screen of the installation procedure, verify that the option Use CDROM Or DVD is selected. If the DVD was found in the disc drive, you'll see the name of the disc in a drop-down list. You can also select the OS type and version in this window. Make sure that the OS Type field is set to Linux and that the version is set to Red Hat Enterprise Linux 6. Click Forward to continue.

6. When prompted for the amount of memory and CPUs, just accept the suggested default. Virtual Machine Manager detects the hardware that you have on board, and it will suggest the optimal amount of RAM and virtual CPUs for your hardware. (Note that you need at least 768MB of RAM to be able to perform a graphical installation.) Click Forward to continue.

7. On the next screen, you'll specify what kind of storage to use. By default, the installer proposes a disk image file with a default size of 8GB. Verify that after creating this 8GB file, you still have enough disk space remaining on your system. If you do, click Forward to continue.

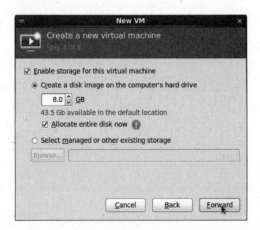

8. In the last window, just click Finish to start the installation. After a short while, you'll see that the installation has started in the Red Hat Enterprise Linux installation window.

9. Perform a basic installation. Select all of the default choices. When you see the Please Name This Computer screen, configure the name `testvm.example.com`. Don't change the network configuration.

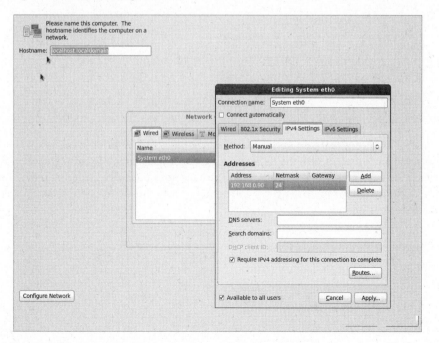

10. When asked to enter the root password, use the password *password*. Click Use Anyway when the installation program indicates that this is a weak password. From there, accept all of the default choices until the window where you select the installation pattern to use is displayed. From this window, click Desktop. Click Next, and wait until all software packages have been copied to the virtual machine.

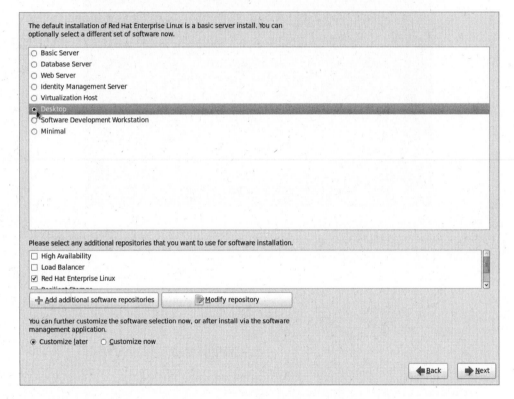

11. Once all of the software packages have been copied, click Reboot to restart the virtual machine. Accept all of the default options until you see the Create User window. In this window, create user *student* with the password *password*. Ignore the warning that you've used a weak password, and continue with the installation, accepting all of the default selections.

Welcome
License
Information
Set Up Software
Updates
▸ Create User
Date and Time
Kdump

Create User

You must create a 'username' for regular (non-administrative) use of your system. To create a system 'username', please provide the information requested below.

Username: student

Full Name: student

Password: ••••••••

Confirm Password: ••••••••

If you need to use network authentication, such as Kerberos or NIS, please click the Use Network Login button.

Use Network Login...

If you need more control when creating the user (specifying home directory, and/or UID), please click the Advanced button.

Advanced...

Back   Forward

12. Finish the installation and start the virtual machine. For the moment, you can leave it running, and there's no need to log in.

Managing KVM Virtual Machines

Your primary management tool for KVM virtual machines is the graphical Virtual Machine Manager. You can start this tool by selecting Applications ➤ System Tools ➤ Virtual Machine Manager or by running the virt-manager command from a console. To manage a virtual machine from a command-line environment, the virsh command is available. In the subsections that follow, you'll learn how to use both methods.

Managing Virtual Machines with Virtual Machine Manager

To manage virtual machines, start the Virtual Machine Manager as described earlier. After starting, the Virtual Machine Manager uses libvirt to detect the available hypervisor on your server. If KVM is available (and the KVM kernel module is loaded), you'll see local-host listed as the hypervisor. To connect to it, you can double-click it, which will show all of the available virtual machines and their current states (see Figure 9.3).

FIGURE 9.3   Virtual Machine Manager shows all virtual machines and their current state

Working on the Virtual Machine Console

In the Virtual Machine Manager main menu, you will also find a toolbar that provides you with the shortcuts needed to create a new virtual machine or to open an existing virtual machine. By default, Virtual Machine Manager doesn't show the console of virtual machines that are running on your host. You have to open it to see what's happening on the virtual machine console. Also, there are buttons to start a virtual machine, to pause a virtual machine in its current state, and to stop a virtual machine.

WARNING   Don't press the Power Off button by accident; it will immediately stop the virtual machine without asking for additional confirmation.

The rightmost button allows you to reboot, shut down, or force off a virtual machine. The last option can be useful if the VM cannot be stopped normally. You'll also find the Save button here, which allows you to save the current state of a virtual machine.

To manage a virtual machine, first you select the VM and next click the Open button. Alternatively, you can double-click the virtual machine from the overview window. By default, this shows the current virtual machine in a window. Figure 9.4 shows an example of this.

FIGURE 9.4   Displaying a Virtual Machine console window

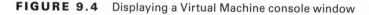
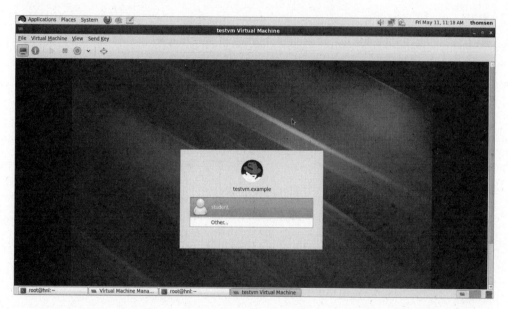

You have many options to manage a virtual machine from the window where it is shown. Some interesting options are in the Virtual Machine menu option. You may find the Clone and Migrate options particularly useful. The Clone option allows you to create a new virtual machine based on the current state of this virtual machine. The Migrate option works in a network environment where more than one KVM host is available. This option allows you to perform a live migration of a virtual machine from one KVM host to another. This is very useful in a datacenter because it allows you to migrate a virtual machine without suffering any downtime.

In the View menu option, you can select how to display the current virtual machine. First you can select between the Console view and the Details view. The latter screen is interesting because it allows you to manage the hardware properties of a virtual machine (see Figure 9.5).

FIGURE 9.5 Displaying virtual machine hardware properties

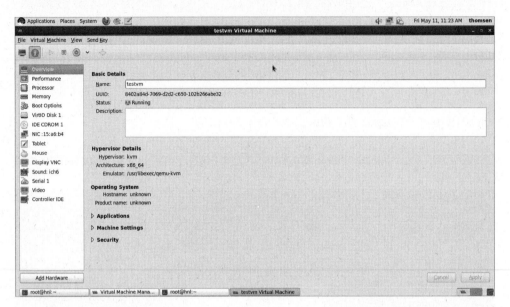

The other options in the View menu allow you to determine how the virtual machine console should be displayed. By default, it is shown in its full size, which may prevent you from seeing the complete VM screen. To fix this, you can run the VM in Full Screen mode, resize the display window to the size of the VM, or select one of the Scale Display options to make the VM fit within the display screen. In Exercise 9.4, you'll learn how to work with a virtual machine in Virtual Machine Manager and to use all relevant display options.

EXERCISE 9.4

Working with Virtual Machine Manager

In this exercise, you'll work with Virtual Machine Manager and explore the different display options.

1. Start Virtual Machine Manager, and double-click the virtual machine you created earlier in this chapter to open its console. If the VM is not currently active, click the Play button to start it.

2. Click in the virtual machine, and log in as user *student* with the password *password*. Try to move the mouse cursor out of the virtual machine. Press Ctrl+Alt, and try to move the mouse cursor out of the virtual machine. Do you notice a difference?

3. From the toolbar above the virtual machine, click the Switch To Full Screen View but-
    ton. This is the rightmost button on the toolbar. Hover your cursor over the buttons
    to see the short descriptions of each.

4. Once you are in Full Screen mode, move the cursor to the top center of the screen.
    You'll see a small floating window offering two options. Click the right button, which
    allows you to leave Full Screen mode.

5. Now select the Send Key menu, and from there, select the Ctrl+Alt+F2 option. You
    have now activated the virtual console on TTY2. Repeat this procedure, and this time
    select Ctrl+Alt+F1 to get back to the graphical mode.

6. Close the testvm Virtual Machine console window. Notice that this just closes the
    virtual machine display; it does not shut down the virtual machine.

Changing Virtual Machine Hardware Settings

After double-clicking a virtual machine, you can click the Show Virtual Hardware Details
button (the second button from the left) to show the current virtual machine hardware
details. You'll see a list of all currently available hardware, and you can change hardware
features and add new hardware from here. In Exercise 9.5, you'll walk through some of the
most interesting options available there.

Before starting to change hardware features, it helps to understand a bit more about the
way hardware is handled by the virtual machine. In KVM, most hardware is addressed by
the *virtio drivers*. These are drivers that allow the virtual machine to communicate directly
with the hardware instead of passing through an emulation layer. This also means you
don't deal with the properties of specific hardware devices but with the virtual hardware
drivers instead. In some cases, working through the virtio drivers allows you to perform
actions that normally are otherwise impossible when working directly on the physical
hardware.

Changing a VM Hardware Configuration

In this exercise, you'll explore some useful options that help you change features of the
virtualized hardware of your virtual machines.

1. Double-click your virtual machine in Virtual Machine Manager. Next click the Show
    Virtual Hardware Details button. Make sure that Overview is selected, and enter a
    description of your virtual machine. Then open the Machine Settings item (still on the
    Overview page), and disable ACPI as well as APIC. These hardware settings, which
    can cause problems on some hardware, are easily switched off this way.

EXERCISE 9.5 *(continued)*

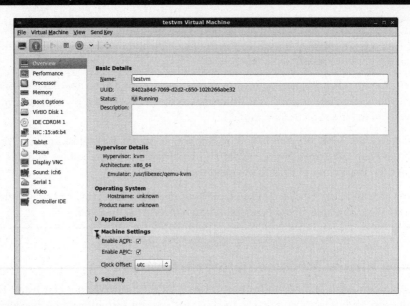

2. Click the Processor button in the pane on the left of the screen. Increase the amount of logical host CPU from one to two (if your hardware supports this). Select CPU Features, and browse down the list until you see the vmx feature. By default, it should be off. Click the feature, and from the drop-down list, select Default to make this a default feature.

3. Still from the Processor item, open Pinning and enter **0,1** as the default pinning. By doing this, you pin this VM down to CPU cores 0 and 1 in your host. This means it will never run on other CPU cores, which can be good for performance.

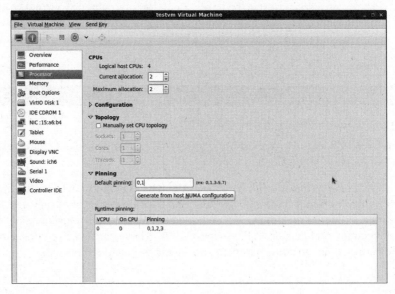

4. Click the Memory icon in the pane on the left. Double the amount of memory that is defined as the Maximum allocation. This doesn't change anything for the current settings, but it allows you to increase the amount of RAM for the virtual machine at a later stage without bringing it down first.

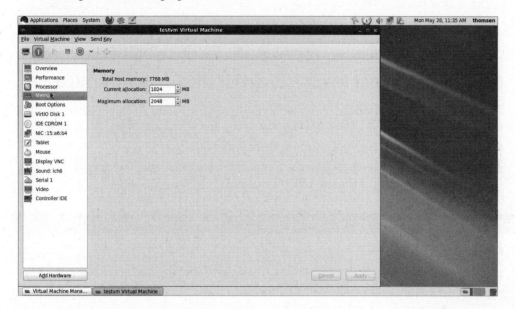

5. Click the Boot Options item. From there, select Start Virtual Machine On Host Boot Up. Also enable Network (PXE) in the boot device order, and make sure it is selected as the second option.

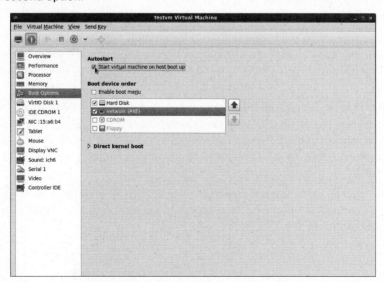

EXERCISE 9.5 *(continued)*

6. Click Apply to save and apply all changes. At this point, switch back to the console of the testvm virtual machine. Reboot the virtual machine.

7. Once the virtual machine has rebooted, log in as root. Use the lscpu command to check the amount of CPU cores, and check the amount of memory that is currently allocated, using free -m.

Managing Virtual Machines from the virsh Interface

To manage virtual machines, you can use Virtual Machine Manager or, alternatively, the powerful virsh command. There are two ways you can use virsh.

- Type **virsh** to open an interactive virsh shell interface.
- Type **virsh**, directly followed by the command you want to run. In Exercise 9.6, you'll explore both ways of working with virsh.

EXERCISE 9.6

Exploring virsh

In this exercise, you'll perform some basic virsh commands and their arguments, and you will also run the virsh interactive shell.

1. Type **virsh list --all**. This displays a list of all virtual machines that are known to your system and the current state of these machines.

2. Type **virsh** to open the interactive virsh shell interface. Notice that the Bash shell prompt changes to virsh #.

3. Type **help** to get a list of all available virsh commands. You can also run each of these commands as an argument while running the virsh command from a Bash shell. That is, from the virsh shell, you can type list for a list of all virtual machines and their current state, or you can also invoke the command as virsh list.

4. From the virsh shell, type **shutdown testvm** to shut down your virtual machine. This is confirmed by the virsh shell with the message Domain testvm is being shut-down. The success of this command depends on the ACPI capabilities of the guest, so if the command does not succeed, check these options.

5. Still from the virsh shell, type **list** after a few moments to confirm that the virtual machine is no longer in the running state. If it still is, use **virsh destroy testvm**. Using this command is comparable to pulling the power plug on a physical server, so use it with caution.

6. Still from the virsh shell, type **start testvm** to start your virtual machine again.

7. Confirm that the virtual machine is now in the running state. Notice that the ID of the virtual machine has been increased by one. Type **exit** to close the virsh shell.

Understanding KVM Networking

When you create a virtual machine in KVM, this virtual machine probably needs to connect to an external network. To accomplish this, NAT is used by default. Using NAT means that the virtual machine can connect to any host on external networks but that the virtual machine cannot be reached from external networks. If your virtual machine needs to be reached by external computers, you need to change the way networking is handled. The following networking modes are available:

Isolated Virtual Network   Use this if you need virtual machines to be able to communicate among each other or with the KVM host when you don't need any external communication.

NAT   Use this if you want to enable your virtual machines to initiate outside traffic but want to protect them from computers on other networks. In this mode, the virtual machines cannot be reached directly by other computers.

Routed   Use this if you want virtual machines to be fully reachable by computers on external networks. If you need this mode, the virtual machine needs to be on its own network and the KVM host is working as a router to route traffic.

To use your virtual machine as a test machine in your network, you need to set it up with an isolated virtual network. This is something you can accomplish while installing the virtual machines by selecting the Advanced configuration mode on the network card. Alternatively, you can reconfigure networking later. The latter is a more complicated method, but it works just as well. In Exercise 9.4, you'll walk through the procedure required to change NAT networking on testvm to isolated networking.

When setting up networking, you always have to be aware of the two parts involved. First there is the host portion, which is the part of the configuration that you'll set up on the KVM host and that puts your network in a specific mode. Next, after setting up a specific kind of network on the KVM host, you need to connect the network card in the virtual machine to this network. In Exercise 9.7, you'll set up the network adapter in the KVM host environment.

EXERCISE 9.7

Changing Virtual Machine Networking

In this mandatory exercise, you'll learn how to switch network configuration for your KVM environment. First you'll set up an isolated virtual network on the host, and then you will connect the network card in the virtual machine to this isolated network. If all goes well, at the end of this exercise you'll be able to ping the host computer from the virtual machine.

1. Log in as root to the KVM host computer. Start Virtual Machine Manager, and select Edit ➢ Connection Details. From there, click the Virtual Networks tab to display currently configured virtual networks. You should see just the default network.

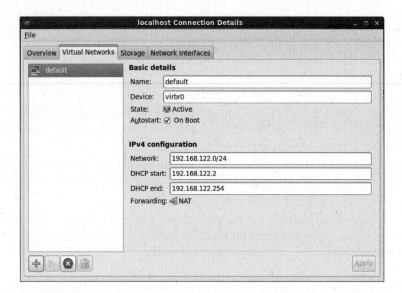

2. Click the + sign in the lower-left corner of the Virtual Networks tab. This starts the Create A Virtual Network Wizard. From the first screen of this wizard, click Forward.

3. Enter a meaningful name for the virtual network (for example, **privatenet**), and click Forward to continue.

EXERCISE 9.7 *(continued)*

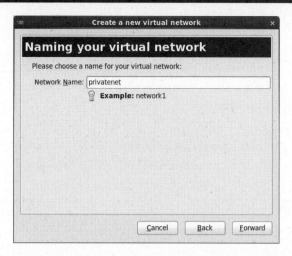

4. Now you need to select a network that is to be used on this private network. By default, an IP network address is selected automatically from the private address ranges. If this address range doesn't conflict with an address already in use at your site, just accept it and click Forward. If it does conflict, select another address before clicking Forward.

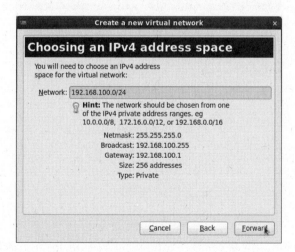

5. By default, DHCP is used to give a network to virtual machines in this network. The DHCP server can use addresses from a default range of IP addresses that is selected. Accept this default suggestion, and click Forward to continue.

EXERCISE 9.7 *(continued)*

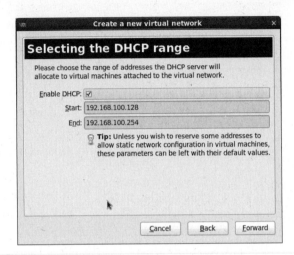

6. In the next window, you'll select how to connect to the physical network. In this exercise, you're setting up an isolated network, so click Isolated Virtual Network and next click Forward to continue.

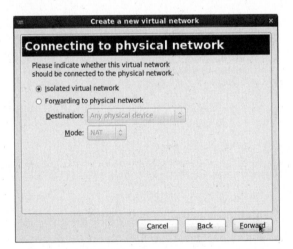

7. Now you'll see the ready to create network window. From there, click Finish to create the new network adapter on the KVM host.

Back in the localhost Connection Details window, you'll see two network adapters. One allows you to connect to an external network using NAT, and the other just offers you a private network. On the virtual host, this network adapter is known as a *virtual bridge adapter.* You can see this adapter if you use the `ip link show` command (see Listing 9.2). Because a default KVM installation already creates a virtual bridge, this new virtual bridge adapter will be known as `virbr1`.

Listing 9.2: The virtual network adapter shows as `virbr1`

```
[root@hnl ~]# ip link show
1: lo: <LOOPBACK,UP,LOWER_UP> mtu 16436 qdisc noqueue state UNKNOWN
    link/loopback 00:00:00:00:00:00 brd 00:00:00:00:00:00
2: p6p1: <BROADCAST,MULTICAST,UP,LOWER_UP> mtu 1500 qdisc mq state UP
qlen 1000
    link/ether b8:ac:6f:c9:35:25 brd ff:ff:ff:ff:ff:ff
3: wlan0: <NO-CARRIER,BROADCAST,MULTICAST,UP> mtu 1500 qdisc mq state
DOWN qlen 1000
    link/ether a0:88:b4:20:ce:24 brd ff:ff:ff:ff:ff:ff
4: virbr0: <BROADCAST,MULTICAST,UP,LOWER_UP> mtu 1500 qdisc noqueue
state UNKNOWN
    link/ether 52:54:00:dc:71:43 brd ff:ff:ff:ff:ff:ff
5: virbr0-nic: <BROADCAST,MULTICAST> mtu 1500 qdisc noop state DOWN qlen 500
    link/ether 52:54:00:dc:71:43 brd ff:ff:ff:ff:ff:ff
10: vnet0: <BROADCAST,MULTICAST,UP,LOWER_UP> mtu 1500 qdisc pfifo_fast
state UNKNOWN qlen 500
    link/ether fe:54:00:15:a6:b4 brd ff:ff:ff:ff:ff:ff
11: virbr1: <BROADCAST,MULTICAST,UP,LOWER_UP> mtu 1500 qdisc noqueue state
UNKNOWN
    link/ether 52:54:00:95:39:26 brd ff:ff:ff:ff:ff:ff
12: virbr1-nic: <BROADCAST,MULTICAST> mtu 1500 qdisc noop state DOWN qlen 500
    link/ether 52:54:00:95:39:26 brd ff:ff:ff:ff:ff:ff
```

At this point, you've finished the network configuration on the host, and you just need to configure the client to use this virtual bridge adapter. In Exercise 9.8, you'll learn how to do this.

EXERCISE 9.8

Reconfiguring Networking in a Virtual Machine

In this exercise, you'll reconfigure the network card in the virtual machine to connect to the private adapter in the host you just configured.

1. Restart the Virtual Machine, and click the Show Virtual Hardware Details button.

2. Select the network card in the pane at the left of the configuration details screen. From the drop-down list at Source device, select Virtual Network 'privatenet' (or whatever meaningful name you used).

3. In the drop-down list at Device Model, the virtio driver is selected by default. This is a good choice because the virtio driver offers a performance that is much better than that of the emulated drivers for other types of network card.

4. Click Apply to save the settings. Click OK when a message appears indicating that you need to restart the virtual machine.

5. Reboot your virtual machine. While it is rebooting, use `ip address show` on the KVM host to find the IP address that is used on the `virbr1` adapter that you created in the previous exercise. If you've used all the suggested values in this exercise, it should have the IP address 192.168.100.1.

6. Log in to the virtual machine, and open a root shell. From this shell, type **ping 192.168.100.1** to verify that you have successfully completed this exercise.

If you don't succeed in changing the network configuration as described in Exercise 9.8, try to apply this procedure while the virtual machine is down.

Summary

In this chapter, you learned how to work with virtual machines in a KVM environment. You learned how to install a virtual machine in KVM and how to manage the virtual machine using Virtual Machine Manager once it was installed. You also learned how to configure nondefault networking in a KVM environment.

Chapter

10

Securing Your Server with iptables

TOPICS COVERED IN THIS CHAPTER:

- ✓ **Understanding Firewalls**
- ✓ **Setting Up a Firewall with system-config-firewall**
- ✓ **Setting Up a Firewall with iptables**
- ✓ **Advanced iptables Configuration**
- ✓ **Configuring NAT**

Red Hat Enterprise Linux is often used to offer services on the Internet. That means that unauthorized users will try to attack your server and get access to parts of the server that you don't want to be available to unauthorized users. To prevent this, you need to install a firewall. In this chapter you'll learn how to install a firewall on Red Hat Enterprise Linux, and thus protect valuable assets on your server.

Understanding Firewalls

Some administrators believe that if they offer only the services that are supposed to be on a server and nothing else, the server is thus secure and no additional security measures are required. They are wrong!

Too often, when a hacker breaks through the security wall of a server, it is done by using ports that are actually allowed on the server. For instance, the hacker can abuse an Apache web server and have it launch a script that opens connections to external machines. In Chapter 8, you learned how SELinux can be used to avoid this scenario. In this chapter, you'll learn how a firewall can be used to make sure that no connections are initiated to nodes that haven't specifically been allowed beforehand.

A firewall works through *packet inspection*. This means that the firewall screens incoming and outgoing packets to check whether the address, protocol, and port of the packet is either allowed or denied. From the perspective of the OSI model, a firewall works on layers 3, 4, and 5. What a firewall typically cannot do is a check on the user that has sent the packet. Also, firewalls normally have a hard time checking the actual data portion of the packet. You'll need a proxy to do that.

Even though a firewall is important, not every server is using one. By default, Red Hat switches it on, but in some cases it doesn't make much sense, and the administrator disables it. Typically, this depends on the configuration of the network in which the server is installed. In large company networks, firewalls are often handled by the router that connects the network to the Internet. Everything behind the router is considered to be secure and doesn't need a firewall of its own. However, if a server is directly connected to the Internet, the server does require a firewall. Also, if a server has a specific role in a company network and you want to configure it for additional security, it's a good idea to configure it with a firewall.

Netfilter is the default firewall offered through the Linux kernel. To configure Netfilter on Red Hat Enterprise Linux, you can use the system-config-firewall tool if you prefer to use a graphical interface or the `iptables` command if you want to work from the command line. In this chapter, you'll learn how to do both.

Setting Up a Firewall with system-config-firewall

If you just need basic firewall services and have a graphical desktop available, system-config-firewall is the simplest way to get started. Using the graphical interface, you can easily select the services you trust on the interfaces you trust. It also allows you to set up some of the more advanced configurations, including IP masquerading and port forwarding (see Figure 10.1). In a text-only mode, you can use the `system-config-firewall-tui` command if you want a menu-driven interface to configure the firewall.

FIGURE 10.1   system-config-firewall offers a graphical interface to configure the firewall.

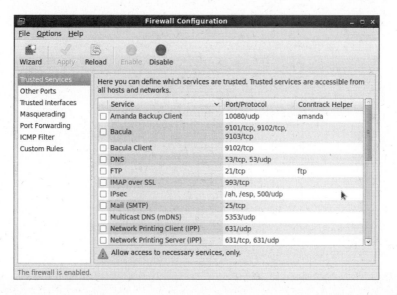

WARNING   Before starting to configure a firewall with system-config-firewall, one important thing to realize is that it wipes clean all configurations you created manually. It warns you about this when you start the utility, but it is better to say it twice because it is frustrating to see the fruits of your hard labor erased with one simple mouse click. Thus, if you plan to set up a sophisticated firewall, it's OK to start with system-config-firewall, but once you've modified it manually, you should never use system-config-firewall again.

Allowing Services

After an installation of Red Hat Enterprise Linux, the firewall is configured by default, and not many services are allowed through the firewall. The simplest way to allow specific services through the firewall is by selecting them using the Trusted Services option in system-config-firewall. This interface offers a list of commonly used services. To enable a service, you just have to select it from the list. After selecting the desired services, you click the Apply button to save the current configuration (see Figure 10.2).

FIGURE 10.2   Allowing services through the firewall

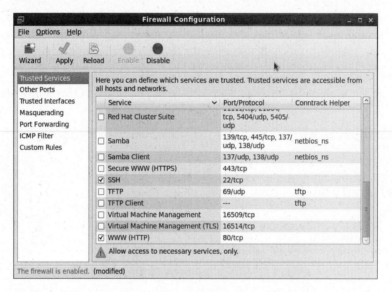

To make the configuration you just created operational, do the following:

1. Check that the iptables service is enabled.
2. Use the `iptables -L` command to verify that the rules have been applied.

In Exercise 10.1, you'll learn how to do this.

EXERCISE 10.1

Allowing Basic Services Through the Firewall

In this exercise, you'll learn how to allow basic services through the firewall using system-config-firewall. You'll also learn how to verify the current operation of the firewall.

1. From the GNOME graphical interface, select System ≻ Administration ≻ Firewall. Review the warning that tells you that all current configurations will be overwritten, and click Close. Also, enter the root password if prompted.

2. From the list of trusted services, select DNS, FTP, SSH, and WWW, and click Apply to save the configuration.

3. Close system-config-firewall, and open a shell prompt.

4. Type **chkconfig | grep iptables**. This command will display the current status of the iptables service in the runlevels on your server. It should read as follows:

   ```
   [root@hnl ~]# chkconfig | grep iptables
   iptables        0:off   1:off   2:on    3:on    4:on    5:on    6:off
   ```

5. If the iptables service that implements your firewall isn't listed as being on in runlevels 2, 3, 4, and 5, use **chkconfig iptables on** to enable it.

6. Type **service iptables status**. This command shows that the current status of iptables is enabled.

7. Type **iptables -L -v**. You'll see a list that displays all of the firewall rules. Listing 10.1 shows what this list looks like if the firewall is currently operational. Listing 10.2 shows what it looks like if the firewall is currently not activated.

Listing 10.1: The firewall configuration as seen with iptables -l -v

```
[root@hnl ~]# iptables -L -v
Chain INPUT (policy ACCEPT 0 packets, 0 bytes)
 pkts bytes target     prot opt in      out     source               destination
   61  4884 ACCEPT     all  --  any     any     anywhere             anywhere
state RELATED,ESTABLISHED
    0     0 ACCEPT     icmp --  any     any     anywhere             anywhere
    0     0 ACCEPT     all  --  lo      any     anywhere             anywhere
    0     0 ACCEPT     tcp  --  any     any     anywhere             anywhere
    state NEW tcp dpt:domain
    4   264 ACCEPT     udp  --  any     any     anywhere             anywhere
    state NEW udp dpt:domain
    0     0 ACCEPT     tcp  --  any     any     anywhere             anywhere
    state NEW tcp dpt:ftp
    1    92 ACCEPT     tcp  --  any     any     anywhere             anywhere
    state NEW tcp dpt:ssh
    0     0 ACCEPT     tcp  --  any     any     anywhere             anywhere
    state NEW tcp dpt:http
  105 17322 REJECT     all  --  any     any     anywhere             anywhere
    reject-with icmp-host-prohibited

Chain FORWARD (policy ACCEPT 0 packets, 0 bytes)
 pkts bytes target     prot opt in      out     source               destination
    0     0 REJECT     all  --  any     any     anywhere             anywhere
    reject-with icmp-host-prohibited

Chain OUTPUT (policy ACCEPT 58 packets, 5304 bytes)
 pkts bytes target     prot opt in      out     source               destination
```

Listing 10.2: Firewall rules list when no firewall is activated

```
[root@hn1 ~]# iptables -L -v
Chain INPUT (policy ACCEPT 0 packets, 0 bytes)
 pkts bytes target     prot opt in     out     source              destination

Chain FORWARD (policy ACCEPT 0 packets, 0 bytes)
 pkts bytes target     prot opt in     out     source              destination

Chain OUTPUT (policy ACCEPT 0 packets, 0 bytes)
 pkts bytes target     prot opt in     out     source              destination
```

The system-config-firewall utility offers an interface to select common services. In some situations, your service might be activated on a nondefault port. If that is the case, you need to use the Other Ports interface in system-config-firewall to open that port. From Other Ports, click Add to open the Port And Protocol window. You'll see a list containing all known port assignments in this window. If the port is not available from this list, you can click User Defined to enter the port or port range manually. You can see what this interface looks like in Figure 10.3.

FIGURE 10.3   Adding nondefault ports to the firewall

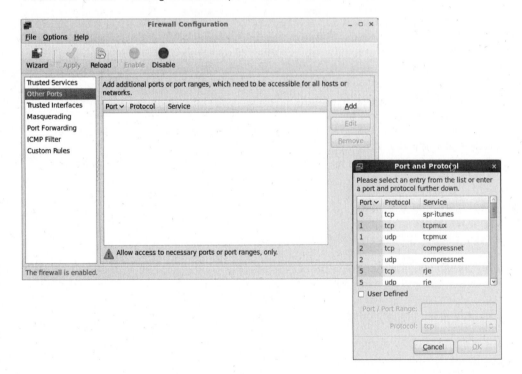

Trusted Interfaces

Typically, there are two use cases for firewalls: on routers and on servers. If the firewall is installed on a server, there is normally just one network interface on which the firewall is operational. If the firewall is on a server that is used as a router, usually there is an internal network interface and an external network interface. Packets are routed between these interfaces by a routing process. In such situations, you need to indicate which interface is a part of the trusted internal network and which is on the untrusted external network.

By default, all network interfaces are considered untrusted. If your server works as a router and you want to specify some interfaces as trusted, from system-config-firewall, click Trusted Interfaces and select the interfaces you want to add. From that moment on, no packets will be filtered on that interface (see Figure 10.4).

FIGURE 10.4   Marking interfaces as trusted

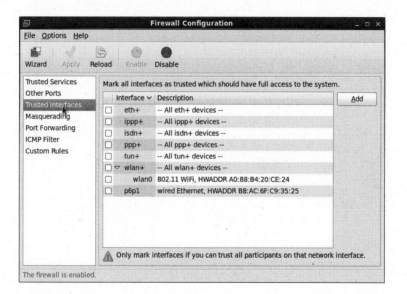

Masquerading

In *IP masquerading*, you can configure a server to connect your local network to the Internet. In this configuration, IP addresses from the private address ranges are used on the private network. These addresses cannot communicate on the Internet, but they will be translated to the public IP address on the interface that faces the Internet. This process is known as IP masquerading, also referred to as *Network Address Translation (NAT)*. The major benefit of using masquerading is that with just one public IP address, you can connect many devices on the private network to the Internet. IP masquerading is commonly used in home and corporate networks.

To enable masquerading, you need to select the public interface (see Figure 10.5). Once this interface is masqueraded, all packets are rewritten with the IP address of the public interface as the source address. To trace the packet back to its original sender, the NAT router maintains a NAT table. A port address is used to trace every connection in this NAT table. Once a reply to the packet comes back and has to be forwarded by the NAT router to the originating host, it will use the NAT table to find the address of the host from which the packet is originating, and it forwards the packet.

FIGURE 10.5   To enable masquerading, you need to select the public network interface on the NAT router.

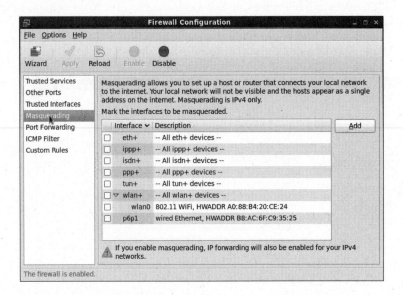

You can also use *port forwarding* in combination with masquerading. This means you assign a port on the public interface of the NAT router and forward everything that comes in on that port to a specific host and port on the private network. You can use this approach if one of the computers on the private network is not directly reachable from the Internet, but it offers a specific service that you want to make available on the Internet. Users that want to use that service address the masquerading router and the specific port that is assigned on that router. Port forwarding will then forward the packet to the destination host.

You select port forwarding to add a port that is to be forwarded from system-config-firewall. Next you click Add and select the interface and port you want to make available (see Figure 10.6). After specifying the source port, you need to assign a destination. You can choose between forwarding to a local port (a port on the masquerading router itself) or you can forward packets to a specific IP address and port on that node. In Exercise 10.2, you'll learn how to configure port forwarding.

FIGURE 10.6 Configuring port forwarding

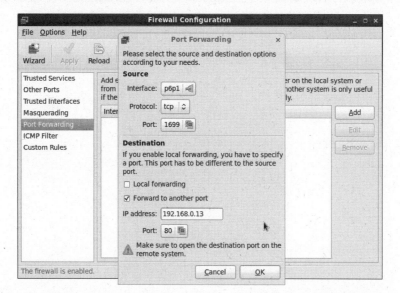

Configuring Port Forwarding

In this exercise, you'll configure port forwarding. To perform this exercise, you need to use the virtual machine you created in Chapter 9.

1. Start the virtual machine you created in Chapter 9. Open Virtual Machine Manager, open a root shell on the virtual machine, and verify that it is configured to use the IP address 192.168.100.176. Use **yum -y install httpd** to install a web server on this computer.

2. On the host computer, open system-config-firewall, and click Port Forwarding. Click Add, and in the Source part of the configuration, select the interface that is used as the physical network card on your host computer.

3. Click Port, and in the Port And Protocol window that opens, select User Defined. Enter port **3333**, and click OK.

4. In the destination part of the Port Forwarding window, select Forward To Another Port. Enter the IP address that is used by your virtual machine, and from the Port list, select port 80. Click OK to save the configuration. Next click Apply to apply the configuration to the firewall.

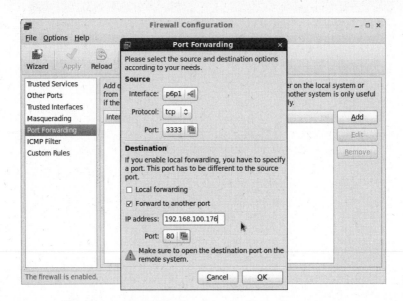

5. On the host computer, type **iptables -L -v** and verify that you see a line with the IP address 192.168.100.176 as its destination in the Forward chain. This is the packet-forwarding rule.

Configuration Files

Everything you do with system-config-firewall is saved to two configuration files that are stored in the directory /etc/sysconfig, which is the case with all configuration files that are read when a service is started. In the file iptables, you'll find all the rules that you've added to the firewall. In the file iptables-config, the configuration of the firewall is stored. Listing 10.3 shows a sample configuration that is stored in the iptables file.

Listing 10.3: Sample contents of the /etc/sysconfig/iptables file

```
[root@hnl ~]# cat /etc/sysconfig/iptables
# Firewall configuration written by system-config-firewall
# Manual customization of this file is not recommended.
*nat
:PREROUTING ACCEPT [0:0]
:OUTPUT ACCEPT [0:0]
:POSTROUTING ACCEPT [0:0]
-A PREROUTING -i p6p1 -p tcp --dport 3333 -j DNAT --to-destination
```

```
 192.168.100.176:80
COMMIT
*filter
:INPUT ACCEPT [0:0]
:FORWARD ACCEPT [0:0]
:OUTPUT ACCEPT [0:0]
-A INPUT -m state --state ESTABLISHED,RELATED -j ACCEPT
-A INPUT -p icmp -j ACCEPT
-A INPUT -i lo -j ACCEPT
-A INPUT -m state --state NEW -m tcp -p tcp --dport 53 -j ACCEPT
-A INPUT -m state --state NEW -m udp -p udp --dport 53 -j ACCEPT
-A INPUT -m state --state NEW -m tcp -p tcp --dport 21 -j ACCEPT
-A INPUT -m state --state NEW -m tcp -p tcp --dport 22 -j ACCEPT
-A INPUT -m state --state NEW -m tcp -p tcp --dport 80 -j ACCEPT
-A FORWARD -m state --state ESTABLISHED,RELATED -j ACCEPT
-A FORWARD -p icmp -j ACCEPT
-A FORWARD -i lo -j ACCEPT
-A FORWARD -i p6p1 -m state --state NEW -m tcp -p tcp -d 192.168.100.176
 --dport 80 -j ACCEPT
-A INPUT -j REJECT --reject-with icmp-host-prohibited
-A FORWARD -j REJECT --reject-with icmp-host-prohibited
COMMIT
```

> **NOTE** system-config-iptables stores the old configuration before it starts, which is very useful. You can find this old configuration in the files /etc/sysconfig/iptables.old and /etc/sysconfig/iptables-config.old. This is good to know if you make a mistake and want to revert to the previous configuration.

If you've also configured firewall rules for IPv6, these have their own configuration files: /etc/sysconfig/ip6tables and /etc/sysconfig/ip6tables-config.

Setting Up a Firewall with iptables

The system-config-firewall tool includes a good utility to set up a basic firewall. However, if you need to configure a firewall that offers advanced features, it's really not good enough. In that case, you're better off using the iptables command. iptables tends to generate rather long commands. However, once you understand what you're doing, it's not very difficult. This section is designed to help you understand how to use the iptables command so that you can create firewall rules yourself whenever necessary.

Understanding Tables, Chains, and Rules

Tables are the basic building blocks of a Netfilter firewall. Specific tables can be created to stipulate the specific functionality of the firewall. By default, the filter table is used. The NAT table is also frequently used.

A table contains chains. A *chain* consists of a set of rules that is sequentially processed for each packet that enters the firewall until it finds a match. The default strategy is "exit on match," which means that the firewall looks no further once the first rule that matches for a specific packet is found. The following chains are used in the filter table:

INPUT   Incoming packets are processed in this chain.

OUTPUT   This chain is used for outgoing packets.

FORWARD   This chain is used on routers, and packets that don't have a process on the firewall as their destination use it.

Of these chains, a server administrator must understand how to use INPUT and OUTPUT. Configuring the FORWARD chain is not as important as it is for routers only. In modern network environments, hardware routers are used more and more frequently, which means that the role of Linux servers as a firewall becomes less important.

Understanding How a Rule Is Composed

Different elements can be used to specify properties of a packet in each rule. You don't have to specify each of these elements, but you are free to use them and make the rule more specific. Some elements are mandatory, though. Here is a list of some of the most common elements you'll find in rules:

Modules   A *module* is an optional element that you can use in a rule. Modules offer enhancements to the Netfilter firewall. They do that by loading a specific kernel module that adds functionality. A very common module in iptables rules is the *state* module, which looks at the state of a packet.

Interface   On a server with multiple network cards, it makes sense to apply rules to specific interfaces only. However, if you're configuring your firewall on a typical server with one network card only, you can safely omit the interface specification.

IP Addresses   In a rule, you can allow or deny access to specific IP addresses or IP network addresses. For example, if you're in a school, you might want to differentiate between a safe internal network, which contains users who typically can be trusted, such as internal staff, and an unsafe internal network that is used by the students. IP addresses are also used in rules that configure port forwarding.

Protocol   Most rules allow or deny access to specific ports. These ports are always connected to the UDP or TCP protocol. Therefore, if you want to state a specific port, you also need to indicate the protocol that is to be used. You can also include ICMP as the protocol to be used.

Target   The target is also a mandatory component in a rule. A *target* specifies what needs to be done with a matching packet. Different targets can be used, of which ACCEPT, DROP, REJECT, and LOG are the most important.

Apart from these common elements found in rules, you need to specify the purpose of the rule. If viewed generically, there are two options: either you can set a policy or you can add a rule to a chain.

A *policy* defines the default behavior. If no specific rule is found in the chain that matches an incoming packet, the policy is applied. It is always good practice to define a policy that denies all access.

After defining a policy, you can start working on the chains. This typically means you'll append or insert rules in the chain. It is very important to be aware that order does matter. That is, if you use -A to append a rule, it is entered at the last position in the chain. However, if you use -I to insert a rule, you can specify where exactly in the chain you want to insert it.

Configuration Example

That's enough talk about how rules and chains are used. Now let's work on an example. In this example, you'll configure a basic firewall. The purpose of this firewall is that FTP, SSH, HTTP, and HTTPS traffic needs to be allowed. Everything else has to be specifically denied.

The previous scenario sketches a typical customer request that a consultant might receive. Before starting to work on the request, it is important to think it through thoroughly because critical information is often lacking. The previous request, for example, is missing some basic elements.

- If all traffic is denied, traffic on the loopback interface is also denied. You'll need to allow everything that's happening on the loopback interface, however, to ensure that internal IP traffic can be handled correctly.

- The customer wants for four specific services. Do these services need to be available on this server for external users only, or is internal access also required?

- The DNS protocol is needed in nearly all situations. Typically, this is not something a customer asks for specifically.

- Apart from allowing incoming packets to the HTTP server, the firewall also needs to be configured to allow replies to be returned to the originator of the request.

Different styles can be used to configure a firewall. If you use system-config-firewall, for example, you'll notice that all outgoing traffic is allowed. This is not always wise because it would allow a hacker to install a malicious script configured to access a common port on your server that opens connections to external machines at will. Therefore, it is a good idea to think about the OUTPUT chain as well as the INPUT chain.

In Exercise 10.3, you'll learn how to build a Netfilter firewall.

EXERCISE 10.3

Building a Netfilter Firewall

In this exercise, you'll build a firewall on your virtual machine. You'll also make sure that no firewall rules are blocking anything on the host machine in order to allow you to test the firewall properly. The purpose of this exercise is to teach you how to configure a firewall from the command line; therefore, you'll also encounter some commonly made mistakes in this exercise.

1.   On the host computer, type **iptables -L -v** to display the current configuration. The purpose of this instruction is to clear any current configuration. Before doing that, however, it's good to know how your firewall is currently configured.

2.   Type the following commands: **iptables -P INPUT ACCEPT**, **iptables -P OUTPUT ACCEPT**, and **iptables -P FORWARD ACCEPT**. Now use **iptables -F** to flush all other rules.

3.   At this point, there should be no firewall on the host computer. Use **iptables -L -v** to verify that the policy is set to ACCEPT for all three chains in the filter table (see Listing 10.4). If this is the case, use **service iptables save** to write the current configuration to the configuration files. This ensures you'll keep this configuration, even after a reboot.

Listing 10.4: Verify that no firewall configuration is used before continuing

```
[root@hnl ~]# iptables -L -v
Chain INPUT (policy ACCEPT 49 packets, 6084 bytes)
 pkts bytes target     prot opt in    out     source               destination

Chain FORWARD (policy ACCEPT 0 packets, 0 bytes)
 pkts bytes target     prot opt in    out     source               destination

Chain OUTPUT (policy ACCEPT 34 packets, 5807 bytes)
 pkts bytes target     prot opt in    out     source               destination
```

4.   Repeat steps 1 to 3 on the virtual machine.

5.   After clearing the firewall on the virtual machine, you must test which services are offered from the virtual machine. Use ping to test whether you can still reach the virtual machine (for example, ping 192.168.100.176).

6.   Next use **yum install -y nmap** on the host to install the nmap network scanner.

7.   After installing it, use nmap, followed by the IP address of the virtual machine to scan available services on the virtual machine (for example, nmap 192.168.100.176). You should see that some services are offered.

Listing 10.5 shows what the nmap output should look like.

Listing 10.5: Testing service availability using nmap

```
[root@hnl ~]# nmap 192.168.100.177

Starting Nmap 5.21 ( http://nmap.org ) at 2012-05-26 18:09 CEST
mass_dns: warning: Unable to determine any DNS servers. Reverse DNS is
 disabled. Try using --system-dns or specify valid servers with
 --dns-servers
Nmap scan report for 192.168.100.177
Host is up (0.00036s latency).
Not shown: 999 filtered ports
PORT   STATE SERVICE
22/tcp open  ssh
MAC Address: 52:54:00:15:A6:B4 (QEMU Virtual NIC)

Nmap done: 1 IP address (1 host up) scanned in 4.97 seconds
```

8. At this point, it is time to start configuring the firewall. Remember, everything you do from this moment on must be done on the virtual machine. The first thing to do is to set a policy for the three chains. To do this, type the following:

```
iptables -P INPUT DROP
iptables -P OUTPUT DROP
iptables -P FORWARD DROP
```

There are two options to block packets. If you use the target REJECT, the sender of a packet gets an error message indicating that the package could not be delivered. If you use DROP, the packet is dropped silently, which is better because it doesn't reveal anything about the presence of the firewall node. You cannot use REJECT in a policy. REJECT is typically used on an internal network to prevent an application from hanging. After setting the policy, you can verify its existence again using iptables -L -v.

9. At this point, all traffic is blocked, so it's time to open your firewall and allow the traffic that you want to permit. Given that not even a ping to localhost (ping localhost) is going to work at this time, open the loopback interface first. Use the following code to accomplish this:

```
iptables -A INPUT -i lo -j ACCEPT
iptables -A OUTPUT -o lo -j ACCEPT
```

Notice the different elements in this command. First, -A is used to add a line to the INPUT and OUTPUT chain. Next, -i is used for the incoming interface in the INPUT chain, and -o is used for the outgoing interface in the OUTPUT chain. In the last part of the commands, the option -j ACCEPT is used to jump to the target ACCEPT. Also, note the use of uppercase and lowercase in the command. After entering these commands, use ping localhost to verify that the internal IP stack is indeed restored.

10. Now that localhost is working again, it's time to open the SSH port. To do this, enter the following command:

```
iptables -A INPUT -p tcp --dport 22 -j ACCEPT
```

Now try to open an SSH session from the host computer. You will see that it doesn't work. This is because your virtual machine is now configured to accept incoming SSH sessions, but it is not configured to send a reply to the originator of the SSH request. To open your virtual machine to also send a reply, use the following command:

```
iptables -A OUTPUT -m state --state ESTABLISHED,RELATED -j ACCEPT
```

This line does much more than simply allowing your server to send replies to SSH packages; it also permits you to send an answer to anything that has been allowed as an incoming connection using TCP. This is because in TCP/IP traffic, the first packet that comes in, initializes the connection. It has the state NEW. Once the incoming packet with the new state has been accepted, an answer is sent. This answer is part of a connection that has now been established. Hence, you're seeking the state ESTABLISHED. At this point, you'll again be able to open an SSH session to your virtual machine.

11. Now that SSH is open, you'll still need to open the HTTP port. To do this, use the following command:

```
iptables -A INPUT -p tcp --dport 80 -j ACCEPT
```

By using this command, you should now be able to reach the web server on the virtual host. No additional action is required because you've already configured a rule that allows all answers to be returned to the originator of the request.

12. Now is a nice moment to check the current configuration. To do this, type **iptables -L -v**. The result is shown in Listing 10.6.

Listing 10.6: Verifying the configuration using iptables -l -v

```
[root@hnl ~]# iptables -L -v
Chain INPUT (policy DROP 12 packets, 3324 bytes)
 pkts bytes target     prot opt in     out    source               destination
   86 17488 ACCEPT     all  --  lo     any    anywhere             anywhere
   62  5028 ACCEPT     tcp  --  any    any    anywhere
 anywhere     tcp dpt:ssh
    0     0 ACCEPT     tcp  --  any    any    anywhere
```

EXERCISE 10.3 *(continued)*

```
    anywhere    tcp dpt:http

Chain FORWARD (policy DROP 0 packets, 0 bytes)
 pkts bytes target      prot opt in      out     source              destination

Chain OUTPUT (policy DROP 0 packets, 0 bytes)
 pkts bytes target      prot opt in      out     source              destination
   86 17488 ACCEPT      all  --  any     lo      anywhere            anywhere
   52  5056 ACCEPT      all  --  any     any     anywhere            anywhere
    anywhere     state RELATED,ESTABLISHED
[root@hnl ~]#
```

In the output of the previous listing, you can see that all traffic is allowed on the lo interface in the INPUT chain and that all traffic that has the destination ssh or http is allowed as well. You can also see a counter that indicates how many packets have already been processed by a specific rule.

13. Now that everything is working as expected, it's time to allow FTP. FTP is a specific type of protocol, because it has a data and a command port. In case you're not sure how a protocol behaves or which port it uses, you can always check the /etc/services file. You'll find a list of all default ports and associated protocols in this file. Listing 10.7 shows a partial output of this file, where you can see that port 20 is used for FTP data and port 21 is used for FTP commands.

Listing 10.7: To find out more about a specific protocol, check /etc/services

```
tcpmux          1/udp                              # TCP port service multiplexer
rje             5/tcp                              # Remote Job Entry
rje             5/udp                              # Remote Job Entry
echo            7/tcp
echo            7/udp
discard         9/tcp           sink null
discard         9/udp           sink null
systat          11/tcp          users
systat          11/udp          users
daytime         13/tcp
daytime         13/udp
qotd            17/tcp          quote
qotd            17/udp          quote
msp             18/tcp                             # message send protocol
msp             18/udp                             # message send protocol
chargen         19/tcp          ttytst source
chargen         19/udp          ttytst source
ftp-data        20/tcp
```

EXERCISE 10.3 *(continued)*

```
ftp-data        20/udp
# 21 is registered to ftp, but also used by fsp
ftp             21/tcp
ftp             21/udp          fsp fspd
ssh             22/tcp                          # The Secure Shell (SSH) Protoco:
```

14. To permit TCP traffic to get through as well, you need to allow both port 21 and port 20 through the INPUT chain. Of course, you could type two different lines to do that, because by default iptables will not allow you to put more than one port on a line. However, you can also use the multiport module. This module is loaded in the kernel, and it allows you to load more than just one port per line.

    ```
    iptables -A INPUT -m multiport -p tcp --port 21,20 -j ACCEPT
    ```

15. At this point, your firewall is fundamentally ready. Type **iptables -L -v** to verify that it appears as you would expect, and then type **service iptables save**. This writes all that you've done to the firewall configuration file in /etc/sysconfig/iptables.

16. Now imagine that you want to create an exception in your firewall. That is, you want to allow one specific IP address to access any service that is available. This is where order matters. Since the first rule that matches in a chain is applied, it makes sense to put such an exception rule on top of the chain to prevent a rule later in the chain from blocking access to a specific port. To do this, use **iptables -I** followed by the name of the CHAIN and the number where you want to insert the rule. To do that, you need to find the correct number first. First retrieve an overview of the current configuration, including the line numbers, by using **iptables -L -v --line-numbers**. Listing 10.8 shows chains with line numbers.

Listing 10.8: Showing chains with line numbers

```
[root@hnl ~]# iptables -L -v --line-numbers
Chain INPUT (policy DROP 88 packets, 19093 bytes)
num   pkts bytes target      prot opt in      out     source
   destination
1        86 17488 ACCEPT     all  --  lo      any     anywhere              anywhere
2       175 13672 ACCEPT     tcp  --  any     any     anywhere
 anywhere            tcp dpt:ssh
3         0     0 ACCEPT     tcp  --  any     any     anywhere
 anywhere               tcp dpt:http
4         0     0 ACCEPT     tcp  --  any     any     anywhere
 anywhere            multiport ports ftp,ftp-data

Chain FORWARD (policy DROP 0 packets, 0 bytes)
```

EXERCISE 10.3 *(continued)*

```
num   pkts bytes target      prot opt in    out    source
   destination

Chain OUTPUT (policy DROP 0 packets, 0 bytes)
num   pkts bytes target      prot opt in    out    source
   destination
1       86 17488 ACCEPT      all  --  any   lo     anywhere            anywhere
2      140 17536 ACCEPT      all  --  any   any    anywhere
   anywhere            state RELATED,ESTABLISHED
[root@hn1 ~]#
```

17. To make sure that the exception for one IP address is placed before anything else, use the following command to create an exception for the IP address used on the host machine:

```
iptables -I INPUT 2 -s 192.168.100.1/24 -j ACCEPT
```

18. The firewall is now ready. Use **service iptables save** to save everything.

Advanced iptables Configuration

In the previous section, you learned how to use iptables to set up a basic firewall. In this section, you'll study some more advanced options. First you'll read how to set up logging in an iptables environment. Next you'll learn how the firewall can be activated using the limit module.

Configuring Logging

Up to now, you've read about how to accept, reject, and drop a package if it matches. Another very useful target is the *LOG target.* As its name suggests, this target allows you to log matching packets. If you need to know exactly what is happening in your firewall, the LOG target is your best friend. Nevertheless, make sure it doesn't log too much, because if it logs every packet that is sent to your machine during a ping flood attack (try ping -f loc- alhost to find out what this does), your log files will be flooded with useless information.

To send a packet to the LOG target, you need to include a line that refers to that target before anything else happens to the packet. If a packet matches a LOG line, it won't be dropped, so you can still perform an action on that packet in the next line. The following two lines show you how to log all packets, which the node with IP address 192.168.0.75 sends to SSH—before SSH traffic is allowed in general:

```
iptables -A INPUT -s 192.168.0.75 -p tcp --dport 22 -j LOG
iptables -A INPUT -p tcp --dport 22 -j ACCEPT
```

When using the LOG target, you should be aware that sequence is very important. That is, you want to make sure that the LOG line comes before the line that actually handles the packet. This is because if you first drop the packet, it isn't processed any further, and it will never encounter the LOG line. In Exercise 10.4, you'll learn how to set up packet logging.

EXERCISE 10.4

Setting Up iptables Logging

In this exercise, you'll set up iptables logging on your virtual machine and see how you can read the results.

1. Type **iptables -L -v --line-numbers**, and determine on which line in the INPUT chain SSH traffic is allowed. For this exercise, assume it is on line 4.

2. Type **iptables -I INPUT 4 -p tcp --dport 22 -j LOG**. This line makes sure all SSH traffic is logged.

3. Open an SSH session to your virtual machine, and run some commands, such as ls and who.

4. Use **less /var/log/messages**, and use **G** to go to the end of the file. You'll see numerous log lines being added to the log file (see Listing 10.9).

Listing 10.9: iptables log lines in /var/log/messages

```
.168.0.75 DST=192.168.0.70 LEN=92 TOS=0x00 PREC=0x00 TTL=128 ID=3763 DF
 PROTO=TCP SPT=64906 DPT=22 WINDOW=16308 RES=0x00 ACK PSH URGP=0
May 27 09:58:16 hnl kernel: IN=p6p1 OUT=
 MAC=b8:ac:6f:c9:35:25:14:fe:b5:a9:9d:e3:08:00 SRC=192.168.0.75
 DST=192.168.0.70 LEN=92 TOS=0x00 PREC=0x00 TTL=128 ID=3765 DF PROTO=TCP
 SPT=64906 DPT=22 WINDOW=16295 RES=0x00 ACK PSH URGP=0
May 27 09:58:16 hnl kernel: IN=p6p1 OUT=
 MAC=b8:ac:6f:c9:35:25:14:fe:b5:a9:9d:e3:08:00 SRC=192.168.0.75
 DST=192.168.0.70 LEN=92 TOS=0x00 PREC=0x00 TTL=128 ID=3766 DF PROTO=TCP
 SPT=64906 DPT=22 WINDOW=16282 RES=0x00 ACK PSH URGP=0
May 27 09:58:16 hnl kernel: IN=p6p1 OUT=
 MAC=b8:ac:6f:c9:35:25:14:fe:b5:a9:9d:e3:08:00 SRC=192.168.0.75
 DST=192.168.0.70 LEN=92 TOS=0x00 PREC=0x00 TTL=128 ID=3767 DF PROTO=TCP
 SPT=64906 DPT=22 WINDOW=16269 RES=0x00 ACK PSH URGP=0
May 27 09:58:16 hnl kernel: IN=p6p1 OUT=
 MAC=b8:ac:6f:c9:35:25:14:fe:b5:a9:9d:e3:08:00 SRC=192.168.0.75
 DST=192.168.0.70 LEN=40 TOS=0x00 PREC=0x00 TTL=128 ID=3768 DF PROTO=TCP
 SPT=64906 DPT=22 WINDOW=16425 RES=0x00 ACK URGP=0
May 27 09:58:16 hnl kernel: IN=p6p1 OUT=
 MAC=b8:ac:6f:c9:35:25:14:fe:b5:a9:9d:e3:08:00 SRC=192.168.0.75
```

```
DST=192.168.0.70 LEN=124 TOS=0x00 PREC=0x00 TTL=128 ID=3769 DF PROTO=TCP
SPT=64906 DPT=22 WINDOW=16425 RES=0x00 ACK PSH URGP=0
May 27 09:58:16 hnl kernel: IN=p6p1 OUT=
MAC=b8:ac:6f:c9:35:25:14:fe:b5:a9:9d:e3:08:00 SRC=192.168.0.75
DST=192.168.0.70 LEN=92 TOS=0x00 PREC=0x00 TTL=128 ID=3770 DF PROTO=TCP
SPT=64906 DPT=22 WINDOW=16425 RES=0x00 ACK PSH URGP=0

May 27 09:58:17 hnl kernel: IN=p6p1 OUT=
MAC=b8:ac:6f:c9:35:25:14:fe:b5:a9:9d:e3:08:00 SRC=192.168.0.75
DST=192.168.0.70 LEN=40 TOS=0x00 PREC=0x00 TTL=128 ID=3771 DF PROTO=TCP
SPT=64906 DPT=22 WINDOW=16416 RES=0x00 ACK URGP=0
(END)
```

As you noticed in Exercise 10.4, when you enable logging, numerous lines are logged. In the next section, you'll learn what you can do about that.

The Limit Module

You just learned that when using logging, numerous lines are written to the log files. On an active system, the number of lines logged can be so high that your log files will suffer a denial-of-service attack, and nothing further will be readable. To protect yourself against this, you can use the *limit module*. This module allows you to jump to a target if a certain number of packets have been matched within a specific period of time. For example, if you want to limit the number of packets logged to one per second for all SSH traffic, use the following line:

```
iptables -I INPUT 3 -p tcp --dport 22 -m limit --limit 1/s -j LOG
```

Another way the limit module can be used to log incoming packets is by including it after all rules that allow incoming traffic. You might be interested to know which traffic is denied by your firewall. The following lines do this for you:

```
iptables -A INPUT -m limit --limit 15/minute -j LOG
iptables -A OUTPUT -m limit --limit 15/minute -j LOG
```

Configuring NAT

Network Address Translation (NAT) is a common technique that can be used on routers to have nodes on the private network go out with one registered IP address on the public network. You can use NAT for three purposes:

- To change the source IP address to the IP address of the firewall before it is sent to the Internet, you need the MASQUERADE target.
- To change the source IP address of a specific host to the IP address of the firewall before it is sent to the Internet, you need the SNAT target.

- To redirect traffic that is sent to a specific IP address and port on the public IP address to an IP address and port on the private network, you need the DNAT target.

Figure 10.7 summarizes the NAT process. It demonstrates what is happening while a packet is being sent and processed by the NAT router. In this packet, you can read a summary of DNAT, which allows you to make a port on the private network available for the Internet.

FIGURE 10.7   Packet processing by a NAT router

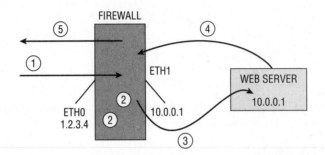

(1) A packet targeted at IP address `1.2.3.4:80` comes in on the NAT router. This packet has to be sent to the web server that listens at IP address `10.0.0.10` on the internal network.

(2) The packet is processed by the firewall. To make sure DNAT is used to send the packet to the web server, use this command: `iptables -t nat -A POSTROUTING -o eth0 -j MASQUERADE`. You also need to enable routing (`echo 1 > /proc/sys/net/ipv4/ip_forward`) and set the policy for the routing chain to ALLOW: `iptables -P FORWARD ALLOW`.

(3) Because of the rule in the PREROUTING chain of the NAT table, here the packet can be delivered to the web server.

(4) The web server sends back the answer. However, the source address of the web server is used in the answer, and this address is unknown on the Internet.

(5) Thus, a masquerading rule has to be defined.

The following command defines the masquerading rule:

```
iptables -t nat -A PREROUTING -i eth0 -p tcp --dport 80 -j DNAT --to-destination
10.0.0.10
```

The masquerading rule makes sure that the source IP address is changed to the source IP address of the NAT router, which allows nodes on the Internet to send the packet back to the appropriate destination.

The previous process described how NAT can be used. A NAT table is used to process packets. In the NAT table, three different chains are available.

- PREROUTING
- POSTROUTING
- OUTPUT

Of these chains, PREROUTING and POSTROUTING are most important. In *PREROUTING*, packets are processed before the routing decision is made. This chain is typically used for incoming packets where the destination address has to be rewritten, which happens in DNAT. In SNAT and MASQUERADE, the source IP address must be rewritten, and that needs to be done after the routing process has been applied. Therefore, the SNAT and MASQUERADE rules are added to the POSTROUTING chain.

To enable any kind of Network Address Translation, there remains one important thing to address: your host must be configured for packet forwarding. By default, the Linux kernel doesn't allow packet forwarding. To make sure that your computer can do packet forwarding, check that the /etc/sysctl.conf file contains the following line:

```
net.ipv4.ip_forward = 1
```

After changing this line, use sysctl -p to read the changed settings. Now your host can be used for NAT. In Exercise 10.5, you'll learn how to configure NAT.

EXERCISE 10.5

Configuring NAT

In this exercise, you'll learn how to set up NAT. You'll use the host computer as the NAT router and the virtual machine as the web server on the private network. All configuration is done on the host computer, but you must make sure that all iptables configuration is erased. (You'll take care of this during the first steps of this exercise.) To test the configuration, you'll need a third machine that is connected to the same network as the RHEL server that you are using as host. If you don't have a third machine available, that's fine; you just can't test the configuration.

1. On the virtual machine, use **iptables -F, iptables -P INPUT ALLOW, iptables -P OUTPUT ALLOW**, and **iptables -P FORWARD ALLOW**. Next use **service iptables save** to save this configuration.

2. Repeat step 1 on the host computer, and use **service httpd stop** followed by **chkconfig httpd off** to make sure the web server is stopped on the host computer.

3. On the host computer, enable routing by opening /etc/sysctl.conf with an editor. Make sure it includes the line net.ipv.ip_forward = 1, and use **sysctl -p** to the sysctl service to make the change effective.

4. On the host, use **iptables -t nat -A PREROUTING -i eth0 -p tcp --dport 80 -j DNAT --to-destination 192.168.100.76**. Make sure that you use the actual name of your network card on the host machine and that the --to-destination option uses the IP address of the virtual machine.

5. Also on the host, use **iptables -t nat -A POSTROUTING -o eth0 -j MASQUERADE** to enable IP masquerading.

EXERCISE 10.5 *(continued)*

6. On another computer connected to the same network as your RHEL host, test that you can reach the HTTP port on the host.

7. After verifying that this works, restart both the host computer and the virtual machine to clear the NAT configuration. *Note*: Don't forget this step, or you will experience problems completing the exercises in upcoming chapters successfully.

Summary

In this chapter, you learned how to configure a firewall on your Red Hat server. You worked with the system-config-firewall tool and the iptables command to configure a basic firewall. You also learned how to extend the functionality of the firewall by using modules. You studied how to configure logging, which lets you analyze when something is not working as expected in the firewall. Finally, you learned how to set up the three different kinds of NAT to make computers on the private network available to the outside world.

Chapter 11

Setting Up Cryptographic Services

TOPICS COVERED IN THIS CHAPTER:

- ✓ **Introducing SSL**
- ✓ **Managing Certificates with openssl**
- ✓ **Working with GNU Privacy Guard**

On a typical Red Hat Enterprise Linux system, there are many services that need to be secured while transmitting packets over the network. SSL is the common solution that is shared between many services, such as LDAP, http, and many more. Before starting to work with these services in subsequent chapters, you'll learn in this chapter how to use SSL. Also, you'll learn how to use GPG as a security solution.

Introducing SSL

For many of the services that are offered on a current-day server, additional security is a requirement. By applying this security, you can make sure that traffic to the server is encrypted and that the identity of the server is guaranteed. To achieve this level of security, you can use SSL. Before learning about SSL, however, you'll learn about how public/private keys are used in cryptography.

When thinking about SSL, many people consider web servers only. Other types of servers also use SSL certificates. Without SSL, anyone can capture passwords that are sent between a POP or IMAP mail client and the mail server. Furthermore, LDAP is commonly protected with SSL to make sure that the passwords sent when authenticating against an LDAP server cannot be captured.

If a user wants to establish a connection to a website, this connection needs to be protected. To ensure a protected connection, public and private keys are used. These keys can be used for three reasons:

- To encrypt traffic to and from a server
- To prove the identity of another party
- To verify that a message has not been tampered with

Let's take an example where public/private keys are used to encrypt traffic that is sent to a server, which is common on the Internet.

1. When the connection to the server is first initialized, the server sends its *public key (PKI) certificate*. This contains the public key of the server, and it is signed with the private key of the certificate authority (CA) used by the owner of the server.

2. To verify that the PKI certificate can be trusted, the signature of the CA in the certificate is checked. If the signature can be traced back to a public key that already is known to the client, the connection is considered to be trusted.

3. Now that the connection is trusted, a symmetric session key generated by the client is sent. The data traffic is encrypted with this session key for performance reasons.

4. Because public/private key encryption is one-way encryption, only the server is capable of decrypting the traffic by using its private key.

As you've seen in this example, to work with SSL, you need a public key certificate. The certificate is required to guarantee the identity of the server that uses it. It contains the public key of the server that users are going to use to establish a secured connection, and it contains a "proof of identity," which is normally provided by a CA. As an alternative, you can work with self-signed certificates. In this chapter, you'll learn how to set up both.

Proof of Authenticity: the Certificate Authority

The use of public/private keys is a great improvement in Internet security. There is a challenge, however: how can the receiver be sure that the public key that it receives actually comes from a trusted server and not from a hacker who has hijacked the connection? This is where the CA comes in.

A CA is used to guarantee the authenticity of a public key. The role of the CA is to sign PKI certificates. Any server can generate a PKI certificate, and it is the role of the CA to sign these PKI certificates with its private key. However, this is useful only if the client that receives the certificate knows the public key of the CA. If this is not the case, users will see a message indicating they are using an untrusted connection, and the client application will probably close the connection. Thus, for common use on the Internet, make sure that the CA is known to everyone. For private internal use, an in-house CA can also be used.

The Trusted Root

If you want to create your own CA, make sure the users who use it can trust it. You can accomplish this by having its certificates signed by a commonly known CA. Because the public keys of these commonly known CAs are available in most client applications, the CA that uses it will be transparently accepted. The only drawback is that, in general, you need to pay money to the CA that is going to sign your certificates. If you don't want or don't need to do that, you can use a self-signed certificate.

If you are creating a certificate that is to be trusted, you need to have it signed. To do this, you'll send a certificate signing request. You'll learn how to do this later in this chapter.

Running Your Own CA

In this chapter, you will learn how to run your own CA. If you do that, you can have its certificates signed by a trusted root. Alternatively, you can use self-signed certificates. This is the "you can trust me because I say so" type of certificate. It's not the kind of security you want to show your customers on the Internet, but it works well for internal use.

If you're using a self-signed certificate anywhere in the chain, the first time it is used, the user will get a message indicating there is a problem with the trustworthiness of the certificate. If your users are mainly internal, you can deal with that by importing the certificates on the users' workstations. If they are external users, you need to convince them that the certificate is to be trusted. If you're offering an SSL-protected web server for your local hockey club, for example, that's not too hard to do, but you don't try want to do this with your e-commerce customers.

Managing Certificates with openssl

To create and manage certificates, you can use the openssl command-line utility. This is a very versatile command that offers many options but is sometimes difficult to use. To begin, you'll learn how to create a self-signed certificate.

Creating a Self-Signed Certificate

In the following procedure, you can read how to create a self-signed certificate.

To begin, you need to store the certificates that you are going to create. You can do this in the home directory of user root if you want them to be well protected, or else you can put the certificates in the directory /etc/pki/tls, which exists for this purpose by default. Within this directory, you need four subdirectories to store the certificates: certs, newcerts, private, and crl. These subdirectories have already been created on Red Hat Enterprise Linux.

Here is an overview of how each of these directories is used:

certs This is the location used to store all signed PKI certificates. The directory can be open for public access because it contains only public keys and no private ones.

newcerts This is where you temporarily store all new certificates until they have been signed. After you've signed them, you can remove them from this location.

private This directory is used to store private keys. You must make sure that this directory is well protected because the private keys that are stored here are the proof of identity for your server. If the private keys are compromised, anyone can pretend to be your server. To protect the private keys, make sure that the private directory has permission mode 700 and that user root is owner of this directory.

crl A *certificate revocation list (CRL)* is a list of certificates that are invalid. If ever you need to revoke certificates, copy them to this directory.

In the procedure below, you'll learn how to create your own Certificate Authority.

1. To create a certificate for your CA server, you can use the configuration file that you'll find in /etc/pki/openssl.cnf. This file contains default settings that are used to facilitate the creation of new certificates. Using this file makes creating certificates easier; all default values that are specified here don't have to be used on the command line. It's a good idea to read through this file so that you know which kinds of settings are available. Take special notice of the directory paths where you can find a reference to all the directories that are used while using the openssl command. If you're planning to put the certificates somewhere else on your server, you can change the HOME and dir variables from this file to reflect the directories you will be using (see Listing 11.1).

Listing 11.1: Partial contents of the /etc/pki/openssl.cnf file

```
HOME      = /root/rootCA
dir       = /root/root-CA
...
certificate = $dir/root-CAcert.pem
...
private-key = $dir/root-CAkey.pem
```

2. After checking the default values you want to use in openssl.cnf, you can start creating your own self-signed certificate. The following command allows you to create a certificate that uses a 1024-bit RSA key with a validity of 10 years:

```
openssl req -newkey rsa:1024 -x509 -days 3650
```

In the previous code snippet, you can see that openssl is used as the master command. It is used with the req command. The openssl command uses subcommands. req is the command that is used to generate a certificate-signing request. With that request, a new key is created with an RSA length of 1024 bits in which x509 and a validity of 10 years is used.

When creating a certificate that is to be used for a CA, it's a good idea to choose a long validity period. It should at least be longer than the period a normal certificate is typically valid, because when the CA certificate expires, all certificates that are signed by it will expire too.

In this command, only a minimal number of parameters are used. The command could have been much longer, but that wasn't necessary, because the default options from openssl.cnf have been used. A more complex example follows, where a specific mention is made of where the private key and certificate must be written.

```
openssl req -newkey rsa:2048 -x509 -days 3650 -keyout private/my-CAkey.pem -out
my-CAcert.pem
```

When you are creating a key, the openssl command prompts for a passphrase. This will always occur, because a passphrase cannot be read from a configuration file. It is very important to select a secure passphrase. If the private key gets stolen, the passphrase is your last protection it has against being abused. If you don't want to be forced to enter a passphrase every time the service is restarted, you can just press Enter when prompted for the passphrase. This will set an empty passphrase, so the user won't be prompted.

 Real World Scenario

Self-Signed Certificates and Security

Creating a self-signed certificate doesn't necessarily guarantee security. In fact, self-signed certificates are not about security—they are about trustworthiness. A self-signed certificate is as secure as a certificate that has been signed by a commercial certificate authority. The only difference is that users risk getting a message when they are setting up a connection with this type of certificate because it is signed by an unknown CA.

In many corporate environments, it makes sense to work with self-signed certificates. For instance, think of an intranet site, where https is a requirement and the data has to be protected when sent to users. Because the users of such a website all can typically be managed by corporate IT, it makes sense to save a lot of money by using self-signed certificates instead of an expensive commercial certificate.

Another way of creating a self-signed certificate is by using the genkey command. This command provides a text user interface that guides the user through the process of creating a certificate. In Exercise 11.1, you'll learn how to use genkey to create such a certificate.

EXERCISE 11.1

Creating a Self-Signed Certificate

In this exercise, you will create a self-signed certificate using the genkey command.

1. Use **yum install -y crypto-utils mod_ssl** to install the RPM package that contains the genkey command.

2. Use the **genkey** command followed by a unique name that is going to be used for the resulting files. It is good to the name of your server as the filename. You must also specify how long you want the key to be valid by using **--days** followed by a number of days. If you omit this option, the key will be valid for one month only. The complete command looks like **genkey --days 365 yourserver.example.com**. Notice that the genkey command automatically places the resulting PKI certificate and private key in the correct directories, which are /etc/pki/tls/private and /etc/pki/tls/certs.

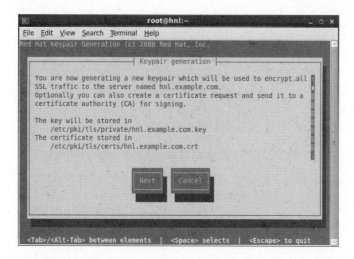

3. On the next screen, select the key size you want to use. The default key size is set to 1024 bits, which works fine in most cases. If you need a higher security level, you can select a bigger key size, but by doing that you will slow your system.

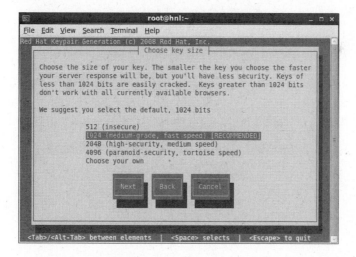

4. After you have selected the key size you want to use, the system will generate some random bits that are necessary to produce the key. This may take a long time, particularly if you've chosen to use a big key size. To speed up this process, it is a good idea to move the mouse and type some command, or in some way make sure your computer is busy.

EXERCISE 11.1 *(continued)*

5. Once the key has been generated, genkey asks whether you want to create a certificate-signing request. This is what you would do if you wanted to have the key signed by an external certificate authority. Because you are creating a self-signed certificate right now, you can skip this step by answering No.

6. Now you can indicate whether you want to set a passphrase for the private key. It is a good idea always to protect your private keys with a passphrase, so select Yes and set a passphrase that is difficult to guess. The longer the passphrase, the harder it gets to guess its value after a private key has become compromised.

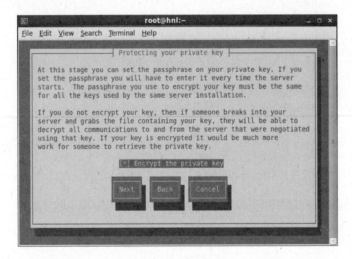

7. Now enter the appropriate information to identify your server. The most important part of the identification consists of the common name. This must match the fully qualified domain name of the server.

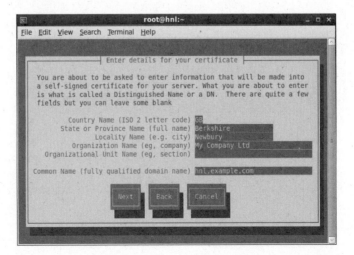

8. After you enter the appropriate identification, the public and private keys are written to the appropriate directories and are ready for use.

In the preceding exercise, you created a new public/private key pair. At this point, it is a good idea to verify the contents of the key. To do this, use the **openssl x509 -text** command and feed as the input file the key you've just created: **openssl x509 -text < /etc/ pki/tls/certs/hnl.example.com.crt.** Listing 11.2 shows the result of this command. In particular, look at the key validity. As you can see in the listing, in some cases this can be set way too short!

Listing 11.2: Validating a PKI certificate

```
[root@hnl ~]# openssl x509 -text < /etc/pki/tls/certs/hnl.example.com.crt
Certificate:
    Data:
        Version: 3 (0x2)
        Serial Number: 2558171526 (0x987a9986)
        Signature Algorithm: md5WithRSAEncryption
        Issuer: C=GB, ST=Berkshire, L=Newbury, O=My Company Ltd,
CN=hnl.example.com
        Validity
            Not Before: Jul  2 08:43:53 2012 GMT
            Not After : Jul  2 08:43:53 2013 GMT
        Subject: C=GB, ST=Berkshire, L=Newbury, O=My Company Ltd,
CN=hnl.example.com
        Subject Public Key Info:
            Public Key Algorithm: rsaEncryption
                Public-Key: (1024 bit)
                Modulus:
                    00:ba:31:99:c1:97:a5:54:e5:51:6e:7d:66:7b:ac:
                    82:7e:73:04:94:32:ad:8f:88:75:5b:9c:50:f7:a6:
                    02:1b:5f:1c:a7:3e:f2:1a:f8:83:a1:76:b4:37:32:
                    47:09:cf:cc:0f:ae:22:95:88:9f:81:ac:9e:ad:a0:
                    f6:fd:f2:ea:11:05:9d:a5:25:de:ab:e7:d9:d1:e0:
                    c9:b4:bc:c4:c2:a0:75:3b:32:ad:81:89:df:d8:4a:
                    10:3e:9f:ee:b2:fa:08:2d:0f:31:91:62:4c:6c:4d:
                    40:50:05:4b:74:65:c0:3c:f0:42:83:3a:be:77:b2:
                    c6:fa:25:cf:55:51:31:ce:53
                Exponent: 65537 (0x10001)
    Signature Algorithm: md5WithRSAEncryption
        7d:0b:07:49:da:5c:29:ea:07:a5:69:ae:68:be:bd:4b:f9:73:
        a6:d2:80:6c:d0:1a:5f:61:c7:9d:45:cb:75:85:9b:08:78:17:
```

```
        6f:d3:7e:34:a1:87:a6:b1:97:f3:c6:17:fa:4c:ca:a3:f3:65:
        aa:5e:fb:f5:4d:a1:7a:61:7b:70:4d:3c:1b:bf:0d:af:ab:3a:
        34:a1:55:0f:59:a3:2e:1f:12:ac:76:62:1f:88:98:2f:da:64:
        33:76:10:a8:fb:78:95:90:2b:23:66:66:61:52:ab:af:f2:35:
        fa:42:61:6b:8d:f6:06:ae:27:f5:e1:07:f0:f4:c1:b4:72:7e:
        0f:20
-----BEGIN CERTIFICATE-----
MIICRDCCAa2gAwIBAgIFAJh6mYYwDQYJKoZIhvcNAQEEBQAwZjELMAkGA1UEBhMC
ROIxEjAQBgNVBAgTCUJlcmtzaGlyZTEQMA4GA1UEBxMHTmV3YnVyeTEXMBUGA1UE
ChMOTXkgQ29tcGFueSBMdGQxGDAWBgNVBAMTD2hubC5leGFtcGxlLmNvbTAeFw0x
MjA3MDIwODQzNTNaFw0xMjA4MDIwODQzNTNaMGYxCzAJBgNVBAYTAkdCMRIwEAYD
VQQIEwlCZXJrc2hpcmUxEDAOBgNVBAcTB05ld2J1cnkxFzAVBgNVBAoTDk15IENv
bXBhbnkgTHRkMRgwFgYDVQQDEw9obmwuZXhhbXBsZS5jb20wgZ8wDQYJKoZIhvcN
AQEBBQADgY0AMIGJAoGBALoxmcGXpVTlUW59Znusgn5zBJQyrY+IdVucUPemAhtf
HKc+8hr4g6F2tDcyRwnPzA+uIpWIn4Gsnq2g9v3y6hEFnaUl3qvn2dHgybS8xMKg
dTsyrYGJ39hKED6f7rL6CCOPMZFiTGxNQFAFS3RlwDzwQoM6vneyxvolz1VRMc5T
AgMBAAEwDQYJKoZIhvcNAQEEBQADgYEAfQsHSdpcKeoHpWmuaL69S/lzptKAbNAa
X2HHnUXLdYWbCHgXb9N+NKGHprGX88YX+kzKo/Nlql779U2hemF7cE08G78Nr6s6
NKFVD1mjLh8SrHZiH4iYL9pkM3YQqPt4lZArI2ZmYVKrr/I1+kJha432Bq4n9eEH
8PTBtHJ+DyA=
-----END CERTIFICATE-----
[root@hnl ~]#
```

Creating a Signing Request

In the procedure described earlier, you created a self-signed certificate. While using genkey, you selected not to create a certificate signing request. If you do want the key to be signed by an external CA, you should indicate this when genkey asks whether you want to create a signing request (see Figure 11.1).

After creating the certificate signing request, send this request to the CA. Once you receive the signed certificate back, you can copy it to the /etc/pki/tls/certs directory and tell your application to use the signed certificate.

Working with GNU Privacy Guard

While PKI certificates and SSL are primarily used with web servers, another way to protect files is by using *GNU Privacy Guard (GPG)*. GPG is commonly used in email communication, and it is also used to encrypt and decrypt files so that they can be securely transported.

FIGURE 11.1   After creating the public/private key pair, genkey asks whether you also want to create a signing request.

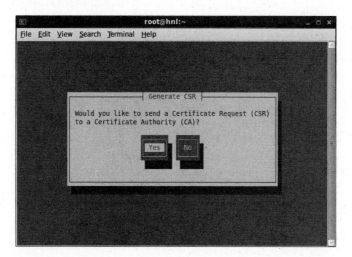

Creating GPG Keys

To create a key pair, you have to use **gpg --gen-key**. This command starts an interactive interface where questions are posed about the identity of the user who is going to use the key. Next you'll need to enter a passphrase to protect the key. Once that has been done, the process that generates the key needs *entropy*. This is random data that you have to generate while the key pair is being created. Note that for longer keys, it will take more time to generate the key, and a lot of disk activity may be required to create it successfully (see Listing 11.3).

Listing 11.3: Generating a GPG key pair

```
[linda@hnl ~]$ gpg --gen-key.gpg (GnuPG) 2.0.14; Copyright (C) 2009 Free
Software Foundation, Inc.
This is free software: you are free to change and redistribute it.
There is NO WARRANTY, to the extent permitted by law.

Please select what kind of key you want:
    (1) RSA and RSA (default)
    (2) DSA and Elgamal
    (3) DSA (sign only)
    (4) RSA (sign only)
```

```
Your selection? 1
RSA keys may be between 1024 and 4096 bits long.
What keysize do you want? (2048) 2048
Requested keysize is 2048 bits
Please specify how long the key should be valid.
         0 = key does not expire
      <n>  = key expires in n days
      <n>w = key expires in n weeks
      <n>m = key expires in n months
      <n>y = key expires in n years
Key is valid for? (0) 0
Key does not expire at all
Is this correct? (y/N) y

GnuPG needs to construct a user ID to identify your key.

Real name: Linda Thomsen
Email address: linda.thomsen@example.com
Comment: non
You selected this USER-ID:
    "Linda Thomsen (non) <linda.thomsen@example.com>"

Change (N)ame, (C)omment, (E)mail or (O)kay/(Q)uit? o
You need a Passphrase to protect your secret key.

can't connect to `/root/.gnupg/S.gpg-agent': No such file or directory
gpg-agent[3118]: directory `/root/.gnupg/private-keys-v1.d' created
We need to generate a lot of random bytes. It is a good idea to perform
some other action (type on the keyboard, move the mouse, utilize the
disks) during the prime generation; this gives the random number
generator a better chance to gain enough entropy.
gpg: key 3CBABF7E marked as ultimately trusted
public and secret key created and signed.

gpg: checking the trustdb
gpg: 3 marginal(s) needed, 1 complete(s) needed, PGP trust model
gpg: depth: 0  valid:   1  signed:   0  trust: 0-, 0q, 0n, 0m, 0f, 1u
pub   2048R/3CBABF7E 2012-06-29
      Key fingerprint = A733 F93E A224 EFEE AB3D  9850 7A07 A037 3CBA BF7E
```

```
uid               Linda Thomsen (non) <linda.thomsen@example.com>
sub   2048R/B398384F 2012-06-29
```

 When you start to create a passphrase, a graphical window opens. If for some reason you get an error while assigning the passphrase, this graphical window will likely not open. In this case, restart the command from a graphical environment. In addition, don't use it from an su – environment, because this is a common cause of errors when creating GPG keys.

While creating the key pair, a keyring is created. This *keyring* consists of two files that are written to the .gnupg directory in the home directory of the user. The public key is written to ~/.gnupg/pubring.gpg, and the private key is written to ~/.gnupg/secring.gpg. Make sure that the private key file is well secured because it contains your identity. Thus, if anyone steals this file, they can pretend to be you. So, always make sure the private key is protected with a passphrase and that unauthorized use is not possible.

Key Transfer

Having a GPG public/private key pair is good, but it is useful only if you can share the key with others. If others are using your public key to send encrypted messages by email or to encrypt files they want to send to you, you can ensure communications in a secure way. To accomplish this, you need to initialize the key transfer.

Initializing a *key transfer* means you have to export the key. To do this, you can use the gpg --export command. For example, use **gpg --export -a** to dump the public key to the STDOUT. You can see the result of this command in Listing 11.4.

Listing 11.4: Exporting your public key

```
sander@SYD:~> gpg --export -a
-----BEGIN PGP PUBLIC KEY BLOCK-----
Version: GnuPG v2.0.9 (GNU/Linux)

mQGiBEmvh28RBADqKXLjFBih2T+Vpq9dARMl6gvxShcHPet4tZ/Pyr/h/NNwiqwP
ZP/K69ki2qCMLLJ8o3S+KlQqXXedkKHbI61A1G3RSnPZIrEoRTMQBjUn3WkTgRU3
W3FXb3YdLezjT+tYGGosaglIkToWr8vDNXbcerOCWYOM5l3jeABWdZzWFwCgppZ3
hpPCyJ8YIbsLMgAKOxdSg20EANZelbPncoPUcOp9INRLIW+Xt1sMbPDtZj1bIqxx
vWTowpMdJMKSekihXAb3sqKMx5LEJGtaOY6qjD3aygt4GzLcedzVmdZAdNUiFS89
xrphg/wejhvZVrGFuofpN9r6jziQ4yyFeuX77rb0aHj2Zj2aWL4nnO9h5KMHaUx7
8ZsrA/0XUwcOL4AT6Z3MdPc5LHxMRSgJqiidh3DJhi6UxN9vCwtksDvMptDuOb/Y
```

```
14hkQSv9R/WfjVAUyLOG6BGmyb7rfc5uyGEib3D6EX7Piu+XCcbgfaJ5RcN8J6VJ
jzjVugLlPRQ/Il8sdlIWkDK4NKkLqFSt77dKu5qD2RwMeR9D1LQnU2FuZGVyIHZh
biBWdWdOIDxtYWlsQHNhbmRlcnZhbnZ3Z3Qubmw+iGAEExECACAFAkmvh28CGwMG
CwkIBwMCBBUCCAMEFgIDAQIeAQIXgAAKCRBv1hNURmbjjcALAKCB8UhUesS+9tbS
rXesTEPVSUz8yQCfWyvpeVw6N2+1OGLeXjjvlvfMT/C5Ag0ESa+HbxAIAPHOD8Ep
Q77oyjcGHMOwFdCQBSO/N2XFRzLcnKrqGfojXMeedQkLSdLxMPuYp16cO4yyBQGo
UgRUEh2q5vR1QQOTm+b2JvnbPTYvqiAqWHEENnaWt3qdAgnGByxLFbTTyi05naSA
Sos9mmcFAkzyz2PwecaGNVjtEIB3dGMAbOckuprYLCNXHxlGFBj13txv3wtbvOQC
jOxVU/TzhQi+PrYEKJuv9baxHgsT+6o35GraBcGHP068R+wYe2zW6o8hBPnv4AIw
EH9vMAstfluYoSFJPHJHaAvr9QASqyJ4gz7HYkOrobw/o3OBeL5o3OYZILVZaTwT
VMGI4tMLzBpeMYsAAwUIAJ9So4DIzbcDlwayYAcydTsiY8dRITO9thOP2n5Ywccn
tUFlq+Od5cgTqaVxbM+YL8vBgBgbB92ajMAFTSXmHOSTcsXHEqBYepBEQla3Yw7h
aG3xomD9x4GOtbw2y2VpnN/5yzBlvXET9fFLeaWw6hVtR2aEILVxfOFN6u2/OTOA
VIMTGirYm3+pWcWhBrmOoQ/4kH2TJz4X/mhCOUnqJIeNm65rogecM2wwfqAc/kSJ
t2S2GWDInTuQLZ1inXU12vyxfOJfbathQw+3agkONMXMVZP9V1ogativGFeUkLvv
TLeACuB+a4TMi3ye3753dlHrEgjsAbrZ/NVgogjzu8SISQQYEQIACQUCSa+HbwIb
DAAKCRBv1hNURmbjjdY3AJ9BZa+3Qck3YooxXQEOa5X/L+k4VwCcD8A2/Os6Mvnw
HcN8OeWmtTDjhl4=
=F5mD
-----END PGP PUBLIC KEY BLOCK-----
```

Exporting a key by using gpg `--export -a` in itself is not that useful. The key is written to the STDOUT. To copy it to a file, redirect the output of the gpg `--export -a` command to a file. Next you can attach that file to a mail message and send it to a user with whom you want to be able to communicate in a secure way. The other user can now import the key using the gpg `--import < keyfile` command. Thus, if Linda has written her key to the `linda.key` file and Lisa needs to import that file, she would run the command gpg `--import < linda.key` (see Listing 11.5). In Exercise 11.2 you'll learn how to create and exchange GPG keys.

Listing 11.5: Importing keys to your keyring

```
[linda@hnl ~]$ gpg --import < /tmp/linda.key
gpg: key 3A6FAE33: "Linda Thomsen <linda.thomsen@example.com>" not changed
gpg: Total number processed: 1
gpg:               unchanged: 1
[linda@hnl ~]$
```

EXERCISE 11.2

Creating and Exchanging GPG Keys

In this exercise, you'll use two user accounts to create a GPG key pair and export it.

1. If they don't exist already, create two users named linda and lisa, and give them the password *password*.

2. Log in to the graphical interface as user linda, and use **gpg --gen-key** to create a GPG key pair. Accept all default values, and assign the password *password12* to the private key. When the gen-key program tells you to generate entropy, use **ls -R /** a couple of times to get you through the procedure faster.

3. Repeat step 2 for user lisa, and use the same parameters.

4. As linda, use the command **gpg --export -a > /tmp/linda.key** to export linda's private key to the /tmp directory.

5. As lisa, use the command **gpg --import < /tmp/linda.key** to import linda's key to lisa's keyring.

6. As lisa, use **gpg --list-keys** to show that the key has been imported correctly.

Managing GPG Keys

Once the keys have been created and you have imported all the keys you need, there are some management tasks of which you must be aware. To begin, you can generate an overview of all the keys that are imported to your account. Please note that GPG keys are always owned by a user account and not by your entire system. To see the keys that are currently available, use **gpg --list-keys** (see Listing 11.6). This command will show you at least your own GPG keys. However, after using GPG for some time, it will also list the GPG keys of other users you have imported.

Listing 11.6: Listing GPG keys imported to your account

```
[lisa@hnl ~]$ gpg --list-keys
/home/lisa/.gnupg/pubring.gpg
----------------------------
pub   2048R/1F16DFE1 2012-06-29
uid                  Lisa Ericson <lisa.ericson@example.com>
sub   2048R/94DE9694 2012-06-29

pub   2048R/3A6FAE33 2012-06-29
uid                  Linda Thomsen <linda.thomsen@example.com>
sub   2048R/FE8A259A 2012-06-29
```

As you can see, gpg --list-keys provides an overview of all keys, including the email address that is assigned to it. You can also see the ID of the key; it is the part after the slash. Thus, for the key of user Linda that is imported to Lisa's account, the key-ID is 3A6FAE33.

When using the gpg --list-keys command, you see only public keys assigned to your account. If you want to check your private key, you can use **gpg --list-secret-keys** instead. This command is useful if you're encountering problems and you want to make sure that a private key has been installed correctly.

Another interesting command, which you can use to manage the keys assigned to your environment, is gpg --fingerprint. Some people who use GPG a lot have their GPG key fingerprint printed on their business card. So, if you need to verify that you're dealing with the right person, you can compare the result of the gpg --fingerprint command with the GPG key fingerprint that you've received from that person on their business card. If the keys match, you're probably dealing with the right person (see Listing 11.7).

Listing 11.7: Checking GPG key fingerprints

```
[lisa@hnl ~]$ gpg --fingerprint
/home/lisa/.gnupg/pubring.gpg
----------------------------
pub   2048R/1F16DFE1 2012-06-29
      Key fingerprint = D8C3 E566 D477 E610 9588  398F 4696 4A11 1F16 DFE1
uid                    Lisa Ericson <lisa.ericson@example.com>
sub   2048R/94DE9694 2012-06-29

pub   2048R/3A6FAE33 2012-06-29
      Key fingerprint = 63C7 DA03 EC3E C194 7792  50BB F0AB DE8F 3A6F AE33
uid                    Linda Thomsen <linda.thomsen@example.com>
sub   2048R/FE8A259A 2012-06-29
```

Encrypting Files with GPG

GPG is commonly used to encrypt files. The base command to do this is easy: **gpg -e yourfile.** The gpg command will next ask for a user ID. This is the ID of the user to which you want to send the encrypted file. This must be a user who is already in your GPG keyring. Enter the name of each user for whom you want to encrypt the file on a separate line. When you're done, just press Enter on an empty line (see Listing 11.8).

Listing 11.8: Using GPG to encrypt a file

```
[lisa@hnl ~]$ gpg -e hosts
You did not specify a user ID. (you may use "-r")

Current recipients:

Enter the user ID.  End with an empty line: Linda Thomsen
gpg: FE8A259A: There is no assurance this key belongs to the named user

pub  2048R/FE8A259A 2012-06-29 Linda Thomsen <linda.thomsen@example.com>
 Primary key fingerprint: 63C7 DA03 EC3E C194 7792  50BB F0AB DE8F 3A6F AE33
```

Subkey fingerprint: F083 D505 E0C9 1548 2C94 A648 A6E6 EE80 FE8A 259A

It is NOT certain that the key belongs to the person named
in the user ID. If you *really* know what you are doing,
you may answer the next question with yes.

Use this key anyway? (y/N) y

Current recipients:
2048R/FE8A259A 2012-06-29 "Linda Thomsen <linda.thomsen@example.com>"

Enter the user ID. End with an empty line:

The receiver of the encrypted file can decrypt it by using the command gpg -d. By
default, this will write the resulting file to the STDOUT, which isn't very useful. To send
it to a new file, make sure to use redirection when specifying the target file. The command gpg -d myfile.gpg > myfile will extract the contents of the GPG encrypted file to
myfile. There is one requirement for extracting a file that has been encrypted with gpg; the
user who decrypts the file needs to enter their passphrase to do this. In Exercise 11.3 you'll
learn how to encrypt and decrypt files using GPG.

EXERCISE 11.3

Encrypting and Decrypting Files

In this exercise, you'll use the user accounts linda and lisa you created in the previous
exercise to practice GPG file encryption and decryption.

1. Open a shell, and use **su - linda** to become user linda.

2. As linda, copy the file /etc/hosts to your home directory using **cp /etc/hosts ~**.

3. Use **gpg --listkeys** to list the keys currently imported in Linda's environment, and
    note the exact name of the user lisa.

4. Encrypt the file using **gpg -e hosts**. When the user account is requested, enter the
    exact name of user lisa as you found it in the previous step of this exercise. Next
    press Enter on an empty line to complete the encryption procedure.

5. Use **cp ~/hosts.gpg /tmp** to copy the gpg file to the tmp directory where lisa can see
    and read it.

6. Use **exit** to log out as linda, and now use **su - lisa** to become user lisa.

7. As lisa, use **gpg -d /tmp/hosts.gpg** to decrypt the hosts file.

 **Real World Scenario**

GPG File Encryption

On occasion, I need to send network security designs to one of my customers. This customer runs a sensitive business, so they want to make sure that nothing can go wrong with it and that the document cannot be intercepted. For that reason, I proposed to my customer to use GPG file encryption. After showing them how easy it is to use, they quickly agreed.

GPG Signing

The purpose of signing is to provide proof that something has actually been transmitted to the intended sender. To sign data, the user's private key is used. The signing process adds a digital signature to a message or file. If the receiver of the message has the public key of the sender in their GPG ring, this can automatically prove that the message actually comes from the intended sender. The procedure of signing is frequently used in email communications, but it can also be used to sign RPM files. You will learn how to do this in Exercise 11.4.

To sign a file, the basic command is `gpg -s file`. This command can also be combined with -e to encrypt the file. Use `gpg -e -s file` if you want to encrypt and sign a file at the same time. Notice that in order to sign a file, you don't need to have the GPG key of the recipient on your system; a signed file can be for anyone, and the verification of the signed file happens with the public key of the person who signed it. If you want to sign and encrypt the same file, you do need the public key of the recipient in your GPG ring of trust for the encryption part of the command.

If you've received a file that is signed with GPG, you can use `gpg -d` to open it. If you have the public key of the sender on your system, it will automatically be opened. If you don't have the public key, that means you cannot verify the signature of the file, but you still are able to open it.

Signing RPM Files

GPG is commonly used when working with RPM files. When installing an RPM file, this is done with root permissions, and since an RPM file may also contain scripts that are executed with root permissions, you must be sure that you can trust it. To ensure that you can trust the RPM files you're installing, many RPMs are signed with a GPG key. By default, yum will always do a GPG check, and if it fails, you cannot install the RPM.

When signing RPM packages, the creator of the RPM package needs to go through a signing procedure. The result is a signature that you can offer together with the RPM package. This signature can then be checked against the GPG key, which should be publicly available and imported by the person who wants to install the package. If the signature matches this publicly available GPG key, the person who downloads the package indeed is guaranteed that the package is signed by the GPG key, which is joined with the package. This procedure is convenient, but it doesn't offer a 100 percent guarantee. If the source offering the package gets compromised, a situation may arise where both the RPM package and the key are falsified. Signing packages, however, does increase confidentiality, because the hacker needs to perform two hacks instead of one before the forged package can be offered. Therefore, if you ever want to publish your own RPM packages, it's a good idea to offer a GPG signature as well. In Exercise 11.4, you'll learn how to use GPG signing on RPM packages.

EXERCISE 11.4

Signing RPM Packages with GPG Keys

In this exercise, you'll learn how to sign an RPM package with a GPG key. There is no need for a specific RPM package to perform this procedure; any RPM that you've copied from one of the default Red Hat repositories will do. All of the steps described in this procedure have to be executed as root.

1. To begin, you need a GPG key pair. To create it, use the **gpg --gen-key** command and specify the properties of the key. Before the key can be created, you need to generate some random data, so make sure to cause some disk activity to speed up the process of key generation.

2. After generating the GPG key pair, you need the key ID, and based on that, you need to create a key file. The key ID is what you see in the output of the gpg command in the pub line. You can also use **gpg --list-keys** to find the key ID for the key you've just created. The following command will create a file in the home directory of the current user, which you can use to sign the key. (Make sure to replace the key ID with the key ID of your GPG key.)

    gpg -a -o ~/RPM-GPG-KEY-test --export 455F7CBF

3. Next, in the home directory of that same user, you have to create an .rpmmacros file that has (at least) the following content. Notice that the GPG key ID is also used in this command:

    %_gpg_name 455F7CBF

4. At this point, you can (re)sign the package. The following command is used to sign an RPM package that has just been created and is available in the RPM build directory:

    rpm --resign ~/rpmbuild/RPMS/x86_64/test-1.0-1.fc14.x86_64.rpm

EXERCISE 11.4 *(continued)*

5. At this point, you have a signed package as well as a key, which the user who wants to verify the package integrity can use. To use it, you should publish the key together with the signed package and put it on a web server, for example. Before you do that, however, it is a good idea to test it to see whether it works. The following two commands perform a local test; the first command imports the GPG package, and in the next command, you use yum localinstall to install the package with the Yum package manager but without the need to set up a repository first:

```
rpm --import ~/RPM-GPG-KEY-test
yum localinstall ~/rpmbuild/RPMS/x86_64/test-1.0-1.fc14.x86_64.rpm
```

Summary

In this chapter, you learned about two different encryption-related commands. First you used the openssl command to create a self-signed SSL certificate. You also read when it is useful to do it this way and in which cases you're better off using a certificate that is signed by an official and widely recognized certificate authority (CA).

In the second part of this chapter, you read how to use GPG to add security to your server. Using GPG helps you sign files and messages so that the receiving party knows that they can be trusted. It also allows you to encrypt files and messages so that they cannot be read by unauthorized people.

Networking Red Hat Enterprise Linux

Chapter

12

Configuring OpenLDAP

TOPICS COVERED IN THIS CHAPTER:

✓ Understanding OpenLDAP

✓ Configuring a Base OpenLDAP Server

✓ Populating the OpenLDAP Database

✓ Using OpenLDAP for Authentication

If you're running a single Red Hat Enterprise Linux Server or even just a few servers, there is no problem in managing configuration files on each individual server. However, if you're responsible for operating dozens of servers, you'll need a solution that helps you maintain essential system information from a single location in your network. An LDAP server is such a solution, and in this chapter you'll learn how to set up OpenLDAP for authenticating users on the network.

Understanding OpenLDAP

The *Lightweight Directory Access Protocol (LDAP)* is a solution to access centrally stored information over a network. This centrally stored information is organized in a directory that follows the X.500 standard.

Apart from being a protocol to access information in a directory, LDAP has developed into a specification to create such a Directory by itself. Because it is an open source solution, in Linux environments, OpenLDAP is one of the most commonly used LDAP directory services.

Apart from OpenLDAP, some proprietary directory services exist as well. One of these is the Fedora directory, which was introduced in 2005 and has been used in previous versions of Red Hat. Development of this directory service has been discontinued in favor of OpenLDAP.

Types of Information in OpenLDAP

An LDAP server like OpenLDAP is typically used to disclose information that is important for many servers and clients in a network. This normally includes users and groups, and it might encompass information about systems in the network as well. However, the scope of OpenLDAP isn't restricted to this type of information. Originally, the X.500 standard was developed as a phone Directory, and some telecom providers still use an online Directory of all their customers that runs on OpenLDAP.

The LDAP Name Scheme

One of the typical properties in OpenLDAP is that it is organized in a hierarchical manner. This hierarchical setup is organized more or less like a DNS hierarchy is organized.

The advantage of this approach is that information can be grouped into containers where it is really needed, and clients can refer to the actual location where this information is stored.

The OpenLDAP hierarchy often follows the way a DNS hierarchy is set up. However, while specifying where a certain item exists in the hierarchy, it is common to refer to the specific type of item in that hierarchy. If, for instance, there is a user linda in the hierarchy `Colorado.example.com`, the fully distinguished name of this user is referred to as `cn=linda, dc=Colorado,dc=example,dc=com`.

Notice that in the fully distinguished names of objects in the LDAP hierarchy, a comma is used as a separator and not a dot, which is common in DNS. Also, notice the way you refer to the type of object. In the example of `cn=linda,dc=Colorado,dc=example,dc=com`, two object types are used.

cn   This is short for *common name*. It is a generic way to refer to *leaf entries*, which are the end objects, such as users and groups, that by themselves cannot contain anything else.

dc   This is short for *domain component*. It is used to refer to one of the container entries in the LDAP hierarchy. If in a setup the LDAP hierarchy is mapped to a DNS hierarchy, typically all the DNS domains are referred to as dc objects.

In this chapter, I'll use the cn and dc entry types only. However, these are not the only entry types that can be used in OpenLDAP; many others are commonly used as well. Although they're interesting, using these other entry types is not a requirement to set up a working OpenLDAP directory server, which can be used for network authentication.

> When learning about OpenLDAP, you'll often hear the word *entry*, which in OpenLDAP is anything that can be used in the LDAP database. In the context of this chapter, where the purpose is to set up an OpenLDAP directory server to be used for authentication, entries are often users and groups. The information that is directly associated with an entry is stored in its attributes. The LDAP schema defines which types of entries use which attributes.

As you've seen, by using the different LDAP entry types, you can set up a hierarchical Directory structure. This is the reason why OpenLDAP is so widely used. You can easily build an OpenLDAP hierarchy where objects in other locations are easily referred to without storing them on local servers. This makes OpenLDAP a lightweight Directory, especially if compared to other directory servers, such as Microsoft's Active Directory.

Replication and Referrals

Among the most important reasons why LDAP has replaced Network Information System (NIS), commonly used on older UNIX and Linux versions, is that it is possible to set up a solution that consists of multiple servers all over the world. This is accomplished by setting up OpenLDAP Directories in a hierarchical way and telling servers that contain a copy of the database for a specific domain how they can contact servers, which contain the information used elsewhere in the hierarchy. To do this, LDAP uses referrals. A *referral* is a specification in the configuration file of an LDAP server that specifies where it can find other LDAP servers that it needs for specific information.

Another very useful feature of OpenLDAP is that it can use *replication*. This means you can set up an OpenLDAP Directory in a way in which there is no single point of failure, because the information is available on multiple servers in the hierarchy. To accomplish this goal, OpenLDAP uses `slurpd`, a daemon that runs on your Linux server to make sure that all the information that is added to a local copy of the database is also replicated to all remote copies of the database.

Configuring a Base OpenLDAP Server

After learning something about LDAP base terminology, you'll now discover how to set up a base OpenLDAP server. The goal is not to do anything very complicated; you'll just learn how to set up a single instance of an LDAP server that can be used by multiple clients in your network for authentication. To configure a base OpenLDAP server, you need to follow these steps:

1. Install the OpenLDAP software.

2. Configure the LDAP process to service your needs.

3. Run the OpenLDAP server.

Once you've completed these steps, you can continue and add information to the LDAP database.

Installing and Configuring OpenLDAP

Installing OpenLDAP is not hard. Just run the following command to install everything you need on your server:

```
yum install -y openldap openldap-clients openldap-servers
```

This will copy about 5MB of files to your server, after which you can start OpenLDAP's configuration. In contrast to the configuration of other services, OpenLDAP doesn't contain a single configuration file. Instead, it uses a configuration directory, which by itself is organized in a way that is typical for LDAP. This means you'll have to run some specific utilities against this directory to configure it in the appropriate manner. In most cases, however, you don't need to make any changes to the default configuration that is specified in /etc/openldap/slapd.d/cn=config.ldif.

The configuration for the LDAP process is stored in a file that is created in the LDIF format. This is the *LDAP Input Format (LDIF)*, a specific format that allows you to enter information into the LDAP Directory. You'll use this format later, while adding entries to the LDAP database. You'll also use this format to change the base configuration of your LDAP server. In Exercise 12.1, you'll learn how to change some base parameters for your LDAP server.

Apart from the basic LDAP parameters that you'll use to specify items such as the number of connections the server can support or the timeouts it should apply, there are also some database-specific settings. These are located in /etc/openldap/slapd.d/cn=config/olcDatabase={2}bdb.ldif and contain parameters like the LDAP root user and the base DN. You'll also learn in the exercise how to change parameters in this file.

EXERCISE 12.1

Changing the Base LDAP Configuration

In this exercise, you'll change a few basic parameters for your LDAP server. This exercise also lets you become familiar with the base procedures for modifying information in the LDAP Directory.

1. Open a root terminal, and type **service slapd stop**. You'll probably get a FAILED message, because the service wasn't running yet. It's important, however, to stop the LDAP service before making modifications to its configuration.

2. Use an editor to open the file /etc/openldap/slapd.d/cn=config.ldif, and find the parameter olcConnMaxPending. This parameter specifies the maximum number of pending requests, which is set to 100. If you want to configure the LDAP server to offer unauthenticated access to its information, you might be better off setting this parameter a bit higher, so change its value to **200**.

3. Now find the olcIdleTimeout parameter. This parameter specifies how long the LDAP server waits before closing an idle session. If your LDAP server suffers performance problems, it's a good idea to set this to a limited amount of time, such as **90**.

4. Next, make sure to include the olcReferral parameter, which is not in the configuration file by default. You're not going to change it, but it is good to know that, with this parameter, you can tell your LDAP server to check another LDAP server if it can't find specific information. Use the URL format to refer to the other server, as in olcReferral: ldap://server.example.com. You can now close the cn=config.ldif file and write your changes.

5. You have finished the generic configuration of your LDAP server. Now you'll need to change some parameters in the LDAP database backend, which is in /etc/openldap/slapd.d/cn=config/olcDatabase={2}bdb.ldif. Open this file with an editor. It's a good idea to create a dedicated root user account first, that is, a user who has permissions to change information in the LDAP database. Look for the parameter olcRootDN and change it to the following: **olcRootDN: cn=linda,dc=example,dc=com**.

6. Open a second terminal window, and from there, use **slappasswd** to create a hash for the root password you want to use. Next, in the cn=config.ldif file, include the olcRootPW parameter, and copy the hashed password to the argument of this parameter. Listing 12.1 shows you what to do.

Listing 12.1: Setting a password for the LDAP root user

```
[root@hn1 ~]# slappasswd
New password:
Re-enter new password:
{SSHA}mrMb/MJ30amKUnP3KYPOMz9KNBfAB8pQ
olcRootPW: {SSHA}mrMb/MJ30amKUnP3KYPOMz9KNBfAB8pQ
```

7. Finally, search the olcSuffix directive, and make sure it has the default fully quali-fied domain name that you want to use to start LDAP searches. To set this domain to dc=example,dc=com, include this: **olcSuffix: dc=example,dc=com**. Next, close the editor with the configuration file.

8. Use **service slapd restart** to restart the LDAP server. At this point, you should be ready to start populating it with entry information.

Your LDAP server is now configured. Only the last step remains. You should make sure that the slapd process is started automatically when your server boots. To do this, use **chkconfig slapd on**, and you're ready to use your server.

Populating the OpenLDAP Database

Now that the slapd process has its basic configuration, you're ready to start populating it. To do this, you need to create LDIF files. These are the standard LDAP input files in which the entries and all the properties that you want to define for these entries are specified. Before adding users and groups that you can use to authenticate on a Linux machine, you first need to create the base structure. In this base structure, you'll create the LDAP domain (which often matches the name your organization uses in DNS). Some organizational units are also often used.

Creating the Base Structure

The use of organizational unit objects can help you in providing additional structure to the LDAP database. Particularly if you're planning on adding in different types of entries, such as users, groups, computers, printers, and more to the LDAP Directory, it makes it easier to put every entry type into its own container. For that purpose, the organizational unit (entry type ou) is used.

To build them, you can create an initial LDIF file similar to the example shown in Listing 12.2. This file allows you to create the base container, which is dc=example,dc=com, and it creates two organizational units with the names users and groups in that container. A minimal number of attributes are used, so if you want to follow this sample configuration, make sure that the attributes mentioned here are used.

Listing 12.2: Sample LDIF file

```
[root@hnl ~]# cat base.ldif
dn: dc=example,dc=com
objectClass: dcObject
objectClass: organization
o: example.com
dc: example

dn: ou=users,dc=example,dc=com
objectClass: organizationalUnit
objectClass: top
ou: users

dn: ou=groups,dc=example,dc=com
objectClass: organizationalUnit
objectClass: top
ou: groups
[root@hnl ~]#
```

In the LDIF file, you can see that each section defines one entry. To begin, you see the top-level entry in this database, which is dc=example,dc=com. For each of these entries, you'll need to define which objectClass they are members of. At the end of the three sections that are added here, the actual object is created. This happens in the line dc: example (which creates the dc example) and in the two lines ou: users and ou: groups (which create these objects in the dc=example,dc=com domain).

To add this information to the LDAP Directory, you'll need to use the ldapadd command. With this command, you'll specify the name of the administrative user you've created while setting up the LDAP Directory and the password you've set for this user. In our case, where the administrator user is cn=linda,dc=example,dc=com, the command would appear as follows:

```
ldapadd -x -D "cn=linda,dc=example,dc=com" -w password -f base.ldif
```

When adding information to an LDAP database, it's also useful if you can verify that the information has been added correctly. The tool to use for this purpose is ldapsearch. This tool requires a number of parameters. You'll need to use the following options at least:

-x Indicates that simple authentication should be used.

-D Specifies the account you want to use to get the requested information from the LDAP Directory.

-w Specifies the password to use. Notice that the password is entered as clear text on the command line.

-b Specifies the base context to use.

When using ldapsearch, you'll also need to specify exactly what it is you are seeking. To see all the information, you can add "(objectclass=*)" to the command. This means that to get the information from the LDAP Directory you've just entered, you can now use the following command:

```
ldapsearch -x -D "cn=linda,dc=example,dc=com" -w password -b "dc=example,dc=com"
"(objectclass=*)"
```

Listing 12.3 shows you what this command and its output should look like.

Listing 12.3: Displaying information from the LDAP Directory

```
[root@hnl ~]# ldapsearch -x -D "cn=linda,dc=example,dc=com" -w password
 -b "dc=example,dc=com" "(objectclass=*)"
# extended LDIF
#
# LDAPv3
# base <dc=example,dc=com> with scope subtree
# filter: (objectclass=*)
# requesting: ALL
#

# example.com
dn: dc=example,dc=com
objectClass: dcObject
objectClass: organization
o: example.com
dc: example

# users, example.com
dn: ou=users,dc=example,dc=com
objectClass: organizationalUnit
objectClass: top
```

```
ou: users

# groups, example.com
dn: ou=groups,dc=example,dc=com
objectClass: organizationalUnit
objectClass: top
ou: groups

# search result
search: 2
result: 0 Success

# numResponses: 4
# numEntries: 3
[root@hnl ~]#
```

In Exercise 12.2, you'll put this all together to create your own base LDAP Directory contents.

EXERCISE 12.2

Creating the Base LDAP Directory Structure

In this exercise, you'll create the base LDAP structure that you're going to use. Follow the examples just discussed to ensure that your LDAP Directory is ready for adding users and groups later.

1. Use an editor to create the LDIF file from Listing 12.2, and save it using the name **base.ldif**.

2. Make sure the slapd process is started.

3. Import the LIDF file using **ldapadd -x -D "cn=linda,dc=example,dc=com" -w password -f base.ldif**.

4. Use **ldapsearch -x -D "cn=linda,dc=example,dc=com" -w password -b "dc=example,dc=com" "(objectclass=*)"** to verify that the information has been added correctly to the LDAP database.

Understanding the Schema

When working with any database, you need to define which kinds of entries you can add to the database. In OpenLDAP, this is done by defining the schema. The *schema* is a collection of files that is found in /etc/openldap/schema. Everything you need to use OpenLDAP for basic functions is available in the schema by default. However, if you want to add functionality, you'll often have to include additional schema files.

One case where you might want to add additional schema files is for the inclusion of DHCP information in the LDAP Directory. Just make sure the dhcp.schema file is installed. To do this, you can use yum whatprovides to find the appropriate file and then install the package from which that file is derived. In Exercise 12.3, you'll install the schema file for DHCP. This provides a good example of how to install schema files in general.

EXERCISE 12.3

Installing the Schema File for DHCP

In this exercise, you'll find and install the schema file for DHCP. Using this procedure teaches you how to install schema files in general, which is useful if you want to include some custom information in your LDAP Directory.

1. Use **yum whatprovides "*/dhcp.schema"** to find the name of the package that contains the schema file for DHCP. It should yield dhcp, which is the generic package used to install a DHCP server. (This topic is covered in Chapter 13, "Configuring Your Server for File Sharing.")

2. Use **yum install dhcp** to install the package.

3. Open a terminal, and use **cd** to go to the /etc/openldap/schema directory. You'll see that the dhcp.schema file is now listed in this directory.

Once the schema files you need are installed, you can view them in the /etc/openldap/schema directory. Even though modifying schema files goes well beyond the scope of this chapter, it is good to know that schema files are just readable text files that define which entries can exist at which location in the LDAP Directory.

Everything in OpenLDAP consists of ASCII text and can thus be tuned to fit your needs, which is exactly the reason why OpenLDAP is such a commonly used Directory server. In Listing 12.4, you'll see the first lines of the dhcp.schema file, which defines which attributes can be used by the DHCP entry in the LDAP database.

Listing 12.4: Schema files are ASCII text files.

```
attributetype ( 2.16.840.1.113719.1.203.4.48
        NAME 'dhcpFailOverPrimaryPort'
        EQUALITY integerMatch
        DESC 'Port on which primary server listens for connections from
 its fail over peer (secondary server)'
        SYNTAX 1.3.6.1.4.1.1466.115.121.1.27  )
```

```
attributetype ( 2.16.840.1.113719.1.203.4.49
        NAME 'dhcpFailOverSecondaryPort'
        EQUALITY integerMatch
        DESC 'Port on which secondary server listens for connections
 from its fail over peer (primary server)'
        SYNTAX 1.3.6.1.4.1.1466.115.121.1.27  )


attributetype ( 2.16.840.1.113719.1.203.4.50
        NAME 'dhcpFailOverResponseDelay'
        EQUALITY integerMatch
        DESC 'Maximum response time in seconds, before Server assumes
 that connection to fail over peer has failed'
        SYNTAX 1.3.6.1.4.1.1466.115.121.1.27  )


attributetype ( 2.16.840.1.113719.1.203.4.51
        NAME 'dhcpFailOverUnackedUpdates'
        EQUALITY integerMatch
        DESC 'Number of BNDUPD messages that server can send before it receives
BNDACK from its fail over peer'
        SYNTAX 1.3.6.1.4.1.1466.115.121.1.27  )


attributetype ( 2.16.840.1.113719.1.203.4.52
        NAME 'dhcpFailOverSplit'
        EQUALITY integerMatch
        DESC 'Split between the primary and secondary servers for fail
 over purpose'
        SYNTAX 1.3.6.1.4.1.1466.115.121.1.27  )


attributetype ( 2.16.840.1.113719.1.203.4.53
        NAME 'dhcpFailOverLoadBalanceTime'
        EQUALITY integerMatch
        DESC 'Cutoff time in seconds, after which load balance is disabled'
        SYNTAX 1.3.6.1.4.1.1466.115.121.1.27  )


attributetype ( 2.16.840.1.113719.1.203.4.54
        NAME 'dhcpFailOverPeerDN'
        EQUALITY distinguishedNameMatch
        DESC 'The DNs of Fail over peers. In case of locator object,
 this will be list of fail over peers in the tree. In case of Subnet
 and pool, it will be a single Fail Over Peer'
        SYNTAX 1.3.6.1.4.1.1466.115.121.1.12  )
```

```
#List of all servers in the tree
attributetype ( 2.16.840.1.113719.1.203.4.55
        NAME 'dhcpServerDN'
        EQUALITY distinguishedNameMatch
        DESC 'List of all  DHCP Servers in the tree. Used by dhcpLocatorObject'
        SYNTAX 1.3.6.1.4.1.1466.115.121.1.12 )


attributetype ( 2.16.840.1.113719.1.203.4.56
        NAME 'dhcpComments'
        EQUALITY caseIgnoreIA5Match
        DESC 'Generic attribute that allows coments  within any DHCP object'
        SYNTAX 1.3.6.1.4.1.1466.115.121.1.26 SINGLE-VALUE )
```

Managing Linux Users and Groups in LDAP

In this section, you'll learn how to manage Linux user and group accounts in an LDAP Directory. You'll learn how to add users and groups, how to set passwords for LDAP users, and how to change the group membership for users. You'll also learn how to delete entries from the LDAP Directory.

Adding LDAP Users

To add anything to an LDAP Directory, you need to create an LDIF file. This file needs to contain definitions for all attributes that are required for the entries you want to create. Once the LDIF file is created, you can use ldapadd to import it into the Directory. In Listing 12.5, you can see what an LDIF file designed to import user accounts into the Directory looks like.

Listing 12.5: LDIF file for user import

```
[root@hnl ~]# cat lisa.ldif
dn: uid=lisa,ou=users,dc=example,dc=com
objectClass: top
objectClass: account
objectClass: posixAccount
objectClass: shadowAccount
cn: lisa
uid: lisa
uidNumber: 5000
gidNumber: 5000
homeDirectory: /home/lisa
```

```
loginShell: /bin/bash
gecos: lisa
userPassword: {crypt}x
shadowLastChange: 0
shadowMax: 0
shadowWarning: 0
[root@hnl ~]#
```

 Real World Scenario

Finding the Admin User

A common problem with openldap is that the admin user is unknown. Using ldapsearch on the Directory doesn't help, because the name of the user who is used to manage data in the Directory isn't in the Directory itself—it's in the database file. If you ever need to find which user is used as the admin user, log in as root to the machine on which Open-LDAP is configured and open the file olcDatabase={2}bdb.ldif. Look for the olcRootDN parameter in this file, which contains the name of the admin account. The olcRootPW parameter contains the hashed password. If you don't know that either, use slappasswd to generate a new hash and copy it to the olcRootDN parameter in olcDatabase={2}bdb .ldif. After doing that, you can log in with the new password.

As you can see, multiple properties of the user are defined in the LDIF file. In the example in Listing 12.4, you can see the following specifications:

Dn   The complete name of the user you want to create.

objectClass   This is used to define the properties of the user account (see the following note).

Cn   The common name, which is the full object definition in the LDAP Directory.

Uid   The username as it is required for every Linux user account. This field corresponds with the username in /etc/passwd. Notice that it is not the numeric UID that is defined in /etc/passwd.

uidNumber   The numeric UID that each Linux user is required to have.

gidNumber   The numeric ID of the primary group of the user.

homeDirectory   The directory in the file system that is to be used as the home directory for the user.

loginShell   The shell that is started after the user has successfully logged in.

gecos The information field that is used to specify additional information for the user.

userPassword The user password. You don't set the real password here. However, for every user you use the text {crypt}x, which indicates that the user is using an encrypted password. To actually set the password, use ldappasswd as discussed in the next section.

shadowLastChange The value that is normally in /etc/shadow that indicates when the password was changed the last time.

shadowMax The value that normally is used in /etc/shadow to specify the maximum number of days the password can be used.

shadowWarning The value that normally is used in /etc/shadow to specify when users should get a warning that they should change their passwords.

> To define the attributes of entries in an LDAP Directory, the entries inherit these from superclasses. A *superclass* is an entry that contains a set of specific attributes that are used by many other entries. Instead of specifying each of these attributes for every individual entry that is added, you'll need to refer only to the superclass that is to be used. In an LDIF file, this is done by including the objectClass lines. In the sample LDIF file in Listing 12.5, for example, you can see that the entries of a user account come from four different superclasses in the schema. This is not something you typically need to change, but it's good to know how it works anyway.

Once you have generated an LDIF for the user accounts you want to create, you can use ldapadd to import it. Assuming the name of the LDIF file is lisa.ldif, the administrator user account cn=linda,dc=example,dc=com would use the following command to complete the import:

```
ldapadd -x -D "cn=linda,dc=example,dc=com" -w password -f lisa.ldif
```

Setting the Password for LDAP Users

Now that you have imported a user account in the LDAP Directory, you still need to set its password. To do this, as the LDAP administrator, you can use the ldappasswd command. The following example shows you how the LDAP administrator linda uses ldappasswd to set the password for user lisa to mypassword:

```
ldappasswd -s mypassword -D "cn=linda,dc=example,dc=com" -w password -x "uid=lisa,
ou=users,dc=example,dc=com"
```

In Exercise 12.4, you'll create a user in the LDAP Directory.

EXERCISE 12.4

Creating an LDAP User

In this exercise, you'll create an LDAP user and set a password for this user. You'll also use ldapsearch to verify that the LDAP user was created successfully.

1. Create an LDIF file with the following contents, and save it to your home directory as lisa.ldif:

```
dn: uid=lori,ou=users,dc=example,dc=com
objectClass: top
objectClass: account
objectClass: posixAccount
objectClass: shadowAccount
cn: lori
uid: lori
uidNumber: 5001
gidNumber: 5001
homeDirectory: /home/lori
loginShell: /bin/bash
gecos: lori
userPassword: {crypt}x
shadowLastChange: 0
shadowMax: 0
shadowWarning: 0
```

2. Use the following command to import the user into the Directory:

```
ldapadd -x -D "cn=linda,dc=example,dc=com" -w password -f lori.ldif
```

3. To set the password for the user lori that you just created to mypassword, use the following command:

```
ldappasswd -s mypasswd -D "cn=admin,dc=example,dc=com" -w password
 "uid=lori,ou=users,dc=example,dc=com"
```

4. To verify that you created the user account successfully, you can use the ldapsearch command. By default, no authentication is required to get user information from an LDAP Directory, so the following command would work and give you the user account information as it is defined in the LDAP Directory:

```
ldapsearch -x -b "dc=example,dc=com" "(cn=lisa)"
```

Using an LDIF Template File

It's a lot of work to create an LDIF file for each individual user you want to create. You can simplify the process by using template files and the search and replace feature in vi to change the default username.

To try this approach, you can create a file with a name such as user.ldif. Don't specify a username, but use the text MYUSER instead. (It's a good idea to capitalize the text so that it is easy to see that it needs to be changed.) Next, if you want to create a user with the name lucy, use :%s/MYUSER/lucy/g in vi, which will change all occurrences of MYUSER to the name of the user you want to create. Don't forget to change the uidNumber and gidNumber as well. Now you're all set.

Creating LDAP Groups

You'll also use an LDIF file to create groups. The LDIF file for a group is easier to create than the typical LDIF file for a user account. In Listing 12.6, you can see what the file looks like to create a group account for user lisa, which you created earlier.

Listing 12.6: Example LDIF file for creating a group in LDAP

```
[root@hnl ~]# cat lisagroup.ldif
dn: cn=lisa,ou=groups,dc=example,dc=com
objectClass: top
objectClass: posixGroup
cn: lisa
userPassword: {crypt}x
gidNumber: 5000
```

Notice that the group has the name lisa. This is not a problem because the group is created in the group's ou. If you tried to add this group to the user's ou, this would produce an error message, because in that ou, an entry with the name lisa already exists.

After creating the LDIF file, you still need to add it to the LDAP Directory.

```
ldapadd -x -D "cn=linda,dc=example,dc=com" -w password -f lisagroup.ldif
```

Once you've created both the user account and its primary group in the LDAP Directory, your user account will be fully operational. In Exercise 12.5, you'll apply the procedure to add a group to the Directory.

EXERCISE 12.5

Adding an LDAP Group

In this exercise, you'll complete the creation of a user account by also adding its primary group to the LDAP Directory.

1. Create an LDIF file with the following contents, and save it as **lorigroup.ldif** to your home directory:

```
dn: cn=lorigroup,ou=groups,dc=example,dc=com
objectClass: top
objectClass: posixGroup
cn: lori
userPassword: {crypt}x
gidNumber: 5000
```

2. Use the following command to import the group into the LDAP Directory:

```
ldapadd -x -D "cn=linda,dc=example,dc=com" -w password -f lorigroup.ldif
```

3. The group has now been added, and this makes the user account lori ready for use.

Adding Users to LDAP Groups

You can also add secondary groups on your Red Hat Enterprise Linux Server. The procedure for this is similar to the creation of primary groups. Just create an LDIF file with all the group information as you saw in Listing 12.6, and add it to the Directory using **ldapadd**.

Once the group is created, you need to add users to it. Listing 12.7 shows you how to create an LDIF to modify an existing group and add some users to it. (The listing assumes you've already created an LDAP group with the name *sales*.)

Listing 12.7: Adding users to an LDAP group

```
dn: cn=sales,ou=groups,dc=example,dc=com
changetype: modify
add: memberuid
memberuid: lisa

dn: cn=sales,ou=groups,dc=example,dc=com
changetype: modify
add: memberuid
memberuid: linda

dn: cn=sales,ou=groups,dc=example,dc=com
changetype: modify
add: memberuid
memberuid: lori
```

As you can see, a definition of what to do is required for every user you want to add to the group. Once the LDIF file is created, you'll need to use the `ldapmodify` command to write the modifications to the Directory.

```
ldapmodify -x -D "cn=linda,dc=example,dc=com" -w password -f groupmod.ldif
```

Deleting Entries from an LDAP Directory

Deleting entries from an LDAP Directory isn't hard either. You just need to be specific when indicating exactly what you want to delete and then delete it using the `ldapdelete` command. The following command, for example, would remove user lisa and all associated properties from the Directory:

```
ldapdelete -D "cn=linda,dc=example,dc=com" -w password
"uid=lisa,ou=users,dc=example,dc=com"
```

Using OpenLDAP for Authentication

At this point, you've set up an OpenLDAP Directory server, and you've created accounts to use it for authentication. Now you'll just have to tell your Linux servers and workstations to use this server to authenticate user accounts. In Chapter 7, you learned how to use `system-config-authentication` or `authconfig` to configure your Red Hat Enterprise Linux machines for LDAP authentication. Review the information provided in that chapter to set up your RHEL machines.

Summary

In this chapter, you learned how to configure an OpenLDAP Server on your Red Hat Enterprise Linux Server. First you read how to set up OpenLDAP and how to use the `slapd` process itself. After that, you learned how to configure the OpenLDAP server as a Directory that can be used on your network for user authentication.

Chapter

13

Configuring Your Server for File Sharing

TOPICS COVERED IN THIS CHAPTER:

- ✓ Configuring NFS4
- ✓ Configuring Automount
- ✓ Configuring Samba
- ✓ Offering FTP Services
- ✓ File Sharing and SELinux

Linux can do great work as a file server. In this chapter, you'll learn about the options for doing so. First you'll read how to configure NFS4, a configuration solution that is often used when files need to be shared between different Linux computers. After learning how to use NFS4, you'll read how to make mounting NFS shares easy by configuring Automount. Next, you'll read how to offer file sharing in a way that is compatible with Windows by setting up a Samba server that offers shared files and printers to CIFS clients. FTP is a good solution for offering file access over the Internet when Samba and NFS are used in local network environments. Therefore, you'll learn how to set up FTP in this chapter. In the last part of this chapter, you'll read how SELinux can make offering file sharing services difficult and what you can do to open it for file sharing.

Configuring NFS4

NFS is the old solution for offering file-sharing services on UNIX platforms. Every brand of UNIX and Linux supports the NFS file system natively, and NFS functionality is offered through the kernel. This makes it a very fast solution. To use NFS, you need to install the NFS server package.

Because it is old, NFS security is not as developed as those in other file-sharing solutions, such as Samba. By default, the security is host-based. This means an administrator will allow or deny access to hosts, not to individual users. Once a host has established a connection, there isn't much to do to configure access for individual users. By default, a user on an NFS client will access files with the same user ID on the NFS server. This means that if on her client machine, user linda uses UID 502, she will access files on the NFS server with that same UID, even if it belongs to a completely different user. As you can imagine, this can be very confusing! Therefore, NFS works best in environments where user identities are shared over the network by using a solution such as LDAP, which you read about in Chapter 12.

NFSv4 is offered on Red Hat Enterprise Linux 6 and newer. This version provides some significant improvements over previous versions, such as the following:

- Filtering NFSv4 in a firewall is much easier than in the past.

- NFSv4 has better security options, including the option to use Kerberos.

- NFSv4 offers the option to make a pseudo-root mount, which allows users to mount everything to which they have access by issuing one mount only.

Setting Up NFSv4

Setting up an NFS server is not difficult. It basically consists of two tasks:

1. Create the configuration file /etc/exports, which contains the shares you want to offer.

2. Start and enable the NFS service.

You'll specify what you want to export in the file /etc/exports. The minimum setup also requires you to specify to whom you want to offer the share and what options you want to use on the share. The following line of code provides an example of a share that you can use in /etc/exports:

```
/data    192.168.1.0/24 (rw,no_root_squash)
```

As you can see, the line consists of three parts. First, there is the name of the directory you want to share, or /data in this example. Next, you specify to whom you want to offer access. In this example, access is offered to the network 192.168.1.0/24. As mentioned previously, the access restriction is always host-based, and many options are available to specify which hosts you want to give access. Here are some examples:

*.example.com   This specifies all hosts in the DNS domain example.com. (This works only if reverse DNS is set up properly.)

*   This specifies all hosts with no restrictions.

server1 server2   This specifies server1 and server2.

The last part of the export line specifies which options to use on the export. Many options are available. For a complete list, consult the man page of exports. Table 13.1 describes some common options.

TABLE 13.1   Commonly used export options

Option	Description
rw	Allows both read and write requests on the NFS volume.
ro	Allows only reads on the NFS share.
async	Improves performance by allowing the server to reply to requests before changes to the share are committed to storage. Using this option is faster but also increases the chance of losing data.
no_root_squash	Allows user root from an NFS client to work as user root on the NFS server as well. This should not be used because of security implications.

TABLE 13.1   Commonly used export options *(continued)*

Option	Description
fsid	Gives each NFS share a unique ID, which makes it easier to track. This option is especially important in high-availability clusters.
all_squash	Maps the user ID of any user to the anonymous user, which ensures that the NFS user has minimum rights on the server.
anonuid	Specifies to which user to map anonymous user requests.

After putting all of the shares in /etc/exports, you just need to (re)start the NFS server to activate them. To do this, use `service nfs restart`. After a successful start of the NFS server, you can use `showmount -e localhost` to check that the shares are available. As an alternative, you can also use the `exportfs -r` command to activate new exports. In Exercise 13.1, you'll apply this procedure to create your own NFS shares.

EXERCISE 13.1

Creating NFS Shares

In this exercise, you'll create a directory and offer access to that directory as an NFS share. You'll also set local permissions to make sure that users indeed have access to the share.

1. Use `mkdir /data` to create a directory with the name /data.

2. After creating the directory you want to share, make sure that incoming users also have permissions on that share. To do this, you'll use regular Linux permissions. In this case, use `chmod 777 /data` to open the share to anyone.

3. Use an editor to open the file /etc/exports, and insert the following line of code to share the /data directory with anyone:

   /data   *(rw,no_root_squash)

4. Use `service nfs restart` to restart the NFS server and have it offer the new share.

5. Use `chkconfig nfs on` to make sure that the NFS server starts at a server reboot.

6. To verify that the share is available, use `showmount -e localhost`, which shows all exported shares on the local computer.

After creating the NFS share, you'll need to make sure it is accessible through the firewall. On previous versions of NFS, this was difficult. In NFSv4, you can allow NFS access by opening port 2049 in the firewall.

Mounting an NFS Share

After creating an NFS share on the NFS server, you can access it from a client. To do this, you'll just mount it as if it were a regular file system. However, for mounting an NFS share, you'll need to include the name or IP address of the NFS server instead of the device name you would normally use to mount devices. Thus, use the following command to mount the NFS share you just created:

```
mount mynfsserver:/data /mnt
```

For temporary mounts, it is fine to use the /mnt directory. If you want to mount your NFS shares in a more persistent way, it makes sense to create a dedicated directory for this purpose.

Before mounting an NFS share, it may be useful to discover which shares are offered by that server. To do this, you can again use the showmount command with the -e option. This command shows all of the NFS shares offered by the server in question:

```
showmount -e mynfsserver
```

In Exercise 13.2, you'll mount an NFS share.

EXERCISE 13.2

Mounting an NFS Share

In this exercise, you'll learn how to access the NFS share you created in the previous exercise. To perform this exercise, use your virtual machine as the client machine.

1. On the client machine, use **showmount -e yournfsserver**. Make sure to replace yournfsserver with the actual name of the server. This shows the names of directories that are shared by the NFS server. In this case, it should show you the /data directory.

2. Mount the share on the local /mnt directory using **mount yournfsserver:/data /mnt**.

3. Type **mount** to verify that the NFS share has been mounted.

Among the cool new features of NFSv4 is the option to mount a *pseudo-root*. Imagine that, on an NFS server, three NFS exports are defined: /home, /data, and /files. Of course, you can use mount to mount each of these directories. However, now you can also mount all of them using a pseudo-root mount by entering the following on the client machine:

```
mount nfsserver:/ /mnt
```

As you can see, you'll mount the root directory of the NFS server. By doing this, you'll see all directories to which you have access appearing in the /mnt directory.

Making NFS Mounts Persistent

In the previous exercise, you mounted the NFS share manually. In some cases, you'll want NFS shares to be mounted automatically. To do this, you can insert a line in /etc/fstab. There is one issue, though: the file /etc/fstab is processed long before the network is available, and you don't want your machine to generate a failure on the NFS share that isn't accessible yet. To achieve this goal, you'll need to include the _netdev option in the NFS mount that you'll put in /etc/fstab. Using this option ensures that your system waits until the network is up before making this mount. The complete line you would put in /etc /fstab would appear as follows:

```
mynfsserver:/data       /data   nfs     _netdev 0 0
```

Configuring Automount

In some cases, putting your NFS mounts in /etc/fstab works just fine. In other cases, it doesn't work well, and you'll need a better way to mount NFS shares.

An example of such a scenario is a network where users are using OpenLDAP to authenticate, after which they get access to their home directories. To make sure users can log in on different workstations and still get access to their home directory, you can't just put an NFS share in /etc/fstab for each user.

Automount is a service that mounts NFS shares automatically. To configure it, you'll need to take care of three different steps:

1. Start the autofs service.

2. Edit the /etc/auto.master file.

3. Create an indirect file to specify what you want Automount to do.

The central configuration file in Automount is /etc/auto.master. You can see the contents of this file in Listing 13.1.

Listing 13.1: Sample /etc/auto.master

```
[root@hnl ~]# cat /etc/auto.master
#
# Sample auto.master file
# This is an automounter map and it has the following format
# key [ -mount-options-separated-by-comma ] location
# For details of the format look at autofs(5).
```

```
#
/misc    /etc/auto.misc
#
# NOTE: mounts done from a hosts map will be mounted with the
#       "nosuid" and "nodev" options unless the "suid" and "dev"
#       options are explicitly given.
#
/net     -hosts
#
# Include central master map if it can be found using
# nsswitch sources.
#
# Note that if there are entries for /net or /misc (as
# above) in the included master map any keys that are the
# same will not be seen as the first read key seen takes
# precedence.
#
+auto.master
[root@hn1 ~]#
```

In /etc/auto.master, directories are specified that Automount should monitor. One very interesting directory is /net, which is monitored by the automount -hosts mechanism. This means that in /net, mounts to hosts that have NFS shares available will be mounted automatically. A small demo shows best how this works. In Exercise 13.3, you'll use the /net directory to access an NFS share.

EXERCISE 13.3

Using /net to Access an NFS Share

In this exercise, you'll use the automount /net directory to access an NFS share.

1. On your virtual machine, use **service autofs restart** to (re)start Automount.

2. Use **cd /net**, and then use ls to monitor the contents of the /net directory. It should normally appear empty.

3. With /net as your current directory, use **cd yournfsserver** (replace yournfsserver with the name of your NFS server) and press Enter. You'll see that you have changed to a subdirectory with the name yournfsserver, which wasn't visible before in /net.

As you saw in the previous exercise, /net is used by Automount to give easy access to NFS servers. Apart from /net, you can also make your own Automount directories. To do that, you'll work with indirect files. This means that in /etc/auto.master, you'll define the directory to monitor and the file that defines the configuration for monitoring that directory. In that file, you'll next define exactly what to do in that directory. In Exercise 13.4, you'll create an Automount configuration for the /data directory. In this configuration, the auto.data file is used to specify what should be done in that directory.

EXERCISE 13.4

Creating an Automount Indirect Map

In this exercise, you'll define a directory that should be monitored by Automount.

1. On the virtual machine that is used as the NFS client, use **mkdir /data** to create a directory with the name /data.

2. Open the file /etc/auto.master with an editor, and include the following line:

   ```
   /data              /etc/auto.data
   ```

   This line defines the indirect map. It tells Automount that it can find the configuration for the /data directory in the file /etc/auto.data.

3. Open the file /etc/auto.data, and give it the following contents:

   ```
   files              -rw    yournfsserver:/data
   ```

4. Use **service autofs restart** to restart autofs. Next use **cd /data** and enter the ls command. You'll see no subdirectories. Now use **cd files** to activate the /data subdirectory files. You'll be in the /data/files directory now, and you'll see the contents of the /data share on the NFS server.

 If the /data directory in the previous example wasn't created, it will be created by the automounter. This reduces the chances that mounts fail.

In Exercise 13.4, you learned how to set up an Automount indirect map. In the auto.data file, you referred to a fixed NFS exported directory. In some cases, however, you'll need Automount to be more dynamic. Let's get back to the example where you configured an OpenLDAP server to handle authentication of clients on a central server in the network. After authenticating successfully, you'll want the clients to get access to their home directories. To accomplish this, you can again use Automount, but you'll need a way to refer to any subdirectory in the directory that is monitored by Automount.

Let's say that the home directories of LDAP users should always be mounted in /home /ldap. So, if LDAP user linda logs in, she would get access to /home/ldap/linda, which is her home directory; and if LDAP user lori logs in, she would get access to /home/ldap

/lori, which is also an NFS mount to her home directory. Assuming the home directories are available through an NFS export on the server with the name nfsserver, you could make the following Automount configuration.

First, in /etc/auto.master, include the following line to monitor the content of /home /ldap:

```
/home/ldap        /etc/auto.ldap
```

This line tells Automount that the additional configuration for /home/ldap is in the file /etc/auto.ldap. In that file, you would need to add the following:

```
*    -rw     nfsserver:/home/ldap/&
```

You can read this line as follows: for * (which is every subdirectory you can imagine) in the directory /home/ldap, a read-writable mount should be made to the & (which is the directory that uses the same name) on nfsserver:/home/ldap. In Exercise 13.5, you'll learn how to bring all of this together.

EXERCISE 13.5

Creating an Automount Configuration for Home Directories

In this exercise, you'll create an NFS share on your host computer, which gives access to user home directories. Next you'll set up Automount on the virtual machine to make mounting these home directories transparent.

1. On the host computer, open /etc/exports, and add the following line:

   ```
   /home              *(rw)
   ```

2. On the host computer, use **service nfs restart** to (re)start the NFS service.

3. On the host computer, use **useradd lucy** to create a user lucy and a directory /home/ lucy.

3. On the virtual machine, use **showmount -e yournfsserver** to verify that the NFS server offers the share.

4. On the virtual machine, open /etc/auto.master, and insert the following line:

   ```
   /home              /etc/auto.home
   ```

5. On the virtual machine, create the file /etc/auto.home, and give it the following contents:

   ```
   *    -rw     yournfsserver:/home/&
   ```

6. Restart Automount on the virtual machine using **service autofs restart**, and use **cd /home/lucy** to access the contents of /home/lucy. You'll now have access to / home/lucy on the NFS server.

Configuring Samba

You just learned how to use NFS for accessing file systems on remote computers. NFS is fast and convenient, but it also has an major disadvantage: it works only between Linux and UNIX machines. To offer access to other types of clients, you'll need to use a file-sharing protocol that is available on those clients as well. The *Common Internet File System (CIFS)* is such a protocol, and it is offered by the Linux Samba server. In this chapter, you'll learn how to set up a Samba server to offer file shares.

Samba is a very versatile service that you can use for different purposes on your network. Apart from sharing files, it can share printers and also offer Windows domain services such as directory services. You can even integrate Samba into an Active Directory domain and make it a member server of Active Directory. This means that all users in Active Directory get easy access to the resources you offer on the Samba server. The most popular use of Samba, however, is as a file server.

Setting Up a Samba File Server

Setting up a Samba file server is fairly straightforward. To set one up, you need to do the following:

1. Create a directory on the Linux file system on the Samba server.

2. If needed, create Linux users and give the appropriate permissions to the directory you just created.

3. Install the Samba server.

4. Define the share in /etc/samba/smb.conf.

5. Create a Samba user account that has access to the share.

6. (Re)start the Samba service.

7. Tell SELinux to give access to the Samba share.

A few of the previous steps require further explanation. Let's start with the user account. There are different ways to offer user access on Samba, which is also further explained in the next section in this chapter. To set up a basic Samba server, as you'll do in the following exercise, you'll need both a Linux user and a Samba user. The Linux user is used for Linux permissions on the local Linux file system. A Windows user cannot authenticate with the credentials of a Linux user, however. This is why you'll also need a Samba user with the same name as the Linux user. Typically, the Windows user needs to work only with the Samba user, which also means that only the password of the Samba user is relevant. The Linux user is for local Linux access only. As an administrator, you only need to make sure that it has the appropriate rights.

To define the Samba share, you'll put it in Samba's main configuration file, which is /etc/samba/smb.conf. The basic share definition is very simple: it gives a name to the share, and it tells Samba what to share. A minimum share definition might appear as follows:

```
[myshare]
```

```
        path=/mysharedfolder
```

When defining a share, you can also use many options to define to whom and with which access permissions the share should be available. It could, for example, appear as follows:

```
[myshare]
        path = /mydatafiles
        comment = some shared files
        allow hosts = 192.168.1.
        writable = yes
        public = yes
        write list = +mygroup
```

In this example share, some options are added. First a comment is specified, which makes it easier for clients to identify the share when they are browsing the network for available services. Next the `allow hosts` parameter restricts access to hosts that have an IP address starting with 192.168.1 only. The option `public = yes` makes it a public share that is accessible by anyone who has a Samba account to authenticate to this server. It is also writable, which is indicated by the option `writable = yes`. To write to the share, though, a user must be a member of the local Linux group `mygroup`.

Apart from the definition of many shares, you'll also find a [global] section in the beginning of each /etc/samba/smb.conf configuration file. In this section, you'll find the generic parameters that your Samba server is using, such as its workgroup name, the network interfaces on which it is listening, and the locations to which it writes its log files. You normally don't have to change anything here to set up a basic Samba server. In Listing 13.2, you can see an example of some of the parameters that are defined in the [global] section. For more details, read man (5) smb.conf.

Listing 13.2: The Samba [global] section defines generic Samba parameters

```
[root@hnl samba]# less smb.conf
[global]

# ---------------------- Network Related Options ----------------------
#
# workgroup = NT-Domain-Name or Workgroup-Name, eg: MIDEARTH
#
# server string is the equivalent of the NT Description field
#
# netbios name can be used to specify a server name not tied to the hostname
#
# Interfaces lets you configure Samba to use multiple interfaces
# If you have multiple network interfaces then you can list the ones
# you want to listen on (never omit localhost)
#
```

```
# Hosts Allow/Hosts Deny lets you restrict who can connect, and you can
# specifiy it as a per share option as well
#
        workgroup = MYGROUP
        server string = Samba Server Version %v

;       netbios name = MYSERVER

;       interfaces = lo eth0 192.168.12.2/24 192.168.13.2/24
;       hosts allow = 127. 192.168.12. 192.168.13.

# -------------------------- Logging Options ---------------------------
#
```

After specifying the directory you want to share and setting Linux permissions to it, you'll also need to create Samba user accounts. Before doing that, however, you need to make sure you have Linux user accounts with the corresponding names. Therefore, if you need a Samba account for Windows user lucy, you'll have to create Linux for user lucy first. To create a Samba user account, you'll use smbpasswd -a. For example, smbpasswd -a lucy would create Samba user named lucy on your system. In Exercise 13.6, you'll set up a Samba server on your host computer.

<hr>

EXERCISE 13.6

Setting Up a Samba Server

In this exercise, you'll walk through all the steps necessary to set up a Samba server. You'll start by creating a directory on the Linux file system and grant the appropriate permissions to this directory. Next, you'll install the Samba packages and create the share in Samba. After completing that, you'll create a Samba account, which makes the Samba server accessible for the designated Samba users.

1. Use **mkdir /sambafiles** to create a directory on the Linux file system.

2. Use **chmod 777 /sambafiles** to grant the appropriate permissions to the /sambafiles share. It's not the most elegant way to set security, but it's not local Linux security that matters here.

3. As root, use **yum -y install samba samba-common samba-client** to install all the required Samba server packages.

4. Open the file /etc/samba/smb.conf with an editor. Locate the workgroup parameter, and change it to workgroup = MYSAMBA.

5. Go to the bottom of the configuration file, and add the following share configuration:

    [sambafiles]

EXERCISE 13.6 *(continued)*

```
comment = samba files
path = /sambafiles
writable = yes
valid user = lucy, linda, lori
```

6. Use **useradd lucy** to create a user account for user lucy. Don't set the password, because Samba users don't need a password on the Linux system.

7. Use **smbpasswd -a lucy** to create Samba user lucy.

8. Use **service smb restart** to (re)start the Samba service and **chkconfig smb on** to make sure that it starts when the server boots.

9. Use **smbclient -L //localhost**. This will show you the current Samba server parameters, and you'll see that the share you just created is listed. The smbclient -L command will show a login prompt that you can ignore. Do this by pressing Enter twice.

Samba and SELinux

You've just created a Samba share, but for now it won't work. This is because you must apply some SELinux settings before being able to use Samba on Red Hat. Apart from some Booleans, which you can use, the most important change required is that you set the directories that you want to share with Samba to the samba_share_t context type. If you want to grant access to a Samba shared directory to other file-sharing services, you can also set the context type to public_content_t.

To set the appropriate Samba context type, use the following two commands:

```
semanage fcontext -a -t samba_share_t "/sambashare(/.*)?"
restorecon -R -v /sambashare
```

After making these changes, the Samba share should now be accessible. In Exercise 13.7, you can practice applying SELinux labels for Samba.

EXERCISE 13.7

Setting SELinux Labels for Samba

In this exercise, you'll set the SELinux labels that are required for directories shared with Samba.

1. As root, use **semanage fcontext -a -t samba_share_t "/sambashare(/.*)?"**.

2. Use **restorecon -R -v /sambashare** to make the new label effective.

Samba Advanced Authentication Options

When working with Samba, you can use different security options. This option is set in the [global] section of the /etc/samba/smb.conf file, and it determines where Samba looks for user authentication information. The default setting is security = user, which means that Samba needs a local Samba user account that is stored in a smbpasswd file.

The following authentication options are available:

security = share When using this option, a user does not need to send a username and password to a share before connecting to it. You can set it up so that a user has to enter a password before connecting. However, this would be a share-level password that is used by every user connecting to the share. Using it can be beneficial on an anonymous share, to where you want users to connect with limited permissions. When using this option, use the guest only parameter in the share. Never use it for shares that contain valuable data.

security = user This is the default security option, where a user must log in to the share before getting access.

security = domain This option works if your Samba server has been added to a Windows domain. (You can use the net utility on Linux to do that.) If used, Samba user account information is obtained from the Windows domain. You still need a local Linux account to handle permissions, though.

security = server This option uses an external server (such as another Samba server) to handle Samba authentication requests. It is best to avoid using this, because it isn't very secure.

security = ads This option makes Samba a member in a Windows Active Directory domain. It does not make it a domain controller but integrates Samba in the AD domain, which makes it easier to access resources in the AD domain or to set up access for AD users to resources in Samba.

Accessing Samba Shares

After setting up the Samba server, you'll need to access it. From Windows, you can set up a network share and point to the Samba server. There's no real difference in accessing a Samba share from Windows than from accessing a Windows share from Windows.

There are also some tools that you can use to access Samba shares on Linux. First you can use graphical tools, such as Nautilus, to connect to a Samba share. To list the Samba shares that are offered by a specific server, you can use smbclient -L (see Listing 13.3). This shows the names of all shares that are offered, and it also provides an option to log in to the Samba server. The smbclient interface is not very easy to use, however. When using smbclient -L to list shares, just press Enter when asked for a password. Entering a password is not required to list available shares.

Listing 13.3: Listing Samba shares

```
[root@hn1 ~]# smbclient -L //localhost
Enter root's password:
Anonymous login successful
Domain=[MYGROUP] OS=[Unix] Server=[Samba 3.5.10-114.el6]


        Sharename       Type        Comment
        ---------       ----        -------
        sambafiles      Disk        sambafiles
        IPC$            IPC         IPC Service (Samba Server Version
3.5.10-114.el6)
Anonymous login successful
Domain=[MYGROUP] OS=[Unix] Server=[Samba 3.5.10-114.el6]


        Server              Comment
        ---------           -------


        Workgroup           Master
        ---------           -------
[root@hn1 ~]#
```

Mounting the Samba share into the local file system is a commonly used option. You can either do this manually by using the `mount` command or make it automatic by putting the mount command in `/etc/fstab`.

When putting a Samba share in `/etc/fstab`, you'll also need to include the username and password required to gain access to the share. Because this is typically not information readable by just anyone in `/etc/fstab`, you can use a credentials file instead of the name and password. To do this, first create the credentials file and store it in a secure place that's not accessible to all users. You need to specify a user and password for every Samba user in the credentials file in the form shown in Listing 13.4.

Listing 13.4: Use a credentials file to automate Samba mounts in `/etc/fstab`

```
user=linda
password=secret
user=lori
password=drowssap
```

After creating a credentials file, you can enter a line in /etc/fstab to mount the Samba share. To refer to the share, you'll need to use the //server/share format. The following sample code snippet shows how you can mount Samba shares from /etc/fstab:

```
//mysambaserver/share   /data/samba   cifs   credentials=/root/credentials 0 0
```

In Exercise 13.8, you will practice mounting Samba shares from /etc/fstab.

EXERCISE 13.8

Mounting a Samba Share Using /etc/fstab

In this exercise, you'll set up your client computer to connect to the Samba share you just created. Perform all steps on the virtual machine that you're using as a client computer.

1. On the client computer, use **smbclient -L //yoursambaserver** to list the Samba shares on your Samba server. You'll see the share you created in Exercise 13.6.

2. Open /etc/fstab with an editor, and add the following line:

    ```
    //sambaserver/sambafiles   /mnt/samba   cifs   credentials=/root/credentials   0 0
    ```

3. Use an editor to create the file /root/credentials with the following content:

    ```
    user=lucy
    password=password
    ```

4. Use **mount -a** to mount the newly created share from /etc/fstab. Type **mount**, and you'll see that the Samba share is mounted on your computer.

Offering FTP Services

Samba and NFS are commonly used services designed to offer access to shared files within the same network. If you also want to share files with external users, FTP is a more suitable option. On Red Hat Enterprise Linux, vsftpd is the preferred FTP server.

Deploying vsftpd to offer access to shared files is easy to do. After installing the vsftpd package, it uses its default home directory, /var/ftp. If you create a /pub subdirectory within that directory, you can start putting files in it that will be accessible for anonymous FTP users. Remember that FTP is clear text, so extra security precautions should be taken.

To open vsftpd for authenticated users, you can change the settings in the configuration file /etc/vsftpd.conf. This is a very readable configuration file, which contains many settings examples and good documentation on how to use these settings. Listing 13.5 shows part of its contents.

Listing 13.5: Use /etc/vsftpd/vsftpd.conf to configure the vsftpd server

```
# Example config file /etc/vsftpd/vsftpd.conf
#
# The default compiled in settings are fairly paranoid. This sample file
# loosens things up a bit, to make the ftp daemon more usable.
# Please see vsftpd.conf.5 for all compiled in defaults.
#
# READ THIS: This example file is NOT an exhaustive list of vsftpd options.
# Please read the vsftpd.conf.5 manual page to get a full idea of vsftpd's
# capabilities.
#
# Allow anonymous FTP? (Beware - allowed by default if you comment this out).
anonymous_enable=YES
#
# Uncomment this to allow local users to log in.
local_enable=YES
#
# Uncomment this to enable any form of FTP write command.
write_enable=YES
#
# Default umask for local users is 077. You may wish to change this to 022,
# if your users expect that (022 is used by most other ftpd's)
local_umask=022
#
# Uncomment this to allow the anonymous FTP user to upload files. This only
# has an effect if the above global write enable is activated. Also, you will
# obviously need to create a directory writable by the FTP user.
#anon_upload_enable=YES
```

Table 13.2 describes some of the most interesting parameters in /etc/vsftpd/vsftpd .conf.

TABLE 13.2   vsftpd settings

Setting	Description
anonymous_enable	Use to enable anonymous users (enabled by default).
local_enable	Use to enable access for authenticated local users (enabled by default). Because it is insecure, this option should be disabled.

TABLE 13.2   vsftpd settings *(continued)*

Setting	Description
write_enable	Allows write access (by default only for authenticated users).
anon_upload_enable	Use this if you want to allow anonymous users to upload files. (Be sure you know what you're doing if you're planning to enable this option because using it has some security risks!)
xferlog_enable	Logs all FTP transfers.
chown_uploads	Change the owner of uploaded files. (This parameter can be useful if you want to allow anonymous users to upload files.)

After applying the required settings to your FTP server, you'll also need to make sure it is accessible. This requires setting the appropriate firewall rules and the SELinux settings as well. The next section in this chapter further explains SELinux and FTP. Before that, however, read what to do on the firewall.

First you'll need to open the firewall. Remember that if you've made custom modifications to your firewall configuration, you shouldn't use system-config-firewall anymore, so make sure to apply the proposed changes manually.

You'll need to load two firewall modules for FTP: nf_conntrack_ftp and nf_nat_ftp. The first allows FTP to track connections, which is an absolute requirement for opening both ports 20 and 21 on the firewall and the higher ports that are needed for active/passive connection. The second module, nf_nat_ftp, is required only if you want to offer FTP services through a NAT. To load these modules at all times when the firewall is initialized, put the following line of code in /etc/sysconfig/iptables_config:

```
IPTABLES_MODULES="nf_conntrack_ftp nf_nat_ftp"
```

After adding these two modules, you'll need to restart the firewall service, so use service iptables restart before continuing. Next you can open the FTP ports in the firewall. The following two commands allow you to do just that:

```
iptables -A INPUT -p tcp --dport 21 -j ALLOW
iptables -A INPUT -m state --state ESTABLISHED,RELATED -j ALLOW
```

If possible, try to determine which services you need to be accessible through the firewall before starting to configure anything. It's much easier to use system-config-firewall just once to open everything you need and then never touch the firewall configuration again.

In Exercise 13.9 you'll learn how to set up an Anonymous FTP Server.

EXERCISE 13.9

Enabling an Anonymous FTP Server

In this exercise, you'll learn how easy it is to set up your server for anonymous FTP access.

1. Use **yum -y install vsftpd**.

2. Use **service vsftpd start** to start the FTP server, and use **chkconfig vsftpd on** to make sure it starts when you reboot your server.

3. Use **yum -y install lftp** to install the lftp FTP client to your computer.

4. From a console, type **lftp localhost**. This opens an anonymous FTP client interface. From this interface, use **ls** to see the contents of the current directory, use **cd** to change directories, and use the **get** and **put** commands to download and upload files.

File Sharing and SELinux

When configuring file-sharing services, you'll also have to deal with SELinux. SELinux normally works with known services and gives them access to their default directories. File-sharing services typically give access to files no matter where they are stored, but you will need to make sure they can in this case.

The first step in configuring access for file-sharing services is to set the appropriate context type on directories. In the section on Samba, you read that public_content_t is a good option for opening a directory for different file-sharing services. Use semanage to set the context type, and use restorecon to apply it before starting to use any of the services discussed in this chapter.

A second step in the configuration process consists of setting the appropriate Booleans. It may not always be clear which Booleans are available for the services you're trying to configure, but there are some easy ways to find out. First you can use getsebool -a to display a list of all Booleans and use grep to filter out the appropriate Booleans. Use semanage boolean -l for more details on what the Booleans are doing. Listing 13.6 shows you how this works for FTP.

Listing 13.6: Finding the appropriate Booleans for your service

```
[root@hnl ~]# getsebool -a | grep ftp
allow_ftpd_anon_write --> off
```

```
allow_ftpd_full_access --> off
allow_ftpd_use_cifs --> off
allow_ftpd_use_nfs --> off
ftp_home_dir --> off
ftpd_connect_db --> off
httpd_enable_ftp_server --> off
tftp_anon_write --> off
[root@hnl ~]#
```

After finding the Boolean you want to set, use `setsebool -P` to set it. Don't forget the `-P` option, which makes the Boolean persistent.

If these generic approaches don't help you gain access to your service, you can also consult the appropriate man pages. If you use the command `man -k _selinux`, you'll see a list of man pages for all service-specific SELinux man pages that are available on your server (see Listing 13.7).

Listing 13.7: Use `man -k _selinux` to get a list of all service-specific SELinux man pages

```
[root@hnl ~]# man -k _selinux
abrt_selinux       (8)  - Security-Enhanced Linux Policy for the ABRT daemon
ftpd_selinux       (8)  - Security-Enhanced Linux policy for ftp daemons
git_selinux        (8)  - Security Enhanced Linux Policy for the Git daemon
httpd_selinux      (8)  - Security Enhanced Linux Policy for the httpd daemon
kerberos_selinux   (8)  - Security Enhanced Linux Policy for Kerberos
mysql_selinux      (8)  - Security-Enhanced Linux Policy for the MySQL daemon
named_selinux      (8)  - Security Enhanced Linux Policy for the
 Internet Name server (named) daemon
nfs_selinux        (8)  - Security Enhanced Linux Policy for NFS
pam_selinux        (8)  - PAM module to set the default security context
rsync_selinux      (8)  - Security Enhanced Linux Policy for the rsync daemon
samba_selinux      (8)  - Security Enhanced Linux Policy for Samba
squid_selinux      (8)  - Security-Enhanced Linux Policy for the squid daemon
ypbind_selinux     (8)  - Security Enhanced Linux Policy for NIS
```

Summary

In this chapter, you learned how to set up file-sharing services on your server. You learned how to work with NFSv4 to make convenient and fast file shares between Linux and UNIX computers. You also learned how to configure `autofs` to make it easy to access files that are offered by an NFS server.

You also read about Samba, which has become the de facto standard for sharing files between any client. All modern operating systems have a CIFS stack, which can communicate with a Samba service.

You also learned about setting up an FTP server in this chapter, which is a convenient way to share files on the Internet. Since when setting up file-sharing services you also need to take care of SELinux, this chapter concluded with a section on SELinux and file-sharing services.

Chapter
14

Configuring DNS and DHCP

TOPICS COVERED IN THIS CHAPTER:

- ✓ Understanding DNS
- ✓ Setting Up a DNS Server
- ✓ Understanding DHCP
- ✓ Setting Up a DHCP Server

In each network, some common services are used. Amongst the most common of these services are DNS and DHCP. DNS is the system that helps clients resolve an IP address in a name and vice versa. DHCP is the service that allows clients to obtain IP related configuration automatically. In this chapter, you'll learn how to set up these services.

Understanding DNS

Domain Name System (DNS) is the system that associates hostnames with IP addresses. Thanks to DNS, users and administrators don't have to remember the IP addresses of computers to which they want to connect but can do so just by entering a name, such as www. example.com. In this section, you'll learn how DNS is organized.

The DNS Hierarchy

DNS is a worldwide hierarchical system. In each DNS name, you can see the place of a server in the hierarchy. In a name like www.example.com, three parts are involved. First, there is the *top-level domain (TLD)* .com. This is one of the top-level domains that have been established by the Internet Assigned Numbers Authority (IANA), the organization that is the ultimate authority responsible for DNS naming. Other common top-level domains are .org, .gov, .edu, .mil, and the many top-level domains that exist for countries, such as .uk, .ca, .in, .cn, and .nl. Currently, the top-level domain system is changing, and a proposal has been released to make many more top domains available.

Each of the top-level domains has a number of *name servers*. These are the servers that have information on the hosts within the domain. The most important piece of information that the name servers of the top-level domain have is that relating to the domains that exist within that domain (the subdomain), such as redhat.com, example.com, and so forth. The name servers of the top-level domains need to know how to find the name servers of these second-tier domains.

Within the second-tier domains, subdomains can also exist, but often this is the level where individual hosts exist. Think of hostnames like www.example.com, ftp.redhat.com, and so on. To find these hosts, the second-tier domains normally have a name server that contains *resource records* for hosts within the domain, which are consulted to find the specific IP address of a host.

The *root domain* is at the top of the DNS hierarchy. This is the domain that is not directly visible in DNS names but is used to connect all of the top-level domains together.

Within DNS, a name server can be configured to administer just the servers within its domain. Often, a name server is also configured to administer the information in subdomains. The entire portion of DNS for which a name server is responsible is referred to as a *zone*. Consider Figure 14.1, where part of the DNS hierarchy is shown. There are a few subzones under `example.com` in this hierarchy. This does not mean that each of these subzones needs to have its own name server. In a configuration such as this, one name server in the `example.com` domain can be configured with resource records for all the subzones as well.

FIGURE 14.1   Part of a DNS hierarchy

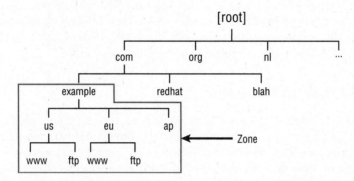

It is also possible to split subzones. This is referred to as the *delegation of subzone authority*. This means a subdomain has its own name server, which has resource records for the subdomain. In addition, the name server of the parent domain does not know which hosts are in the subdomain. This is the case between the `.com` domain and the `example.com` domain. You can imagine that name servers of the `.com` domain don't want to know everything about all that happens in the subzones. Therefore, the name server of a parent domain can delegate subzone authority. This means that the name server of the parent domain is configured to contact the name server of the subdomain to find out which resource records exist within that subdomain.

As an administrator of a DNS domain, you will not configure subzones frequently, that is, unless you are responsible for a large domain in which many subdomains exist that are managed by other organizations.

DNS Server Types

The DNS hierarchy is built by connecting name servers to one another. You can imagine that it is useful to have more than one name server per domain. Every zone has at least a *primary name server*, also referred to as the *master name server*. This is the server that is responsible for a zone and the one on which modifications can be made. To increase redundancy in case the master name server goes down, zones are also often configured with a *secondary* or *slave name server*. One DNS server can fulfill the role of both name server types. This means that an administrator can configure a server to be the primary name server for one domain and the secondary name server for another domain.

To keep the primary and secondary name servers synchronized, a process known as *zone transfer* is used. In a zone transfer, a primary server can push its database to the secondary name server, or the secondary name server can request updates from the primary name server. How this occurs depends on the way that the administrator of the name server configures it.

In DNS traffic, both primary and secondary name servers are considered to be *authoritative name servers*. This means that if a client gets an answer from the secondary name server about a resource record within the zone of that name server, it is considered to be an authoritative reply. This is because the answer comes from a name server that has direct knowledge of the resource records in that zone.

Apart from authoritative name servers, there are also *recursive name servers*. These are name servers that are capable of giving an answer, but they don't get the answer from their own database. This is possible because, by default, every DNS name server caches its most recent request. How this works is explained in the following section.

The DNS Lookup Process

To get information from a DNS server, a client computer is configured with a DNS resolver. This is the configuration that tells the client which DNS server to use. If the client computer is a Linux machine, the DNS resolver is in the configuration file /etc/resolv.conf.

When a client needs to get information from DNS, it will always contact the name server that is configured in the DNS resolver to request that information. Because each DNS server is part of the worldwide DNS hierarchy, each DNS server should be able to handle client requests. In the DNS resolver, more than one name server is often configured to handle cases where the first DNS server in the list is not available.

Let's assume that a client is in the example.com domain and wants to get the resource record for www.sander.fr. The following will occur:

1. When the request arrives at the name server of example.com, this name server will check its cache. If it has recently found the requested resource record, the name server will issue a recursive answer from cache, and nothing else needs to be done.

2. If the name server cannot answer the request from cache, it will first check whether a forwarder has been configured. A forwarder is a DNS name server to which requests are forwarded that cannot be answered by the local DNS server. For example, this can be the name server of a provider that serves many zones and that has a large DNS cache.

3. If no forwarder has been configured, the DNS server will resolve the name step-by-step. In the first step, it will contact the name servers of the DNS root domain to find out how to reach the name servers of the .fr domain.

4. After finding out which name servers are responsible for the .fr domain, the local DNS server, which still acts on behalf of the client that issued the original request, contacts a name server of the .fr domain to find out which name server to contact to obtain information about the sander domain.

5. After finding the name server that is authoritative for the sander.fr domain, the name server can then request the resource record it needs. It will cache this resource record and send the answer back to the client.

DNS Zone Types

Most DNS servers are configured to service at least two zone types. First there is the regular zone type that is used to find an IP address for a hostname. This is the most common use of DNS. In some cases, however, it is needed to find the name for a specific IP address. This type of request is handled by the in-addr.arpa zones.

In in-addr.arpa zones, PTR resource records are configured. The name of the in-addr .arpa zone is the reversed network part of the IP address followed by in-addr.arpa. For example, if the IP address is 193.173.10.87, the in-addr.arpa zone would be 87.10.173 .in-addr.arpa. The name server for this zone would be configured to know the names of all IP addresses within that zone.

Although in-addr.arpa zones are useful, they are not always configured. The main reason is that DNS name resolving also works without in-addr.arpa zones; reverse name resolution is required in specific cases only.

Setting Up a DNS Server

The Berkeley Internet Name Domain (BIND) service is used to offer DNS services on Red Hat Enterprise Linux. In this section, you'll learn how to set it up. First you'll read how to set up a cache-only name server. Next you'll learn how to set up a primary name server for your own zone. Then you'll learn how to set up a secondary name server and have it synchronize with the primary name server.

If you want to set up DNS in your own environment for testing purposes, use the example.com domain. This domain is reserved as a private DNS domain on the Internet. Thus, you can be assured that nothing related to example.com will ever go out on the Internet so that it doesn't give you any conflicts with other domains. As you have already noticed, nearly every example in this book is based on the example.com domain.

Setting Up a Cache-Only Name Server

Running a cache-only name server can be useful when optimizing DNS requests in your network. If you run a BIND service on your server, it will do the recursion on behalf of all clients. Once the resource record is found, it is stored in cache on the cache-only name server. This means that the next time a client needs the same information, it can be provided much faster.

Configuring a cache-only name server isn't difficult. You just need to install the BIND service and make sure that it allows incoming traffic. For cache-only name servers, it also makes sense to configure a forwarder. In Exercise 14.1, you'll learn how to do this.

EXERCISE 14.1

Configuring a Cache-Only Name Server

In this exercise, you'll install BIND and set it up as a cache-only name server. You'll also configure a forwarder to optimize speed in the DNS traffic on your network. To complete this exercise, you need to have a working Internet connection on your RHEL server.

1. Open a terminal, log in as root, and run **yum -y install bind-chroot** on the host computer to install the bind package.

2. With an editor, open the configuration file /etc/named.conf. Listing 14.1 shows a portion of this configuration file. You need to change some parameters in the configuration file to have BIND offer its services to external hosts.

Listing 14.1: By default, BIND offers its services only locally

```
[root@hnl ~]# vi /etc/named
named/                    named.iscdlv.key      named.root.key
named.conf                named.rfc1912.zones
[root@hnl ~]# vi /etc/named.conf
// See /usr/share/doc/bind*/sample/ for example named configuration files.
//

options {
        listen-on port 53 { 127.0.0.1; };
        listen-on-v6 port 53 { ::1; };
        directory        "/var/named";
        dump-file        "/var/named/data/cache_dump.db";
        statistics-file "/var/named/data/named_stats.txt";
        memstatistics-file "/var/named/data/named_mem_stats.txt";
        allow-query      { localhost; };
        recursion yes;

        dnssec-enable yes;
        dnssec-validation yes;
        dnssec-lookaside auto;

        /* Path to ISC DLV key */
        bindkeys-file "/etc/named.iscdlv.key";
};

logging {
        channel default_debug {
```

EXERCISE 14.1 *(continued)*

3. Change the file to include the following parameters: `listen-on port 53 { any; };` and `allow-query { any; };`. This opens your DNS server to accept queries on any network interface from any client.

4. Still in `/etc/named.conf`, change the parameter `dnssec-validation;` to `dns-server-validation no;`.

5. Finally, insert the line `forwarders x.x.x.x` in the same configuration file, and give it the value of the IP address of the DNS server you normally use for your Internet connection. This ensures that the DNS server of your Internet provider is used for DNS recursion and that requests are not sent directly to the name servers of the root domain.

6. Use the **`service named restart`** command to restart the DNS server.

7. From the RHEL host, use **`dig redhat.com`**. You should get an answer, which is sent by your DNS server. You can see this in the SERVER line in the dig response. Congratulations, your cache-only name server is operational!

Setting Up a Primary Name Server

In the previous section, you learned how to create a cache-only name server. In fact, this is a basic DNS server that doesn't serve any resource records by itself. In this section, you'll learn how to set up your DNS server to serve its own zone.

To set up a primary name server, you'll need to define a zone. This consists of two parts. First you'll need to tell the DNS server which zones it has to service, and next you'll need to create a configuration file for the zone in question.

To tell the DNS server which zones it has to service, you need to include a few lines in `/etc/named.conf`. In these lines, you'll tell the server which zones to service and where the configuration files for that zone are stored. The first line is important. It is the directory line that tells `named.conf` in which directory on the Linux file system it can find its configuration. All filenames to which you refer later in `named.conf` are relative to that directory. By default, it is set to `/var/named`. The second relevant part tells the `named` process the zones it services. On Red Hat Enterprise Linux, this is done by including another file with the name `/etc/named.rfc192.conf`. Listing 14.2 shows a `named.conf` for a name server that services the `example.com` domain. All relevant parameters have been set correctly in this example file.

Listing 14.2: Example `named.conf`

```
[root@rhev ~]# cat /etc/named.conf
//
// named.conf
//
// Provided by Red Hat bind package to configure the ISC BIND named(8) DNS
```

```
// server as a caching only nameserver (as a localhost DNS resolver only).
//
// See /usr/share/doc/bind*/sample/ for example named configuration files.
//

options {
        listen-on port 53 { any; };
        listen-on-v6 port 53 { ::1; };
        directory       "/var/named";
        dump-file       "/var/named/data/cache_dump.db";
        statistics-file "/var/named/data/named_stats.txt";
        memstatistics-file "/var/named/data/named_mem_stats.txt";
        allow-query     { any; };
        forwarders { 8.8.8.8; };
        recursion yes;

        dnssec-enable yes;
        dnssec-validation no;
        dnssec-lookaside auto;

        /* Path to ISC DLV key */
        bindkeys-file "/etc/named.iscdlv.key";

        managed-keys-directory "/var/named/dynamic";
};

logging {
        channel default_debug {
                file "data/named.run";
                severity dynamic;
        };
};

zone "." IN {
        type hint;
        file "named.ca";
};

include "/etc/named.rfc1912.zones";
include "/etc/named.root.key";
```

As indicated, the configuration of the zones themselves is in the include file /etc/named. rfc1912.zones. Listing 14.3 shows you what this file looks like after a zone for the example.com domain has been created.

Listing 14.3: Example of the named.rfc1912.zones file

```
[root@rhev ~]# cat /etc/named.rfc1912.zones
// named.rfc1912.zones:
//
// Provided by Red Hat caching-nameserver package
//
// ISC BIND named zone configuration for zones recommended by
// RFC 1912 section 4.1 : localhost TLDs and address zones
// and http://www.ietf.org/internet-drafts/draft-ietf-dnsop-default-
local-zones-02.txt
// (c)2007 R W Franks
//
// See /usr/share/doc/bind*/sample/ for example named configuration files.
//

zone "localhost.localdomain" IN {
        type master;
        file "named.localhost";
        allow-update { none; };
};

zone "localhost" IN {
        type master;
        file "named.localhost";
        allow-update { none; };
};

zone "example.com" IN {
        type master;
        file "example.com";
};

zone "1.0.0.0.0.0.0.0.0.0.0.0.0.0.0.0.0.0.0.0.0.0.0.0.0.0.0.0.0.0.0.0.
ip6.arpa" IN {
        type master;
        file "named.loopback";
```

```
        allow-update { none; };
};

zone "1.0.0.127.in-addr.arpa" IN {
        type master;
        file "named.loopback";
        allow-update { none; };
};

zone "0.in-addr.arpa" IN {
        type master;
        file "named.empty";
        allow-update { none; };
};
```

As you can see, some sections exist by default in the named.rfc1912.zone file. These sections ensure that localhost name resolving is handled correctly by the DNS server. To tell the DNS server that it also has to service another zone, add the following few lines:

```
zone "example.com" IN {
        type master;
        file "example.com";
};
```

The first line, zone "example.com" IN, tells named that it is responsible for a zone with the name example.com that is of the type IN. This means this zone is servicing IP addresses. (In theory, DNS also supports other protocols.) After the zone declaration, you can find further definition of the zone between braces. In this case, the definition consists of just two lines. The first line tells named that this is the master server. The second line tells named that the configuration file is example.com. This file can, of course, be found in the directory /var/named, which was set in /etc/named.conf as the default directory.

DNS as provided by BIND has had its share of security problems in the past. That is why named is by default started as a chroot service. That means the content of /var/named/chroot is set as the root directory for named. It cannot see anything above this directory level! This is a good protection mechanism that ensures that if a hacker breaks through the system, the hacker cannot access other parts of your server's file system. As an administrator, you don't have to deal with the contents of the chroot directory, and you can simply access the configuration files at their regular locations. These configuration files are actually links to the files in the chrooted directory.

Now that named knows where to find the zone configuration file, you'll also need to create a configuration for that zone file. Listing 14.4 provides an example of the contents of this file.

A zone file consists of two parts. The first part is the *header*, which provides generic information about the timeouts that should be used for this zone. Just two parameters really matter in this header. The first is `$ORIGIN example.com`. This parameter tells the zone file that it is the zone file for the `example.com` domain. This means that anywhere a domain name is not mentioned, `example.com` will be assumed as the default domain name. Notice that the file writes `example.com.` with a dot at the end of the hostname and not `example.com`. This is to define `example.com` as an absolute path name that is relative to the root of the DNS hierarchy.

The second important part in the header file is where the SOA is defined. This line specifies which name server is authoritative for this DNS domain:

```
@       1D      IN      SOA     rhev.example.com.
        hostmaster.example.com. (
```

As you can see, the host with the name `rhev.example.com.` (notice the dot at the end of the hostname) is SOA for this domain. Notice that "this domain" is referenced with the @ sign, which is common practice in DNS configurations. The email address of the domain administrator is also mentioned in this line. This email address is written in a legacy way as `hostmaster.example.com` and not `hostmaster@example.com`.

In the second part of the zone file, the resource records themselves are defined. They contain the data that is offered by the DNS server. Table 14.1 provides an overview of some of the most common resource records.

TABLE 14.1 Common resource records

Resource record	Stands for	Use
A	Address	Matches a name to an IP address
PTR	Pointer	Matches an IP address to a name in reverse DNS
NS	Name server	Tells DNS the name of name servers responsible for subdomains
MX	Mail exchange	Tells DNS which servers are available as SMTP mail servers for this domain
SRV	Service record	Used by some operating systems to store service information dynamically in DNS
CNAME	Canonical name	Creates alias names for specific hosts

In the example configuration file shown in Listing 14.4, you can see that first an NS record is defined to tell DNS which are the name servers for this domain. In this example, just one name server is included. However, in a configuration where slave name servers are also configured, you might find multiple NS lines.

After the NS declaration, you can see that there's a number of address resource records. This is often the most important part of DNS because it matches hostnames to IP addresses.

The last part of the configuration tells DNS the mail exchanges for this domain. As you can see, one is an internal server that is within the same DNS domain, and the other is a server that is hosted by some provider in an external domain. In Exercise 14.2, you'll practice setting up your own DNS Server.

Listing 14.4: Example zone file

```
[root@rhev named]# cat example.com
$TTL 86400
$ORIGIN example.com.
@       1D      IN      SOA     rhev.example.com.
        hostmaster.example.com. (
                                20120822
                                3H ; refresh
                                15 ; retry
                                1W ; expire
                                3h ; minimum
)
        IN NS rhev.example.com.


rhev    IN      A       192.168.1.220
rhevh   IN      A       192.168.1.151
rhevh1  IN      A       192.168.1.221
blah    IN      A       192.168.1.1
router  IN      CNAME   blah
        IN      MX      10      blah.example.com.
        IN      MX      20      blah.provider.com.
```

Real World Scenario

Why Bother Creating Your Own DNS?

If you have servers hosted with your provider, the easiest way of setting up a DNS configuration is likely by using the provider interface and host of the DNS database of your provider. This is excellent when you want to make sure your DNS records are accessible for external users. In some cases, however, you will not want to do that, and you'll need only the DNS records in your internal network. In such cases, you can use what you've learned in this book to create your own DNS server.

One reason I've come across for setting up my own DNS occurred while I was setting up a Red Hat Enterprise Virtualization (RHEV) environment. In RHEV, DNS is essential because all the nodes communicate by names only, and there is no way to access a shell on an RHEV hypervisor node, which is a minimal operating system with no option to log in as root. On my first attempt to set up the environment without DNS, it failed completely. On the second attempt, with a correctly configured and operational DNS, RHEV worked smoothly.

EXERCISE 14.2

Setting Up a Primary DNS Server

In this exercise, you'll learn how to set up a primary DNS server. You'll configure the name server for the example.com domain and then put in some resource records. At the end of the exercise, you'll check that it's all working as expected.

1. Make sure that the bind package is installed on your host computer.

2. Open the /etc/named.conf file, and make sure the following parameters are included:

   ▪ directory is set to /var/named

   ▪ listen-on port 53 is set to any

   ▪ allow-query is set to any

   ▪ forwarders contains the IP address of your Internet provider's DNS name server

   ▪ dns-sec validation is set to *no*

3. Open the /etc/named.rfc1912.zones file, and create a definition for the example.com domain. You can use the same configuration shown in Listing 14.3.

4. Create a file /var/named/example.com, and give it contents similar to those in Listing 14.4. Change it to match the hostnames in your environment.

5. Make sure that the DNS resolver in /etc/resolv.conf is set to your own DNS server.

6. Use **dig yourhost.example.com**, and verify that your DNS server gives the correct information from your DNS database.

Configuring an in-addr.arpa Zone

In the previous section, you learned how to set up a normal zone, which is used to resolve a name to its IP address. It is often a good idea also to set up an in-addr.arpa zone. This allows external DNS servers to find the name that belongs to an incoming IP address. Setting up an in-addr.arpa zone is not a strict requirement, however, and your DNS server will work fine without an in-addr.arpa zone.

Creating an in-addr.arpa zone works similarly to the creation of a regular zone in DNS. You'll need to modify the /etc/named.rfc1912.zones file to define the in-addr.arpa zone. This definition might appear as follows:

```
zone "100.173.193.in-addr.arpa" {
        type master;
        file "193.173.100.zone";
};
```

Notice that in in-addr.arpa, you'll always use the reverse network part of the IP address. In this case, the network is 193.173.100.0/24, so the reverse network part is

`100.173.193.in-addr.arpa`. For the rest, you just need to create a zone file, as you've done when creating a regular DNS zone. In the `in-addr.arpa` zone file, you'll define PTR resource records. In the first part of the resource record, you'll enter the node part of the IP address. Thus, if the IP address of the node is `193.173.100.1`, you'll just enter a 1 in there. Then you will use PTR to indicate that it is a reverse DNS record. For the last part, you'll use the complete node name, ending with a dot. Such a line might appear as follows:

```
1        PTR      router.example.com
```

The rest of the file that contains the resource records is not much different. You'll still need the header part in which the SOA and name servers are specified, as well as the time-outs. Don't put any other resource record in it other than the PTR resource record.

Setting Up a Secondary Name Server

After setting up a primary name server, you should add at least one secondary name server. A *secondary server* is one that synchronizes with the primary. Thus, to enable this, you must first allow the primary to transfer data. You do this by setting the `allow-transfer` parameter for the zone as you previously defined it in the `/etc/named.rfc1912.conf` file. It's also a good idea to set the `notify yes` parameter in the definition of the master zone. This means that the master server automatically sends an update to the slaves if something has changed. After adding these lines, the definition for the `example.com` zone should appear as shown in Listing 14.5.

Listing 14.5: Adding parameters for master-slave communication

```
zone "example.com" IN {
        type master;
        file "example.com";
        notify yes;
        allow-update { 192.168.1.70; };
};
```

Once you have allowed updates on the primary server, you need to configure the slave. This means that in the `/etc/named.rfc1912.conf` file on the Red Hat server, which you're going to use as DNS slave, you also need to define the zone. The example configuration in Listing 14.6 will do that for you.

Listing 14.6: Creating a DNS slave configuration

```
zone "example.com" IN {
        type slave;
        masters {
                192.168.1.220;
        };
        file "example.com.slave";
};
```

After creating the slave configuration, make sure to restart the named service to get it working.

> **NOTE** This chapter hasn't presented any information about key-based DNS communication. If you truly need security in a DNS environment, it is important to secure the communication between the master and slave servers by using keys. Working with DNS keys is complicated, and you don't need it for internal use. If you want to know more about key-based DNS communication, look for information about TSIG keys, which is what you need to set up DNS in a highly secured environment.

Understanding DHCP

The *Dynamic Host Configuration Protocol (DHCP)* is used to assign IP-related configuration to hosts in your network. Using a DHCP server makes managing a network a lot easier, because it gives the administrator the option to manage IP-related configuration on a single, central location on the network, instead of on multiple different hosts.

Counter to common belief, DHCP offers much more than just the IP address to hosts that request its information. A DHCP server can be configured to assign more than 80 different parameters to its clients, of which the most commonly used are IP addresses, default gateways, and the IP address of the DNS name servers.

When a client comes up, it will send a DHCP request on the network. This DHCP request is sent as a broadcast, and the DHCP server that receives the DHCP request will answer and assign an available IP address. Because the DHCP request is sent as a broadcast, you can have just one DHCP server per subnet. If multiple DHCP servers are available, there is no way to determine which DHCP server assigns the IP addresses. In such cases, it is common to set up failover DHCP, which means that two DHCP services together are servicing the same subnet, and one DHCP server completely takes over if something goes wrong.

It is also good to know that each client, no matter which operating system is used on the client, remembers by default the last IP address it has used. When sending out a DHCP request, it will always request to use the last IP address again. If that IP address is no longer available, the DHCP server will give another IP address from the pool of available IP addresses.

When configuring a DHCP server, it is a good idea to think about the default lease time. This is the amount of time that the client can use an IP address it has received without contacting the DHCP server again. In most cases, it's a good idea to set the default lease time to a rather short amount of time, which means it doesn't take too long for an IP address to be given back to the DHCP server. This makes sense especially in an environment where users connect for a short period of time, because within the max-lease-time (two hours by default), the IP address is claimed and cannot be used by another client. In many cases, it makes sense to set the max-lease-time to a period much shorter than 7,200 seconds.

Setting Up a DHCP Server

To set up a DHCP server, after installing the dhcp package, you need to change common DHCP settings in the main configuration file: /etc/dhcp/dhcpd.conf. After installing the dhcp package, the file is empty, but there is a good annotated example file in /usr/share /doc/dhcp-<version>/dhcpd.conf.sample. You can see the default parameters from this file in Listing 14.7.

Listing 14.7: Example dhcpd.conf file

```
[root@hnl dhcp-4.1.1]# cat dhcpd
dhcpd6.conf.sample  dhcpd.conf.sample   dhcpd-conf-to-ldap
[root@hnl dhcp-4.1.1]# cat dhcpd.conf.sample
# dhcpd.conf
#
# Sample configuration file for ISC dhcpd
#

# option definitions common to all supported networks...
option domain-name "example.org";
option domain-name-servers ns1.example.org, ns2.example.org;

default-lease-time 600;
max-lease-time 7200;

# Use this to enble / disable dynamic dns updates globally.
#ddns-update-style none;

# If this DHCP server is the official DHCP server for the local
# network, the authoritative directive should be uncommented.
#authoritative;

# Use this to send dhcp log messages to a different log file (you also
# have to hack syslog.conf to complete the redirection).
log-facility local7;

# No service will be given on this subnet, but declaring it helps the
# DHCP server to understand the network topology.

subnet 10.152.187.0 netmask 255.255.255.0 {
```

```
}

# This is a very basic subnet declaration.

subnet 10.254.239.0 netmask 255.255.255.224 {
  range 10.254.239.10 10.254.239.20;
  option routers rtr-239-0-1.example.org, rtr-239-0-2.example.org;
}

# This declaration allows BOOTP clients to get dynamic addresses,
# which we don't really recommend.

subnet 10.254.239.32 netmask 255.255.255.224 {
  range dynamic-bootp 10.254.239.40 10.254.239.60;
  option broadcast-address 10.254.239.31;
  option routers rtr-239-32-1.example.org;
}

# A slightly different configuration for an internal subnet.
subnet 10.5.5.0 netmask 255.255.255.224 {
  range 10.5.5.26 10.5.5.30;
  option domain-name-servers ns1.internal.example.org;
  option domain-name "internal.example.org";
  option routers 10.5.5.1;
  option broadcast-address 10.5.5.31;
  default-lease-time 600;
  max-lease-time 7200;
}

# Hosts which require special configuration options can be listed in
# host statements.   If no address is specified, the address will be
# allocated dynamically (if possible), but the host-specific information
# will still come from the host declaration.

host passacaglia {
  hardware ethernet 0:0:c0:5d:bd:95;
  filename "vmunix.passacaglia";
  server-name "toccata.fugue.com";
}
```

```
# Fixed IP addresses can also be specified for hosts.   These addresses
# should not also be listed as being available for dynamic assignment.
# Hosts for which fixed IP addresses have been specified can boot using
# BOOTP or DHCP.   Hosts for which no fixed address is specified can only
# be booted with DHCP, unless there is an address range on the subnet
# to which a BOOTP client is connected which has the dynamic-bootp flag
# set.
host fantasia {
  hardware ethernet 08:00:07:26:c0:a5;
  fixed-address fantasia.fugue.com;
}


# You can declare a class of clients and then do address allocation
# based on that.   The example below shows a case where all clients
# in a certain class get addresses on the 10.17.224/24 subnet, and all
# other clients get addresses on the 10.0.29/24 subnet.

class "foo" {
  match if substring (option vendor-class-identifier, 0, 4) = "SUNW";
}

shared-network 224-29 {
  subnet 10.17.224.0 netmask 255.255.255.0 {
    option routers rtr-224.example.org;
  }
  subnet 10.0.29.0 netmask 255.255.255.0 {
    option routers rtr-29.example.org;
  }
  pool {
    allow members of "foo";
    range 10.17.224.10 10.17.224.250;
  }
  pool {
    deny members of "foo";
    range 10.0.29.10 10.0.29.230;
  }
}
```

Here are the most relevant parameters from the dhcpd.conf file and a short explanation of each:

option domain-name   Use this to set the DNS domain name for the DHCP clients.

option domain-name-servers   This specifies the DNS name servers that should be used.

default-lease-time   This is the default time in seconds that a client can use the IP address that it has received from the DHCP server.

max-lease-time   This is the maximum time that a client can keep on using its assigned IP address. If within the max-lease-time timeout it hasn't been able to contact the DHCP server for renewal, the IP address will expire, and the client can't use it anymore.

log-facility   This specifies which syslog facility the DHCP server uses.

subnet   This is the essence of the work of a DHCP server. The subnet definition specifies the network on which the DHCP server should assign IP addresses. A DHCP server can serve multiple subnets, but it is common for the DHCP server to be directly connected to the subnet it serves.

range   This is the range of IP addresses within the subnet that the DHCP server can assign to clients.

option routers   This is the router that should be set as the default gateway.

As you see from the sample DHCP configuration file, there are many options that an administrator can use to specify different kinds of information that should be handed out. Some options can be set globally and also in the subnet, while other options are set in specific subnets. As an administrator, you need to determine where you want to set specific options.

Apart from the subnet declarations that you make on the DHCP server, you can also define the configuration for specific hosts. In the example file in Listing 14.7, you can see this in the host declarations for host passacaglia and host fantasia. Host declarations will work based on the specification of the hardware Ethernet address of the host; this is the MAC address of the network card where the DHCP request comes in.

At the end of the example configuration file, you can also see that a class is defined, as well as a shared network in which different subnets and pools are used. The idea is that you can use the class to identify a specific host. This works on the basis of the vendor class identifier, which is capable of identifying the type of host that sends a DHCP request. Once a specific kind of host is identified, you can match it to a class and, based on class membership, assign specific configuration that makes sense for that class type only.

At the end of the example dhcpd.conf configuration file, you can see that, on a shared network, two different subnets are declared where all members of the class foo are assigned to one of the subnets and all others are assigned to the other class. In Exercise 14.3, you'll learn how to set up your own DHCP Server.

EXERCISE 14.3

Setting Up a DHCP Server

In this exercise, you'll set up a DHCP server. Because of the broadcast nature of DHCP, you'll run it on the virtual machine so that it doesn't interfere with other computers in your network. To test the operation of the DHCP server, you'll also need a second virtual machine.

1. Start the virtual machine, and open a root shell. From the root shell, use the command **yum -y dhcp** to install the DHCP server.

2. Open the file /etc/dhcp/dhcpd.conf with an editor, and give it the following contents. Make sure that the names and IP addresses used in this example match your network:

   ```
   option domain-name "example.com";
   option domain-name-servers YOUR.DNS.SERVERNAME.HERE;

   default-lease-time 600;
   max-lease-time 1800;

   subnet 192.168.100.0 netmask 255.255.255.0 {
       range 192.168.100.10 192.168.100.20;
       options routers 192.168.100.1;
   }
   ```

3. Start the DHCP server by using the command **service dhcpd start**, and enable it using **chkconfig dhcpd on**.

4. Start the second virtual machine. Make sure that the network card is set to get an IP address from a DHCP server. After starting it, verify that the DHCP server has indeed handed out an IP address.

Summary

In this chapter, you learned how to set up a DNS server and a DHCP server. Using these servers allows you to offer network services from your Red Hat Enterprise Linux server. The use of your own Red Hat–based DNS server, in particular, can be of great help. Many products require having an internal DNS server, and by running your own DNS on Linux, you're free to configure whatever resource records you need in your network environment.

Chapter

15

Setting Up a Mail Server

TOPICS COVERED IN THIS CHAPTER:

✓ Using the Message Transfer Agent

✓ Setting Up Postfix as an SMTP Server

✓ Configuring Dovecot for POP and IMAP

✓ Further Steps

It's hard to imagine the Internet without email. Even if new techniques to communicate, such as instant messaging, tweeting, and texting, have established themselves, email is still an important means of communicating on the Internet. To configure an Internet mail solution, Red Hat offers Postfix as the default mail server. Before learning how this mail server works, this chapter is a short introduction into the domain of Internet mail.

Using the Message Transfer Agent

Three components play a role in the process of Internet mail. First there is the *message transfer agent (MTA)*. The MTA uses the *Simple Mail Transfer Protocol (SMTP)* to exchange mail messages with other MTAs on the Internet. If a user sends a mail message to a user on another domain on the Internet, it's the responsibility of the MTA to contact the MTA of the other domain and deliver the message there. To find out which MTA serves the other domain, the DNS MX record is used.

Upon receiving a message, the MTA checks whether it is the final destination. If it is, it will deliver the message to the local *message delivery agent (MDA)*, which takes care of delivering the message to the mailbox of the user. If the MTA itself is not the final destination, the MTA relays the message to the MTA of the final destination.

Relaying is a hot item in email delivery. Normally, an MTA doesn't relay messages for just anyone, but only for authenticated users or users who are known in some other way. If messages were relayed for everyone, this would likely mean that the MTA was being abused by spammers on the Internet.

If, for some reason, the MTA cannot deliver the message to the other MTA, it will queue it. *Queuing* means that the MTA stores the message in a local directory and will try to deliver it again later. As an administrator, you can flush the queues, which means that you can tell the MTA to send all queued messages now.

Upon delivery, it sometimes happens that the MTA, which contacted an exterior MTA and delivered the message there, receives it back. This process is referred to as *bouncing*. In general, a message is bounced if it doesn't comply with the rules of the receiving MTA, but it can also be bounced if the destination user simply doesn't exist. Alternatively, it's nicer if an MTA is configured simply to generate an error if the message couldn't be delivered.

Understanding the Mail Delivery Agent

Upon receiving a message, the MTA typically delivers it at the mail delivery agent. This is the software component that takes care of delivering the mail message to the destination user. Typically, the MDA delivers mail to the recipient's local message store, which by default on Red Hat Enterprise Linux is the directory /var/spool/mail/$USER. In the Postfix mail server, an MDA is included in the form of the local program.

You should be aware that the MDA is only the software part that drops the message somewhere the recipient can find it. It is not the POP or IMAP server, which is an addition to a mail solution that makes it easier for users to get their messages (if they're not on the same machine where the MDA is running). In the early days of the Internet, message recipients typically logged in to the machine where the MDA functioned; nowadays, it is common for users to get their messages from a remote desktop on which they are working. To facilitate this, you need a POP server that allows users to download messages or an IMAP server that allows users to connect to the mail server and read the messages while they're online.

Understanding the Mail User Agent

Finally, the mail message arrives in the *mail user agent (MUA)*. This is the mail client that end users use to read their messages or to compose new messages. As a mail server administrator, you typically don't care much about the MUA. It is the responsibility of users to install an MUA, which allows them to work with email on their computer, tablet, or smartphone. Popular MUAa are Outlook, Evolution, and the Linux command-line Mutt tool, which you'll work with in this chapter.

Setting Up Postfix as an SMTP Server

Setting up a Postfix mail server can be easy, depending on exactly what you want to do with it. If you only want to enable Postfix for local email delivery, you just have to set a few security parameters and be aware of a minimal number of administration commands. If you want to set up Postfix for mail delivery to other domains on the Internet, that is a bit more involved.

In both cases, you will do most of the work in the /etc/postfix/main.cf file. This is the Postfix configuration file in which you'll tune some of the many parameters that are available in this file.

For troubleshooting the message delivery process, the /var/log/maillog file is an important source of information. In this file, you'll find status information about the message delivery process, and just by reading it, you will often find out why you are experiencing problems.

Another common task you'll use in both configuration scenarios is checking the mail queue. The *mail queue* is the list of messages that haven't been sent yet because there was some kind of problem. As an administrator, you can use the `mailq` command to check the current contents of the mail queue or use the `postfix flush` command to flush the entire mail queue. This means that you'll tell Postfix to process all messages that are currently in the mail queue and try to deliver them now.

Before I go into detail about the basic configuration and the configuration you'll need to connect your mail server to the Internet, you'll read about using the Mutt mail client, not because it is the best mail client that's available, but foremost because it's an easy tool that as an administrator you'll appreciate when handling problems with email delivery.

Working with Mutt

The Mutt MUA is available in the default Red Hat Enterprise Linux repositories, but you'll have to install it. You'll acquire basic Mutt skills by performing Exercise 15.1.

EXERCISE 15.1

Getting to Know Mutt

In this exercise, you'll acquire some basic Mutt skills. The purpose of this exercise is to teach you how to use Mutt to test and configure the Postfix mail server as an administrator.

1. Log in as root, and use **yum -y install mutt** to install Mutt.

2. Still as root, use the command **mail -s hello linda <**. This sends an empty message to user linda, because it is useful if the test user has at least one message in their mailbox.

3. Use **su - linda** to become linda, and type **mutt**. If you get a message that the mail directory for linda doesn't exist, type **y** to create it. You'll now see the Mutt interface.

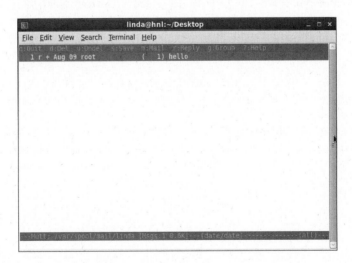

4. Press Enter to open the mail message. Because it doesn't contain any content, you'll just see the message header.

5. Type **q** once you've finished reading the message.

6. To reply to the message, type **r**. Mutt will prompt you to choose which user you want to send the message and which subject line you want to use. Press Enter twice to accept the default suggestions.

7. The message composition window opens next. This is a vi window, so use **o** to open a new line and start writing the message. Once you are finished writing, use the vi command **:wq!** to close the message-editing interface.

8. Now you'll see the message summary. From there, type **y** to send it to root. Next type **q** to quit Mutt.

9. Exit linda's su shell, and as root type **mutt**. You'll see that linda's message has been delivered to her inbox.

At this point, you know everything about Mutt that you need to know as a mail server administrator. You've seen that it's not difficult to send mail messages with Mutt, and because the recipient is on the local machine, it works perfectly.

In Exercise 15.2, you're going to try to send an email message to a user on the virtual machine testvm.

Sending a Message to an External User

In this exercise, you're going to send an email message to a user on another computer. This means that two instances of Postfix will need to communicate with one another. Make sure to follow all of the instructions so that all prerequisites have been set properly.

1. On the host computer, use **virsh list**. If you performed all previous exercises, you'll see a virtual machine with the name testvm. Use **virsh start testvm** to start this virtual machine.

2. On the host computer, start the Virtual Machine Manager using the **virt-manager** command. Open a console on the virtual machine, and note its IP address.

3. On both the host and the virtual machine, edit the /etc/hosts file and include a line for the host computer and the virtual machine. The purpose for doing this is that these two computers can then resolve one another.

4. On the virtual machine, use **useradd lisa** to create a user with the name lisa.

5. On the host computer, use **su - linda** to become linda and start Mutt. From the Mutt interface, type **m** to start composing a new mail message. Enter **lisa@testvm .example.com** in the to field. In the Subject field, enter test message 1. Enter some text in the mail message, and press **y** to send it.

EXERCISE 15.2 *(continued)*

6. Open a shell on testvm, and as root, use `yum -y install mutt` to install Mutt. Next, use `su - lisa` to log in as lisa and start Mutt. You'll notice that lisa's mailbox is empty, and the message that user linda sent from the other machine has not yet been sent.

That's all for now. As you've noticed, you cannot send a message yet. You'll learn how to fix this in the next section.

Basic Configuration

As you noticed from the previous exercise, your Postfix mail server cannot receive messages from other computers after a default installation. That is because, by default, Postfix binds to the loopback IP address only. You can verify this by using the `netstat -tulpen | grep 25` command. In Listing 15.1 you can see what the result of this command looks like.

Listing 15.1: By default, your Postfix server is bound to the local loopback address only.

```
[root@hn1 ~]# netstat -tulpen | grep 25
tcp    0   0 127.0.0.1:25     0.0.0.0:*     LISTEN  0   18453  2561/master
tcp    0   0 ::1:25     :::*  LISTEN  0    18456   2561/master
```

To configure Postfix for basic email delivery, you need to open the server to the outside world to make sure that it binds to ports other than the loopback port. To do this, you'll have to change a parameter in the `/etc/postfix/main.cf` file. You can see part of the contents of this file in Listing 15.2.

Listing 15.2: Partial contents of `/etc/postfix/main.cf`

```
# RECEIVING MAIL

# The inet_interfaces parameter specifies the network interface
# addresses that this mail system receives mail on.  By default,
# the software claims all active interfaces on the machine. The
# parameter also controls delivery of mail to user@[ip.address].
#
# See also the proxy_interfaces parameter, for network addresses that
# are forwarded to us via a proxy or network address translator.
#
# Note: you need to stop/start Postfix when this parameter changes.
#
#inet_interfaces = all
#inet_interfaces = $myhostname
```

```
#inet_interfaces = $myhostname, localhost
inet_interfaces = localhost

# Enable IPv4, and IPv6 if supported
inet_protocols = all

# The proxy_interfaces parameter specifies the network interface
# addresses that this mail system receives mail on by way of a
:
```

In the receiving mail section of the main.cf file, you'll notice that by default the inet_interfaces parameter is set to localhost. This is very secure, and it's also the reason why lisa never received her email message on testvm in the previous exercise. In Exercise 15.3, you'll learn how to change this and also enable the mail server on testvm to receive email messages from external sources.

EXERCISE 15.3

Opening Your Mail Server for External Mail

In this exercise, you'll learn how to open your mail server to receive mail messages from external sources. It doesn't really make it an Internet mail server just yet, but at least you'll be able to receive messages from others.

1. On the testvm virtual machine, open the /etc/postfix/main.cf file with an editor.

2. Find the parameter inet_interfaces = localhost, and put a hash sign in front of it.

3. Enable the parameter inet_interfaces = all by removing the pound sign in front of the line.

4. Still on testvm, use **service postfix restart** to restart the Postfix process. If a firewall is active, make sure that port 25 is open on it.

5. On testvm, use **su - lisa** to become user lisa and start Mutt. You'll notice that lisa still hasn't received her message yet.

6. As root on the host computer, type **mailq** to type the current content of the mail queue. As with the first attempt, the message couldn't be sent; the message that linda tried to send to lisa is stuck in the queue.

7. Type **postfix flush** to flush the mail queue. Postfix will now try to send the message again.

In the previous exercise, you enabled your mail server to receive messages from other servers. It still doesn't work, however, and that is because of DNS. Typically, in a DNS domain, only one or a few servers are solely responsible for mail message handling. The clients in the domain are set up to fetch their messages from this *mail exchange (MX)* host.

In the exercise that you just completed, you worked with two hosts within the same DNS domain, and that simply isn't how it works.

To create a fully functional mail environment, you need to set up two different DNS domains so that in each domain one server can be assigned as the mail exchange. This will allow you to send mail messages to users in different domains.

Now that you know what to do to set up message delivery in a simple environment, you'll learn how to set up more complex environments in the next section.

Internet Configuration

There are a few more steps to take to configure a mail server, which is going to handle messages from the Internet. Most of the additional tasks relate to security. You'll need to make sure your mail server has at least a minimum level of protection against spam and other email abuses. To make a secure Internet configuration, you need to set some additional parameters. All of these will be set in the /etc/postfix/main.cf file. The following are the relevant parameters:

myhostname This parameter specifies the name of this host. If not specified, it is set to the full DNS domain name (FQDN) of this host. This parameter is used as a variable in other parameters in the main.cf file, so it is useful to set it.

mydomain This parameter specifies the domain of this host. If not set, the domain name part of the FQDN is used.

myorigin This parameter determines the domain seen by the email recipient when receiving messages. The default is to use the FQDN of this host. This means that if user linda on server dfw.example.com sends a message, the recipient will see a message coming in from linda@dfw.example.com. This is often not what you want. To append the domain name only and not the entire FQDN, use myorigin = $mydomain.

inet_interfaces This parameter specifies the IP addresses of the mail server to which it binds. By default, it is set to localhost only, which means that your mail server cannot receive messages from the Internet. This is fine if the mail server only has to send messages and another server is used for email reception. However, you'll normally want to enable all inet_interfaces using inet_interfaces = all.

mydestination This parameter contains a list of all domains for which this server will receive messages. Messages that are addressed to users in other domains will be rejected. Make sure that this parameter contains a list of all domains serviced by this server. Also notice that in the default setting, message reception for $mydomain is off, so you'll need to change this.

mynetworks This parameter is optional. You can use it to specify the network address from which your MTA accepts messages for relaying without further authentication. It's a good idea to set this to your trusted network.

relayhost This parameter contains the name of a host that is used to relay all messages to. Use this if, for example, you want the mail server of your ISP to take care of all message delivery.

To change any of these parameters (or one of the many other parameters that you'll find in /etc/postfix/main.cf), you can change the configuration file by hand and restart Postfix after doing so. Alternatively, you can use the postconf command to monitor and set parameters. Use postconf mydestination to see the current setting of the postconf parameter, and use postconf -e "mydestination = $mydomain" to change its current value.

Configuring Dovecot for POP and IMAP

After installing and configuring the Postfix MTA, users can connect to your server and read mail messages using an MUA such as Mutt. To allow users to handle mail on their own computers, you need a service that offers POP or IMAP mail access. Dovecot is the default service to do that on Red Hat Enterprise Linux.

When using POP, users can connect to the mail server and download messages to their own computers. When using IMAP, users connect to the mail server and edit their messages on that mail server. POP works fine for users who have one device to handle mail. IMAP works better for users who have multiple devices to handle their mail.

After a default installation of Dovecot, it will offer POP and IMAP. To configure POP, you'll tune the /etc/dovecot/dovecot.conf file. There aren't many changes that need to be done in this file. By default, Dovecot offers POP and IMAP over both a secure and an unsecure port. All you need to do after installing Dovecot is to make sure it is started by using service dovecot start and chkconfig dovecot on.

By default messages are sent unencrypted in Dovecot. This means that passwords and other sensitive information can be captured while in transit. For that reason, you should also always offer POP3S and IMAPS. Offering these services is not hard; you just need to create and sign an SSL certificate as discussed in Chapter 12 and copy it to the right locations.

The default Dovecot certificate and private key are in the files /etc/pki/dovecot/certs /dovecot.pem and /etc/pki/dovecot/private/dovecot.pem. If you ever create your own certificates and have them signed, make sure to copy the new .pem files to these locations. After putting the certificates there, you should restart Dovecot. You can also use the /usr /libexec/dovecot/mkcert.sh script to generate some self-signed certificates for Dovecot and put them in the right locations. In Exercise 15.4, you'll create your own base Dovecot configuration.

EXERCISE 15.4

Creating a Base Dovecot Configuration

In this exercise, you'll install Dovecot and create a base configuration that can be used by users to connect and get their email.

1. As root on the host computer, use **yum -y install dovecot** to install the Dovecot service.

2. Run **/usr/libexec/dovecot/mkcert.sh** to create some self-signed certificates for Dovecot, and install them in the right locations.

3. Use **service dovecot start** to start Dovecot.

4. As root, make sure that user linda has a message in her mailbox by entering the following command: **mail -s hello linda** <. This sends an empty message to user linda that has only a subject line.

5. Use **su** - to become linda, and as linda, start Mutt.

6. From Mutt, hit **c** to change the mailbox you're accessing, and enter the URL **pop://linda@localhost**. This should give you access to your mailbox on the local computer.

7. Use **c** once more, and enter the URL **pop3://linda@localhost**. You'll now have access to the mailbox using the TLS version of POP3.

In the previous exercise, you learned that it really is very easy to set up a basic mail server for internal users. You now have Dovecot running and offering POP and IMAP mail, including the TLS-secured versions of these mail protocols.

Further Steps

The purpose of this chapter was to teach you how to set up a simple mail environment that is good for internal use. The steps discussed here aren't good enough to set up a reliable and secure email infrastructure for external use, however. One important aspect that hasn't been covered is spam/antivirus security. To accomplish this, you'll need additional solutions that require different licenses, such as Spam Assassin. Configuring these programs, however, is beyond the scope of this book. Nevertheless, don't forget to address these issues if you want to set up a reliable infrastructure for email handling.

Summary

In this chapter, you learned how to set up a basic environment for handling email. You configured Postfix for email handling and Dovecot to offer POP3 and IMAP access to user mailboxes. Your server is now ready to start servicing mail messages.

Chapter

16

Configuring Apache on Red Hat Enterprise Linux

TOPICS COVERED IN THIS CHAPTER:

✓ Configuring the Apache Web Server

✓ Working with Virtual Hosts

✓ Securing the Web Server with TLS Certificates

✓ Configuring Authentication

✓ Setting Up MySQL

LAMP is amongst the most common uses of Linux. LAMP stands for Linux, Apache, MySQL, and PHP. In this chapter, you'll learn how to set up a LAMP server. Well, a LAM server actually, because PHP is too big a subject to summarize in this chapter. You'll first learn how to set up an Apache web server, including information about setting up virtual hosts, using TLS Certificates, and the configuration of authentication. At the end of the chapter, you'll also learn how to set up a basic MySQL server.

Configuring the Apache Web Server

Apache is one of the most used services on Red Hat Enterprise Linux. A basic installation of an Apache website is easy to perform, but by using modules you can make Apache as sophisticated as you need. In this section, you'll learn how to set up a basic Apache web server, which offers access to a simple website. Later sections teach you how to work with more advanced options, such as virtual hosts, security, and TLS certificates.

Creating a Basic Website

Configuring an Apache server that services just one website is not hard to do—you just have to install the Apache software and create some content in the Apache document root. The default document root is set to /var/www/html on a Red Hat Enterprise Linux server. Just put a file in this directory with the name index.html, and it will be served by your Apache server. In Exercise 16.1, you'll learn how to install a basic Apache web server and have it serve a basic website.

EXERCISE 16.1

Creating a Basic Website

In this exercise, you'll learn how to configure Apache to serve a basic website.

1. Use **yum -y install httpd** to install the Apache web server.

2. Use **chkconfig httpd on** to put the Apache web server in your server's runlevels, and have it start at boot in your runlevels.

3. Open a root shell, and go to the directory /var/www/html. In this directory, create a file with the name index.html. In this file, put the content "welcome to my website" and then use **service httpd start** to start the Apache web server.

4. Still from the root shell, use **elinks http://localhost** to access the website you just created. You'll notice that your web server is up and running!

Understanding the Apache Configuration Files

As you've seen, it's easy to set up a basic Apache web server, as long as you can retain all of the default settings. Later in this chapter, you'll see that it's not so easy once you go beyond the default settings. To be able to configure the web server in more complex scenarios, you'll need to understand how the Apache configuration files are organized.

Everything related to the configuration of your Apache server is in the /etc/httpd directory. In this directory, you'll find two subdirectories: conf and conf.d. In /etc/httpd /confd, you'll find the main Apache configuration file httpd.conf. From the httpd.conf file, many configuration files are included, and by default, they are in /etc/httpd/conf.d. This httpd.conf file is designed to contain the entire Apache configuration. However, because Apache can take advantage of many additional features, parts of the configuration are stored in additional configuration files in Red Hat Enterprise Linux.

To understand how these additional configuration files are organized, you need to appreciate that Apache is modular. Installing additional modules can extend the functionality of the httpd process. An example of this is the mod_ssl module that you'll use later in this chapter to make the Apache server work with TLS encryption.

Many modules are available for Apache to provide different kinds of functionality. Each module normally has its own configuration file, which is stored in the /etc/httpd/conf.d directory. The names of these modules have to end with .conf to ensure they are included by your web server.

Creating configuration files where the name does not end in .conf is a common error made by some administrators. Make sure that the names of configuration files always end in .conf. Otherwise, they won't be included by your Apache server.

As mentioned earlier, the main configuration file of Apache is /etc/httpd/conf/httpd.conf. Listing 16.1 shows part of its configuration. The original httpd.conf file is more than 1,000 lines long. Listing 16.1 shows some of its more relevant parts.

Listing 16.1: Example httpd.conf file

```
[root@hnl conf]# cat httpd.conf.svv
ServerTokens OS
```

```
ServerRoot "/etc/httpd"
PidFile run/httpd.pid
Timeout 60
KeepAlive Off
MaxKeepAliveRequests 100
KeepAliveTimeout 15

<IfModule prefork.c>
StartServers        8
MinSpareServers     5
MaxSpareServers    20
ServerLimit       256
MaxClients        256
MaxRequestsPerChild 4000
</IfModule>

<IfModule worker.c>
StartServers         4
MaxClients         300
MinSpareThreads     25
MaxSpareThreads     75
ThreadsPerChild     25
MaxRequestsPerChild  0
</IfModule>

#Listen 12.34.56.78:80
Listen 80

LoadModule auth_basic_module modules/mod_auth_basic.so
LoadModule auth_digest_module modules/mod_auth_digest.so
LoadModule authn_file_module modules/mod_authn_file.so
LoadModule authn_alias_module modules/mod_authn_alias.so
LoadModule authn_anon_module modules/mod_authn_anon.so
LoadModule authn_dbm_module modules/mod_authn_dbm.so
LoadModule authn_default_module modules/mod_authn_default.so
LoadModule authz_host_module modules/mod_authz_host.so
LoadModule authz_user_module modules/mod_authz_user.so
LoadModule authz_owner_module modules/mod_authz_owner.so
...

Include conf.d/*.conf
```

```
User apache
Group apache
ServerAdmin root@localhost
UseCanonicalName Off
DocumentRoot "/var/www/html"

<Directory />
    Options FollowSymLinks
    AllowOverride None
</Directory>

<Directory "/var/www/html">
    Options Indexes FollowSymLinks
    AllowOverride None
    Order allow,deny
    Allow from all
</Directory>


<IfModule mod_userdir.c>
   UserDir disabled
</IfModule>

DirectoryIndex index.html index.html.var
AccessFileName .htaccess

<IfModule mod_mime_magic.c>
#    MIMEMagicFile /usr/share/magic.mime
     MIMEMagicFile conf/magic
</IfModule>

HostnameLookups Off

ErrorLog logs/error_log
LogLevel warn
CustomLog logs/access_log combined
ServerSignature On
Alias /icons/ "/var/www/icons/"

<Directory "/var/www/icons">
```

```
    Options Indexes MultiViews FollowSymLinks
    AllowOverride None
    Order allow,deny
    Allow from all
</Directory>

ScriptAlias /cgi-bin/ "/var/www/cgi-bin/"

<Directory "/var/www/cgi-bin">
    AllowOverride None
    Options None
    Order allow,deny
    Allow from all
</Directory>
```

Generic Parameters

The example configuration file from Listing 16.1 starts with some generic configuration settings. An important directive is `ServerRoot`. This defines the root of the configuration directory. On Red Hat Enterprise Linux, by default the server root is set to `/etc/httpd`. It is important to be aware of this because other filenames that are referenced later in the configuration file are all relative to the server root directory. An example is the `PidFile` (a file that contains the PID of the httpd process), which is set to `run/httpd.pid`. This filename must be related to the server root directory; hence, the full name is `/etc/httpd/run/httpd.pid`.

Another important parameter in the beginning of the configuration file is the `Listen` parameter. In this example, it directs httpd to listen at port 80. Because no specific IP addresses are mentioned, it will bind to port 80 on all IP addresses that are available. You can include a specific IP address if you want httpd to bind to just that one and to no other IP addresses.

The next list of generic parameters is a bit lower in the `httpd.conf` file. These are the parameters `User` and `Group`, which specify the user and group that should be used to run the Apache server. Apache is normally started as root and, once started, will run as this user and group with fewer privileges. By default, both are set to `apache`. The most important thing to remember here is that Apache should never offer its services as root!

Another important directive is the `DocumentRoot`. This specifies where Apache should look for its content. Documents that are stored in the `DocumentRoot` are served by default. The standard behavior on Red Hat Enterprise Linux is to show the contents of the `index.html` file that is created in the `DocumentRoot`. However, there are some parameters behind that behavior, which are explained later in this chapter.

Apache Mode

Apache can be started in two different modes: the prefork mode and the worker mode. The prefork mode is the default mode. In this mode, a master httpd process is started, and this master process will start different httpd servers. As an alternative, the worker mode can be used. In this mode, one httpd process is active, and it uses different threads to serve client requests. Even if the worker mode is a bit more efficient with regard to resource usage, some modules cannot handle it, and therefore the prefork mode is used as default.

However, if you need the best performance that httpd can offer and you don't use modules that are incompatible with worker mode, it's a good idea to use worker mode instead. Worker mode can be configured to serve more simultaneous processes.

To change the default mode that Apache uses, you can modify the HTTPD parameter in `/etc/sysconfig/httpd`. To use the worker mode, you have to start the `/usr/sbin/httpd.worker` binary instead of `/usr/sbin/httpd`. To accomplish this, just remove the pound sign in front of the example line in `/etc/sysconfig/httpd` and restart the httpd process using `service httpd restart`.

For both modes, you can set some performance parameters:

`StartServers`   This is the number of server processes httpd should always start.

`MinSpareServers`   This is the minimum amount of spare server processes that are kept. It is good to have a certain minimum because it allows httpd to serve client requests really fast. However, the minimum shouldn't be too high because each server uses system resources.

`MinSpareThreads`   In worker mode, this is the minimum amount of spare threads that httpd should keep. You can see that it is set considerably higher than the `MinSpareServers` parameter in prefork mode.

`MaxSpareServers` and `MaxSpareThreads`   This is the maximum amount of spare servers or threads that httpd should keep.

`ServerLimit`   This is the total amount of server processes that can be started as a maximum. Note that the value of 256 is pretty high, and it should be sufficient for most servers.

`MaxClients`   This is the maximum number of clients that can be connected. Note that in worker mode, one client can have several concurrent requests, which are opened simultaneously.

`MaxRequestPerChild`   This is the number of requests that can be opened by a server process. In prefork mode, the maximum is capped at 4,000; in worker mode, there is no maximum setting.

Modules

Among the features that make the Apache web server attractive is the fact that it is modular. By including modules, functionality can be added to Apache. To include Apache modules, they first need to be installed. By default, some of the most common modules are installed to the `/etc/httpd/modules` directory. To tell Apache that it should load a specific module, you need to use the `LoadModule` directive. By default, this directive is used to include many modules.

If a module is loaded, it can also have a specific configuration. There are three ways to load additional configurations for modules:

- Use the IfModule directive in httpd.conf.

- Put it in an include file.

- If a module is common, its parameters can be entered in httpd.conf without further specification.

By default, some modules put their configuration in a separate configuration file and store that file in the directory /etc/httpd/conf.d. The directive include conf.d/*.conf ensures that all configuration files where the name ends in .conf are included by default when Apache starts. Later in this chapter, you'll read about the mod_ssl module, which creates its own configuration file in /etc/httpd/conf.d.

Another approach to include parameters that are relevant for specific modules is by using the IfModule parameter in the httpd.conf file. This approach is more practical for modules that have a limited number of specific directives.

If a module is very common and almost always used, its parameters can simply be entered in the httpd.conf file. An example of this is the DirectoryIndex option discussed next. This option is provided by the mod_dir module, which is included in nearly all Apache configurations and therefore requires no further specification.

Setting Directory Options

The administrator can also set different directory options on an Apache web server. These options are used to define how the contents of a directory on the httpd server should be presented to users who access that directory. The default behavior is that the httpd processes look in the document root to see whether there is a file whose name starts with index. The DirectoryIndex directive can be used to specify that other files should also be considered. If this is the case, it will show the contents of this file, and if not, a list of files in the directory is shown.

To modify this behavior, the DirectoryIndex and Options directives can be used. By default, the DirectoryIndex directive specifies that Apache should look for a file with the name index.html or index.html.var. The Options directive within a directory definition (as you can see in the /var/www/icons directory statement) can further fine-tune the options that are used to display the contents of a directory. You can also use Options to determine which server features are available in a particular directory.

A useful argument for the Options directive is Indexes. If you use this option, you will see a list of files in the directory if no index.html is available. Related to this option is FollowSymLinks. This option will ensure that symbolic links are followed if they exist in the document directory. Don't use this because it is considered a security threat.

Handling Basic Directory Restrictions

In a directory served by Apache, some basic restrictions can be used. First, there is the AllowOverride directive. This directive is related to the .htaccess file that an administrator can use to restrict access to a given directory. If AllowOverride is set to none, the contents of any .htaccess file that is found anywhere in a subdirectory of the current directory will be ignored. If you don't want the owners of subdirectories to restrict access to their directories, you should set AllowOverride to none. If you want to allow users to restrict access to subdirectories, set it to All. In high-performance environments, don't use it at all because this will force Apache to recurse through the entire directory tree on every request.

Another basic way to handle access restrictions is by using the Order directive. With this directive, you'll specify the order in which allow and deny commands are used. The order is not defined by how the rules appear in your configuration file but by how you've used the Order directive. The default order is deny and then allow. This means that if a client is excluded by deny, it will be excluded unless it matches allow. If neither is matched, the client gets access. As you see, this is a rather open approach that doesn't put many restrictions on a directory.

Look at this example:

```
order allow, deny
allow from 10.100
deny from all
```

In this line, the allow rules are read first and give access to any host that has an IP address starting with 10.100. However, after reading the deny line that denies access to all, the site would be closed, even for devices that have an IP address starting with 10.100. If you want to make sure that everyone is denied with the exception of devices that have an IP address starting with 10.100, you should rewrite the statement as follows:

```
order deny, allow
allow from 10.100
deny from all
```

Put this way, the httpd process first reads the deny line, which denies access to all, and then handles all exceptions as stated on the allow lines.

Apache Log Files

To help you troubleshoot Apache issues, two log files are used by default. You can find these files in the /var/log/httpd directory. The access_log file contains information about users who have accessed your server. Note that it can grow very fast on busy web servers! The error_log file has error messages that can be useful in troubleshooting your Apache web server.

Apache and SELinux

As an administrator, SELinux can often be an annoyance. This is because it defines in a very strict way what is allowed and what isn't allowed. Moreover, if anything happens that isn't allowed specifically in the policy, SELinux will deny it. You already learned this while working on Exercise 8.6.

To make sure that Apache runs smoothly with SELinux, there are a few things that need to be addressed. First you'll need to make sure that the appropriate context types have been applied. Typically, these are httpd_sys_content_t on directories where Apache can access documents, and httpd_sys_script_exec_t on directories from where Apache needs to run scripts. But some other context types are also available. Here are the context types that are defined for httpd:

httpd_sys_content_t Set this on directories that should be accessible by the httpd process.

httpd_sys_script_exec_t Set this on directories that contain scripts that are allowed to run from the httpd process.

httpd_sys_rw_content_t This context type is useful if you want to run scripts from the httpd process and allow the httpd process to write the resulting data to a directory.

httpd_sys_ra_content_t Use this if you want to allow scripts to append to existing files.

httpd_unconfined_script_exec_t Use this to allow a script to run without any SELinux protection. Use this only as a last resort if nothing else works!

public_content_t Use this to allow access to a directory from the httpd process but also by other services like Samba and NFS.

public_content_rw_t Use this to allow shared read-write access to a directory.

To change the context type in the policy, you can use the `semanage fcontext` command. For example, use `semanage fcontext -a -t httpd_sys_content_t "/www(/.*)"` to label the /www directory for the specified context type. Next use `restorecon -r /www` to apply the new context to the file system.

Apart from the context types that can be used for Apache, there are numerous Booleans as well. These behave as on/off switches for specific features. To get a list of all available Booleans for httpd, use `getsebool -a | grep httpd`. Alternatively, you can read the man page `httpd_selinux` for Apache SELinux-specific information. The command `semanage Boolean -l` will also yield a nice, short description of all Booleans. In Exercise 16.2, you will configure SELinux for Apache.

EXERCISE 16.2

Configuring SELinux for Apache

In this exercise, you'll run Apache on a different port. SELinux will deny this, but you'll apply the appropriate fix to ensure that Apache is allowed to listen on this port.

1. Open a root shell. Copy the file /etc/httpd/conf/httpd.conf to httpd.conf.bak, which allows you easily to revert to the original situation later.

2. Open the /etc/httpd/conf/httpd.conf file in an editor.

3. Look up the parameter Listen 80, and change it to **Listen 888**. Save the changes, and use **service httpd restart** to restart the httpd process. It will give you an error message.

4. Use **tail -f /var/log/messages** to read the log message that was written when Apache tried to start on port 888. If you don't see a line that instructs you to use the sealert command, use **yum -y install setroubleshoot-server**. Also make sure that the auditd process is running, and restart Apache.

EXERCISE 16.2 *(continued)*

5. In /var/log/messages, you will find a `sealert` command that you can run. This is the line that starts with run `sealert -l`, followed by a long UUID. Copy this line, and paste it on a console so that the command can run.

6. Read the message that `sealert` displays. It tells you that you need to change the port type for port 888 so that Apache can run on it. Because it cannot determine exactly what you want to do, it suggests a few port types from which to choose. Because you are trying to run Apache, you'll need to set the `http_port_t` port type.

7. Use **semanage port -a -t http_port_t -p tcp 888** to flag port 888 with the appropriate port type.

8. Restart httpd. It should now run without any problems.

9. Stop httpd and copy the `httpd.conf.bak` file you created in step 1 of this exercise to /etc/httpd/conf/httpd.conf. This restores the original situation.

Getting Help

The number of options that Apache offers can be overwhelming for a new user. Fortunately, there is excellent documentation available in the `httpd-manual` package. Every task an Apache administrator will ever undertake is documented in the online documentation that is available on your web server after installing the `httpd-manual` package. In Figure 16.1, you can see what the documentation looks like. In Exercise 16.3, you'll learn how to install and use the manual.

FIGURE 16.1   All the Apache documentation you'll ever need is in the `httpd-manual`.

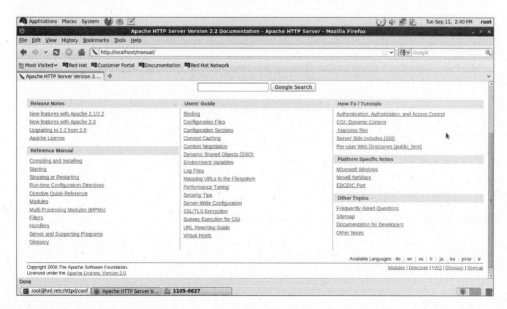

EXERCISE 16.3

Installing and Using the Apache Documentation

There is no need to try to remember all of the options Apache has to offer—just install the manual. In this exercise, you'll learn how to install and use the Apache documentation.

1. Open a root shell, and use **yum -y install httpd-manual** to install the Apache documentation.

2. Use **service httpd restart** to restart the httpd process.

3. Open a browser, and enter the URL **http://localhost/manual**. This will show the Apache documentation containing all of the information you'll ever need about Apache.

Working with Virtual Hosts

One Apache installation can handle more than one Apache website. To handle more than one site from an Apache server, you can create virtual hosts. A *virtual host* is a definition of different websites to be served by the Apache web server. You can include this definition in the main Apache configuration file /etc/httpd/conf/httpd.conf or in separate files that you'll create in the /etc/httpd/conf.d/ directory. If you chose the latter solution, make sure the name of each of these files ends in .conf.

Before you can start working with virtual hosts, you'll need to make sure that hostname resolving works. That means you'll need to make sure the virtual host can be reached by its name. This means you'll either have to create A records or CNAME records in DNS or have to create an entry in the /etc/hosts file that tells the client computer which IP address to connect to in order to reach the virtual host. In a test environment like the one you're using in this book, it is a very common error to forget to set up name resolving.

When setting up virtual hosts, you'll have to choose which type to use. You can configure either a name-based virtual host, an IP-based virtual host, or both. Name-based virtual hosts are the default, and they are easier to set up because you can run multiple Apache sites on one IP address. IP-virtual hosts are often used if SSL is needed on a website, because in SSL it is beneficial if a connection can be traced back to its original unique IP address. So, you must set up IP-based virtual hosting to get SSL working.

When setting up a virtual host, you can use almost any Apache directive. In Listing 16.2, you can see an example of some of the most common directives that are used while setting up virtual hosts.

Listing 16.2: Example virtual host configuration

```
<VirtualHost *:80>
        ServerAdmin webmaster@dummy-host.example.com
```

```
    DocumentRoot /www/docs/dummy-host.example.com
    ServerName dummy-host.example.com
    ErrorLog logs/dummy-host.example.com-error_log
    CustomLog logs/dummy-host.example.com-access_log common
</VirtualHost>
```

The example in Listing 16.2 starts by defining the port on which the virtual host should listen. This is set to *:80, which means that it is available on any IP address on this machine on port 80. Next, the ServerAdmin directive is used to tell users whom to contact if they need to get in touch with the administrator of this web server.

The most important parameter that you'll use when defining a virtual host is a DocumentRoot that is specific for that virtual host. In this example, a DocumentRoot in /www is used, which means you'll also need to set the appropriate SELinux context type. Next the ServerName is specified, and as the last bit of the configuration, some dedicated log files for this virtual host are defined.

WARNING   When setting up virtual hosts, you should be aware of one thing. Either you configure all hosts as virtual hosts or you don't. This means that if you set up some virtual hosts on an Apache server that also already has a normal host definition, the normal host definition will fail after installing the virtual hosts.

When configuring virtual hosts, you should consider creating separate .conf files for the virtual hosts in /etc/httpd/conf.d. Working with separate .conf files makes managing virtual hosts easier, especially if you're planning on creating many of them. In Exercise 16.4, you'll learn how to set up two virtual hosts.

EXERCISE 16.4

Configuring Virtual Hosts

In this exercise, you'll create two virtual hosts. Before setting up virtual hosts, you'll first set up name resolving. After that, you'll create the virtual hosts configuration. You'll also need to change the SELinux configuration to make this work. You will use both the host computer and the virtual machine for this exercise.

1. On your host computer, open the file /etc/hosts with an editor and add two lines that make it possible to resolve the names of the virtual host you are going to create to the IP address of the virtual machine.

2. On the virtual machine, open a root shell and create a configuration file with the name server1.example.com.conf in the directory /etc/httpd/conf.d. Give this file the following content:

```
<VirtualHost *:80>
    ServerAdmin webmaster@server1.example.com
```

```
        DocumentRoot /www/docs/server1.example.com
        ServerName server1.example.com
        ErrorLog logs/server1/example.com-error_log
        CustomLog logs/server1.example.com-access_log common
    </VirtualHost>
```

3. Close the configuration file, and from the root shell, use **mkdir -p /www/docs/ server1.example.com**.

4. Create a file with the name index.html in the server1 document root, and make sure its contents read "Welcome to server1."

5. Use **semanage fcontext -a -t httpd_sys_content_t "/www(/.*)"**, followed by restorecon -r /www.

6. Open the /etc/httpd/conf/httpd.conf file with your editor, and take out the # sign at the front of the line NameVirtualHost *:80.

7. Use **service httpd restart** to restart the Apache web server.

8. Use **elinks http://server1.example.com**. You should now see the server1 welcome page.

9. Back on the root shell, copy the /etc/httpd/conf.d/server1.example.com.conf file to a file with the name /etc/httpd/conf.d/server2.example.com.conf.

10. Open the server2.example.com.conf file in vi, and use the vi command **:%s/ server1/server2/g**. This should replace all instances of server1 with the text server2.

11. Create the /www/docs/server2.example.com document root, set the SELinux labels, and create a file index.html in it containing the text "Welcome to server2."

12. Restart httpd, and verify that both server1 and server2 are accessible.

In the previous exercise, you created two virtual hosts and verified that both are working as expected. With the creation of the virtual hosts, the web server you've configured in Exercise 16.1 is no longer working. If you try to access this web server by using the command elinks http://localhost, for example, you'll get access to the first virtual web server that Apache finds. This process goes in alphabetical order, and because httpd finds the server1 configuration file first, it will show you the server1 configuration by default.

When configuring a server with multiple web servers, make sure your most important website comes first. That is, make sure that httpd loads the configuration of the most important website if it can't find the site the user is trying to access. You can do this by having the name of the configuration file come first alphabetically; this website will be used as the default one.

Securing the Web Server with TLS Certificates

For some web servers, protection isn't an issue; for others, it is a major issue. For example, if you're running an ecommerce site, a website where users need to be sure they are connected to the correct site or a website where traffic simply must be protected, you'll need to use encryption. TLS security guarantees that sensitive data can be encrypted while in transit. At the same time, it can be used to prove the identity of servers on the Internet.

To use TLS in an Apache environment, you need mod_ssl. This Apache module is not installed by default, so you'll need to do the installation yourself. After installing mod_ssl, you'll find its configuration file ssl.conf in the /etc/httpd/conf.d directory. Listing 16.3 shows the directives that are used in this configuration file.

Listing 16.3: The ssl.conf configuration file

```
[root@hnl conf.d]# cat ssl.conf
LoadModule ssl_module modules/mod_ssl.so
Listen 443

##   SSL Global Context
SSLPassPhraseDialog  builtin
SSLSessionCache         shmcb:/var/cache/mod_ssl/scache(512000)
SSLSessionCacheTimeout  300
SSLMutex default

SSLRandomSeed startup file:/dev/urandom  256
SSLRandomSeed connect builtin
#SSLRandomSeed startup file:/dev/random  512
#SSLRandomSeed connect file:/dev/random  512
#SSLRandomSeed connect file:/dev/urandom 512

SSLCryptoDevice builtin
#SSLCryptoDevice ubsec

## SSL Virtual Host Context
<VirtualHost _default_:443>
#DocumentRoot "/var/www/html"
#ServerName www.example.com:443
ErrorLog logs/ssl_error_log
TransferLog logs/ssl_access_log
LogLevel warn
```

```
SLEngine on
SSLProtocol all -SSLv2
SSLCipherSuite ALL:!ADH:!EXPORT:!SSLv2:RC4+RSA:+HIGH:+MEDIUM:+LOW
SSLCertificateFile /etc/pki/tls/certs/localhost.crt
SSLCertificateKeyFile /etc/pki/tls/private/localhost.key
#SSLCertificateChainFile /etc/pki/tls/certs/server-chain.crt
#SSLCACertificateFile /etc/pki/tls/certs/ca-bundle.crt
#SSLVerifyClient require
#SSLVerifyDepth  10
<Files ~ "\.(cgi|shtml|phtml|php3?)$">
    SSLOptions +StdEnvVars
</Files>
<Directory "/var/www/cgi-bin">
    SSLOptions +StdEnvVars
</Directory>

SetEnvIf User-Agent ".*MSIE.*" \
        nokeepalive ssl-unclean-shutdown \
        downgrade-1.0 force-response-1.0

CustomLog logs/ssl_request_log \
        "%t %h %{SSL_PROTOCOL}x %{SSL_CIPHER}x \"%r\" %b"

</VirtualHost>
```

In the ssl.conf file, many directives are used to specify how the SSL protocol should be configured. In most cases, you are just fine using the default values. The important values for configuring a site with SSL are as follows:

```
LoadModule ssl_module modules/mod_ssl.so
```

This line makes sure that the SSL module is loaded. Note the path that is used. It is relative to the ServerRoot directive that defines the path in httpd.conf **to** /etc/httpd.

Listen 443   This line tells mod_ssl to offer TLS services on port 443.

SSLCertificateFile   This line refers to the file that is used for the server certificate. By default, the localhost.crt file is used. This is the default configuration file that is created while installing Red Hat Enterprise Linux.

SSLCertificateKeyFile   This line tells mod_ssl where it can find the private key for the server. By default, the localhost.key file is used, which is generated during the installation of Red Hat Enterprise Linux.

Apart from these four directives, all of the other directives are OK as is. However, there is an important change that you should apply when using SSL. The `localhost.crt` certificate doesn't include the name of the server for which you are using it. For that reason, it will be rejected by most SSL clients. Therefore, you'll need to replace it with a self-generated certificate that contains the name of the server for which you are using it. In Exercise 16.5, you'll learn how to set up an SSL-based virtual host. Self-signed certificates will also be rejected unless the public key of the signer is known in the browser. Read Chapter 13, "Configuring Your Server for File Sharing," for more details about PKI certificates.

EXERCISE 16.5

Setting Up an SSL-Based Virtual Host

In this exercise, you'll set up an SSL-based virtual host. You'll use the `server1.example.com` host that you set up in Exercise 16.3 and also make it accessible over the SSL port.

1. Open a root shell, and use **cd** to go to the directory `/etc/httpd/conf.d`. In this directory, create a file with the name `server1_ssl.conf`, and give it the following contents:

```
<VirtualHost *:443>
DocumentRoot "/www/docs/server1.example.com"
ServerName server1.example.com:443
ErrorLog logs/server1_ssl_error_log
TransferLog logs/server1_ssl_access_log
LogLevel warn

SSLEngine on
SSLProtocol all -SSLv2
SSLCipherSuite ALL:!ADH:!EXPORT:!SSLv2:RC4+RSA:+HIGH:+MEDIUM:+LOW
SSLCertificateFile /etc/pki/tls/certs/localhost.crt
SSLCertificateKeyFile /etc/pki/tls/private/localhost.key
</VirtualHost>
```

2. Use **service httpd restart** to restart Apache. You may get an error message about overlapping virtual hosts. You can ignore this message.

3. Start a browser, and enter the URL **https://server1.example.com**. You will get a message that the connection is untrusted. Open the technical details. There you'll see that server1 uses an invalid security certificate. The browser mentions that the certificate is untrusted because it is self-signed, and you'll get a message that it is valid only for ..., which is followed by the name of the host machine and not the virtual web server. You're going to fix this problem in the steps that follow in this exercise. For now, you can close the browser.

EXERCISE 16.5 *(continued)*

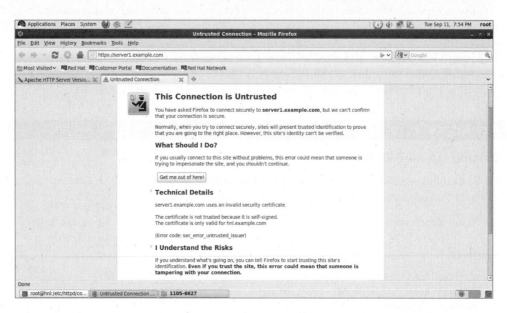

4. Use **yum -y install crypto-utils** to install the genkey utility on your server. Next, use **genkey server1.example.com** to start the genkey utility, which will create certificates for your server.

5. From the first screen, note the location where genkey will store the certificate and the key files, and click Next to continue.

6. Select a key size of 512 bits. This doesn't produce a secure key, but it minimizes the time you'll have to wait to create the key pair.

7. When you see the Generating Random Bits screen, move your mouse or cause some other activity on your server. This makes the process go faster.

8. When asked if you would like to send a CSR to a CA, select No. To get a completely secure key that doesn't display error messages to your user, normally you would select Yes and send the key to an external CA. Since there is no external CA available in the test environment that you've built in this book, select No here.

9. Select Encrypt the private key to protect the private key with a passphrase, and click Next.

10. In the Set Private Key Passphrase dialog box, type the passphrase **password** twice, and click Next.

11. You'll now enter the details of your certificate. It is important to make sure the common name matches the name of your server. It is also a good habit to specify the rest of the information that is requested so that users of your web server can see who is behind it.

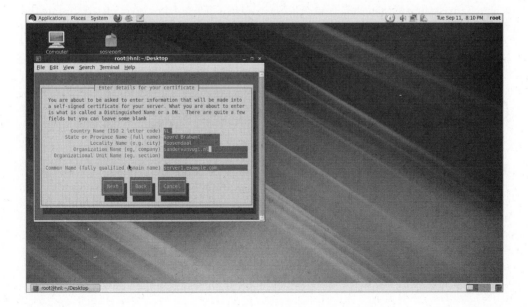

12. At this point you've generated a key pair that at least matches the name of your server. Open the /etc/httpd/conf.d/server1_ssl.conf file again with an editor. Look up the directives SSLCertificateFile and SSLCertificateKeyFile, and make sure the key you've just generated is referenced as shown in the following two example lines:

    ```
    SSLCertificateFile /etc/pki/tls/certs/server1.example.com.crt
    SSLCertificateKeyFile /etc/pki/tls/private/server1.example.com.key
    ```

13. Use the command **service httpd restart**. When starting, httpd will prompt you for a password. Enter the passphrase to finish starting your web server.

14. Use your browser to connect to https://server1.example.com again. You'll still get a certificate error message because you're using a self-signed certificate, but you will no longer see the error about the name used in the certificate.

In Exercise 16.5, you configured your server to use a certificate. You also entered a passphrase to protect the private key. This is normally recommended because without a passphrase on the private key, an intruder would only have to steal the private key to be able to forge your entire website. Therefore, in production environments, TLS-protected websites should always have a passphrase on the private key. The drawback, however, is that it has to be reentered on every restart, and for that reason it is also often omitted.

You also witnessed a significant disadvantage of using a private key; that is, you'll need to enter a passphrase when the httpd process is started. This makes it very hard to start the web server automatically from the runlevels while booting your server. Therefore, if you want to shield your web server with a private key that is protected with a passphrase, you have to remove it from the runlevels.

Configuring Authentication

You already learned how to protect your Apache server from access by unauthorized devices. You can also configure Apache to allow access only to specific users. To do this, you can configure your server to use authentication. In this section, you'll learn how to configure authentication based on a flat file that contains usernames and hashed passwords and how to configure authentication for user accounts that are stored in an LDAP directory server.

In both cases, you need to be aware that authentication settings are related to a directory or web context that you want to protect. This means that the settings discussed in this chapter are always placed in a block that opens with <Directory> and ends with

</Directory>. This allows you to set up authentication for specific directories on only the web server. If you want to set up authentication for the entire website, you need to set it up for a directory as well. If this is the case, just set it up for the root directory in that case.

Setting Up Authentication with .htpasswd

The easiest way to set up authentication is to create a file with the name .htpasswd that contains the names of users and their hashed passwords. If you do this, make sure that the file is in a directory where web users will never find it to read its contents! The directory /etc/httpd is a reasonably secure directory in which to put this file.

To add user accounts to the .htpasswd file, use the htpasswd command. In the following two example lines, the first line creates the file (option -c) and adds a user linda with an MD5 hashed password. The second line adds user leo to the existing file. Make sure to use -c only for the first user you add to the file. If not, you'll overwrite all of the existing content in the file.

```
htpasswd -cm /etc/httpd/.htpasswd linda
htpasswd -m /etc/httpd/.htpasswd leo
```

After creating the file and adding some user accounts, you'll need to configure your web server to work with one or more restricted directories. If you need several restricted directories, you will have to repeat this procedure for every directory that you want to configure for user authentication. Listing 16.4 shows you what to include in your web server configuration to create a protected directory.

Listing 16.4: Configuring a restricted directory

```
<Directory />
AuthName geheim
AuthType basic
AuthUserFile /etc/httpd/.htpasswd
Require valid-user
</Directory>
```

The example in Listing 16.4 uses four different directives:

AuthName   Specifies a name that is displayed when a user tries to access the restricted directory.

AuthType   Specifies the authentication type. Use basic for all cases discussed in this chapter.

AuthUserFile   Tells Apache which file to use to find the user accounts and passwords.

Require valid-user   Tells Apache which users are allowed access. Use valid-user to allow access for any user in the authuserfile, or use a list of users to allow access only for specific users.

In Exercise 16.6, you'll learn how to set up your SSL-protected virtual host server1 so that users can view its contents only after entering the username and password.

EXERCISE 16.6

Setting Up a Protected Web Server

In this exercise, you'll use the SSL-protected web server that you created in Exercise 16.5 as a restricted web server where user authentication is required.

1. Open a root shell, and use an editor to open the /etc/httpd/conf.d/server1_ssl. conf file.

2. Include the following lines anywhere in the VirtualHost definition:

   ```
   <Directory />
   AuthName Protected website, please enter your credentials
   AuthType basic
   AuthUserFile /etc/httpd/.htpasswd
   Require valid-user
   </Directory>
   ```

3. From the root shell, enter the following commands to add two users to the configuration file. Set the password for both users to *password* when prompted:

   ```
   htpasswd -cm /etc/httpd/.htaccess lisa
   htpasswd -m /etc/httpd/.htaccess luigi
   ```

4. Use **service httpd restart** to restart Apache, and enter the passphrase when prompted. Once it has successfully started, use a browser to connect to https:// server1.example.com. You'll be prompted for a password before you get access.

Configuring LDAP Authentication

As you've seen in the previous section, handling authentication based on a flat user file works, but it's hard to maintain if you have many users to whom you want to grant access. In such cases like this, it might be interesting to add user accounts to an LDAP server and configure your Apache server to get the credentials from LDAP. This type of authentication can be handled by using the mod_authnz_ldap module and associated parameters. The only requirement from the LDAP side of the configuration is that the user account to which you'll refer has to exist.

To configure an Apache server to use LDAP, the administrator needs to address two things. First the Apache server must be able to handle the LDAP certificate, and the basic authentication provider must be set to LDAP. This section of the configuration is in the generic part of httpd.conf so that it is available for all virtual servers' services of your

Apache instance. Next the (virtual) server itself must be configured to use LDAP for authentication. To take care of this, you'll need to include the following in your `httpd.conf` file:

```
LDAPTrustedGlobalCert CA_BASE64 /etc/httpd/your-ldap-server-certificate.crt
AuthBasicProvider ldap
```

The important part of the general segment of the configuration is the `LDAPTrustedGlobalCert` parameter that tells Apache which LDAP certificate to use. This assumes that your LDAP server has its own certificate, which you have already copied to the appropriate location. After setting this up, you'll need to include the parameters shown in Listing 16.5 in your web server configuration.

Listing 16.5: Configuring Apache for LDAP authentication

```
<Directory />
AuthName Enter your credentials for access
AuthType basic
AuthBasicProvider ldap
AuthLDAPUrl "ldap://yourserver.example.com/dc=example,dc=com" TLS
Require valid-user
</Directory>
```

The only parameter from Listing 16.5 that hasn't been discussed previously is `AuthLDAPUrl`. This parameter specifies the URL to use to get access to the LDAP user information. Note how this URL is comprised. The first part is the fully qualified DNS name of the server, followed by the LDAP base context that is used to access user information. All other parameters are similar to the configuration of the basic user authentication that was discussed in the previous section.

Setting Up MySQL

Apache is often used in the LAMP stack. This means that it also uses a database, which is commonly the MySQL database. In this section, you will read how to install MySQL and configure it with basic user information. The rest of the setup is the domain of the database administrator (DBA), which is beyond the scope of this book. In Exercise 16.7, you'll learn how to install MySQL and perform some basic user configuration tasks.

EXERCISE 16.7

Installing MySQL and Creating User Accounts

In this exercise, you'll learn how to install MySQL. You'll also set the MySQL root password and create a user account for a user who is allowed to manage databases.

EXERCISE 16.7 *(continued)*

1. Use **yum install -y mysql mysql-server** to install the MySQL core components.

2. Use **service mysqld start** to start MySQL.

3. Add a MySQL root user (this is an internal MySQL account and has nothing to do with the Linux root user). Use **mysqladmin -u root password 'password'** to perform this task.

4. At this stage, you're ready to authenticate in MySQL as root. Use **mysql -u root -p**, and enter the root password. You'll now enter a MySQL prompt.

5. Now you will use one of the many available SQL commands to check the MySQL internal users. At the MySQL prompt, enter **SELECT User, Host, Password FROM mysql.user;** (be sure to include the semicolon at the end of the command). This should yield the following result:

```
[root@hn1 ~]# mysql -u root -p
Enter password:
Welcome to the MySQL monitor.  Commands end with ; or \g.
Your MySQL connection id is 5
Server version: 5.1.52 Source distribution

Copyright (c) 2000, 2010, Oracle and/or its affiliates. All rights reserved.
This software comes with ABSOLUTELY NO WARRANTY. This is free software,
and you are welcome to modify and redistribute it under the GPL v2 license

Type 'help;' or '\h' for help. Type '\c' to clear the current input statement.

mysql> SELECT User, Host, Password FROM mysql.user;
+------+-----------------+-------------------------------------------+
| User | Host            | Password                                  |
+------+-----------------+-------------------------------------------+
| root | localhost       | *2470C0C06DEE42FD1618BB99005ADCA2EC9D1E19 |
| root | hn1.example.com |                                           |
| root | 127.0.0.1       |                                           |
|      | localhost       |                                           |
|      | hn1.example.com |                                           |
+------+-----------------+-------------------------------------------+
5 rows in set (0.00 sec)
```

6. Now create a MySQL User with the following command (still from the MySQL prompt): **CREATE USER 'mysqlUser'@'localhost' IDENTIFIED BY 'mysqlpassword';**.

7. Now that `mysqlUser` is created, you'll need to give this user some management permissions. The following command gives this user all of the permissions that a DBA typically wants to have to create databases: **GRANT ALL PRIVILEGES ON *.* TO 'mysqlUser'@'localhost' WITH GRANT OPTION;**.

8. At this point, you're done and ready to leave the MySQL management interface. Type **exit**.

9. Now test that you can log into MySQL using the user account you just created. From the bash shell prompt, use **mysql -u mysqlUser -p** to log in, and use **exit** to log out again.

Summary

In this chapter, you learned how to configure Apache on your server. You read how to perform most of the common configuration tasks, including virtual web servers, SSL protection, and authentication using user accounts. You also learned how to fix SELinux issues that might occur when managing Apache and how the Apache configuration files are handled on Red Hat Enterprise Linux. At the end of the chapter, you had a short introduction to MySQL management in an Apache environment.

Advanced Red Hat Enterprise Linux Configuration

PART

V

Chapter

17

Monitoring and Optimizing Performance

TOPICS COVERED IN THIS CHAPTER:

- ✓ Interpreting What's Going On: The top Utility
- ✓ Analyzing CPU Performance
- ✓ Analyzing Memory Usage
- ✓ Monitoring Storage Performance
- ✓ Understanding Network Performance
- ✓ Optimizing Performance

Running a server is one thing; running a server that works well is something else. On a server installed with the default settings, performance may not be up to where you need it to be. Finding a performance problem on a Linux server is not that easy. You need to know exactly what is going on, and you also need to know how to interpret performance-monitoring data. In this chapter, you will first learn how to monitor performance. After that, you'll learn how to optimize your server.

Interpreting What's Going On: The top Utility

Before examining details, you need a general overview of the current state of your server. The top utility is an excellent tool to help you get this information.

Let's start by looking at a server that is restoring a workstation from an image file using the Clonezilla imaging solution. (This is merely a random example of a tool that produces some workload on the machine.) The top window in Listing 17.1 shows how busy the server is doing this task.

Listing 17.1: Analyzing top on a somewhat busy server

```
top - 09:19:12 up 21 min,  3 users,  load average: 0.55, 0.21, 0.13
Tasks: 140 total,   1 running, 139 sleeping,   0 stopped,   0 zombie
Cpu(s):  0.0%us,  1.0%sy,  0.0%ni, 90.1%id,  3.9%wa,  0.0%hi,  5.0%si,  0.0%st
Mem:   4083276k total,   989152k used,  3094124k free,    15712k buffers
Swap:  2097144k total,        0k used,  2097144k free,   862884k cached


  PID USER      PR  NI  VIRT  RES  SHR S %CPU %MEM    TIME+  COMMAND
 5350 root      20   0     0    0    0 S    0  0.0   0:00.05 nfsd
 5356 root      20   0     0    0    0 S    0  0.0   0:00.07 nfsd
 5359 root      20   0     0    0    0 S    0  0.0   0:00.08 nfsd
    1 root      20   0  1804  760  548 S    0  0.0   0:01.19 init
    2 root      15  -5     0    0    0 S    0  0.0   0:00.00 kthreadd
    3 root      RT  -5     0    0    0 S    0  0.0   0:00.00 migration/0
    4 root      15  -5     0    0    0 S    0  0.0   0:00.00 ksoftirqd/0
    5 root      RT  -5     0    0    0 S    0  0.0   0:00.00 watchdog/0
```

```
 6 root      RT  -5    0    0    0 S    0  0.0   0:00.00 migration/1
 7 root      15  -5    0    0    0 S    0  0.0   0:00.00 ksoftirqd/1
 8 root      RT  -5    0    0    0 S    0  0.0   0:00.00 watchdog/1
 9 root      15  -5    0    0    0 S    0  0.0   0:00.00 events/0
10 root      15  -5    0    0    0 S    0  0.0   0:00.00 events/1
11 root      15  -5    0    0    0 S    0  0.0   0:00.00 khelper
46 root      15  -5    0    0    0 S    0  0.0   0:00.00 kblockd/0
47 root      15  -5    0    0    0 S    0  0.0   0:00.00 kblockd/1
50 root      15  -5    0    0    0 S    0  0.0   0:00.00 kacpid
```

CPU Monitoring with top

When analyzing performance, you start with the first line of the top output. The load average parameters are of special interest. There are three of them, indicating the load average for the last minute, last five minutes, and the last fifteen minutes. The *anchor value* is 1.00. You will see 1.00 on a single CPU system where the system is completely busy but all is running smoothly and there is no queuing; 1.00 is the anchor value for each CPU core in your system. Thus, on a dual quad-core processor system, the anchor value would be 8.00.

NOTE   The load average is for your system, not for your CPU. It is definitively possible to have a load average far above 1.00 while your CPU is doing next to nothing. For example, the system can be busy waiting for I/O.

Having a system that works exactly at the anchor value may be good but not necessarily. You need to understand more about typical workloads before being able to determine whether a workload of 1.00 is good.

For example, think about a task that is running completely on the CPU. You can force such a task by entering the following code line:

```
while true; do true; done
```

This task will completely claim one CPU core, thus causing a workload of 1.00. However, since this is a task that doesn't do any I/O, it does not have waiting times. Therefore, for a task such as this, 1.00 is considered a heavy workload because if another task is started, processes will have to be queued because of a lack of available resources.

Now let's consider a task that is I/O intensive, such as one in which your hard drive is completely copied to the null device (dd if=/dev/sda of=/dev/null). This task also easily results in a workload that is 1.00 or greater, but since it involves a lot of waiting time for I/O, it's not as bad as the while true task. This is because while waiting for I/O, the CPU can do something else. Thus, don't draw conclusions too quickly from the load line.

When you see that your servers' CPUs are quite busy, you should pursue further analysis. First you should relate the load average to the number of CPUs in your server. By default, top gives a summary for all of the CPUs in your server. Press the **1** on the keyboard to show a line for each CPU core in your server. Since all modern servers are multicore, you should apply this option because it also provides information about the multiprocessing environment. Listing 17.2 shows usage statistics on a quad-core server.

Listing 17.2: Monitoring performance on a quad-core server

```
[root@hn1 ~]# top
top - 18:38:28 up 17 min,  3 users,  load average: 0.22, 0.32, 0.18
Tasks: 205 total,   1 running, 204 sleeping,   0 stopped,   0 zombie
Cpu0  :  1.1%us,  2.0%sy,  0.0%ni, 94.2%id,  2.5%wa,  0.0%hi,  0.1%si,  0.0%st
Cpu1  :  0.6%us,  1.1%sy,  0.0%ni, 97.5%id,  0.7%wa,  0.0%hi,  0.1%si,  0.0%st
Cpu2  :  0.7%us,  1.4%sy,  0.0%ni, 95.8%id,  2.0%wa,  0.0%hi,  0.0%si,  0.0%st
Cpu3  :  0.6%us,  1.1%sy,  0.0%ni, 97.6%id,  0.6%wa,  0.0%hi,  0.0%si,  0.0%st
Mem:   1016928k total,   560572k used,   456356k free,    60092k buffers
Swap:  2064376k total,        0k used,  2064376k free,   198728k cached

  PID USER      PR  NI  VIRT  RES  SHR S %CPU %MEM    TIME+  COMMAND
 3255 root      20   0 15088 1320  960 R  1.4  0.1  0:00.27 top
   42 root      20   0     0    0    0 S  0.7  0.0  0:00.12 ata/1
    1 root      20   0 19404 1568 1252 S  0.0  0.2  0:04.31 init
    2 root      20   0     0    0    0 S  0.0  0.0  0:00.03 kthreadd
    3 root      RT   0     0    0    0 S  0.0  0.0  0:00.04 migration/0
    4 root      20   0     0    0    0 S  0.0  0.0  0:00.00 ksoftirqd/0
    5 root      RT   0     0    0    0 S  0.0  0.0  0:00.00 migration/0
    6 root      RT   0     0    0    0 S  0.0  0.0  0:00.00 watchdog/0
    7 root      RT   0     0    0    0 S  0.0  0.0  0:00.15 migration/1
    8 root      RT   0     0    0    0 S  0.0  0.0  0:00.00 migration/1
    9 root      20   0     0    0    0 S  0.0  0.0  0:00.00 ksoftirqd/1
   10 root      RT   0     0    0    0 S  0.0  0.0  0:00.00 watchdog/1
   11 root      RT   0     0    0    0 S  0.0  0.0  0:00.05 migration/2
   12 root      RT   0     0    0    0 S  0.0  0.0  0:00.00 migration/2
```

When thinking about exactly what your server is doing, the CPU lines are an important indicator. There you can monitor CPU performance, divided into different performance categories. The following list summarizes these options:

us   This refers to a workload in user space. Typically, this relates to processes that are started by end users and don't run with root priorities. If you see a high load here, this means your server is heavily used by applications.

sy   This refers to the work that is done in system space. These are important tasks in which the kernel of your operating system is also involved. In general, load average here should not be too high. You can see that it is elevated when particular jobs are executed, such as for the creation of a 4096 private key in which a large amount of random data is read.

ni This indicator relates to the number of jobs that have been started with an adjusted nice command value.

id Here you can see how busy the idle loop is. This special loop indicates the amount of time your CPU is doing nothing. Thus, a high percentage in the idle loop time means a CPU that is not too busy.

wa This is an important indicator. The wa parameter refers to the amount of time that your CPU is waiting for I/O. If the value you observe is frequently greater than 30 percent, this could indicate a problem on the I/O channel that involves storage and network. See the sections on storage and network performance monitoring later in this chapter to find out what may be causing this.

hi The hi parameter relates to the time the CPU spends handling hardware interrupts. You will see some utilization here when a device is particularly busy (optical drives, for instance, stress this parameter from time to time), but normally you won't ever see it above a few percentage points.

si This parameter relates to software interrupts. Typically, these are lower-priority interrupts that are created by the kernel. You will likely never see a high utilization in this field.

st The st parameter relates to an environment where virtualization is used. In some virtual environments, a virtual machine can take, or "steal" (hence st), CPU time from the host operating system. If this happens, you will see some utilization in the st field. If the utilization becomes very high, consider offloading virtual machines from your server.

Memory Monitoring with top

The second piece of information you get from top are the lines relating to memory and swap usage. The memory lines contain five parameters. The last parameter is in the swap line. The five parameters are as follows:

total The total amount of physical memory installed in your server.

used The amount of memory that is currently in use by something. This includes memory in buffers and cache.

free The amount of memory that is currently not in use. On a typical server, which is operational for more than a couple of hours, you will always see that this value is rather low.

buffers This parameter relates to the write cache that your server uses. It also contains file system tables and other structures that the server needs to have in memory. All data that a server must write to disk is written to the write cache first. From there, the disk controller takes care of this data when it has the time to write it. The advantage of using write cache is that, from the perspective of the end user, the data is written so that the application the user is using does not need to wait for it to be available. However, this buffer cache is memory used for nonessential purposes, and when an application needs more memory and can't allocate it from the pool of free memory, the write cache can be written to disk (flushed) so that memory that had been used by the write cache is then available for other purposes. Essentially, write cache is a good thing that makes your server perform faster.

cached   When a user requests a file from the server, the file normally has to be read from the hard disk. Since a hard disk is typically about 1,000 times slower than RAM, this process causes major delays. For this reason, the file is stored in cache every time after fetching a file from the server hard drive. This is a read cache and has only one purpose: to speed up reads. When memory that is currently allocated to the read cache is needed for other purposes, the read cache can be freed instantly so that more memory can be added to the pool of available ("free") memory.

Your server will typically see a high amount of cached memory, especially if it is used mostly for reads. This is considered good because it will speed up your server. In case your server is used mostly for reads and this parameter falls below 40 percent of total available memory, you will most likely slow down performance. Add more RAM if this happens. Be aware, however, that there are exceptions. Servers running large databases typically don't have a very high read cache, because the data is stored in memory, which is claimed by the database. It is not managed by the Linux kernel.

Apart from the Mem: line, which gives information about memory usage, there is the Swap: line. This relates to the usage of swap space. *Swap space* is emulated RAM on a hard disk, typically on a swap partition that you create when installing your server. If your server starts using swap, this can be bad because it is about 1,000 times slower than RAM. Swap isn't always that bad, however, because the kernel can use it to move data to swap that it doesn't really need at the moment, and this action frees memory for data that is needed more often. Also, there are some applications, such as Oracle databases or SAP applications, that use swap in a clever way. So, swap isn't always a bad thing. In Exercise 17.1, you'll learn how to monitor buffer and cache memory.

EXERCISE 17.1

Monitoring Buffer and Cache Memory

In this exercise, you'll monitor how buffer and cache memory is used. To start with a clean image, first you'll restart your server so that no old data is in buffers or cache. Next, you'll run some commands that will fill the buffer and cache memory. Finally, you'll clear the total amount of buffer and cache memory by using /proc/sys/vm/drop_caches.

1.   Reboot your server.

2.   After rebooting, open two root console windows. In one window, start top so that you'll have a real-time overview of what's happening. Note the current memory allocation. Buffers and cache should be low, and your server should have a relatively large amount of free memory available.

3.   Run the following script to read data, which will fill your server cache:

```
cd /etc
for I in *
```

```
do
    cat $I
done
```

4. You should see an increase in cache (probably not much, because the contents of the /etc directory typically aren't that high).

5. Run the following command to fill the buffer cache: **ls -Rl / > /dev/null &**.

6. Notice that the buffer cache has also filled somewhat.

7. Optionally, you can run some additional commands that will fill buffers as well as cache, such as **dd if=/dev/sda of=/dev/null &**.

8. Once finished, type **free -m** to observe the current usage of buffers and cache.

9. Tell the kernel to drop all buffers and cache that it doesn't need at this time by using echo 2 > /proc/sys/vm/drop_caches.

Process Monitoring with top

The last part of top is reserved for information about the most active processes. In this section, you'll see a few parameters that are related to these processes.

PID   The process ID of the process.

USER   The user who started the process.

PR   The priority of the process. The priority of any process is determined automatically, and the process with the highest priority is eligible to be serviced first from the queue of runnable processes. Some processes run with a real-time priority, which is indicated as RT. Processes with this priority can claim CPU cycles in real time, which means they will always have the highest priority.

NI   The nice value with which the process was started. This refers to an adjusted priority that has been set using the nice command.

VIRT   The amount of memory that was claimed by the process when it first started.

RES   This stands for resident memory. It relates to the amount of memory that a process is actually using. You will see that, in some cases, this is considerably lower than the parameter mentioned in the virt column. This is because many process like to over-allocate memory, which means that they claim more memory than they really need.

SHR   The amount of memory this process uses that is shared with another process.

S   The status of a process.

%CPU Relates to the percentage of CPU time that this process is using. You will normally see the process with the highest CPU utilization mentioned on top of this list.

%MEM The percentage of memory that this process has claimed.

TIME+ The total amount of time that this process has been using CPU cycles.

COMMAND The name of the command that relates to this process.

Analyzing CPU Performance

The top utility offers a good starting point for performance tuning. However, if you need to dig more deeply into a performance problem, top does not offer adequate information, and more advanced tools are required. In this section, you'll learn what you can do to find out more about CPU performance-related problems.

Most people tend to start analyzing a performance problem at the CPU, since they think CPU performance is the most important factor in server performance. In most situations, this is not true. Assuming that you have an up-to-date CPU, you will rarely see a performance problem related to the CPU. In most cases, a problem that appears to be CPU-related is caused by something else. For instance, your CPU may be waiting for data to be written to disk. In Exercise 17.2, you'll learn how to analyze CPU performance.

EXERCISE 17.2

Analyzing CPU Performance

In this exercise, you'll run two different commands that both affect CPU performance. You'll notice a difference in behavior between both commands.

1. Log in as root, and open two terminal windows. In one of the windows, start top.

2. In the second window, run the command **dd if=/dev/urandom of=/dev/null**. You will see the usage percentage increasing in the us column. Press **1** if you have a multicore system. You'll notice that one CPU core is completely occupied by this task.

3. Stop the dd job, and write a small script in the home directory of user root with the following content:

```
[root@hnl ~]# cat wait
#!/bin/bash

COUNTER=0

while true
do
        dd if=/dev/urandom of=/root/file.$COUNTER bs=1M count=1
```

```
                    COUNTER=$(( COUNTER + 1 ))
                        [ COUNTER = 1000 ] && exit
    done
```

4. Run the script. You'll notice that first the sy parameter in top goes up, and the wa parameter also goes up after a while. This is because the I/O channel gets too busy, and the CPU has to wait for data to be committed to I/O.

5. Make sure that both the script and the dd command have stopped, and close the root shells.

Understanding CPU Performance

To monitor what is happening on your CPU, you should know how the Linux kernel works with it. A key component is the run queue. Before being served by the CPU, every process enters the *run queue*. There's a run queue for every CPU core in the system. Once a process is in the run queue, it can be *runnable* or *blocked*. A *runnable process* is one that is competing for CPU time.

The Linux scheduler decides which runnable process to run next based on the current priority of the process. A blocked process doesn't compete for CPU time. The load average line in top summarizes the workload that is caused by all runnable and blocked processes combined. If you want to know how many of the processes are currently in either a runnable or blocked state, use the vmstat utility. The columns *r* and *b* show the number of runnable and blocked processes. Listing 17.3 shows what this looks like on a system where vmstat has polled the system five times with a two-second interval.

Listing 17.3: Use vmstat to see how many processes are in runnable or blocked state

```
[root@hn1 ~]# vmstat 2 5
procs -----------memory---------- ---swap-- -----io---- --system-- -----cpu-----
 r  b   swpd   free   buff  cache   si   so    bi    bo   in   cs us sy id wa st
 2  0      0  82996 372236 251688    0    0    61     3   36   29  1  1 98  1  0
 2  0      0  66376 493776 143932    0    0 76736     0 3065 1343 25 27 45  3  0
 2  0      0  71408 491088 142924    0    0 51840     0 2191  850 29 15 54  2  0
 2  0      0  69552 495568 141128    0    0 33536     0 1914  372 31 13 56  0  0
 2  0      0  69676 498000 138900    0    0 34816    16 1894  507 31 12 57  0  0
```

Context Switches and Interrupts

A modern Linux system is a multitasking system. This is true for every processor architecture because the Linux kernel constantly switches between different processes. To perform this switch, the CPU needs to save all the context information for the old process and retrieve the context information for the new process. Therefore, the performance price of these context switches is heavy.

In the ideal world, you would limit the number of context switches. You can do this by using a multicore CPU architecture, a server with multiple CPUs, or a combination of both. However, you would need to ensure that processes are locked to a dedicated CPU core to prevent context switches. Processes that are serviced by the kernel scheduler, however, are not the only reason for context switching. Another important reason for a context switch is hardware interrupts.

When you work on your server, the timer interrupt plays a role. The process scheduler uses this *timer interrupt* to ensure that each process gets a fair amount of processor time. Normally, the number of context switches should be lower than the number of timer interrupts. In some cases, however, you will see that there are more context switches than there are timer interrupts. If this is the case, it may indicate that there is just too much I/O to be handled by your server or that some long-running intense system call is causing this load. It is useful to know this because the relationship between timer interrupts and context switches provides a hint on where to look for the real cause of your performance problem.

Use `vmstat -s` to get an overview of the number of context switches and timer interrupts. It is also useful to look at the combination of a high amount of context switches and a high `IOWAIT`. This might indicate that the system tries to write a lot, but it cannot. Listing 17.4 shows the output of this command.

Listing 17.4: The relationship between timer interrupt and context switches provides a sense of what your server is doing

```
[root@hnl ~]# vmstat -s
   1016928  total memory
    907596  used memory
    180472  active memory
    574324  inactive memory
    109332  free memory
    531620  buffer memory
     59696  swap cache
   2064376  total swap
         0  used swap
   2064376  free swap
     23283 non-nice user cpu ticks
        54 nice user cpu ticks
     15403 system cpu ticks
   1020229 idle cpu ticks
      8881 IO-wait cpu ticks
        97 IRQ cpu ticks
       562 softirq cpu ticks
         0 stolen cpu ticks
```

```
  7623842 pages paged in
    34442 pages paged out
        0 pages swapped in
        0 pages swapped out
   712664 interrupts
   391869 CPU context switches
1347769276 boot time
     3942 forks
```

Another performance indicator for what is happening in your CPU is the interrupt counter. You can find this in the file /proc/interrupts (see Listing 17.5). The kernel receives interrupts by devices that need the CPU's attention. For the system administrator, it is important to know how many interrupts there are because, if the number is very high, the kernel will spend a lot of time servicing them, and other processes will get less attention.

Listing 17.5: The /proc/interrupts file shows you exactly how many of each type of interrupt have been handled

```
[root@hn1 ~]# cat /proc/interrupts
```

	CPU0	CPU1	CPU2	CPU3		
0:	264	0	0	0	IO-APIC-edge	timer
1:	52	0	0	0	IO-APIC-edge	i8042
3:	2	0	0	0	IO-APIC-edge	
4:	1116	0	0	0	IO-APIC-edge	
7:	0	0	0	0	IO-APIC-edge	parport0
8:	1	0	0	0	IO-APIC-edge	rtc0
9:	0	0	0	0	IO-APIC-fasteoi	acpi
12:	393	0	0	0	IO-APIC-edge	i8042
14:	0	0	0	0	IO-APIC-edge	ata_piix
15:	6918	0	482	0	IO-APIC-edge	ata_piix
16:	847	0	0	0	IO-APIC-fasteoi	Ensoniq AudioPCI
NMI:	0	0	0	0	Non-maskable interrupts	
LOC:	257548	135459	149931	302796	Local timer interrupts	
SPU:	0	0	0	0	Spurious interrupts	
PMI:	0	0	0	0	Performance monitoring interrupts	
PND:	0	0	0	0	Performance pending work	
RES:	11502	19632	8545	13272	Rescheduling interrupts	
CAL:	2557	9255	29757	2060	Function call interrupts	
TLB:	514	1171	518	1325	TLB shootdowns	
TRM:	0	0	0	0	Thermal event interrupts	
THR:	0	0	0	0	Threshold APIC interrupts	

```
MCE:          0         0         0         0   Machine check exceptions
MCP:         10        10        10        10   Machine check polls
ERR:          0
MIS:          0
[root@hnl ~]#
```

As mentioned previously, in a multicore environment, context switches can result in performance overhead. You can see how often these occur by using the top utility. It can provide information about the CPU that was last used by any process, but you need to switch this on. To do that, from the top utility, first press the **f** command and type **j**. This will switch the option Last Used CPU (SMP) on for an SMP environment. Listing 17.6 shows the interface that allows you to do this.

Listing 17.6: After pressing the **f** key, you can switch different options on or off in top

```
Current Fields: AEHIOQTWKNMbcdfgjplrsuvyzX  for window 1:Def
Toggle fields via field letter, type any other key to return
```

```
* A: PID        = Process Id            u: nFLT      = Page Fault count
* E: USER       = User Name             v: nDRT      = Dirty Pages count
* H: PR         = Priority              y: WCHAN     = Sleeping in Function
* I: NI         = Nice value            z: Flags     = Task Flags <sched.h>
* O: VIRT       = Virtual Image (kb)  * X: COMMAND   = Command name/line
* Q: RES        = Resident size (kb)
* T: SHR        = Shared Mem size (kb)  Flags field:
* W: S          = Process Status        0x00000001  PF_ALIGNWARN
* K: %CPU       = CPU usage             0x00000002  PF_STARTING
* N: %MEM       = Memory usage (RES)    0x00000004  PF_EXITING
* M: TIME+      = CPU Time, hundredths  0x00000040  PF_FORKNOEXEC
  b: PPID       = Parent Process Pid    0x00000100  PF_SUPERPRIV
  c: RUSER      = Real user name        0x00000200  PF_DUMPCORE
  d: UID        = User Id               0x00000400  PF_SIGNALED
  f: GROUP      = Group Name            0x00000800  PF_MEMALLOC
  g: TTY        = Controlling Tty       0x00002000  PF_FREE_PAGES (2.5)
  j: P          = Last used cpu (SMP)   0x00008000  debug flag (2.5)
  p: SWAP       = Swapped size (kb)     0x00024000  special threads (2.5)
  l: TIME       = CPU Time              0x001D0000  special states (2.5)
  r: CODE       = Code size (kb)        0x00100000  PF_USEDFPU (thru 2.4)
  s: DATA       = Data+Stack size (kb)
```

After switching the last used CPU option on, you will see the column P in top that displays the number of the CPU that was last used by a process.

Using vmstat

top offers a very good starting point for monitoring CPU utilization. If it doesn't provide you with all the information that you need, you may want to try the vmstat utility. First you may need to install this package using `yum -y install sysstat`. With vmstat, you get a nice, detailed view on what is happening on your server. The CPU section is of special interest because it contains the five most important parameters of CPU usage.

cs The number of context switches

us The percentage of time the CPU has spent in user space

sy The percentage of time the CPU has spent in system space

id The percentage of CPU utilization in the idle loop

wa The percentage of utilization where the CPU was waiting for I/O

There are two ways to use `vmstat`. Probably the most useful way to run it is in the so-called *sample mode*. In this mode, a sample is taken every *n* seconds. You must specify the number of seconds for the sample as an option when starting `vmstat`. Running performance-monitoring utilities in this way is always beneficial, since it will show you progress over a given amount of time. You also may find it useful to run vmstat for a certain number of times only.

Another useful way to run vmstat is with the `-s` option. In this mode, vmstat shows you the statistics since the system was booted. Apart from the CPU-related options, vmstat also shows information about processors, memory, swap, i/o, and system. These options are covered later in this chapter.

Analyzing Memory Usage

Memory is also an essential component of your server. The CPU can work smoothly only if processes are ready in memory and can be offered from there. If this is not the case, the server has to get its data from the I/O channel, which is about 1,000 times slower to access than memory. From the processor's point of view, even system RAM is relatively slow. Therefore, modern server processors contain large amounts of cache, which are even faster than memory.

You learned how to interpret basic memory statistics provided by top earlier in this chapter. In this section, you will learn about some more advanced memory-related information.

Page Size

A basic concept in memory handling is the memory *page size*. On an i386 system, 4KB pages are typically used. This means that everything that happens does so in 4KB chunks.

There is nothing wrong with that if you have a server handling large numbers of small files. However, if your server handles huge files, it is highly inefficient if small 4KB pages are used. For that purpose, your server can take advantage of huge pages with a default size of 2MB a page. Later in this chapter, you'll learn how to configure huge pages.

A server can run out of memory. When this happens, it uses swapping. *Swap memory* is emulated RAM on the server's hard drive. Since the hard disk is involved in swap, you should avoid it if possible. Access times to a hard drive are about 1,000 times slower than access times to RAM. If your server is slow, swap usage is the first thing to examine. You can do this using the command `free -m`, which will show you the amount of swap that is currently being used, as shown in Listing 17.7.

Listing 17.7: `free -m` provides information about swap usage

```
[root@hn1 ~]# free -m
             total       used       free     shared    buffers     cached
Mem:           993        893         99          0        528         57
-/+ buffers/cache:        307        685
Swap:         2015          0       2015
```

As you can see in Listing 17.7, nothing is wrong on the server where this sample is derived. There is no swap usage at all, which is good.

On the other hand, if you see that your server is swapping, the next thing you need to know is how actively it is doing so. The `vmstat` utility provides useful information about this. This utility provides swap information in the `si` (swap in) and `so` (swap out) columns.

If you see no activity at all, that's not too bad. In that case, swap space has been allocated but is not being used. However, if you see significant activity in these columns, you're in trouble. This means that swap space is not only allocated but is also being used, and that will really slow down your server. The solution? Install more RAM or find the most memory-intensive process and move it somewhere else.

Active vs. Inactive Memory

To determine which memory pages should be swapped, a server uses active and inactive memory. *Inactive memory* is memory that hasn't been used for some time. *Active memory* is memory that has been used recently. When moving memory blocks from RAM to swap, the kernel makes sure that only blocks from inactive memory are moved. You can see statistics about active and inactive memory using `vmstat -s`. In Listing 17.8, for example, you can see that the amount of active memory is relatively small compared to the amount of inactive memory.

Listing 17.8: Use `vmstat -s` to get statistics about active vs. inactive memory

```
[root@hn1 ~]# vmstat -s
    1016928  total memory
```

```
   915056  used memory
   168988  active memory
   598880  inactive memory
   101872  free memory
   541564  buffer memory
    59084  swap cache
  2064376  total swap
        0  used swap
  2064376  free swap
   142311  non-nice user cpu ticks
      251  nice user cpu ticks
    30673  system cpu ticks
  1332644  idle cpu ticks
    24256  IO-wait cpu ticks
      371  IRQ cpu ticks
     1175  softirq cpu ticks
        0  stolen cpu ticks
 21556610  pages paged in
    56830  pages paged out
        0  pages swapped in
        0  pages swapped out
  2390762  interrupts
   695020  CPU context switches
1347791046 boot time
     6233  forks
```

Kernel Memory

When analyzing memory usage, you should also take into account the memory that is used by the kernel itself. This is called *slab memory*. You can see the amount of slab currently in use in the /proc/meminfo file. Listing 17.9 provides an example of the contents of this file that gives you detailed information about memory usage.

Listing 17.9: The /proc/meminfo file provides detailed information about memory usage

```
[root@hnl ~]# cat /proc/meminfo
MemTotal:        1016928 kB
MemFree:           99568 kB
Buffers:          541568 kB
Cached:            59092 kB
SwapCached:            0 kB
```

```
Active:             171172 kB
Inactive:           598808 kB
Active(anon):        69128 kB
Inactive(anon):     103728 kB
Active(file):       102044 kB
Inactive(file):     495080 kB
Unevictable:             0 kB
Mlocked:                 0 kB
SwapTotal:         2064376 kB
SwapFree:          2064376 kB
Dirty:                  36 kB
Writeback:               0 kB
AnonPages:          169292 kB
Mapped:              37268 kB
Shmem:                3492 kB
Slab:                90420 kB
SReclaimable:        32420 kB
SUnreclaim:          58000 kB
KernelStack:          2440 kB
PageTables:          27636 kB
NFS_Unstable:            0 kB
Bounce:                  0 kB
WritebackTmp:            0 kB
CommitLimit:       2572840 kB
Committed_AS:       668328 kB
VmallocTotal:    34359738367 kB
VmallocUsed:        272352 kB
VmallocChunk:    34359448140 kB
HardwareCorrupted:       0 kB
AnonHugePages:       38912 kB
HugePages_Total:         0
HugePages_Free:          0
HugePages_Rsvd:          0
HugePages_Surp:          0
Hugepagesize:         2048 kB
DirectMap4k:          8192 kB
DirectMap2M:       1040384 kB
```

In Listing 17.9, you can see that the amount of memory that is used by the Linux kernel is relatively small. If you need more details about what the kernel is doing with that memory, you may want to use the slabtop utility. This utility provides information about the different parts (referred to as *objects*) of the kernel and what exactly they are doing. For normal performance-analysis purposes, the SIZE and NAME columns are the most interesting ones. The other columns are of interest mainly for programmers and kernel developers, and thus they are not discussed in this chapter. Listing 17.10 shows an example of the type of information provided by slabtop.

Listing 17.10: The slabtop utility provides information about kernel memory usage

```
[root@hnl ~]# slabtop
 Active / Total Objects (% used)    : 1069357 / 1105539 (96.7%)
 Active / Total Slabs (% used)      : 19402 / 19408 (100.0%)
 Active / Total Caches (% used)     : 110 / 190 (57.9%)
 Active / Total Size (% used)       : 71203.09K / 77888.23K (91.4%)
 Minimum / Average / Maximum Object : 0.02K / 0.07K / 4096.00K

  OBJS ACTIVE   USE OBJ SIZE   SLABS OBJ/SLAB CACHE SIZE NAME
480672 480480   99%    0.02K    3338      144    13352K avtab_node
334096 333912   99%    0.03K    2983      112    11932K size-32
147075 134677   91%    0.10K    3975       37    15900K buffer_head
 17914  10957   61%    0.07K     338       53     1352K selinux_inode_security
 15880  10140   63%    0.19K     794       20     3176K dentry
 15694  13577   86%    0.06K     266       59     1064K size-64
 14630  14418   98%    0.20K     770       19     3080K vm_area_struct
 11151  11127   99%    0.14K     413       27     1652K sysfs_dir_cache
  8239   7978   96%    0.05K     107       77      428K anon_vma_chain
  6440   6276   97%    0.04K      70       92      280K anon_vma
  6356   4632   72%    0.55K     908        7     3632K radix_tree_node
  6138   6138  100%    0.58K    1023        6     4092K inode_cache
  5560   5486   98%    0.19K     278       20     1112K filp
  4505   4399   97%    0.07K      85       53      340K Acpi-Operand
  4444   2537   57%    1.00K    1111        4     4444K ext4_inode_cache
  4110   3596   87%    0.12K     137       30      548K size-128
```

The most interesting information a system administrator gets from slabtop is the amount of memory that a particular slab is using. If this amount seems too high, there may be something wrong with this module, and you might need to update your kernel. The slabtop utility can also be used to determine the number of resources a certain kernel module is using. For instance, you'll find information about the caches your file system driver is using, and if these appear too high, it can indicate you might have to tune some file system parameters. In Exercise 17.3, you'll learn how to analyze kernel memory.

EXERCISE 17.3

Analyzing Kernel Memory

In this exercise, you'll induce a little bit of stress on your server, and you'll use slabtop to find out which parts of the kernel are getting busy. Because the Linux kernel is sophisticated and uses its resources as efficiently as possible, you won't see huge changes, but you will be able to observe some subtle changes.

1. Open two terminal windows in which you are root.

2. In one terminal window, type **slabtop**, and look at what the different slabs are currently doing.

3. In the other terminal window, use **ls -lR /**. You should see the *dentry cache* increasing, which refers to the part of memory where the kernel caches directory entries.

4. Once the ls -R command has finished, type **dd if=/dev/sda of=/dev/null** to create some read activity. You'll see the buffer_head parameter increasing. These are the file system buffers that are used to cache the information the dd command uses.

Using ps for Analyzing Memory

When tuning memory utilization, the ps utility is one you should never forget. The advantage of ps is that it provides memory usage information for all processes on your server, and it is easy to grep on its results to locate information about particular processes.

To monitor memory usage, the ps aux command is very useful. It displays memory information in the VSZ and the RSS columns. The VSZ (Virtual Size) parameter provides information about the virtual memory that is used. This relates to the total amount of memory that is claimed by a process. The RSS (Resident Size) parameter refers to the amount of memory that is actually in use. Listing 17.11 provides an example of some lines of ps aux output.

Listing 17.11: ps aux displays memory usage information for particular processes

```
[root@hnl ~]# ps aux | less
USER       PID %CPU %MEM    VSZ   RSS TTY      STAT START   TIME COMMAND
root         1  0.0  0.1  19404  1440 ?        Ss   00:27   0:04 /sbin/init
root         2  0.0  0.0      0     0 ?        S    00:27   0:00 [kthreadd]
root         3  0.0  0.0      0     0 ?        S    00:27   0:00 [migration/0]
root         4  0.0  0.0      0     0 ?        S    00:27   0:00 [ksoftirqd/0]
root         5  0.0  0.0      0     0 ?        S    00:27   0:00 [migration/0]
root         6  0.0  0.0      0     0 ?        S    00:27   0:00 [watchdog/0]
root         7  0.0  0.0      0     0 ?        S    00:27   0:00 [migration/1]
```

```
root             8  0.0  0.0       0     0 ?          S    00:27   0:00 [migration/1]
root             9  0.0  0.0       0     0 ?          S    00:27   0:00 [ksoftirqd/1]
root            10  0.0  0.0       0     0 ?          S    00:27   0:00 [watchdog/1]
root            11  0.0  0.0       0     0 ?          S    00:27   0:00 [migration/2]
root            12  0.0  0.0       0     0 ?          S    00:27   0:00 [migration/2]
root            13  0.0  0.0       0     0 ?          S    00:27   0:00 [ksoftirqd/2]
root            14  0.0  0.0       0     0 ?          S    00:27   0:00 [watchdog/2]
root            15  0.0  0.0       0     0 ?          S    00:27   0:00 [migration/3]
root            16  0.0  0.0       0     0 ?          S    00:27   0:00 [migration/3]
root            17  0.0  0.0       0     0 ?          S    00:27   0:00 [ksoftirqd/3]
root            18  0.0  0.0       0     0 ?          S    00:27   0:00 [watchdog/3]
root            19  0.0  0.0       0     0 ?          S    00:27   0:00 [events/0]
root            20  0.0  0.0       0     0 ?          S    00:27   0:00 [events/1]
root            21  0.0  0.0       0     0 ?          S    00:27   0:00 [events/2]
root            22  0.0  0.0       0     0 ?          S    00:27   0:00 [events/3]
:
```

When reviewing the output of ps aux, you may notice that there are two different kinds of processes. The names of some are between square brackets, while the names of others are not. If the name of a process is between square brackets, the process is part of the kernel. All other processes are "normal."

If you need to know more about a process and what exactly it is doing, there are two ways to get that information. First you can check the /proc directory for the particular process. For example, /proc/5658 yields information for the process with PID 5658. In this directory, you'll find the maps file that gives you some more insight on how memory is mapped for this process. As you can see in Listing 17.12, this information is rather detailed. It includes the exact memory addresses that this process is using, and it even tells you about subroutines and libraries that are related to this process.

Listing 17.12: The /proc/PID/maps file provides detailed information on memory utilization of particular processes

```
root@hnl:~# cat /proc/5658/maps
b7781000-b78c1000 rw-s  00000000  00:09  14414     /dev/zero (deleted)
b78c1000-b78c4000 r-xp  00000000  fe:00  5808329   /lib/security/pam_limits.so
b78c4000-b78c5000 rw-p  00002000  fe:00  5808329   /lib/security/pam_limits.so
b78c5000-b78c7000 r-xp  00000000  fe:00  5808334   /lib/security/pam_mail.so
b78c7000-b78c8000 rw-p  00001000  fe:00  5808334   /lib/security/pam_mail.so
b78c8000-b78d3000 r-xp  00000000  fe:00  5808351   /lib/security/pam_unix.so
b78d3000-b78d4000 rw-p  0000b000  fe:00  5808351   /lib/security/pam_unix.so
b78d4000-b78e0000 rw-p  b78d4000  00:00  0
...
```

```
b7eb7000-b7eb8000 r-xp  00000000  fe:00  5808338  /lib/security/pam_nologin.so
b7eb8000-b7eb9000 rw-p  00000000  fe:00  5808338  /lib/security/pam_nologin.so
b7eb9000-b7ebb000 rw-p  b7eb9000  00:00  0
b7ebb000-b7ebc000 r-xp  b7ebb000  00:00  0             [vdso]
b7ebc000-b7ed6000 r-xp  00000000  fe:00  5808145  /lib/ld-2.7.so
b7ed6000-b7ed8000 rw-p  00019000  fe:00  5808145  /lib/ld-2.7.so
b7ed8000-b7f31000 r-xp  00000000  fe:00  1077630  /usr/sbin/sshd
b7f31000-b7f33000 rw-p  00059000  fe:00  1077630  /usr/sbin/sshd
b7f33000-b7f5b000 rw-p  b7f33000  00:00  0             [heap]
bff9a000-bffaf000 rw-p  bffeb000  00:00  0             [stack]
```

Another way of finding out what particular processes are doing is by using the pmap command. This command mines the /proc/PID/maps file for information and also addresses some other information, such as the summary of memory usage displayed by ps aux. pmap also lets you see which amounts of memory are used by the libraries involved in this process. Listing 17.13 provides an example of the output of this utility.

Listing 17.13: The pmap command mines /proc/PID/maps to provide its information

```
[root@hnl 2996]# pmap -d 2996
2996:   /usr/libexec/pulse/gconf-helper
Address            Kbytes Mode  Offset            Device     Mapping
0000000000400000        8 r-x-- 0000000000000000 0fd:00000  gconf-helper
0000000000601000       16 rw--- 0000000000001000 0fd:00000  gconf-helper
0000000001bc6000      136 rw--- 0000000000000000 000:00000  [ anon ]
00000037de400000      128 r-x-- 0000000000000000 0fd:00000  ld-2.12.so
00000037de61f000        4 r---- 000000000001f000 0fd:00000  ld-2.12.so
00000037de620000        4 rw--- 0000000000020000 0fd:00000  ld-2.12.so
00000037de621000        4 rw--- 0000000000000000 000:00000  [ anon ]
00000037de800000        8 r-x-- 0000000000000000 0fd:00000  libdl-2.12.so
00000037de802000     2048 ----- 0000000000002000 0fd:00000  libdl-2.12.so
00000037dea02000        4 r---- 0000000000002000 0fd:00000  libdl-2.12.so
00000037dea03000        4 rw--- 0000000000003000 0fd:00000  libdl-2.12.so
00000037dec00000     1628 r-x-- 0000000000000000 0fd:00000  libc-2.12.so
00000037ded97000     2048 ----- 0000000000197000 0fd:00000  libc-2.12.so
00000037def97000       16 r---- 0000000000197000 0fd:00000  libc-2.12.so
00000037def9b000        4 rw--- 000000000019b000 0fd:00000  libc-2.12.so
00000037def9c000       20 rw--- 0000000000000000 000:00000  [ anon ]
00000037df000000       92 r-x-- 0000000000000000 0fd:00000  libpthread-2.12.so
...
00007f9a30bf4000        4 r---- 000000000000c000 0fd:00000  libnss_files-2.12.so
```

```
00007f9a30bf5000       4 rw--- 000000000000d000  0fd:00000  libnss_files-2.12.so
00007f9a30bf6000      68 rw--- 0000000000000000  000:00000  [ anon ]
00007f9a30c14000       8 rw--- 0000000000000000  000:00000  [ anon ]
00007fffb5628000      84 rw--- 0000000000000000  000:00000  [ stack ]
00007fffb57b9000       4 r-x-- 0000000000000000  000:00000  [ anon ]
ffffffffff600000       4 r-x-- 0000000000000000  000:00000  [ anon ]
mapped: 90316K     writeable/private: 792K     shared: 0K
```

One of the advantages of the pmap command is that it presents detailed information about the order in which a process does its work. You can see calls to external libraries and additional memory allocation (malloc) requests that the program is doing, as shown in the lines that have [anon] at the end.

Monitoring Storage Performance

One of the hardest things to do properly is to monitor storage utilization. The reason is that the storage channel is typically at the end of the chain. Other elements in your server can have either a positive or a negative influence on storage performance. For example, if your server is low on memory, this will be reflected in storage performance because if you don't have enough memory, there can't be a lot of cache and buffers, and thus your server has more work to do on the storage channel.

Likewise, a slow CPU can have a negative impact on storage performance because the queue of runnable processes can't be cleared fast enough. Therefore, before jumping to the conclusion that you have bad performance on the storage channel, you should also try to consider other factors.

It is generally hard to optimize storage performance on a server. The best behavior generally depends on your server's typical workload. For example, a server that does a lot of reads has other needs than a server that mainly handles writes. A server that is doing writes most of the time can benefit from a storage channel with many disks because more controllers can work on clearing the write buffer cache from memory. However, if your server is mainly reading data, the effect of having many disks is just the opposite. Because of the large number of disks, seek times will increase, and performance will thus be negatively impacted.

Here are some indicators for storage performance problems. Is one of these the cause of problems on your server? If it is, analyze what is happening:

- Memory buffers and cache are heavily used, while CPU utilization is low.

- The disk or controller utilization is high.

- The network response times are long while network utilization is low.

- The wa parameter in top is very high.

Understanding Disk Activity

Before trying to understand storage performance, you should consider another factor, and that is the way that disk activity typically takes place. First, a storage device in general handles large sequential transfers better than small random transfers. This is because, in memory, you can configure read-ahead and write-ahead, which means that the storage controller already moves to the next block where it likely has to go. If your server handles mostly small files, read-ahead buffers will have no effect at all. On the contrary, they will only slow it down.

From the tools perspective, three tools really count when doing disk performance analysis. The first tool to start your disk performance analysis is vmstat. This tool has a couple of options that help you see what is happening on a particular disk device, such as -d, which gives you statistics for individual disks, or -p, which gives partition performance statistics. As you have seen, you can use vmstat with an interval parameter and also a count parameter. In Listing 17.14, you can see the result of the command vmstat -d, which gives detailed information on storage utilization for all disk devices on your server.

Listing 17.14: To understand storage usage, start with vmstat

```
[root@hnl ~]# vmstat -d
disk- ------------reads------------ ------------writes----------- -----IO------
         total    merged    sectors      ms    total   merged   sectors       ms    cur    sec
ram0        0         0         0         0      0        0         0          0      0      0
ram1        0         0         0         0      0        0         0          0      0      0
ram2        0         0         0         0      0        0         0          0      0      0
ram3        0         0         0         0      0        0         0          0      0      0
ram4        0         0         0         0      0        0         0          0      0      0
ram5        0         0         0         0      0        0         0          0      0      0
ram6        0         0         0         0      0        0         0          0      0      0
ram7        0         0         0         0      0        0         0          0      0      0
ram8        0         0         0         0      0        0         0          0      0      0
ram9        0         0         0         0      0        0         0          0      0      0
ram10       0         0         0         0      0        0         0          0      0      0
ram11       0         0         0         0      0        0         0          0      0      0
ram12       0         0         0         0      0        0         0          0      0      0
ram13       0         0         0         0      0        0         0          0      0      0
ram14       0         0         0         0      0        0         0          0      0      0
ram15       0         0         0         0      0        0         0          0      0      0
loop0       0         0         0         0      0        0         0          0      0      0
loop1       0         0         0         0      0        0         0          0      0      0
loop2       0         0         0         0      0        0         0          0      0      0
loop3       0         0         0         0      0        0         0          0      0      0
```

disk-	------------reads------------				------------writes------------				-----IO-----	
	total	merged	sectors	ms	total	merged	sectors	ms	cur	sec
loop4	0	0	0	0	0	0	0	0	0	0
loop5	0	0	0	0	0	0	0	0	0	0
loop6	0	0	0	0	0	0	0	0	0	0
loop7	0	0	0	0	0	0	0	0	0	0
sr0	0	0	0	0	0	0	0	0	0	0
sda	543960	15236483	127083246	1501450	8431	308221	2533136	4654498	0	817
dm-0	54963	0	1280866	670472	316633	0	2533064	396941052	0	320
dm-1	322	0	2576	1246	0	0	0	0	0	0

You can see detailed statistics about the reads and writes that have occurred on a disk in the output of this command. The following parameters are displayed when using vmstat -d.

Reads

total   The total number of reads requested.

merged   The total amount of adjacent locations that have been merged to improve performance. This is the result of the read-ahead parameter. High numbers are good. A high number here means that within the same read request, a couple of adjacent blocks have also been read.

sectors   The total amount of disk sectors that have been read.

ms   Total time spent reading from disk.

Writes

total   The total amount of writes

merged   The total amount of writes to adjacent sectors

sectors   The total amount of sectors that have been written

ms   The total time in milliseconds that your system has spent writing data

I/O

cur   The total number of I/O requests currently in process

sec   The total amount of time spent waiting for I/O to complete

Another way to monitor disk performance with vmstat is by running it in sample mode. For example, vmstat 2 15 will run 15 samples with a 2-second interval. Listing 17.15 shows the result of this command.

Listing 17.15: In sample mode, you can get a real-time impression of disk utilization

```
root@hn1:~# vmstat 2 15
procs -----------memory---------- ---swap-- -----io---- -system-- ----cpu----
 r  b  swpd    free   buff  cache  si so   bi  bo   in    cs  us sy id wa
 0  0    0 3666400  14344 292496  0  0   56   4   579   70   0  0 99  0
 0  0    0 3645452  14344 313680  0  0 10560   0 12046 2189   0  4 94  2
 0 13    0 3623364  14344 335772  0  0 11040   0 12127 2221   0  6 92  2
 0  0    0 3602032  14380 356880  0  0 10560  18 12255 2323   0  7 90  3
 0  0    0 3582048  14380 377124  0  0 10080   0 11525 2089   0  4 93  3
 0  0    0 3561076  14380 398160  0  0 10560  24 12069 2141   0  5 91  4
 0  0    0 3539652  14380 419280  0  0 10560   0 11913 2209   0  4 92  4
 0  0    0 3518016  14380 440336  0  0 10560   0 11632 2226   0  7 90  3
 0  0    0 3498756  14380 459600  0  0 9600    0 10822 2455   0  4 92  3
 0  0    0 3477832  14380 480800  0  0 10560   0 12011 2279   0  3 94  2
 0  0    0 3456600  14380 501840  0  0 10560   0 12078 2670   0  3 94  3
 0  0    0 3435636  14380 523044  0  0 10560   0 12106 1850   0  3 93  4
 0  0    0 3414824  14380 544016  0  0 10560   0 11989 1731   0  3 92  4
 0  0    0 3393516  14380 565136  0  0 10560   0 11919 1965   0  6 92  2
 0  0    0 3370920  14380 587216  0  0 11040   0 12378 2020   0  5 90  4
```

The columns that count in Listing 17.15 are io: bi and io: bo because they show the number of blocks that came in from the storage channel (bi) and the number of blocks that were written to the storage channel (bo). It is clear in Listing 17.15 that the server is busy servicing some heavy read requests and works on nearly no writes at all. It is not always this easy, however. In certain situations, you will find that some clients are performing heavy read requests while your server shows nearly no activity in the io: bi column. If this happens, it is probably because the data that was read is still in cache.

Another tool for monitoring performance on the storage channel is iostat. It provides an overview for each device of the number of reads and writes. In Listing 17.16, you can see the following device parameters displayed:

tps The number of transactions (read plus writes) handled per second

Blk_read/s The number of blocks read per second

Blk_wrtn/s The rate of disk blocks written per second

Blk_read The total number of blocks read since start-up

Blk_wrtn The total number of blocks that were written since start-up

Listing 17.16: The iostat utility provides information about the number of blocks that were read and written per second

```
[root@hn1 ~]# iostat
Linux 2.6.32-220.el6.x86_64 (hn1.example.com)   09/16/2012 _x86_64_   (4 CPU)

avg-cpu:  %user   %nice %system %iowait  %steal   %idle
          13.49    0.01    2.64    1.52    0.00   82.35
```

Device:	tps	Blk_read/s	Blk_wrtn/s	Blk_read	Blk_wrtn
sda	77.16	17745.53	366.29	127083390	2623136
dm-0	53.46	178.88	366.28	1281026	2623064
dm-1	0.04	0.36	0.00	2576	0

If used in this way, iostat doesn't provide you with enough detail. Therefore, you can also use the -x option. This option provides much more information, so it doesn't fit on the screen as nicely as iostat alone in most cases. In Listing 17.17, you can see an example iostat used with the -x option.

Listing 17.17: `iostat -x` provides a lot of information about what is happening on the storage channel

```
[root@hnl ~]# iostat -x
Linux 2.6.32-220.el6.x86_64 (hnl.example.com)   09/16/2012 _x86_64_   (4 CPU)

avg-cpu:  %user   %nice %system %iowait  %steal   %idle
          13.35    0.01    2.88    1.51    0.00   82.26
```

Device:	rrqm/s	wrqm/s	r/s	w/s	rsec/s	wsec/s	avgrq-sz
avgqu-sz	await	svctm	%util				
sda	2104.75	61.00	75.14	1.33	17555.25	498.66	236.07
0.86	11.19	1.51	11.56				
dm-0	0.00	0.00	7.60	62.33	177.05	498.65	9.66
55.55	794.39	0.67	4.69				
dm-1	0.00	0.00	0.04	0.00	0.36	0.00	8.00
0.00	3.87	2.04	0.01				

When using the -x option, iostat provides the following information:

rrqm/s Reads per second merged before being issued to disk. Compare this to the information in the r/s column to find out how much of a gain in efficiency results because of read-ahead.

wrqm/s Writes per second merged before being issued to disk. Compare this to the w/s parameter to see how much of a performance gain results because of write-ahead.

r/s The number of real reads per second.

w/s The number of real writes per second.

rsec/s The number of 512-byte sectors read per second.

wsec The number of 512-byte sectors written per second.

avgrq-sz The average size of disk requests in sectors. This parameter provides important information because it shows the average size of the files that were requested from disk. Based on the information that you get from this parameter, you can optimize your file system.

avgqu-sz The average size of the disk request queue. This should be low at all times because it gives the number of pending disk requests. If it yields a high number, this means the performance of your storage channel cannot cope with the performance of your network.

await   The average waiting time in milliseconds. This is the time the request has been waiting in the I/O queue, plus the time it actually took to service this request. This parameter should also be low in all cases.

svctm   The average service time in milliseconds. This is the time it took before a request could be submitted to disk. If this parameter is less than a couple of milliseconds (never more than 10), nothing is wrong with your server. However, if this parameter is greater than 10 milliseconds, something is wrong, and you should consider performing some storage optimization.

%util   The percentage of CPU utilization related to I/O.

Finding Most Busy Processes with iotop

The most useful tool for analyzing performance on a server is iotop. This tool hasn't been around for a long time, because it requires relatively new functionality in the kernel, which allows administrators to find out which processes are causing the heaviest weight on I/O performance.

Running iotop is as easy as running top. Just start the utility, and you will see which process is causing you an I/O headache. The busiest process is listed at the top, and you can also see details about the reads and writes that this process performs.

Within iotop, you'll see two different kinds of processes, as shown in Listing 17.18. There are processes where the name is written between square brackets. These are kernel processes that aren't loaded as a separate binary but are part of the kernel itself. All other processes listed are normal binaries.

Listing 17.18: Analyzing I/O performance with iotop

```
[root@hnl ~]# iotop
Total DISK READ: 0.00 B/s | Total DISK WRITE: 0.00 B/s
  TID  PRIO  USER     DISK READ   DISK WRITE  SWAPIN      IO>     COMMAND
 2560 be/4 root       0.00 B/s     0.00 B/s   0.00 %    0.00 % console-k~-no-daemon
    1 be/4 root       0.00 B/s     0.00 B/s   0.00 %    0.00 % init
    2 be/4 root       0.00 B/s     0.00 B/s   0.00 %    0.00 % [kthreadd]
    3 rt/4 root       0.00 B/s     0.00 B/s   0.00 %    0.00 % [migration/0]
    4 be/4 root       0.00 B/s     0.00 B/s   0.00 %    0.00 % [ksoftirqd/0]
    5 rt/4 root       0.00 B/s     0.00 B/s   0.00 %    0.00 % [migration/0]
    6 rt/4 root       0.00 B/s     0.00 B/s   0.00 %    0.00 % [watchdog/0]
    7 rt/4 root       0.00 B/s     0.00 B/s   0.00 %    0.00 % [migration/1]
    8 rt/4 root       0.00 B/s     0.00 B/s   0.00 %    0.00 % [migration/1]
    9 be/4 root       0.00 B/s     0.00 B/s   0.00 %    0.00 % [ksoftirqd/1]
   10 rt/4 root       0.00 B/s     0.00 B/s   0.00 %    0.00 % [watchdog/1]
   11 rt/4 root       0.00 B/s     0.00 B/s   0.00 %    0.00 % [migration/2]
   12 rt/4 root       0.00 B/s     0.00 B/s   0.00 %    0.00 % [migration/2]
```

```
13 be/4 root          0.00 B/s    0.00 B/s  0.00 %  0.00 % [ksoftirqd/2]
14 rt/4 root          0.00 B/s    0.00 B/s  0.00 %  0.00 % [watchdog/2]
15 rt/4 root          0.00 B/s    0.00 B/s  0.00 %  0.00 % [migration/3]
16 rt/4 root          0.00 B/s    0.00 B/s  0.00 %  0.00 % [migration/3]
17 be/4 root          0.00 B/s    0.00 B/s  0.00 %  0.00 % [ksoftirqd/3]
18 rt/4 root          0.00 B/s    0.00 B/s  0.00 %  0.00 % [watchdog/3]
19 be/4 root          0.00 B/s    0.00 B/s  0.00 %  0.00 % [events/0]
20 be/4 root          0.00 B/s    0.00 B/s  0.00 %  0.00 % [events/1]
21 be/4 root          0.00 B/s    0.00 B/s  0.00 %  0.00 % [events/2]
```

Normally, you would start to analyze I/O performance because of an abnormality in the regular I/O load. For example, you may find a high wa indicator in top. In Exercise 17.4, you'll explore an I/O problem using this approach.

EXERCISE 17.4

Exploring I/O Performance

In this exercise, you'll start a couple of I/O-intensive tasks. First you'll see abnormal behavior occurring in top, after which you'll use iotop to explore what is going on.

1. Open two root shells. In one shell, run top. In the second shell, start the command **dd if=/dev/sda of=/dev/null**. Run this command four times.

2. Observe what happens in top. You will notice that the wa parameter increases. Press 1. If you're using a multicore system, you should also see that the workload is evenly load-balanced between the cores.

3. Start **iotop**. You will see that the four dd processes are listed at the top, and you'll also notice that no other kernel processes are significantly high in the list.

4. Use **find / -exec xxd {} \;** to create some read activity. In iotop, you should see the process itself listed earlier but no further significant workload.

5. Create a script with the following content:

    ```
    #!/bin/bash

    while true
    do
            cp -R / blah.tmp
            rm -f /blah.tmp
            sync
    done
    ```

6. Run the script, and observe the list of processes in iotop. Occasionally, you should see the flush process doing a lot of work. This is to synchronize the newly written files back from the buffer cache to disk.

Setting and Monitoring Drive Activity with hdparm

The hdparm utility can be used to set drive parameters or display parameters that are currently set for the drive. It has lots of options that you can use to set many features, not all of which are useful in every case. To see the default settings for your disk, use hdparm /dev/sda. This yields the result shown in Listing 17.19.

Listing 17.19: Use hdparm to see disk parameters

```
[root@hnl ~]# hdparm /dev/sda

/dev/sda:
 multcount     = 16 (on)
 IO_support    =  1 (32-bit)
 readonly      =  0 (off)
 readahead     = 256 (on)
 geometry      = 30401/255/63, sectors = 488397168, start = 0
```

The hdparm utility has some optimization options. For example, the -a option can be used to set the default drive read-ahead in sectors. Use hdparm -a 64, for example, if you want the disk to read ahead a total of 64 sectors. Some other management options are also useful, such as -f and -F, which allow you to flush the buffer cache and the write cache for the disk. This ensures that all data on the disk has been written to disk.

Understanding Network Performance

On a typical server, network performance is as important as disk, memory, and CPU performance. After all, the data has to be delivered over the network to the end user. The problem is, however, that things aren't always as they seem. In some cases, a network problem can be caused by misconfiguration in server RAM. For example, if packets get dropped on the network, the reason may very well be that your server just doesn't have an adequate number of buffers reserved for receiving packets, which may be because your server is low on memory. Again, everything is related, and it's your job to find the real cause of the troubles.

When considering network performance, you should always ask yourself what exactly you want to know. As you know, several layers of communication are used on a network. If you want to analyze a problem with your Samba server, this requires a completely different approach from analyzing a problem with dropped packets. A good network performance analysis always goes from bottom up. This means that you first need to check what is happening at the physical layer of the OSI model and then go up through the Ethernet, IP, TCP/UDP, and protocol layers.

When analyzing network performance, you should always start by checking the network interface itself. Good old ifconfig offers excellent statistics to do just that. For example, consider Listing 17.20, which shows the result of ifconfig on the eth0 network interface.

Listing 17.20: Use ifconfig to see what is happening on your network board

```
[root@hnl ~]# ifconfig
eth0      Link encap:Ethernet  HWaddr 00:0C:29:6D:CE:44
          inet addr:192.168.166.10  Bcast:192.168.166.255  Mask:255.255.255.0
          inet6 addr: fe80::20c:29ff:fe6d:ce44/64 Scope:Link
          UP BROADCAST RUNNING MULTICAST  MTU:1500  Metric:1
          RX packets:46680 errors:0 dropped:0 overruns:0 frame:0
          TX packets:75079 errors:0 dropped:0 overruns:0 carrier:0
          collisions:0 txqueuelen:1000
          RX bytes:3162997 (3.0 MiB)  TX bytes:98585354 (94.0 MiB)

lo        Link encap:Local Loopback
          inet addr:127.0.0.1  Mask:255.0.0.0
          inet6 addr: ::1/128 Scope:Host
          UP LOOPBACK RUNNING  MTU:16436  Metric:1
          RX packets:16 errors:0 dropped:0 overruns:0 frame:0
          TX packets:16 errors:0 dropped:0 overruns:0 carrier:0
          collisions:0 txqueuelen:0
          RX bytes:960 (960.0 b)  TX bytes:960 (960.0 b)
```

As you can see from Listing 17.19, the eth0 network board has been a bit busy with 3 MiB of data received and 94 MiB of data transmitted. This is the overview of what your server has been doing since it started up. You will note that these can be much higher for a server that has been up and running for a long time. You can also see that IPv6 (inet6) has been enabled for this network card. There is nothing wrong with that, but if you don't use it, there's no reason to enable it.

 The last IPv4 network addresses are being handed out as you read this. Thus, you will probably need IPv6 soon.

Next, in the lines RX packets and TX packets, you can see send (transmit, TX) and receive (RX) statistics. The number of packets is of special interest here, particularly the number of erroneous packets. In fact, all of these parameters should be 0 at all times. If you see anything other than 0, you should check what is going on. The following error indicators are displayed using ifconfig:

Errors The number of packets that had an error. Typically, this is because of bad cabling or a duplex mismatch. In modern networks, duplex settings are detected automatically, and most of the time that goes quite well. Thus, if you see a number that is increasing here, it might be a good idea to replace the patch cable to your server.

Dropped A packet gets dropped if no memory is available to receive the packet on the server. Dropped packets also occur on a server that runs out of memory. Therefore, make sure you have enough physical memory installed in your server.

Overruns   An overrun will occur if your NIC becomes overwhelmed with packets. If you are using up-to-date hardware, overruns may indicate that someone is conducting a denial-of-service attack on your server. Also, they can be the result of too many interrupts, a bad driver, or hardware problems.

Frame   A frame error is one that is caused by a physical problem in the packet at the Ethernet Frame level, such as a CRC check error. You may see this error on a server with a bad connection link.

Carrier   The carrier is the electrical wave used for modulation of the signal. It is the actual component that carries the data over your network. The error counter should be 0 at all times. If it isn't, you probably have a physical problem with the network board, so it's time to replace the board itself.

Collisions   You may see this error in Ethernet networks where a hub is used instead of a switch. Modern switches make packet collisions impossible, so you will likely never see this error. You will see them on hubs, however.

If you see a problem when using ifconfig, the next step is to check your network board settings. Use **ethtool eth0** to determine the settings you're using currently, and make sure they match the settings of other network components, such as the switches. Listing 17.21 shows what you can expect when using ethtool to check the settings of your network board.

Listing 17.21: Use ethtool to check the settings of your network board

```
[root@hnl ~]# ethtool eth0
Settings for eth0:
        Supported ports: [ TP ]
        Supported link modes:   10baseT/Half 10baseT/Full
                                100baseT/Half 100baseT/Full
                                1000baseT/Full
        Supports auto-negotiation: Yes
        Advertised link modes:  10baseT/Half 10baseT/Full
                                100baseT/Half 100baseT/Full
                                1000baseT/Full
        Advertised pause frame use: No
        Advertised auto-negotiation: Yes
        Speed: 1000Mb/s
        Duplex: Full
        Port: Twisted Pair
        PHYAD: 0
        Transceiver: internal
        Auto-negotiation: on
        MDI-X: Unknown
```

```
Supports Wake-on: d
Wake-on: d
Current message level: 0x00000007 (7)
Link detected: yes
```

Typically, there are only two parameters from the `ethtool` output that are of interest: the Speed and Duplex settings. They show you how your network board is talking to the switch.

Another nice tool that is used to monitor what is happening on the network is IPTraf (start it by typing `iptraf`). This is a real-time monitoring tool that shows what is happening on the network using a graphical interface. Figure 17.1 shows the IPTraf main menu.

FIGURE 17.1   IPTraf allows you to analyze network traffic from a menu interface.

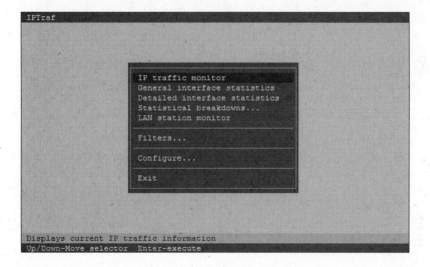

Before starting to use IPTraf, invoke the configure option. From there, you can specify exactly what you want to see and how you want it to be displayed. For example, a useful setting to change is the additional port range. By default, IPTraf shows activity on privileged TCP/UDP ports only. If you have a specific application that you want to monitor that doesn't use one of these privileged ports, select Additional Ports from the configuration interface and specify the additional ports you want to monitor.

After telling IPTraf how to do its work, use the IP traffic monitor to start the tool. Next, you can select on which interface you want to listen, or just hit Enter to listen on all interfaces. Following that, IPTraf asks you in which file you want to write log information. Note that it isn't always a smart choice to configure logging, since logging may fill up your file systems quite fast. If you don't want to log, press Ctrl+X now. This will start the IPTraf interface (see Figure 17.2), which gives you an idea of what kind of traffic is going on. To analyze that traffic, you need a network analyzer, such as the WireShark utility.

FIGURE 17.2 IPTraf provides a quick overview of the kind of traffic sent on an interface.

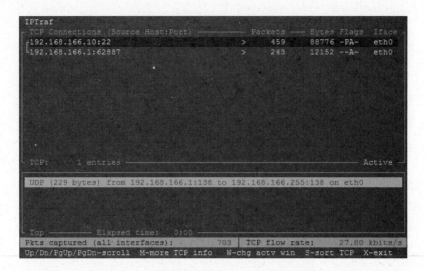

If you are not really interested in the performance on the network board but more of what is happening at the service level, `netstat` is a good basic network performance tool. It uses different parameters to show you what ports are open and on what ports your server sees activity.

My personal favorite way of using `netstat` is by issuing the `netstat -tulpn` command. This yields an overview of all listening ports on the server, and it even tells you what other node is connected to a particular port. See Listing 17.22 for an overview.

Listing 17.22: With netstat, you can see what ports are listening on your server and who is connected

```
[root@hnl ~]# netstat -tulpn
Active Internet connections (only servers)
Proto Recv-Q Send-Q Local Address     Foreign Address   State      PID/Program name
tcp        0      0 0.0.0.0:111       0.0.0.0:*         LISTEN     1959/rpcbind
tcp        0      0 0.0.0.0:22        0.0.0.0:*         LISTEN     2232/sshd
tcp        0      0 127.0.0.1:631     0.0.0.0:*         LISTEN     1744/cupsd
tcp        0      0 127.0.0.1:25      0.0.0.0:*         LISTEN     2330/master
tcp        0      0 0.0.0.0:59201     0.0.0.0:*         LISTEN     2046/rpc.statd
tcp        0      0 0.0.0.0:5672      0.0.0.0:*         LISTEN     2373/qpidd
tcp        0      0 :::111            :::*              LISTEN     1959/rpcbind
```

tcp	0	0 :::22	:::*	LISTEN	2232/sshd
tcp	0	0 :::42998	:::*	LISTEN	2046/rpc.statd
tcp	0	0 ::1:631	:::*	LISTEN	1744/cupsd
tcp	0	0 ::1:25	:::*	LISTEN	2330/master
udp	0	0 0.0.0.0:950	0.0.0.0:*		2046/rpc.statd
udp	0	0 0.0.0.0:39373	0.0.0.0:*		2046/rpc.statd
udp	0	0 0.0.0.0:862	0.0.0.0:*		1959/rpcbind
udp	0	0 0.0.0.0:42464	0.0.0.0:*		2016/avahi-daemon
udp	0	0 0.0.0.0:5353	0.0.0.0:*		2016/avahi-daemon
udp	0	0 0.0.0.0:111	0.0.0.0:*		1959/rpcbind
udp	0	0 0.0.0.0:631	0.0.0.0:*		1744/cupsd
udp	0	0 :::47801	:::*		2046/rpc.statd
udp	0	0 :::862	:::*		1959/rpcbind
udp	0	0 :::111	:::*		1959/rpcbind

When using netstat, many options are available. Here is an overview of the most interesting ones:

-p Shows the PID of the program that has opened a port

-c Updates the display every second

-s Shows statistics for IP, UDP, TCP, and ICMP

-t Shows TCP sockets

-u Shows UDP sockets

-w Shows RAW sockets

-l Shows listening ports

-n Resolves addresses to names

Many other tools are available to monitor the network. Most of them fall beyond the scope of this chapter because they are rather protocol- or service-specific, and they will not be very helpful in determining performance problems on the network.

There is one very simple performance testing method that I use at all times when analyzing a performance problem. All that really counts when analyzing network performance is how fast your network can copy data to and from your server. To measure this, I like to create a big file (1GB, for example) and copy it over the network. To measure the time expended, I use the time command, which gives a clear impression of how long it actually took to copy the file. For example, time scp server:/bigfile /localdir will yield a summary of the total time it took to copy the file over the network. This is an excellent test, especially when you start optimizing performance, because it will immediately show you whether you have achieved your goals.

Optimizing Performance

Now that you know what to look for in your server's performance, it's time to start optimizing. Optimizing performance is a complicated job. While the tips provided in this chapter cannot possibly cover everything about server performance optimization, it's good to know at least some of the basic approaches you can use to make your server perform better.

You can look at performance optimization in two different ways. For some people, it is simply a matter of changing some parameters and seeing what happens. This is not the best approach. A much better approach to performance optimization occurs when you first start performance monitoring. This gives you some crystal-clear ideas on what exactly is happening with performance on your server.

Before optimizing anything, you should know exactly what to optimize. For example, if the network performs badly, you should know whether it is because of problems on the network itself or simply because you don't have enough memory allocated for the network. Therefore, make sure you know exactly what to optimize, using the methods you've read about in the previous sections.

Once you know what to optimize, it comes down to doing it. In many situations, optimizing performance means writing a parameter to the /proc file system. This file system is created by the kernel when your server comes up, and it normally contains the settings your kernel is using.

Under /proc/sys, you'll find many system parameters that can be changed. The easy way to do this is by echoing the new value to the configuration file. For example, the /proc/sys/vm/swappiness file contains a value that indicates how willing your server is to swap. The range of this value is between 0 and 100. A low value means that your server will avoid swapping as long as possible, while a high value means that your server is more willing to swap. The default value in this file is 60. If you think your server is too eager to swap, you can change it as follows:

```
echo "30" > /proc/sys/vm/swappiness
```

This method works well, but there is a problem. As soon as the server restarts, you will lose this value. Thus, the better solution is to store it in a configuration file and make sure that configuration file is read when your server restarts. A configuration file exists for this purpose, and the name of the file is /etc/sysctl.conf. When booting, your server starts the sysctl service, which reads this configuration file and applies all of the settings in it.

In /etc/sysctl.conf, you refer to files that exist in the /proc/sys hierarchy. Thus, the name of the file to which you are referring is relative to this directory. Also, instead of using a slash as the separator between directories, subdirectories, and files, it is common to use a dot (even if the slash is also accepted). This means that to apply the change to the swappiness parameter as explained earlier, you should include the following line in /etc/sysctl.conf:

```
vm.swappiness=30
```

This setting is applied the next time your server reboots only. Instead of just writing it to the configuration file, you can apply it to the current sysctl settings as well. To do that, the following command can be used to apply this setting immediately:

```
sysctl -w vm.swappiness=30
```

Using sysctl -w does exactly the same as using the echo "30" > /proc/sys/vm/swap-piness command—it does *not* also write the setting to the sysctl.conf file. The most practical way of applying these settings is to write them to /etc/sysctl.conf first and then activate them using sysctl -p /etc/sysctl.conf. Once activated in this manner, you can also get an overview of all current sysctl settings using sysctl -a. In Listing 17.23, you can see a portion of the output of this command.

Listing 17.23: sysctl -a shows all current sysctl settings

```
net.nf_conntrack_max = 31776
net.bridge.bridge-nf-call-arptables = 1
net.bridge.bridge-nf-call-iptables = 1
net.bridge.bridge-nf-call-ip6tables = 1
net.bridge.bridge-nf-filter-vlan-tagged = 0
net.bridge.bridge-nf-filter-pppoe-tagged = 0
net.unix.max_dgram_qlen = 10
abi.vsyscall32 = 1
crypto.fips_enabled = 0
sunrpc.rpc_debug = 0
sunrpc.nfs_debug = 0
sunrpc.nfsd_debug = 0
sunrpc.nlm_debug = 0
sunrpc.transports = tcp 1048576
sunrpc.transports = udp 32768
sunrpc.transports = tcp-bc 1048576
sunrpc.udp_slot_table_entries = 16
sunrpc.tcp_slot_table_entries = 16
sunrpc.min_resvport = 665
sunrpc.max_resvport = 1023
sunrpc.tcp_fin_timeout = 15
```

The output of sysctl -a is overwhelming, because all of the kernel tunables are shown, and there are hundreds of them. I recommend you to use it in combination with grep to locate the information you need. For example, sysctl -a | grep xfs shows you only lines that have xfs in their output. In Exercise 17.5 later in this chapter, you'll apply a simple performance optimization test in which the /proc file system and sysctl are used.

Using a Simple Performance Optimization Test

Although sysctl and its configuration file sysctl.conf are very useful tools to change performance-related settings, you shouldn't use them immediately. Before writing a parameter to the system, make sure that this really is the parameter you need. The big question, however, is how to be certain of this. There's only one answer: testing.

Before starting any test, remember that tests always have their limitations. The test proposed here is far from perfect, and you shouldn't use this test alone to make definitive conclusions about the performance optimization of your server. Nevertheless, it provides a good idea of the write performance on your server in particular.

The test consists of creating a 1GB file using the following code:

```
dd if=/dev/zero of=/root/1GBfile bs=1M count=1024
```

By copying this file several times and measuring the time it takes to copy it, you will get a decent idea of the effect of some of the parameters. Many of the tasks you perform on your Linux server are I/O-related, so this simple test can give you an good idea of whether there is any improvement. To measure the time it takes to copy this file, use the time command, followed by cp, as in time cp /root/1GBfile /tmp. Listing 17.24 shows what this looks like when doing this task on your server.

Listing 17.24: By timing how long it takes to copy a large file, you can get a good idea of the current performance of your server

```
[root@hnl ~]# dd if=/dev/zero of=/1Gfile bs=1M count=1024
1024+0 records in
1024+0 records out
1073741824 bytes (1.1 GB) copied, 16.0352 s, 67.0 MB/s
[root@hnl ~]# time cp /1Gfile /tmp

real    0m20.469s
user    0m0.005s
sys     0m7.568s
```

Time gives you three different indicators: the real time, the user time, and the sys time it took to complete the command. The *real time* is the time from starting to completion of the command. The *user time* is the time the kernel spent in user space, and the *sys time* is the time the kernel spent in system space. When doing a test like this, it is important to interpret it in the right way. Consider, for example, Listing 17.25 in which the same command was repeated a couple of seconds later.

Listing 17.25: The same test, 10 seconds later

```
[root@hnl ~]# time cp /1Gfile /tmp


real    0m33.511s
user    0m0.003s
sys     0m7.436s
```

As you can see, it now performs slower than the first time the command was used. This is only in real time, however, and not in sys time. Is this the result of a performance parameter that I've changed in between tests? No, but look at the result of free -m as shown in Listing 17.26.

Listing 17.26: free -m might indicate why the second test went faster

```
root@hn1:~# free -m
                total      used      free    shared   buffers    cached
Mem:             3987      2246      1741         0        17      2108
-/+ buffers/cache:  119      3867
Swap:            2047         0      2047
```

Do you have any idea what has happened here? The entire 1GB file was put into cache. As you can see, free -m shows almost 2GB of data in cache that wasn't there beforehand, and this influences the time it takes to copy a large file.

So, what lesson can you learn from these examples? Performance optimization is complex. You have to take into account many factors that influence the performance of your server. Only when this is done the right way will you truly see how your server performs currently and whether you have succeeded in improving its performance. If you fail to examine the data carefully, you may miss things and think you have improved performance while in actuality worsening it.

CPU Tuning

In this section, you'll learn what you can do to optimize the performance of your server's CPU. First you'll learn about some aspects of the workings of the CPU that are important when trying to optimize its performance parameters. Then you'll read about some common techniques that are employed to optimize CPU utilization.

Understanding CPU Performance

To be able to tune the CPU, you must know what is important about this part of your system. To understand the CPU, you should know about the *thread scheduler*. This part of the kernel makes sure that all process threads get an equal amount of CPU cycles. Since most processes will also do some I/O, it's not really a problem that the scheduler puts process threads on hold at a given moment. While not being served by the CPU, the process thread can handle its I/O. The scheduler operates by using *fairness*, meaning that all threads are moving forward in an even manner. By using fairness, the scheduler makes sure there is not too much latency.

The scheduling process is pretty simple in a single–CPU core environment. However, if multiple cores are used, it is more complicated. To work in a multi-CPU or multicore environment, your server will use a specialized *Symmetric Multiprocessing (SMP)* kernel. If needed, this kernel is installed automatically. In an SMP environment, the scheduler makes sure that some kind of *load balancing* is used. This means that process threads are spread over the available CPU cores. Some programs are written to be used in an SMP environment and are able to use multiple CPUs by themselves. Most programs can't do this, however, and depend on the capabilities of the kernel to do it.

One specific concern in a multi-CPU environment is that the scheduler should prevent processes and threads from being moved to other CPU cores. Moving a process means that the information the process has written in the CPU cache needs to be moved as well, and that is a relatively expensive process.

You may think that a server will always benefit from installing multiple CPU cores, but this is not true. When working on multiple cores, chances increase that processes are swapped among cores, taking their cached information with them, and that slows down performance in a multiprocessing environment. When using multicore systems, you should always optimize your system for such a configuration.

Optimizing CPU Performance

CPU performance optimization is about two things: priority and optimization of the SMP environment. Every process gets a static priority from the scheduler. The scheduler can differentiate between real-time (RT) processes and normal processes. However, if a process falls into one of these categories, it will be equal to all other processes in the same category. Note that some real-time processes (most of them are part of the Linux kernel) will run at highest priority, while the rest of available CPU cycles must be divided among the other processes. In this procedure, it's all about fairness: the longer a process is waiting, the higher its priority. You have already learned how to use the nice command to tune process priority.

If you are working in an SMP environment, one important utility used to improve performance is the taskset command. You can use taskset to set CPU affinity for a process to one or more CPUs. The result is that your process is less likely to be moved to another CPU. The taskset command uses a hexadecimal bitmask to specify which CPU to use. In this bitmap, the value 0x1 refers to CPU0, 0x2 refers to CPU1, 0x4 to CPU2, 0x8 to CPU3, and so on. Notice that these numbers combine, so use 0x3 to refer to CPUs 0 and 1.

Therefore, if you have a command that you would like to bind to CPU 2 and CPU 3, you would use the command taskset 0x12 somecommand.

You can also use taskset on running processes by using the -p option. With this option, you can refer to the PID of a process; for instance, taskset -p 0x3 7034 would set the affinity of the process using PID 7034 to CPU 0 and CPU 1.

You can specify CPU affinity for IRQs as well. To do this, you can use the same bitmask that you used with taskset. Every interrupt has subdirectory in /proc/irq/, and in that subdirectory there is a file called smp_affinity. Thus, if your IRQ 5 is producing a very high workload (check /proc/interrupts to see whether this is the case) and therefore you want that IRQ to work on CPU 1, use the command echo 0x2 > /proc/irq/3/smp_affinity.

Another approach to optimizing CPU performance is by using cgroups. *cgroups* provide a new way to optimize all aspects of performance, including CPU, memory, I/O, and more. Later in this chapter, you'll learn how to use cgroups.

Tuning Memory

System memory is a very important part of a computer. It functions as a buffer between CPU and I/O, and by tuning memory you can really get the best out of it. Linux works with the concept of *virtual memory*, which is the total of all memory available on a server. You can tune virtual memory by writing to the /proc/sys/vm directory. This directory contains lots of parameters that help you tune the way your server's memory is used.

WARNING   As always, when tuning the performance of a server, there are no solutions that work in all cases. Use the parameters in /proc/sys/vm with caution, and use them one by one. Only by tuning each parameter individually will you be able to determine whether it achieved the desired result.

Understanding Memory Performance

In a Linux system, virtual memory is used for many purposes. First, there are processes that claim their amount of memory. When tuning for processes, it helps to know how these processes allocate memory. For example, a database server that allocates large amounts of system memory when starting up has different needs than a mail server that works with small files only. Also, each process has its own memory space that may not be addressed by other processes. The kernel ensures that this never happens.

When a process is created using the fork() system call, which basically creates a child process from the parent, the kernel creates a virtual address space for the process. The part of the kernel that handles this is known as the *dynamic linker.* The virtual address space that is used by a process consists of pages. On a 64-bit server, the default page size is 4KB. For applications that need lots of memory, you can optimize memory by configuring huge pages. It needs to be supported by the application, however. Think of large databases, for example. Also note that memory, which has been allocated for huge pages, cannot be used for any other purpose.

Another important aspect of memory usage is caching. In your system, there is a read cache and a write cache. It may not surprise you that a server that handles read requests most of the time is tuned in a different way than a server that primarily handles write requests.

Configuring Huge Pages

If your server is heavily used for one application, it may benefit from using large pages (also referred to as *huge* pages). A *huge page* by default is 2MB in size, and it may be useful in improving performance in high-performance computing environments and with memory-intensive applications. By default, no huge pages are allocated, because they would be wasteful for a server that doesn't need them. Typically, you set huge pages from the Grub boot loader when starting your server. Later, you can check the amount of huge pages in use with the /proc/sys/vm/nr_hugepages parameter. In Exercise 17.5, you'll learn how to set huge pages.

EXERCISE 17.5

Configuring Huge Pages

In this exercise, you'll configure huge pages. You'll set them as a kernel argument, and then you'll verify their availability. Notice that, in this procedure, you'll specify the number of huge pages as a boot argument to the kernel. You can also set it from the /proc file system as explained later.

1.   Using an editor, open the Grub menu configuration file in /boot/grub/menu.1st.

2.   Find the section that starts your kernel, and add **hugepages=64** to the kernel line.

3.   Save your settings, and reboot your server to activate them.

4.   Use **cat /proc/sys/vm/nr_hugepages** to confirm that there are 64 huge pages set on your system. Notice that all of the memory that is allocated in huge pages is not available for other purposes.

Be careful, though, when allocating huge pages. All memory pages that are allocated as huge pages are no longer available for other purposes. Thus, if your server needs a heavy read or write cache, you will suffer from allocating too many huge pages up front. If you determine that this is the case, you can change the number of huge pages currently in use by writing to the /proc/sys/vm/nr_hugepages parameter. Your server will pick up this new amount of huge pages immediately.

Optimizing Write Cache

The next couple of parameters all relate to the buffer cache. As discussed earlier, your server maintains a write cache. By putting data in that write cache, the server can delay writing data. This is useful for more than one reason. Imagine that just after committing the write request to the server, another write request is made. It will be easier for the server to handle the second write request if the data is not yet written to disk but is still in memory. You may also want to tune the write cache to balance between the amount of memory reserved for reading data and the amount that is reserved for writing data.

The first relevant parameter is in /proc/sys/vm/dirty_ratio. This parameter is used to define the percentage of memory that is maximally used for the write cache. When the percentage of buffer cache in use rises above this parameter, your server will write memory from the buffer cache to disk as soon as possible. The default of 10 percent works fine for an average server, but in some situations you may want to increase or decrease the amount of memory used here.

Related to dirty_ratio are the dirty_expire_centisecs and dirty_writeback_centisecs parameters, which are also in /proc/sys/vm. These parameters determine when data in the write cache expires and has to be written to disk, even if the write cache hasn't yet reached the threshold defined in dirty_ratio. By using these parameters, you reduce the chances of losing data when a power outage occurs on your server. Furthermore, if you want to use power more efficiently, it is useful to give both of these parameters a 0 value, which actually disables them and keeps data as long as possible in the write cache. This is useful for laptop computers because the hard disk needs to spin up in order to write these data, and that uses a lot of power.

The last parameter that is related to writing data is nr_pdflush_threads. This parameter helps determine the amount of threads the kernel launches for writing data from the buffer cache. This is fairly simple in concept: more of these means faster write back. Thus, if you think that buffer cache on your server is not cleared fast enough, increase the amount of pdflush_threads using the command sysctl -w vm.nr_pdflush_threads=4.

When using this option, respect the limitations. By default, the minimum amount of pdflush_threads is set to 0, and there is a maximum of 8 so that the kernel still has a dynamic range to determine what exactly it has to do.

Next, there is the issue of overcommitting memory. By default, every process tends to claim more memory than it really needs. This is good because it makes the process faster if some spare memory is available. It can then access it much faster when it needs it because it doesn't have to ask the kernel if it has some more memory to give.

To tune the behavior of overcommitting memory, you can write to the /proc/sys/vm/overcommit_memory parameter. You can set this parameter's values. The default value is 0, which means that the kernel checks to see whether it still has memory available before granting it. If this doesn't give you the performance you need, you can consider changing it to 1, which means that the system thinks there is enough memory in all cases. This is good for the performance of memory-intensive tasks but may result in processes getting killed automatically. You can also use the value of 2, which means that the kernel fails the memory request if there is not enough memory available.

This minimum amount of memory that is available is specified in the /proc/sys/vm/overcommit_ratio parameter, which by default is set to 50 percent of available RAM. Using the value of 2 ensures that your server will never run out of available memory by granting memory demanded by a process that needs huge amounts of memory. (On a server with 16GB of RAM, the memory allocation request would be denied only if more than 8GB is requested by one single process!)

Another nice parameter is /proc/sys/vm/swappiness. This indicates how eager the process is to start swapping out memory pages. A high value means that your server will swap very quickly, and a low value means that the server will wait some more before starting to swap. The default value of 60 works well in most situations. If you still think that your server starts swapping too quickly, set it to a somewhat lower value, like 40.

Optimizing Interprocess Communication

The last relevant parameters are those that relate to shared memory. *Shared memory* is a method that the Linux kernel or Linux applications can use to make communication between processes (also known as *Interprocess Communication*, or *IPC*) as fast as possible. In database environments, it often makes sense to optimize shared memory. The cool thing about shared memory is that the kernel is not involved in the communication among the processes using it, because data doesn't even have to be copied since the memory areas can be addressed directly. To get an idea of shared memory-related settings that your server is currently using, use the `ipcs -lm` command, as shown in Listing 17.27.

Listing 17.27: Use the `ipcs -lm` command to get an idea of shared memory settings

```
root@hnl ~]# ipcs -lm

------ Shared Memory Limits --------
max number of segments = 4096
max seg size (kbytes) = 67108864
max total shared memory (kbytes) = 17179869184
min seg size (bytes) = 1
```

When your applications are written to use shared memory, you can benefit from tuning some of its parameters. If on the other hand your applications don't know how to handle it, it doesn't make a difference if you change the shared memory-related parameters. To find out whether on your server shared memory is used and, if so, in what amount it is used, use the `ipcs -m` command. Listing 17.28 provides an example of this command's output on a server where just one shared memory segment is used.

Listing 17.28: Use `ipcs -m` to find out if your server is using shared memory segments

```
[root@hnl ~]# ipcs -m

------ Shared Memory Segments --------
key        shmid      owner      perms      bytes      nattch     status
0x00000000 0          gdm        600        393216     2          dest
0x00000000 32769      gdm        600        393216     2          dest
0x00000000 65538      gdm        600        393216     2          dest
```

The first /proc parameter that is related to shared memory is `shmmax`. This defines the maximum size in bytes of a single shared memory segment that a Linux process can allocate. You can see the current setting in the configuration file /proc/sys/kernel/shmmax.

```
root@hnl:~# cat /proc/sys/kernel/shmmax
33554432
```

This sample was taken from a system that has 4GB of RAM. The `shmmax` setting was automatically created to allow processes to allocate up to about 3.3GB of RAM. It doesn't make sense to tune the parameter to use all available RAM, since the RAM also has to be used for other purposes.

The second parameter that is related to shared memory is shmmni, which is not the minimal size of shared memory segments as you might think but rather the maximum number of the shared memory segments that your kernel can allocate. You can get the default value from /proc/sys/kernel/shmmni. It should be set to 4096. If you have an application that relies heavily on the use of shared memory, you may benefit from increasing this parameter, as follows:

```
sysctl -w kernel.shmmni=8192
```

The last parameter related to shared memory is shmall. It is set in /proc/sys/kernel/shmall, and it defines the total amount of shared memory pages that can be used system-wide. Normally, the value should be set to the value of shmmax, divided by the current page size your server is using. On a 32-bit processor, finding the page size is easy; it is always set to 4096. On a 64-bit computer, you can use the getconf command to determine the current page size.

```
[root@hnl ~]# getconf PAGE_SIZE
4096
```

If the shmall parameter doesn't contain a value that is big enough for your application, change it as needed. For example, use the following command:

```
sysctl -w kernel.shmall=2097152
```

Tuning Storage Performance

The third element in the chain of Linux performance is the storage channel. Performance optimization on this channel can be divided in two parts: journal optimization and I/O buffer performance. Apart from that, there are also some file system parameters that can be tuned to optimize performance. You already read how to do this using the tune2fs command.

Understanding Storage Performance

To determine what happens with I/O on your server, Linux uses the I/O scheduler. This kernel component sits between the block layer that communicates directly with the file systems and the device drivers. The block layer generates I/O requests for the file systems and passes those requests to the I/O scheduler. This scheduler in turn transforms the request and passes it on to the low-level drivers. The drivers then forward the request to the actual storage devices. Optimizing storage performance starts with optimizing the I/O scheduler. Figure 17.3 gives an overview of everything involved in analyzing I/O performance.

FIGURE 17.3   I/O Performance overview

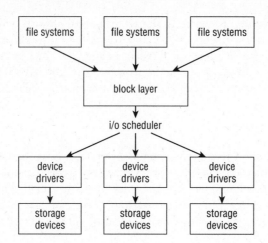

Optimizing the I/O Scheduler

Working with an I/O scheduler makes your computer more flexible. The I/O scheduler can prioritize I/O requests and also reduce data searching time on the hard disk. Also, the I/O scheduler makes sure that a request is handled before it times out.

An important goal of the I/O scheduler is to make hard disk seek times more efficient. The scheduler does this by collecting requests before committing them to disk. Because of this approach, the scheduler can do its work more efficiently. For example, it may choose to order requests before committing them to disk, which makes hard disk seeks more efficient.

When optimizing the performance of the I/O scheduler, there is a dilemma you will need to address: You can optimize either read performance or write performance, but not both at the same time. Optimizing read performance means that write performance will be not as good, whereas optimizing write performance means you have to pay a price in read performance. So, before starting to optimize the I/O scheduler, you should analyze the workload that is generated by your server.

There are four different ways for the I/O scheduler to do its work:

Complete Fair Queuing   In the *Complete Fair Queuing (CFG)* approach, the I/O scheduler objectively tries to allocate I/O bandwidth. This approach offers a good solution for machines with mixed workloads, and it offers the best compromise between latency, which is relevant for reading data, and throughput, which is relevant in an environment where there is a lot of file writes.

Noop Scheduler   The *noop scheduler* performs only minimal merging functions on your data. There is no sorting, and therefore this scheduler has minimal overhead. The noop scheduler was developed for non-disk-based block devices, such as memory devices. It also works well with storage media that have extensive caching, virtual machines (in some cases), and intelligent SAN devices.

Deadline Scheduler   The *deadline scheduler* works with five different I/O queues and thus is very capable of making a difference between read requests and write requests. When using this scheduler, read requests get a higher priority. Write requests do not have a deadline, and therefore data to be written can remain in cache for a longer period. This scheduler works well in environments where both good read and good write performance are required but where they have a higher priority for reads. This scheduler does particularly well in database environments.

Anticipatory Scheduler   The *anticipatory scheduler* tries to reduce read response times. It does so by introducing a controlled delay in all read requests. This increases the possibility that another read request can be handled in the same I/O request, and therefore it makes reads more efficient.

The results of switching among I/O schedulers heavily depends on the nature of the workload of the specific server. The previous summary is merely a guideline, and before changing the I/O scheduler, you should test intensively to find out whether it really leads to the desired results.

There are two ways to change the current I/O scheduler. You can echo a new value to the /sys/block/<YOURDEVICE>/queue/scheduler file. Alternatively, you can set it as a boot parameter using elevator=yourscheduler on the GRUB prompt or in the GRUB menu. The choices are noop, anticipatory, deadline, and CFQ.

Optimizing Reads

Another way to optimize the way your server works is by tuning read requests. This is something you can do on a per-disk basis. First there is read_ahead, which can be tuned in /sys/block/<YOURDEVICE>/queue/read_ahead_kb. On a default Red Hat Enterprise Linux installation, this parameter is set to 128 KB. If you have fast disks, you can optimize your read performance by using a higher value; 512 KB is a starting point, but make sure always to test before making a new setting final. Also, you can tune the number of outstanding read requests by using /sys/block/<YOURDEVICE>/queue/nr_requests. The default value for this parameter also is set to 128 KB, but a higher value may optimize your server significantly. Try 512 KB, or even 1024 KB, to get the best read performance. Always observe, however, that it doesn't introduce too much latency while writing files. In Exercise 17.6 you'll learn how to change scheduler parameters.

Optimizing read performance works well, but remember that while improving read performance, you also introduce latency on writes. In general, there is nothing wrong with that, but if your server loses power, all data that is still in the memory buffers and yet hasn't been written will be lost.

EXERCISE 17.6

Changing Scheduler Parameters

In this exercise, you'll change the scheduler parameters and try to see a difference. Note that complex workloads will normally better show the differences, so don't be surprised if you don't see much of a difference based on the simple tests proposed in this exercise.

1. Open a root shell. Use the command **cat /sys/proc/sda/queue/scheduler** to find out the current setting of the scheduler. If it's a default Red Hat installation, it will be set to CFQ.

2. Use the command **dd if=/dev/urandom of=/dev/null** to start some background workload. The idea is to start a process that is intense on reads but doesn't write a lot.

3. Write a script with the name reads that reads the contents of all files in /etc.

   ```
   cd /etc
   for i in *
   do
       cat $i
   done
   ```

4. Run the script using **time reads**, and note the time it takes for the script to complete.

5. Run the command **time dd if=/dev/zero of=/1Gfile bs=1M count=1000**, and note the time it takes for the command to complete.

6. Change the I/O scheduler setting to noop, anticipatory and deadline, and repeat steps 4 and 5. To change the current I/O scheduler setting, use **echo noop > /sys/proc/sda/queue/scheduler**. You now know which settings work best for this simple test environment.

7. Use **killall dd** to make sure all dd jobs are terminated.

Changing Journal Options

By default, most file systems in Linux use journaling, which logs an upcoming transaction before it happens to speed up repair actions if they are needed after a system crash. For some specific workloads, the default journaling mode will cause you a lot of problems. You can find out whether this is the case for your server by using iotop. If you see kjournald high in the list, you have a journaling issue that you need to optimize.

You can set three different journaling options by using the data=journaloption mount option:

data=writeback   This option guarantees internal file system integrity, but it doesn't guarantee that new files have been committed to disk. In many cases, it is the fastest but also the most insecure journaling option.

data=ordered   This is the default mode. It forces all data to be written to the file system before the metadata is written to the journal.

data=journaled   This is the most secure journaling option, where all data blocks are journaled as well. The performance price for using this option is high, but it does offer the best security for your files.

 Real World Scenario

Saving Lots of Money Through Performance Optimization

A customer once contacted me about a serious issue on one of their servers. At the end of the day, the server received about 50GB of database data, and then it completely stalled because it was working so hard on these database files. This took about half an hour, and then the server started reacting again. At the moment the customer contacted me, they were about to replace the entire 8TB of storage in their server with SSD disks at an estimated cost of about $50,000. Before spending that much money on a solution they weren't certain would fix the problem, they called me and asked to analyze the server.

At the moment the problem normally occurred, I logged in to the server, and on the first attempt, I noticed that it became completely unresponsive. Even a command like ls took more than five minutes to produce a result in a directory with only a small number of files. top showed that the server was very busy with I/O, however. The second day I prepared iotop to see which process was responsible for the high I/O load, and kjournald, the kernel process responsible for journaling, showed up very high in the list. I changed the journal setting from data=ordered to data-writeback, and the next day the server was perfectly capable of handling the 50GB of data it received at the end of the day. My actions thus saved the customer about $50,000 for the purchase of new hardware.

Network Tuning

Among the most difficult items to tune is network performance. This is because, in networking, multiple layers of communication are involved, and each is handled separately on Linux. First there are buffers on the network card itself that deal with physical frames. Next, there is the TCP/IP protocol stack, and then there is also the application stack. All work together, and tuning one has consequences on the other layer. While tuning the network, always work upward in the protocol stack. That is, start by tuning the packets themselves, then tune the TCP/IP stack, and after that, examine the service stacks that are in use on your server.

Tuning Kernel Parameters

While it initializes, the kernel sets some parameters automatically based on the amount of memory that is available on your server. So, the good news is that, in many situations, there is no work to be done. By default, some parameters are not set in the most optimal way, so in those cases there is some performance to be gained.

For every network connection, the kernel allocates a socket. The socket is the end-to-end line of communication. Each socket has a receive buffer and a send buffer, also known as the *read* (receive) and *write* (send) buffers. These buffers are very important. If they are full, no more data can be processed, so the data will be dropped. This will have important consequences for the performance of your server, because if data is dropped, it needs to be sent and processed again.

The basis of all reserved sockets on the network comes from two /proc tunables.

```
/proc/sys/net/core/wmem_default
/proc/sys/net/core/rmem_default
```

All kernel-based sockets are reserved from these sockets. However, if a socket is TCP based, the settings in here are overwritten by TCP-specific parameters, in particular the `tcp_rmem` and `tcp_wmem` parameters. In the next section, you will read about how to optimize them.

The values of the `wmem_default` and `rmem_default` are set automatically when your server boots. If you have dropped packets on the network interface, you may benefit by increasing them. For some workloads, the values that are used by default are rather low. To set them, tune the following parameters in /etc/sysctl.conf:

```
net.core.wmem_default
net.core.rmem_default
```

Particularly if you have dropped packets, try doubling them to find out whether the dropped packets go away by doing so.

Related to the default read and write buffer size is the maximum read and write buffer size, `rmem_max` and `wmem_max`. These are also calculated automatically when your server comes up. For many situations, however, they are far too low. For example, on a server that has 4GB of RAM, the sizes of these are set to 128KB only! You may benefit from changing their values to something that is much larger, such as 8MB instead.

```
sysctl -w net.core.rmem_max=8388608
sysctl -w net.core.wmem_max=8388608
```

When increasing the read and write buffer size, you also have to increase the maximum amount of incoming packets that can be queued. This is set in `netdev_max_backlog`. The default value is set to 1000, which is insufficient for very busy servers. Try increasing it to a much higher value, such as 8000, especially if you have lots of connections coming in or if there are lots of dropped packets.

```
sysctl -w net.core.netdev_max_backlog=8000
```

Apart from the maximum number of incoming packets that your server can queue, there also is a maximum amount of incoming connections that can be accepted. You can set them from the `somaxconn` file in /proc.

```
sysctl -w net.core.somaxconn=512
```

By tuning this parameter, you will limit the amount of new connections that are dropped.

Optimizing TCP/IP

Up until now, you have tuned kernel buffers for network sockets only. These are generic parameters. If you are working with TCP, some specific tunables are also available. By default, some TCP tunables have a value that is too low. Many are self-tunable and adjust their values automatically, if needed. Chances are that you can gain a lot by increasing them. All relevant options are in proc/sys/net/ipv4.

To begin, there is a read buffer size and a write buffer size that you can set for TCP. They are written to tcp_rmem and tcp_wmem. Here again the kernel tries to allocate the best possible values when it boots. In some cases, however, it doesn't work out very well. If this happens, you can change the minimum size, the default size, and the maximum size of these buffers. Notice that each of these two parameters contains three values at the same time, for minimum, default, and maximum size. In general, there is no need to tune the minimum size. It can be interesting, though, to tune the default size. This is the buffer size that will be available when your server boots. Tuning the maximum size is also important, because it defines the upper threshold above which packets will get dropped. Listing 17.29 shows the default settings for these parameters on my server with 4GB of RAM.

Listing 17.29: Default settings for TCP read and write buffers

```
[root@hnl ~]# cat /proc/sys/net/ipv4/tcp_rmem
4096    87380    3985408
[root@hnl ~]# cat /proc/sys/net/ipv4/tcp_wmem
4096    16384    3985408
```

In this example, the maximum size is quite good. Almost 4MB is available as the maximum size for read and write buffers. The default write buffer size is limited. Imagine that you want to tune these parameters in a way that the default write buffer size is as big as the default read buffer size, and the maximum for both parameters is set to 8MB. You can do that with the next two commands:

```
sysctl -w net.ipv4.tcp_rmem="4096 87380 8388608"
sysctl -w net.ipv4.tcp_wmem="4096 87380 8388608"
```

Before tuning options such as these, you should always check the availability of memory on your server. All memory that is allocated for TCP read and write buffers can no longer be used for other purposes, so you may cause problems in other areas while tuning these. It's an important rule in tuning that you should always make sure that the parameters are well balanced.

Another useful set of parameters is related to the acknowledged nature of TCP. Let's look at an example to understand how this works. Imagine that the sender in a TCP connection sends a series of packets numbered 1, 2, 3, 4, 5, 6, 7, 8, 9, and 10. Now imagine that the receiver receives all of them, with the exception of packet 5. In the default setting, the receiver would acknowledge receiving up to packet 4, in which case the sender would send packets 5, 6, 7, 8, 9, and 10 again. This is a waste of bandwidth since packets 6, 7, 8, 9, and 10 have already been received correctly.

To handle this acknowledgment traffic in a more efficient way, the setting /proc/sys/ net/ipv4/tcp_sack is enabled (that is, it has the value of 1). This means that in cases such as the previous one, only missing packets have to be sent again and not the complete packet stream. For your network bandwidth, this is good because only those packets that actually need to be retransmitted are retransmitted. Thus, if your bandwidth is low, you should always leave it on. However, if you are on a fast network, there is a downside. When using this parameter, packets may come in out of order. This means you need larger TCP receive buffers to keep all of the packets until they can be defragmented and put in the right order. This means that using this parameter requires more memory to be reserved, and from that perspective, on fast network connections you had better switch it off. To accomplish that, use the following code:

```
sysctl -w net.ipv4.tcp_sack=0
```

When disabling TCP selective acknowledgments as described earlier, you should also disable two related parameters: tcp_dsack and tcp_fack. These parameters enable selective acknowledgments for specific packet types. To enable them, use the following two commands:

```
sysctl -w net.ipv4.tcp_dsack=0
sysctl -w net.ipv4.tcp_fack=0
```

In case you prefer to work with selective acknowledgments, you can also tune the amount of memory that is reserved to buffer incoming packets that have to be put in the right order. Two parameters are relevant to accomplish this: ipfrag_low_tresh and ipfrag_high_tresh. When the amount specified in ipfrag_high_tresh is reached, new packets to be defragmented are dropped until the server reaches ipfrag_low_tresh. Make sure that the value of both of these parameters is set high enough at all times if your server uses selective acknowledgments. The following values are reasonable for most servers:

```
sysctl -w net.ipv4.ipfrag_low_tresh=393216
sysctl -w net.ipv4.ipfrag_high_tresh=524288
```

Next, there is the length of the TCP Syn queue that is created for each port. The idea is that all incoming connections are queued until they can be serviced. As you can probably guess, when the queue is full, connections get dropped. The situation is that the tcp_max_ syn_backlog that manages these per port queues has a default value that is too low, because only 1024 bytes are reserved for each port. For good performance, you should allocate 8192 bytes per port using the following:

```
sysctl -w net.ipv4.tcp_max_syn_backlog=8192
```

There are also some options that relate to the time an established connection is maintained. The idea is that every connection that your server has to keep alive uses resources. If your server is very busy at a given moment, it will run out of resources and tell new incoming clients that no resources are available. Since it is easy enough for a client to reestablish a connection in most cases, you probably want to tune your server in a way that it detects failing connections as soon as possible.

The first parameter that relates to maintaining connections is `tcp_synack_retries`. This parameter defines the number of times the kernel will send a response to an incoming new connection request. The default value is 5. Given the current quality of network connections, three is probably enough, and it is better for busy servers because it makes a connection available sooner. Use the following to change it:

```
sysctl -w net.ipv4.tcp_synack_retries=3
```

Next, there is the `tcp_retries2` option. This relates to the number of times the server tries to resend data to a remote host, which has an established session. Since it is inconvenient for a client computer if a connection is dropped, the default value of 15 is a lot higher than the default value for `tcp_synack_retries`. However, retrying it 15 times means while your server is retrying to send the data, it can't use its resources for something else. Therefore, it is best to decrease this parameter to a more reasonable value of 5.

```
sysctl -w net.ipv4.tcp_retries2=5
```

The parameters just discussed relate to sessions that appear to be gone. Another area where you can do some optimization is in maintaining inactive sessions. By default, a TCP session can remain idle forever. You probably don't want that, so use the `tcp_keepalive_time` option to determine how long an established inactive session will be maintained. By default, this will be 7,200 seconds, or two hours. If your server tends to run out of resources because too many requests are coming in, limit it to a considerably shorter period of time, as shown here:

```
sysctl -w net.ipv4.tcp_keepalive_time=900
```

Related to the `keepalive_time` is the number of packets that your server will send before deciding that a connection is dead. You can manage this by using the `tcp_keepalive_probes` parameter. By default, nine packets are sent before a server is considered dead. Change it to 3 if you want to terminate dead connections faster, as shown here:

```
sysctl -w net.ipv4.tcp_keepalive_probes=3
```

Related to the amount of `tcp_keepalive_probes` is the interval you use to send these probes. By default, this happens every 75 seconds. So, even with three probes, it still takes more than three minutes before your server sees that a connection has failed. To reduce this period, give the `tcp_keepalive_intvl` parameter the value of 15, as follows:

```
sysctl -w net.ipv4.tcp_keepalive_intvl=15
```

To complete the story of maintaining connections, you need two more parameters. By default, the kernel waits a bit before reusing a socket. If you run a busy server, performance will benefit from switching this off. To do this, use the following two commands:

```
sysctl -w net.ipv4.tcp_tw_reuse=1
sysctl -w net.ipv4.tcp_tw_recycle=1
```

Generic Network Performance Optimization Tips

Up to this point, I have only discussed kernel parameters. There are also some more generic hints to follow when optimizing performance on the network. You probably have applied all of them already, but just to be sure, let's repeat some of the most important tips:

- Make sure you have the latest network driver modules.

- Use network card teaming to make a bond interface in which two physical network cards are used to increase the performance of the network card in your server.

- Check the Ethernet configuration settings, such as the frame size, MTU, speed, and duplex mode, on your network. Make sure that all devices involved in network communications use the same settings.

Optimizing Linux Performance Using cgroups

Among the latest features for performance optimization that Linux offers is cgroups (short for control groups). Using *cgroups* is a technique that allows you to create groups of resources and allocate them to specific services. With this solution, you can make sure that a fixed percentage of resources on your server are always available for those services that need it.

To start using cgroups, first make sure the `libcgroup` RPM package is installed. Once you have confirmed its installation, you need to start the `cgconfig` and `cgred` services. Make sure to put these in the runlevels of your server, using `chkconfig cgconfig on` and `chkconfig cgred on`. Next make sure to start these services. This will create a directory `/cgroup` with a couple of subdirectories in it. These subdirectories are referred to as *controllers*. The *controllers* refer to the system resources that you can limit using cgroups. Some of the most interesting controllers include the following:

blkio   Use this to limit the amount of I/O that can be handled.

cpu   This is used to limit CPU cycles.

memory   Use this to limit the amount of memory that you can grant to processes.

There are additional controllers, but they are not as useful as those described.

Now let's assume you're running an Oracle database on your server, and you want to make sure that it runs in a cgroup where it has access to at least 75 percent of available memory and CPU cycles. The first step would be to create a cgroup that defines access to CPU and memory resources. The following command would create this cgroup with the name `oracle`: `cgcreate -g cpu,memory oracle`. After defining the cgroups this way, you'll see that in the `/cgroups/cpu` and `/cgroups/memory` directories, a subdirectory with the name `oracle` is created. In this subdirectory, different parameters are available to specify the resources you want to make available to the `cgroup` (see Listing 17.30).

Listing 17.30: In the subdirectory of your `cgroup`, you'll find all tunables

```
[root@hn1 ~]# cd /cgroup/cpu/oracle/
[root@hn1 oracle]# ls
cgroup.procs            cpu.rt_period_us       cpu.stat
cpu.cfs_period_us       cpu.rt_runtime_us      notify_on_release
cpu.cfs_quota_us        cpu.shares                   tasks
```

To specify the amount of CPU resources available for the newly created cgroup, you'll use the `cpu.shares` parameter. This is a relative parameter that makes sense only if everything is in cgroups, and it defines the amount of shares available in this cgroup. This means that if in the cgroup `oracle` you give it the value 80 and in the cgroup `other`, which contains all other processes, you give it the value of 20, the `oracle` cgroup gets 80 percent of available CPU resources. To set the parameter, you can use the `cgset` command: `cgset -r cpu.shares=80 oracle`.

After setting the amount of CPU shares for this cgroup, you can put processes into it. The best way to do this is to start the process you want to put in the cgroup as an argument to the `cgexec` command. In this example, that would mean you'd run `cgexec -g cpu:/oracle /path/to/oracle`. At this time, the `oracle` process and all its child processes will be visible in the `/cgroups/cpu/oracle/tasks` file, and you have assigned `oracle` to its specific cgroup.

In this example, you've read how to create cgroups manually, make resources available to the cgroup, and put a process in it. The disadvantage of this approach is that, after a system restart, all settings will be lost. To make the cgroups permanent, you have to use the `cgconfig` service and the `cgred` service. The `cgconfig` service reads its configuration file `/etc/cgconfig.conf` in which the cgroups are defined, including defining the resources you want to assign to that cgroup. Listing 17.31 shows what it would look like for the `oracle` example.

Listing 17.31: Example `cgconfig.conf` File

```
group oracle {
        cpu {
                cpu.shares=80
        }
        memory {
        }
}
```

Next, you need to create the `cgrules.conf` file, which specifies the processes that have to be put into a specific cgroup automatically. This file is read when the `cgred` service is starting. For the `oracle` group, it would have the following contents:

```
*:oracle        cpu,memory      /oracle
```

If you have made sure that both the `cgconfig` service and the `cgred` service are starting from the runlevels, your services will automatically be started in the appropriate cgroup.

Summary

In this chapter, you learned how to tune and optimize performance on your server. You read that for both the tuning and the optimization parts, you'll always look at four different categories: CPU, memory, I/O, and network. For each of these, several tools are available to optimize performance.

Performance optimization is often done by tuning parameters in the /proc file system. Apart from that, there are also different options that can be very diverse, depending on the optimization you're trying to achieve. cgroups is an important new instrument designed to optimize performance. It allows you to limit resources for services on your server in a very specific way.

Chapter

18

Introducing Bash Shell Scripting

TOPICS COVERED IN THIS CHAPTER:

- ✓ Getting Started
- ✓ Working with Variables and Input
- ✓ Performing Calculations
- ✓ Using Control Structures

Once you are at ease working with the command line, you'll want more. You already learned how to combine commands using piping, but if you really want to get the best from your commands, there is much more you can do. In this chapter, you'll be introduced to the possibilities of Bash shell scripting, which helps you accomplish difficult tasks easily. Once you have a firm grasp of shell scripting, you'll be able to automate many tasks and thus be able to complete your work more than twice as fast as you could before.

Getting Started

A *shell script* is a text file that contains a sequence of commands. Basically, anything that can run a bunch of commands is considered a shell script. Nevertheless, there are some rules to ensure that you create quality shell scripts—scripts that not only work well for the task for which they are written but that also will be readable by others. At some point, you'll be happy to write readable shell scripts. Especially as your scripts get longer, you'll agree that if a script does not meet the basic requirements of readability, even you won't be able to understand what it is doing.

Elements of a Good Shell Script

When writing a script, make sure it meets the following recommendations:

- Has a unique name
- Includes the shebang (#!) to tell the shell which subshell should execute the script
- Includes *comments*—lots of comments
- Uses the `exit` command to tell the shell executing the script that it has executed successfully
- Is executable

Let's talk about the name of the script first. You'll be amazed how many commands exist on your computer. Thus, you have to be sure that the name of your script is unique. For example, many people like to name their first script `test`. Unfortunately, there's already a command with the name `test`, which will be discussed later in this chapter. If your script has the same name as an existing command, the existing command will be executed and not your script, unless you prefix the name of the script with a backslash (/) character. So, make sure that the name of your script is not in use already. You can find out whether the name of your script already exists by using the which command. For example, if you want to use the name hello and want to be sure that it's not in use already, type which hello. Listing 18.1 shows the result of this command.

Listing 18.1: Use which to find out whether the name of your script is already in use

```
nuuk:~ # which hello
which: no hello in
(/sbin:/usr/sbin:/usr/local/sbin:/opt/gnome/sbin:/root/bin:/usr/local/bin:
/usr/bin:/usr/X11R6/bin:/bin
:/usr/games:/opt/gnome/bin:/opt/kde3/bin:/usr/lib/mit/bin:/usr/lib/mit/sbin)
```

In Exercise 18.1, you'll create your first shell script.

EXERCISE 18.1

Creating Your First Shell Script

Type the following code, and save it with the name hello in your home directory.

```
#!/bin/bash
# this is the hello script
# run it by typing ./hello in the directory where you've found it

clear
echo hello world
exit 0
```

You have just created your first script. This script uses several ingredients that you'll use in many shell scripts to come.

Look at the content of the script you created in Exercise 18.1. In the first line of the script, you can find the *shebang*. This scripting element tells the shell executing this script which subshell should execute this script. This may sound rather cryptic but is not difficult to understand.

- If you run a *command* from a shell, the command becomes the child process of the shell. The pstree command demonstrates this perfectly (see Figure 18.1).
- If you run a *script* from the shell, it also becomes a child process of the shell.

This means that it is not necessary to run the same shell as your current one to run the script. If you want to run a different subshell in a script, use the shebang to tell the parent shell which subshell to execute. The shebang always starts with #! and is followed by the name of the subshell that should execute the script. In Exercise 18.1, I used /bin/bash as the subshell, but you can use any other shell you like. For instance, use #!/bin/perl if your script contains Perl code.

FIGURE 18.1   Use pstree to show that commands are run as a subshell.

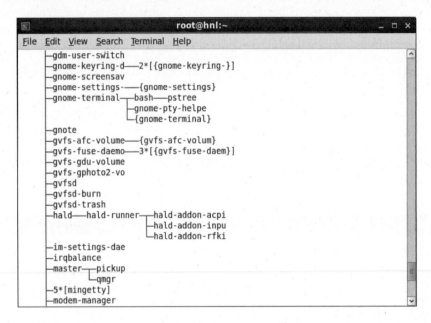

You will notice that not all scripts include a shebang. Without a shebang, the shell just executes the script using the same shell for the subshell process. This makes the script less portable; however, if you try to run it from a different parent shell than the shell for which the script was written, you'll risk that the script will fail.

The second part in the script in Exercise 18.1 consists of two lines of comments. As you can see, these comment lines explain to the user the purpose of the script and how to use it.

Comment lines should be clear and explain what's happening. A comment line always starts with a #.

You may ask why the shebang, which also starts with a #, is not interpreted as a comment. This is because of its position and the fact that it is immediately followed by an exclamation mark. This combination at the very start of a script tells the shell that it's not a comment but rather a shebang.

Back to the script that you created in Exercise 18.1. The body of the script follows the comment lines, and it contains the code that the script should execute. In the example, the code consists of two simple commands: first the screen is cleared, and next the text hello world is echoed on the screen.

The command `exit 0` is used as the last part of the script. It is good habit to use the `exit` command in all of your scripts. This command exits the script and then tells the parent shell how the script has executed. If the parent shell reads `exit 0`, it knows the script has executed successfully. If it encounters anything other than `exit 0`, it knows that there was a problem. In more complex scripts, you could even start working with different exit codes; that is, use `exit 1` as a generic error message, `exit 2` to specify that a specific condition was not met, and so forth. Later, when applying conditional loops, you'll see that it is very useful to work with exit codes.

Executing the Script

Now that you have written your first shell script, it's time to execute it. There are three different ways of doing this.

- Make it executable, and run it as a program.
- Run it as an argument of the `bash` command.
- Source it.

Making the Script Executable

The most common way to run a shell script is by making it executable. To do this with the `hello` script from Exercise 18.1, use the following command:

```
chmod +x hello
```

After making the script executable, you can run it just like any other command. The only limitation is the exact location in the directory structure of your script. If it is in the search path, you can run it by typing any command. If it is not in the search path, you have to run it from the exact directory where it is located. This means that if user linda created a script with the name `hello` in /home/linda, she has to run it using the command /home/linda/hello. Alternatively, if she is already in /home/linda, she could use `./hello` to run the script. In the latter example, the dot and slash tell the shell to run the command from the current directory.

 Not sure if a directory is in the path or not? Use echo $PATH to find out. If the directory is not in the path, you can add it by redefining it. When defining it again, mention the new directory followed by a call to the old path variable. For instance, to add the directory /something to the PATH, use PATH=$PATH:/something.

Running the Script as an Argument of the Bash Command

The second option for running a script is to specify its name as the argument of the `bash` command. For example, the script `hello` would run using the command `bash hello`. The advantage of running the script this way is that there is no need to make it executable first.

There's one additional benefit too: if you run it this way, you can specify an argument to the bash command while running it.

Make sure you are using a complete path to the location of the script when running it this way. It has to be in the current directory, or you would have to use a complete reference to the directory where it is located. This means that if the script is /home/linda/hello and your current directory is /tmp, you should run it using bash /home/linda/hello.

Sourcing the Script

The third way of running a script is completely different. You can source the script. By sourcing a script, you don't run it as a subshell. Rather, you include it in the current shell. This can be useful if the script contains variables that you want to be active in the current shell. (This often happens in the scripts that are executed when you boot your computer.)

If you source a script, you need to know what you're doing, or you may encounter unexpected problems. For example, if you use the exit command in a script that is sourced, it closes the current shell. Remember, the exit command exits the current script. To be more specific, it doesn't exit the script itself, but rather it tells the executing shell that the script is over and it has to return to its parent shell. Therefore, don't source scripts that contain the exit command.

There are two ways to source a script. These two lines show you how to source a script that has the name settings:

```
. settings
source settings
```

It doesn't really matter which one you use because both are completely equivalent. When discussing variables in the next section, I'll provide more examples of why sourcing is a very useful technique.

Working with Variables and Input

What makes a script so flexible is the use of variables. A *variable* is a value you get from somewhere that will be dynamic. The value of a variable normally depends on the circumstances. For example, you can have your script get the variable itself by executing a command, making a calculation, specifying it as a command-line argument for the script, or modifying a text string. In this section, you'll learn about the basic variables.

Understanding Variables

You can define a variable somewhere in a script and use it in a flexible way later. Though you can do this in a script, you don't absolutely have to. You can also define a variable in a shell. To define a variable, use varname=value to get the value of a variable. Later, you can call its value using the echo command. Listing 18.2 provides an example of how a variable is set on the command line and how its value is used in the next command.

Listing 18.2: Setting and using a variable

```
nuuk:~ # HAPPY=yes
nuuk:~ # echo $HAPPY
yes
```

The method described here works for the bash command. Not every shell supports this. For example, on tcsh, you need to use the set command to define a variable. For instance, use set HAPPY=yes to give the value yes to the variable HAPPY.

Variables play a very important role on your server. When booting, lots of variables are defined and used later as you work with your computer. For example, the name of your computer is in a variable, the name of the user account that you used to log in is in a variable, and the search path is also defined in a variable. You get shell variables, or so-called environment variables, automatically when logging in to the shell. You can use the env command to get a complete list of all the variables that are set for your computer.

Most environment variables appear in uppercase. This is not a requirement, however. Using uppercase for variable names has the benefit that it makes it a lot easier to recognize them. Particularly if your script is long, using uppercase for variable names makes the script a lot more readable. Thus, I recommend using uppercase for all variable names you set.

The advantage of using variables in shell scripts is that you can use them in different ways to treat dynamic data. Here are some examples:

- A single point of administration for a certain value
- A value that a user provides in some way
- A value that is calculated dynamically

When looking at some of the scripts that are used in your computer's boot procedure, you'll notice that, in the beginning of the script, there is often a list of variables that are referred to several times later in the script. Let's look at a simple script in Listing 18.3 that shows the use of variables that are defined within the script.

Listing 18.3: Understanding the use of variables

```
#!/bin/bash
#
# dirscript
#
# Script that creates a directory with a certain name
# next sets $USER and $GROUP as the owners of the directory
# and finally changes the permission mode to 770

DIRECTORY=/blah
```

```
USER=linda
GROUP=sales

mkdir $DIRECTORY
chown $USER $DIRECTORY
chgrp $GROUP $DIRECTORY
chmod 770 $DIRECTORY

exit 0
```

As you can see, after the comment lines, the script starts by defining all of the variables that are used. They are specified in uppercase to make them more readable. In the second part of the script, the variables are all preceded by a $ sign. While defining it, there is no need to put a $ in front of the variable name to tell the shell that something that it uses is a variable.

You will observe that quite a few scripts work this way. There is a disadvantage, however—it is a rather static way of working with variables. If you want a more dynamic way to work with variables, you can specify them as arguments to the script when executing it on the command line.

Variables, Subshells, and Sourcing

When defining variables, be aware that a variable is defined for the current shell only. This means that if you start a subshell from the current shell, the variable will not be there. Moreover, if you define a variable in a subshell, it won't be there anymore once you've quit the subshell and returned to the parent shell. Listing 18.4 shows how this works.

Listing 18.4: Variables are local to the shell where they are defined

```
nuuk:~/bin # HAPPY=yes
nuuk:~/bin # echo $HAPPY
yes
nuuk:~/bin # bash
nuuk:~/bin # echo $HAPPY

nuuk:~/bin # exit
exit
nuuk:~/bin # echo $HAPPY
yes
nuuk:~/bin #
```

In Listing 18.4, I've defined a variable with the name HAPPY. You can then see that its value is correctly echoed. In the third command, a subshell is started, and as you can see, when asking for the value of the variable HAPPY in this subshell, it isn't there because it simply doesn't exist. But when the subshell is closed using the exit command, you're back in the parent shell where the variable still exists.

In some cases, you may want to set a variable that is present in all subshells as well. If this is the case, you can define it using the export command. For example, the command export HAPPY=yes defines the variable HAPPY and makes sure that it is available in all subshells from the current shell forward until the computer is rebooted. However, there is no way to define a variable and make it available in the parent shells in this manner.

Listing 18.5 shows the same commands used in Listing 18.4 but now includes the value of the variable being exported.

Listing 18.5: By exporting a variable, you can also make it available in subshells

```
nuuk:~/bin # export HAPPY=yes
nuuk:~/bin # echo $HAPPY
yes
nuuk:~/bin # bash
nuuk:~/bin # echo $HAPPY
yes
nuuk:~/bin # exit
exit
nuuk:~/bin # echo $HAPPY
yes
nuuk:~/bin #
```

So much for defining variables that are also available in subshells. A technique that you'll also often come across related to variables is the sourcing of a file that contains variables. The idea is that you keep a common file that contains variables somewhere on your computer. For example, consider the file vars in Listing 18.6.

Listing 18.6: By putting all your variables in one file, you can make them easily available

```
HAPPY=yes
ANGRY=no
SUNNY=yes
```

The main advantage of putting all variables in one file is that you can also make them available in other shells by sourcing them. To do this with the example file from Listing 18.6, you would use the . vars command (assuming that the name of the variable file is vars).

> The command . vars is not the same as ./vars. With . vars, you include the contents of vars in the current shell. With ./vars, you run vars from the current shell. The former doesn't start a subshell, while the latter does.

You can see how sourcing is used to include variables from a generic configuration file in the current shell in Listing 18.7. In this example, I've used sourcing for the current shell, but it is quite common to include common variables in a script as well.

Listing 18.7: Example of sourcing usage

```
nuuk:~/bin # echo $HAPPY

nuuk:~/bin # echo $ANGRY

nuuk:~/bin # echo $SUNNY

nuuk:~/bin # . vars
nuuk:~/bin # echo $HAPPY
yes
nuuk:~/bin # echo $ANGRY
no
nuuk:~/bin # echo $SUNNY
yes
nuuk:~/bin #
```

Working with Script Arguments

In the preceding section, you learned how to define variables. Up until now, you've seen how to create a variable in a static way. In this section, you'll learn how to provide values for your variables dynamically by specifying them as an argument for the script when running it on the command line.

Using Script Arguments

When running a script, you can specify arguments to the script on the command line. Consider the script dirscript from Listing 18.3. You could run it with an argument on the command line like this: dirscript /blah.

Now wouldn't it be nice if, in the script, you could do something with its argument /blah? The good news is that you can. You can refer to the first argument used in the script as $1 in the script, the second argument as $2, and so on, up to $9. You can also use $0 to refer to the name of the script itself. In Exercise 18.2, you'll create a script that works with such arguments.

EXERCISE 18.2

Creating a Script That Works with Arguments

In this exercise, you'll create a script that works with arguments.

1. Type the following code, and execute it to find out what it does.

2. Save the script using the name argscript.

3. Run the script without any arguments.

4. Observe what happens if you put one or more arguments after the name of the script.

```
#!/bin/bash
#
# argscript
#
# Silly script that shows how arguments are used

ARG1=$1
ARG2=$2
ARG3=$3
SCRIPTNAME=$0

echo The name of this script is $SCRIPTNAME
echo The first argument used is $ARG1
echo The second argument used is $ARG2
echo The third argument used is $ARG3
exit 0
```

In Exercise 18.3, you'll rewrite the script dirscript to use arguments. This changes dirscript from a rather static script that can create only one directory to a very dynamic one that can create any directory and assign any user and any group as the owner of that directory.

Referring to Command-Line Arguments in a Script

The following script is a rewrite of dirscript. In this new version, the script works with arguments instead of fixed variables, which makes it a lot more flexible.

1. Type the code from the following example script.

2. Save the code to a file with the name dirscript2.

3. Run the script with three different arguments. Also try running it with more arguments.

4. Observe what happens.

```
#!/bin/bash
#
# dirscript
```

```
#
# Silly script that creates a directory with a certain name
# next sets $USER and $GROUP as the owners of the directory
# and finally changes the permission mode to 770
# Provide the directory name first, followed by the username and
# finally the groupname.

DIRECTORY=$1
USER=$2
GROUP=$3

mkdir /$DIRECTORY
chown $USER $DIRECTORY
chgrp $GROUP $DIRECTORY
chmod 770 $DIRECTORY

exit 0
```

To execute the script from this exercise, use a command such as dirscript /some-dir kylie sales. Using this line clearly demonstrates how dirscript has been made more flexible. At the same time, however, it also demonstrates the most important disadvantage of arguments, which is somewhat less obvious. You can imagine that, for a user, it is very easy to mix up the correct order of the arguments and to type dirscript kylie sales /somedir instead. Thus, it is important to provide good help on how to run this script.

Counting the Number of Script Arguments

Occasionally, you'll want to check the number of arguments provided with a script. This is useful if you expect a certain number of arguments and want to make sure that this number is present before running the script. To count the number of arguments provided with a script, you can use $#. Basically, $# is a counter that just shows you the exact number of arguments used when running a script. Used only by itself, that doesn't make a lot of sense. When used with an if statement, it makes perfect sense. (You'll learn about the if statement later in this chapter.) For example, you could use it to show a help message if the user hasn't provided the correct number of arguments. In Exercise 18.4, the script countargs does this using $#. There is a sample running of the script directly after the code listing.

EXERCISE 18.4

Counting Arguments

One useful technique for checking to see whether the user has provided the required number of arguments is to count these arguments. In this exercise, you'll write a script that does just that.

1. Type the following script:

```
#!/bin/bash
#
# countargs
# sample script that shows how many arguments were used

echo the number of arguments is $#

exit 0
```

2. If you run the previous script with a number of arguments, it will show you how many arguments it has seen. The expected results are as follows:

```
nuuk:~/bin # ./countargs a b c d e
the number of arguments is 5
nuuk:~/bin #.
```

Referring to All Script Arguments

So far, you've seen that a script can work with a fixed number of arguments. The script you created in Exercise 18.3 is hard-coded to evaluate arguments as $1, $2, and so on. But what happens when the number of arguments is not known beforehand? In that case, you can use $@ or $* in your script. Both refer to all arguments that were specified when starting the script. However, there is a difference. To explain the difference, you need to create a small loop with for.

Let's start with the difference between $@ and $*. $@ refers to a collection of all arguments that is treated as all individual elements. $* also refers to a collection of all arguments, but it cannot distinguish between the individual arguments that are used. A *for loop* can be used to demonstrate this difference.

First let's look at their default output. As noted previously, both $@ and $* are used to refer to all arguments used when starting the script. Listing 18.8 provides a small script that shows this difference.

Listing 18.8: Showing the difference between $@ and $*

```
#!/bin/bash
# showargs
```

```
# this script shows all arguments used when starting the script

echo the arguments are $@
echo the arguments are $*

exit 0
```

Let's look at what happens when you launch this script with the arguments a b c d. The result appears in Listing 18.9.

Listing 18.9: Running showargs with different arguments

```
nuuk:~/bin # ./showargs a b c d
the arguments are a b c d
the arguments are a b c d
```

So far, there seems to be no difference between $@ and $*. However, there is an important difference: the collection of arguments in $* is seen as one text string, and the collection of arguments in $@ is seen as separate strings. In the section that explains for loops, you will see proof of that.

At this point, you've learned how to handle a script that has an infinite number of arguments. You just tell the script that it should interpret each argument one by one. The next section shows you how to count the number of arguments.

Asking for Input

Another way to get input is simply to ask for it. To do this, you can use read in the script. When using read, the script waits for user input and puts that into a variable. In Exercise 18.5, you will create a simple script that first asks for input and then reflects the input provided by echoing the value of the variable. You can see what happens when you run the script directly after the sample code.

EXERCISE 18.5

Asking for Input with read

In this exercise, you'll write a script that handles user input. You'll use read to do this.

1. Type the following code, and save it to a file with the name askinput.

    ```
    #!/bin/bash
    #
    # askinput
    # ask user to enter some text and then display it

    echo Enter some text
    read SOMETEXT
    ```

EXERCISE 18.5 *(continued)*

```
echo -e "You have entered the following text:\t $SOMETEXT"

exit 0
```

2. Run the script, and when it gives the message "Enter some text," type some text.

3. Observe what happens. Also try running the script without providing input but by just pressing **Enter**.

As you can see from Exercise 18.5, the script starts with an echo line that explains what it expects the user to do. Next, in the line read SOMETEXT, it will stop to allow the user to enter some text. This text is stored in the variable SOMETEXT. In the line that follows, the echo command is used to show the current value of SOMETEXT. As you see, echo -e is used in this sample script. This option allows you to use special formatting characters. In this case, it's \t is used, which enters a tab in the text. You can make the result display in an attractive manner using formatting characters in this way.

As you can see in the line that contains the command echo -e, the text that the script displays on the screen because of the use of the echo command appears between double quotes. This is to prevent the shell from interpreting the special character \t before echo does. Again, if you want to make sure the shell does not interpret special characters such as this one, put the string between double quotes.

You may be confused here because there are two different mechanisms at work. First there is the mechanism of *escaping*. Escaping is a solution that you can use to make sure the following characters are not interpreted. This is the difference between echo \t and echo "\t". In the former case, \ is treated as a special character with the result that only the letter t is displayed. In the latter case, double quotes are used to tell the shell not to interpret anything that is between the double quotes; hence, it shows as \t.

The second mechanism is the special formatting character \t. This is one of the special characters that you can use in the shell, and this one tells the shell to display a tab. However, to make sure it is not interpreted by the shell when it first parses the script (which would result in the shell displaying a t), you have to put these special formatting characters between double quotes. In Listing 18.10, you can see the differences between all the possible ways of escaping characters.

Listing 18.10: Escaping and special characters

```
SYD:~ # echo \t
t
SYD:~ # echo "\t"
\t
SYD:~ # echo -e \t
t
```

```
SYD:~ # echo -e "\t"

SYD:~ #
```

When using echo -e, use the following special characters:

\0NNN This is the character whose ASCII code is NNN (octal).

**** Use this if you want to show just a backslash.

\a If supported by your system, this will let you hear a beep.

\b This is a backspace.

\c This suppresses a trailing newline.

\f This is a form feed.

\n This is a new line.

**** This is a carriage return.

\t This is a horizontal tab.

\v This is a vertical tab.

Using Command Substitution

Another way of putting a variable text in a script is by using command substitution. In *command substitution*, you use the result of a command in the script. This is useful if the script has something to do with the result of a command. For example, you can use this technique to tell a script that it should execute only if a certain condition is met (using a conditional loop with if to accomplish this). To use command substitution, put the command that you want to use between backquotes (also known as *backticks*). As an alternative, you can put the command substitution between braces with a $ sign in front of the (. The following sample code shows how this works:

```
nuuk:~/bin # echo "today is $(date +%d-%m-%y)"
today is 04-06-12
```

In this example, the date command is used with some of its special formatting characters. The command date +%d-%m-%y tells date to present its result in the day-month-year format. In this example, the command is just executed. However, you can also put the result of the command substitution in a variable, which makes it easier to perform a calculation on the result later in the script. The following sample code shows how to do that:

```
nuuk:~/bin # TODAY=$(date +%d-%m-%y)
nuuk:~/bin # echo today=$TODAY
today is 27-01-09
```

There is also an alternative method to using command substitution. In the previous examples, the command was put between $(and). Instead, you can also place the command between backticks. This means that $(date) and `date` will have the same result.

Substitution Operators

It may be important to verify that a variable indeed has a value assigned to it within a script before the script continues. To do this, bash offers substitution operators. *Substitution operators* let you assign a default value if a variable doesn't have a currently assigned value and much more. Table 18.1 describes substitution operators and their use.

TABLE 18.1   Substitution operators

Operator	Use
${*parameter*:-*value*}	This shows a value if a parameter is not defined.
${*parameter*=*value*}	This assigns a value to a parameter if a parameter does not exist. This operator does nothing if a parameter exists but doesn't have a value.
${*parameter*:=*value*}	This assigns value if a parameter currently has no value or if a parameter doesn't exist.
${*parameter*:?*value*}	This shows a message that is defined as the value if a parameter doesn't exist or is empty. Using this construction will force the shell script to be aborted immediately.
${*parameter*:+*value*}	If a parameter has a value, the value is displayed. If it doesn't have a value, nothing happens.

Substitution operators can be difficult to understand. To make it easier to see just how they work, Listing 18.11 provides some examples. Something happens to the $BLAH variable in all of these examples. Notice that the result of the given command is different depending on the substitution operator that is used. To make it easier to understand what happens, I've added line numbers to the listing. (Omit the line numbers when trying this yourself.)

Listing 18.11: Using substitution operators

```
1. sander@linux %> echo $BLAH
2.
3. sander@linux %> echo ${BLAH:-variable is empty}
4 variable is empty
5. sander@linux %> echo $BLAH
6.
7. sander@linux %> echo ${BLAH=value}
8. value
9. sander@linux %> echo $BLAH
10. value
11. sander@linux %> BLAH=
```

```
12. sander@linux %> echo ${BLAH=value}
13.
14. sander@linux %> echo ${BLAH:=value}
15. value
16. sander@linux %> echo $BLAH
17. value
18. sander@linux %> echo ${BLAH:+sometext}
19. sometext
```

Listing 18.11 starts with the command echo $BLAH.

This command reads the variable BLAH and shows its current value. Because BLAH doesn't yet have a value, nothing is shown in line 2. Next a message is defined in line 3 that should be displayed if BLAH is empty. This occurs with the following command:

```
sander@linux %> echo ${BLAH:-variable is empty}
```

As you can see, the message is displayed in line 4. However, this doesn't assign a value to BLAH, which you see in line 5 and line 6 where the current value of BLAH is again requested:

```
3. sander@linux %> echo ${BLAH:-variable is empty}
4 variable is empty
5. sander@linux %> echo $BLAH
6.
```

BLAH finally gets a value in line 7, which is displayed in line 8 as follows:

```
7. sander@linux %> echo ${BLAH=value}
8. value
```

The shell remembers the new value of BLAH, which you can see in line 9 and line 10 where the value of BLAH is referred to and displayed as follows:

```
9. sander@linux %> echo $BLAH
10. value
```

BLAH is redefined in line 11, but it gets a null value.

```
11. sander@linux %> BLAH=
```

The variable still exists; it just has no value here. This is demonstrated when echo ${BLAH=value} is used in line 12. Because BLAH has a null value at that moment, no new value is assigned.

```
12. sander@linux %> echo ${BLAH=value}
13.
```

Next, the construction echo ${BLAH:=value} is used to assign a new value to BLAH. The fact that BLAH actually gets a value from this is shown in line 16 and line 17:

```
14. sander@linux %> echo ${BLAH:=value}
15. value
16. sander@linux %> echo $BLAH
17. value
```

Finally, the construction in line 18 is used to display sometext if BLAH currently has a value.

```
18. sander@linux %> echo ${BLAH:+sometext}
19. sometext
```

Note that this doesn't change the value that is assigned to BLAH at that moment; sometext just indicates that it indeed has a value.

Changing Variable Content with Pattern Matching

You've just seen how substitution operators can be used to supply a value to a variable that does not have one. You can view them as a rather primitive way of handling errors in your script. A *pattern-matching operator* can be used to search for a pattern in a variable and, if that pattern is found, modify the variable. This is very useful because it allows you to define a variable in exactly the way you want. For example, think of the situation in which a user enters a complete path name of a file but only the name of the file (without the path) is needed in your script.

You can use the pattern-matching operator to change this. Pattern-matching operators allow you to remove part of a variable automatically. In Exercise 18.6, you'll write a small script that uses pattern matching.

EXERCISE 18.6

Working with Pattern-Matching Operators

In this exercise, you'll write a script that uses pattern matching.

1. Write a script that contains the following code, and save it with the name stripit.

   ```
   #!/bin/bash
   # stripit
   # script that extracts the file name from a filename that includes the path
   # usage: stripit <complete file name>

   filename=${1##*/}
   echo "The name of the file is $filename"

   exit 0
   ```

2. Run the script with the argument /bin/bash.

3. Observe the result. You will notice that, when executed, the code you've just written will show the following result:

   ```
   sander@linux %> ./stripit /bin/bash
   the name of the file is bash
   ```

Pattern-matching operators always try to locate a given string. In this case, the string is */. In other words, the pattern-matching operator searches for a / preceded by another character *. In this pattern-matching operator, ## is used to search for the longest match of the provided string starting from the beginning of the string. So, the pattern-matching operator searches for the last / that occurs in the string and removes it and everything that precedes it. How does the script come to remove everything in front of the /?. It does so because the pattern-matching operator refers to */ and not to /. You can confirm this by running the script with a name like /bin/bash as an argument. In this case, the pattern that is sought is in the last position of the string and the pattern-matching operator removes everything.

This example explains the use of the pattern-matching operator that looks for the longest match. By using a single #, you can let the pattern-matching operator look for the shortest match, again starting from the beginning of the string. For example, if the script you created in Exercise 18.6 used filename=${1#*/}, the pattern-matching operator would look for the first / in the complete filename and remove it and everything that came before it.

The * is important in these examples. The pattern-matching operator ${1#*/} removes the first / found and anything in front of it. The pattern-matching operator ${1#/} removes the first / in $1 only if the value of $1 starts with a /. However, if there's anything before the /, the operator will not know what to do.

In the preceding examples, you've seen how a pattern-matching operator is used to search from the beginning of a string. You can search from the end of the string as well. To do so, a % is used instead of a #. The % refers to the shortest match of the pattern, and %% refers to the longest match. Listing 18.12 shows how this works.

Listing 18.12: Using pattern-matching operators to start searching at the end of a string

```
#!/bin/bash
# stripdir
# script that isolates the directory name from a complete file name
# usage: stripdir <complete file name>

dirname=${1%%/*}
echo "The directory name is $dirname"

exit 0
```

You will notice that this script has a problem when executing.
```
sander@linux %> ./stripdir /bin/bash
The directory name is
```

As you can see, the script does its work somewhat too enthusiastically and removes everything. Fortunately, this problem can be remedied by first using a pattern-matching operator that removes the / from the start of the complete filename (but only if that / is provided) and then removing everything following the first / in the complete filename. Listing 18.13 shows how this is done.

Listing 18.13: Fixing the example in Listing 18.12

```
#!/bin/bash
# stripdir
# script that isolates the directory name from a complete file name
# usage: stripdir <complete file name>

dirname=${1#/}
dirname=${1%%/*}
echo "The directory name is $dirname"

exit 0
```

As you can see, the problem is solved by using ${1#/}. This construction searches from the beginning of the filename to a /. Because no * is used here, it looks only for a / at the very first position of the filename and does nothing if the string starts with anything else. If it finds a /, it removes it. Thus, if a user enters usr/bin/passwd instead of /usr/bin /passwd, the ${1#/} construction does nothing at all. In the line after that, the variable dirname is defined again to do its work on the result of its first definition in the preceding line. This line does the real work and looks for the pattern /*, starting at the end of the filename. This construction makes sure that everything after the first / in the file-name is removed and that only the name of the top-level directory is echoed. Of course, you can easily edit this script to display the complete path of the file by just using dirname=${dirname%/*}instead.

Listing 18.14 provides another example using pattern-matching operators to make sure you are comfortable. This time, however, the example does not work with a filename but with a random text string. When running the script, it gives the result shown in Listing 18.15. In Exercise 18.17 you'll learn how to apply pattern matching.

Listing 18.14: Another example of pattern matching

```
#!/bin/bash
#
# generic script that shows some more pattern matching
# usage: pmex
BLAH=babarabaraba
echo BLAH is $BLAH
echo 'The result of ##ba is '${BLAH##*ba}
echo 'The result of #ba is '${BLAH#*ba}
echo 'The result of %%ba is '${BLAH%ba*}
echo 'The result of %ba is '${BLAH%%ba*}

exit 0
```

Listing 18.15: The result of the script in Listing 18.14

```
root@RNA:~/scripts# ./pmex
BLAH is babarabaraba
The result of ##ba is
The result of #ba is barabaraba
The result of %%ba is babarabara
The result of %ba is
root@RNA:~/scripts#
```

EXERCISE 18.7

Applying Pattern Matching on a Date String

In this exercise, you'll apply pattern matching on a date string. You'll see how to use pattern matching to filter out text in the middle of a string. The goal is to write a script that works on the result of the command date +%d-%m-%y. Next, it should show three separate lines, echoing today's day is ..., the month is ..., and the year is ....

1. Write a script that uses command substitution on the command date +%d-%m-%y and saves the result in a variable with the name DATE. Save the script using the name today.

2. Modify the script so that it uses pattern matching on the $DATE variable to show three different lines.

    ```
    today is 22
    this month is september
    this year is 2012
    ```

3. Verify that the script you've written looks more or less like the following example script:

    ```
    #!/bin/bash
    #
    DATE=$(date +%d-%m-%y)
    TODAY=${DATE%%-*}
    THISMONTH=${DATE%-*}
    THISMONTH=${THISMONTH#*-}
    THISYEAR=${DATE##*-}
    echo today is $TODAY
    echo this month is $THISMONTH
    echo this year is $THISYEAR
    ```

Performing Calculations

bash offers some options that allow you to perform calculations from scripts. Of course, you're not likely to use them as a replacement for your spreadsheet program, but performing simple calculations from bash can be useful. For example, you can use bash calculation options to execute a command a number of times or to make sure that a counter is incremented when a command executes successfully. Listing 18.16 provides an example of how counters can be used.

Listing 18.16: Using a counter in a script

```
#!/bin/bash
# counter
# script that counts until infinity
counter=1
     counter=$((counter + 1))
     echo counter is set to $counter
exit 0
```

This script consists of three lines. The first line initializes the variable counter with a value of 1. Next, the value of this variable is incremented by 1. In the third line, the new value of the variable is shown.

Of course, it doesn't make much sense to run the script this way. It would make more sense if you include it in a conditional loop to count the number of actions that are performed until a condition is true. In the section "Working with while" later in this chapter, there is an example that shows how to combine counters with while.

So far, we've dealt with only one method to do script calculations, but there are other options as well. First, you can use the external expr command to perform any kind of calculation. For example, this line produces the result of 1 + 2: sum=`expr 1 + 2`; echo $sum.

As you can see, a variable with the name sum is defined, and this variable calculates the result of the command expr 1 + 2 by using command substitution. A semicolon is then used to indicate that what follows is a new command. (Remember the generic use of semicolons? They're used to separate one command from the next command.) After the semicolon, the command echo $sum shows the result of the calculation.

The expr command can work with addition and other calculations. Table 18.2 summarizes these options.

All of these options work fine with the exception of the multiplication operator (*). Use of this operator results in a syntax error:

```
linux: ~> expr 2 * 2
expr: syntax error
```

This seems curious, but it can be easily explained. The * has a special meaning for the shell, as in ls -l *. When the shell parses the command line, it interprets the *, and you don't want it to do that here. To indicate that the shell shouldn't touch it, you have to escape it. Therefore, change the command to expr 2 * 2.

TABLE 18.2   expr operators

Operator	Meaning
+	Addition (1 + 1 = 2).
-	Subtraction (10 - 2 = 8).
/	Division (10 / 2 = 5).
*	Multiplication (3 * 3 = 9).
%	Modulus; this calculates the remainder after division. This works because expr can handle integers only (11 % 3 = 2).

Another way to perform calculations is to use the internal command let. Just the fact that let is internal makes it a better solution than the external command expr. This is because it can be loaded from memory directly, and it doesn't have to come from your computer's relatively slow hard drive. let can perform your calculation and apply the result directly to a variable like this: let x="1 + 2".

The result of the calculation in this example is stored in the variable x. The disadvantage of using let is that it has no option to display the result directly like expr. For use in a script, however, it offers excellent capabilities. Listing 18.17 shows a script that uses let to perform calculations.

Listing 18.17: Performing calculations with let

```
#!/bin/bash
# calcscript
# usage: calc $1 $2 $3
# $1 is the first number
# $2 is the operator
# $3 is the second number

let x="$1 $2 $3"
echo $x

exit 0
```

Here you can see what happens if you run this script:

```
SYD:~/bin # ./calcscript 1 + 2
3
SYD:~/bin #
```

If you think that I've already covered all the methods used to perform calculations in a shell script, then you're wrong. Listing 18.18 shows another method that you can use to perform calculations.

Listing 18.18: Another way to calculate in a bash shell script

```
#!/bin/bash
# calcscript
# usage: calc $1 $2 $3
# $1 is the first number
# $2 is the operator
# $3 is the second number

x=$(($1 $2 $3))
echo $x

exit 0
```

If you run the above script, the result is as follows:

```
SYD:~/bin # ./calcscript
1 + 2
3
SYD:~/bin #
```

You saw this construction previously when you read about the script that increases the value of the variable counter. Note that the double pair of parentheses can be replaced with one pair of square brackets instead, assuming the preceding $ is present.

Using Control Structures

Up until now, I haven't discussed the way in which the execution of commands can be made conditional. The technique for enabling this in shell scripts is known as *flow control*. bash offers many options to use flow control in scripts.

if   Use if to execute commands only if certain conditions are met. To customize the working of if further, you can use else to indicate what should happen if the condition isn't met.

case   Use case to handle options. This allows the user to specify further the working of the command as it is run.

for   This construction is used to run a command for a given number of items. For example, you can use for to do something for every file in a specified directory.

while   Use while as long as the specified condition is met. For example, this construction can be very useful to check whether a certain host is reachable or to monitor the activity of a process.

until   This is the opposite of while. Use until to run a command until a certain condition is met.

Flow control is covered in more detail in the sections that follow. Before going into detail, however, I will first cover the `test` command. This command is used to perform many checks to see, for example, if a file exists or if a variable has a value. Table 18.3 shows some of the more common `test` options.

TABLE 18.3   Common options for the test command

Option	Use
test -e $1	Checks whether $1 is a file, without looking at what particular kind of file it is.
test -f $1	Checks whether $1 is a regular file and not, for example, a device file, a directory, or an executable file.
test -d $1	Checks whether $1 is a directory.
test -x $1	Checks whether $1 is an executable file. Note that you can also test for other permissions. For example, –g would check to see whether the SGID permission is set.
test $1 -nt $2	Controls whether $1 is newer than $2.
test $1 -ot $2	Controls whether $1 is older than $2.
test $1 -ef $2	Checks whether $1 and $2 both refer to the same inode. This is the case if one is a hard link to the other.
test $1 -eq $2	Sees whether the integer values of $1 and $2 are equal.
test $1 -ne $2	Checks whether the integers $1 and $2 are not equal.
test $1 -gt $2	Is true if integer $1 is greater than integer $2.
test $1 -lt $2	Is true if integer $1 is less than integer $2.
test -z $1	Checks whether $1 is empty. This is a very useful construction to find out whether a variable has been defined.
test $1	Gives the exit status 0 if $1 is true.
test $1=$2	Checks whether the strings $1 and $2 are the same. This is most useful to compare the value of two variables.
test $1 != $2	Checks whether the strings $1 and $2 are not equal to each other. You can use ! with all other tests to check for the negation of the statement.

You can use test command in two ways. First you can write the complete command as in test -f $1. You can also rewrite this command as [-f $1]. You'll often see the latter option used because people who write shell scripts like to work as efficiently as possible.

Using if...then...else

The classic example of flow control consists of constructions that use if...then...else. Especially when used in conjunction with the test command, this construction offers many interesting possibilities. You can use it to find out whether a file exists, whether a variable currently has a value, and much more.

The basic construction is if condition then command fi. Therefore, you'll use it to check one specific condition, and if it is true, a command is executed. You can also extend the code to handle all cases where the condition was not met by also including an else statement.

Listing 18.19 provides an example of a construction using if...then.

Listing 18.19: Using if...then to perform a basic check

```
#!/bin/bash
# testarg
# test to see if argument is present

if [ -z $1 ]
then
     echo You have to provide an argument with this command
     exit 1
fi

echo the argument is $1

exit 0
```

The simple check from Listing 18.19 is used to see whether the user who started your script provided an argument. Here's what you would see when you run the script:

```
SYD:~/bin # ./testarg
You have to provide an argument with this command
SYD:~/bin #
```

If the user didn't provide an argument, the code in the if loop becomes active, in which case it displays the message that the user needs to provide an argument and then terminates the script. If an argument has been provided, the commands within the loop aren't executed, and the script will run the line echo the argument is $1 and, in this case, echo the argument to the user's screen.

Also notice how the syntax of the if construction is organized. First you open it with if. Next, then is used, separated on a new line (or with a semicolon). Finally, the if loop is closed with a fi statement. Make sure that all these ingredients are used all the time or your loop won't work.

The example in Listing 18.19 is a rather simple one. It's also possible to make more complex if loops and have them test for more than one condition. To do this, use else or elif. By using else within the control structure, you can make sure that some action occurs if the condition is met. However, it allows you to check another condition if the condition is not met. You can even use else in conjunction with if (elif) to open a new control structure if the first condition isn't met. If you do that, you have to use then after elif. Listing 18.20 is an example of the latter construction.

Listing 18.20: Nesting if control structures

```
#!/bin/bash
# testfile

if [ -f $1 ]
then
     echo "$1 is a file"
elif [ -d $1 ]
then
     echo "$1 is a directory"
else
     echo "I don't know what \$1 is"
fi

exit 0
```

Here is what happens when you run this script:
```
SYD:~/bin # ./testfile /bin/blah
I don't know what $1 is
SYD:~/bin #
```

In this example, the argument that was entered when running the script is checked. If it is a file (if [-f $1]), the script informs the user. If it isn't a file, the part beneath elif is executed, which opens a second control structure. In this second control structure, the first test performed is to see whether $1 is a directory. Note that this second part of the control structure becomes active only if $1 is not a file. If $1 isn't a directory, the part following else is executed, and the script reports that it has no idea about what the function of $1 is. Notice that, for this entire construction, only one fi is needed to close the control structure, but after every if or elif statement, you need to use then.

if...then...else constructions are used in two different ways. You can write out the complete construction as shown in the previous examples, or you can use constructions that use && and ||. These *logical operators* are used to separate two commands and establish a conditional relationship between them. If **&&** is used, the second command is executed only if the first command is executed successfully; in other words, if the first command is true. If **| |** is used, the second command is executed only if the first command isn't true. Thus, with one line of code you can find out whether $1 is a file and echo a message if it is, as follows:

```
[ -f $1 ] && echo $1 is a file
```

This can also be rewritten differently, as follows:

```
[ ! -f $1 ] || echo $1 is a file
```

The previous example works only as part of a complete shell script. Listing 18.21 shows how the example from Listing 18.20 is rewritten to use this syntax.

The code in the second example (where **| |** is used) performs a test to see whether $1 is not a file. (The **!** is used to test whether something is not the case.) Only if the test fails (which is the case if $1 is a file), it executes the part after the **| |** and echoes that $1 is a file.

Listing 18.21: The example from Listing 18.20 rewritten with **&&** and **| |**

```
([ -z $1 ] && echo please provide an argument; exit 1) || (([ -f $1 ]
&& echo $1 is a file) || ([ -d $1 ] && echo $1 is a directory || echo
I have no idea what $1 is))
```

Basically, the script in Listing 18.21 does the same thing as the script in Listing 18.20. However, there a few differences. First, I've added a [-z $1] test to give an error if $1 is not defined. Next, the example in Listing 18.21 is all on one line. This makes the script more compact, but it also makes it a little harder to see what is going on. I've used parentheses to increase the readability a little bit and also to keep the different parts of the script together. The parts between parentheses are the main tests, and those within the main tests are some smaller ones.

Let's have a look at some other examples with if...then...else. Consider the following line:

```
rsync -vaze ssh --delete /var/ftp 10.0.0.20:/var/ftp || echo "rsync failed" |
mail admin@mydomain.com
```

In this single script line, the **rsync** command tries to synchronize the content of the directory **/var/ftp** with the content of the same directory on some other machine. If this succeeds, no further evaluation of this line is attempted. If it does not, however, the part after the **||** becomes active, and it makes sure that user **admin@mydomain.com** gets a message.

The following script presents another, more complex example, which checks whether available disk space has dropped below a certain threshold. The complex part lies in the sequence of pipes used in the command substitution.

```
if [ `df -m /var | tail -n1 | awk '{print $4} '` -lt 120 ]
then
     logger running out of disk space
fi
```

The important part of this piece of code is in the first line where the result of a command is used in the if loop by using backquoting. That result is compared with the value 120. If the result is less than 120, the section that follows becomes active. If the result is greater than 120, nothing happens. As for the command itself, it uses the df command to check available disk space on the volume where /var is mounted, filters out the last line of that result, and, from that last line, filters out the fourth column only, which in turn is compared to the value 120. If the condition is true, the logger command writes a message to the system log file. The example isn't very well organized. The following rewrite does the same things but uses a different syntax:

```
[ `df -m /var | tail -n1 | awk '{print $4}'` -lt $1 ] && logger running out of
disk space
```

This rewrite demonstrates the challenge in writing shell scripts: you can almost always make them better.

Using case

Let's start with an example this time. In Exercise 18.8, you'll create the script, run it, and then try to explain what it has done.

EXERCISE 18.8

Example Script Using case

In this exercise, you'll create a "soccer expert" script. The script will use case to advise the user about the capabilities of their preferred soccer teams.

1. Write a script that advises the user about the capabilities of their favorite soccer team. The script should contain the following components:

    ▪   It should ask the user to enter the name of a country.

    ▪   It should use case to test against different country names.

    ▪   It should translate all input to uppercase to make evaluation of the user input easier.

    ▪   It should tell the user what kind of input is expected.

2. Run your script until you're happy with it, and apply fixes where needed.

3. Compare your solution to the following one suggested, which is only an example of how to approach this task:

```
#!/bin/bash
# soccer
# Your personal soccer expert
# predicts world championship football

cat << EOF
```

```
Enter the name of the country you think will be world soccer champion in 2010.
EOF

read COUNTRY
# translate $COUNTRY into all uppercase
COUNTRY=`echo $COUNTRY | tr a-z A-Z`

# perform the test
case $COUNTRY in
     NEDERLAND | HOLLAND | NETHERLANDS)
     echo "Yes, you are a soccer expert "
     ;;
     DEUTSCHLAND | GERMANY | MANNSCHAFT)
     echo "No, they are the worst team on earth"
     ;;
     ENGLAND | AUSTRALIA | FRANCE | BRAZIL)
     echo "hahahahahahaha, you must be joking"
     ;;
     *)
     echo "Huh? Do they play soccer?"
     ;;
esac

exit 0
```

As you can see in the example script from Exercise 18.8, this script is used to predict the results of the next World Cup championship. (Of course, you can modify it for any sports event that you like.) First, it asks the person who runs the script to enter the name of the country that they think will be the next World Cup champion. This country is put into the $COUNTRY variable. Notice the use of uppercase for this variable; it's a good way to identify variables easily as your script grows.

Because the case statement that is used in this script is case-sensitive, the user input in the first part is translated into all uppercase using the tr command. Then, using command substitution, the current value of $COUNTRY is read, translated to all uppercase, and assigned again to the $COUNTRY variable. Also note that I've made it easier to distinguish the different parts of this script by adding some extra comments.

The body of this script consists of the case command, which is used to evaluate the input the user has entered. The generic construction used to evaluate the input is as follows:

```
alternative1 | alternative2)
command
;;
```

The first line evaluates everything the user can enter. Notice that more than one alternative is used on most lines, which makes it easier to handle typos and other situations where the user has entered input incorrectly. Then, on separate lines, come all the commands you want the script to execute. In the example, just one command is executed, but if you like, you can enter 100 lines to execute commands. Finally, the test is closed with ;;. Don't forget to close all items with double semicolons; otherwise, the script won't understand what you want. The ;; can be on a line by itself, but you can also put them directly after the last command line in the script.

When using case, make it a habit to handle all options to accommodate the unexpected. Ideally, when the script is run, the user will enter something that you expect. But what if the user enters something unexpected? In that case, you probably want the user to see some result or message. This is handled by the *) at the end of the script. In the case of the script in Exercises 18.8, for everything the user enters that isn't specifically mentioned as an option in the script, the script will echo "Huh? Do they play soccer?" to the user.

Using while

You can use while to run a command as long as a condition is met. Listing 18.22 shows how while can be used to monitor the activity of an important process.

Listing 18.22: Monitoring process activity with while

```
#!/bin/bash
# procesmon
# usage: monitor <processname>

while ps aux | grep $1
do
     sleep 1
done

logger $1 is no longer present

exit 0
```

The body of this script consists of the command ps aux | grep $1. This command monitors the availability of the process whose name was entered as an argument at the start of the script. As long as the process is detected, the condition is met, and the commands in the loop are executed. In this case, the script waits one second and then repeats its action. When the process is no longer detected, the logger command writes a message to syslog.

As you can see from this example, while offers an excellent method for checking whether something (such as a process or an IP address) still exists. If you combine it with the sleep command, you can start your script with while as a kind of daemon and perform a check repeatedly. In Exercise 18.9, you'll write a message to syslog if, because of an error, the IP address suddenly gets lost.

EXERCISE 18.9

Checking Whether the IP Address Is Still There

In this exercise, you'll write a script that uses while to test the availability of an IP address.

1. Write a script with the name ipmon that monitors whether a specific IP address is still available on a computer. Use the following directions:

   - Use the ip a s command to grep for an IP address.

   - The IP address should be provided as an argument or using read.

   - The script should check every five seconds and do nothing if the IP address is available.

2. Run the script until you're satisfied with the result. Once you are, compare the result with the following example code:

   ```
   #!/bin/bash
   # ipmon
   # script that monitors an IP address
   # usage: ipmon <ip-address>

   while ip a s | grep $1/ > /dev/null
   do
           sleep 5
   done

   logger HELP, the IP address $1 is gone.

   exit 0
   ```

Using until

Whereas while works *as long as* a certain condition is met, until is just the opposite; that is, it runs *until* the condition is met. This is demonstrated in Listing 18.23 where the script monitors whether the user, whose name is entered as the argument, is logged in.

Listing 18.23: Monitoring user login

```
#!/bin/bash
# usermon
# script that alerts when a user logs in
# usage: ishere <username>

until who | grep $1 >> /dev/null
do
        echo $1 is not logged in yet
        sleep 5
done

echo $1 has just logged in

exit 0
```

In this example, the until who | grep $1 command is executed repeatedly. The result of the who command, which lists users currently logged in to the system, is grepped for the occurrence of $1. As long as the until... command is not true (which is the case if the user is not logged in), the commands in the loop are executed. As soon as the user logs in, the loop is broken, and a message is displayed to say that the user has just logged in. Notice the use of redirection to the null device in the test. This ensures that the result of the who command is not echoed on the screen.

Using for

Sometimes it's necessary to execute a series of commands, either for a limited number of times or for an unlimited number of times. In such cases, for loops offer an excellent solution. Listing 18.24 shows how you can use for to create a counter.

Listing 18.24: Using for to create a counter

```
#!/bin/bash
# counter
# counter that counts from 1 to 9

for (( counter=1; counter<10; counter++ )); do
        echo "The counter is now set to $counter"
done

exit 0
```

The code used in this script isn't difficult to understand. The conditional loop determines that, as long as the counter has a value between 1 and 10, the variable counter must be automatically incremented by 1. To do this, the construction counter++ is used. As long as the incrementing of the variable counter continues, the commands between do and done are executed. When the specified number is reached, the loop is exited, the script terminates, and it indicates to the system with exit 0 that it has completed its work successfully.

Loops with for can be pretty versatile. For example, you can use it to do something on every line in a text file. The example in Listing 18.25 illustrates how this works. (As you will see, it has some problems, however.)

Listing 18.25: Displaying lines from a text file

```
#!/bin/bash
# listusers
# faulty script that tries to show all users in /etc/passwd

for i in `cat /etc/passwd`
do
     echo $i
done


exit 0
```

In this example, for is used to display all lines in /etc/passwd one by one. Of course, just echoing the lines is a rather trivial example, but it's enough to show you how a for statement works. If you're using for in this manner, notice that it cannot handle spaces in the lines. A space is interpreted as a field separator, so a new field would begin after the space.

 **Real World Scenario**

Finding All Available IP Addresses

In this example, for is used to ping a range of IP addresses. This is a script that one of my customers likes to run to see whether a range of machines is up and running. Because the IP addresses are always in the same range, starting with 192.168.1, there's no harm in including these first three bits in the IP address itself.

```
#!/bin/bash
for i in $@
do
     ping -c 1 192.168.1.$i
done
```

Notice the use of $@ in this script. This operator allows you to refer to all arguments specified when the script was started, no matter how many arguments there are.

Remember how $* and $@ were used to treat arguments that were used with a script? Now it is time to show you the exact difference between the two by using the for loop. Using for, you can perform an action on each element in a string. You can see a simple example that demonstrates this in Listing 18.26.

Listing 18.26: Using for to distinguish different elements in a string

```
nuuk:~/bin # for i in 1 2 3; do echo $i; done
1
2
3
```

The command line in Listing 18.26 consists of three different parts, separated by the semicolon. The first part is for i in 1 2 3, which you can interpret as "for each element in the string 1 2 3." While evaluating the for loop, each of these elements is stored in the temporary variable i. In the second part, a command is executed for each of these elements. In this case, the command is do echo $i, which echoes the elements one by one. You can clearly see this in the output of the command used in Listing 18.26. Finally, the third part of this for loop is the word done, which closes the for loop. Every for loop starts with for, followed by do, and closed by done. Now let's change the showargs script that you worked with at the beginning of this chapter to include a for loop for both $@ and $*. Listing 18.27 demonstrates what the new script looks like.

Listing 18.27: Evaluating $@ and $* using for

```
#!/bin/bash
# showargs
# this script shows all arguments used when starting the script

echo showing for on \$@
for i in "$@"
do
        echo $i
done

echo showing for on \$*
for i in "$*"
do
        echo $i
done

exit 0
```

Let's consider a few comments before running this script. In this script, a technique called *escaping* is used. The purpose of *escaping* is to make sure that the shell doesn't interpret certain elements. Consider for instance the line `echo showing for on $@`. If you run it this way, the shell interprets `$@` and shows you its current value. In this case, since you don't want that, the shell just displays the characters `$@`. To do that, the shell does not interpret the `$` sign, which you enforce by adding a slash in front of it. By using a slash, you tell the shell not to interpret the next character.

A few lines of code later, there are the lines `for i in "$@"` and `for i in "$*"`. Here I've used double quotes to prevent the shell from interpreting `$@` and `$*` *before* executing the code lines in the script. You want the shell to interpret these the moment it runs the script, and therefore I put both in double quotes. I recommend at this point that you to try the difference yourself. Run the script once without the double quotes and once with them.

When running the script without the double quotes, you start the script with a command like `./showargs a b c d`. The shell already interprets `$*` before it comes at the line `for i in $*`. Thus, it would execute `for i in a b c d` and next show four different lines containing a, b, c, and d. However, that's not what you want: you want the shell to show the result of `for i in $*`. To make sure that this happens, put `$*` in double quotes. Listing 18.28 shows the result of running the example script from Listing 18.26.

Listing 18.28: Result of running the example script from Listing 18.26

```
nuuk:~/bin # ./showargs a b c d
showing for on $@
a
b
c
d
showing for on $*
a b c d
nuuk:~/bin #
```

Summary

In this chapter, you learned how to write shell scripts. You worked with some of the basic shell scripting technologies, which will allow you to use shell scripting and to start experimenting with this technique and creating your own, more advanced scripts. Also, based on the information provided in this chapter, you should now be able to understand most of the start-up scripts that are on your server.

Chapter

19

Understanding and Troubleshooting the Boot Procedure

TOPICS COVERED IN THIS CHAPTER:

✓ Introduction to Troubleshooting the Boot Procedure

✓ Configuring Booting with GRUB

✓ Common Kernel Management Tasks

✓ Configuring Service Startup with Upstart

✓ Basic Red Hat Enterprise Linux Troubleshooting

Many things can go wrong on a Linux system. Often, if something goes wrong it is related to the startup of the server. Linux servers can be used a long time without ever being restarted, so if after years of uninterrupted functioning a server is restarted, problems may appear. In this chapter for that reason you'll read about the startup procedure and how problems can occur and be fixed.

Introduction to Troubleshooting the Boot Procedure

On some occasions, your server may not want to start. If this happens, you'll need a minimal understanding of the server boot procedure in order to fix the problems. In this chapter, you'll learn about the different phases of the server startup procedure and how to fix them if something goes wrong.

First you'll learn how the server uses GRUB for booting. *GRUB* is the boot loader that is installed on the bootable disk in your server. It takes care of starting the Linux kernel. Once successfully loaded, GRUB will start a kernel and all of the associated drivers. Once this is complete, Upstart is started. *Upstart* is responsible for starting all the services on your server.

In this chapter, you will also learn what to do if things go wrong. You will learn how to boot using a rescue system on a server which is still capable of booting. You will also learn how to recover your server using a rescue disk. In Figure 19.1 you'll see a schematic overview of the Red Hat Enterprise Linux boot procedure.

FIGURE 19.1   Schematic overview of the Red Hat Enterprise Linux boot procedure

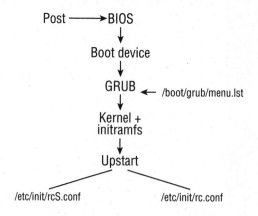

Configuring Booting with GRUB

When your server starts, it needs to know which operating system to start. A *boot loader* is loaded for this purpose. On Red Hat Enterprise Linux, the GRUB boot loader is used. On a standard installation, the first part of the boot loader program is installed in the master boot record, and from there the rest of the boot procedure is executed.

Understanding the grub.conf Configuration File

An important part of GRUB is the configuration file /boot/grub/grub.conf. Listing 19.1 shows you what this file looks like.

Listing 19.1: Sample /boot/grub/grub.conf file

```
[root@hn1 ~]# cat /boot/grub/grub.conf
# grub.conf generated by anaconda
#
# Note that you do not have to rerun grub after making changes to this file
# NOTICE: You have a /boot partition. This means that
#         all kernel and initrd paths are relative to /boot/, eg.
#         root (hd0,0)
#         kernel /vmlinuz-version ro root=/dev/mapper/vg_hn1-lv_root
#         initrd /initrd-[generic-]version.img
#boot=/dev/sda
default=0
timeout=5
splashimage=(hd0,0)/grub/splash.xpm.gz
hiddenmenu
title Red Hat Enterprise Linux (2.6.32-220.el6.x86_64)
        root (hd0,0)
        kernel /vmlinuz-2.6.32-220.el6.x86_64 ro root=/dev/mapper/vg_hn1-
lv_root rd_NO_LUKS LANG=en_US.UTF-8  KEYBOARDTYPE=pc KEYTABLE=us-acentos
 rd_NO_MD quiet SYSFONT=latarcyrheb-sun16 rhgb crashkernel=128M
 rd_LVM_LV=vg_hn1/lv_swap rd_LVM_LV=vg_hn1/lv_root rd_NO_DM
        initrd /initramfs-2.6.32-220.el6.x86_64.img
```

The purpose of GRUB is to load the kernel and the initial RAM file system. The kernel is the heart of the operating system, which ensures that the hardware in the computer can be used. The initial RAM file system contains modules that are needed by the kernel to access the file system and load other modules.

To load the kernel and initial RAM file system, different sections can be included in grub.conf. Only one section is used in the sample file in Listing 19.1. It is defined in the line that starts with title Red Hat Enterprise Linux and the three lines beneath that one.

The first thing that happens in each section is that the root device is referenced. This is *not* the device that contains the root file system; it is the device that GRUB will use to find all the files that are referenced in the grub.conf configuration file. The root device is referred to by its BIOS name, which in this case is hd0,0. This refers to the first partition on the first hard disk, which from the perspective of the kernel is known as /dev/sda1. GRUB has to use the BIOS name of the device because, at the initial boot stage when this file is read, the kernel name /dev/sda1 is unknown yet.

Next the kernel is loaded on the line that starts with kernel /vmlinuz..., and it is followed by a number of options that specify exactly how the kernel should be loaded. The name of the referenced file (/vmlinuz) is relative to the root that is defined in the first line. This means it is obtained from the partition root of the device /dev/sda1.

After specifying the name of the kernel, some kernel load options are specified. All options that appear in uppercase are variables that are passed to the init. If you're starting your server in troubleshooting mode, you can safely omit all of these parameters. The important boot parameters are listed next.

There are many boot parameters you can use. For a complete overview, read the man page bootparam(7).

ro   This parameter indicates that the root file system should be mounted as read-only.

root=   This parameter specifies the name of the device that contains the root file system. On Red Hat Enterprise Linux, this is typically an LVM device.

quiet   This parameter hides the messages that are generated while booting. For better insight into what your server is doing when it boots, consider removing it.

rhgb   This parameter loads the Red Hat Graphical Boot, which displays a logo graphic when booting. Because this hides the messages that are generated while your server is booting, consider removing it.

The last parameter in the section that specifies what should be loaded indicates the name of the initial RAM file system. The parameter name is initrd, and the name of the file is initramfs. This line ensures that an automatically generated file is loaded, which contains all of the required hardware drivers to boot your server and also some important other drivers, such as the Ext4 file system driver.

Apart from the specific sections that specify which kernel to load, in grub.conf you'll also find a generic section that specifies how to load it. You will find the following parameters in the example file in Listing 19.1:

default   This specifies which of the proposed operating systems to load, and it refers to the sections that are defined below the generic section in grub.conf. In Listing 19.1, section 0 is referenced. This refers to the first (and only) section in the example listing.

timeout   During boot, the user can press Tab to open the GRUB menu and add or change kernel parameters. The timeout boot option is used to specify how much time a user has to get into the GRUB menu.

splashimage   This parameter refers to a file containing a graphical background, which is loaded while GRUB is displayed.

hiddenmenu   This option makes sure that no GRUB menu is shown while booting. To enter the GRUB menu, the administrator has to press the Enter key at the right moment.

Apart from the default options in the grub.conf menu, there are other options that can also be used. One of them is the GRUB password. Using a password is a good choice when you want to add an extra layer of security to your system. By default, anyone with physical access to a server can open the GRUB menu and change the boot parameters. By using a GRUB password, you can restrict such modifications only to users who have entered the correct password.

To set a GRUB password, you first need to generate a password that is hashed with the MD5 hashing algorithm. This password is then included in the grub.conf configuration file using the password parameter in the general section of GRUB (see Figure 19.2). In Exercise 19.1 you'll learn how to apply a GRUB password to your server.

FIGURE 19.2   Protecting GRUB with a password

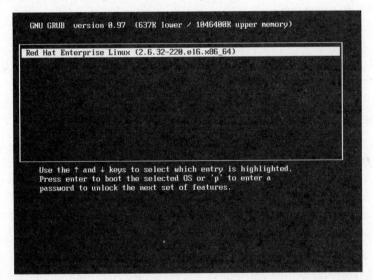

EXERCISE 19.1

Adding a GRUB Boot Password

In this exercise, you'll learn how to generate an MD5 hashed password string and include it in GRUB in order to add an extra layer of protection that ensures that only users who know the password can make modifications to the password file.

1.   Open a root shell.

2.   Use the **grub-md5-crypt** command. This command asks you to enter a password. This is the password that you will use to add an additional layer of protection to GRUB. Enter this password twice.

3. Copy the password hash that is shown on the screen of your computer using your mouse (you need to be able to paste it in the next step).

4. Open /boot/grub/grub.conf with an editor, and in the general section of the file, add the line password=. Paste the password hash after the = sign so that the complete line appears as follows:

   password --md5 $1$6XWaoO$98FkjAkEJWBB/

5. Remove the line that contains the hiddenmenu parameter. Then save the changes to the grub.conf file, and close your editor.

6. Reboot your computer.

7. When the GRUB menu shows, press **p**. You'll then be prompted for the password that you used to protect GRUB. Enter the password to unlock the mode where you can change GRUB parameters.

8. You'll now see that the GRUB menu asks you to press **a**, **c**, or **e** to apply changes to the boot procedure. In the next section, you'll learn more about useful boot options you can use. For now, press Enter to continue the normal boot procedure.

Changing Boot Options

In the previous section, you learned how to change the GRUB configuration file from a running system. Occasionally, your server may have a problem booting normally, and you'll need to enter the GRUB prompt to change the GRUB parameters from there. Here are some common reasons:

- You've made an error in the grub.conf file, which prevents your server from booting.
- There is a problem while booting your server, and you need to boot it in maintenance mode.

If you are having trouble booting your server, there are several options you can use to change the way GRUB is loading. To use these options, you need to enter the GRUB menu while booting (see Figure 19.3).

The exact procedure to enter the GRUB boot menu while booting depends on the GRUB configuration.

- If the hiddenmenu option is used, press the Escape key after the computer's power-on self-test (POST) and before the operating system starts loading.
- If the GRUB menu is password-protected, press **p** and enter the GRUB password to unlock the editing features.
- From the GRUB menu, press **a** if you want to change only the boot parameters for the kernel. This can be useful if, for instance, instead of booting into the default runlevel 5, you want to boot into another runlevel, such as runlevel 3.

- From the GRUB menu, press **e** to edit the lines from the configuration file. This is useful if you know there is an error somewhere in the GRUB configuration file.

- Press **c** to open a GRUB command line. This is the most difficult option, but it is also the most powerful one that you can use. It helps when entering GRUB parameters manually to perform a manual boot of your server.

FIGURE 19.3   Changing GRUB boot options

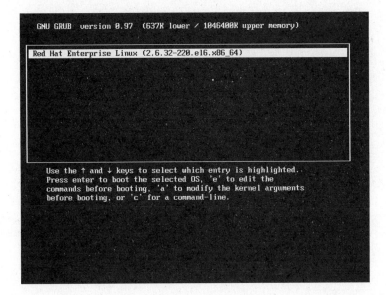

The most versatile way to modify GRUB parameters is by entering the edit mode from the GRUB prompt. To do this, first select the GRUB menu entry that you want to modify and then press **e**. This displays the edit menu shown in Figure 19.4.

In the edit menu, you first select the line that you want to change, and then you press **e** to open this line in edit mode. By default, the editor opens at the end of the line. You can then use the arrow keys to move to the exact position where the changes are needed. It is also possible to use Bash-like shortcuts such as Ctrl+a for the beginning of a line or Ctrl+e to go to the end of a line. Tab completion also works. Next apply the changes you want to make, and press Enter (not Escape!) to get back to the main edit menu. From there, you can enter **b** to boot your server. In Exercise 19.2 you'll learn how to boot using alternate boot options.

Anything you change from the GRUB editor interface is not permanent. After booting your server by applying GRUB changes from the GRUB menu, don't forget to apply the modifications to the grub.conf file as well!

From the main edit menu shown in Figure 19.4, a few other options are available. Some of these include **d** to delete a line, **o** to open a line, or Escape to get back into the main GRUB menu, as shown in Figure 19.3.

FIGURE 19.4   Editing GRUB menu options

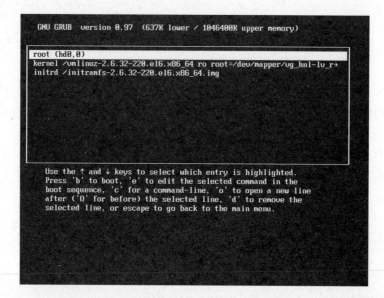

```
 GNU GRUB  version 0.97  (637K lower / 1046400K upper memory)

 ┌────────────────────────────────────────────────────────────────────┐
 │ root (hd0,0)                                                         │
 │ kernel /vmlinuz-2.6.32-220.el6.x86_64 ro root=/dev/mapper/vg_hnl-lv_r→│
 │ initrd /initramfs-2.6.32-220.el6.x86_64.img                          │
 │                                                                      │
 │                                                                      │
 │                                                                      │
 │                                                                      │
 └────────────────────────────────────────────────────────────────────┘

      Use the ↑ and ↓ keys to select which entry is highlighted.
      Press 'b' to boot, 'e' to edit the selected command in the
      boot sequence, 'c' for a command-line, 'o' to open a new line
      after ('O' for before) the selected line, 'd' to remove the
      selected line, or escape to go back to the main menu.
```

EXERCISE 19.2

Booting with Alternative Boot Options

In this exercise, you'll create an error in the grub.conf file, which prevents your server from booting properly. Next you'll fix this error from the GRUB editor interface.

1. Make sure that your server is booted, and open a root shell.

2. Open /boot/grub/grub.conf with an editor, and go to the line where the kernel is loaded. Change the word root that loads the root file system to **rot** on this line, and reboot your server.

3. Observe what happens while your server is booting. You'll notice that it loads the kernel and then halts and displays a panic message. The kernel doesn't know what to do, and therefore it stops booting completely and hangs your computer.

4. Use the power button to switch off your computer, and boot it again. This time, enter the options in the GRUB menu. If you still have a GRUB password, first use **p** to enter the password. Next type **e** to enter the editor mode.

5. Select the kernel line, and while this line is selected, press **e**. Now move your cursor to the position where the word is misspelled and correct it.

6. Press Enter to confirm the corrected line, and from the main GRUB menu, press **b** to boot your server.

7. Once your server has booted, log in as root. Open /boot/grub/menu.1st in an editor, and correct the kernel line where the word root is still misspelled.

Using the GRUB Command Line

In the previous section, you changed GRUB from the menu interface. This is a convenient option to correct small issues in the grub.conf file. In other instances, the problems can be much more serious. In such cases, it's good to know that you can also open a GRUB shell to enter everything by hand that GRUB needs to boot.

To open a GRUB shell, from the GRUB menu that is shown at system boot, press **c**. For GRUB maintenance on a running system, you can also open the GRUB shell interface by typing the grub command. This opens a shell interface, as shown in Figure 19.5.

FIGURE 19.5   The GRUB shell interface

```
   GNU GRUB  version 0.97  (637K lower / 1046400K upper memory)

[ Minimal BASH-like line editing is supported.  For the first word, TAB
  lists possible command completions.  Anywhere else TAB lists the possible
  completions of a device/filename.  ESC at any time exits.]

grub> █
```

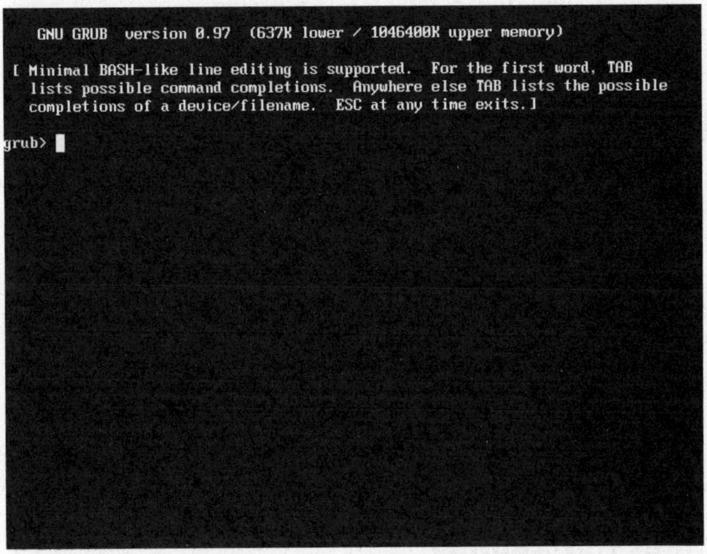

Different commands are available from the GRUB shell interface. For a complete overview, you can type the help command after entering the GRUB shell. The sequence of commands that allows you to start the kernel and initial RAM fs manually from the GRUB command line interface. To do this, you'll basically enter all commands that are normally started from the GRUB configuration file /boot/grub/grub.conf. You'll perform this procedure in Exercise 19.3.

EXERCISE 19.3

Manually Starting GRUB

In this exercise, you'll learn how to start GRUB manually. This is a useful procedure to repair a damaged GRUB installation.

1. Restart your computer; when the GRUB menu displays, type **p** to enter the password. After entering the password, type **c** to open the GRUB shell.

2. Type **cat /grub/grub.conf**. This command tries to read the GRUB configuration file, which is useful if the file is still accessible. If successful, it shows the current configuration.

3. Now enter all of the boot parameters by hand. The commands listed here might need to be adjusted to suit your environment. First type **root (hd0,0)**.

4. Now type **kernel vmlinuz-[tab] ro root=/your/root/filesystem**. Notice the use of the Tab key in the command. Command completion works from the GRUB prompt, and in this case, it will show you the available kernel versions and make it easier to start the kernel version you need.

5. Type **initrd /initramfs-[tab]**.

6. Type **boot**, and press Enter. Your computer will now start.

Reinstalling GRUB

In some situations your GRUB configuration might be so badly damaged that you need to reinstall it. There are two ways of doing this: from the GRUB shell or from a Bash shell environment on a rescue system. The easiest way to reinstall GRUB is from the GRUB shell. All you need to do is to run the command setup followed by the BIOS name of the device where you want to install the GRUB boot loader. For example, setup (hd0) installs GRUB in the master boot record of your computer.

An alternative is to use the grub-install command from a Bash shell. You can do this on a running system (but why would you want to reinstall GRUB if you are able to boot it into a running system?). Alternatively, you can also use this approach from a rescue disk. In a later section, you will learn how to boot a rescue system.

GRUB behind the Scenes

It helps to understand how GRUB works in order to manage it. GRUB consists of different parts. The first part is installed in the master boot record (MBR) of your hard disk or in the boot sector of the active partition. By default, Red Hat Enterprise Linux installs it in the MBR. This part is very small, just 446 bytes, and it is called the *GRUB stage 1 boot loader.*

The 446 bytes in the MBR are not enough to start an entire operating system, however, and that is the reason behind the stage 2 part of GRUB. This part is in the first megabyte of your hard disk—an area used to store metadata needed to start the computer. With the use of the stage 2, GRUB is capable of reading files directly from the file system, as long as the file system is supported. You can find a list of supported file systems in the /boot/grub directory. The minimal file system drivers in this directory all have a name that ends with stage1_5.

An important file also used by GRUB is /boot/grub/device.map. This file contains the mapping between kernel device names and BIOS device names. If you're ever having a problem recognizing the boot disk correctly, the reason might be a misconfiguration of this file.

On a server that experiences severe problems with GRUB, it can be useful to check whether GRUB is still present in the MBR. To do this, the tool xxd can be useful. xxd is a hexadecimal viewer, and if you use xxd -1 512 /dev/sda on your computer, it will show you the contents of the MBR. Even if the contents are completely hexadecimal, you'll easily recognize the GRUB error message, which indicates that a GRUB boot loader has been installed. Listing 19.2 shows a typical MBR that contains GRUB.

Listing 19.2: Showing the contents of an MBR with xxd

```
[root@hnl ~]# xxd -1 512 /dev/sda
0000000: eb48 9010 8ed0 bc00 b0b8 0000 8ed8 8ec0  .H..............
0000010: fbbe 007c bf00 06b9 0002 f3a4 ea21 0600  ...|.........!..
0000020: 00be be07 3804 750b 83c6 1081 fefe 0775  ....8.u........u
0000030: f3eb 16b4 02b0 01bb 007c b280 8a74 0302  .........|...t..
0000040: ff00 0020 0100 0000 0002 fa90 90f6 c280  ... ............
0000050: 7502 b280 ea59 7c00 0031 c08e d88e d0bc  u....Y|..1......
0000060: 0020 fba0 407c 3cff 7402 88c2 52f6 c280  . ..@|<.t...R...
0000070: 7454 b441 bbaa 55cd 135a 5272 4981 fb55  tT.A..U..ZRrI..U
0000080: aa75 43a0 417c 84c0 7505 83e1 0174 3766  .uC.A|..u....t7f
0000090: 8b4c 10be 057c c644 ff01 668b 1e44 7cc7  .L...|.D..f..D|.
00000a0: 0410 00c7 4402 0100 6689 5c08 c744 0600  ....D...f.\..D..
00000b0: 7066 31c0 8944 0466 8944 0cb4 42cd 1372  pf1..D.f.D..B..r
00000c0: 05bb 0070 eb7d b408 cd13 730a f6c2 800f  ...p.}....s.....
00000d0: 84f0 00e9 8d00 be05 7cc6 44ff 0066 31c0  ........|.D..f1.
00000e0: 88f0 4066 8944 0431 d288 cac1 e202 88e8  ..@f.D.1........
00000f0: 88f4 4089 4408 31c0 88d0 c0e8 0266 8904  ..@.D.1......f..
0000100: 66a1 447c 6631 d266 f734 8854 0a66 31d2  f.D|f1.f.4.T.f1.
0000110: 66f7 7404 8854 0b89 440c 3b44 087d 3c8a  f.t..T..D.;D.}<.
0000120: 540d c0e2 068a 4c0a fec1 08d1 8a6c 0c5a  T.....L......l.Z
0000130: 8a74 0bbb 0070 8ec3 31db b801 02cd 1372  .t...p..1......r
0000140: 2a8c c38e 0648 7c60 1eb9 0001 8edb 31f6  *....H|`......1.
0000150: 31ff fcf3 a51f 61ff 2642 7cbe 7f7d e840  1.....a.&B|..}.@
0000160: 00eb 0ebe 847d e838 00eb 06be 8e7d e830  .....}.8.....}.0
0000170: 00be 937d e82a 00eb fe47 5255 4220 0047  ...}.*...GRUB .G
0000180: 656f 6d00 4861 7264 2044 6973 6b00 5265  eom.Hard Disk.Re
0000190: 6164 0020 4572 726f 7200 bb01 00b4 0ecd  ad. Error.......
00001a0: 10ac 3c00 75f4 c300 0000 0000 0000 0000  ..<.u...........
00001b0: 0000 0000 0000 0000 6123 0500 0000 8020  ........a#.....
00001c0: 2100 83dd 1e3f 0008 0000 00a0 0f00 00dd  !....?..........
00001d0: 1f3f 8efe ffff 00a8 0f00 00b0 0c1d 0000  .?..............
00001e0: 0000 0000 0000 0000 0000 0000 0000 0000  ................
00001f0: 0000 0000 0000 0000 0000 0000 0000 55aa  ..............U.
[root@hnl ~]#
```

Apart from the GRUB error message that is shown in Listing 19.2, in the lines that start with 1c0 and 1d0, you can also recognize the partition table. The second columns of these lines clearly mark the existence of a partition of type 83 and 8e.

GRUB 2

The GRUB boot loader is used on Red Hat Enterprise Linux 6. In recent versions of Fedora, GRUB has been replaced with GRUB 2, which is organized in a completely different way. GRUB 2 is going to be introduced in Red Hat Enterprise Linux 7.

Common Kernel Management Tasks

The main task of GRUB is to load the kernel. The kernel is the heart of the operating system, and it is the layer that addresses the hardware directly. To access different hardware components, the kernel uses initrd, which contains everything needed to access the file system from which the other modules can be loaded. As an administrator, you will occasionally have to manage these kernel drivers.

The Linux kernel that is used in Red Hat Enterprise Linux 6 is feature rich, and it offers support for the most common server hardware. This support is added by using open source drivers, which are included with the kernel itself. In some cases, as an administrator you'll have to give the kernel a little help to get the appropriate driver loaded. If you've purchased server hardware that is certified for Red Hat Enterprise Linux, this will rarely be the case. If you're installing Red Hat on noncertified hardware, you may end up with unsupported hardware components.

As an administrator, there are a few tasks that you'll need to be able to perform with regard to hardware management.

- Analyze your server to find out whether a specific module is loaded.

- Load and unload kernel modules.

- Load kernel modules with specific options.

In the early days of Linux, kernels occasionally needed to be recompiled to include specific functions. In a modern, supported Linux server operating system like Red Hat Enterprise Linux, you should never have to do that. You may even lose support if you recompile your kernel! To include functionality in the kernel, you'll typically make sure that the correct supporting modules are loaded.

Analyzing Availability of Kernel Modules

If you have a problem addressing hardware correctly, the first step is to make sure the supporting kernel module is loaded. lspci -v is a useful command for doing this. This command shows all devices that are found on the PCI bus, and if a kernel module was also found for the device, you'll see it listed on the last line for the specific device. In Listing 19.3, you can see an example where the i915 module is loaded to address the graphical card in the computer.

Listing 19.3: The lspci -v command is useful for finding out whether kernel modules are loaded.

```
[root@hnl ~]# lspci -v | less
00:00.0 Host bridge: Intel Corporation 2nd Generation Core Processor Family
 DRAM Controller (rev 09)
        Subsystem: Dell Device 049a
        Flags: bus master, fast devsel, latency 0
        Capabilities: [e0] Vendor Specific Information <?>
        Kernel driver in use: agpgart-intel

00:02.0 VGA compatible controller: Intel Corporation 2nd Generation Core
 Processor Family Integrated Graphics Controller (rev 09) (prog-if 00 [VGA
 controller])
        Subsystem: Dell Device 049a
        Flags: bus master, fast devsel, latency 0, IRQ 29
        Memory at e1c00000 (64-bit, non-prefetchable) [size=4M]
        Memory at d0000000 (64-bit, prefetchable) [size=256M]
        I/O ports at 7000 [size=64]
        Expansion ROM at <unassigned> [disabled]
        Capabilities: [90] MSI: Enable+ Count=1/1 Maskable- 64bit-
        Capabilities: [d0] Power Management version 2
        Capabilities: [a4] PCI Advanced Features
        Kernel driver in use: i915
        Kernel modules: i915

00:16.0 Communication controller: Intel Corporation 6 Series/C200 Series Chipset
Family MEI Controller #1 (rev 04)
```

Another useful way to find out what the kernel has done to initialize a new device is with the dmesg command. This command is particularly useful for detecting devices that were newly attached to the system. With dmesg, you'll read the *kernel ring buffer*, a specific area in memory that contains just kernel messages. Listing 19.4 shows the results of the dmesg command after connecting a USB disc to the system (see Listing 19.4). Some kernel module names can be recognized as the part of the dmesg lines before the colon.

Listing 19.4: Using dmesg to show recent kernel messages

```
usb 2-1.4: New USB device strings: Mfr=1, Product=2, SerialNumber=3
usb 2-1.4: Product: DataTraveler 2.0
usb 2-1.4: Manufacturer: Kingston
usb 2-1.4: SerialNumber: 5B711B8EA1FB
usb 2-1.4: configuration #1 chosen from 1 choice
Initializing USB Mass Storage driver...
scsi6 : SCSI emulation for USB Mass Storage devices
usbcore: registered new interface driver usb-storage
USB Mass Storage support registered.
usb-storage: device found at 3
usb-storage: waiting for device to settle before scanning
usb-storage: device scan complete
scsi 6:0:0:0: Direct-Access     Kingston DataTraveler 2.0 PMAP PQ: 0 ANSI: 0 CCS
sd 6:0:0:0: Attached scsi generic sg2 type 0
sd 6:0:0:0: [sdb] 4030464 512-byte logical blocks: (2.06 GB/1.92 GiB)
sd 6:0:0:0: [sdb] Write Protect is off
sd 6:0:0:0: [sdb] Mode Sense: 23 00 00 00
sd 6:0:0:0: [sdb] Assuming drive cache: write through
sd 6:0:0:0: [sdb] Assuming drive cache: write through
 sdb: sdb1
sd 6:0:0:0: [sdb] Assuming drive cache: write through
sd 6:0:0:0: [sdb] Attached SCSI removable disk
SELinux: initialized (dev sdb1, type vfat), uses genfs_contexts
```

Loading and Unloading Kernel Modules

As an administrator, you rarely have to load kernel modules manually. This is because the Linux kernel by itself detects which hardware is available, and it will normally automatically load the modules. Nevertheless, sometimes you will indeed have to load kernel modules manually.

To load a kernel module, use the modprobe command followed by the name of the specific kernel module. For example, use modprobe cdrom to load the kernel module that is used to access the optical drive in your computer. To unload the same kernel module manually, you would use modprobe -r cdrom.

To see which kernel modules have been loaded, you can use the `lsmod` command. This produces a list of all modules that are currently loaded, and it will also show you if other kernel modules are dependent on it.

Listing 19.5 shows what the output of the `lsmod` command looks like.

Listing 19.5: Listing kernel modules with `lsmod`

```
sr_mod                16228  1
cdrom                 39771  1 sr_mod
sd_mod                39488  6
crc_t10dif             1541  1 sd_mod
sdhci_pci              8191  0
sdhci                 20595  1 sdhci_pci
mmc_core              72991  1 sdhci
firewire_ohci         24901  0
firewire_core         51229  1 firewire_ohci
crc_itu_t              1717  1 firewire_core
ahci                  40455  3
wmi                    6287  0
i915                 545923  2
drm_kms_helper        33236  1 i915
drm                  230675  3 i915,drm_kms_helper
i2c_algo_bit           5762  1 i915
i2c_core              31276  5 i2c_i801,i915,drm_kms_helper,drm,i2c_algo_bit
video                 21032  1 i915
output                 2505  1 video
dm_mirror             14101  0
dm_region_hash        12170  1 dm_mirror
dm_log                10122  2 dm_mirror,dm_region_hash
dm_mod                81500 16 dm_mirror,dm_log
```

You may have heard of the `insmod` and `rmmod` commands. These are older commands and should no longer be used. The modprobe command analyzes the dependencies of a kernel module, and it will also load all module dependencies. This is not the case for `insmod` and `rmmod`.

Loading Kernel Modules with Specific Options

As is the case for drivers in other operating systems, kernel modules can also be loaded with specific driver options. This is useful if you need to enable specific options for the module in question. To find out which options are available for a specific module, use the modinfo command followed by the name of the module. At the end of the modinfo output, you'll see a list of parameters, each of which starts with parm. These are the module-specific options that can be used. Listing 19.6 shows an example of what this looks like.

Listing 19.6: Use modinfo to find out which options are available for a module.

```
alias:          pci:v00008086d000027A2sv*sd*bc03sc*i*
alias:          pci:v00008086d00002772sv*sd*bc03sc*i*
alias:          pci:v00008086d00002592sv*sd*bc03sc*i*
alias:          pci:v00008086d0000258Asv*sd*bc03sc*i*
alias:          pci:v00008086d00002582sv*sd*bc03sc*i*
alias:          pci:v00008086d00002572sv*sd*bc03sc*i*
alias:          pci:v00008086d0000358Esv*sd*bc03sc*i*
alias:          pci:v00008086d00003582sv*sd*bc03sc*i*
alias:          pci:v00008086d00002562sv*sd*bc03sc*i*
alias:          pci:v00008086d00003577sv*sd*bc03sc*i*
depends:        drm,drm_kms_helper,i2c-core,video,i2c-algo-bit
vermagic:       2.6.32-220.el6.x86_64 SMP mod_unload modversions
parm:           modeset:int
parm:           fbpercrtc:int
parm:           panel_ignore_lid:int
parm:           powersave:int
parm:           semaphores:int
parm:           i915_enable_rc6:int
parm:           i915_enable_fbc:int
parm:           lvds_downclock:int
parm:           lvds_use_ssc:int
parm:           vbt_sdvo_panel_type:int
parm:           reset:bool
[root@hnl ~]#
```

Unfortunately, module options normally aren't documented very well. Generally, you can search the Internet to find out more about the function of a specific module.

To enable specific module features, you can create a configuration file in the directory /etc/modprobe.d. The name of the file doesn't really matter, as long as it ends with the .conf extension. The kernel will find it while loading kernel modules. In this file, you'll create a line that appears as follows:

options b43 nohwcrypt=1 qos=0

In this example line, options are specified for the b43 module. These options will be loaded the next time the module is activated. Thus, after changing a kernel module's option, use **modprobe -r** and **modprobe** to reload the module. You'll apply this technique in Exercise 19.4.

EXERCISE 19.4

Applying Kernel Module Options

In this exercise, you'll change the kernel module for the CD-ROM drive. By default, it will physically eject an optical disc that has been ejected by software. By changing a kernel module, you'll disable this option.

1. Insert a CD-ROM disc in your optical drive. It will automatically be mounted in the graphical interface, and you'll see an icon on the desktop that enables you to access it easily.

2. Use `modinfo cdrom`, and look at the parm section at the end of the command. You can see that there is an auto-eject option in that section.

3. Create a file with the name **/etc/modprobe.d/cdrom.conf**, and make sure it has the following contents:

    `options cdrom autoeject=0`

4. Use `modprobe -r cdrom`. You'll notice that it fails. This is because a CD-ROM is currently mounted. If the command still fails after unmounting the CD-ROM, restart your computer. (Occasionally, you will need to do this to reload a kernel module.)

5. If you didn't restart the computer, use `modprobe cdrom` to load the kernel module for the CD-ROM.

6. Insert the CD-ROM disc again. It will automatically be mounted. Try to eject it again. You'll notice that this no longer works.

Upgrading the Kernel

On occasion, Red Hat releases a newer version of the kernel. To make sure you will benefit from all its new features, it's a good idea to install the newer version of the kernel using **yum install kernel**. This will install the newer version without removing the older version of the kernel. This is a useful feature because, if something doesn't work well once you install the new kernel on your system, you can still select the old kernel from the GRUB boot menu.

Configuring Service Startup with Upstart

Much work has been done recently on the way that Linux boots. After using systemv-init to start services for many years, Upstart appeared to be a worthy successor. However, the first Linux distributions had only just begun to use Upstart as the default boot solution when a new method named systemd began to conquer the world. systemd will absolutely be the standard on most, if not all, Linux distributions released in the next several months and years. In the meantime, however, as an administrator, you will still have to deal with Upstart. Upstart is the default method for starting services on Red Hat Enterprise Linux 6.

Speed was the most important design goal for the developers when creating Upstart. The old method started services sequentially, and that took up a lot of time. Upstart uses an event-driven approach. In this approach, the Upstart process (implemented by the /sbin/init daemon) is the first thing started when the Linux kernel is booted. After starting, it executes a few scripts that take care of starting all the processes that your server needs. These scripts are in the /etc/init directory.

An event-driven start-up method was needed mostly for desktop environments, which were taking too long to start. On servers, the effective speed gain in starting up is minimal. However, physical servers take a long time to boot no matter what because of their extensive hardware checks.

An easy way to understand exactly what is happening is by examining the contents of the /etc/inittab file, as shown in Listing 19.7. This file was used to configure the entire systemv boot procedure in previous versions of Red Hat Enterprise Linux. To make it easy for administrators to understand how to work with Upstart, it now contains hints on the different files that are used in the Upstart procedure.

Listing 19.7: Check /etc/inittab if you want to know which Upstart configuration file is used for a given purpose.

```
[root@hnl ~]# cat /etc/inittab
# inittab is only used by upstart for the default runlevel.
#
# ADDING OTHER CONFIGURATION HERE WILL HAVE NO EFFECT ON YOUR SYSTEM.
#
# System initialization is started by /etc/init/rcS.conf
#
# Individual runlevels are started by /etc/init/rc.conf
#
# Ctrl-Alt-Delete is handled by /etc/init/control-alt-delete.conf
#
# Terminal gettys are handled by /etc/init/tty.conf and /etc/init/serial.conf,
# with configuration in /etc/sysconfig/init.
#
# For information on how to write upstart event handlers, or how
# upstart works, see init(5), init(8), and initctl(8).
#
# Default runlevel. The runlevels used are:
#   0 - halt (Do NOT set initdefault to this)
#   1 - Single user mode
```

```
#    2 - Multiuser, without NFS (The same as 3, if you do not have networking)
#    3 - Full multiuser mode
#    4 - unused
#    5 - X11
#    6 - reboot (Do NOT set initdefault to this)
#
id:5:initdefault:
```

The only thing still relevant in /etc/inittab is that it defines the default runlevel. This happens on the last line. In Listing 19.3, you can see that id:5:initdefault: is used to set runlevel 5 as the default. If ever you want your server to start in a different runlevel, like the nongraphical runlevel 3, you can change it here. (You can also add it for one-time use as a kernel argument from the GRUB prompt.)

The main part of the Upstart configuration is handled by different scripts in the /etc/ init directory. Of these, two are particularly important in the boot procedure. The /etc/ init/rcS.conf file is used for system initialization, and the /etc/init/rc.conf file is used to start the runlevel services. Examining these scripts reveals that Red Hat hasn't changed that much since it used systemv in the old days. The most important line in /etc/init/ rcS.conf is the one that starts rc.sysinit, a script that takes care of starting everything your server needs to do its job, such as mounting file systems and initializing proc and swap.

The other script is /etc/init/rc.conf, which takes care of starting services in the runlevels. Upstart on RHEL 6 is still fully compliant with runlevels as they were used in system-init. The scripts that start the services themselves are in the directory /etc/init.d. These are the scripts that you can start with a command like service nameofthescript start.

To automate the start of these scripts during the boot procedure, Upstart executes symbolic links that start with S in the directory /etc/rcX.d, where X is the current runlevel to be started. Thus, if your server is configured to start runlevel 3 from the /etc/init/ rc.conf file, the rc script is started, and it executes all symbolic links in order. On my system, this means that /etc/rc3.d/S01sysstat is the first thing that is executed, and /etc/ rc3.d/S99local is the last script that is executed. At the end of the procedure, all services that are configured to be started are started using this approach. As an administrator, you can use the chkconfig command to put the services in the runlevels where they are typically needed. While switching runlevels, all symbolic links that have a name that starts with K are also executed—called *kill scripts*. This is because you could be switching to another runlevel where services that were needed previously are no longer needed.

After processing the runlevels, a few minor scripts are executed. These are, for example, the /etc/init/start-ttys.conf script, which prepares all TTYs on your server, or prefdm.conf, which runs the graphical interface in case you use it. As an administrator, it is interesting to know these scripts exist, but you'll never really change anything in them.

For your daily work as an administrator of a Red Hat Enterprise Linux server, you don't need to go into the Upstart scripts very often. If after installing a service your server refuses to boot, it can be useful, though, to know how Upstart works. Having knowledge of its workings allows you to correct errors that are related to misconfiguring the Upstart scripts.

Basic Red Hat Enterprise Linux Troubleshooting

Things don't go wrong too often on your Red Hat Enterprise Linux server. If things do go wrong, it is frequently related to the boot procedure. You have already learned how to enter the GRUB shell to perform some basic troubleshooting tasks from there, such as manually loading the kernel and initial RAM file system files. In this section, you'll learn about some other techniques that can be useful in fixing boot-related problems on your server.

Booting in Minimal Mode

If your server refuses to boot properly, it may very well be because a service has been installed that cannot start. To fix such problems, it is helpful to start your server in a minimal mode. There are two minimal modes that you can use under specific circumstances.

- Runlevel 1 is the mode entered for troubleshooting problems when you're sure they are located in the runlevels and not in the initial phase of the boot procedure. In runlevel 1, all of the essential services are started, and only a minimal number of services are started in the runlevels. You can see which services these are by examining all symbolic links that start with S in the /etc/rc1.d directory.

- If your server still doesn't boot after entering runlevel 1, the problem might be in the initial boot phase. If this is the case, you can skip the entire Upstart-related part of the boot procedure by using the init=/bin/bash command as a kernel argument on the GRUB prompt. This brings you into a minimal mode where only the root file system is mounted and not much else has been started. From this mode, you can start all of the essential services yourself, which allows you to analyze where things go wrong and to fix them.

Another useful troubleshooting mode is the interactive mode, which you can activate by pressing I once the services start loading. In *interactive mode* you can start every script one by one so that you can see exactly where it goes wrong if problems do occur. To use interactive mode, your system needs to have loaded the init process successfully.

In general, it's a good idea to use runlevel 1 before trying to fix your problems from an init=/bin/bash shell. The reason is simple: many parts of your system have been started in runlevel 1, whereas not very much is started when you use init=/bin/bash. This makes troubleshooting from runlevel 1 a lot easier. In Exercise 19.5 you'll practice how to do this.

EXERCISE 19.5

Starting Your Server in Minimal Mode

In this exercise, you'll learn how to start your server in minimal mode using the `init=/bin/bash` kernel argument.

1. Restart your server, and when the GRUB menu shows, press **a** to enter a kernel argument.

2. As the kernel argument, type **init=/bin/bash**. This tells the kernel to bypass the entire Upstart procedure and just drop a root shell.

3. Once you have shell access, use the command **touch blah** to create a file with the name *blah*. You will get an error message indicating that you're on a read-only file system.

4. Use **mount -o remount,rw /** to remount the root file system in read-write mode. At this point, you can modify files on the root file system.

5. If you also need access to other file systems, type **mount -a** to mount them. You might get an error message on some file systems.

6. Once you're done, type **exec /sbin/init** to start your server in normal mode.

As you noticed in the previous exercise, using the `init=/bin/bash` kernel argument gives you a minimal environment for troubleshooting. That's why you are better off using runlevel 1.

No Root Password?

As you noticed in Exercise 19.5, you didn't have to enter a root password to enter the shell environment. This is not a security leak—it's a feature. In contrast to other operating systems, Linux allows you to set a password on the boot loader, which makes it hard to enter the init=/bin/bash kernel argument (or any other GRUB argument for that matter). In addition, console access to your server should be secured at all times. Servers should be behind a locked door. If an intruder succeeds in physically accessing your server, the intruder will get access to the data on your server no matter what you try to do.

Resetting the Root Password

As an administrator of a Linux system, it can sometimes happen that you need to change settings on a server where you don't know the root password. Fortunately, it's not difficult to reset the root password as long as you have physical access and you can enter GRUB boot options. To do this, you have to enter runlevel 1 for maintenance mode. After that, you'll need to disable SELinux and then reset the root password. In Exercise 19.6, you'll apply this procedure.

EXERCISE 19.6

Resetting the Root Password

In this exercise, you'll learn how to reset the password for the root user.

1. Reboot your server. When GRUB shows, press **a** to open the interface where you can enter kernel parameters, and type **1** at the end of the line.

2. Your server now starts in runlevel 1 and drops you into a root shell without the need to enter a password.

3. Enter the command **setenforce 0** to set SELinux to permissive mode.

4. Type **passwd**, and enter the new password you want to use for the root user.

 Real World Scenario

How Real Is All This?

Normally, you shouldn't experience too many problems with your Linux server. This is especially true because many Linux servers keep running for years without ever restarting. If after years a server is shut down, for instance, because it has to be moved to another location and it is started again at its new location, problems can manifest themselves because of mechanical problems with the hard disk. Most of these problems happen during the boot procedure. In my practice as a consultant, I have seen many occasions where boot problems have occurred, or even entire GRUB configurations have disappeared. The knowledge that you've acquired in this chapter will help you if this ever happens on one of your servers.

Using a Rescue Environment to Recover System Access

If you can still start GRUB, the kernel, and an initial RAM file system, you can enter a kernel option to start an environment where you can troubleshoot your server. In some cases, you can't do this because something is wrong with one of these three items. If that happens, it's good to know how you can start a rescue system.

A Linux installation that allows you to start from external media can be used as a rescue system. For example, if you have a Knoppix DVD, you can use it to repair your Red Hat Enterprise Linux server. Just start from the Knoppix DVD, mount the Red Hat file systems from your server's hard disk, and start troubleshooting.

You can also use the Rescue System option that is on the Red Hat Enterprise Linux installation disc. There is a major benefit to using this option: it uses the same software that you have installed on your server's hard disk, and therefore you're less likely to encounter problems because of different kernel versions or other parts of the system that are not the same.

In Exercise 19.7, you'll learn how to start a rescue system and mount it in a way that you can repair anything on your Red Hat Enterprise Linux server.

EXERCISE 19.7

Starting a Rescue System

In this exercise, you'll start a rescue system that allows you to repair anything on your server's hard disk if it fails to boot normally. You'll need the installation DVD of your Red Hat server to perform this procedure.

1. Insert the installation disc in the optical drive of your server, and reboot the server.

2. Make sure the server boots from the DVD; from the DVD menu, select the Rescue Installed System option. It will take a while before the initial rescue image is loaded from the appropriate initrd image file on the installation disc.

3. In the Choose A Language menu, select English. Next select the keyboard type you're using.

4. When asked what type of media contains the rescue image, select Local CD/DVD.

5. In the Setup Networking screen, select No. You normally don't need networking to repair issues that prevent your server from booting properly.

6. On the next screen, press Enter to select the Continue option. This option tries to find a Red Hat Enterprise Linux installation on the disks of your current machine, and mount this on the directory /mnt/sysimage.

7. Once the rescue system has successfully discovered your current installation, it will tell you so on a screen that states that your system has been mounted. Click OK to acknowledge this, and on the screen that follows, click OK again.

8. Now select the shell option to start a shell and click OK. This drops you into a Bash shell environment.

9. Use **chroot /mnt/sysimage** to make the root of your installation on disk your current root directory. This ensures that all path references are right, and you can perform any repair action you like.

Summary

In this chapter, you learned about the parts of your computer that are involved in the boot procedure. You learned how GRUB is configured and what you can do to specify specific boot options. You also learned how Upstart is used to start essential services on your computer. At the end of this chapter, you read about some common scenarios that can help you troubleshoot your server if it fails to start normally.

Chapter

20

Introducing High-Availability Clustering

TOPICS COVERED IN THIS CHAPTER:

- ✓ Understanding High-Availability Clustering
- ✓ Configuring Cluster-Based Services
- ✓ Installing the Red Hat High Availability Add-on
- ✓ Creating Resources and Services
- ✓ Configuring GFS2 File Systems

High-availability clustering is often used in conjunction with Red Hat Enterprise Linux. In this chapter, you'll learn how to set up a high-availability cluster using the Red Hat High Availability add-on. Using such a cluster lets you guarantee that vital services are available at all times and, if something bad happens to your servers, that the services monitored by high availability are restarted on another node as soon as possible.

Understanding High-Availability Clustering

The purpose of a server is to offer services to users. In some cases, it doesn't matter if the services are briefly unavailable. In other cases, it will cost a lot of money if a service cannot be reached temporarily. For example, think of a highly popular ecommerce site; if it is down, the customer will shop somewhere else. For those important services, high availability is a requirement.

Lab Hardware Requirements

The labs described in this chapter require the use of three different machines. The easiest way to prepare for the labs is by creating a second virtual machine on your KVM host. The KVM host itself can then be used as the iSCSI SAN, as described in Exercise 20.1, whereas the virtual machines can be used as nodes in the HA cluster. You may also run the labs on three different virtual machines. In this chapter, the SAN node will be referred to as san, and the nodes in the cluster are referred to as node1 and node2.

The Workings of High Availability

In a high-availability (HA) cluster, at least two servers are involved when offering high availability of vital services. A typical HA cluster is dedicated to just that service. This means that other services, which are not involved in the HA setup, are not offered by that cluster.

The service in an HA setup is a group of resources. Be sure that you're thinking about this correctly: what on a stand-alone server is typically referred to as a *service* (think of those that are started from the runlevels) is referred to as a *resource* in an HA environment. A service in an HA environment consists of different resources that are treated as one by the cluster.

To make sure that the service is available, the HA cluster continuously monitors the servers that are involved in the cluster (the nodes). If a node goes down, the cluster makes sure the service is started as soon as possible on another node. This means in any HA cluster, there *will always* be a small amount of time that the service is not available after a failure. The goal is to make sure that this amount of time is as small as possible.

Apart from node monitoring, the service itself can also be monitored. This often happens by default. In some cases, you'll need to set up service monitoring manually. This is because the cluster software doesn't always know how to monitor the availability of specific services, especially if custom software is involved.

High-Availability Requirements

Several components are involved in setting up an HA cluster. In its simplest form, two servers are connected to each other by a network cable. But a cluster that is configured in a simple, nonredundant way like this can create some unpleasant surprises. Imagine, for instance, that the network cable breaks. In that case, both nodes in the cluster would no longer see each other, and there would be no way for one node to find out what the other node is doing. This also means that, in such a scenario, there would be no way to make sure that the cluster service is started on the right machine and that its services would continue to be offered. That is why a typical Red Hat cluster involves more than just two nodes.

The following items are typically used in HA clusters:

- Multiple nodes
- Fence devices
- Ethernet bonding
- Shared storage

Let's take a closer look at each of these standard components.

Multiple Nodes

Obviously, it doesn't make much sense to create a cluster that consists of one node only.

> **NOTE**   You can actually create a one-node cluster. In a test environment, a one-node cluster allows you to become familiar with the software, and if the monitored resource becomes unavailable, the one-node cluster will make sure that it is restarted on the same node.

A typical cluster uses at least two nodes, with a maximum number of 16 nodes. Sixteen-node clusters are not very common, but they can be deployed to ensure the high availability of a large number of services.

In this chapter, I'll use the two-node cluster as an example because it is typically enough to ensure that one service can be offered at high availability. Some administrators like to work with three nodes as the minimum. This is to ensure that *quorum* can be maintained at all times.

Quorum is also an important element in an HA cluster. It is the minimum number of nodes that must be available to continue offering services. Typically, the quorum consists of half-plus-one nodes. That is, a node needs majority in the cluster to be able to continue offering services. Later you'll learn that, instead of using a third node, you can also configure a quorum device to get quorum in the cluster.

Fence Devices

To maintain the integrity of the cluster, a failing node must be stopped at all times. The "Using Fencing to Prevent Disaster" example explains why.

 Real World Scenario

Using Fencing to Prevent Disaster

Imagine a service that consists of an IMAP mail server process and a file system that is offered by one of the nodes in the cluster. Picture that it currently is running on node1, but at a given moment, communication in the cluster fails and node1 no longer can see node2. From the perspective of node1, nothing would happen because it is already servicing the mail server. From the perspective of node2, however, node1 is considered to be down, so it would also start the mail server service. The result would be that the mail server process is running on two different nodes in the cluster, and it is writing to the same file system at the same time from these two different nodes. In the case of a normal file system, like Ext4 or XFS, this would definitely cause file system corruption. That is why you need a solution to shut down a failed node before taking over its resources. To accomplish this goal, you'll need a fencing device.

A *fencing device* is typically a hardware device, which is available to shut down another node, even if the node itself has failed. Common solutions include power switches or integrated management cards, such as HP ILO or Dell DRAC. Before taking over a resource, the cluster can instruct the fencing device to make sure the failing node is actually shut down. A power switch can do that by shutting down the physical port(s) to which the node is connected, and a management board can do that by halting the failing node.

If you're using an integrated management card for fencing, you'll need to make sure that ACPI is disabled on the hosts that you want to fence. If enabled, ACPI can cause the fencing process to fail.

The problem with fencing is that you'll need specific hardware to shut down a failing node, and that hardware isn't always available. The good news is that you can create a cluster without fencing or have a cluster that uses a dummy fence device, such as fence_manual.

The bad news is that by doing so, you will risk that services in the cluster will be corrupted. Thus, when planning the purchase of cluster hardware, make sure to include fencing hardware as well!

Fencing is also referred to as *STONITH*, which stands for Shoot The Other Node In The Head. This is exactly what STONITH will do if a node needs to be shut down to prevent corruption from occurring on your cluster.

A Dedicated Cluster Interface

To make sure that cluster traffic is not interrupted by anything—for example, a spike in the number of packets sent on the user network—a dedicated cluster network is often created. This ensures that cluster packets will always get through no matter what happens on the user network. To increase fault tolerance, the user network can serve as a backup for the cluster traffic, which is used in case something physically goes wrong on the cluster network interface.

In the lab setup described in this chapter, you will not use a dedicated cluster interface and send packets over the user network.

Ethernet Bonding

A network card can always fail. To minimize the impact of this and to get more bandwidth, Ethernet bonding is often used in HA cluster environments. An *Ethernet bond* is a logical device that groups at least two network cards. When configuring this, you choose a protocol that specifies how the bond should work. A round-robin algorithm is often used, which means that, under normal operation, frames are distributed across all network interfaces involved in the bond. However, if one of the interfaces goes down, the other interface is capable of handling all the traffic. Other algorithms are also available, such as active/passive or LACP, but these often depend on the features that are offered by the switch.

Setting up bonding is rather essential because without a bond, if one interface in the cluster goes down, the service that the cluster is hosting may become unavailable.

Shared Storage

Most services that run in your cluster will need access to files. When the service fails over, these files will also need to be available on the target server. Of course, you can use rsync or another synchronization tool to synchronize these files, but it's much more convenient to use shared storage to accomplish this goal.

Many companies have a proprietary Fibre Channel or iSCSI SAN that is used as shared storage. However, you don't have to make the large investment required for a shared SAN. Software-based shared storage options are also available, including iSCSI and NFS. Even though both are capable of providing access to the same files from different machines, a shared storage solution that offers block instead of file access is generally considered better, more resilient, and faster. Thus, you will learn how to configure an iSCSI target as a shared storage device in this chapter.

Typically with shared storage, you'll also want to use a storage network. This is to make sure the packets that are sent over the storage network cannot interfere with the packets on the user network, which normally is the network on which cluster traffic is sent. If packets did interfere, it could lead to cluster traffic no longer coming through, and this can cause failures on the cluster.

If you're using a proprietary iSCSI or Fibre Channel SAN, you probably already have a storage network that was installed with the SAN. If you're first setting up an iSCSI SAN as described later in this chapter, you'll need to set up this shared storage network yourself. Figure 20.1 gives an overview of a typical cluster configuration.

FIGURE 20.1 Typical cluster configuration overview

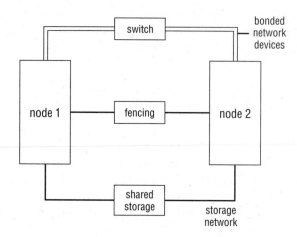

Red Hat High-Availability Add-on Software Components

When working with Red Hat high-availability add-ons, you'll use several different software components. The following sections introduce these components in order to prepare you to build the cluster.

Corosync

Corosync takes care of the lower layers of the cluster. It uses the Totem protocol to ensure that all nodes in the cluster are still available. If something goes wrong on the Corosync layer, it will notify the upper layers of the cluster, where the placement of services and resources is addressed. You'll also encounter the name OpenAIS, which is what was used before Corosync was adopted. The OpenAIS developers halted their work and joined forces with the Corosync developers.

Rgmanager

Rgmanager refers to the upper layers of the cluster. It consists of different processes, which ensure that services are running where they should be. If Corosync detects a failure on the cluster, the Rgmanager layer will move the services to a node where they can continue to do their work.

Pacemaker

Rgmanager is the traditional Red Hat HA cluster stack. There is another Linux-based HA solution, however, which is known as *Pacemaker.* It is a broadly adopted HA project, and Red Hat has also contributed to it. In RHEL 6, it is available as an unsupported technology preview solution. If testing goes well, it is likely that Pacemaker will be the default solution for the upper layers in the cluster in Red Hat Enterprise Linux 7. Because Rgmanager is still the standard in RHEL 6, Pacemaker is not discussed in this chapter.

Conga

Conga is the management interface that is used to create and manage clusters. It consists of two parts: ricci and luci. *Ricci* is the agent that should be installed on all nodes in the cluster, and *luci* is the management application that talks to ricci. As an administrator, you'll log in to the luci web interface to create and manage your cluster.

The names come from the 1950s comedy "I Love Lucy," starring Lucille (Lucy) Ball and Desi (Ricky) Arnez, where Ricky played the conga drums in a nightclub.

Apart from Conga, you can also manage your cluster from the command line. In RHEL 6 the cssadmin tool is used extensively as a command-line interface and allows you to manage all aspects of the cluster.

Configuring Cluster-Based Services

As you've read in the previous sections, a typical cluster includes shared storage as well as network bonding. Before starting the configuration of the cluster, you'll learn how to set up these components in order to ensure that the cluster you are building is a redundant and resilient cluster.

Setting Up Bonding

To set up a bonded network interface, you'll have to accomplish these steps:

1. Identify the physical network cards that you want to configure in the bonding interface.
2. Change the configuration for the physical network cards to make them slaves for the bonding interface.
3. Create a configuration file for the bonding interface.
4. Make sure the bonding kernel module is loaded.

In Exercise 20.1, you will learn how to create a bond device.

EXERCISE 20.1

Creating a Bond Device

In this exercise, you'll set up a bond device. You'll do this on one network interface only, which doesn't really matter for the procedure, because it still stays the same.

1. Nowadays, a typical server is configured with several physical network cards. If there are only two cards that you want to put in the bonding device, it's easy to use them, and there is no particular need to determine which is which. If you have several network cards, it can be hard to find out which physical card corresponds to which logical device. There are a few tricks that can help, however. First, if you plug or unplug a network cable, you'll see a message in /var/log/messages indicating that a cable has been (un)plugged for that specific device. You can also use the command ethtool -p em1 30. This will blink the LEDs on the specific network card (em1, in this example) for 30 seconds, which also makes it easy to identify the appropriate network card.

2. After finding out which network card you want to use, you need to put it in slave mode. You'll also need to remove all configurations on the network card, because they will be set on the bonding device instead. Thus, if the network card em1 is going to be used in a bonded configuration, make sure that its configuration file follows the example shown here:

   ```
   DEVICE=em1
   BOOTPROTO=none
   ONBOOT=yes
   MASTER=bond0
   SLAVE=yes
   USERCTL=no
   ```

3. After creating the appropriate configuration for the devices you want to put in slave mode, you'll need to create a configuration for the bond device itself. Typically, these devices will use names bond0, bond1, and so on, and the configuration file (which would be /etc/sysconfig/network-scripts/ifcfg-bond0 for bond device bond0) would appear as follows:

   ```
   DEVICE=bond0
   IPADDR=192.168.1.100
   PREFIX=24
   ONBOOT=yes
   BOOTPROTO=none
   USERCTL=no
   BONDING_OPTS="mode=1 miimon=100"
   ```

While most of the parameters in the `ifcfg-bond0` file should be clear, you can see that there are also a few bonding options included. First there is the bonding mode, which is set to mode `1` in this example. `mode 1` is the active-backup configuration in which only one interface is active at a time, and the other interface takes over in case it fails. Other popular modes include mode `0` (balance-rr) where frames are transmitted in round-robin fashion across interfaces, and mode `3`, where packets are broadcast to all interfaces at all times. Another bonding option is `miimon`, the monitoring interval that is specified in milliseconds. In this example, the interface is monitored every 100 milliseconds. If that causes problems on your network, you might consider setting it lower; for example, to 50 milliseconds to make sure that the bond device reacts faster if a physical connection drops.

4. After creating the configuration for the bond device, you'll need to make sure that the bonding kernel module is loaded. To do this, create a file with the name `/etc/modprobe.d/bonding.conf`, and put in the line `alias bond0 bonding`.

After performing all of these steps, your bond device is ready for use. Restart the network, and use the `ip a` command to verify that it is indeed available.

Setting Up Shared Storage

Now that you've set up bonding, you're ready to take the next step, which is to set up the shared storage. In this section, you'll learn how to set up a software-based iSCSI SAN. You will set up a central SAN machine that is configured to offer shared storage to the other nodes. This machine is referred to as the *iSCSI target*.

Next you'll connect the two other nodes in your lab to communicate with the iSCSI target. To accomplish this, you'll need to set them up as the iSCSI initiator. After successfully connecting the iSCSI initiator to the iSCSI target, you will see additional disk devices on the cluster nodes. These disk devices exist on the iSCSI target and not on the iSCSI initiators. For that reason, everything you write to these disk devices is also accessible by the other node.

When creating services later in this chapter, you will set up a file system resource that is managed by the cluster. This file system resource will be running on one of the nodes, and if that node experiences a problem, it will fail over to the other node to ensure that, even after a failure, the file system is still accessible. Figure 20.2 gives an overview of an iSCSI configuration.

Setting Up the iSCSI Target

To set up an iSCSI target, you'll need a few things. First you'll need something to share. This can be any storage device, such as a complete disk, an LVM logical volume, a partition, or a sparse file. In Exercise 20.2, first you will create an LVM volume to use as a shared storage device.

After taking care of the shared storage, you'll need to install and configure the iSCSI target process. This means you'll have to install the software, after which you can create a configuration in the file /etc/tgt/targets.conf. You will execute all of these steps and learn how to do this in the exercise.

FIGURE 20.2   iSCSI configuration overview

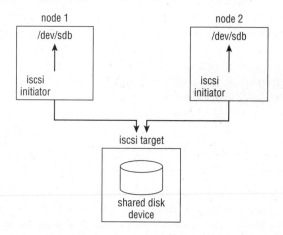

EXERCISE 20.2

Creating an iSCSI Target Configuration

In this exercise, you'll create an LVM device as a shared storage device. Next, you will install the scsi-target-utils package and create the /etc/tgt/targets.conf file that exports the shared storage device. Execute all steps that are described in this exercise on the san node.

If you don't have available disk space to create a new LVM volume, as an alternative you can configure a USB flash drive as the iSCSI target device.

1. Use the command **vgs** to verify that you still have unallocated storage in your volume group.

2. After verifying that you have unallocated storage, use **lvcreate -n iscsivol -L 10G /dev/yourvgname**. In this example, you'll create a 10GB volume, which is ideal. If you don't have that much storage available, try to allocate at least 1GB of storage to the volume. Use **lvs** to verify that the volume has been created.

3. Use **yum install -y scsi-target-utils** to install the iSCSI target software.

4. Open the file /etc/tgt/targets.conf. This file contains some sample iSCSI target configurations. Each configuration consists of a unique name for the target (the so-called iqn name) and a specification of what exactly to share. Add the example configuration lines to the end of the targets.conf file, and make sure you replace

the name of the volume group and logical volume to match the names of the volume group and logical volume you are using:

```
<target iqn.2012-12.com.example.san:mytarget>
    backing-store /dev/myvolumegroup/iscsivol
</target>
```

5. Use **service tgtd start** to start the iSCSI target software. Once you've done that, run **chkconfig tgtd on** to enable the iSCSI target.

Setting Up the iSCSI Initiator

At this point, your iSCSI target is ready for use. Now it's time to create the iSCSI initiator configuration. You can think of the iSCSI initiator as an SCSI controller. The only difference between an iSCSI SCSI controller and a regular SCSI controller is that in an iSCSI controller, you're using a network cable instead of a SCSI flat cable. In an iSCSI controller, IP packets are used to send the SCSI commands to the iSCSI target.

Before establishing a connection with the iSCSI initiator, your nodes will show local disk devices only. Once the iSCSI connection has been established, you'll also see the iSCSI disk devices. In Exercise 20.3, you will use the lsscsi command to see this.

To create the iSCSI connections, you'll use the iscsiadm command. This command stores its configuration in a database, not in a text file. For that reason, you need to use the iscsiadm command for everything you want to do with your iSCSI connections. First, you'll have to discover the LUNs that are offered by a specific target. Next, you'll need to log in to the target and, in case you don't need the iSCSI connection anymore, you'll need to log out. If you don't log out from an iSCSI connection, it will be reestablished every time the iSCSI initiator process is started.

To manage connections to an iSCSI SAN, you'll need four different iSCSI commands.

iscsiadm --mode discoverydb --type sendtargets --portal 192.168.1.70 --discover   This command connects to the IP address that is specified with the --portal option and discovers all iSCSI targets and LUNS offered by the targets that are available. See Listing 20.1 for an example of its output.

Listing 20.1: Discovering iSCSI targets

```
[root@node2 ~]# iscsiadm --mode discoverydb --type sendtargets --portal
192.168.1.70 --discover
Starting iscsid:                                          [  OK  ]
192.168.1.70:3260,1 iqn.2012-8.com.example.san:mytarget

[root@node2 ~]#
```

iscsiadm --mode node --targetname iqn.2012-8.com.example.san:mytarget --portal 192.168.1.70 --login   This command uses the target name that was discovered with the previous command to make a connection to the iSCSI target. In Listing 20.2, you can see the results of this command.

Listing 20.2: Connecting to an iSCSI target

```
[root@node2 ~]# iscsiadm --mode node --targetname iqn.2012-8.com.example
.san:mytarget --portal 192.168.1.70 --login
Logging in to [iface: default, target: iqn.2012-8.com.example.san:mytarget,
portal: 192.168.1.70,3260] (multiple)
Login to [iface: default, target: iqn.2012-8.com.example.san:mytarget,
portal: 192.168.1.70,3260] successful.

[root@node2 ~]#
```

iscsiadm --mode node --targetname iqn.2012-8.com.example.san:mytarget --portal 192.168.1.70 -logout This command logs you out from a currently connected target. After restarting the iSCSI initiator software, the connection will be restored because it is still in the database.

iscsiadm --mode node --targetname iqn.2012-8.com.example.san:mytarget --portal 192.168.1.70 --delete Use this command to delete a current connection. After restarting the iSCSI initiator, the connection won't be reestablished because the configuration that was created before is now deleted from the server.

After connecting to an iSCSI target, you can request current status parameters about the connection. To do this, use one of the following commands:

iscsiadm --mode discoverydb Shows information about the targets that have been discovered

iscsiadm --mode node Shows which targets this node is configured to connect to

iscsiadm --mode session Shows all sessions that are currently existing

In Exercise 20.3, you will connect the servers that you want to use as nodes in the cluster to the iSCSI target you created in Exercise 20.2.

EXERCISE 20.3

Connecting to an iSCSI Target

In this exercise, you'll connect all cluster nodes to the storage using the iscsiadm commands you just learned. Make sure to execute the following steps on all computers that will be connected to the cluster.

1. Use **yum install iscsi-initiator-utils** to install the iSCSI initiator on all nodes.

2. Use **iscsiadm --mode discoverydb --type sendtargets --portal 192.168.1.70** to get a list of targets that are available on that IP address. Notice the exact name of the target, because you'll need it for the next step. Also make sure to replace the IP address used in the example by the IP address that your iSCSI target is actually using.

3. Using the name of the target that you just discovered, log in to it using the following command: **iscsiadm --mode node --targetname iqn.2012-8.com .example.san:mytarget --portal 192.168.1.70 --login**.

4. Use **yum -y install lsscsi** to install the lsscsi package, and enter **lsscsi** to verify that you are connected to the target. You should see the iSCSI disk listed as disk type VIRTUAL-DISK.

```
[root@node2 ~]# lsscsi
[0:0:0:0]    disk     ATA      WDC WD2500BEKT-7 01.0   /dev/sda
[1:0:0:0]    cd/dvd   TEAC     DVD-ROM DV-28SW  3.2C   /dev/sr0
[6:0:0:0]    storage  IET      Controller       0001   -
[6:0:0:1]    disk     IET      VIRTUAL-DISK     0001   /dev/sdb
```

5. Reboot the nodes, and ensure that the iSCSI target connection comes up after the reboot.

If all goes well, you'll have two working iSCSI target connections at this point. In some cases, it may refuse to come up after a restart. If that happens, use the following checklist for troubleshooting:

- Is the tgtd process in the runlevels on the iSCSI target?
- Is port 3260 open in the firewall?
- Is the iSCSI initiator process started automatically on the nodes?

Now that you've set up the iSCSI configuration and you know how to set up bonding, it's time to move ahead and start the installation of the cluster itself.

Installing the Red Hat High Availability Add-on

Once you've set up all of the base requirements, you're just about ready to start the installation of the Red Hat High Availability add-on on the two nodes. Before you start doing that, however, there's one more thing you need to address: all nodes should be able to reach each other by name. This means you have to create entries in DNS or create an /etc/hosts file and distribute it among the nodes. Follow the steps in Exercise 20.4 to make sure that all the hosts recognize each other.

Creating an /etc/hosts File

Creating an /etc/hosts file so that all hosts in the cluster are capable of resolving each other by name is an essential part of the cluster setup. Without proper name resolution, your cluster setup will assuredly fail.

This exercise helps you create the /etc/hosts file and distribute it to all servers in the cluster. Make sure that both the names and IP addresses match the setup you are using.

1. On one of the nodes, create an /etc/hosts file with the following contents:

    ```
    192.168.1.70   san.example.com     san
    192.168.1.80   node1.example.com   node1
    192.168.1.90   node2.example.com   node2
    ```

2. Use scp to copy the file to all other nodes in the cluster. This means you'll typically have to execute a line as shown in the following example twice:

    ```
    scp /etc/hosts 192.168.1.80:/etc
    ```

After copying the /etc/hosts file, you're ready to start setting up the cluster. To do this, you'll use Conga. Conga consists of ricci, an agent that runs on all nodes in the cluster, and luci, the management platform that should be available somewhere but not necessarily in the cluster. By using these components, you'll generate a file with the name /etc/cluster /cluster.conf and distribute it to all nodes. You can also create and manage this file manually. To make it easy to get started, however, you'll first set up the cluster using Conga. Exercise 20.5 describes exactly what you need to do to create the cluster.

Building the Initial State of the Cluster

Before starting to create the cluster, you should consider multicasting. By default, the Red Hat High Availability add-on uses network multicasting, and this means it has to be supported on all nodes in the cluster, including switches. Therefore, make sure both IGMP and multicasting are enabled on the switch. If for some reason this is not possible, you can use UDP Unicast as an alternative. (Note: this works only on RHEL 6.2 and newer.) It is still recommended to use multicasting, however. If you need to use unicasting, after creating the base cluster, add the following parameter to cluster.conf:

```
cman transport="udpu"
```

You can set this parameter manually and also from the network configuration section in the luci management interface.

Creating a Cluster with Conga

In this exercise, you'll walk through the steps that are needed to set up a cluster with Conga. Read carefully where to perform these steps, because some have to be executed on each cluster node, while others have to be executed on one cluster node only.

1. The cluster cannot run if you have NetworkManager enabled or if it is running. Therefore, before doing anything else, use **service NetworkManager stop** and **chkconfig NetworkManager off** on all nodes.

2. On all nodes, use **yum install -y ricci** to install ricci. If you get an error message claiming that ricci is already installed, you can safely ignore it. Next, use **service ricci start** to start the service, and use **chkconfig ricci on** to make sure that it is started when rebooting on all nodes. Finally, again on all nodes, use **passwd ricci** to set a password for the user *ricci* and set the password to *password*.

3. In this chapter, you'll use the SAN node to host luci. Use **yum install luci** to install it. Then start luci using the **service luci start** command. While starting luci for the first time, a public/private key pair is generated and installed. The name of this certificate is /var/lib/luci/certs/hosts.pem, and it is referred to in the configuration file /var/lib/luci/etc/cacert.config. If you want to replace these certificates with certificates that are signed by an external CA, you can just copy the host certificate to the /var/lib/luci/certs directory. After generating the certificates, luci will start and offer its services on HTTPS port 8084.

4. Launch a browser, and connect to https://yourserver:8084 to get access to the luci management interface. You can safely ignore the certificate warning that is displayed. From the login page, log in using your root credentials. You'll now get access to the luci home page.

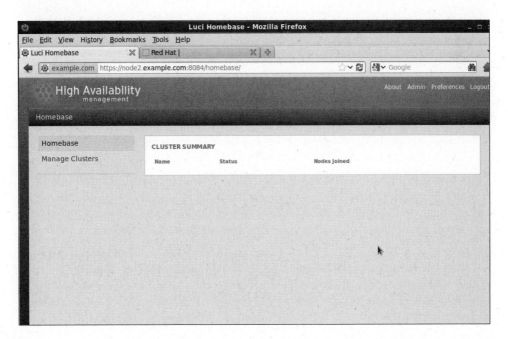

5.   After logging in to Luci, you need to create a cluster. Click Manage Cluster, and then click the Create button. This opens the Create New Cluster interface.

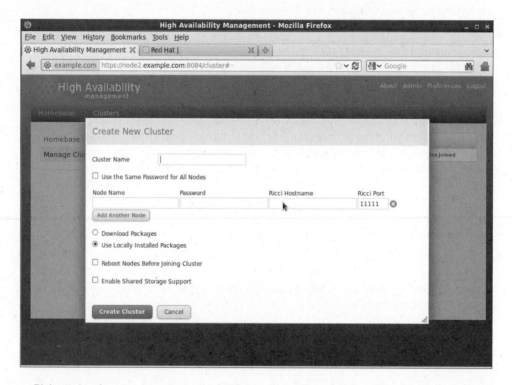

Pick a name for your new cluster in the Create New Cluster dialog. The name cannot be longer than 15 characters, and it cannot be called *cluster*. Next, you need to specify the nodes that you want to add to the cluster. The password to which the dialog refers is the ricci password, which is probably the same on all nodes. The node name is the normal node name of the cluster. If your cluster is configured to use a dedicated network for cluster traffic, use the name of the host on that specific network as the Ricci hostname.

By default, you'll see one line to add nodes only. For each node you want to add, click Add Another Node, and specify the name and Ricci password of that node. If you want the cluster nodes to download all updates for cluster packages, select Download Packages. If you don't, you can just leave the default Use Locally Installed Packages option selected. In both cases, required software will be installed.

The option Reboot Nodes Before Joining Cluster isn't really necessary. However, by selecting it, you'll ensure that the nodes are capable of booting with cluster support. If you're planning to use a cluster-aware file system like GFS, you should also select Enable Shared Storage Support to make sure the packages you'll need for that are installed.

EXERCISE 20.5 *(continued)*

After entering all parameters, click Create Cluster to start the cluster creation. It will take a while for this procedure to complete. Once it finishes, you'll see that the cluster has been created successfully and that all nodes have been able to join the cluster.

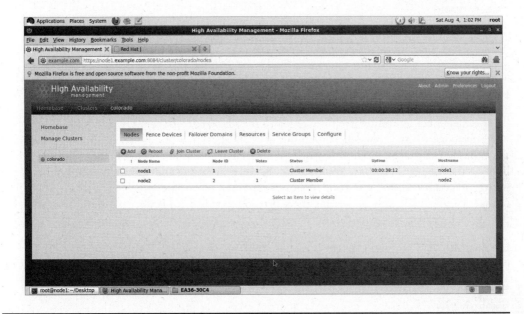

Normally, you should now have a cluster. It often happens that something went wrong, and the cluster refuses to start correctly. If that's the case, take a look at the following checklist to see whether that can help you fix your problems:

- Make sure that the nodes in the cluster can recognize each other by name.

- Reboot both nodes after they've joined the cluster.

- Stop the firewall to ensure it doesn't block any cluster traffic.

- Make sure that at least the ricci and cman services are running and enabled in your runlevels. The cman service is responsible for starting many elements of the cluster, including corosync.

- Check /var/log/cluster/corosync.log for additional messages.

At this point, your cluster should be operational. You can verify this from the luci management interface or by using the clustat command as root from a terminal (see Listing 20.3). This command should show you that all nodes in the cluster are up and available and that the cluster has *quorum*, which means that the majority of nodes are available and the cluster is ready to start offering services to the network.

Listing 20.3: Use clustat to verify the current state of the cluster

```
[root@node1 ~]# clustat
Cluster Status for colorado @ Fri Aug  3 20:58:15 2012
Member Status: Quorate

 Member Name                             ID   Status
 ------ ----                             ---- ------
 node1                                    1 Online, Local
 node2                                    2 Online

[root@node1 ~]#
```

The cluster configuration itself is written to the file /etc/cluster/cluster.conf. This XML file contains the complete configuration of the cluster, and it is synchronized between the nodes in the cluster. At the moment, it is still small, because nothing but the nodes have been configured thus far. You'll notice, however, that the configuration you create is written to cluster.conf. It is good habit to keep track of this file, especially because some changes can be made only by writing them directly to this file. Listing 20.4 shows you what the file looks like in its current state.

Listing 20.4: The /etc/cluster/cluster.conf file contains the configuration of the cluster

```
[root@node1 ~]# cat /etc/cluster/cluster.conf
<?xml version="1.0"?>
<cluster config_version="1" name="colorado">
        <clusternodes>
                <clusternode name="node1" nodeid="1"/>
                <clusternode name="node2" nodeid="2"/>
        </clusternodes>
        <cman expected_votes="1" two_node="1"/>
        <fencedevices/>
        <rm/>
</cluster>
```

Configuring Additional Cluster Properties

Now that you've created the initial state of the cluster, it's time to fine-tune it a bit. To do this, from the Homebase ➢ Clusters interface in luci, select your cluster and click Configure. You'll see six tabs where you can specify all generic properties of the cluster (see Figure 20.3).

FIGURE 20.3   Click Configure to specify the cluster properties you want to use.

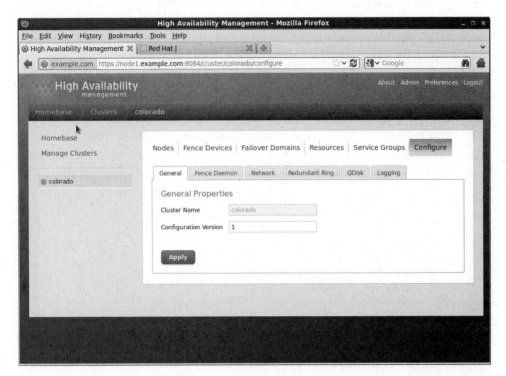

On the General tab, you'll see the Cluster Name and Configuration Version fields. The configuration version number is updated automatically every time the cluster is changed in Conga. If you've manually changed the cluster.conf file, you can increase it from here so that the changes can be synchronized to other nodes.

If your network does not offer multicast services, you can set the Network Transport Type option on the Network tab. The default selection is UDP Multicast, with an automatic selection of the multicast address. If required, you can elect to specify the multicast address manually or to use UDP Unicast, which is easier for many switches (see Figure 20.4). Remember to click the Apply button to write the modification to the cluster.

On the Redundant Ring tab (see Figure 20.5), you can specify an additional interface on which to send cluster packets. You'll need a second network interface to do this. To specify the interface you want to use, select the alternate name. This is an alternative node name that is assigned only to the IP address that is on the backup network. This way, the cluster knows automatically where to send this redundant traffic. Of course, you must make sure that this alternate name resolves to the IP address that the node uses to connect to the backup network. Tune DNS or /etc/hosts accordingly.

The last generic option that you can specify here is Logging. Use the options on this tab to specify to where log messages need to be written. The options on this tab allow you to specify exactly which file the cluster should log to and what kind of messages are logged. It also offers an option to create additional configurations for specific daemons.

FIGURE 20.4 Select UDP Unicast if your network does not support multicasting.

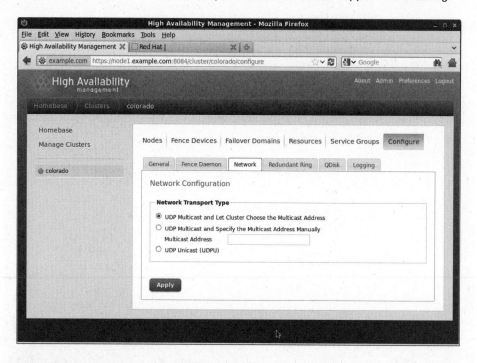

FIGURE 20.5 Specifying a redundant ring

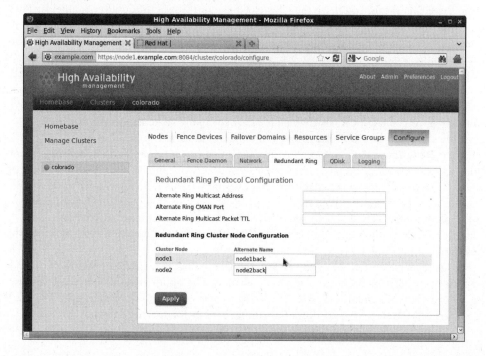

Configuring a Quorum Disk

As you have learned, quorum is an important mechanism in the cluster that helps nodes determine whether they are part of the majority of the cluster. By default, every node has one vote, and if a node sees at least half of the nodes plus one, then there is quorum. An exception exists for two-node clusters, where the <cman two_node="1"> parameter is set in /etc/cluster /cluster.conf to indicate that it is a two-node cluster in which the quorum rules are different because otherwise the cluster could never have quorum if one of the nodes is down.

Particularly in a two-node cluster but also in other clusters that have an even number of nodes, a situation of a *split brain* can arise. That is a condition where two parts of the cluster, which have an equal amount of cluster votes, can no longer reach one another. This would mean that the services could not run anywhere. To prevent situations such as this, using a quorum disk can be useful.

A *quorum disk* involves two parts. First you'll need a shared storage device that can be accessed by all nodes in the cluster. Then you'll need heuristics testing. *Heuristics* testing consists of at least one test that a node has to perform successfully before it can connect to the quorum disk.

If a situation of split brain arises, the nodes will all poll the quorum disk. If they're capable of performing the heuristics test, the node can count an extra vote toward its quorum. If the heuristics test cannot be executed successfully, the node will not have access to the vote offered by the quorum disk, and it will therefore lose quorum and know that it has to be terminated.

To set up a quorum disk, you have to perform these steps:

1. Create a partition on the shared disk device.

2. Use mkqdisk to mark this partition as a quorum disk.

3. Specify the heuristics to use in the Conga management interface.

In Exercise 20.6, you'll perform these steps.

EXERCISE 20.6

Creating a Quorum Disk

In this exercise, you'll set up your cluster to use a quorum disk. Access to the shared iSCSI device is needed in order to perform this exercise.

1. On one cluster node, use **fdisk** to create a partition on the iSCSI device. It doesn't need to be big—100MB is sufficient.

2. On the other cluster node, use the **partx -a** command to update the partition table. Now check /proc/partitions on both nodes to verify that the partition on the iSCSI disk has been created.

3. On one of the nodes, use the following command to create the quorum disk: **mkqdisk -c /dev/sdb1 -l quorumdisk**. Before typing this command, make sure to double-check the name of the device you are using.

4. On the other node, use **mkqdisk -L** to show all quorum disks. You should see the quorum disk with the label quorumdisk that you just created.

EXERCISE 20.6 *(continued)*

5. In Conga, open the Configuration ➢ QDisk tab. On this tab, select the option Use A Quorum Disk. Then you need to specify the device you want to use. The best way to refer to the device is by using the label that you created when you used `mkqdisk` to format the quorum disk. That would be `quorumdisk` in this case.

Next, you'll need to specify the heuristics. This is a little test that a node must perform to get access to the vote of the quorum disk. In this example, you'll use a `ping` command that pings the default gateway. So, in the Path to Program field, enter **`ping -c 1 192.168.1.70`**. The interval specifies how often the test should be executed. Five seconds is a good value to start with. The score specifies what result this test yields if executed successfully. If you connect several different heuristics tests to a quorum disk, you can work with different scores. In the case of this example, however, that wouldn't make much sense, so you can use score 1.

The TKO is the time to knock out, which specifies the tolerance for the quorum test. Set it to 12 seconds, which means that a node can fail the heuristics test no more than two times.

The last parameter is Minimum Total Score. This is the score that a node can add when it is capable of executing the heuristics properly. Click Apply to save and use these values.

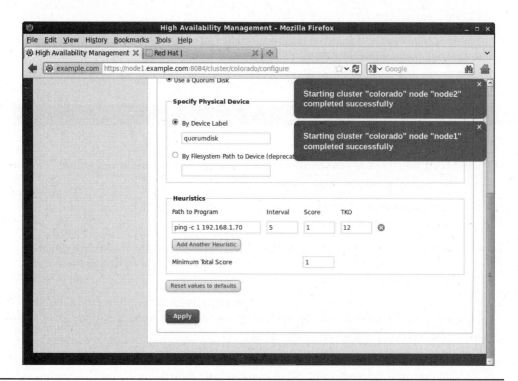

After creating the quorum device, you can use the `cman_tool status` command to verify that it works as expected (see Listing 20.5). Look at the number of nodes (which is set to 2) and the number of expected nodes (which is set to 3). The reason for this can be found in the quorum device votes, which as you can see is set to 1. This means that the quorum device is working, and you're ready to move on to the next step.

Listing 20.5: Use `cman_tool status` to verify the working of the quorum device

```
[root@node1 ~]# cman_tool status
Version: 6.2.0
Config Version: 2
Cluster Name: colorado
Cluster Id: 17154
Cluster Member: Yes
Cluster Generation: 320
Membership state: Cluster-Member
Nodes: 2
Expected votes: 3
Quorum device votes: 1
Total votes: 3
Node votes: 1
Quorum: 2
Active subsystems: 11
Flags:
Ports Bound: 0 11 177 178
Node name: node1
Node ID: 1
Multicast addresses: 239.192.67.69
Node addresses: 192.168.1.80
```

Setting Up Fencing

After setting up a quorum disk, you'll need to address fencing. *Fencing* is what you need to maintain the integrity of the cluster. If the Totem protocol packets sent out by Corosync can no longer reach another node, before taking over its services, you must make sure that the other node is really down. The best way to achieve this is by using hardware fencing.

Hardware fencing means that a hardware device is used to terminate a failing node. Typically, a power switch or integrated management card, such as HP ILO or Dell Drac, is used for this purpose.

To set up fencing, you need to perform two different steps. First you need to configure the fence devices, and then you associate the fence devices to the nodes in the network. To define the fence device, you open the Fence Devices tab in the Conga management interface. After clicking Add, you'll see a list of all available fence devices. A popular fence device type is IPMI LAN. This fence device can send instructions to many integrated management cards, including the HP ILO and Dell Drac.

After selecting the fence device, you need to define its properties. These properties are different for each fence device, but they commonly include a username, a password, and an IP address. After entering these parameters, you can submit the device to the configuration (see Figure 20.6).

FIGURE 20.6 Defining the fence device

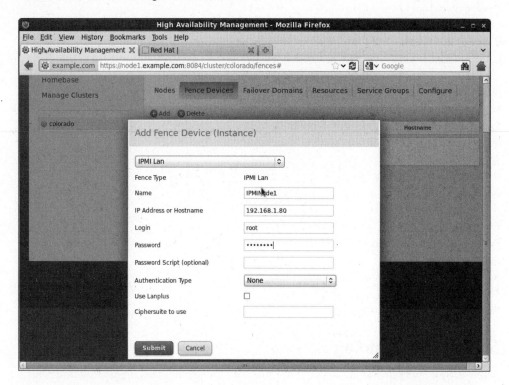

After defining the fence devices, you need to connect them to the nodes. From the top of the Luci management interface, click Nodes, and then select the node to which you want to add the fence device. Scroll down on the node properties screen, and click the Add Fence Method button (see Figure 20.7). Next, enter a name for the fence method you're using, and for each method, click Add Fence Instance to add the fence device you just created. Submit the configuration, and repeat this procedure for all the nodes in your cluster.

You just learned how to add a fence device to a node. For redundancy reasons, you can also add multiple fence devices to one node. The benefit is that this guarantees that, no matter what happens, there will always be one fence device that works, which can fence your nodes if anything goes wrong.

FIGURE 20.7   Adding fence devices to nodes

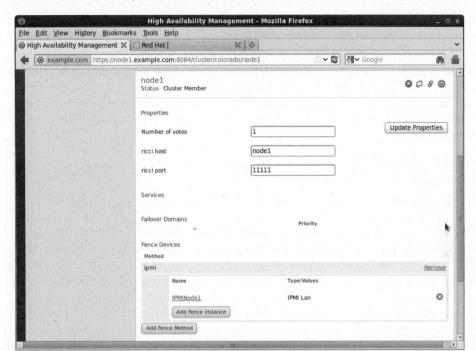

Real World Scenario

Alternative Solutions

It's good to have a quorum disk and fencing in your cluster. In some cases, however, the hardware just doesn't allow this. For a customer who had neither the hardware for fencing nor a shared disk device, I created a mixed fencing/quorum disk solution myself. The solution consisted of a script, which I called SMITH (Shoot Myself In The Head). The purpose of the script was to self-terminate once the connection had been lost to the rest of the network. The contents of this script were as follows:

```
DEFAULT_GATEWAY=192.168.1.1
while true
do sleep 5
      ping -c 1 $DEFAULT_GATEWAY || echo b > /proc/sysrq-trigger
done
```

As you can see, the script runs indefinitely. Every five seconds, it tries to ping the default gateway. (The goal is to ping a node that should be present at all times.) If the ping replies, that's good; if it fails, the command echo b > /proc/sysrq-trigger is used to self-fence the node in question.

Creating Resources and Services

At this point, the base cluster is ready for use. Now it is time to create the services that the cluster will offer. The Red Hat High Availability add-on supports many services, but in this chapter, you'll examine the Apache web server as an example. The purpose here is to design a solution where the Apache web server keeps running at all times.

When creating a high-availability solution for a service, you need to find out exactly what the service needs to continue its services. In the case of many services, this consists of three things:

- The service itself
- An IP address
- A location where the configuration file and data for the service are stored

To define a service in the cluster, you'll need to make sure that the cluster offers all of the required parts. In the case of an Apache web server that fails over, this means you first need to make sure the web server can be reached after it has failed over. Thus, you'll need a unique IP address for the Apache web server that fails over with it and that is activated before it is started.

Next, your web server probably needs access to its DocumentRoot, the data files that the web server offers to clients in the network. This means you'll need to make sure these data files are available on whatever physical node the web server is currently running. To accomplish this, you'll create a file system on the SAN and make sure that it is mounted on the node that runs the web server. Once these two conditions have been met, you can start running the web server itself.

Even with regard to the service itself, be mindful that it's a bit different from a stand-alone web server. For example, the service needs access to a configuration file, which has to be the same on all nodes where you want to run the service. To make sure that services can run smoothly in a cluster, Red Hat provides a number of service scripts. These scripts are in the directory /usr/share/cluster, and they are developed to make sure that specific services run well in a clustered environment. The services that have a corresponding script are available as resources in the Conga management interface. For everything that's not available by default, there is the /usr/share/cluster /script.sh script. This is a generic script that you can modify to run any service that you want in the cluster.

To create a service for Apache in the cluster, you start by adding the resources for the individual parts of the service. In the case of Apache, these are the IP address, the file system, and the Apache service itself. Once these resources have been created, you'll put them together in the service, which allows you to start running the service in the cluster. In Exercise 20.7, you'll learn how to create an Apache service for your cluster.

EXERCISE 20.7

Creating an HA Service for Apache

In this exercise, you'll create an HA service for Apache. First, you'll configure resources for the IP address, shared storage, and Apache itself, and then you'll group them together in the service.

1. In the Conga management interface, select Resources, and click Add. From the Resource Type drop-down list, select IP Address. You'll use this resource to add a unique IP address to the cluster, so make sure that the IP address you're using is not yet in use on the network. In the properties window that opens, enter the IP address and the number of bits to use in the network mask, and click Submit to write it to the cluster.

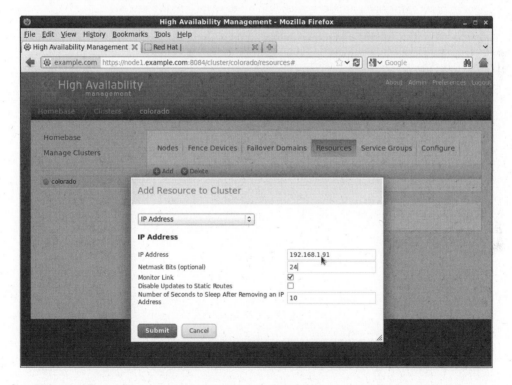

2. Before adding a file system as a resource to the cluster, you need to create it. Use fdisk on one of the cluster nodes to create a 500MB partition on the SAN device and format it as an Ext4 file system. Because this file system will be active on one node at a time only, there is no need to make it a clustered file system. On both nodes, use **partx -a /dev/sdb** to make the new partition known to the kernel. Use **mkfs.ext4 -L apachefs /dev/sdb2** to create a file system on the device. (Make sure to verify the name of the device. It might be different on your system.)

3. Next, from Conga, click Resources ➢ Add, and from the Resource Type drop-down list, select Filesystem. You first need to give the resource a name to make it easier to identify in the cluster. Use ApacheFS. Leave Filesystem Type set to Autodetect, and set the mount point to /var/www/html, the default location for the Apache document root. Next, you need to specify the device, FS label, or UUID. Because the name of the device can change, it is a good idea to use something persistent. That's why while you created the Ext4 file system, you added the file system label apachefs. Enter this label in the Device, FS Label, or UUID field. Everything else is optional, but it's a good idea to select the option Reboot Host If Unmount Fails. This ensures that the file system resource will be available at all times if it needs to be migrated. After entering all of these parameters, click Submit to write it to the cluster.

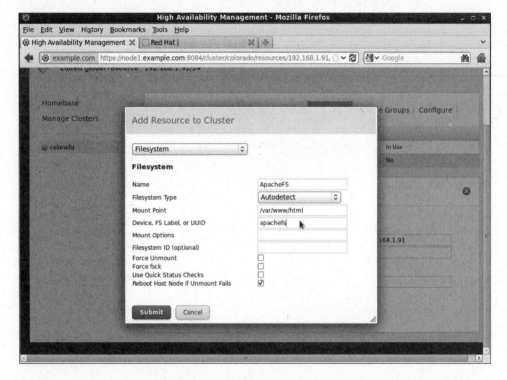

4. At this point, you can create the resource for the Apache web server. From the Conga management interface, select Resources, click Add, and select the resource type Apache. The only thing you need to do is give it a unique name; the server root and config file are already set up in a way that will work. Note that although these parameters are typically in the Apache configuration itself, they are now managed by the cluster. This is done to make it easier for you to specify an alternative location for the Apache configuration—that is, a location that is on a shared file system in your cluster. After verifying that everything is set correctly, click Submit to write the configuration to disk.

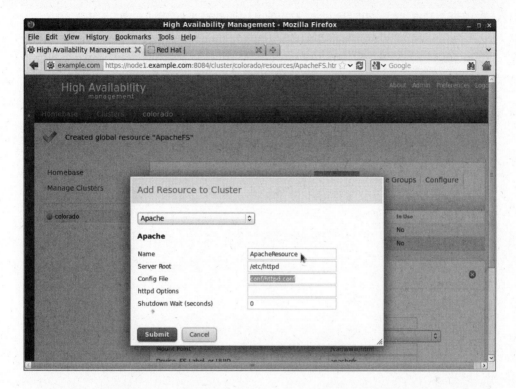

5. You now have created all resources you need. Now it's time to add them to a service group. From the Conga management interface, click Service Group ➤ Add to add a new service group to the cluster. Give it a name (Apache makes sense in this case), and select the option to start the service automatically. You can leave the other service group parameters as they are, but you need to add resources.

    Click Add Resource, and select the IP address resource you created earlier. You'll notice that the resource and all of its properties are now included in the service group. Next you need to enter the file system resource. To do this, click Add Resource again and select the File system resource. (An alternative approach would be to select Add Child Resource, which allows you to create a dependency between resources. This means the child resource will never be started if the parent resource is not available. In the case of the Apache service group, this isn't really necessary.) Add the Apache resource, and then click Submit to write the configuration to the cluster. You're now back at the top of the Service Groups screen where you can see the properties of the service group. Verify that everything appears as you would expect it to be.

6. Select the service group, and click Start to start it.

EXERCISE 20.7 *(continued)*

7. Be aware that the Conga status information isn't always correct. Use clustat on both nodes to find out the status of your cluster service.

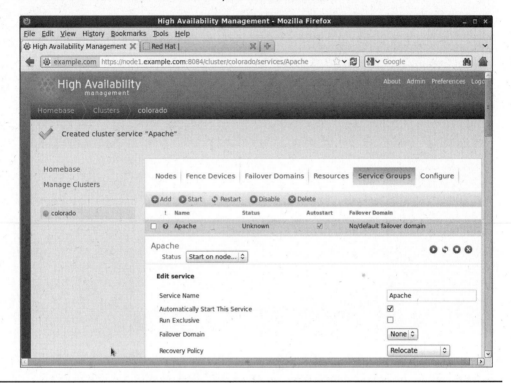

Troubleshooting a Nonoperational Cluster

At this point, everything should be running smoothly. The fact is that, in some cases, it won't. Setting up a cluster involves connecting many components in the right way, and a small mistake may have huge consequences. If you don't succeed in getting the service operational, apply the following tips to try to get it working:

▪ Check the log files. The cluster writes many logs to /var/log/cluster, and one of them may contain a valuable hint as to why the service isn't working. In particular, make sure to check /var/log/cluster/rgmanager.log.

▪ Don't perform your checks from the Conga interface only, because the information it gives may be faulty. Also, use clustat on both nodes to check the current service status, and verify that individual components have actually been started or not.

▪ From the Conga interface, disable the resource and try to activate everything manually. That is, use ip a a to add the IP address. Use mount to mount the file system, and use service `httpd start` to start the Apache service. This will probably allow you to narrow down the scope of the problem to one particular resource.

- If you have a problem with the file system resource, make sure to use /dev/disk naming, instead of device names like /dev/sdb2, which can change if something changes to the storage topology.

- If a service appears as disabled in both Conga and in clustat, use clusvcadm -e servicename to enable it. It may also help to relocate the service to another node. Use clusvcadm -r servicename -m nodename to relocate a service.

- Don't use the service command on local nodes to verify whether services are running. (You haven't started them from the runlevels, so the service command won't work.) Use ps aux and grep for the process you are seeking.

Configuring GFS2 File Systems

You now have a working cluster and a service running within it. You used an Ext4 file system in this service. Ext4 is fine for services that fail over between nodes. If multiple nodes in the cluster need access to the same file system at the same time, you'll need a cluster file system. Red Hat offers the *Global File System 2 (GFS2)* as the default cluster file system. Using GFS2 lets you to write to the same file system from multiple nodes at the same time.

To use GFS2, you need to have a running cluster. Once you have that, you'll need to install the cluster version of LVM2 and make sure that the accompanying service is started on all nodes that are going to run the GFS2 file system. Next, you will make a cluster-aware LVM2 volume and create the GFS2 file system on it. Once created, you can mount the GFS file system from /etc/fstab on the affected nodes or create a cluster resource that mounts it automatically for you. In Exercise 20.8, you'll learn how to set up the GFS file system in your cluster.

EXERCISE 20.8

Creating a GFS File System

In this exercise, you'll create a GFS file system. To do this, you'll enable cluster LVM, create the file system, and, on top of that, create the GFS file system that will be mounted from fstab.

1. On one of the nodes, use fdisk to create a partition on the SAN device, and make sure to mark it as partition type 0x8e. Reboot both nodes to make sure the partitions are visible on both nodes, and verify this is the case before continuing.

2. On both nodes, use **yum install -y lvm2-cluster gfs2-utils** to install cLVM and the GFS software.

3. On both nodes, use **service clvmd start** to start the cLVM service and **chkconfig clvmd on** to enable it.

4. On one node, use **pvcreate /dev/sdb3** to mark the LVM partition on the SAN device as a physical volume. Before doing this, however, verify that the name of the partition is correct.

5. Use **vgcreate -c y clusgroup /dev/sdb3** to create a cluster-enabled volume group.

6. Use **lvcreate -l 100%FREE -n clusvol clusgroup** to create a cluster-enabled volume with the name clusvol.

7. On both nodes, use **lvs** to verify that the cluster-enabled LVM volume has been created.

8. Use **mkfs.gfs2 -p lock_dlm -t name_of_your_cluster:gfs -j 2 /dev /clusgroup/clusvol**. This will format the clustered LVM volume as a GFS2 file system. The -p option tells mkfs to use the lock_dlm lock table. This instructs the file system to use a distributed lock manager so that file locks are synchronized to all nodes in the cluster. The option -t is equally important, because it specifies the name of your cluster, followed by the name of the GFS resource you want to create in the cluster. The option -j 2 tells mkfs to create two GFS journals; you'll need one for each node that accesses the GFS volume.

9. On both nodes, mount the GFS2 file system temporarily on /mnt, using mount /dev /clusgroup/clusvol /mnt. On both nodes, create some files on the file system. You'll notice that the files also appear immediately on the other nodes.

10. Use **mkdir /gfsvol** to create a directory on which you can mount the GFS volume.

11. Make the mount persistent by adding the following line to /etc/fstab:

    /dev/clusgroup/clusvol   /gfsvol   gfs2   _netdev 0 0

12. Use **chkconfig gfs2 on** to enable the GFS2 service, which is needed to mount GFS2 volumes from /etc/fstab.

13. Reboot both nodes to verify that the GFS file system is mounted automatically.

Summary

In this chapter, you learned how to create a high-availability cluster using the Red Hat High Availability add-on. After reading about the base requirements to set up a cluster, you created a two-node cluster that uses iSCSI as a shared disk device. You learned how to set up cluster essentials, such as a quorum disk and fencing, and you created a service for Apache, which ensures that the cluster ensures that your Apache process will always be running. Finally, you learned how to set up cLVM and GFS2 to use the GFS2 cluster-aware file system in your cluster.

Chapter

21

Setting Up an Installation Server

TOPICS COVERED IN THIS CHAPTER:

✓ Configuring a Network Server As an Installation Server

✓ Setting Up a TFTP and DHCP Server for PXE Boot

✓ Creating a Kickstart File

In this chapter, you'll learn how to set up an installation server. This is useful if you need to install several instances of Red Hat Enterprise Linux. By using an installation server, you can avoid installing every physical server individually from the installation DVD. Also, it allows you to install servers that don't have optical drives, such as blade servers.

Setting up an installation server involves several steps. To begin, you need to make the installation files available. To do this, you'll configure a network server. This can be an NFS, FTP, or HTTP server. Next, you'll need to set up PXE boot, which provides a boot image to your client by working together with the DHCP server.

The last step in setting up a completely automated installation is to create a kickstart file. This is an answer file that contains all the settings that are needed to install your server.

Configuring a Network Server As an Installation Server

The first step in setting up an installation server is to configure a network server as an installation server. This involves copying the entire installation DVD to a share on a network server. After doing this, you can use a client computer to access the installation files. In Exercise 21.1, you'll set up a network installation server. After setting it up, you'll test it. For now, the test is quite simple: you'll boot the server from the installation DVD and refer to the network path for installation. Once the entire installation server has been completely set up, the procedure will become much more sophisticated, because the TFTP server will provide a boot image. Because there is no TFTP server yet, you'll have to use the installation DVD instead.

EXERCISE 21.1

Setting Up the Network Installation Server

In this exercise, you'll set up the network installation server by copying over all the files required for installation to a directory that is offered by an HTTP server. After doing this, you'll test the installation from a virtual machine. To perform this exercise, you need the server1.example.com virtual Apache web server you created in Exercise 16.3 of this book.

1. Insert the Red Hat Enterprise Linux installation DVD in the optical drive of your server.

2. Use `mkdir /www/docs/server1.example.com/install` to create a subdirectory in the Apache document root for server1.example.com.

3. Use **cp -R * /www/docs/server1.example.com/install** from the directory where the Red Hat Enterprise Linux installation DVD is mounted to copy all of the files on the DVD to the install directory in your web server document root.

4. Modify the configuration file for the server1 virtual host in /etc/httpd/conf.d/ server1.example.com, and make sure that it includes the line Options Indexes. Without this line, the virtual host will show the contents of a directory only if it contains an index.html file.

5. Use **service httpd restart** to restart the Apache web server.

6. Start a browser, and browse to http://server1.example.com/install. You should now see the contents of the installation DVD.

7. Start Virtual Machine Manager, and create a new virtual machine. Give the virtual machine the name testnetinstall, and select Network Install when asked how to install the operating system.

8. When asked for the installation URL, enter **http://server1.example.com/install**. The installation should now be started.

9. You may now interrupt the installation procedure and remove the virtual machine. You have seen that the installation server is operational. It's time to move on to the next phase in the procedure.

Setting Up a TFTP and DHCP Server for PXE Boot

Now that you've set up a network installation server, it's time to configure PXE boot. This allows you to boot a server you want to install from the network card of the server. (You normally have to change default boot order, or press a key while booting, to activate PXE boot). The PXE server then hands out a boot image, which the server you want to install uses to start the initial phase of the boot.

Two steps are involved:

1.   You need to install a TFTP server and have it provide a boot image to PXE clients.

2.   You need to configure DHCP to talk to the TFTP server to provide the boot image to PXE clients.

Installing the TFTP Server

The first part of the installation is easy: you need to install the TFTP server package using yum -y install tftp-server. TFTP is managed by the xinetd service, and to tell xinetd that it should allow access to TFTP, you need to open the /etc/xinetd.d/tftp file and change the disabled parameter from Yes to No (see Listing 21.1). Next, restart the xinetd service using service xinetd restart. Also make sure to include xinetd in your start-up procedure, using chkconfig tftp on.

Listing 21.1: The xinetd file for TFTP

```
 [root@hnl ~]# cat /etc/xinetd.d/tftp
# default: off
# description: The tftp server serves files using the trivial file transfer \
#        protocol.  The tftp protocol is often used to boot diskless \
#        workstations, download configuration files to network-aware printers, \
#        and to start the installation process for some operating systems.
service tftp
{
        socket_type             = dgram
        protocol                = udp
        wait                    = yes
        user                    = root
        server                  = /usr/sbin/in.tftpd
        server_args             = -s /var/lib/tftpboot
        disable                 = yes
        per_source              = 11
        cps                     = 100 2
        flags                   = IPv4
}
```

At this point, the TFTP server is operational. Now you'll have to configure DHCP to communicate with the TFTP server to hand out a boot image to PXE clients.

Configuring DHCP for PXE Boot

Now you'll have to modify the DHCP server configuration so that it can hand out a boot image to PXE clients. To do this, make sure to include the boot lines in Listing 21.2 in your dhcpd.conf file, and restart the DHCP server.

Listing 21.2: Adding PXE boot lines to the dhcpd.conf file

```
option space pxelinux;
option pxelinux.magic code 208 = string;
option pxelinux.configfile code 209 = text;
option pxelinux.pathprefix code 210 = text;
option pxelinux.reboottime code 211 = unsigned integer 32 ;

subnet 192.168.1.0 netmask 255.255.255.0 {
        option routers 192.168.1.1 ;
        range 192.168.1.200 192.168.1.250 ;

        class "pxeclients" {
                match if substring (option vendor-class-identifier, 0, 9) =
"PXEClient";
                next-server 192.168.1.70;
                filename "pxelinux/pxelinux.0";
        }
}
```

The most important part of the example configuration in Listing 21.2 is where the class pxeclients is defined. The match line ensures that all servers that are performing a PXE boot are recognized automatically. This is done to avoid problems and to have DHCP hand out the PXE boot image only to servers that truly want to do a PXE boot. Next, the next-server statement refers to the IP address of the server that hands out the boot image. This is the server that runs the TFTP server. Finally, a file is handed out. In the next section, you'll learn how to provide the right file in the right location.

Creating the TFTP PXE Server Content

The role of the PXE server is to deliver an image to the client that performs a PXE boot. In fact, it replaces the task that is normally performed by GRUB and the contents of the boot directory. This means that to configure a PXE server, you'll need to copy everything needed to boot your server to the /var/lib/tftpboot/pxelinux directory. You'll also need to create a PXE boot file that will perform the task that is normally handled by the grub.conf file. In Exercise 21.2, you'll copy all of the required contents to the TFTP server root directory.

The file default plays a special role in the PXE boot configuration. This file contains the boot information for all PXE clients. If you create a file with the name default, all clients that are allowed to PXE boot will use it. You can also create a configuration file for a specific host by using the IP address in the name of the file. There is one restriction, however; it has to be the IP address in a hexadecimal notation. To help you with this, a host that is performing a PXE boot will always show its hexadecimal IP address on the console while booting.

Alternatively, you can calculate the hexadecimal IP address yourself. If you do so, make sure to calculate the hexadecimal value for the four parts of the IP address of the target host. The calculator on your computer can help you with this. For example, if the IP address is 192.168.0.200, the hexadecimal value is C0.A8.0.C8. Thus, if you create a file with the name C0A80C8, this file will be read only by that specific host. If you want to use this solution, it also makes sense to create host-specific entries in the dhcpd.conf file. You learned how to do this in Chapter 14, "Configuring DNS and DCHP."

EXERCISE 21.2

Configuring the TFTP Server for PXE Boot

To set up a TFTP server, you'll configure a DHCP server and the TFTP server. Be aware that the configuration of a DHCP server on your network can cause problems. An additional complicating factor is that the KVM virtual network environment probably already runs a DHCP server. This means you cannot use the DHCP server, which you'll configure to serve virtual machines. To succeed with this exercise, make sure your Red Hat Enterprise Linux Server is disconnected from the network and connect it to only one PC, which is capable of performing a PXE boot.

1. Use **yum install -y tftpserver** to install the TFTP server. Because TFTP is managed by xinetd, use **chkconfig xinetd on** to add xinetd to your runlevels.

2. Open the configuration file /etc/xinetd.d/tftp with an editor, and change the line disabled = yes to disabled = no.

3. If not yet installed, install a DHCP server. Open the configuration file /etc/dhcp/dhcpd.conf, and give it the exact contents of the example shown in Listing 21.2.

4. Copy syslinux<version>.rpm from the Packages directory on the RHEL installation disc to /tmp. You'll need to extract the file pxelinux.0 from it. This is an essential file for setting up the PXE boot environment. To extract the RPM file, use **cd /tmp** to go to the /tmp directory, and from there, use **rpm2cpio syslinux<version>.rpm | cpio -idmv** to extract the file.

5. Copy the /usr/share/syslinx/pxelinux.0 file to /var/lib/tftpboot/pxelinux.

6. Use `mkdir /var/lib/tftpboot/pxelinux/pxelinux.cfg` to create the directory in which you'll store the pxelinux configuration file.

7. In /var/lib/tftpboot/pxelinux/pxelinux.cfg, create a file with the name default that contains the following lines:

```
default Linux
prompt 1
timeout 10
display boot.msg
label Linux
    menu label ^Install RHEL
    menu default
    kernel vmlinuz
    append initrd=initrd.img
```

8. If you want to use a splash image file while doing the PXE boot, copy the /boot/grub/splash.xpm.gz file to /var/lib/tftptboot/pxelinux/.

9. You can find the files vmlinuz and initrd.img in the directory images/pxeboot on the Red Hat installation disc. Copy these to the directory /var/lib/tftpboot/pxe-linux/.

10. Use `service dhcpd restart` and `service xinetd restart` to restart the required services.

11. Use `tail -f /var/log/message` to trace what is happening on the server. Connect a computer directly to the server, and from that computer, choose PXE boot in the boot menu. You will see that the computer starts the PXE boot and loads the installation image that you have prepared for it.

12. If you want to continue the installation, when the installation program asks "What media contains the packages to be installed?" select URL. Next, enter the URL to the web server installation image you created in Exercise 21.1: http://server1.example.com/install.

In Exercise 21.2, you set up a PXE server to start an installation. You can also use the same server to add some additional sections. For example, the rescue system is a useful section, and it also might be useful to add a section that allows you to boot from local disk. The example contents for the default file in Listing 21.3 show how to do that.

If you're adding more options to the PXE menu, it also makes sense to increase the timeout to allow users to make a choice. In Listing 21.3, using the timeout 600 value does this. You should, however, note that this is not typically what you need if you want to use the PXE server for automated installations using a kickstart file, as described in the following section.

Listing 21.3: Adding more options to the PXE boot menu

```
default Linux
prompt 1
timeout 600
display boot.msg
label Linux
        menu label ^Install RHEL
        menu default
        kernel vmlinuz
        append initrd=initrd.img
label Rescue
        menu label ^Rescue system
        kernel vmlinuz
        append initrd=initrd.img rescue
label Local
        menu label Boot from ^local drive
localboot 0xffff
```

Creating a Kickstart File

You have now created an environment where everything you need to install your server is available on another server. This means you don't have to work with optical discs anymore to perform an installation, however you still need to answer all the questions which are part of the normal installation process. Red Hat offers an excellent solution for this challenge: the kickstart file. In this section, you'll learn how to use a kickstart file to perform a completely automated installation and how you can optimize the kickstart file to fit your needs.

Using a Kickstart File to Perform an Automated Installation

When you install a Red Hat system, a file with the name anaconda-ks.cfg is created in the home directory of the root user. This file contains most settings that were used while installing your computer. It is a good starting point if you want to try an automated kickstart installation.

To specify that you want to use a kickstart file to install a server, you need to tell the installer where to find the file. If you want to perform an installation from a local Red Hat installation disc, add the linux ks= boot parameter while installing. (Make sure you include the exact location of the kickstart file after the = sign.) As an argument to this parameter, add a complete link to the file. For example, if you copied the kickstart file to the server1.example.com web server document root, add the following line as a boot option while installing from a DVD:

linux ks=http://server1.example.com/anaconda-ks.cfg

To use a kickstart file in an automated installation from a TFTP server, you need to add the kickstart file to the section in the TFTP default file that starts the installation. In this case, the section that you need to install the server would appear as follows:

```
label Linux
        menu label ^Install RHEL
        menu default
        kernel vmlinuz
        append initrd=initrd.img
        ks=http://server1.example.com/anaconda-ks.cfg
```

You can also use a kickstart file while installing a virtual machine using Virtual Machine Manager. In Exercise 21.3, you'll learn how to perform a network installation without PXE boot and to configure this installation to use the anaconda-ks.cfg file.

EXERCISE 21.3

Performing a Virtual Machine Network Installation Using a Kickstart File

In this exercise, you'll perform a network installation of a virtual machine that uses a kickstart file. You'll use the network installation server that you created in Exercise 21.1. This network server is used to access the installation files and also to provide access to the kickstart file.

Note: In this exercise, you're using the DNS name of the installation server. If the installation fails with the message Unable to retrieve http://server1.example.com/ install/images/install.img, this is because server1.example.com cannot be resolved with DNS. Use the IP address of the installation server instead.

1. On the installation server, copy the anaconda-ks.cfg file from the /root directory to the /www/docs/server1.example.com directory. You can just copy it straight to the root directory of the Apache virtual host. After copying the file, set the permissions to mode 644, or else the Apache user will not be able to read it.

2. Start Virtual Machine Manager, and click the Create Virtual Machine button. Enter a name for the virtual machine, and select Network Install.

3. On the second screen of the Create A New Virtual Machine Wizard, enter the URL to the web server installation directory: http://server1.example.com/install. Open the URL options, and enter this Kickstart URL: **http://server1.example .com/anaconda-ks.cfg**.

4. Accept all the default options in the remaining windows of the Create A New Virtual Machine Wizard, which will start the installation. In the beginning of the procedure, you'll see the message `Retrieving anaconda-ks.cfg`. If this message disappears and you don't see any error messages, this indicates that the kickstart file has loaded correctly.

5. Stop the installation after the kickstart file has loaded. The kickstart file wasn't made for virtual machines, so it will ask lots of questions. After stopping the installation, remove the kickstart file from the Virtual Machine Manager configuration.

Modifying the Kickstart File with system-config-kickstart

In the previous exercise, you started a kickstart installation based on the kickstart file created after the installation of your server finished. You may have noticed that many questions were asked despite finishing the installation. This is because your kickstart file didn't match the hardware of the virtual machine you were trying to install. In many cases, you'll need to fine-tune the kickstart configuration file. To do this, you can use the `system-config-kickstart` graphical interface (see Figure 21.1).

Using `system-config-kickstart`, you can create new kickstart files. You can also read an existing kickstart file and make all the modifications you need. The `system-config-kickstart` interface looks like the one used to install an RHEL server, and all options are offered in different categories, which are organized similar to the screens that pose questions during an installation of Red Hat Enterprise Linux. You can start building everything yourself, and you can use the File ➢ Open option to read an existing kickstart file.

FIGURE 21.1   Use system-cofig-kickstart to create or tune kickstart files

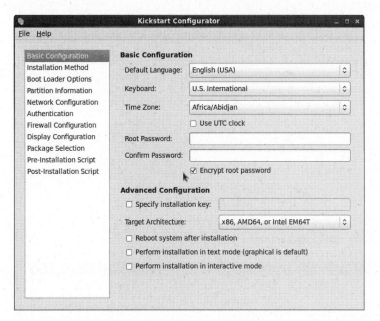

Under the Basic Configuration options, you can find choices such as the type of keyboard to be used and the time zone in which your server will be installed. Here you'll also find an interface to set the root password. Under Installation Method, you'll find among other options, such as the installation source. For a network installation, you'll need to select the type of network installation server and the directory used on that server. Figure 21.2 shows you what this looks like for the installation server you created in Exercise 21.1.

Under Boot Loader Options, you can specify that you want to install a new boot loader and where you want to install it. If specific kernel parameters are needed while booting, you can also specify them there. Partition Information is an important option (see Figure 21.3). There you can tell kickstart which partitions you want to create on the server. Unfortunately, the interface doesn't allow you to create logical volumes, so if you need these, you'll need to add them manually. How to do this is explained in the section that follows.

FIGURE 21.2 Specifying the network installation source

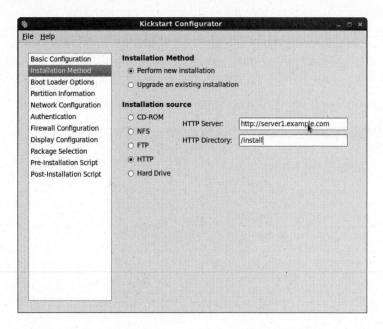

FIGURE 21.3 Creating partitions

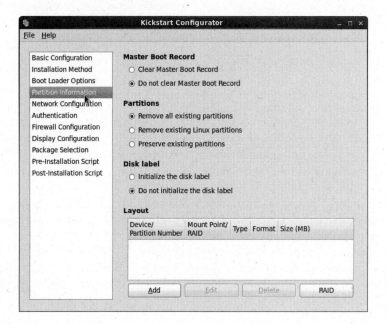

By default, the Network Configuration option is empty. If you want networking on your server, you'll need to use the Add Network Device option to indicate the name of the device and how you want it to obtain its network configuration. The Authentication option offers tabs to specify external authentication services such as NIS, LDAP, Kerberos, and some others. If you don't specify any of these, you'll default to the local authentication mechanism that goes through /etc/passwd, which is fine for many servers.

If you don't like SELinux and firewalls, activate the Firewall Configuration option. SELinux is on by default, which is good in most cases, and the firewall is switched off by default. If your server is connected directly to the Internet, turn it on and select all of the trusted services that you want to allow. For the Display Configuration option, you can tell the installer whether your server should install a graphical environment.

An interesting option is Package Selection. This option allows you to select package categories, however it does not allow you to select individual packages. If you need to select individual packages, you'll have to create a manual configuration. Finally, there are the Pre-Installation Script and Post-Installation Script options that allow you to add scripts to the installation procedure to execute specific tasks while installing the server.

Making Manual Modifications to the Kickstart File

There are some modifications that you cannot make to a kickstart file using the graphical interface. Fortunately, kickstart is an ASCII text file that can be edited manually. You can make manual modifications to configure features, including LVM logical volumes or individual packages, which are tasks that cannot be accomplished from the system-config-kickstart interface. Listing 21.4 shows the contents of the anaconda-ks.cfg file that is generated upon installation of a server. This file is interesting because it shows examples of everything that cannot be done from the graphical interface.

Listing 21.4: Contents of the anaconda-ks.cfg file

```
[root@hnl ~]# cat anaconda-ks.cfg
# Kickstart file automatically generated by anaconda.

#version=DEVEL
install
cdrom
lang en_US.UTF-8
keyboard us-acentos
network --onboot no --device p6p1 --bootproto static --ip 192.168.0.70 --netmask
 255.255.255.0 --noipv6 --hostname hnl.example.com
network --onboot no --device wlan0 --noipv4 --noipv6
rootpw  --iscrypted
 $6$tvvRd3Vd2ZBQ26yi$TdQs4ndaKXnyOCkvtmENBeFkCs2eRnhzeobyGR50BENO2OdKCmr.
x0yAkY9nhk.
```

```
0fuMWB7ysPTqjXzEOzv6ax1
firewall --service=ssh
authconfig --enableshadow --passalgo=sha512
selinux --enforcing
timezone --utc Europe/Amsterdam
bootloader --location=mbr --driveorder=sda --append=" rhgb crashkernel=auto
quiet"
# The following is the partition information you requested
# Note that any partitions you deleted are not expressed
# here so unless you clear all partitions first, this is
# not guaranteed to work
#clearpart --none

#part /boot --fstype=ext4 --onpart=sda1 --noformat
#part pv.008002 --onpart=sda2 --noformat

#volgroup vg_hnl --pesize=4096 --useexisting --noformat pv.008002
#logvol /home --fstype=ext4 --name=lv_home --vgname=vg_hnl --useexisting
#logvol / --fstype=ext4 --name=lv_root --vgname=vg_hnl --useexisting
#logvol swap --name=lv_swap --vgname=vg_hnl --useexisting --noformat
#logvol  --name=target --vgname=vg_hnl --useexisting --noformat

repo --name="Red Hat Enterprise Linux"  --baseurl=cdrom:sr0 --cost=100

%packages
@base
@client-mgmt-tools
@core
@debugging
@basic-desktop
@desktop-debugging
@desktop-platform
@directory-client
@fonts
@general-desktop
@graphical-admin-tools
@input-methods
@internet-browser
@java-platform
@legacy-x
@network-file-system-client
```

```
@perl-runtime
@print-client
@remote-desktop-clients
@server-platform
@server-policy
@x11
mtools
pax
python-dmidecode
oddjob
sgpio
genisoimage
wodim
abrt-gui
certmonger
pam_krb5
krb5-workstation
libXmu
perl-DBD-SQLite
%end
```

The `anaconda-ks.cfg` file starts with some generic settings. The first line that needs your attention is the network line. As you can see, it contains the device name `--device p6p1`. This device name is related to the specific hardware configuration of the server on which the file was created, and it will probably not work on many other hardware platforms. So, it is better replace this with `--device eth0`. Also, it is not a very good idea to leave a fixed IP address in the configuration file. So, you should replace `--bootproto static --ip 192.168.0.70 --netmask 255.255.255.0` with `--bootproto dhcp`.

The next interesting parameter is the line that contains the root password. As you can see, it contains the encrypted root password that was used while installing this server. If you want the installation process to prompt for a root password, you can remove this line completely.

An important part of this listing is where partitions and logical volumes are created. You can see the syntax that is used to accomplish these tasks, and you can also see that no sizes are specified. If you want to specify the size that is to be used for the partitions, add the `--size` option to each line where a partition or a logical volume is created. Also, consider the syntax that is used to create the LVM environment, because this cannot be done from the graphical interface.

After the definition of partitions and logical volumes, the repository to be used is specified. This is also a parameter that also generally needs to be changed. The `--baseurl` parameter contains a URL that refers to the installation URL that you want to use. For example, it can read --baseurl=http://server1.example.com/install to refer to an HTTP installation server.

In the next section, the packages that are to be installed are specified. Everything that starts with an @ (like @base) refers to an RPM package group. At the bottom of the list, individual packages are added simply by mentioning the name of the packages.

Summary

In this chapter, you learned how to configure an installation server. First, you learned how to configure a web server as an installation server by copying all packages to this server. Based on this, you were able to start an installation from a standard installation disk and then refer to the installation server to continue the installation process.

The next step involved configuring a DHCP/TFTP server to deliver a boot image to clients that boot from their network card. On the DHCP server, you created a section that tells the server where it could find the TFTP server, and in the TFTP document root, you copied all files that were needed to start the installation process, including the important file default, which contains the default settings for all PXE clients.

In the last part of this chapter, you learned how to create a kickstart file to automate the installation of your new server. You worked with the system-config-kickstart graphical utility and the options that can be added by modifying a kickstart configuration file manually. Putting all of this together, you can now set up your own installation server.

Appendix A

Hands-On Labs

Chapter 1: Getting Started with Red Hat Enterprise Linux

Exploring the Graphical Desktop

In this lab, you'll explore the GNOME graphical desktop interface. This lab helps you find where the essential elements of the GNOME desktop are located.

1. Log in to the graphical desktop as user "student."

2. Change the password of user student to "password," using the tools available in the graphical desktop.

3. Open a terminal window, and type `ls` to display files in the current directory.

4. Use Nautilus to browse to the contents of the /etc directory. Can you open the files in this directory? Can you create new files in this directory?

5. Configure your graphical desktop to have four available workspaces.

6. Open the NetworkManager application, and find out the current IP address configuration in use on your computer.

7. Use the graphical help system, and see what information you can find about changing a user's password.

Chapter 2: Finding Your Way on the Command Line

1. Use man and man -k to find out how to change the current date on your computer. Set the date to yesterday (and don't forget to set it back when you're done with the exercise).

2. Create a directory with the name /tempdir. Copy all files from the /etc directory that start with an a, b, or c to this directory.

3. Find out which command and which specific options you will need to show a time-sorted list of the contents of the directory /etc.

4. Create a file in your home directory, and fill it all with errors that are generated if you try to run the command `grep -R root *` from the /proc directory as an ordinary user. If necessary, refer to the man page of `grep` to find out how to use the command.

5. Find all files on your server that have a size greater than 100 MB.

6. Log in as root, and open two console windows in the graphical environment. From console window 1, run the following commands: `cpuinfo`, `cat /etc/hosts`,

and w. From console window 2, use the following commands: `ps aux`, `tail -n 10 /etc/passwd`, and `mail -s hello root <`. Can you run the commands that you've entered in console window 1 from the history in console window 2? What do you need to do to update the history with the commands that you've used from both environments?

7. Make a copy of the file `/etc/passwd` to your home directory. After copying it, rename the file `~/passwd` to `~/users`. Use the most efficient method to delete all lines in this file in which the third column has a number less than 500. Next, replace the text `/bin/bash` all throughout the file with the text `/bin/false`.

Chapter 3: Performing Daily System Administration Tasks

Managing Processes

In this lab, you'll explore process management options.

1. Start the command `dd if=/dev/sda of=/dev/zero` three times as a background job.
2. Find the PID of the three dd processes you just started, and change the `nice` value of one of the processes to -5.
3. Start the command `dd if=/dev/zero of=/dev/sda` as a foreground job. Next, use the appropriate procedure to put it in the background. Then verify that it indeed runs as a background job.
4. Use the most efficient procedure to terminate all of the dd commands.

Working with Storage Devices and Links

In this lab, you'll mount a USB key and create symbolic links.

1. Find a USB flash drive, and manually mount it on the `/mnt` directory.
2. Create a symbolic link to the `/etc` directory in the `/tmp` directory.

Making a Backup

In this lab, you'll use tar to make a backup of some files.

1. Create a backup of the `/tmp` directory in an archive with the name `/tmp.tar`. Check if it contains the symbolic link you just created.
2. Use the `tar` man page to find the `tar` option that allows you to archive symbolic links.

3. Create an `rsyslog` line that writes a message to user root every time that a user logs in. This line shouldn't replace the current configuration for the given facility; it should just add another option.

4. Use the `man` page of `logrotate` to find out how to rotate the `/var/log/messages` file every week, but only if it has a size of at least 1MB.

Chapter 4: Managing Software

Creating a Repository

1. Copy all package files on your installation disc to a directory with the name /packages, and mark this directory as a repository.

2. Configure your server to use the `/packages` repository.

Using Query Options

1. Search and install the package that contains the `winbind` file.

2. Locate the configuration file from the `winbind` package, and then delete it.

Extracting Files From RPMs

1. Extract the package that contains the `winbind` file so that you can copy the original configuration file out of the package to its target destination.

Chapter 5: Configuring and Managing Storage

In this lab, you will apply all the skills you have learned in this chapter. You will create two partitions on the `/dev/sdb` device that you worked with in previous exercises. Also, make sure that all currently existing partitions and volumes are wiped before you begin.

Both partitions have to be 500MB in size and created as primary partitions. Use the first partition to create an encrypted volume with the name `cryptvol`. Format this volume with the Ext4 file system, and make sure it mounts automatically when your server reboots.

Use the second partition in an LVM setup. Create a logical volume with the name `logvol`, in the VG `vgroup`. Mount this as an Ext4 file system on the `/logvol` directory. Make sure that this file system also mounts automatically when you reboot your server.

Chapter 6: Connecting to the Network

1. Using the command line, display the current network configuration on your server. Make sure to document the IP address, default gateway, and DNS server settings.

2. Manually add the secondary IP address `10.0.0.111` to the Ethernet network card on your server. Do this in a nonpersistent way.

3. Change the IP address your server uses by manipulating the appropriate configuration file. Do you also need to restart any service?

4. Query DNS to find out which DNS server is authoritative for `www.sandervanvugt.com`. (This works only if you can connect to the Internet from your server.)

5. Change the name of your server to `myserver`. Make sure that the name still exists after a reboot of your server.

6. Set up SSH in such a way that the user root cannot log in directly to it and so that user linda is the only allowed user.

7. Set up key-based authentication to your server. Use keys that are not protected with a passphrase.

8. Configure your client so that X-Forwarding over SSH is enabled by default.

9. Set up a VNC Server for user linda on session 1.

10. From the client computer, establish a VNC session to your server.

Chapter 7: Working with Users, Groups, and Permissions

This lab is scenario-based. That is, imagine you're a consultant and have to create a solution for the customer request that follows.

Create a solution for a small environment where shared groups are used. The environment needs four users: Bob, Bill, Susan, and Caroline. The users work in two small departments: support and sales. Bob and Bill are in the group support, and Susan and Caroline are in the group sales.

The users will store files in the directories /data/support and /data/sales. Each of these groups needs full access to its directory; the other group needs read access only. Make sure that group ownership is inherited automatically and that users can only delete files that they have created themselves.

Caroline is the leader of the sales team and needs permissions to manage files in the sales directory. Bill is the leader of the support team and needs permissions to manage files in the support directory. Apart from the members of these two groups, all others need to be excluded from accessing these directories.

Set default permissions on all new files that allow the users specified to do their work.

Chapter 8: Understanding and Configuring SELinux

Install an Apache web server that uses the directory /srv/web as the document root. Configure it so that it can also serve up documents from user home directories. Also, make sure you can use the sealert command in case anything goes wrong.

Chapter 9: Working with KVM Virtualization

First make sure you have completed at least Exercises 9.1, 9.2, 9.6, and 9.7. You need the configuration that is created in these labs to complete labs that will come later in this book successfully.

This additional end-of-chapter lab requires you to configure a Yum repository. The repository is to be configured on the host computer, and the virtual machine should have access to this repository. You need to complete this task in order to be able to install software on the virtual machine in the next chapter.

To complete this lab, do the following:

1. Install an FTP server on the host computer. Then create a share that makes the /repo directory accessible over the network.

2. Configure the virtual machine so that it can reach the host computer based on its name.

3. Create a repository file on the virtual machine that allows access to the NFS shared repository on the host computer.

Chapter 10: Securing Your Server with iptables

In Exercise 10.3, you opened the firewall on the virtual machine to accept incoming DNS, SSH, HTTP, and FTP traffic. It's impossible, however, to initiate this traffic from the firewall. This lab has you open the firewall on the virtual machine for outgoing DNS, SSH, and HTTP traffic.

Chapter 11: Setting Up Cryptographic Services

1. Create a self-signed certificate, and copy it to the directory /etc/pki. Make sure that the certificate is accessible to the services that need access to it, while the private key is in a well-secured directory where it isn't accessible to other users.

2. Create two user accounts: ronald and marsha. Create a GPG key pair for each. As Marsha, create a file with the name secret.txt. Make sure to store it in Marsha's home directory. Encrypt this file, and send it to Ronald. As Ronald, decrypt it and verify that you can read the contents of the file.

Chapter 12: Configuring Open LDAP

In this chapter, you read how to set up an OpenLDAP server for authentication. This lab exercise provides an opportunity to repeat all of the previous steps and to set up a domain in your slapd process. Make sure to complete the following tasks:

1. Create all that is needed to use a base context example.local in LDAP. Create an administrative user account with the name admin.example.local, and give this user the password *password*.

2. Set up two organizational units with the names users and groups.

3. In ou=users, create three users: louise, lucy, and leo. The users should have a group with their own name as the primary group.

4. In ou=groups, create a group called sales and make sure louise, lucy, and leo are all members of this group.

5. Use `ldapsearch` to verify that all is configured correctly.

6. Start your virtual machine, and configure it to authenticate on the LDAP server. You should be able to log in from the virtual machine using any of the three user accounts you created in step 3.

Chapter 13: Configuring Your Server for File Sharing

1. Set up an NFS server on your virtual machine. Make sure it exports a directory `/nfsfiles` and that this directory is accessible only for your host computer.

2. Set up `autofs` on your host. It should make sure that when the directory `/mnt/nfs` is used, the NFS share on the other machine is accessed automatically.

3. Set up a Samba server that offers access to the `/data` directory on your virtual machine. It should be accessible only by users linda and lisa.

4. Set up an FTP server in such a way that anonymous users can upload files to the server. However, after uploading, the files should immediately become invisible to the users.

Chapter 14: Configuring DNS and DHCP

This lab exercise consists of two tasks:

1. Configure a DNS zone for `example.net`. You can add this zone as an extra one to the DNS server you configured earlier while working through the exercises in this chapter. Configure your DNS as master server, and also set up a slave server in the virtual machine. Add a few resource records, including an address record for `blah.example.org`. You can test the configuration by using dig. It should give you the resource record for `blah.org`, even if the host does not exist.

2. Use `ifconfig` to find out the MAC address in use on your second virtual machine. Configure a DHCP server that assigns the IP address `192.168.100.2` to this second virtual machine. Run this DHCP server on the first virtual machine. You can modify the configuration of your current DHCP server to accomplish this task.

Chapter 15: Setting Up a Mail Server

In Exercise 15.3, you saw how email delivery failed because DNS wasn't set up properly. In this lab, you'll set up a mail environment between two DNS domains. For the DNS portion of the configuration requirements, please consult the relevant information in Chapter 14.

1. Configure your virtual machine to be in the DNS domain `example.local`. It should use the host server as the DNS server.

2. Set up your host computer to be the DNS server that serves both `example.local` and `example.com`, and make sure you have resource records for at least the mail servers.

3. On both servers, configure Postfix to allow the receipt of mail messages from other hosts. Also make sure that in messages, which originate from these services, just the DNS domain name is shown and not the FQDN of the originating host.

4. On both servers, make sure that Dovecot is started, and users can use only POP3 and POP3S to access their mail messages.

5. On the host, use Mutt to send a message to user lisa on the `testvm` computer. As lisa on the `testvm` computer, start Mutt and verify that the message has arrived.

Chapter 16: Configuring Apache on Red Hat Enterprise Linux

In this lab, you'll configure an Apache web server that has three virtual hosts. To do this lab, you'll also need to enter records in DNS, because the client must always be able to resolve the name to the correct IP address in virtual host configurations. The names of the virtual hosts are `public.example.com`, `sales.example.com`, and `accounting.example.com`. Use your virtual machine to configure the httpd server, and use the host computer to test all access. Make sure to implement the following functions:

1. The servers must have a document root in `/web`, followed by the name of the specific server (that is, `/web/public`, `/web/sales`, and `/web/accounting`).

2. Make sure the document roots of the servers have some content to serve. It will work best to create an `index.html` file for each server showing the text `welcome to <servername>`. This helps you identify the server easily when connecting to it at a later stage.

3. For each server, create a virtual server configuration that redirects clients to the appropriate server.

4. Ensure that only hosts from the local network can access the accounting website and that access is denied to all other hosts.

5. Configure user authentication for the sales server. Only users leo and lisa should get access, and all others should be denied access.

Chapter 17: Monitoring and Optimizing Performance

In this lab, you'll work on a performance-related case. You can perform the steps of this lab on your virtual computer to make sure that the host computer will keep running properly.

A customer has problems with the performance of her server. While analyzing the server, you see that no swap is used. You also notice that the server is short on memory, with just about 10 percent of total memory used by cache and buffers, while there are no specific applications that require a large memory allocation. You also notice that disk I/O is slow.

Which steps are you going to take to optimize these problems? Use a simple test procedure, and try all of the settings that you want to apply.

Chapter 18: Introducing Bash Shell Scripting

Writing a Script to Monitor Activity on the Apache Web Server

1. Write a script that monitors the availability of the Apache web server. The script should check every second to see whether Apache is still running. If it is no longer running, it should restart Apache and write a message that it has done so to syslog.

Using the select Command

2. As a Red Hat Certified professional, you are expected to be creative with Linux and apply solutions that are based on things that you have not worked with previously. In this exercise, you are going to work with the bash shell statement select, which allows you to present a menu to the user. Use the available help to complete this exercise.

Write a simple script that asks the user to enter the name of an RPM or file that the user wants to query. Write the script to present a menu that provides different options that allow the user to do queries on the RPM database. The script should offer some options, and it should run the task that the user has selected.

The following options must be presented:

a. Find the RPM from which this file originates.

b. Check that the RPM where the user has provided the name is installed.

c. Install this RPM.

d. Remove this RPM.

Chapter 19: Understanding and Troubleshooting the Boot Procedure

In this lab, you'll break and (ideally) fix your server. You must perform this lab on your virtual machine, because it is easier to reinstall if things go wrong. The lab is at your own risk, things might seriously go wrong, and you might not be able to fix it.

1. Open the /etc/fstab file with an editor, and locate the line where your home directory is mounted. In the home directory device name, remove one letter and reboot your server. Fix the problems you encounter.

2. Open the /etc/inittab file, and set the default runlevel to 6. Reboot your server, and fix the problem.

3. Use the command dd if=/dev/zero of=/dev/sda bs=446 count=1. (Change /dev/sda to /dev/vda if you're on your virtual machine.) Reboot your server, and fix the problem.

Chapter 20: Introducing High-Availability Clustering

Before starting this lab, you need to do some cleanup on the existing cluster. To do so, perform the following tasks:

1. Use the iscsiadm logout function on the cluster nodes to log out from the iSCSI target device.

2. Use Conga to delete the current cluster.

3. Make sure that the following services are no longer in your runlevels: cman, rgmanager, ricci, clvmd, and gfs2.

After cleaning everything up, create a cluster that meets the following requirements:

1. Use iSCSI as shared storage. You can use the iSCSI target you created in an earlier exercise.

2. Use Conga to set up a base cluster with the name Wyoming.

3. Create a quorum disk that pings the default gateway every 10 seconds. (Don't configure fencing.)

4. Create a service for FTP.

Chapter 21: Setting Up an Installation Server

Create an installation server. Make sure that this server installs from a dedicated virtual web server, which you will need to create for this purpose. Also, configure DHCP and TFTP to hand out an installation image to clients. Create a simple kickstart installation file that uses a 500MB /boot partition and that adds the rest of the available disk space to a partition that is going to be used to create some LVM logical volumes. Also, make sure that the nmap package is installed and that the network card is configured to use DHCP on eth0.

WARNING If you want to test the configuration, you'll need to use an external system and connect it to the installation server. Be warned that everything that is installed on this test system will be wiped out and replaced with a Red Hat Enterprise Linux installation!

Appendix B

Answers to Hands-On Labs

Chapter 1: Getting Started with Red Hat Enterprise Linux

Exploring the Graphical Desktop

1. In the login screen, click the login name "student" and type the password.

2. In the upper-right corner you can see the name of the user who is currently logged in. Click this username to get access to different tools, such as the tool that allows you to change the password.

3. Right-click the graphical desktop, and select Open in terminal. Next, type **ls**.

4. On the graphical desktop, you'll find an icon representing your home folder. Click it and navigate to the /etc folder. You'll notice that as a normal user, you have limited access to this folder.

5. Right-click a workspace icon, and select the number of workspaces you want to be displayed.

6. Right-click the NetworkManager icon in the upper-right corner of the desktop. Next, click Connection Information to display information about the current connection.

7. Press F1 to show the help system. Type the keyword you want to search for and browse the results.

Chapter 2: Finding Your Way on the Command Line

1. For instance, use `man -k time | grep 8`. You'll find the `date` command. Use `date mmddhhmm` to set the date.

2. `mkdir /tempdir, cp /etc/[abc]* /tempdir`

3. Use `man ls`. You'll find the -t option, which allows you to sort `ls` output on time.

4. `cd /proc; grep -R root * 2> ~/procerrors.txt`

5. `find / -size +100M`

6. This doesn't work because the history file gets updated only when the shell is closed.

7. `cp /etc/passwd ~. mv ~/passwd ~/users`

Chapter 3: Performing Daily System Administration Tasks

Managing Processes

1. Run dd `if=/dev/sda of=/dev/zero` three times.

2. Use `ps aux | grep dd`, and write down the PIDs. A useful addition to show just the PIDs and nothing else is found by piping the results of this command through awk '{ print $2 }'. Next, use `nice -5 $PID` (where $PID is replaced by the PIDs you just found).

3. To put a foreground job in the background, use the Ctrl+Z key sequence to pause the job. Next, use the `bg` command, which restarts the job in the background. Then use `jobs` to show a list of current jobs, including the one you just started.

4. Use `killall dd`.

Working with Storage Devices and Linkx

1. First use `dmesg` to find out the device name of the USB flash drive. Next, assuming that the name of the USB drive is /dev/sdb, use `fdisk -cul` to show the partitions on this device. It will probably show just one partition with the name /dev/sdb1. Mount it using `mount /dev/sdb1 /mnt`.

2. The link is `ln -s /etc /tmp`.

Making a Backup

1. Use `tar czvf /tmp.tar /tmp`. To verify the archive, use `tar tvf /tmp.tar`. You'll see that the archive doesn't contain the symbolic link.

2. This is the h option. Use `tar czhvf /tmp.tar /tmp` to create the archive.

3. Add the following to /etc/rsyslog.conf:
    `authpriv.info root`.
    Next, use `service restart rsyslog` to restart the syslog service.

4. Remove the /var/log/messages line from the /etc/logrotate.d/syslog file. Next, create a file with the name /etc/logrotate.d/messages, containing the following contents:

    ```
    /var/log/messages
    {
        weekly
        rotate 2
        minsize 1M
    }
    ```

Chapter 4: Managing Software

Creating Repositories

1. Use `mkdir /packages`. Next, copy all RPMs from the installation DVD to this directory. Then install `createrepo`, using `rpm -ivh createrepo[Tab]` from the directory that contains the packages (assuming that createrepo hasn't yet been installed). If you get messages about dependencies, install them as well. Use `createrepo /packages` to mark the /packages directory as a repository.

2. Create a file with the name /etc/yum.repos.d/packages.repo, and make sure it has the following contents:
   ```
   [packages]
   name=packages
   baseurl=file:///packages
   gpgcheck=0
   ```

Using Query Options

1. Use `yum provides */winbind`. This shows that `winbind` is in the `samba-winbind` package. Use `yum install samba-winbind` to install the package.

2. `rpm -qc samba-winbind` reveals after installation that the only configuration file is /etc/security/pam_winbind.conf.

Extracting Files from RPMs

1. Copy the `samba-winbind-[version].rpm` file to /tmp. From there, use `rpm2cpio samba-winbind[tab] | cpio -idmc` to extract it. You can now copy it to its target destination.

Chapter 5: Configuring and Managing Storage

1. Use `dd if=/dev/zero of=/dev/sdb bs=1M count=10`.

2. Use `fdisk -cu /dev/sdb` to create two partitions. The first needs to be of type 83, and the second needs to be type 8e. Use `+500M` twice when asked for the last cylinder you want to use.

3. Use `pvcreate /dev/sdb2`.

4. Use `vgcreate vgroup /dev/sdb2`.

5. Use `lvcreate -n logvol1 -L 500M /dev/vgroup`.

6. Use `mkfs.ext4 /dev/vgroup/logvol1`.

7. Use `cryptsetup luksFormat /dev/sdb1`.

8. Use `cryptsetup luksOpen /dev/sdb1 cryptvol`.

9. Use `mkfs.ext4 /dev/mapper/cryptvol`.

10. Add the following line to /etc/crypttab: `cryptvol    /dev/sdb1`.

11. Add the following lines to /etc/fstab: `/dev/mapper/cryptvol /cryptvol ext4 defaults 1 2` and `/dev/vgroup.logvol1 /logvol ext4 defaults 1 2`.

Chapter 6: Connecting to the Network

1. Use `ip addr show`, `ip route show`, and `cat /etc/resolv.conf`.

2. Use `ip addr add dev <yourdevicehere> 10.0.0.111/24`.

3. Change the IPADDR line in /etc/sysconfig/network-scripts/yourinterface. The NetworkManager service picks up the changes automatically.

4. `dig www.sandervanvugt.com` will give you the answer.

5. Change the `HOSTNAME` parameter in /etc/sysconfig/network.

6. Modify the contents of /etc/ssh/sshd_config. Make sure these two lines are activated: `PermitRootLogin no` and `AllowUsers linda`.

7. Use `ssh-keygen` to generate the public/private key pair. Next, copy the public key to the server from the client using `ssh-copy-id server`.

8. Modify the /etc/sysconfig/ssh_config file to include the line `ForwardX11 yes`.

9. Install `tigervnc-server`, and modify the /etc/sysconfig/vncservers file to include the lines VNCSERVERS="1:linda" and VNCSERVERARGS[1]="-geometry 800x600 -nolisten tcp -localhost". Next, use `su - linda` to become user linda, and as linda use vncpasswd to set the VNC password and start the vncserver using `service vncserver start`.

10. Use `vncviewer -via linda@server localhost:1`. Make sure that an entry that defines the IP address for the server is included in /etc/hosts on the client.

Chapter 7: Working with Users, Groups, and Permissions

1. Use `useradd BobBillSusanCaroline` to create the users. Don't forget to set the password for each of these users using the `passwd` command.

2. Use `groupadd {support,sales}` to create the groups.

3. Use `mkdir -p /data/sales /data/support` to create the directories.

4. Use `chgrp sales /data/sales` and `chgrp support /data/support` to set group ownership.

5. Use `chown Caroline /data/sales` and `chown Isabelle /data/account` to change user ownership.

6. Use `chmod 3770 /data/*` to set the appropriate permissions.

Chapter 8: Understanding and Configuring SELinux

1. Use `yum -y install httpd` (if it hasn't been installed yet), and change the Document-Root setting in /etc/httpd/conf/httpd.conf to /srv/www.

2. Use `ls -Zd /var/www/htdocs` to find the default type context that Apache needs for the document root.

3. Use `semanage -f -a "" -t http_sys_content_t /srv/www(/.*)?` to set the new type context.

4. Use `restorecon -R /srv` to apply the new type context.

5. Use `setsebool -P httpd_enable_homedirs on` to allow httpd to access web pages in user home directories.

6. Install the setroubleshoot-server package using `yum -y install setroubleshoot-server`.

Chapter 9: Working with KVM Virtualization

1. On the host, run `yum install -y vsftpd`.

2. On the host, create a bind mount in /var/ftp/pub/repo to /repo.

   a. To perform this mount manually, use `mount -o bind /repo /var/ftp/pub/repo`.

   b. To have this mount activated automatically on reboot, put the following line in /etc/fstab:

   ```
   /repo  /var/ftp/pub/repo  none  bind  0 0
   ```

3. On the host, run `service vsftpd start`.

4. On the host, run `chkconfig vsftpd on`.

5. On the virtual machine, open the file /etc/hosts with an editor and include a line that reads <yourhostipaddress> <yourhostname>.example.com, as in the following:

```
192.168.100.1       hnl.example.com
```

6. Make sure that the network is up on the virtual machine, and use ping.yourhostname.example.com to verify that you can reach the host at its IP address.

7. On the virtual machine, create a file with the name /etc/yum.repos.d/hostrepo.repo, and give it the following contents:

```
[hostrepo]
name=hostrepo
baseurl=ftp://hnl.example.com/pub/repo
gpgcheck=0
```

8. Use yum repolist on the virtual machine to verify that the repository is working.

Chapter 10: Securing Your Server with iptables

Perform the same steps as you did in Exercise 10.3, but now open the OUTPUT chain to send packets to DNS, HTTP, and SSH. These lines do that for you:

```
iptables -A OUTPUT -p tcp --dport 22 -j ACCEPT
iptables -A OUTPUT -p tcp --dport 53 -j ACCEPT
iptables -A OUTPUT -p tcp --dport 80 -j ACCEPT
iptables -A OUTPUT -p tcp --dport 21 -j ACCEPT
```

Just opening these ports in the output chain is not enough, however. You need to make sure that answers can also get back. To do this, use the following command:

```
iptables -A INPUT -m state --state ESTABLISHED,RELATED -j ACCEPT
```

Now save the configuration to make it persistent.

```
service iptables restart.
```

Chapter 11: Setting Up Cryptographic Services

1. You can easily perform this exercise by using the genkey command. Just be sure you indicate the amount of days you want the certificate to be valid (the default value is set to one month only), and include the FQDN of the server for which you are creating the certificate.

2. Start by using the gpg --gen-key command for both users. Next, have both users export their key using gpg --export > mykey. Then have both users import each other's keys by using gpg --import < mykey. Use gpg --list-keys to verify that the keys are visible.

   You can now create the encrypted file using gpg -e secret.txt. Type the name of the other user to whom you want to send the encrypted file. As the other user, use gpg -d secret.txt to decrypt the file.

Chapter 12: Configuring OpenLDAP

1. Open the file /etc/openldap/slapd.d/cn=config/olcDatabase={2}bdb.ldif. Change the parameter olcRootDN: to specify which user to use as the root account. Next, open a second terminal window, and from there, use slappasswd to create a hash for the root password you want to use. Next, in the cn=config.ldif file, find the olcRootPW parameter and copy the hashed password to the argument of this parameter. Finally, search the olcSuffix directive, and make sure it has the default fully qualified domain name that you want to use to start LDAP searches.

   To set this domain to dc=example,dc=com, include this: olcSuffix: dc=example,dc=com. Next, close the editor with the configuration file. Use service slapd restart to restart the LDAP server. At this point, you should be ready to start populating it with entry information.

2. Create a file with the following content, and use ldapadd to import it into the Directory:
   ```
   dn: dc=example,dc=local
   objectClass: dcObject
   objectClass: organization
   o: example.local
   dc: example

   dn: ou=users,dc=example,dc=local
   objectClass: organizationalUnit
   objectClass: top
   ou: users

   dn: ou=groups,dc=example,dc=local
   objectClass: organizationalUnit
   objectClass: top
   ou: groups
   ```

3. Create an LDIF file to import the users and their primary groups. The content should look like the following example file. Use ldapadd to import the LDIF file.

```
dn: uid=lisa,ou=users,dc=example,dc=local
objectClass: top
objectClass: account
objectClass: posixAccount
objectClass: shadowAccount
cn: lisa
uid: lisa
uidNumber: 5001
gidNumber: 5001
homeDirectory: /home/lisa
loginShell: /bin/bash
gecos: lori
userPassword: {crypt}x
shadowLastChange: 0
shadowMax: 0
shadowWarning: 0

dn: cn=lisa,ou=groups,dc=example,dc=com
objectClass: top
objectClass: posixGroup
cn: lisa
userPassword: {crypt}x
gidNumber: 5000
```

4. Make an LDIF file to create the group sales, and use ldapadd to add it to the Directory.
```
dn: cn=sales,ou=groups,dc=example,dc=com
objectClass: top
objectClass: posixGroup
cn: sales
userPassword: {crypt}x
gidNumber: 600
```

5. Use ldapmodify to modify the group, and add the users you just created as the new group members.
```
dn: cn=sales,ou=groups,dc=example,dc=com
changetype: modify
add: memberuid
memberuid: lisa

dn: cn=sales,ou=groups,dc=example,dc=com
changetype: modify
add: memberuid
memberuid: linda
```

```
dn: cn=sales,ou=groups,dc=example,dc=com
changetype: modify
add: memberuid
memberuid: lori
```

6. The `ldapsearch` command should appear as follows:
    ```
    ldapsearch -x -D "cn=linda,dc=example,dc=com" -w password -b
    "dc=example,dc=com" "(objectclass=*)"
    ```

7. Use `system-config-authentication` for an easy interface to set up the client to authenticate on LDAP.

Chapter 13: Configuring Your Server for File Sharing

1. Make sure the directory you want to create exists in the file system, and copy some random files to it. Next, create the file `/etc/exports`, and put in the following line:
    ```
    /nfsfiles   192.168.1.70(rw)
    ```

    Use service `nfs start` to start the NFS server, and use `chkconfig nfs on` to enable it. Use `showmount -e localhost` to verify that it is available.

2. On the host, edit `/etc/auto.master` and make sure it includes the following line:
    ```
    /mnt/nfs    /etc/auto.nfs
    ```

    Create the file `/etc/auto.nfs`, and give it the following contents:
    ```
    *    -rw      192.168.1.70/nfsfiles
    ```

    Access the directory `/mnt/nfs`, and type `ls` to verify that it works.

3. Use `mkdir /data` to create the data directory, and put some files in there. Make a Linux group `sambausers`, make this group owner of the directory `/data`, and give it rwx permissions. Install the samba and samba-common packages and edit the `/etc/samba/smb.conf` file to include the following minimal share configuration:
    ```
    [sambadata]
    path = /data
    writable = yes
    ```

    Set the SELinux context type to `public_content_t` on the `/data` directory, and then use `smbpasswd -a` to create Samba users linda and lisa. They can now access the Samba server.

4. Install vsftpd. Create a directory /var/ftp/upload, and make sure the user and group owners are set to ftp.ftp. Set the permission mode on this directory to 730. Use semanage to label this directory with public_content_rw_t, and use setsebool -P allow_ftpd_anon_write on. Next, include the following parameters in /etc/vsftpd/ vsftpd.conf:

```
anon_upload_enable = YES
chown_uploads = YES
chown_username = daemon
```

To get your traffic through the firewall, edit the /etc/sysconfig/iptables_config file to include the following line:

```
IPTABLES_MODULES="nf_conntrack_ftp nf_nat_ftp"
```

Add the following lines to the firewall configuration, and after adding these lines, use service iptables save to make the new rules persistent:

```
iptables -A INPUT -p tcp --dport 21 -j ALLOW
iptables -A INPUT -m state --state ESTABLISHED,RELATED -j ALLOW
```

Chapter 14: Configuring DNS and DCHP

1. In /etc/named.rfc1912.zones, create a zone declaration. It should appear as follows on the master server:

```
zone "example.com" IN {
    type master;
    file "example.com";
    notify yes;
    allow-update { IP-OF-YOUR-SLAVE };
};
```

On the slave server, also create a zone declaration in /etc/named.rfc19212.zones that looks like the following:

```
zone "example.com" IN {
    type slave;
    masters {
            192.168.1.220;
    };
    file "example.com.slave";
};
```

On the master, create the example.com file in /var/named following the example in Listing 14.4. Make sure to add the DNS server to your runlevels using chkconfig named on on both servers, and start the name servers using .service named start. To test this, it works best if you set the local DNS resolver on both machines to the local DNS server. That is, the slave server resolves on itself, and the master server resolves on itself. Next use dig to test any of the servers to which you've given a resource record in the zone configuration file.

2. Use ifconfig to find out the MAC address in use on your second virtual machine. Configure a DHCP server that assigns the IP address 192.168.100.2 to this second virtual machine. Run this DHCP server on the first virtual machine. You can modify the configuration of your current DHCP server to accomplish this task.

3. If you completed Exercise 14.3, all you need to do is to add a host declaration, following the example here. The example assumes that there is an entry in DNS for the host that can be used to assign the IP address.

```
host yourhost {
    hardware ethernet aa:bb:cc:00:11:22;
    fixed-address yourhost.example.com;
}
```

Don't forget the semicolons at the end of each line—it's a common error that people make.

Chapter 15: Setting Up a Mail Server

1. Edit /etc/resolv.conf on both your host and your virtual machines. Set the domain and search parameters to the appropriate domains and, in the nameserver field, put the IP address of the host computer.

2. On the host computer, create a DNS configuration that identifies the host and the virtual machine as the mail exchange for their domains.

3. On both hosts, edit /etc/postfix/main.cf. First make sure that inet_interfaces is set to all. Next change the myorigin parameter to the local domain name.

4. Install Dovecot on both servers, and edit the protocols line so that only POP3 is offered. Run /usr/libexec/dovecot/mkcert.sh to create self-signed certificates, and install them to the appropriate locations.

5. In Mutt, press m to compose a mail message. On the other server, use c to change the mailbox to which you want to connect. Enter the URL pop://testvm.example.local to access POP on the testvm computer, and verify that the message has been received.

6. In addition, make sure that the firewall, if activated, has been adjusted. Ports 143, 993, 110, and 995 need to be open for POP and IMAP to work.

7. To identify the mail server for your domain, you'll also need to set up DNS. Create a zone file containing the following to do this:

```
[root@rhev named]# cat example.com
$TTL 86400
$ORIGIN example.com.
@      1D      IN      SOA     rhev.example.com.        hostmaster.example.
com. (
                               20120822
                               3H ; refresh
                               15 ; retry
                               1W ; expire
                               3h ; minimum
)
        IN NS rhev.example.com.

rhev   IN    A      192.168.1.220
rhevh  IN    A      192.168.1.151
rhevh1 IN    A      192.168.1.221
blah   IN    A      192.168.1.1
router IN    CNAME  blah
       IN    MX    10    blah.example.com.
       IN    MX    20    blah.provider.com.
```

Chapter 16: Configuring Apache on Red Hat Enterprise Linux

Make sure to perform the following tasks:

1. After creating the directories, use semanage fcontext -a -t httpd_sys_content_t "/web(/.*)" followed by restorecon -r /web. This ensures that SELinux allows access to the nondefault document roots.

2. Use an editor to create a file index.html in the appropriate document roots.

3. In /etc/httpd/conf.d, create a configuration file for each of the virtual hosts. Make sure that at least the following directives are used in these files:

```
<VirtualHost *:80>
    ServerAdmin webmaster@server1.example.com
    DocumentRoot /www/docs/server1.example.com
    ServerName server1.example.com
    ErrorLog logs/server1/example.com-error_log
    CustomLog logs/server1.example.com-access_log common
</VirtualHost>
```

4. Put the following lines in the virtual host configuration for the accounting server:

```
order deny,allow
allow from 192.168
deny from all
```

5. Use htpasswd -cm /etc/httpd/.htpasswd leo and htpasswd -m /etc/httpd/.
    htpasswd linda to create the user accounts. Next, include the following code block in
    the sales virtual server configuration file:

```
<Directory />
AuthName Authorized Use Only
AuthType basic
AuthUserFile /etc/httpd/.htpasswd
Require valid-user
</Directory>
```

Chapter 17: Monitoring and Optimizing Performance

The solutions sketched out here will work on a server that has the performance issues discussed in the lab exercise. In your test environment, however, you probably won't see much of a difference.

Before starting your test, use the command dd if=/dev/zero of=/1Gfile to create a file that you can use for testing. Copy the file to /tmp and time how long it takes using time cp /1Gfile /tmp.

The tricky part of this exercise is swap. While in general the usage of too much swap is bad, a server that is tight on memory benefits from it by swapping out the least recently used memory pages.

The first step is to create some swap space. You can do this by using a swap file. First, use dd if=/dev/zero of=/1Gfile bs=1M count=1024. This creates a 1GB swap file. Use mkswap /1Gfile to format this file as swap, and then use swapon /1Gfile to switch it on. Verify that it is available with free -m. Also consider tuning the swappiness parameter by making the server more eager to swap, for example, by adding vm.swappiness = 80 to /etc/sysctl.conf.

The second challenge is disk I/O. This can be caused by the elevator settings that are in the file /sys/block/sda/queue/scheduler. It can also be because of journaling, which is set too heavy for the workload of the server. Try the data=writeback mount option in /etc/fstab.

After making the adjustments, run test time cp /1Gfile /tmp again to see whether you can discern any improvement in performance.

Chapter 18: Introducing Bash Shell Scripting

Writing a Script to Monitor Activity on the Apache Web Server

1. Here's the answer:

```
#!/bin/bash
#
# Monitoring process httpd
#
COUNTER=0
while ps aux | grep httpd | grep -v grep > /dev/null
do
     COUNTER=$((COUNTER+1))
     sleep 1
     echo COUNTER is $COUNTER
done

logger HTTPMONITOR: httpd stopped at `date`
/etc/init.d/apache2 start
mail -s Apache server just stopped root < .
```

Using the select Command

2. Here's the answer:

```
#!/bin/bash
#
# RPM research: query the RPM database

echo 'Enter the name of an RPM or file'
read RPM
echo 'select a task from the menu'
select TASK in 'Check from which RPM this file comes' 'Check if
 this RPM is installed' 'Install this RPM' 'Remove this RPM'
do
case $REPLY in
        1) TASK="rpm -qf $RPM";;
        2) TASK="rpm -qa | grep $RPM";;
```

```
        3) TASK="rpm -ivh $RPM";;
        4) TASK="rpm -e $RPM;;
        *) echo error && exit 1;;
    esac

        if [ -n "TASK" ]
        then
                clear
                echo you have selected TASK
                $TASK
                break
        else
                echo invalid choice
        fi
    done
```

Chapter 19: Understanding and Troubleshooting the Boot Procedure

1. Your server will issue an error while booting, and it will tell you to "Enter root pass-word for maintenance mode." Enter the root password to get access to a shell environment. The file system is mounted as read-only at this point. Use `mount -o remount,rw` / to mount the root file system in read-write mode, and fix your `/etc/fstab`.

2. Your server will keep on rebooting. To fix this, you first need to enter the GRUB prompt when the server reboots. From there, enter 3 or 5 to enter a normal runlevel. Don't forget to fix the `/etc/inittab` file as well.

3. You have wiped your GRUB configuration. This is an issue you can repair only from the rescue disk. Boot the rescue disc, and make sure to mount your Linux installation on `/mnt/sysimage`. Next, use `chroot /mnt/sysimage` to change the current root directory. Also verify that your `/boot` directory has been mounted correctly. If it has, use `grub-install /dev/sda` to reinstall GRUB.

Chapter 20: Introducing High-Availability Clustering

1. Use `iscsiadm` to discover the iSCSI target, and log in to it.

2. Make sure to run ricci on all nodes, and set a password for the ricci user. Then start luci on one node, and create the cluster.

3. Make sure you have a partition on the SAN that you can use for the quorum disk. Use mkqdisk to format the quorum disk, and then switch it on from Conga. Also in Conga, define the heuristics test, which consists of the ping -c 1 yourgateway command.

4. Create the service group for FTP, and assign at minimum the resources for a unique IP address, a file system, and the FTP service. Make sure to mount the file system on /var/ftp/pub.

Chapter 21: Setting Up an Installation Server

Complete the following tasks:

1. Create a virtual web server, and add the name of this web server to DNS if you want to be able to use URLs to perform the installation.

2. Copy all files from the installation DVD to the document root of that web server.

3. Set up DHCP and TFTP. You can use the examples taken from the code listings in this chapter.

4. Use the anaconda-ks.cfg file that was created while installing your host machine, and change it to match the requirements detailed previously.

Glossary

A

active memory   This is memory that has recently been used by the kernel and that can be accessed relatively fast.

anchor value   This is a value used in performance optimization that can be used as the default value to which the results of performance tests can be compared.

anticipatory scheduler   This is the I/O scheduler that tries to predict the next read operation. In particular, this scheduler is useful in optimizing read requests.

authoritative name servers   In DNS, this is a name server that has the authority to give information about resource records that are in the DNS database.

automount   This is a system implemented using the autofs daemon and that allows file systems to be mounted automatically when they are needed.

B

Bash   This is the default shell environment that is used in Linux. The Bash shell takes care of interpreting the commands that users will run. Bash also has an extensive scripting language that is used to write shell scripts to automate frequent administrator tasks.

Booleans   These are on/off switches that can be used in SELinux. Using Booleans makes modifying settings in the SELinux policy easy, which would be extremely complex without the use of Booleans.

boot loader   This is a small program of which the first part is installed in the master boot record of a computer, which takes care of loading an operating system kernel. On Red Hat Enterprise Linux, GRUB is used as the default boot loader. Others are also available but rarely used.

bouncing   In email, this is a solution that returns an error message to another MTA after having received a message for a user who doesn't exist in this domain.

C

caching   Caching is employed to keep frequently used data in a faster memory area. Caching occurs on multiple levels. On the CPU, there is a fast but expensive cache that keeps the most frequently used code close to the CPU. In memory, there is a cache that keeps the most frequently used files from hard disk in memory.

certificate revocation list (CRL)   In TLS certificates, a CRL can be used to keep a list of certificates that are no longer valid. This allows clients to verify the validity of TLS certificates.

cgroups   In performance optimization, a cgroup is a predefined group of resources. By using cgroups, system resources can be grouped and reserved for specific processes only. It is possible to configure cgroups in such a way in which only allowed processes can access its resources.

chain   In a Netfilter firewall, a chain is a list of filtering rules. The rules in a chain are always sequentially processed until a match is found.

Common Internet File System (CIFS)   The Common Internet File System is a file-sharing solution that is based on the Server Message Block (SMB) protocol specification, which was developed by IBM for its OS/2 operating system and adapted by Microsoft, which published the specifications in 1995. On Linux, CIFS is implemented in the Samba server, which is commonly used to share files in corporate environments. CIFS is also a common solution on NAS appliances.

command substitution   This is a technique in shell scripting that uses the result of a command in the script. By using command substitution, a flexible shell script can be created to execute on the results of a specific command that may be different given the conditions under which it is executed.

complete fair queuing (CFQ)   In kernel scheduler optimization, CFQ is an approach where read requests have the same priority as write requests. CFQ is the default scheduler setting that treats read and write requests with equal priority. Because of the equal treatment between these requests, it may not be the best approach for optimal performance on a server, which is focused either on read requests or on write requests.

Conga   In the Red Hat High Availability add-on, Conga is the name for the web-based management platform, which consists of the ricci agents and luci management interface.

context   In LDAP, a context is a location in the LDAP directory. An LDAP client is typically configured with a default context, which is the default location in LDAP where the client has to look for objects in the directory.

controllers   In cgroups, different kinds of system resources can be controlled. cgroups use controllers to define to which type of system resource access is provided. Different controllers are available for memory, CPU cycles, or I/O, for example.

copyleft license   A copyleft license is the open source alternative to a copyright license. In a copyright license, the rights are claimed by an organization. In a copyleft license, the license rights are not claimed but are left for the general public.

Corosync   This is the part of the Red Hat High Availability add-on that takes care of the lower layers of the cluster. Corosync uses the Totem protocol to verify whether other nodes in the cluster are still available.

cron daemon   Cron is a daemon (process) that is used to schedule tasks. The cron daemon does this based on the settings that are defined in the `/etc/crontab` file.

D

daemons   Daemons are service processes on Linux. To launch them, you'll typically use the `service` command.

deadline scheduler   This is a scheduler setting that waits as long as possible before it writes data to disk. By doing this, it ensures that writes are performed as efficiently as possible. Using the deadline scheduler is recommended for optimizing servers that do more writing than reading.

default gateway   On IP networks, a default gateway is the router that connects this network to the outside world. Every computer needs to be configured with a default gateway; otherwise, no packets can be sent to exterior networks.

dentry cache   This is an area in kernel memory that is used to cache directory entries. These are needed to find files and directories on disk. On systems that read a lot, the dentry cache will be relatively high.

dig   Dig is a utility that can be used to query DNS name servers.

Domain Name System (DNS)   DNS allows users of networks to use easy-to-remember names instead of hard-to-remember IP addresses. Every computer needs to be configured with at least one DNS server.

Dynamic Host Configuration Protocol (DHCP)   DHCP is a protocol that is used to provide computers on the network with IP addresses and other IP-related information automatically. Using this as an alternative to the tedious manual assignment of IP addresses makes managing network-related configuration on hosts in an IP network relatively easy.

dynamic linker   Library files need to be connected to the program files that use them. This can be done statically or dynamically. In the latter case, the dynamic linker is used to do this. It is a software component that tracks needed libraries, and if a function call is made to the library, it will be loaded.

E

entropy   Entropy is random data. When generating encryption keys, you'll need lots of random data, particularly if you're using large encryption keys (such as 4096-bit keys). Entropy is typically created by causing random action on your computer, such as moving the mouse or displaying large directory listings.

entry   In LDAP, an entry is an object in the LDAP database. The LDAP schema defines the different entries that can be used. Typical entries are users and groups that are created in LDAP to handle authentication.

environment variables   An environment variable is one that is in a shell environment. Shells like Bash use local variables, which are available in the current shell only, and environment variables, which are available in this shell and also in all of its subshells. Many environment variables are automatically set when your server starts.

escaping   In a shell environment, escaping is the technique that makes sure that the next character or set of characters is not interpreted. This is needed to ensure that the shell takes the next character solely as a character and that it does not interpret its function in the shell. Typical characters that are often escaped are the asterisk (*) and dollar ($) sign.

Ethernet bond   An Ethernet bond is a set of network cards that are bundled together. Ethernet bonding is common on servers, and it is used to increase the available bandwidth or add redundancy to a network connection.

execute permission   The execute permission is used on program files in Linux. Without execute permission, it is not possible to run the program file or enter a directory.

extent   Traditionally, file systems used blocks of 4KB as the minimum unit for allocating files. This took up many blocks for large files, which increased the overhead for these types of files. To make large file systems more efficient, modern file systems like ext4 use extents. An extent often has a default size of 2MB.

F

fairness   This is the principle that ensures that all process types are treated by the kernel scheduler with equal priority.

fdisk tool   This tool is used to create partitions.

Fedora   This is an open source Linux distribution that is used as a development platform for Red Hat Enterprise Linux. Before new software solutions are offered in Red Hat Enterprise Linux, they are already thoroughly tested in Fedora.

fencing   This is a solution in a high-availability cluster that is used to make sure that erroneous nodes are stopped.

fencing device   This hardware device used to fence erroneous nodes in a high-availability cluster. Fencing devices can be internal, such as integrated management boards, or external to the server, which is the case for power switches.

file system label   File system labels can be used as an easy method for identifying a file system. Instead of using the device name, which can change depending on the order in which the kernel detects the device, the file system label can be used to mount the devices.

for loop   This is a conditional statement that can be used in shell scripts. A for loop is performed as long as a certain condition is met. It is an excellent structure to process a range of items.

G

Global File System 2 (GFS2)   GFS2 is the Red Hat Cluster File System. The nice thing about GFS2 is that multiple nodes can write it to simultaneously. On a noncluster file system, such as ext4, if multiple nodes try to write to the same file system simultaneously, this leads to file system corruption.

Gnu Privacy Guard (GPG)   GPG is a public/private key-based encryption solution. It can be used for multiple purposes. Some common examples include the encryption of files or RPM checksums. By creating a checksum on the RPM package, the user who downloads a package can verify that the package has not been tampered with.

group owner   Every file and every directory on Linux has a group owner to which permissions are assigned. All users who are members of the group can access the file or directory using the permissions of the group.

H

hard link   A hard link is a way to refer to a file. Basically, it is a second name that is created for a file. Hard links make it easy to refer to multiple files in a flexible way.

hardware fencing   In high-availability clustering, hardware fencing is a method used for stopping failing nodes in the cluster to maintain the integrity of the resources, which are serviced by the cluster node in question. To implement this method, specific hardware is used, such as a management board or manageable power switch.

heuristics   In high-availability clusters, a quorum disk can be used to verify that a node still has quorum. This means that it still is part of the majority of the cluster, and therefore it can serve cluster resources. To define the quorum disk, certain tests are assigned to it, and these are defined in the quorum disk heuristics.

hidden file   A hidden file is a file that cannot be seen in a normal directory listing. To create a hidden file, the user should create a file in which the filename starts with a dot.

huge page   By default, memory is allocated in 4KB pages. For applications such as databases that need to allocate huge amounts of memory, this is very inefficient. Therefore, the operating system can be configured with huge pages, which by default are 2MB in size. Using huge pages in some cases makes the operating system much more efficient.

I

inactive memory   Inactive memory is memory that hasn't been used recently. Pages that are in inactive memory are moved to swap before the actively used pages in active memory.

inode   An inode contains the complete administration of a file. In fact, a file is the inode. In actuality, names are assigned to files only for our convenience. The kernel itself works with inode numbers. Use `ls -i` to find the inode number of a particular file.

insert mode   In the editor vi, the insert mode is the one in which text can be entered. This is in contrast to the command mode, which is the one in which commands can be entered, such as the command needed to save a document.

Inter-Process Communication (IPC)   Inter-Process Communication is that communication that occurs directly between processes. The kernel allocates sockets and named pipes to have IPCs transpire.

internal command   An internal command is one that is part of the Bash shell binary. It cannot be found on disk, but it is loaded when the Bash shell is loaded.

IP masquerading   IP masquerading is the technique where on the public side of the network, a registered IP address is used, and on the private side of the network, non-Internet-routable private IP addresses are used. IP masquerading is used to translate these private IP addresses to the public IP address, which nevertheless allows all private addresses to connect to the Internet.

iSCSI   iSCSI is the protocol that is used to send SCSI commands over IP. It is a common SAN solution that implements shared storage, which is often required in high-availability clusters.

K

Kdump   Kdump is a special version of the kernel that is loaded if a core dump occurs. This situation is rare in Linux, and it happens when the kernel crashes and dumps a memory core. The Kdump kernel takes the memory core dump, and it makes sure that it is written to disk.

key distribution center (KDC)   A KDC is used in Kerberos to hand out tickets. After successful authentication, a KDC ticket allows a client to connect to one of the services that is made available by Kerberos.

key transfer   Key transfer is the process where a shared security key has to be transferred to the communication partner. This is often done by using public/private key encryption.

key-based authentication   Key-based authentication is an authentication solution where no passwords are exchanged. However, the authentication takes place by users who prove their identity by signing a special packet with their private key. Based on the public key, which also is publicly available to the authentication partner, a user can be authenticated. Key-based authentication is frequently used in SSH environments.

keyring In GPG encryption, the key ring is the collection of all the keys that a user has collected. This includes keys from other users, as well as the key that belongs to the particular user.

kickstart file A kickstart file is one that contains all of the answers needed to install the server automatically.

L

LDAP Input Format (LDIF) LDIF is the default format used to enter information in an LDAP directory.

leaf-entries In LDAP, a leaf entry is one that cannot contain any entries by itself. This is in contrast to a container entry, which is used to create structure in the LDAP database.

library A library is a file that contains shared code. Libraries are used to make programming more efficient. Common code is included in the library, and the program files that use these libraries need to be linked to the library.

Libvirt Libvirt is a generic interface that is used for managing virtual environments. Common utilities like virsh and Virtual Machine Manager use it to manage virtualization environments like KVM, the default virtualization solution in Red Hat Enterprise Linux.

Lightweight Directory Access Protocol (LDAP) LDAP is a directory service. This is a service that is used to store items, which are needed in corporate IT environments. It is frequently used to create user accounts in large environments because LDAP is much more flexible than flat authentication databases.

link See *hard link* and *soft link*.

load average Load average is the average workload on a server. For performance optimization, it is important to know the load average that is common for a server.

load balancing Load balancing is a technique that is used to distribute a workload between different physical servers. This technique is often used in combination with high-availability clustering to ensure that high workloads are handled efficiently.

log target In rsyslog, a log target defines where log messages should be sent. This can be multiple destinations, such as a file, console, user, or central log server.

logical operators Logical operators are used in Bash scripts to execute commands depending on the result of previously executed commands. There are two such logical operators: a || b executes b only if a didn't complete successfully, and a && b executes b only if a was executed successfully.

Logical Volume Manager (LVM)   Logical volumes are a flexible method for organizing disk storage. They provide benefits over the use of partitions, for example, in that it is much easier to increase or decrease a logical volume in size than a partition.

Linux Unified Key Setup (LUKS)   LUKS is a method used to create encrypted disks and volumes. LUKS adds a level of security, and it ensures that data on the device cannot be accessed without entering the correct passphrase if the device is connected to another machine.

luci   Management interface for high-availability clusters. As a part of the Conga solution, it probes the ricci agents that are used on cluster nodes to exchange information with them.

M

mail exchange (MX)   A mail exchange is a mail server, which is responsible for handling email for a specific DNS domain.

mail queue   Email that is sent is first placed in the mail queue. From there, it will be picked up by a mail process, which sends it to its destination. Sometimes messages keep "hanging" in the queue. If this happens, it helps to flush the queue or wait for the mail server process to try again to send the message.

mail user agent (MUA)   The MUA is the user program used to send and read email messages.

master name server   A master DNS name server, also referred to as a *primary name server*, is the server responsible for the resource records in a DNS domain. It communicates with slave or secondary DNS name servers to synchronize data for redundancy purposes.

memory over-allocation   Memory over-allocation is the situation where a process claims more memory than that which is actually needed, just in case it might require it later. The total amount of claimed but not necessarily used memory is referred to as *virtual memory*.

message delivery agent (MDA)   The MDA is the part of a mail server, which ensures that messages are delivered to the mailbox of the end user after it has been received by the message transfer agent.

message transfer agent (MTA)   The MTA is the part of the mail server, which sends out a message to the mail server of the recipient. To find that mail server, it uses the MX record in DNS.

meta package handler   A meta package handler is a solution that uses repositories to resolve dependency problems while installing RPM software packages. On Red Hat Enterprise Linux, the yum utility is used as the meta package handler.

mkfs utility   The mkfs utility is used to create a file system on a storage device, which can be a partition or an LVM logical volume. This process is referred to as *formatting* on other operating systems.

module   Modules are pieces of software that can easily be included in a bigger software framework. Modules are used by different software solutions. The Linux kernel and the Apache web server are probably the best-known module solutions.

mounting   Mounting is the process of connecting a storage device to a directory. Once it has been mounted, users can access the storage device to work with the data on that device.

N

name servers   A (DNS) name server is a server that is contacted to translate DNS names like www.example.com, which are easy to use, to IP addresses, which are required to communicate over an IP network. Every client computer needs to be configured with the IP address of at least one DNS name server.

ncurses   ncurses is the generic way to refer to a menu-driven interface. On Red Hat Enterprise Linux, there are some menu-driven interfaces that are useful for configuring a server, which doesn't run a graphical user interface.

Neighbor Discovery Protocol (NDP)   NDP is a protocol used in IPv6 to discover other nodes that are using IPv6. Based on this information, a node can find out in which IPv6 network it is used and, subsequently, add its own MAC address to configure the IPv6 address that it should use automatically.

Netfilter   Netfilter is the name of the kernel-level firewall that is used in Linux. To configure the Netfilter firewall, the administrator uses the iptables command or the system-config-firewall menu-driven interface.

Network Address Translation (NAT)   NAT is a solution used to hide internal nodes on the private network from the outside world. The nodes use the public IP address of the NAT router or firewall to gain access to external servers. Accordingly, only external servers can send answers to these internal hosts without accessing them directly.

Network Manager Service   The Network Manager Service is one that simplifies managing IP addresses. It monitors the IP configuration files and applies changes to these files immediately. It also uses a graphical user interface to make the management of IP addresses and related information easier for the administrator.

network service   The network service is used to manage network interfaces.

noop scheduler   The noop scheduler is an I/O scheduler that performs no operations on I/O transactions. Use this scheduler on advanced hardware, which optimizes I/O requests in a good enough way so that no further Linux OS-level optimization is required.

O

objects   An object is a generic name in IT for an independent entity. Objects occur everywhere, such as in programming, but they also exist in LDAP where the entries in an LDAP directory are also referred to as *objects*.

P

pacemaker   Pacemaker is used in high-availability clusters to manage resources. Pacemaker is the name for the suite of daemons and utilities that help you run cluster resources where they need to be running.

packet inspection   Packet inspection is a technique that is used, among others, by firewalls for looking at the content of a packet. In general, packet inspection refers to an approach that goes beyond solely looking at the header of a packet but also looks into its data.

page size   Memory is allocated in blocks. These blocks are referred to as pages, and they have a default size of 4KB. For applications that need large amounts of memory, it makes sense to use huge pages, which have a default size of 2MB.

Palimpsest tool   Palimpsest is the utility used to manage partitions and file systems on a hard disk.

partition   A partition is the base allocation unit that is needed to create file systems with the mkfs utility.

pattern-matching operator   In shell scripting, a pattern-matching operator is one that analyzes patterns and, if required, modifies patterns in strings that are evaluated by the script.

physical volume   In LVM, a physical volume is the physical device that is added to the LVM volume group. Typically, physical volumes are disks and partitions.

piping   Piping is the solution where the output of one command is sent to another command for further processing. It is often used for filtering, as in `ps aux | grep http`.

Pluggable Authentication Modules (PAM)   Authentication on Linux is modular, and the system used to manage these modules is called Pluggable Authentication Modules (PAM). The benefit of using PAM is that it is easy to insert a module in it, which enables a new way of authenticating without the need to rewrite the complete program.

policy   In a Netfilter firewall, the policy defines the default behavior. If no specific rule matches a packet, which is processed in any of the chains, the policy is applied. In SELinux, the policy is the total collection of SELinux rules that are applied.

port forwarding   On a firewall, port forwarding is used to send all packets, which are received on a public port, on a router to a specific host and port on the internal network.

POSIX standard   POSIX is an old standard from the UNIX world, which was designed to reach a higher level of uniformity between UNIX operating systems. This standard is very comprehensive, including defining the behavior of specific commands. Many Linux commands also comply with the POSIX standard.

pre-routing   In a Netfilter firewall, the pre-routing chain applies to all outgoing packets, and it is applied before the routing process determines how to send them forward.

primary name server   See *master name server.*

priorities   In performance optimization, the priority determines when a specific request is handled. The lower the priority; the sooner the request is handled. Requests that need immediate attention will get real-time priority.

process ID (PID)   Every process has a unique identifier, which is referred to as the process ID (PID). PIDs are used to manage specific processes.

processes   A process is a task that runs on a Linux server. Every process can be managed by its specific PID, and it allocates its own runtime environment, which includes the total amount of memory that is reserved by the process. Within a process, multiple subtasks can be executed. These are referred to as *threads.* Some services, like httpd, can be configured to start multiple processes or just one process that starts multiple tasks.

pseudo-root   In the NFS file-sharing protocol, a pseudo-root is a common directory that contains multiple exported directories. The NFS client can mount the pseudo-root to gain access to all of these directories instead of mounting the individual directories one by one.

Public Key Certificate (PKC)   In TLS secure communications, a public key certificate is used to hand out the public key of nodes to other machines. The public key certificate contains a signature that is created by a certificate authority, which guarantees the authenticity of the public key that is in the certificate.

Q

queue   A queue is a line in which items are placed before they are served. Queues are used in email, and they are also by the kernel in handling processes.

queuing   This is the process of placing items in a queue.

quorum   In high-availability clustering, the quorum refers to the majority of the cluster. Typically, nodes cannot run services if the node is not part of a cluster that has a quorum. This approach is used to guarantee the integrity of services that are running in the cluster.

quorum disk   A quorum disk is a solution that a cluster can use to get quorum. Quorum disks are particularly useful in a two-node cluster, where normally one node cannot have quorum if the other node goes down. To fix this problem, the quorum disk adds another quorum vote to the cluster.

R

read permission   This is the permission given to read a file. If applied to a directory, the read permission allows the listing of items in the directory.

real time   A real-time process is one that is serviced at the highest-level priority. This means that it will go through before any other processes that are currently in the process queue, and it has to wait only for other real-time processes to occur.

realm   A realm is a domain in the Kerberos authentication protocol. The realm is a collection of services that share the same Kerberos configuration.

Red Hat Enterprise Virtualization (RHEV)   RHEV is a KVM-based virtualization solution. It is a separate product that distinguishes itself by offering an easy-to-use management interface, with added features such as high availability, which are not available in default KVM.

Red Hat Package Manager (RPM)   RPM is a standard used to bundle software packages in RPM files. An RPM file contains an archive of packages, as well as metadata that describes what is in the RPM package.

referral   In LDAP, a referral is a pointer to another LDAP server. Referrals are used to find information that isn't managed by this LDAP server.

relaying   In email, relaying is a solution where email is forwarded to another message transfer agent that ensures that it reaches its destination.

replication   In LDAP, replication is creating multiple copies of the same database. In replication, there is a process that ensures that modifications applied to one of the databases are also synchronized to all copies of that database.

repositories   In RPM package management, a repository is an installation source. It can be a local directory or offered by a remote server, and it contains a collection of RPMs and metadata that describes exactly what is in the repository.

resource records   In DNS, resource records are those that are in the DNS database. There are multiple types of resource records, like *A*, which resolves a name in an IP address, or *PTR*, which resolves an IP address into a name.

RGManager   In high-availability clustering, RGManager is the resource group manager. It determines where in the cluster certain resources will be running.

RHEV Manager (RHEV-M)   In Red Hat Enterprise Virtualization, the RHEV-M host offers the management platform that is used to manage virtual machines.

RHEV-H   In Red Hat Enterprise Virtualization, RHEV-H is the hypervisor host. It is the host that runs the actual KVM virtual machines.

ricci   In high-availability clustering, Conga is the platform that provides a web-based management interface. Ricci is the agent that runs on all cluster nodes, and it is managed by the luci management platform. The administrator logs in to the luci management interface to perform management tasks.

root domain   In DNS, the root domain is the starting point of all name resolution. It is at the top of the hierarchy that contains the top-level domains, such as `.com`, `.org`, and many more.

rotating a log file   Rotating a log file is the process where an old log file is closed and a new log file is opened, based on criteria such as the age or size of the old log file. Log rotation is used to ensure that a disk is not completely filled up by log files, which grow too big.

rsyslogd process   The rsyslogd process takes care of logging system messages. To specify what it should log, it uses a configuration file where facilities and priorities are used to define exactly where the messages are logged.

run queue   See *queue*.

runlevel   A runlevel is the status in which a server is started. It determines the amount of services that should be loaded on the server.

S

Samba   Samba is the open source file server that implements the Common Internet File System (CIFS) protocol to share files. It is a popular solution because all Windows clients use CIFS as their native protocol.

Satellite   Red Hat Satellite is an installation proxy. It can be used on large networks, and it is located between the RHN installation repositories and local servers. The Satellite server updates from RHN, and the local servers will install updates from Red Hat Satellite.

scheduler   The scheduler is the part of the kernel that divides CPU cycles between processes. The scheduler takes into consideration the priority of the processes, and it will make sure that the process with the lowest priority number is serviced first. Between processes with equal priority, CPU time will be evenly divided.

schema   In LDAP, the schema defines the objects that can exist in the database. In some cases, when new solutions are implemented, a schema extension is necessary.

secondary server   In DNS, a secondary server is one that receives updates from a primary server. Clients can use a secondary server for name resolving.

Set group ID (SGID)   SGID is a permission, which makes sure that the person who executes a file executes it with the permissions of the group that is owner of the file. Also, when applied to a directory, SGID sets the inheritance of group ownership on that directory forward. This means that all items that are created in that directory and its subdirectories will get the same group owner.

Set user ID (SUID) permission   SUID permission makes sure that a user who executes a file will execute it with the permissions of the owner of the file. This is a potentially dangerous permission, and for that reason, it normally isn't used by system administrators.

shared memory   Shared memory is memory that is shared between processes. Using shared memory is useful if, for example, multiple processes need access to the same library. Instead of loading the library multiple times, it can be shared between the processes.

shebang   The shebang (`#!/bin/bash`) is used on the first line of a shell script. It indicates the shell that should be used to interpret the commands in the shell script.

shell   The shell is the user interface that interprets user commands and interfaces to the hardware in the computer.

shell script   A shell script is a file that contains a series of commands in which conditional statements can be used in order that certain commands are executed only in specific cases.

shell variable   A shell variable is a name that points to an area in memory that contains a dynamic value. Because shell variables are dynamic, they are often used in shell scripts, because they make the shell script flexible.

Simple Mail Transfer Protocol (SMTP)   SMTP is the default protocol that is used by MTAs to make sure that mail is forwarded to the mail exchange, which is responsible for a specific DNS domain.

slab memory   Slab memory is memory that is used by the kernel.

slave name server   See *secondary name server*.

snapshot   In LVM, a snapshot is a "photo" of the state of a logical volume at a specific point in time. Using snapshots makes it much easier to create backups, because there will be never open files in a snapshot.

software dependency   Programmers often use libraries or other components that are necessary for the program to function but are external to the program itself. When installing the program, these components also need to be installed. The installation program will therefore look for these software dependencies.

STDERR   STDERR is standard error, or the default location to which a process will send error messages.

sticky bit permission   The sticky bit permission can be used on directories. It has no function on files. If applied, it makes sure that only the user of a file, or the user of the parent directory, can delete files.

Streamline Editor (SED)   SED is a powerful command-line utility that can be used for text file processing.

substitution operators   Substitution operators are those that change an item in a script dynamically, depending on factors that are external to that script.

superclass   In LDAP, a superclass is used to define entries in the LDAP schema. The superclass contains attributes that are needed by multiple entries. Instead of defining these for every entry that needs them, the attributes are defined on the superclass, and the specific entry in the schema is connected to the superclass so that it inherits all of these attributes.

swap memory   Swap memory is simulated RAM memory on disk. The Linux kernel can use swap memory if it is short on physical RAM.

swap space   See *swap memory*.

symbolic link   A symbolic link is used to point to a file that is somewhere else. Symbolic links are used to make it easier to use remote files.

symmetric multiprocessing (SMP)   SMP is what the kernel uses to divide tasks between multiple processors.

sys time   When the time utility is used to measure the time it takes to execute a command, it will distinguish between real time and sys time. Real time is the time that has passed between the start and the completion of the command. This also includes the time that the processor has been busy servicing other tasks. Sys time, also referred to as *system time*, is the time that the process actually has been using the CPU.

system-config   To make configuring a system easy, Red Hat includes many utilities where the name starts with `system-config`. To find them, type **system-config** and, before pressing Enter, press the Tab key twice.

T

tar ball   A tar ball is an archive file that has been created using the tar utility.

top-level domain (TLD)   A TLD is one of the domains in DNS that exists on the upper level. These are commonly known domains, such as `.com`, `.org`, and `.mil`.

U

Upstart   Upstart is the Linux system used for starting services.

user owner   To calculate file system permissions, the user owner is the first entity that is considered. Every file has a user owner, and if the user who is the owner accesses that file, the permissions of that user are applied.

user space   When a program is executed, it can run in user space and in kernel space. In user space, it has limited permissions. In kernel space (also referred to as *system space*), it has unrestricted permissions.

V

variable   A variable is a name that is connected to a specific area in memory where a changeable value is stored. Variables are frequently used in shell scripts, and they are defined when calling the script, or from within the script, by using statements such as the read statement.

virtio drivers   Virtio drivers are those that are used in KVM virtual machines. A virtio driver allows the virtual machine to communicate directly with the hardware. These drivers are used most frequently for network cards and disks.

virtual bridge adapter   To connect virtual machines to the network, a virtual bridge is used. The virtual bridge at one end is connected to the physical Ethernet card. At the other end, it is connected to the virtual network cards within the virtual machines, and it allows all of these network cards to access the same physical network connection.

virtual host   A virtual host is a computer that is installed as a virtual machine in a KVM environment. This is also referred to as a *virtual guest*. Another context where virtual hosts are used is the Apache web server where one Apache service can serve multiple web services, referred to as *virtual hosts*.

virtual memory   Virtual memory is the total amount of memory that is available to a process. It is not the same as all memory that is in use; rather, it's just the memory that could be used by the process.

volume group   In LVM, the volume group is used as the abstraction of all available storage. It provides the storage needed to create logical volumes, and it gets this storage from the underlying physical volumes.

W

write permission   The write permission is the one that allows users to change the content of existing files. If applied to a directory, it allows the user who has write permissions to create or delete files and subdirectories in that directory.

Y

yum   See *meta package handler*.

Z

zone   This is the connected domains and subdomains for which a DNS server is responsible.

zone transfer   This is the update of changes in DNS zones between master and slave DNS servers.

Index

N

O

Q

S

T